WAR,
PEACE, and
INTERNATIONAL
POLITICS

WAR, PEACE, and INTERNATIONAL POLITICS

FOURTH EDITION

David W. Ziegler

WESTERN WASHINGTON UNIVERSITY

LITTLE, BROWN AND COMPANY
BOSTON   TORONTO

Library of Congress Cataloging-in-Publication Data

Ziegler, David W.
  War, peace, and international politics.

  Includes bibliographical references and index.
    1. International relations.   2. War (International
law) 3. Peace. I. Title.
JX1391.Z53   1987   327'.09'04   86-20884
ISBN 0-316-98775-1

Library of Congress Catalog Card Number 86-20884

ISBN 0-316-98775-1

9 8 7 6 5 4 3 2

MV

Published simultaneously in Canada
by Little, Brown & Company (Canada) Limited

Printed in the United States of America

Produced by R. David Newcomer Associates

This book is for
my beloved wife Rena

אֵשֶׁת־חַיִל מִי יִמְצָא

Preface

Who reads prefaces?

Perhaps you are a student. It may even be that you are a student who is trying to avoid getting started on a reading assignment from this book. If so, I warn you that the preface is less interesting than the book itself. With help from my own students, I have tried to be simple enough to be understood, detailed enough to be vivid, and coherent enough to hold your attention.

Perhaps you are a teacher, considering whether to use this book in your classes. If so, I want to set out the assumptions on which the book was written.

First, most students today, while intellectually capable, are deficient in factual knowledge about the historical and contemporary world. As a rule they have no trouble grasping concepts, but one cannot assume that they have an extensive historical background. Therefore the book tries to provide as much background as is feasible in a limited space.

Second, most students enroll in international relations courses to meet a graduation requirement or to satisfy their curiosity about the world—not because they expect to become either the Secretary of State or a professor of international relations. Thus a heavy emphasis on the latest academic trends is irrelevant to their needs. Questions of methodology and sophisticated tools of analysis are at best of only passing interest. This book draws on recent research (for example, Robert Axelrod's work on the Prisoner's Dilemma) only where substantive results are of interest to the nonspecialist.

Third, students will learn more from a coherent story than from an encyclopedia. Rather than try to cover everything that goes under the name of international relations, I have tried to fit major topics into the framework of war and peace. War is not the only topic in international relations, but it is a central and major one. Large defense budgets and the debate over the threat of nuclear war attest to its current relevance.

In this book I have tried to avoid faddishness. Not so long ago, the demise of the nation-state was widely heralded; the state-centric approach was condemned as obsolete. Such topics as human rights, Eurocommunism, multinational corporations, and international regimes were deemed more important. The claims made for some of these topics now appear to have been exaggerated. This book takes a conservative approach. It seeks to begin at the beginning, with nineteenth-century wars and nineteenth-century views of international politics. Modern trends are more easily understood in the context in which they appear. Even if fads change, students will be left with a foundation in history and traditional concepts. This is not to say that the book ignores all trends. Most topics of current interest and relevance are discussed but they do not form the central theme.

Because the reader of this preface may be someone who comes across this book accidentally, let me explain it briefly. This book is about international relations, which is the study of interactions among states and other actors in global politics. It starts by examining a unique characteristic of international relations—war. It seeks first to discover the causes of war by looking at historical cases. From these cases it makes some generalizations about causes of war. It then looks at suggested approaches to eliminating war or, if not eliminating it, reducing its incidence or ameliorating its effects. Ten different approaches are assessed for weakness and strength. Finally, the book examines the possible causes of war in the world today. You may not find the book as gripping as the average novel but it is hoped that you find it considerably more interesting than the average textbook.

I would like to thank people who were helpful to me in writing this book. Patrick Morgan of Washington State University provided me with a model of light style and solid content in his *Theories and Approaches to International Politics*. He also read and commented on the manuscript, as did Daniel R. Kempton of the University of Illinois at Urbana-Champaign, John D. Molloy of Michigan State University, and James H. Toner of Norwich University. I found their suggestions helpful, even though I did not accept them all.

I am especially grateful to my wife Rena for the time and energy she took from her own professional life to read and comment on many drafts of the manuscript. I was fortunate to have an alert and intelligent reader without any training in the field of international relations who could tell me when I was being clear and when I wasn't. For whatever clarity this book may have, she deserves equal credit.

Contents

INTRODUCTION   1

**PART I
CAUSES OF WAR: HISTORICAL CASES
AND HYPOTHESES**   5

CHAPTER 1   THE WARS FOR GERMAN UNIFICATION   7
The German National Problem   8
Otto von Bismarck and the "Realistic" Analysis   10
The Use of War Against Denmark and Austria   11
The Decisive Role of Technology   14
The Use of War Against France   15
Bismarck as a Political Realist   17

CHAPTER 2   WORLD WAR I AND WORLD WAR II   20
War as "Total War"   21
Technology and the Outbreak of World War I   23
Other Causes of World War I   24

The Role of Technology in Warfare: Poison Gas, Submarines   26
The Results of World War I: The Versailles Treaty   28
German Reaction to Versailles and the Rise of Hitler   31
Hitler's Foreign Policy and Western Appeasement   32
Escalation into Total War   35
The Role of Technology in Warfare: Airplanes, the Atomic Bomb   36
The Results of World War II   38

CHAPTER 3   THE COLD WAR AND THE KOREAN WAR   **41**
Origins of United States–Soviet Rivalry: Iran, Greece, Turkey   41
The Truman Doctrine and the Marshall Plan   45
The Cold War in Europe: Poland, Berlin   47
Bipolarity   49
Hot War in Korea   50
Causes of the Korean War   51
The Course of the Korean War   54
The Practice of Limited War   57

CHAPTER 4   WARS IN THE MIDDLE EAST   **61**
Zionism   61
Arab Nationalism   63
Issues Leading to War   65
The 1948 War   66
The 1956 War   66
The 1967 War   69
The 1973 War   72
Israel and Lebanon   75

CHAPTER 5   WAR IN THE 1970's   **79**
Pakistan and the Bengalis   79
India's Preparation for War   82
War Between India and Pakistan   83
The Problem of Cyprus   84
Crisis in 1974: The Coup Against Makarios   86
War Between Turkey and Cyprus   87
Uganda and Tanzania   90
Cambodia and Vietnam   91

**CHAPTER 6   THE PRINCIPLES OF
INTERNATIONAL RELATIONS**   **94**
The Traditional State-Centric View   95
State and Nation   97

Sovereignty   98
Recognition   100
Non-State Actors   103
Implications of International Anarchy   105

CHAPTER 7   CAUSES OF WAR   **110**
Causal Explanation   110
Causation and War   112
Human Nature: Konrad Lorenz   112
"Troublemakers": Power Groups, Merchants of Death, Wicked
   States   116
Critique of Troublemakers as the Cause of War   117
Nationalism: Mazzini   120

**PART II
APPROACHES TO PEACE**   **125**

CHAPTER 8   WORLD GOVERNMENT   **127**
World Government Theory   127
Arguments in Favor of World Government   131
Advocates of World Government   133
Practical Details of the World State   134
Resistance to World Government   138
Consensus Versus Coercion   140
A World Police Force   142

CHAPTER 9   INTERNATIONAL LAW   **146**
What Law Is   146
Examples of International Law   147
Sources of Law   151
Reasons for Observing Treaties   153
Difficulties with International Law   156
Two Revolutions and Their Effects   159
World Peace Through World Law?   161

CHAPTER 10   BALANCE OF POWER   **165**
The Balance of Power as International System   165
The System in Operation, 1740–1763   168
Balance of Power and the Control of International Violence   173
A Return to the Balance of Power?   174
The Balance of Power in the Contemporary World   176

CHAPTER 11   COLLECTIVE SECURITY   **181**
What Collective Security Is   181
The Advantages of Collective Security   182
An Attempt to Implement Collective Security: The League of
    Nations   184
Reasons for the Failure of the League   190
The Problems of Collective Security   191
Regional Collective Security   198

CHAPTER 12   ARMAMENTS   **204**
"If You Want Peace, Prepare for War"   204
Quantitative Arms Races: The Pre–World War I Race and
    Worst-Case Estimation   207
Technological Arms Race: SALT I and the Interim Agreement   208
Arms Races as Action–Reaction   211
Other Sources of Arms Races   213
Arms Races and War   215
Costs and Hazards of the Arms Race   216

CHAPTER 13   THE BALANCE OF TERROR   **221**
The Nature of Nuclear Weapons   221
The Difference That Nuclear Weapons Made   223
Deterrence   226
Minimum Deterrence   227
MAD and Its Critics   229
Damage Limitation   231
Nuclear Winter   233
Strategic Defense Initiative: A Way Out?   235

CHAPTER 14   ARMS CONTROL   **240**
Accidental and Unauthorized Attacks: The Hot Line,
    Reconnaissance   241
Excessive Collateral Damage and Thresholds   246
War Termination and Cost Reduction   248
Difficulties with Arms Control   249
A Farewell to Arms Control? SALT II   250

CHAPTER 15   DISARMAMENT   **256**
Ways to Disarm   256
A History of Disarmament Agreements: From Rush–Bagot to
    General and Complete Disarmament   261
Obstacles to Disarmament   264

Unilateral Initiatives   267
Charles Osgood's GRIT   268
The Evolution of Cooperation   273

CHAPTER 16   DIPLOMACY   277
The Structure of Diplomacy   278
Modern Technology and Diplomacy   279
Duties of Diplomats   282
Diplomatic Procedure   285
The Value of Diplomacy   288
The New Diplomacy and Its Problems   291
Limitations of Diplomacy   294

CHAPTER 17   THIRD PARTIES   297
The Value of Third Parties   298
Mediation: Cyprus, Indo-China, the Middle East   300
Arbitration: The Rann of Cutch, the *Alabama* Claims   303
Adjudication: The "Lobster War," The Corfu Channel   304
An Evaluation: El Chamizal, Spanish Sahara   308

CHAPTER 18   THE UNITED NATIONS   313
The UN and State Sovereignty: Charter Provisions   313
The UN and Collective Security   315
The UN and the Korean War   316
The UN and Prevention of War   318
Contributions of the UN to Peace   322
UN Peacekeeping Forces: UNEF, ONUC, UNFICYP   326
Limitations of Peacekeeping   329

CHAPTER 19   FUNCTIONALISM   334
Functionalism's Three-Pronged Attack   335
Robbers' Cave and Middle East Water   337
A Critique of Functionalism   338

PART III
SOURCES OF CONFLICT IN THE
CONTEMPORARY WORLD   345

CHAPTER 20   THE SOVIET UNION   347
Declaratory Policy: Marxism–Leninism   347
Declaratory Policy: Peaceful Coexistence   349

Soviet Foreign Policy   350
Military Capability   352
Conventional and Theater Capability   355

CHAPTER 21   THE UNITED STATES   **358**
United States Declaratory Policy: Human Rights   358
United States Declaratory Policy: The Reagan Doctrine   361
United States Declaratory Policy: A Sense of Mission   362
United States Capabilities: Military Power   364
United States Policy: Covert Action   366
United States Policy: Inconsistencies   368

CHAPTER 22   CHINA, JAPAN, EUROPE   **373**
China as a Threat to World Peace   373
China's Prospects   376
Japan: A Resurgence of Power?   377
Japanese Military Capability and Intentions   380
Europe and the Beginning of Integration   383
The Europe of the Six: ECSC, Euratom, EEC   385
The Enlargement of the European Community   387

CHAPTER 23   THE THIRD WORLD   **391**
Rise to Prominence   391
Definition of "Third World"   392
Third World Influence on War and Peace   394
Sources of Conflict Within the Third World   395
Primordial Ties as a Source of Conflict   397
Nationalism and War   398
Nuclear Proliferation   399

CHAPTER 24   NON-STATE ACTORS   **403**
The Multinational Enterprise: Growth and Influence   404
Criticism of Multinational Enterprises   405
The Multinational Enterprise Versus the State   406
Producers' Cartels   408
International Terrorism   411
Incidence of International Terrorism   413
International Action Against Terrorism   416

CHAPTER 25   ECONOMIC ISSUES   **420**
Trade Wars   420
GATT and Free Trade   422

Nontariff Barriers to Trade   423
Domestic Pressures   424
A Specific Case: United States Versus Japan   425
The International Monetary System   426
The Bretton Woods System   429
The New International Economic Order   432
Weaknesses of the NIEO   434
The Fate of the NIEO   436
Third World Debt   437

   CHAPTER 26   GLOBAL ISSUES   **441**
Population   441
Consequences of Population Growth   443
Food   445
Nonrenewable Resources   448
Environmental Pollution   449
Predicted Consequences for International Politics   452
An Evaluation   455

   CONCLUSION   **458**

   INDEX   **465**

WAR,
PEACE, and
INTERNATIONAL
POLITICS

Introduction

Between 1939 and 1945 about 60 million people—3 per cent of the world's population at the time—died as a result of World War II.[1] It was the greatest catastrophe, natural or man-made, in human history. Most of the death and destruction was caused by weapons that we now call conventional. The much more destructive atomic weapon was used only in the closing days of the war. Today nuclear weapons have become standard in the arsenal of major states—the United States alone has about 30,000 of them.[2]

Since the first two atomic bombs were dropped on Japan in 1945, no more atomic weapons have been used in war. Yet the damage such weapons could do if they were used makes their mere existence a threat to human survival. We worry about mercury in the sea water, phosphates in the drainpipes, and photochemical smog in the atmosphere, but smog over Los Angeles is a minor irritant compared to radioactive fallout.

The existence of nuclear weapons has not prevented non-nuclear wars. At least a dozen have been fought since 1945, with the United States involved in two of them.[3] And if states have not spent all of their time fighting wars, they have spent much of it preparing to fight them. In 1985 the total expenditure of all countries on all kinds of weapons was estimated at $940 billion.[4] Furthermore, the resources that states devote to preparing for war have been increasing. Military spending in 1983 was more than 30 per cent higher than it was ten years earlier.[5]

We must conclude that war remains a major problem in the last quarter of the twentieth century. My intention in this book is to introduce you to international relations by focusing on this problem. War is not the only problem of international relations, and so this book does not exhaust the field. But war is a central problem, and the possibility of resort to war affects other aspects of international relations. Whatever else we may look at, we cannot avoid looking at war. In fact, in looking at war, we will touch on most of the other subjects important in international relations.

War is conflict among states carried on by their armed forces.[6] To distinguish war from border skirmishes and other minor incidents we usually say it must reach a certain magnitude (for example, at least 1,000 soldiers killed in battle over a year).[7] It would be ideal if we could systematically study all the wars in the last hundred years, but such an exhaustive study would be out of place here. At the same time we cannot discuss such subjects as the cause of war or proposals for preventing it without some knowledge about actual wars. We must test theories against historical facts. What follows in Part I is a somewhat detailed history of seven wars (or groups of wars) fought in the last hundred years. These include the most destructive of the wars—World War I (1914–1918), World War II (1939–1945), and the Korean War (1950–1953). By way of background to World War I, we will look at the wars of German unification (1864–1871), which preceded and in some ways prepared the way for it. To balance our account, we will also look at several recent wars—India and Pakistan (1971), the Middle East (1948, 1956, 1967, 1973, 1982), Turkey and Cyprus (1974), Uganda and Tanzania (1978–1979), and Cambodia, Vietnam, and China (1978–1980).

After looking at some of the major wars of the last hundred years, we will look at what people have said about the causes of war in general. Then in Part II we will critically examine some of the proposed ways to put an end to war. Finally, in Part III, we will examine some sources of tension in the world today that keep the possibility of a war a major concern in international politics.

NOTES

1. Quincy Wright, *A Study of War,* 2nd ed. (Chicago: University of Chicago Press, 1965), p. 1543.

2. Thomas B. Cochran, William M. Arkin, and Milton M. Hoenig, *Nuclear Weapon Databook,* Vol. 1: *U.S. Nuclear Forces and Capabilities* (Cambridge: Ballinger, 1984), pp. 38–40. The arsenal was estimated at 26,000 in 1983; the Department of Defense announced it expected the number to grow by several thousand.

3. These include Palestine (1948), Korea (1950–1953), Hungary (1956), Middle East (1956), India and China (1962), India and Pakistan (1965), Middle East (1967), Honduras and El Salvador (1969), India and Pakistan (1971), Middle East (1973), Cyprus (1974), Vietnam (1965–1975), Uganda and Tanzania (1978–1979), China and Vietnam (1979), and three wars

---

continuing through the early 1980's—Vietnam and Cambodia, Russia and Afghanistan, and Iran and Iraq. See Melvin Small and J. David Singer, *Resort to Arms* (Beverly Hills: Sage, 1982), p. 59.

4. U.S. Arms Control and Disarmament Agency, *World Military Expenditures and Arms Transfers, 1985* (Washington, D.C., 1985), p. 3.

5. Ibid., p. 4.

6. This brief definition by Quincy Wright appears in his article "War" in the *Encyclopedia of the Social Sciences*. He gives a more detailed definition in *A Study of War*, pp. 8–13.

7. This criterion was used by J. David Singer and Melvin Small, *The Wages of War, 1816–1965* (New York: John Wiley, 1972).

PART I

CAUSES OF WAR: HISTORICAL CASES AND HYPOTHESES

Chapter 1

The Wars for German Unification

War is a normal instrument of state policy. It is a means for achieving goals in the same way as diplomacy is. When diplomacy fails a state turns to war.

If you are a typical reader in the second part of the twentieth century, these views probably seem immoral and irrational as well. Yet only a hundred years ago, they would have seemed obvious wisdom to include in a book on international politics. Writers frequently quoted the formulation of these ideas by a German military writer at the beginning of the nineteenth century, Carl von Clausewitz. "War," he wrote, "is mere continuation of policy by other means . . . a real political instrument . . . a continuation of political commerce."[1]

One reason Clausewitz's ideas were so widely accepted one hundred years ago is that they seemed to be finding their perfect expression in the policy of Chancellor Otto von Bismarck of Prussia. The goal he was pursuing was the unification of Germany under Prussian leadership. On three occasions between 1864 and 1870, Prussia resorted to war to achieve this goal. The reason for going to war in those days was self-evident: War enabled a state to get what it wanted. You might say that wars were viewed no differently from the way we view superhighways. Both are used to obtain something desirable. Wars take a toll in human lives; superhighways do the same. We could save lives by abolishing superhighways, but then we would have to do without the benefits that superhighways bring. Wars are the same. To see why wars were viewed as useful instruments of policy, we must turn to historical circumstances in the second half of the nineteenth century.

THE GERMAN NATIONAL PROBLEM

The Europe of 1848 was different in many ways from the Europe of today. Among the countries active in international politics, only England and France were much as we know them now (see Figure 1.1). Russia was much larger, including at that time parts of the lands that are today Finland, Poland, Rumania, and Turkey. Austria was also much larger, including parts of what are today Italy, Yugoslavia, Hungary, and Czechoslovakia. On the other hand, Italy and Germany were not single states at all but were divided into much smaller units. The area called Germany was more like a miniature United Nations—a confederation of thirty-eight states held together in a very loose organization. Some of these thirty-eight states were tiny, no larger than

Figure 1.1   Europe in 1848

a typical county in the United States; others were good-sized countries, such as Prussia and Austria. The constitution of the German Confederation required unanimity of all thirty-eight states on important matters, guaranteeing only that most of the time it did nothing.

Events in Europe in the nineteenth century had encouraged many Germans to think of creating a single state in which all Germans could be combined. This was the meaning of their national hymn, *Deutschland, Deutschland über alles*. The words seem threatening when translated into English as "Germany, Germany over all," but to those who heard it in the nineteenth century it meant they should put aside their parochial feelings as Bavarians or Saxons or Prussians and think of themselves as Germans above all. There were several reasons for this growth of national feeling. Throughout Europe the idea of nationalism was winning acceptance. More and more people accepted it as right that those who speak the same language and share the same customs belong together in the same state. The example of the Italians, who developed this feeling some years earlier, was a big influence on the Germans. German nationalism also grew because of the belief that only when the many small German states were united would they be able to keep other countries from pushing them around, both dictating policy to them and using their territory as a battlefield. Napoleon had had an easy time taking over Germany in 1806, running into real trouble only when he reached Russia. The obvious power of a unified French or Russian national state was not lost on the Germans.

If agreement was growing on the need for a German state, disagreement continued on how to go about achieving it. Part of the argument was on leadership—would it be Prussian or Austrian? Prussia had a reputation for being militaristic and rigid. Many smaller German states supported Austrian leadership because they expected that under Austria more local rights would be respected. On the other hand some Germans (as well as some outsiders such as the English) favored Prussian leadership because they saw that only Prussian leadership would be dynamic enough to fashion a state strong enough to balance the French. But Prussia's conservative leaders were not sure they wanted to lead a national movement. Today we associate nationalism with right-wing conservatives, but in the nineteenth century things were reversed. German nationalists usually were liberals who believed in constitutional government, guaranteed civil liberties, and participation by citizens in government decisions. Prussian conservatives viewed with suspicion a movement that would have given more power to the masses even if it would have increased the size of the Prussian state. They also believed that the conservative principle of monarchic solidarity called for their cooperation with the monarchy of Austria, even if Austria was Prussia's major rival for German leadership.[2]

German liberal nationalists assembled in the city of Frankfurt in 1848 and drew up a petition asking for a new unified German state with the king of Prussia as its head. The king rejected the offer. As a conservative he could not accept an initiative from the people. He said he didn't want a crown offered from the gutter. With the failure of this attempt, the liberals were at a loss as to what to do next and the movement toward German unification under their leadership died out.

OTTO VON BISMARCK AND THE "REALISTIC" ANALYSIS

Bismarck was no liberal. He had been active in 1848 but had spent his time heaping scorn on the liberal efforts. It was because he had a reputation as an outspoken conservative that the king of Prussia named him chancellor in 1862. The king had been trying to get the Prussian Parliament to approve funds for building a bigger army and the Parliament was trying in return to get some voice in governmental decisions. Bismarck, on becoming chancellor, broke the deadlock by simply instituting the changes in the army and collecting the taxes without parliamentary approval. Before he took this direct approach, he appeared before the Parliament's budget committee and tried to distract the liberal deputies with the prospect of using the enlarged army for foreign conquest. His words, although they failed at that time to win over the liberals, indicate his own philosophy: "It is not by speeches and resolutions that the great questions of the time are decided . . . but by iron and blood."

Bismarck was unquestionably conservative in his aims. It would be more accurate to call him a patriot than a nationalist. He came from a class of aristocrats known as Junkers and, like them, his loyalty was to the state and its ruling dynasty, not to German culture. He did want to build up the power of the Prussian state, but not in order to unite all German-speaking people. He wanted only to increase Prussia's security.

But in his choice of methods Bismarck was not doctrinaire. "I am still a Junker," he said, "but I recognize realities." One reality in the 1860's was that increasingly a monarch needed popular support. The mid-nineteenth century was a period of growth for the German states, in both population and economics. To cite just one statistic: In 1846 Germany had 1,416 steam engines; in 1861, 10,113. The growth of the economy was accompanied by an increase in the number of groups that crossed the political boundaries of the individual German states. Lawyers, school teachers, and booksellers held conventions of their members representing many states, and these conventions increased national sentiment. National festivals were held by choral societies, hunting societies, and gymnastic societies, at which were emphasized German history and culture. This feeling was so advanced in 1861 that an assassin tried to kill the king of Prussia for not doing enough to bring about German unity. Bismarck recognized that this national sentiment was a source of power and could be used to achieve a unified state, even though he did not share it.

Bismarck also realized that Austria was the major obstacle to German unification. The problem was that the Austrian monarch ruled many non-German lands—Hungary, Czechoslovakia, and Italy, among others—and could not create a strongly centralized state. It would, for one thing, never be able to agree on a common language. A state in which the Hungarians could be happy would not satisfy the aspirations of the German Nationalists; a state that would satisfy them would drive out the Hungarians. Furthermore, Austria was the only other major power in the German Confederation. A new German state could be shaped and dominated by Prussia only if Austria were excluded. Therefore Bismarck was willing to violate a cardinal principle of Prussian conservatives: solidarity with Austria. His willingness to utilize German nationalism even though he did not share it, and to forsake conservative solidarity with Austria, are the basis for what is called Bismarck's "realism." Feelings and even principles were put aside if they got in the way of achieving a major state goal.

Bismarck's speech to the budget committee of the Prussian Parliament, using the phrase "iron and blood" to describe military power, hinted at another element in his realism: his willingness to make use of the army that Prussia was building up. He believed, as Clausewitz had written, that war is an instrument of state policy. But he saw war as only one of several instruments. He also made use of diplomacy, winning over allies, making promises, trading concessions, and all the other devices he could think of. It would be accurate to say that Bismarck did not want war, if he could achieve his aims without it. But that is no better than saying, as you hold up the corner store with your pistol, "I don't want to use this pistol." The important question is: What if the goal cannot be achieved in any other way? For Bismarck, the answer was that using force was preferable to going without achieving his goal.

THE USE OF WAR AGAINST DENMARK AND AUSTRIA

Historians say that Bismarck fought three wars to achieve his aim. This statement suggests a lot more calculation and planning than he actually engaged in. In each case, war was a continuation of a policy already being pursued by other means. War was chosen because the other means were not working and because an opportunity presented itself in which military force could be useful.

The first of these wars was with Denmark, fought in 1864, over the duchies of Schleswig and Holstein (see Figure 1.2). These two duchies, although ruled personally by the Danish king, were not constitutionally a part of Denmark. Complex arrangements such as that were frequent in the nineteenth century. Because large numbers of Germans lived in Holstein and Schleswig, separation of the duchies from Denmark was a passionate issue for German nationalists. Bismarck wanted them separated too, but not, like the liberal nationalists, to be turned into more tiny German states. He wanted to incorporate them into Prussia. They would enlarge Prussia, of course, but more important to Bismarck's long-range plans, they could be used as an issue to separate Austria from political cooperation with the other German states.

Bismarck's chance came when the king of Denmark died without a direct heir and the question arose: Will Schleswig and Holstein go to the new Danish king along with the rest of Denmark, or is another ruler available with a better claim to rule these two states? The German nationalists thought

Figure 1.2   Schleswig and Holstein in 1863

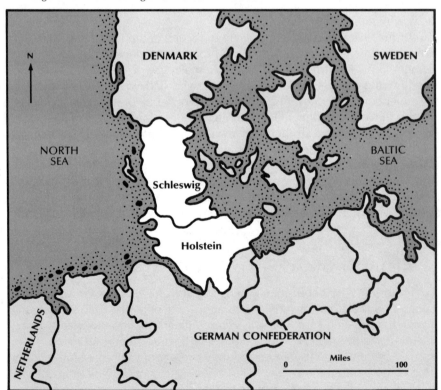

there was in the person of the prince of Augustenburg. Bismarck was willing to use the issue as an excuse to go to war, although he had no intention of letting the prince of Augustenburg ever rule the duchies as an independent state. The new Danish king made matters easier for Bismarck by not only claiming the duchies but also annexing the northern one (Schleswig) to the Danish state, a clear violation of an international treaty. Bismarck used this treaty violation as his reason for going to war. By clever diplomacy he got Austria to join with Prussia alone, making the war a joint Austro–Prussian undertaking rather than one of the whole German Confederation. This was his first move in detaching Austria from the other German states. The small states might have followed Austria, as they would not have followed Prussia, but Austria offered no lead. The war was over quickly, the two big German states being more than a match for little Denmark, and after the war Bismarck's diplomatic moves succeeded again. First he got the Austrians to agree to joint sovereignty over the two duchies, instead of turning them into an independent state. Then he got the Austrians to agree to separate administrations for them, with Prussia taking Schleswig and Austria taking Holstein.

All this, we can see now, was designed to maneuver Austria into a more isolated position. But it would be a mistake to believe that Bismarck had a carefully worked out plan for going to war with Austria. War was only one of several possibilities. If he could have accomplished his aims by diplomacy alone he undoubtedly would have done so. The agreement dividing the administration of the duchies merely provided a rich source of friction between the two countries that could be exploited if the occasion arose.

The moment came two years later, but only after Bismarck's diplomacy had isolated Austria internationally. The major European powers he had to worry about were Russia, England, and France. Prussia had won Russia to its side because of a common concern over Polish nationalism, which threatened both states. Prussia had the support of Britain because the British saw Prussia as a potential balance to an enemy they feared more, France. Yet Prussia also had the support of France, both because the French ruler was eager to do anything that would help the Italian nationalists struggling against Austria and because Bismarck hinted to the French ruler that an Austrian defeat just might be followed by some territorial expansion for the French somewhere along the Rhine. Austria made Bismarck's job easier. Because it considered itself militarily superior to Prussia it did not assiduously search for allies.

By the military standards of the time, Austria's smugness was justified. Yet we call the war that Prussia fought against Austria in 1866 the Seven Weeks' War because it took Prussia only that long to defeat Austria. The startling Prussian victory was made possible by a factor that has loomed increasingly large in every war since then—modern industrial technology.

In addition to showing the use of war as an instrument of policy, Bismarck's wars also mark the entrance of that technology as a decisive factor in international politics. The development that led to the atomic bomb and the intercontinental missile had its beginnings here.

THE DECISIVE ROLE OF TECHNOLOGY

Three major technological developments contributed to the Prussian victory. The most important one may surprise you. It was not some new type of cannon or explosive but the railroad. It was so important to the Prussian army that the general staff had a special Railway Subsection. It was important in two ways. It made possible rapid mobilization of troops from reserve status to front line units. Soldiers who were to be used in combat did not have to be kept in a perpetually combat-ready status in fortifications along the frontier. They could be held in reserve at home, even while working at civilian occupations. When war was declared, the railroads could transport them and their equipment rapidly to the front. The railroad also enabled the Prussians, who lacked overall superiority in numbers, nevertheless to achieve superiority in the one spot where it counted, the battlefield. Rapid transportation meant that the Prussian general staff could achieve the condition that wins battles—concentrated firepower—without leaving other areas of their frontier long exposed to the numerically superior but much slower-moving enemy.

Closely linked to the railroad was a second technological innovation, the telegraph. It enabled mobilization orders to go out rapidly. It enabled the Railway Subsection to control trains. Most important, it enabled one general to control a much larger army than had been possible in the past. Pictures of Napoleon at Waterloo or Lee at Gettysburg show how it used to be done: a general sitting on a horse on high ground, overseeing the entire battlefield. When more men were engaged than could easily be seen from one spot, battles got out of control (as both Napoleon and Lee discovered). The telegraph expanded the commander's control of his troops so much that the Prussian commander, Helmut von Moltke, was able to direct the entire Prussian campaign without leaving Berlin, yet with firmer control over military operations than Napoleon or Lee could have hoped for. The railroads gave the advantage to the smaller Prussian army. The telegraph had the potential, in future wars, of making it advantageous to use much larger armies than ever before.

The third technological innovation was a new kind of rifle, loaded not from the muzzle but from the back. An obvious advantage was that it took less time to feed a shell into the breech of a rifle than it did to ram powder and lead balls down the muzzle. Another was that it enabled Prussian soldiers to fire repeatedly while lying flat. Commanders could concentrate fire-power by placing soldiers very close to each other, some standing, some crouching, and some lying flat.[3]

Prussia won the war in seven weeks. As a result, Austria gave up its membership in the German Confederation and its influence among the small German states. Prussia incorporated a few of the small German states, although by no means all. The remaining ones in the northern part of Germany were brought together in a North German Confederation. Unlike the old German Confederation it replaced, no absolute veto was granted to each state. Rather, voting was weighted, with Prussia getting the clear advantage.

chassepotAlmost as important as what Prussia did after its victory is what it did not do. After defeating the Austrian army at the decisive battle of Sadowa, the Prussian army did not pursue the Austrian army across the Danube River. It did not hold a victory parade through the streets of Vienna, although the king of Prussia would have been happy to get back at Austria in this way for past humiliations. (The principle of conservative solidarity seems to have been forgotten in the heady experience of victory.) Prussia did not annex portions of Austria near its own borders, even though some justification could have been made for incorporation. This policy of restraint was achieved by some effort on Bismarck's part, against the desires of the king and some of his advisers. Bismarck realized, as the king did not, that the work of German unification was not yet completed, and a humiliated and bitter Austria would be a potential ally for the country that now stood in Prussia's way, France.

THE USE OF WAR AGAINST FRANCE

France opposed a takeover of the remaining south German states (those not incorporated into the North German Confederation) and Bismarck saw that only if French power were somehow nullified would German unification be possible. For four years he tried to eliminate French influence and finally in 1870 he had his chance. France, mainly because of the erratic policies of its ruler, Napoleon III, was diplomatically isolated. The French populace, well aware of growing Prussian military and economic strength, was eager to go to war to demonstrate that they were still "number one" in power on the continent. By the simple device of editing a telegram to make a normal diplomatic interview look like an insulting one, Bismarck provoked the French into declaring war on Germany.

The Franco–Prussian War, which began in 1870, consisted of six weeks of fighting, followed by six months of chaos. The German army won so startling a victory that there was no French government left to surrender. Again the new technology was decisive. Two weeks after war was declared, the Germans by using their railroads had mobilized and sent to the front 1,180,000 troops. The French in this time had mobilized only 330,000.

The Franco–Prussian War revealed another lesson of modern technology: It was not the mere possession of advanced weapons that was decisive, but the practiced ability to use them and the knowledge to use them well. For the French lost the war although they had two weapons superior to those of the Germans. The French version of the breech-loading rifle (the *chassepot*) was twice as efficient as the German one (the needle-gun), but the French were not as well instructed in using their weapon. Furthermore, the French used a weapon the Germans did not even have, the machine gun. But they used it poorly; they treated machine guns like artillery pieces and deployed them singly in the midst of infantry. The Germans simply concentrated their artillery on a machine gun until it was destroyed, then advanced. Only in World War I did the French learn to group machine guns so that each could defend the others.

Figure 1.3   Alsace, Lorraine, and the Saar

Eventually the Germans found someone with whom they could make peace and a peace agreement was signed. But this time Bismarck was not able to exercise the restraint over the king and army that he had after the war with Austria. The euphoria of victory was too much. A new German Empire was proclaimed, which was certainly justifiable, but the site chosen for the proclamation was not. It was not in Germany, as you might expect, but in France, in the palace of the most magnificent of the French kings, the Versailles Palace of Louis XIV. (The French did not forget this humiliation. The Germans had to sign the treaty acknowledging their defeat in 1919 in the Palace of Versailles.) On top of this the Germans held a victory parade through the streets of Paris. The French had to pay an indemnity to Germany of 6 billion French francs, to cover the cost of the war. All these were one-time occurrences that were soon over (although not entirely forgotten). But the Germans went on to create a permanent source of resentment by annexing French territory.

The Germans annexed the French provinces of Alsace and Lorraine (see Figure 1.3). They had some justification for annexing Alsace; most of its people could speak German; it had belonged to German kings before 1648. In the case of Lorraine, Germany had no nationalist justification. The people spoke French and wanted to remain part of France. But Lorraine had a major iron and steel industry, as well as some major forts. The Germans annexed it for the contribution it would make to German military strength. Bismarck did successfully oppose some of the more extreme demands the Prussian army made, so that French fortifications were not dismantled and the strength of the French army was not restricted. But what was done was enough. The slogan of the French politicians, contemplating their day of revenge, was, "Never speak of it, always think of it." In 1914, when the fighting began between Germany and France, one of the first gestures of an enthusiastic French population was to remove the mourning crepe that had decked the statue to Lorraine in Paris.

BISMARCK AS A POLITICAL REALIST

Bismarck is a controversial figure for historians, especially for his role in internal German developments. But even among his critics the characteristics of his foreign policy are often held up for admiration. One of these was his ability to keep war limited to achieving specific political goals. Clausewitz, in one of his formulations, wrote that "war is an act of violence to compel an opponent to fulfill our will." Wars are not fought to extend a country's winning streak but to accomplish some purpose. When that purpose is achieved, the war stops. Prussia's war with Austria was not fought to dismantle the Austrian Empire or to gain Austrian territory but simply to exclude Austrian influence from German affairs. The war with Austria lasted only seven weeks because that was long enough to achieve that limited purpose. All three wars were fought to achieve German unification and once that was accomplished, in 1871, Bismarck engaged in no more wars. Prussia did not embark on a program of conquest, as Napoleon had done earlier and Hitler was to do later. To use modern terminology, Bismarck had a plan for "war termination." Unlike the Japanese after their brilliant tactical victory at Pearl Harbor, he had plans for the war beyond the action on the opening day. War was a coherent part of his policy, not a rash or desperate act.[4]

Bismarck is also admired for his diplomatic flexibility. He recognized the need to prepare diplomatically for any use of force. He was careful to isolate potential opponents before beginning a war. He was also careful to avoid treating a defeated country as a permanent enemy. Austria was treated generously after the Seven Weeks' War, not out of benevolence on Bismarck's part but to encourage Austria to remain neutral in what he already saw would be the coming struggle between France and Prussia.

In choosing allies Bismarck was not motivated by principle or sentiment but by the interest of the state. At one time he refused to side with France in supporting Italian nationalists in the state of Sardinia. Such a refusal might have been expected of him, because he was a conservative and conservatives were hostile to nationalism, but Bismarck's explanation was, "I do not go with France and Sardinia—not because I hold it to be morally wrong, but because I consider it harmful to the interest of our security."[5] This overriding concern with the interests of the state, and particularly with interests defined in terms of power, was the essence of his realism. Realists are usually contrasted with idealists. For the realists the power of armies, railroads, and heavy industry is decisive; the idealists base their policy on ideals and principles, whether monarchic solidarity or democratic nationalism. The success of Bismarck's policies converted many people to realism.

The accomplishments of Bismarck in achieving German unification were

Table 1.1 BATTLE DEATHS IN WARS FOR GERMAN
          UNIFICATION

Wars	Total battle deaths	Prussian battle deaths
War with Denmark, 1864	4,500	1,000
War with Austria, 1866	36,100	10,000
War with France, 1870–71	187,500	40,000

Source: Data from J. David Singer and Melvin Small, *The Wages of War, 1816–1965* (New York: John Wiley, 1972), pp. 62–63.

not unnoticed by the other states of Europe. The three wars that led to unification provided a number of obvious lessons, which other states dutifully learned and applied to their own policies. As time passed, it turned out that these lessons were wrong, but that did not make them less influential.

First was the lesson that Clausewitz was right, that war is a useful instrument of policy. Bismarck, with his policy of iron and blood, had accomplished what the liberals with their petitions and assemblies had not. To be sure, the wars were destructive, as you see in Table 1.1. Large numbers of soldiers died (although the number was lower if you were on the winning side). But wars were not disruptive because they were so rapid. That was another lesson of these wars. The fighting was measured in mere weeks. Too long a war, people feared, would disrupt the industrial economies of the countries fighting them. This was seen as a barrier to any drawn-out war. Among the demands imposed by war was that armies depended on reservists who had to be drawn away from their civilian jobs for the duration of the war. If they were gone too long, industrial strength would decline and industrial strength was seen as the basis for military prowess. That was the third lesson. The German military victory had depended on the German railroad network, the German steel industry, and all the other advances of the new industrial technology. Technology was considered decisive; not only the possession of modern weapons such as breech-loading rifles but practice in using them and careful planning long in advance were necessary.

The years following the wars of Bismarck were peaceful ones for Europe. Some wars did occur, but on the fringes—the Boer War in South Africa, the wars in the Balkans. In the meantime the military staffs were busily applying the lessons of the Bismarck wars, acquiring new weapons, training soldiers in their use, drawing up detailed mobilization schedules, all in an effort to be among the winners and not the losers of the next rapid war.

NOTES

1. *Vom Kriege (On War),* originally published 1832, Chapter I, Part 24.

2. There are a number of standard works on Bismarck and the creation of modern Germany. A very readable one is by Hajo Holborn, *A History of Modern Germany, 1840–1945* (New York: Alfred A. Knopf, 1969).

3. Bernard Brodie and Fawn Brodie, *From Crossbow to H-Bomb* (Bloomington, Ind.: Indiana University Press, 1973), Chapter 6; Richard A. Preston, Sydney F. Wise, and Herman O. Werner, *Men in Arms* (New York: Frederick A. Praeger, 1962), Chapter 15.

4. A general discussion of this problem, although without specific reference to Bismarck, is Fred Charles Iklé, *Every War Must End* (New York: Columbia University Press, 1971).

5. Otto Pflanze, *Bismarck and the Development of Germany* (Princeton: Princeton University Press, 1963), p. 134.

Chapter 2

World War I and World War II

For the forty years following the wars of Bismarck, the military staffs of all the major European countries based their planning on three lessons learned in those wars. Wars are an inexpensive means of attaining foreign policy goals. Because they are short, they do not disrupt economic and political life back home. The side that strikes first with the latest weapons will win. World War I showed that all these lessons were wrong.

The war that began in August 1914 was a great shock. It came after four decades when major European countries had not been at war with each other; it followed more than a century of no wars at all in the heartland of Europe involving all the major countries. It also cruelly violated the assumption that war was a useful instrument of policy. In the first full month of war, the French demonstrated that they had learned the lessons of rapid mobilization by putting 1,300,000 troops into combat. From that number they suffered in August 1914 alone 600,000 casualties (casualties are troops no longer capable of fighting because they are dead, seriously wounded, captured by the enemy, or missing). On one day alone, July 1, 1916, the British attacked with 140,000 troops and suffered 60,000 casualties. On another occasion it cost the French 160,000 casualties to gain 7,000 yards. At Passchendaele it cost the British 370,000 casualties for no gain at all.

People tend to form their beliefs about social and political conditions

20

on the basis of very little evidence. This was the case in the years before 1914. The peace that Europe had enjoyed in the decades before World War I was not seen as the result of luck (the chance combination of a number of favorable circumstances) but as proof of theories about society. We might call the two most popular views the Myth of Socialist Solidarity and the Myth of Capitalist Solidarity. The socialists, all good followers of Karl Marx, took seriously Marx's statement that "the workingmen have no country."[1] They believed that a German worker, exploited as he was by the German ruling class, would have more sympathy for a French worker than for a German capitalist. Many leaders of the various national parties of socialists believed that a war on a world scale was not possible because the workers would simply refuse to fight. A declaration of war by governments would be met by a declaration of a general strike by socialists, making war impossible. You couldn't run a war without foot soldiers, any more than you could run a factory without workers. The actual outbreak of war quickly shattered this myth—French socialists and German socialists marched off to war against each other, each singing their socialist songs, each convinced that victory by their country would hasten world socialism.

Paralleling the Myth of Socialist Solidarity was the Myth of Capitalist Solidarity, articulated by British writer Norman Angell in his international best seller *The Great Illusion*. Angell argued, convincing millions of readers, that war was not profitable and in fact was harmful to capitalism. Far from making greater profits in time of war, capitalists did much better in peacetime. War interrupted access to international markets and sources of raw materials. A war that lasted any length of time, Angell believed, would destroy the capitalist system. Therefore, there could be no great war—it would be irrational.

WAR AS "TOTAL WAR"

It quickly became apparent that the war that began in August 1914 was not going to be another of the quick, decisive wars of the late nineteenth century. As months passed and no decisive victories were achieved, more and more men were conscripted into the armies. More and more resources were devoted to war production. Civilians far from the front were affected as much as the soldiers by such things as rationing food, mobilization into munitions production, and (later in the war) air raids from dirigibles. The German economy was put under a central direction so pervasive that it was called "war socialism." A German first used the name for this new experience: "total war."

Before all this became apparent, many people in all countries welcomed

At first
War was welcomed

the coming of the war. Crowds gathered in Paris to cheer the reservists marching off to their units. Germans gathered in a square and sang, "Now Thank We All Our God." A British poet wrote, "Now, God be thanked Who has matched us with His hour."[2] The myth of the short, decisive war was even more entrenched than those about Socialist Solidarity or Capitalist Solidarity. Yet it was held on the basis of equally flimsy evidence. True, the three wars Prussia had fought for German unification were short and decisive. But there had been other wars which did not conform to this model; as with many pieces of evidence that do not fit a hypothesis, they were ignored. The American Civil War (1861–1865) was long and destructive, although in the end decisive. The British began fighting the Dutch settlers (Boers) in South Africa in 1899 and found it difficult to inflict a decisive defeat on them despite Britain's clear industrial superiority. The Russians and Japanese fought each other in 1904 and 1905. Although the decisive engagements took place at sea, the land warfare was a war for position rather than one of movement, dominated by trenches and barbed wire and other features that would become familiar during World War I.

When military observers brought back reports of these wars, their assessments were dismissed with the argument that the experience did not apply to Europe.[3] The planners went ahead trying to create the conditions that would have led to a perfect victory in the wars of the nineteenth century. The problem was that when both sides were prepared, with rapid mobilization using railroads, central direction using the telegraph, and concentrated firepower using breech-loading rifles, neither could win a decisive, sudden victory. The Germans with their Schlieffen Plan intended to pour into France toward the north along the English Channel; the French with their Plan 17 prepared to pour into Germany toward the south near the Swiss Alps. If both plans had succeeded the armies would have passed each other as in a revolving door. In fact, both plans failed, mostly because of a further technological development that nullified the great advantage the offensive side had enjoyed in the Prussian wars. That development was the machine gun, a model improved over the one used unsuccessfully by the French in the Franco–Prussian War and, more important, now correctly deployed. The bold assaults of the French and, to a lesser extent, of the Germans ground to a bloody halt against the concentrated firepower of this new piece of technology. In this transformation in the first weeks of World War I from a war of movement to one of position we see a lesson that was not to be proved false by future wars: Political leaders and military planners cannot fully comprehend the new technology with which they must work. The one consistent winner of modern warfare has been technology; the consistent loser has been humanity.

Winner in War: Technology
Loser: Humanity

Start of WWI (Assassination Exp)

TECHNOLOGY AND THE OUTBREAK OF WORLD WAR I

Technology, you could argue, was even responsible for the war in the first place. The typical explanation of World War I begins with the assassination of Archduke Franz Ferdinand in Sarajevo on June 28, 1914. But how did this event result in the German invasion of France on August 3, 1914? The connection is not at all obvious and needs to be carefully traced. Archduke Franz Ferdinand was heir to the throne of the Austrian Empire. It was widely believed that when his aging uncle, Emperor Franz Josef, died it would be difficult to keep the diverse nationalities of the empire together. Germans in Austria, Czechs in Bohemia, Magyars in Hungary, Serbs in Bosnia—each would want their own state. The problem in Bosnia, where Franz Ferdinand was visiting when he was shot, was acute because its inhabitants made up only about half of the Serb nation; the rest were in the neighboring independent state of Serbia. To make matters worse, Archduke Franz Ferdinand was visiting the Bosnian capital of Sarajevo on June 28, a day of national importance to the Serbs, commemorating a national defeat centuries before. Sending the archduke to visit on this day was like having the Prince of Wales visit Dublin on Easter Sunday. It is not surprising that young Serb nationalists, with weapons acquired from a semiofficial Serbian organization, sneaked across the border and assassinated him.

The Austrians were aware that this was part of the Serbian nationalist attack on their control of Bosnia and on July 23, 1914, sent an ultimatum to Serbia, demanding that that country curb nationalist agitation for the liberation of the Serbs in Bosnia. An ultimatum is a demand for some kind of behavior coupled with a threat that will be implemented after a set time has elapsed if the demand is not met. Despite a basically conciliatory reply by Serbia, when the time ran out Austria chose to declare war on Serbia. The Serbs had been issued a similar ultimatum in 1909 and had complied fully with it then, but in 1914 they were less willing to be totally subservient because they were receiving more support from Russia. Russia, in the name of Slavic solidarity, encouraged the Serbs to stand up to the Austrians and, to back them up, on July 29 ordered mobilization of the Russian army to be held in readiness for possible use against Austria. The Russian tsar showed some hesitation, at first agreeing to mobilization and then canceling it, but the next day (July 30) Russian mobilization went into effect. It was this act that brought in the Germans.

German preparation for war followed the Schlieffen Plan, which rested on several assumptions. One was that any major war in Europe would be for the Germans a two-front war, against Russia in the east and against France

German preparation for the war.

France / Russia
> Germany

Voto

(allied to Russia) in the west. Another assumption was that the huge Russian army would be impossible to defeat; the most the Germans could hope to do would be to keep the Russian army from defeating them. The one advantage that the Germans had, the Schlieffen Plan assumed, was technological superiority, particularly the ability to mobilize quickly. They assumed they could mobilize in two weeks; the Russians, with more territory and a less-developed railway network, would need six weeks. Therefore, the Schlieffen Plan called for a major offensive first against France, to knock it out of the war, before turning the German army to the more difficult task of fighting the Russian army. For this reason, the Russian mobilization was greeted with alarm in Berlin. If the Schlieffen Plan were to work (and for all practical purposes it was the only plan the Germans had), then it was essential that the Germans begin mobilizing as soon as the Russians did. Otherwise they would lose the advantage afforded them by their superior technology. Never mind that the Russian mobilization was directed against Austria. The crucial factor, in German eyes, was mobilization.

Thus when the Germans in their turn delivered an ultimatum to Russia on July 31, demanding that they demobilize, it was not so much in defense of Austria as in defense of their own strategic situation. When Russia declined to demobilize, the Germans mobilized. The French, realizing what was coming, did so too. On August 1, Germany declared war on Russia; on August 3, Germany declared war on France. The advance of troops began two weeks later; the first battle of the war was fought within three weeks of its declaration.

Mutual Distrust

The connecting thread, from the assassination in Sarajevo to the German attack on France, was military planning. Yet no one thought anything was wrong with military planning. Because wars were expected to be swift, planning in advance was believed necessary. There would be no time to improvise once war had been declared. Once the best conceivable plan was devised, preparation and practice were geared to it. That war broke out over an event that had not been foreseen, over an issue indirectly related to the major countries fighting, was not important. Each state had expected war to come sooner or later and had prepared for it. Preparations in one country had only increased the suspicions of neighboring countries, leading them to preparation of their own. In such a climate of mutual distrust, a minor incident like the assassination of Franz Ferdinand could trigger a war.

OTHER CAUSES OF WORLD WAR I

No one can deny how important military planning and military preparation were in the outbreak of World War I.[4] Yet scholars have identified other causes as well. The literature on the causes of the war is enormous, with many authors of books and articles working as hard to attack the theories of others as to advance their own. The war is a rich hunting ground for those looking for evidence to prove some theory. Probably the all-time best seller on the causes of World War I is *Imperialism*, by V. I. Lenin.[5] He argued that the capitalist system in general and the leading capitalist countries in particular were responsible for the war. The essence of capitalism, wrote Lenin (drawing on Karl Marx) is constant expansion. Profits must be reinvested to produce more profits or the system collapses. The collapse of capitalism had not come about as rapidly as Marx had predicted, Lenin wrote, because the capitalist countries had found a new outlet for their surplus capital in investments overseas. This newest form of capitalism, in which banks rather than manufacturers took a leading role, Lenin called "imperialism." At first it worked, giving capitalism a respite, but by 1914 all the unclaimed areas of the world had been divided into colonies or spheres of influence. The countries that were left out, particularly Germany (which had no colonies to speak of), wanted to see the world redivided for their benefit. As Lenin put it, the war was to decide whether "the British or German group of financial marauders was to receive the lion's share."[6]

Lenin, who was writing at the time of the war, blamed the whole system as it then existed. But many writers at that time picked out particular states and attributed the war to them. A typical book from the early days of the war is by James Beck, an American political figure, *The Evidence in the Case in the Supreme Court of Civilization as to the Moral Responsibility for the War*, published in 1914.[7] As we would expect of a man who wanted the United States to enter the war on the side of the British, Beck found that Germany and Austria were guilty of starting the war. He accused them "in a time of profound peace" of secretly conspiring "to impose their will upon Europe in a matter affecting the balance of power."[8] Beck believed Austria was guilty of going to war with Serbia, thereby threatening the Russians in the Balkans, and Germany was guilty of not stopping Austria. England, France, Italy, and Russia, on the other hand, were all sincerely working for peace. The crucial event of Russian mobilization, Beck argued, was no justification for Germany's declaration of war because it was *legal*. A sovereign state, Beck declared, has the right to mobilize so long as its troops do not cross the border.

This extremely legalistic view, which dominated much of the writing about the war while it was being fought and in the years immediately following, provoked a reaction among academic historians in the 1920's. Because they were trying to revise the standard view of World War I—Germany crossed the frontier first, therefore Germany was guilty—they called themselves Revisionists. Most prominent among them was Sidney B. Fay, whose book *The Origins of the World War*, published in 1928, was the monument of this school.[9] Fay's primary point was that all the major powers were more or less responsible, but because no one was deliberately working to bring about a general European war, none was guilty.[10] But after making this claim, Fay went on to apportion some blame anyhow. France and Italy were accused of being at least pleased that war did break out because it gave them the chance to acquire territory. That the French territory (Alsace and Lorraine) had been seized by Germany in the last war was not a mitigating factor in Fay's eyes. Serbia was blamed for the assassination of Franz Ferdinand and Russia was blamed for backing up Serbia; the claims of Serbian nationalism got little sympathy from Fay. On the other hand, Austria and Germany were forgiven for their part in the events of 1914 because Fay believed they were acting in self-defense, Austria from the threat of dismemberment voiced in the nationalist claims of the Serbs and Germany from the threat posed by Russian mobilization.[11]

All this scholarly debate is not very satisfying to the student who wants a clear answer to the question, "What caused World War I?" But there is no agreement on an answer, and for whatever view you prefer, you can find an authority to back you up (although in some places Lenin might not be considered an authority and in other places anyone other than Lenin might not be considered an authority). This lack of agreement on the causes of war goes back to the years of the war itself. It has been argued, in fact, that this is one of the reasons the conflict escalated to total war: no country ever specified exactly what it was fighting for, and in the absence of such information each country assumed the worst of its enemies. The French never said, "We are fighting only to get back Alsace and Lorraine," so the Germans assumed they were trying to turn the clock back past 1870 and split the German Empire into small states again. The Germans never said, "We are fighting only to annex Luxembourg," so the French assumed they were going to annex Luxembourg, Belgium, and a slice of France as well. But whatever the ultimate goals of the war, no one doubted that they had to keep fighting for the immediate goal of not losing.

THE ROLE OF TECHNOLOGY IN WARFARE: POISON GAS, SUBMARINES

The new military technology decisively influenced the outbreak of war in 1914. The Germans attacked when and how they did because their strategy was based on exploiting their industrial superiority. The war failed to develop as preceding wars had because of even newer technology, particularly the machine gun. Technology continued to influence the war throughout its duration. New forms of warfare made their appearance, although they were introduced with little understanding of what they could accomplish or how effective they would be.

One of these technological innovations was poison gas. As industry developed and expanded during the nineteenth century, dangerous industrial chemicals such as chlorine went into widespread use. Before long some planner began thinking about how such chemicals could be applied to warfare. The idea was already so widespread in 1899 that in a conference that year at The Hague, many states agreed to outlaw artillery shells designed to fire poison gas. But sixteen years later, frustrated by seeing their plans fail as mobile warfare turned into war of position, with lines of trenches facing each other from Switzerland to the North Sea, the Germans began to consider whether the use of poison gas might break the stalemate. On April 22, 1915, the Germans used chlorine gas against the French along the front in Belgium, releasing it from canisters in the ground so that technically they did not violate the Hague Gas Declaration. The gas was successful beyond German expectations. French troops fled, leaving a gap 4 miles wide through which the Germans could have marched to Paris. But because the Germans were not expecting any such success, they were not prepared to follow it up. By the time they had completed the necessary preparations and were ready to use gas again, on May 1, 1915, they found the French were equipped with gas masks and able to stop the assault. From then on, both sides began to use gas (and gas masks) in increasing quantities, in artillery shells and grenades as well as in buried canisters, until in the 1918 German offensive, 50 per cent of the shells fired carried gas.[12] The initial advantage of surprise on April 22, 1915, was not exploited and from then on the war was stalemated again, only at a higher level of violence. During World War I, 1.3 million casualties were attributed to gas, 91,000 of them fatalities (although debate has raged over whether this low ratio of those killed to those merely wounded makes it a more or a less humane weapon).[13]

The Germans also pioneered another weapon, the submarine. As with poison gas, the weapon was not decisive. Despite the role that German–British naval competition had played in creating tensions between the two countries in the years preceding the war, when the fighting broke out the Germans found that their navy was useless. In any encounter with the larger British navy, it would have been decisively defeated. Therefore the Germans turned to submarines, which could damage the British in an area vital to the British Isles: importation of food, munitions, and other materials needed to fight the war. The submarine proved an effective weapon in sinking ships but the Germans were limited by international law in how far they could apply this weapon. According to law, attacks on neutral ships were illegal, and it was neutral ships, particularly those under the American flag, that were carrying a large part of the goods. After much debate in German policy-making circles, the general staff convinced the political leaders to agree to "unrestricted" submarine warfare—attacks on all ships going to England, neutral or not.

The German military's justification for this policy illustrates again the difficulty of comprehending the effects of technology even when the utmost care is given to calculation. The German general staff argued that they would be able to sink 600,000 tons of shipping a month and that after six months the British economy would collapse. They also predicted that unrestricted submarine warfare would bring the United States into the war on the side of the British but that it would not matter because America would take a year to mobilize and even then German submarines could sink United States troop transport ships before they reached Europe.[14]

The German technical predictions were remarkably accurate. The average amount of shipping sunk during the crucial first five months was 658,000 tons a month, a little over the predicted average. The Germans went wrong in their prediction of what effect these losses would have on British policy. Perhaps if the British had been fighting alone they would have accepted the hopelessness of their position and given up. But the other German prediction—that America would enter the war—came true, and this changed the British calculation. They decided they could hold out until American help arrived. The German technical prediction was correct but their estimation of the effect of technical factors on political decisions was entirely wrong.[15]

United States entry into the war was one of the factors (although not the only one) that eventually led to victory by the Western Allies. Several times during the war changes in tactics or technical improvements in weapons were introduced that might have made a decisive difference even if the United States had not entered. It is easier to see the effect today, with the benefit of hindsight, than it was then. In 1918, when the German military finally panicked and insisted that their politicians make peace, it was easier to draw a more obvious conclusion, that the United States with its large industrial capacity and its reserve of manpower was the decisive factor in the Western victory.

THE RESULTS OF WORLD WAR I: THE VERSAILLES TREATY

The results of World War I were embodied in the Versailles Peace Treaty of 1919. The treaty was quite long, running to several hundred clauses, but we can summarize its four most important features.

1. New Borders for Germany. In the west, the provinces of Alsace and Lorraine were returned to France, removing one of the grievances that had made the French eager for war in 1914. But at the same time the French ignored the obvious lesson that this exchange seemed to teach about the price a state pays for detaching territory from another and proceeded to

detach territory from Germany for their own benefit. This was the Saar, bordering on Lorraine and like Lorraine a coal and steel producing area but just as German in its population as Lorraine was French (see Figure 1.3). The French did not go quite as far as the Germans had; they did not annex the Saar but put it under the administration of the new League of Nations, taking over control of its mines and industry.

In the east, new boundaries between Germany and Poland were drawn but the problem was too complex to be settled so simply. Germans lived among Poles. Polish villages were scattered among German villages, and no border could be totally satisfactory. The 1919 border was no more fair than any other; it differed from the prewar border only by including more Germans under Polish jurisdiction.

2. New States. The Versailles Treaty with Germany was only one of several negotiated at the end of the war. The whole package, which we might call the Versailles Settlement, created a number of new states in central and eastern Europe on the principle of national self-determination, replacing the old multinational empire of the Austrian rulers. Under this principle, nationalities or closely related groups of nationalities were given states of their own. The Serbs were united with Bosnia and other Slavic areas to form Yugoslavia or the "South Slavs" state. Slavic peoples in the middle of Europe, the Czechs and the Slovaks, were put together in the state of Czechoslovakia. The states of Poland, Hungary, and Austria were also given borders on the principle of national self-determination. But this principle was not applied to the Germans. First, the state of Austria, although consisting primarily of German-speaking members of the old Austrian Empire, was forbidden to unite with Germany. Second, the new state of Czechoslovakia included about 2 million people who spoke German. They lived in the border regions in the Sudeten Mountains and were known as the Sudeten Germans. Before World War I they had been part of the Austrian Empire but now they were put under a government controlled by Slavs instead of being allowed to join either Germany or Austria. Third, the southern portion of the Austrian province of Tyrol was put under Italian rule mainly as a reward to the Italians for joining the war on the side of the British and French.

3. German Disarmament. The Versailles Settlement imposed severe limitations on German armaments, justifying this restriction as the first step toward general European disarmament. Germany would go first, for after all, Germany had lost the war, but the other states would follow. The army was limited to 100,000 men, and each soldier had to serve a minimum of twelve years (to keep the Germans from using the army as a training school for reserves). The navy was limited to 15,000 men and a few ships. An air force was forbidden altogether. Portions of Germany were turned into a demilitarized zone, where no troops could be stationed and no fortifications

built. This area extended 50 kilometers on the east bank of the Rhine along the stretch of river that formed the boundary with France and on the entire west bank of the Rhine for the rest of its length (see Figure 2.1).

4. Reparations. The issue that probably held the greatest interest for the public was reparations. The Germans had imposed reparations on the French after 1871, to make them pay for the war, and in 1919 a number of French and British politicians were determined to make the Germans pay for this much more expensive war just completed. In the end the demands were so extravagant, far beyond any reasonable ability on the part of the Germans to pay, that no figure was set and the treaty merely set forth the principle that the Germans would pay. The part of the treaty that laid down this principle, Clause 231, was similar to an economic liability clause in a commercial contract but became known as the "war guilt" clause. The section on reparations also specified that Germany could be occupied by foreign

Figure 2.1   The Demilitarized Zone Along the Rhine

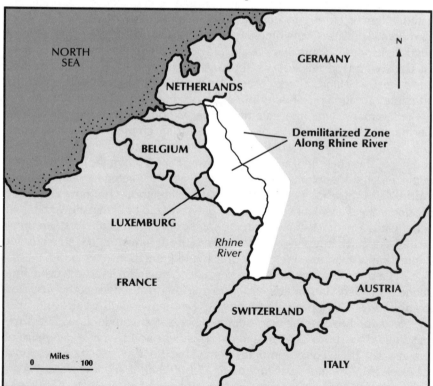

troops if it failed to meet its payments, as the French in fact did in 1923 when a great inflation led to the collapse of the Germany economy.

GERMAN REACTION TO VERSAILLES
AND THE RISE OF HITLER

Imagine that you are a German radical looking for topics for beer hall speeches. What a gold mine you would find in the Versailles Treaty. Alsace and Lorraine are taken away (on the argument that it is wrong to detach territory from another state) at the same time that the Saar is being detached from Germany. New states are being set up everywhere on the principle of national self-determination but Germans in the Sudetenland, Austria, and South Tyrol are denied this right. Germany must disarm and pay for the war because of "war guilt." You could add that it was a dictated peace—Germany was not invited to participate in the Versailles conference but was instead handed the completed treaty and told to sign within seven days.

It is easy to construct an argument that the Versailles Treaty was responsible for the rise of Hitler and hence for World War II. But this is not the only argument you could make. You could also say the Versailles Treaty was a mistake, assuming the victors had no will to enforce it. If it had been enforced with the same sternness with which it was drawn up, it might have worked. We will never know, because the only part ever to be enforced was the least essential: the provisions for reparations, not those for disarmament. And even when the French occupied the industrial area of the Ruhr in 1923 they discovered that they could not mine coal with bayonets. Right-wing extremists and communists cooperated to resist foreign occupation and in the end the French had to withdraw without getting any reparations.

The French effort in 1923 failed, yet it was at least an effort to enforce the treaty, more than the victors did to prevent rearmament. It was something of an open secret in Germany that rearmament was going on. Germany was not allowed to have an air force but the government was encouraging "sport flying" clubs. The airline Lufthansa opened six "pilot schools," turning out 100 pilots a year in a system of education that had many military elements. The Germans set up factories abroad in return for some of the production. In the Soviet Union they set up two airplane factories, three artillery shell factories, and a poison gas factory.[16]

As time went on the Western democracies became less and less interested in enforcing the Versailles Treaty. Partly it was because of the nature of these societies, which gave priority to pursuit of private happiness over the concerns of state; there was no public support for maintaining a large army of occupation in Germany. Partly it was the result of widespread pacifism, particularly encouraged by left-wing political parties. And partly it was the result of influence exerted by academic historians such as Sidney Fay, who were arguing that no one country (and certainly not Germany) was guilty of starting the war. With no war guilt, the justification for such a harsh treaty was hard to find.

The decline in Western self-confidence was paralleled in Germany by the rise to power of a political leader with total self-confidence, Adolf Hitler. Hitler had first come to world attention in 1923, when, imitating Benito Mussolini, he tried to take over the government in Munich. But unlike Mussolini, whose march on Rome had been successful, Hitler failed and went to jail. While there, he wrote a book he called *Four and a Half Years of Struggle Against Lies, Stupidity, and Cowardice.* (His publisher got him to cut the title down to *My Struggle*—in German, *Mein Kampf.*) Consciously echoing Bismarck he wrote, "We must clearly recognize the fact that the recovery of the lost territories is not won through solemn appeals to the Lord or through pious hopes in a League of Nations, but only by force of arms."[17] By 1933 he was chancellor of Germany.

HITLER'S FOREIGN POLICY AND WESTERN APPEASEMENT

Hitler's own statements and the policies he later followed are grounds for saying that he alone was responsible for World War II. But on closer examination, it is not quite so simple. For one thing, his views on the treatment of Germany after World War I were widely shared. The unwillingness of Western political leaders to make any concessions to Hilter's more moderate predecessors made more plausible his argument that only force of arms would bring change—Germany had not even been admitted to the League of Nations until 1926. For another, had Western political leaders followed different policies once Hitler did take office, he never would have gotten a weak and disarmed Germany into a position from which it could hope to make war against all the other countries of Europe with any chance of success.

Yet without question the story of the outbreak of World War II is in large part the personal story of Hitler and his diplomacy. This diplomacy may for convenience be divided into two phases. Phase I begins with Hitler's accession to power in January 1933. His first years were spent consolidating domestic control and he made few foreign policy moves. One thing he did was to take Germany out of the League of Nations in October 1933, on the argument that Germany was being denied equal rights on the question of arms. Germany had disarmed but the other states had not followed. Now, said Hitler, either the others disarm down to our level or we have the right to arm up to theirs. The League, which was sponsoring a disarmament conference at this time, was unable to give an answer and so Germany withdrew. Hitler's next move, in January 1934, was to sign a Non-Aggression Pact with Poland. It was something no moderate German leader would have dared without risking a venomous attack from right-wingers such as the Nazis. But Hitler's patriotism was above criticism and the Nazis by now had eliminated most critics. The treaty with Poland served two purposes: it strengthened Hitler's peace image (and he was later to refer to it as proof of his sincere desire for peace with his neighbors), and it lulled the Poles into thinking they could pursue a policy of independent neutrality and thus made them less willing to cooperate with France against Germany.

In January 1935, Hitler got the kind of foreign policy victory that, had it come five years earlier, might have meant a Hitler never would have come to power. The League of Nations conducted a plebiscite in the Saar to see whether its citizens wanted to return to Germany. (They did, overwhelmingly.) Hitler had little to do with bringing about this vote. A plebiscite had been scheduled for fifteen years after the Saar was detached from Germany. But Hitler got all the credit for recovering this piece of "lost territory." The final piece of Hitler's policy in Phase I was his announcement, in March 1935, of compulsory universal military service; in other words, his denunciation of the disarmament clauses of the Versailles Treaty.

At any time during Phase I it would have been easy for the Western democracies to move against Hitler. Germany was still disarmed and Hitler's own postion in Germany was not totally secure. Yet nothing Hitler did was unequivocally threatening to the Western countries. Rather than make the effort to stop Hitler, it was easier to find a justification for each of his actions. Even denouncing the Versailles Treaty could be justified. Far from fulfilling the pledge of Versailles to disarm down to the German level, France had just doubled the term of service for its soldiers. Hitler himself was careful to keep his announced intentions limited; although he was introducing universal military service he pledged not to rearm the demilitarized zone of the Rhineland. Hitler's tactics are an example of what a contemporary strategist has called, "Give me that last piece of toast or I'll blow my brains out on your new suit!" Of course if you called his bluff, it would hurt him more than it hurt you, but if you calculate rationally you will decide that a piece of toast is less expensive than a dry cleaning bill.[18]

In Phase II Hitler engaged in foreign policy acts that were increasingly threatening to Germany's neighbors. In March 1936, he ordered German troops into the demilitarized zone along the Rhine, even though he had explicitly promised not to do so only a year earlier. In March 1938, he annexed Austria, against both the prescriptions of the Versailles Treaty and the wishes of most of the Austrian people. In September 1938, his threat to go to war against Czechoslovakia led to the surrender of the Sudetenland to Germany. In March 1939, Germany annexed the remaining non-German part of Czechoslovakia.

We might wonder why Hitler was able to get away with these acts. In part it was because Western political leaders were carefully avoiding the conditions that led to World War I. In the postwar analysis everyone agreed that the pre-1914 arms race had been a major source of tension. Spending for arms therefore was kept low after the war. Although the Western democracies were stubbornly refusing to disarm completely, they were also failing to keep up with weapons development, particularly once Germany began open rearmament in 1935. At the time of the Sudetenland crisis in 1938, England had only one operational wing of modern fighter aircraft.[19] The French chief of staff of the air force had been so impressed by his visits to German airplane factories that he warned in August 1938, "If war comes this autumn, as you fear, there will not be one French plane left after fifteen days."[20] As it became ever clearer that Hitler did not keep his promises, France and Britain did begin to rearm, but rearmament with modern weapons is a lengthy process and years were required before new weapons would provide backing for strong diplomatic actions.

Another important cause of World War I was the failure of the major states to conciliate states that had grievances, particularly those caused by national feelings. It was the quarrel over nationalism between the Serbs and the Austrians that set the armies in motion. After World War I Western political leaders listened sympathetically to demands for redressing national grievances. This policy of being conciliatory in the face of justified demands was known as "appeasement," a word that at the time had only favorable connotations. To be against appeasement was to be rigid, inflexible, in favor of the policies that had led to World War I.

The most famous example of appeasement was the Munich conference, at which the Sudetenland was transferred from Czechoslovakia to Germany. Hitler had used a branch of the Nazi Party to stir up trouble in the Sudetenland, telling them always to ask for so much that they could never be satisfied. He then used these incidents as a pretext for demanding that the Sudeten Germans be put under German rule. The Czechs refused to be bullied and mobilized their reserves, but the rest of the world was afraid of war and insisted on an international conference instead. The conference, so eagerly sought as an alternative to war by Western leaders (including the American president), was far from a model of impartiality. It was held in the German city of Munich, site of the Nazi Party's headquarters. It was attended by Britain, France, Italy, and Germany but not by the country most directly threatened, Czechoslovakia. As a result of the conference, the Czechs were ordered to hand over the Sudetenland, including border fortifications and economic resources as well as about 700,000 Czechs who would now go under German rule. Yet Neville Chamberlain, the British prime minister, came back from Munich with his black umbrella in one hand and a piece of paper in the other, saying, "I believe it is peace for our time."[21] The paper was important because Chamberlain had on it Hitler's own promise that this was his last territorial demand in Europe. And it was reasonable to believe him. The German claim to rule Germans in the Sudetenland and Austria was justified by the principle of national self-determination. The issue of Germans in South Tyrol and Germans in the areas along the Polish border remained, but Hitler had concluded treaties with both Italy and Poland.

The Western political leaders quickly discovered that their appeasement policy was mistaken when, only six months later, Hitler took over the rest of Czechoslovakia in clear violation of his pledges at Munich. War had become inevitable. In retrospect most Western policy-makers agreed that they should have gone to war to aid Czechoslovakia. But it was too late for that. The next country to be threatened by Hitler was Poland. Its cause was less just, its regime less compatible with Western ideas of democracy or even human decency, and its terrain a lot harder to defend. It was, in fact, as Hitler calculated, irrational for the French and British to get into a major war with Germany over Poland. Nevertheless, the British and French leaders made that irrational choice and World War II began.

ESCALATION INTO TOTAL WAR

Hitler was aware that military action against Poland was a gamble that could turn into a major war. Like Bismarck before him in 1870 and the German general staff in 1914, he faced the threat of a two-front war. Germany, at the center of Europe, could be attacked simultaneously from east and west. The German general staff had tried to solve the problem in 1914 by careful military planning—a knockout blow to the west, followed by an extended campaign in the east—but the plan had failed. Hitler chose to imitate Bismarck and prevent a two-front war by diplomacy. In August 1939, Germany signed a Non-Aggression Pact with Russia. (Anyone who believed that Mein Kampf was a blueprint for Hitler's actions would have been misled here; Hitler had written that he would never ally with the Bolsheviks or, as he put it, use the devil to drive out Beelzebub.)[22]

With the threat of Russian reaction out of the way, Germany went to war against Poland in September 1939, the date we usually give for the opening of World War II. (In one sense the war in the Pacific had begun in 1937 with the fighting between China and Japan; in another sense it did not truly become a world war until the Japanese attacked Pearl Harbor in 1941.)

The Germans were staging a victory parade through the streets of Poland's capital long before French and British forces could come to Poland's aid. Hitler hoped that the French and British would see how unreasonable it was to continue in a state of war with Germany, once Poland was defeated. After a winter with no fighting, when he was unable to persuade the French and British to make peace, Hitler launched a lightning campaign against France in the spring of 1940. Within six weeks France surrendered. Hitler now seriously undertook to defeat England. As a London news vendor put it, "French sign peace treaty: we're in the finals."[23] But before any invasion could be undertaken, the Germans felt they had to destroy British defenses, and so mounted an aerial campaign that became known as the Battle of Britain.

Subduing England from the air was more difficult than many prewar advocates of air power had predicted. Paradoxically, the British had an advantage precisely because they had delayed so long in rearming. If they had heeded the warnings of men such as Winston Churchill and rearmed in 1933, they would have been massively equipped with inferior aircraft. The British won the Battle of Britain in large part because of their superior fighter aircraft, but the prototype of the Hurricane was first flown only in November 1935, the prototype of the Spitfire in March 1936.[24]

The decisive role of technology in the Battle of Britain reinforced the pessimistic conclusions that had emerged from studies of the conduct of World War I, one of which was the increasing importance of technology. Another was the decreasing ability of human beings to manage technology. Britain won the Battle of Britain because of superior airplanes; Germany would have won if it had developed its jet planes a little sooner. But the British succeeded by luck, not careful planning. The crucial question in modern warfare is: When do we stop developing new weaponry and go into production? The Germans were a bit too early. At the other extreme, the French were a bit too late; their aircraft were still on the assembly lines when the Germans attacked. The British got it right, but only by luck.

THE ROLE OF TECHNOLOGY IN WARFARE: AIRPLANES, THE ATOMIC BOMB

Before fighting began in 1939 many predicted how horrible the coming war would be because of the new technology. On the horror of the war the predictions were correct but not on much else. The most popular prewar version was that poison gas would be widely used, most likely dropped from airplanes onto cities. At the time of the Sudeten crisis in 1938, 38 million gas masks were distributed in Britain. Yet during World War II poison gas was not used at all between major belligerents. (The one exception was its limited use in 1941 by the Japanese against the technologically less advanced Chinese.)

The prediction that airplanes would attack cities was correct (although they did it with high-explosive bombs, not gas). But the prediction that these attacks would be decisive was wrong. World War II was eventually won on the ground, not from the air. Airplanes were decisive when used tactically (that is, coordinated with ground action), but not when used strategically. There were a number of reasons for this. One was that anti-aircraft defense was more effective than expected; a loss of more than 10 per cent in planes for each attack (such as the Germans suffered in the Battle of Britain) was enough to make air raids too costly. British and American raids in 1942 and 1943 often suffered losses much higher than that. Another reason was the gross inaccuracy of bombing. In 1941, the Royal Air Force of Britain determined that fewer than 20 per cent of the bombers it sent out had bombed within a circle 75 square miles in area around the designated target area. In heavily defended areas such as industrial targets, only 7 per cent were dropping bombs within 75 square miles. News stories of "pinpoint" attacks were nothing more than war propaganda.[25] Still another reason for the failure of strategic bombing was that the United States and Britain did not devise a successful strategy for employing bombers. Only in June 1944 did they finally begin to use them in a way that would be decisive, in a single-minded concentration on destroying petroleum products to deprive the German armed forces of fuel. But by the time this aerial strategy began to take hold the war had already begun to turn against the Germans on the ground.[26]

Predictions of the horror of aerial warfare were finally vindicated on August 6, 1945, when the United States dropped the first atomic bomb on Hiroshima. This was not the most destructive raid of the war—raids with high-explosive and incendiary bombs on Tokyo and Dresden killed more people. But the atomic raid required only one airplane and one bomb; the amount of destruction for the area it covered was much greater than that of conventional bombs. Yet the dropping of the atomic bomb is only a further illustration of human inability to come to terms with modern technology. One question has troubled many people since Hiroshima: Was the use of the atomic bomb necessary at all? It was built, after all, out of fear that the Germans would develop one first. It turned out that the Germans had made managerial mistakes and were nowhere close to having a bomb by the time they surrendered. If the United States had been at war with Japan alone there never would have been an expensive crash program to build an atomic bomb. But once the time and money had been invested, it seemed easiest to go on and use it on Japan.

But why, people ask, did we use it to kill people instead of in a harmless way that would still have demonstrated its destructive power? The answer is that scientists could not think of a convincing technical demonstration. Robert Oppenheimer, scientific director of the project that built the bomb, did not think exploding one of them like a firecracker over the desert would be impressive.[27] Another nuclear scientist, Isador Rabi, said it would have required very detailed instructions to the Japanese, more than were possible during the war. "You would have to tell them what instruments to bring," Rabi said, "and where to stand, and what to measure. Otherwise, it would look like a lot of pyrotechnics. It would take someone who understood the theory to realize what he was seeing."[28] Part of this inability to devise an appropriate demonstration came from gross underestimation of the new weapon's power. General Groves, the top administrator of the atomic project, estimated in December 1944 that the bomb would have a force equivalent to 500 tons of TNT. By May 1945 the heads of the Los Alamos laboratories were predicting 700 to 1,500 tons of TNT. The actual power of the Hiroshima explosion was close to 14,000 tons of TNT, or ten times what scientists were saying in the crucial days when the decision was being made.[29]

THE RESULTS OF WORLD WAR II

The dropping of the first atomic bomb on Japan on August 6, 1945 (and another on Nagasaki three days later) was followed in less than a week by the Japanese decision to surrender. It was convincing proof to much of the world that technology was the decisive winner of World War II. If a scientific breakthrough had given the Germans the bomb first, the outcome of the war would surely have been different. The lesson people drew was that a modern industrial economy and a scientific establishment were the major components of military power. In these the United States excelled. The old term "great power" was replaced by a new one, "superpower," implying that all other states of the world combined could not prevail against such a state armed with the latest weapons.

In another way World War II changed the structures of world politics. It marked the emergence from self-imposed isolation of the United States. It also marked the emergence of the Soviet Union from an externally imposed isolation. Soviet ground forces fighting in eastern Europe had reversed the German tide of fortune in the war. Now, although weakened by losses in the war—10 per cent of its population, 25 per cent of its industry—Russia was a major world power second only to the United States. Russia's traditional enemies, Japan in Asia and Germany in Europe, had been eliminated as major rivals by defeat in war. The other traditional powers in Europe had been removed as major factors as well. Italy was among the defeated countries, France was a winner in a technical sense only, having been defeated and occupied by the Germans in 1940. Britain was so weakened by the war that it had to give up most of its overseas interests and concentrate on rebuilding at home. In a few years large portions of the overseas possessions of France and Britain were to receive independence and others were to move into positions from which they could demand it.

Germany was treated far more harshly after World War II than after World War I, yet because the Germans were psychologically more prepared to acknowledge defeat, there was almost no resistance. In 1918, Germany had not even been entered by enemy troops; in 1945, Germany was devastated and occupied. Without even the benefit of a peace treaty this time, Germany was divided into three parts (one part was annexed by the Soviet Union and Poland, the other two parts became separate states). All of Germany was put under foreign administration and, in the zones occupied by the Russians and the French, looted of food and industrial equipment. The troublesome border problems with Poland and Czechoslovakia were solved with brutal finality by simply expelling all Germans from areas now governed by Poland and Czechoslovakia. About 10 million Germans became refugees, most eventually finding their way into West Germany where they made up 25 per cent of the population. Although it was brutal, it did solve the troubled border issue that had caused friction between Germany and its neighbors after World War I. The Germans accepted this solution and successfully absorbed the huge refugee population. In the years after World War II it was not from the defeated but from the victors that the seeds of the next conflict would come.

The two great wars of the twentieth century seemed to demonstrate that the precepts of Clausewitz and the optimism of the age of Bismarck were no longer valid. Instead of being short, useful instruments of state policy, wars turned out to be long and enormously destructive. Battle deaths in World War I numbered around 9 million, yet the political goals were so unclear that we still are debating the reasons for the war. The reasons for World War II seem clearer, yet the destruction was much greater. In addition to about 15 million battle deaths, large numbers of civilians were killed, so that deaths from World War II were around 60 million, or 3 per cent of the world's population.[30] The destructiveness of the two wars convinced many people that war was no longer a useful means for settling disputes between states. The development of nuclear weapons during World War II made the need to find an alternative to war a matter of urgency.

NOTES

1. Karl Marx and Friedrich Engels, *Manifesto of the Communist Party* (first published in 1848), Part II.

2. The British, French, and German reactions are described by Barbara Tuchman in *The Guns of August* (New York: Dell, 1962), pp. 94, 111; the British poet was Rupert Brooke, who wrote "The 1914 Sonnets."

3. A dramatic illustration of the military establishment's reluctance to accept the lessons of the recent wars is provided by Edward L. Katzenbach, Jr., "The Horse Cavalry in the Twentieth Century," *Public Policy: A Yearbook of the Graduate School of Public Administration, Harvard University*, ed. Carl J. Friedrich and Seymour E. Harris, 1958.

4. The importance of military planning is the main thesis of Tuchman's book cited above.

5. *Imperialism: The Highest Stage of Capitalism*, first published in 1917 (New York: International Publishers, 1939).

6. Lenin, p. 11.

7. New York: G. P. Putnam's Sons.

8. Beck, p. 198.

9. New York: Macmillan (2 volumes).

10. Fay, Vol. I, pp. 2, 34.

11. Fay, Vol. I, pp. 124, 403; Vol. II, pp. 550−552, 554.

12. Frederick J. Brown, *Chemical Warfare* (Princeton: Princeton University Press, 1968), p. 43.

13. Seymour M. Hersh, *Chemical and Biological Warfare* (Garden City, N. Y.: Anchor Books, 1969), p. 2.

14. Fred Charles Iklé, *Every War Must End* (New York: Columbia University Press, 1971), pp. 42−50.

15. Ibid.

16. S. William Halperin, *Germany Tried Democracy: A Political History of the Reich from 1918 to 1933* (New York: W. W. Norton, 1946), p. 211.

17. Chapter 13. The most accessible edition in English is translated by Ralph Manheim (Boston: Houghton Mifflin, 1943), p. 627.

18. Thomas Schelling, *The Strategy of Conflict* (New York: Oxford University Press, 1963), p. 127.

19. Iain Macleod, *Neville Chamberlain* (New York: Atheneum, 1962), p. 261.

20. William L. Shirer, *The Collapse of the Third Republic* (New York: Simon and Schuster, 1969), p. 352.

21. For a defense of Chamberlain, see Macleod, cited above.

22. Hitler, Chapter 14 (p. 662 in Houghton Mifflin edition).

23. Alistair Horne, *To Lose a Battle* (Boston: Little, Brown, 1969), p. 579.

24. Winston Churchill, *The Gathering Storm* (Boston: Houghton Mifflin, 1948), p. 128.

25. Charles Kinsley Webster and Noble Frankland, *The Strategic Air Offensive Against Germany, 1939−1945* (London: H.M. Stationery Office, 1961), Vol. I, p. 247.

26. Bernard Brodie, *Strategy in the Missile Age* (Princeton: Princeton University Press, 1959), Chapter 4.

27. Len Giovannitti and Fred Freed, *The Decision to Drop the Bomb* (New York: Coward-McCann, 1965), p. 123.

28. *The New Yorker*, October 20, 1975, p. 61.

29. Herbert Feis, *The Atomic Bomb and the End of World War II* (Princeton: Princeton University Press, 1966), p. 29.

30. Quincy Wright, *A Study of War*, 2nd ed. (Chicago: University of Chicago Press, 1965), p. 1543.

Chapter 3

The Cold War and the Korean War

Today Cold War is a term of disapproval, contrasted unfavorably with "relaxation of tensions" or "détente." Even those who question the wisdom of former Secretary of State Henry Kissinger's policy of détente are careful to say they don't want a return to the Cold War. Yet when the term was first used, the emphasis was on the adjective "cold," not the noun "war." Cold War was contrasted with "hot war" or "shooting war," and its most vocal opponents were those who wanted to get it over with by launching a preventive war against the Soviet Union (USSR).

Despite the intense rivalry between the United States and the USSR in the late 1940's and early 1950's, the struggle never did turn into all-out war between them. But the Cold War period did include a highly destructive war in Korea (2 million battle deaths), which was widely viewed at the time as a war between the United States and the USSR (with the North Koreans and the Chinese acting as Soviet proxies). We will look first at the Cold War to see how a local dispute in the Korean peninsula became a conflict involving major powers.

ORIGINS OF UNITED STATES–SOVIET RIVALRY: IRAN, GREECE, TURKEY

The search for the origins of the Cold War is a major scholarly industry. There are vast numbers of books and articles on the subject to choose from.

Some trace the origins of the war back to 1917 and the Bolshevik victory in Russia. Others see the origin in the policies of one country or another during World War II. In our introduction to the subject, we will concentrate on only the more immediate causes.[1]

During World War II the United States pursued a single goal—to remove the threat to United States interests posed by German and Japanese power. All other goals were subordinated to this one. As a result, the Americans consistently rejected Winston Churchill's suggestions to fight with more attention to political goals. He wanted to invade the Balkans in order to cut off a Russian advance into that region. The Americans replied that this area would be too costly to invade and that such an invasion would not lead to the defeat of Germany any more speedily than an invasion in Italy or France.

The Soviet Union, on the other hand, had a number of foreign policy goals that could be fulfilled by the war. The Russians worried just as much about German power as the Western democracies did. They were less concerned about Japan because they had been able to pursue a successful appeasement policy toward Japan on their own far eastern border from 1930 to 1945. They had also tried an appeasement policy toward Germany in 1939, signing a Non-Aggression Pact a few weeks before Germany invaded Poland and then taking control over a portion of Poland (as provided for in a secret portion of the Pact) as their reward. But Hitler doublecrossed Stalin in 1941 and invaded Russia so that by the time the United States entered the war Russia was lined up with Britain in opposition to Germany. But the Soviet desire for expansion, illustrated in Poland by the secret deal with the Germans, extended to other areas as well. The old empire of the Russian tsar had extended much farther than the boundaries of the Soviet Union in 1939. Some areas under tsarist control had been able to achieve national independence when the Russian Empire collapsed; other parts had been claimed by Russia's neighbors and annexed by them while the new Bolshevik regime was too weak to do anything about it. But the Soviet government had never given up its claims to areas once ruled by the tsar and saw an opportunity in the war to regain this territory.

As a result of World War II, Russia acquired (or reacquired) large amounts of territory in Europe along its eastern borders—parts of Finland; the entire countries of Estonia, Latvia, and Lithuania; parts of Poland, Germany, and Rumania (see Figure 3.1). This acquisition of territory was passively accepted by the Western democracies, in part because they felt Russia deserved something in return for its losses in fighting the Germans and also because the Red Army was firmly in control of these areas and nothing could be done to remove them short of starting World War III. Along its southern border, however, the USSR encountered resistance. One area into which it wished to expand was the northern province of Iran called Azerbaijan. An

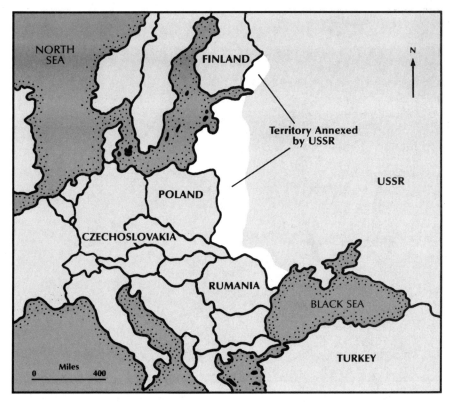

Figure 3.1   Soviet Acquisitions in Europe During World War II

"Azerbaijani Soviet Republic" had existed briefly at the time of the Russian revolution. It was subsequently divided, with part incorporated into Iran and part into the Soviet Union. In 1941, acting out of fear of losing Iran's oil resources to the Germans because of the pro-German sympathies of the shah of Iran, Russia and Britain together occupied Iran, removed the shah, and established their own troops in the country, the Russians in the north, the British in the south. They agreed to remove the troops as soon as the war ended.

The British did remove their troops, the Russians did not. Instead they sponsored an autonomous Azerbaijani Republic, ruled by the local communist party (see Figure 3.2). By 1946, the situation was tense. If the pattern of Europe were to be repeated, then the Red Army would not withdraw but stay to support a puppet regime. After a period of diplomatic maneuvering, in April 1946 the Russians agreed to withdraw, in return for promises of reform in Azerbaijan and the establishment of a Soviet–Iranian oil company.

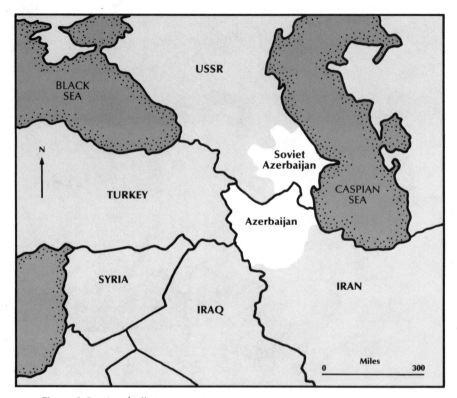

Figure 3.2   Azerbaijan

In May 1946, the Soviet troops did withdraw. The Iranian army promptly occupied the province, executed the leaders of the autonomous republic, and suppressed the communist party. Furthermore, the Iranian parliament refused to ratify the Soviet–Iranian Oil Company, so that the Russians gained nothing at all.

Like so many other events in the Cold War, the Azerbaijan incident can be cited to prove different contentions. It could be used as evidence that Stalin was not committed to expansion. Or it could be evidence that Stalin's expansionist desires could be checked only by vigorous resistance. Credit for bringing about the Russian withdrawal has been given to the United Nations (then just getting started and still meeting in London), to the British who sent a note of protest, to the Americans who talked about extending the draft, to the British and Americans together who showed their solidarity through Churchill's "Iron Curtain" speech at Fulton, Missouri, or to the skillful diplomacy of the premier of Iran. What is significant is that Soviet policy in Azerbaijan was perceived at the time as an attempt at Soviet expansion that was repulsed by Western policy. It was taken as a model of how to deal with the Russians.[2]

THE TRUMAN DOCTRINE AND
THE MARSHALL PLAN

A seemingly parallel situation appeared in two other countries to the south of Russia, Turkey, and Greece. Turkey, like many of the other countries bordering on Russia, had taken advantage of Russian weakness during the Bolshevik revolution and the civil war that followed it in the 1920's to reclaim some disputed territory, in particular the province of Khars. Following the end of the war in Europe in 1945, the Soviet foreign minister requested that the Turks hand this territory over to the Soviet Union (see Figure 3.3). The diplomatic note was backed up by "routine military maneuvers" in the

Figure 3.3   Soviet Claims on Turkey

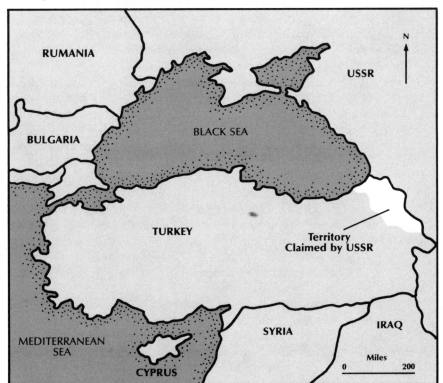

bordering areas of the Soviet Union. The Turks rejected the Soviet request but were uneasy about how far Russian pressure would go.

In the case of Greece, there was no claim to territory by the Soviet Union or actual occupation of territory by the Red Army; rather the Greek government was fighting a civil war against communist guerrillas who, it was assumed, were controlled by Stalin. Both Greece and Turkey had traditionally looked to Britain as the great power that supported them against their powerful northern neighbor. But Britain, weakened by the burden of fighting the Germans during the war, was suffering a financial crisis that made it impossible for it to continue to play the role of a great power in this part of the world. The British approached the Americans and asked them if they would consider abandoning their traditional policy of isolation and provide aid to Turkey and Greece.

This British request was followed by weeks of feverish activity in Washington as government officials debated whether the United States should assume the role traditionally played by great powers and whether the American people would accept this departure from traditional policy. This second question was much more important in the minds of the officials. Everyone remembered how Woodrow Wilson had failed to win the support of the Congress for his plan for a League of Nations, with the result that the United States made no contribution to world politics in the two decades that led up to World War II. In an effort to avoid repeating Wilson's error, it was decided that President Truman should address both houses of Congress, outlining the new American policy of involvement abroad and giving the broadest possible justification for it. On March 12, 1947, President Truman made the address that became known as the "Truman Doctrine." This was a United States pledge to "support free peoples who are resisting attempted subjugation by armed minorities or by outside pressures."[3] The Truman Doctrine was clearly a turning point in American foreign policy and as disenchantment has grown in recent years with American involvement abroad, critics have concentrated on it as a source of much of our trouble. Even some who agreed at the time with the policy of extending aid to Greece and Turkey objected to the universal language in which the policy was couched. Why "free peoples," they asked. Why not just say "Greece and Turkey" and reserve the right to decide whether other countries will get aid at some time in the future?

The ease with which the Truman Doctrine gained acceptance by Congress and the support it got from leaders of both parties in subsequent years make it easy to forget the genuine fears that troubled the planners in 1947. It seemed a realistic possibility that such a departure from traditional policies might be rejected, on the one hand by traditional isolationists, on the other by a new group of idealists who wanted to rely totally on the United Nations.

The Truman Doctrine was widely thought at the time to be a step toward a more mature and responsible foreign policy than the one that America had followed in the years between the two world wars.

The Truman Doctrine, seen by Americans as a program to prevent Soviet interference in Greece and Turkey, was immediately interpreted by the Soviet Union as a "fresh intrusion of the USA into the affairs of other states."[4] This became the typical pattern of Cold War exchanges. Each side interpreted its own moves as defensive and those of its rival as aggressive.

Convinced of Soviet aggressive intentions, the West reacted with defensive measures, first in Azerbaijan, then in Greece and Turkey. The weak condition of the European economies became a cause for concern, not only for humanitarian reasons but also because it was believed that weak economies would make these countries more susceptible to communist takeovers. A few months after President Truman had announced that the United States would give military assistance to Greece and Turkey, his secretary of state, George Marshall, announced that the United States would make available economic assistance to all the countries of Europe. This offer of aid was open to all, but it seemed likely to the planners in Washington that the Russians would find such aid incompatible with the rigid control and secrecy they were accustomed to exercising over their own economy. The Washington planners were correct. Marshall Plan aid was rejected both by the USSR and by countries under its control.

Whatever suspicions Stalin had could only be confirmed by these policies. Measures that the West interpreted as defensive were, from the Russian perspective, preparations for aggression. Whatever Stalin's original intentions for the countries of Eastern Europe, there was no longer any possibility of independent development. Perhaps it had been his intention all along, perhaps Western policy had only speeded up his schedule, perhaps Western policy provoked him into it. Whatever the origin, Stalin now proceeded to eliminate anyone with pro-Western leanings in countries liberated from the Nazis by the Red Army—Bulgaria, Rumania, and Hungary.

THE COLD WAR IN EUROPE: POLAND, BERLIN

It was in Poland that relations with the West became most strained. Poland was different from the other countries of East Europe—it was the country for which Britain and France had originally gone to war against the Germans, it had fought against the Nazis instead of collaborating with them, and enough Poles had immigrated to the United States to make events in Poland a matter of some national concern. Poland had been one of the main topics at the conferences held at Yalta (February 1945) and Potsdam (July 1945) by the three major victors to decide the political fate of Europe after the German defeat. The West had asked in general for the guarantee of fundamental rights and freedoms in East Europe; specifically it asked that the communist government installed in Poland by the Red Army be broadened to include Poles who had spent the war either in exile in London or fighting the Germans in the underground inside Poland. Although the Russians had promised this at Yalta and reaffirmed it at Potsdam the promises were not kept. Perhaps the Russians did not believe that the United States was sincere in its solicitude for the Poles. They were aware that concentrations of Poles in cities such as Chicago and Milwaukee gave them some importance in domestic politics in America. Perhaps they thought that these voters would be satisfied if Presidents Roosevelt and Truman obtained promises on paper.

In fact, the Americans made their demands on idealistic grounds. The war against the Nazis had been fought to guarantee democratic freedoms to the people of Europe and the Americans wanted to see this principle applied. This idea contrasted with the British approach under Churchill. He had agreed in a realistic way in 1944 to a rough division of Europe into spheres of influence, reflecting the relative power of each side. Under this division, the West was to have predominant influence in Greece, whereas Russia would predominate in Rumania and Bulgaria. In fact, in 1944 when the British had harshly repressed the Greek communists on behalf of an autocratic Greek regime, the Russians made no move to aid the communists. The Churchill–Soviet agreement did not cover northern Europe, but when the British and Americans complained about what was happening inside Poland, Stalin replied, in effect, "Did we say anything to you about Greece?"[5]

The Americans' professed dislike of "spheres of influence" must have seemed like hypocrisy to the Russians as long as the Americans professed the Monroe Doctrine, for that Doctrine certainly appeared to reserve a sphere of influence for the United States in Latin America. But words did not speak as loud as actions. In July 1945, the United States Army withdrew 100 miles from the westernmost point it had reached in Germany, to allow the Russians to move up to a line arranged long in advance of the German defeat. Throughout 1945 the strength of the United States Army in Europe was rapidly running down, as the American government tried to meet the popular demand for as rapid a demobilization as possible. On V-E day (Victory in Europe, May 7, 1945) the United States Army in Europe numbered 3,100,000. A year later it was down to 391,000.[6] Anyone interested in power (and as good Leninists the Soviet leaders were obliged to be) could see that whatever the United States might say about events in Poland, it was in no position to do anything about them. Pulling troops back 100 miles was more eloquent than any diplomatic protest.

By 1947 it was clear that Poland would be ruled by the Polish

Communist Party in a way acceptable to Russia. In February 1948, the government of Czechoslovakia was expunged of its pro-Western parties. In June 1948 the city of Berlin, itself under four-power administration but totally within the Soviet Zone of Occupation, was cut off from contact with the rest of Germany by a Soviet blockade.

The United States wished to react strongly to the Berlin Blockade, because it believed that its legal right to be in Berlin was unassailable, but it lacked the military means to do much. Only one combat-ready division in the entire United States Army was not committed to occupation duty. General Marshall said, "We did not have enough to defend the airstrip at Fairbanks."[7] President Truman decided to airlift supplies into Berlin, but it took all the available transport aircraft in the Air Force to accomplish that. As a gesture to show United States firmness, President Truman made one of the few moves available to him and sent a number of B-29 bombers to Britain. This was the first time since the end of the war that bombers (ones capable of carrying the atomic bomb) were stationed outside the United States. The move was followed by discussion within the government of assistance to a rearmed Europe, eventually including Germany. In June 1948 the United States Senate passed a bipartisan resolution supporting collective defense in Western Europe and in April 1949 the North Atlantic Treaty was signed, by which "the Parties agree that an armed attack against one or more of them in Europe or North America shall be considered an attack against them all." From this treaty developed the North Atlantic Treaty Organization, or NATO.

BIPOLARITY

Whatever one considers to be the beginning of the Cold War, by 1949, when the North Atlantic Treaty was signed, we were clearly deeply involved in it. A number of features set this period off from times of peace. One was a high level of hostility between East and West, as manifested in public statements and propaganda. Another was recurring international crises provoked by incidents of violence, such as the shooting down of United States airplanes flying near the border of the Soviet Union. Still another feature was the spread of East–West rivalry into nearly every area of life. Anything that hurt our side helped them and vice versa. Richard Nixon, then vice president, welcomed the Supreme Court decision of 1954 outlawing school segregation as our greatest victory in the Cold War.[8]

As more and more areas of life were affected by the rivalry between the United States and the USSR, a new form of international politics took shape, unlike the system of the nineteenth or first half of the twentieth centuries. Instead of a number of major states, there were only two, and these so exceeded in power all the others that they were known as superpowers. Each acted as a pole around which all the other countries in the world aligned themselves, giving this form of international politics its name, bipolarity. Each superpower and its surrounding client states were known as a "bloc"— the Soviet bloc or the Western bloc. These blocs were held together by military alliances (NATO in the West, the Warsaw Pact in the East), by economic organizations (the Organization for European Economic Cooperation in the West, the Council for Mutual Economic Assistance in the East), and by political values shared by the political leaders. Countries not part of either bloc were of two types—those explicitly neutral by choice or imposition (Sweden, Switzerland, and Austria, for example), and the "nonaligned" states of Africa, Asia, and Latin America that became known as the Third World. In the early days of the Cold War, both superpowers looked on nonalignment as immoral. The Soviet Union saw no difference in India after the British departed in 1947. If a country was not with them, it was against them. The Soviet attitude toward the Third World began to shift around the time of the death of Stalin in 1953. From then on, Third World countries were wooed by the communists. But the United States persisted for several years more in condemning neutralism. John Foster Dulles, secretary of state under President Eisenhower, called nonalignment "an immoral and shortsighted conception."[9] Only under President Kennedy did the United States adopt the same policy as the Soviet Union, arguing now that if they weren't against us, they were for us.

The Cold War was a period of intense rivalry stopping short of all-out war. Preparations for war were made and the enemy in a potential war was clearly identified, but the weapons were not used. Each side engaged in propaganda warfare, in such forums as the United Nations and radio broadcasts. Each side practiced subversion; that is, contacts with citizens of other countries without the approval of their government. Each side maintained sizable armed forces; the United States for the first time continued the draft into peacetime. But United States troops never went into combat against Soviet troops.

HOT WAR IN KOREA

One characteristic of the Cold War was that events in all parts of the world were interpreted as facets of the United States–USSR rivalry. Thus, when fighting broke out in Korea in June 1950, Americans saw it as a new episode in the Cold War. Because the Russians, though not themselves fighting, were supplying material and advisers to the North Koreans, Americans often referred to the conflict as "war by proxy." For its part, however, the United States did not leave all the fighting to its proxy but sent troops to assist South Korea, ultimately committing about 250,000 men. Yet, despite this outbreak of a shooting war, the conflict remained limited and did not escalate into World War III, as everyone feared it would.

Korea had been a virtual protectorate of Japan ever since the Russo–Japanese War ended in 1905. After Japan was defeated in 1945, Korea was divided in the middle, at the 38th parallel, to facilitate the Japanese surrender. The Russians (who had been fighting the Japanese north of Korea in Manchuria) occupied the northern half; the Americans occupied the southern. Koreans in both parts of the country stated that they wanted reunification, but an American–Soviet commission was unable to agree on means for achieving it. In 1947 a United Nations resolution called for countrywide elections to a single Korean parliament, which would then set up a provisional government. The Russians refused entry to the UN commission that was to supervise these elections, and in May 1948 elections were held by the UN in the South alone. Three months later Soviet-style elections were conducted by the Russians in the North.

With the Communist Party firmly in control in the North, the Russians announced withdrawal of their occupation forces, which was completed by January 1949. This move increased pressure on the Americans to withdraw from the South, a move that was being considered already for other reasons. One of these reasons was the hostility of the Koreans to foreign occupation; United States military leaders anticipated demonstrations, riots, and other acts of violence that would make continued occupation difficult. Another reason was budgetary pressure from domestic sources to cut back all military spending. Military leaders did not see any great need for retaining troops in Korea. They considered the peninsula to be a liability in any future war, which they were convinced would be fought globally with nuclear weapons. Therefore, in June 1949, the United States withdrew its troops, leaving behind (as the Russians had in the North) military advisers—a total of 500 for the army of 60,000. But to keep the South from going to war and reunifying the country by force, the United States took with its departing forces all weapons that could be used offensively—airplanes, tanks, and heavy artillery.

CAUSES OF THE KOREAN WAR

A year after the United States withdrawal, on June 25, 1950, the North Koreans launched a massive attack on the South. It was not the low-level violence that had characterized past episodes in the Cold War, such as guerrilla warfare in Greece or harassment of planes airlifting supplies to Berlin during the Blockade, but conventional warfare—armed troops in tanks crossing a well-demarcated frontier. The attack was obviously carefully planned, and because there were 3,000 Russian advisers with the North Korean army (and because supplies such as gasoline were coming from

Russia), it was assumed that the Russians were responsible for the attack.[10]

But the reason behind the attack was a subject of debate in Washington. A number of interpretations were offered at the time.[11] The most popular was the belief that the Korean attack was a feint, a diversionary move to weaken the defense of Europe. The rearmament of Europe was just getting under way, and American attention was concentrated there. Even General Charles de Gaulle of France, not noted for being pro-American or anti-Russian, expected a Russian attack in Europe. The analogy between divided Korea and divided Germany was compelling. In each case the section of the country occupied by the Russians had built up military forces and was issuing belligerent statements, while the section occupied by the West was still weak, underarmed, and inadequately protected.

Another popular explanation for the attack was that it was a Soviet probe for soft spots. After all, Secretary of State Dean Acheson just six months before had declared that the United States would not defend Korea. He had defined a "defensive perimeter" for the United States in the Pacific, running from the Aleutian Islands through Japan and then the Ryukyu Islands (Okinawa) and the Philippines (see Figure 3.4). Outside the perimeter were the island of Formosa, where the Nationlist Chinese were holding out against the Communists, and Korea. "It must be clear," Acheson said, "that no person can guarantee these areas against attack."[12] One could explain the Korean War by saying the North Koreans were simply taking Acheson at his word. When you draw a line in the dirt and warn the other guy not to cross it, you expect at the least that he will step up to the line.

Although some Americans interpreted the attack in this way, others held the contradictory view that the Russians were testing the West's resolve, just as Hitler had done at Munich. President Truman said we had been tough in Iran, Berlin, and Greece, and we must show the same toughness in Asia. Chairman of the Joint Chiefs of Staff Omar Bradley said, "We have to draw the line somewhere."[13] Evidently Bradley and Truman forgot that Acheson had drawn a line only six months before.

Some of the president's advisers saw this attack as more serious, the opening of a Soviet move for world conquest. General Douglas MacArthur, head of United States occupation forces in Japan, wrote that "here in Asia is where the Communist conspirators have elected to make their play for global conquest."[14] John Foster Dulles, a Republican then working for the Truman Administration to prepare a peace treaty with Japan, saw the Korean attack as a move to head off a Pacific version of NATO. Russia already owned Sakhalin Island and the Kurile Islands to the north of Japan. A communist Korea, Dulles believed, would threaten Japan from the south, so Russia's strategic move would place Japan "between the upper and lower jaws of the Russian bear."[15] From such a dominating position Russia could exert

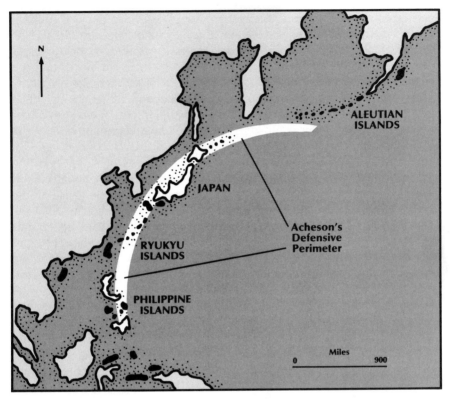

Figure 3.4   Secretary of State Acheson's Defensive Perimeter

diplomatic pressure to keep Japan, at the very least, neutral between East and West.

No one in 1950 seems to have considered a theory for the start of the war that has come to seem more plausible: The simple desire by the North Koreans for reunification. Stalin's power and position in relation to North Korea makes it unlikely that the North Koreans could have started the war without his permission, but it is possible that the North Korean leader Kim Il Sung was able to convince Stalin that he could win a quick and easy victory, and Stalin agreed to go along with him. In this interpretation, responsibility for beginning the war rests primarily with the North Koreans, and the war seems less closely related to the global Cold War.

Despite Acheson's speech putting Korea outside the American defensive perimeter, the United States did go to the aid of South Korea, first with air and naval units, then with ground troops brought over from Japan.[16] As the decision to aid South Korea was being made, it was also decided to go to the United Nations and request Security Council action. Because Russia was then boycotting the Security Council to protest its failure to seat the new communist regime in China, it was not present to use its veto, and the Council supported the United States position. Thus, United States military action in Korea became United Nations military action, although the United States provided by far the largest contingent of UN forces, and all UN forces were under United States command. UN involvement further broadened the war and placed it more firmly in the context of global rivalry between East and West.

From the perspective of thirty years we might say that nationalism and the nationalist desire to have a unified country were the basic causes of the Korean War. But what leaders believed at the time about the causes of the war was what determined policy. Because events in Korea were seen as part of the Cold War, the United States made some changes in its policies in Asia—changes that were to have consequences lasting for decades. The United States reversed itself on the issue of Formosa (or Taiwan, as we have come to call it), putting that island and the Nationalist Chinese on it inside the American defensive perimeter by sending the Seventh Fleet to patrol the Straits of Formosa. The United States also abandoned its opposition to colonial regimes and increased American aid to the French, who were fighting a Vietnamese Communist-Nationalist movement in Indo-China. Aid to the French had begun in early 1950, and because of the Korean War the program was enlarged and intensified. By 1951 it had the second highest priority, just behind the Korean War program itself.[17]

THE COURSE OF THE KOREAN WAR

Lacking substantial weapons, the South Koreans were unable to resist the North Korean army and fell back to the south, almost before United States troops arrived. But the United States was able to maintain a toehold on the Korean peninsula inside a small perimeter around the port of Pusan (see Figure 3.5). Then on September 15, 1950, in a bold and risky move, General MacArthur staged an amphibious landing in the center of the west coast of Korea at Inchon. The landing was a success, and the United States and its allies were able to drive in from Inchon toward the capital of Seoul, trapping North Korean forces as reinforced United Nations troops broke out of the Pusan perimeter. The success of this move reversed the fortunes of the war and encouraged United States leaders to consider a more ambitious aim than the one they had started with (which was merely the expulsion of the North Koreans from the South). The United States now decided to push on across the 38th parallel and reunite the entire country by force.

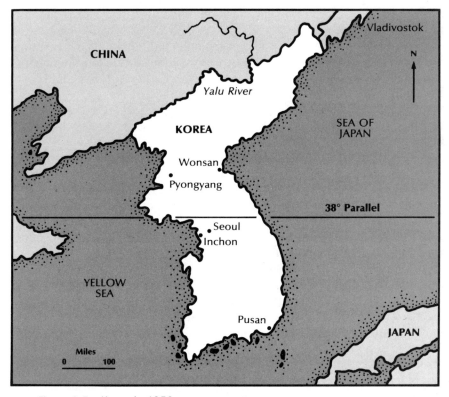

Figure 3.5   Korea in 1950

The major objection to this move within the Truman Administration was that it might provoke China to intervene in the war. China had signaled its concern about the course of events in Korea, and the United States gave serious consideration to the possibility of Chinese intervention. In November 1950, the Chinese did intervene massively, inflicting a grave defeat on United States forces, provoking an increased United States commitment, and prolonging the war for almost three more years. Chinese entry, as observers at the time recognized, created an entirely new and avoidable war.

The second part of the Korean conflict appears to have been a case where nobody wanted war—at least not the specific kind of war that developed between American and Chinese troops. The United States certainly did not. Reuniting Korea was indeed a foreign policy goal of the Truman Administration, but it was far down on Truman's list of priorities. It was not a goal important enough to be worth committing the kind of resources necessary to defeat a large Chinese army in Korea. And it was not a goal of

American foreign policy to fight China or to undo the Chinese revolution by force.[18]

For the Chinese, war in Korea risked escalation to an attack on China itself, possibly with atomic weapons. Even without escalation the fighting was highly costly to the Chinese. More important, Chinese goals could have been achieved without actual fighting.

China's goals have been a topic of debate since 1950. For a time the accepted interpretation was that the Chinese Communists desired to keep in being the communist regime on Korean soil. But recently it has been persuasively argued that an equally important if not overriding goal for the Chinese was simply national security. The Chinese had seen alarming shifts in the United States policy—from Acheson's defensive perimeter to engagement in Korea, from a hands-off policy to support of the nationalist regime on Formosa, and from limited goals in Korea to more ambitious ones. According to the new interpretation, the Chinese wanted to prevent further shifts that would threaten China more directly.[19]

Undeniably the United States had allowed success on the battlefield to encourage it to pursue more ambitious aims. Troops were sent to South Korea initially to repel the North Korean invaders. But with the easy success of the Inchon landing the goal shifted to reunification. United States policy had shifted from containment of communism to rollback of the Iron Curtain. Who was to say that, once reunification was accomplished, American troops wouldn't keep going right into Manchuria and try to undo the Chinese Communist revolution? Perhaps, as the French proverb puts it, the appetite comes with eating.

In fact the United States had no intention of invading China. The conflict resulted from failures to signal intentions and read signals properly. President Truman's limited aims in Korea were undermined by belligerent statements by members of his Administration, including General MacArthur himself (statements that ultimately led to the general's dismissal in April 1951). The Chinese had trouble deciding who really did speak for the United States.

The Chinese suffered from lack of direct contact with the United States. They had no diplomats and no permanent representatives at the United Nations. When they did issue an explicit warning to the United States not to allow American troops to cross the 38th parallel, they sent it through the Indian ambassador, K. M. Pannikar. But because Pannikar and other Indians had shown sympathy for the Chinese Communists in the past, the United States found it easy to dismiss the warnings. The Chinese warning did not come until the eve of the UN vote on a resolution to approve the expansion of the war, and United States effort was concentrated on getting the resolution approved. American leaders did not have time or energy to listen to a signal that would have made them reassess their entire policy.

The United States greatly underestimated China's military capability and willingness to take risks. In part this was because the Chinese had prepared for military entry into the war with great secrecy, moving great numbers of men at night and keeping them carefully hidden from United States reconnaissance aircraft during the day. The movement of large numbers of Chinese troops into Korea in an open way before United States troops crossed the 38th parallel could have prevented escalation of the war. MacArthur had authority to conduct operations in North Korea only as long as there was "no entry into North Korea by major Soviet or Chinese Communist forces, no announcement of an intended entry, and no threat by Russian or Chinese Communists to counter our military operations militarily in North Korea."[20] By keeping the entry of their forces secret, the Chinese were able to win a great tactical victory. If they had entered Korea openly, they might have been able to achieve their strategic goals by avoiding fighting altogether.[21]

Even so, the Chinese gave the Americans one last chance. On October 26 and November 2, Chinese forces in Korea met United States and South Korean forces in several sharp engagements but then disengaged on November 8. Very likely this was intended as a signal that, although they wished to avoid full-fledged war, they were willing to fight to keep United States forces away from China. The United States interpreted China's action as a symbolic objection and pressed on to the Yalu River. On November 26, Chinese forces numbering over 240,000 (over four times the number United States intelligence had estimated) launched an all-out attack that drove the UN forces back south of the 38th parallel.[22]

Once United States prestige was involved in this way, it was unlikely that the Americans would quit (any more than that they would have capitulated to Japan after the Japanese victory at Pearl Harbor). If the United States had carried the war into China, as some American leaders were advocating, the results would have been disastrous for China. Even as it was, the Chinese suffered severely from the fighting in Korea.[23] But the worst did not come to pass. The war remained limited. China's entry resulted in a United States retreat to the south, then a counterattack north that resulted in a stabilized line in about the middle of the peninsula. Armistice talks began in 1951; they were completed in July 1953, when an armistice line similar to the one achieved in 1951 was agreed on.

THE PRACTICE OF LIMITED WAR

During all this time the war remained limited in a number of important ways.[24] Of foremost importance was the limitation on weapons: No type of atomic weapon was used. At the time the Korean War broke out, both sides had the potential to use these weapons, although not to the extent they would later. The Russians had only recently acquired a nuclear capability: President Truman announced in September 1949 that they had exploded an atomic device. The United States had of course exploded its first atomic devices in 1945, but since that time had been building weapons very slowly without any sense of urgency. The conviction of many military leaders that the Korean action was only a feint led them to recommend saving the relatively scarce atomic bombs for use where greater United States interests were at stake, in a potential European war.[25]

Thus one could say that the limitation on weapons in Korea was not clear proof that wars could be kept limited, because it is not certain that either side was in a position to use them. But other limitations were significant, for they were observed despite advantages to one side or the other in ignoring them. The war was limited geographically to the Korean peninsula. The United States did not bomb across the Yalu River into China or even pursue aircraft over it into Chinese territory. Nor did it extend the war to the part of the Soviet Union that borders a tiny strip of Korea in the northeast. The Communist forces, for their part, did not broaden the war to include Japan, which the United States was using as its supply base and staging area.

Another limitation, treated as frivolous at the time, seems from our viewpoint to have greater significance, and that was the legal limitation. The participants in the Korean War did not declare war on each other (although there was a report of a declaration of war by radio by North Korea on the first day). The United States preferred to call it a "military police action." The Chinese claimed they were sending not their regular army but "volunteers." By itself this restraint of language would not have meant much, but given the real limitations in geography and weapons, the legal restraints can be seen as recognizing and reinforcing other restraints.

It is clear why the United States wanted to keep the war limited. As the chairman of the Joint Chiefs of Staff said, a wider war would be "at the wrong place, at the wrong time, and with the wrong enemy."[26] There was a widespread feeling that getting bogged down in a land war in Asia impaired American ability to help Europe withstand a Russian invasion. For the same reason the small stockpile of atomic bombs was hoarded for use against targets more substantial than peasant huts and dirt roads. The United States was also restrained by fighting in a coalition with other UN members. Even though their numbers were not significant (in June 1951, in addition to 250,000 Americans and 275,000 South Koreans, there were only 28,000 others, and they came from fifteen countries), the United States was concerned about their opinion on our policy.

It is harder to understand why the Communist forces observed these limits. After all, they started the fighting. On reflection it appears that they assumed there would be at the most only token resistance. They expected to achieve a quick, decisive takeover of all of Korea, or what we call a *fait accompli*. Once they had control of Korea, the West would have found it extremely difficult to retake the peninsula, by, say, an amphibious invasion, and the rest of the world in all likelihood would have accepted the takeover. That is the advantage of the technique of the fait accompli: If you can achieve your ends quickly, before the other side can organize to stop you, chances are they won't want to go to the trouble of undoing what you have done. Putting the other side in the position where the next move is up to them always gives your side an advantage. But having failed to achieve a fait accompli in Korea, the Communists were willing to accept a stalemate.

The Cold War continued after the armistice in Korea, although there is no agreement for just how long. Some writers have used the Cuban missile crisis of October 1962, or the Partial Test Ban Treaty of the following summer as termination dates. Perhaps in some ways the Cold War continues to the present. But the Korean War was its most violent stage and the limits to violence observed in it were the limits on great power rivalry observed throughout the Cold War: Soldiers of the two major powers would not face each other on the battlefield and atomic weapons would not be employed.

NOTES

1. A staggering number of books have been published on the Cold War. Among the most readable of the traditional interpretations is Adam Ulam, *The Rivals* (New York: Viking Press, 1971). A brief and readable version of the radical reinterpretation is by Carl Oglesby and Richard Shaull, *Containment and Change* (New York: Macmillan, 1967). A very literate moderate view is Louis Halle, *The Cold War as History* (New York: Harper and Row, 1967).

2. One account of events in Azerbaijan is Joseph Marion Jones, *The Fifteen Weeks* (New York: Viking Press, 1955), pp. 48–58.

3. The entire speech is printed as an appendix in Jones's book, pp. 269–274.

4. *Izvestia* (March 13, 1947), quoted in Alvin Z. Rubinstein, ed., *The Foreign Policy of the Soviet Union,* 2nd ed. (New York: Random House, 1966), p. 231.

5. Harry S. Truman, *Memoirs,* Vol. 1: *Year of Decisions* (Garden City, N.Y.: Doubleday, 1955), pp. 85–86.

6. Robert W. Coakley and Richard M. Leighton, *The United States Army in World War II. The War Department. Global Logistics and Strategy 1943–1945* (Washington, D.C.: Office of the Chief of Military History, Department of the Army, 1968), p. 836.

7. Quoted in John C. Sparrow, *History of Personnel Demobilization in the United States Army* (Washington, D.C.: Office of the Chief of Military History, Department of the Army, 1951), p. 380.

8. Cited by Kenneth Waltz, "The Stability of a Bipolar World," *Daedalus,* Vol. 93, No. 3 (Summer 1964), p. 883.

9. Commencement address at Iowa State College, Ames, Iowa, June 9, 1956, in *Department of State Bulletin,* Vol. 34, No. 886 (June 18, 1956), pp. 99–100.

10. David Rees, *Korea: The Limited War* (New York: St. Martin's Press, 1964), pp. 19–20.

11. Contemporary interpretations are described by Alexander L. George in "American Policy-Making and the North Korean Aggression," *World Politics,* Vol. 7, No. 2 (January 1955), pp. 209–232.

12. The speech was published in *Department of State Bulletin,* Vol. 22, No. 551 (January

23, 1950), pp. 111–118. For Acheson's justification of his speech, see his *Present at the Creation* (New York: Signet Books, 1969), p. 467.

13. Harry Truman, *Memoirs,* Vol. 2: *Years of Trial and Hope* (Garden City, N.Y.: Doubleday, 1956), p. 335.

14. Ibid., p. 445.

15. John Spanier, *The Truman–MacArthur Controversy and the Korean War* (Cambridge: Harvard University Press, 1959), p. 25.

16. For an explanation of why the United States responded in spite of its declared policy not to, see Ernest May, "The Nature of Foreign Policy: The Calculated versus the Axiomatic," *Daedalus,* Vol. 91, No. 4 (Fall 1962), pp. 633–667.

17. *The Pentagon Papers* (Senator Gravel Edition), Vol. 1 (Boston: Beacon Press, 1971), p. 83.

18. Richard Neustadt, *Presidential Power* (New York: Signet Books, 1964), especially p. 131.

19. Allen S. Whiting, *China Crosses the Yalu* (Stanford: Stanford University Press, 1960), p. 155; Edward Friedman, "Problems in Dealing with an Irrational Power: America Declares War on China," in *America's Asia: Dissenting Essays on Asian–American Relations,* ed. Edward Friedman and Mark Selden (New York: Pantheon Books, 1969), pp. 207–252.

20. Truman, Vol. 2, p. 360.

21. Thomas C. Schelling, *Arms and Influence* (New Haven: Yale University Press, 1966), p. 55 n.

22. Friedman, pp. 228–238.

23. Frank E. Armbruster, "China's Conventional Military Capability," in Frank E. Armbruster et al., *China Briefing* (Chicago: University of Chicago Center for Policy Study, 1968), pp. 59–60.

24. For a thorough discussion of this point, see Morton H. Halperin, *Limited War in the Nuclear Age* (New York: John Wiley, 1963), Chapter 3.

25. Bernard Brodie, *Strategy in the Missile Age* (Princeton: Princeton University Press, 1959), pp. 319–321.

26. Testimony at the "MacArthur Hearings," published as *Military Situation in the Far East,* quoted by Rees, p. 274.

Chapter 4

Wars in the Middle East

The Middle East has had more than its share of tension and conflict among states. The conflict that is most serious both in the casualties it has produced and in the threat it poses to world peace is the ongoing one between Israel and the Arab states. The basic issue is simple: Two separate groups of people want to build a state on the same piece of land. The complexity of the problem emerges when we examine how both Jews and Arabs happened to claim the same land.

ZIONISM

Through centuries when nations appeared, merged, and disappeared, the Jews distinguished themselves by maintaining a separate identity. In part their separateness was forced on them by persecution, especially by the Christian church. But it was reinforced by the basic tenets of their religion, which stressed codes of behavior. Various dietary laws—for example, no mixing of milk and meat—made it simpler for Jews to avoid eating with non-Jews and thus cut off one common avenue of social interchange.

Judaism also stressed membership in a community, belonging to a people. The sacred writings of Judaism were as much the history of the Jews as anything else, and that history took place on a particular piece of land, which the Jews called the land of Israel and we today know as Palestine. Even though most Jews had been expelled from their historic homeland by the Romans, over the centuries Jews everywhere kept alive their ties to the land by religious practices. Many of their religious holidays were intimately connected with the seasons in Palestine. The spring holiday of Shavuot, for example, was basically a harvest festival. For Jews celebrating Shavuot in the cold, wet spring of Poland and Russia, the holiday made sense only if they remembered the spring harvest of grain in the land of Israel.

Ties to the historic homeland of the Jews—sometimes poetically called Zion—were thus kept alive in a form we call religious Zionism. It had few practical consequences. Pious Jews wished to be buried in the land of Israel and hoped that someday a Messiah would come to restore the glories of the ancient kingdom of David.

For centuries the Jews were the victims of anti-Semitism, or prejudice, because of their religion. They were disliked because of their beliefs. If they changed their beliefs and converted to Christianity, they were accepted. Attitudes toward Jews changed in the nineteenth century, and the changes brought changes to Zionism. In the nineteenth century, anti-Semitism came to be based on race. Jews were disliked because of what they were, and no change could make them acceptable. Racial anti-Semitism accompanied the rise of extreme nationalism. Russian nationalists reemphasized the Slavic language and race. The French emphasized their origins in ancient Gaul. Outsiders, even converted and assimilated Jews, could never hope to become members of these nations.

With people around them emphasizing their own historic origins, Jews too began thinking about their roots. When their neighbors began telling them they were outsiders, they began to look for a part of the world they could call home. Religious Zionism provided the answer. By the end of the nineteenth century, young Jews began forming societies to encourage a return to their historic homeland. The first such groups appeared in Russia around 1880. Zionism became an international political movement after the publication in 1896 of a pamphlet called *The Jewish State* by an Austrian Jew, Theodore Herzl. The following year Herzl organized the first World Zionist Congress to provide an organizational structure for the movement.

A small number of Jews left Europe to escape anti-Semitic persecution and set up the beginnings of their own state. They were able to establish colonies in Palestine because national currents had not yet reached the people living in that part of the world (a condition that was to make possible their initial success but lay the foundation for later tragedy). To the Arabs living in Palestine, Europeans arriving to set up settlements were objects of curiosity but not alarm. Although not empty, the land was not nearly as populous as it would become later. Maladministration by the Turks, who had ruled the area for centuries, had not encouraged population growth. In the late nineteenth century, Palestine was a home for many utopian schemers, including Russian Orthodox pilgrims and German Pietists. Zionists were just one more group.[1]

ARAB NATIONALISM

The same national stirrings that hit the European Jews in the late nineteenth century affected the Arabs about twenty-five years later. Some of the first writings about an Arab state appeared in the first years of the twentieth century.[2] But the major impetus came from World War I. The Turks had joined the war on the side of the Germans, and the British were fearful for their possessions in the Middle East, particularly the Suez Canal. The British, hoping to protect their holdings by exploiting Arab resentment against the Turks, who were still the nominal rulers, promoted an Arab revolt. In return for British military support and the promise of an Arab state after the war, the Arabs were to rise up against the Turks.

Sherif Hussein of Mecca, the great-great-grandfather of King Hussein, the current ruler of Jordan, led the revolt. He expected that after the war he would head an Arab state centered in Damascus and including the area today known as Syria, Lebanon, Israel, and Jordan. But the Arab revolt did not proceed fast enough for the Arabs to be firmly in control of this territory by the time the war ended. The Arabs then discovered that the British, in addition to promising this land to them, had promised a portion of the area to the Jews (in the Balfour Declaration of 1917) and another portion to the French (in the Sykes–Picot agreement of 1916).

The Arab forces were no match for the French and British troops, and by 1922 the European powers had a new system firmly in place, sanctioned by the new League of Nations as mandates that were to train the natives for self-government. The dividing line between the French and British mandates separated what has become Syria from what has become Jordan. Within each mandate, the European powers made further divisions. The French divided the Christian area of Lebanon from Syria; the British divided the strictly Arab area of Trans-Jordan from the area of Palestine, where Jews were allowed to settle (see Figure 4.1).

Arab nationalists were left with many grievances. In addition to a betrayal of promises and foreign domination, they saw European rulers allowing European Jews to settle on Arab land. Such settlement was in conflict with the widespread belief that nations must have exclusive control of a state. Indeed, it was just this belief that made the Jews insist on creating a state entirely under their own control. The most persistent demand of Arab nationalists during the 1920's and 1930's was a halt to Jewish immigration and land sales.

When the British established their mandate in Palestine, the conflict between Arabs and Jews was not yet acute. Total Zionist immigration to that time numbered only 90,000. The Zionists had paid for all the land they bought, and they were improving the economic life of the country, providing employment and improving standards of living.

But life in Palestine was hard, and most European Jews were not Zionists. Far more wanted to emigrate to America. In the period when fewer than 100,000 were leaving for Palestine, over a million and a half left Russia for America. The Zionist settlement of Palestine might have become no more than a footnote in history had it not been for two major events, both external to the Middle East. First, Britain and then America severely restricted immigration from Russia and Eastern Europe (meaning, above all, Jewish immigration). Second, the rise to power of the Nazis made the need to emigrate all the more urgent. Despite obstacles created by the Nazis and immigration restrictions imposed by the British Mandate authorities, over 350,000 Jews

Figure 4.1   The Middle East, 1947

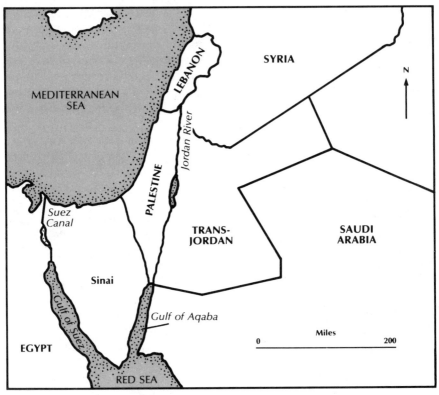

moved to Palestine during the Nazi era. Palestine, with a population that was 30 per cent Jewish, had the densest concentration of Jews in the world.

ISSUES LEADING TO WAR

The stake in the conflict was clear. Two groups wanted to set up a state on the same piece of land. For the Zionists, the justification was that Jews everywhere were being told they were not welcome because they were outsiders. In effect, governments were saying to them, "Why don't you people go back where you came from?" Where they came from was Palestine or, as they called it, the land of Israel, and to there they had returned in significant numbers. No place on earth was better qualified to be the site for a Jewish state, and recent political events had demonstrated that without a state of their own they were doomed. For the Arabs, the justification was much simpler. They wanted a state in Palestine because that is where they were living, and, despite the large numbers of Jews, they still formed the majority.

Underlying this desire for a state were several basic ideas of modern political thought. Both sides believed they needed an exclusive state. Only a small minority among Jews and Arabs were willing to try other arrangements, such as a confederation of provinces or a dual-nationality state. The Jews had experienced centuries of insecurity as a minority. They knew too well that the firmest constitutional guarantees could be terminated overnight by a ruler such as Hitler. The Arabs had suffered centuries of misrule as a province of the Turks in the Ottoman Empire. For them foreign rule had meant exploitation. According to modern notions of national self-determination held by Jews and Arabs alike, it was no longer feasible for two separate peoples to live side by side within one nation as they had in many cases in the past.

A final factor leading to war in 1948 was involvement of the great powers. The Zionists had powerful support in the United States, especially from Congress and the president. The Arabs found support with the British, who valued their good relations with the Arabs and wanted to protect their economic interests, including oil, in the several Arab states. In the UN debate about what to do with Palestine, the Americans were backed by the Soviet Union, not because Stalin had any concern for the plight of the Jews but because he saw the issue as a wedge that could be driven between his two most powerful capitalist enemies. Thus, in November 1947 the UN General Assembly passed a resolution, jointly sponsored by the United States and the Soviet Union, calling for the establishment of two states in the British Mandate of Palestine, a Jewish state and an Arab one.

THE 1948 WAR

On May 14, 1948, Zionist leaders declared independence for their new state, naming it Israel. The Arabs, who had bitterly opposed the UN vote, had no intention of letting a Jewish state come into existence in their midst. On May 15, Arab armies attacked.

Because the issues were so clear, war had been expected. The Israelis were fighting for the survival of their state and, most of them believed, for their physical survival as well. The Arab states opposing Israel were united in their goal of preventing such a state from coming into existence. Beyond that negative goal, however, the Arabs did not agree, and their lack of agreement was the fundamental cause of their defeat.

The strongest Arab force was the Arab Legion of Trans-Jordan (now Jordan). But the king of Trans-Jordan, Abdullah, was not fighting on behalf of a Palestinian state. He intended to annex the area to his own kingdom. It was primarily to keep this from happening that Egypt entered the war. All the Arabs assumed the Israelis would be easy to defeat. Egypt's primary concern in deploying its armies was to keep the Arab Legion from gaining control over the entire territory. Egypt favored a separate Palestinian state because it believed such a state would be weak and would quickly become an Egyptian client. Syria and Lebanon also participated, partly out of feelings of solidarity, partly in the hope of adding to their own territory. Iraq sent some troops as well. The weakest contingents of all were the armed bands of Arabs from Palestine itself.

By skillful fighting and skillful diplomacy, taking advantage of Arab divisions, the Israelis were able to prevail. The war consisted of short periods of violent fighting, each lasting a few weeks, interspersed with truces. The Israelis were able to get their foes to break the truces; then they defeated them one by one in short, well-planned campaigns. Because of Arab distrust, the Arab Legion stood aside while the Israelis defeated the Egyptians in the south; then the Egyptians stood aside while the Israelis defeated the Arab Legion. Finally, in early 1949, Egypt concluded an armistice with Israel. In the next few months the other Arab belligerents followed except for Iraq, which had no borders in common with Israel and thus needed no formal agreement.

•

THE 1956 WAR

For Israel, the 1948 war was a tentative success, a first step toward security. But the victory was not complete. Israel had no internationally recognized boundaries, only armistice lines. Arab neighbors still considered themselves in a state of war. All the states of the Middle East felt that the basic issue of the existence of a Jewish state was not yet resolved. Another armed clash would come; the only question was when.

Partly as a result of their defeat in the 1948 war, a group of Egyptian army officers in 1952 deposed their king, whom they blamed for the corruption and inefficiency in their society. The most important of these officers was Gamal Abdel Nasser, who became president in 1954. The elimination of the state of Israel was always a goal of Nasser's foreign policy. As he was to put it, the very existence of the state of Israel was an act of aggression.[3] What determines a state's actual policy, however, is not what its leaders wish but how much they are willing to sacrifice to see their wishes realized. In the first years of Nasser's rule, he seemed content to give only lip service to the goal of eliminating Israel, concentrating instead on strengthening Egypt's political system and economy.

Nasser's policies changed after February 1955, when Israeli troops crossed the armistice line into the Gaza Strip (a section of Palestine under Egyptian control) in retaliation for a terrorist attack. Arab attacks across the armistice line into Israel were common, but before February 1955 they were individual efforts not sponsored by any Arab government. After the Gaza Strip raid, however, Nasser set up an organization to conduct raids into Israel. The existence of terrorist bases in territory controlled by Egypt became a serious concern to Israel, serious enough that it was willing to contemplate war to see them eliminated.

A second reason for Israel to contemplate war was Nasser's restrictions on Israeli shipping. When Britain gave control of the Suez Canal to Egypt in a treaty signed in October 1954, all cargo destined for or coming from Israel, even in non-Israeli ships, was prohibited by Egypt from going through the canal. This meant that if Israel wished to trade with countries around the Indian Ocean or in the Pacific, it had to use the long route around the southern tip of Africa. The only other possibility was to use the Israeli port of Elat and travel through the Gulf of Aqaba out into the Red Sea. But Egypt controlled the strategic heights of Sharm el Sheik, which overlooked the Strait of Tiran, the exit from the Gulf of Aqaba into the Red Sea. Thus Egypt was able to prevent Israeli shipping from using that route as well (see Figure 4.2). In September 1955, in response to another Israeli retaliatory raid, Nasser announced that even air travel over the Gulf of Aqaba was prohibited.

Meanwhile, quite independently of the conflict between Egypt and Israel, British troops were withdrawing from the Suez Canal zone under the terms of the October 1954 treaty. Even though the British were not friendly toward Israel, the presence of their troops had provided a buffer between Egyptian forces and Israel. With the British withdrawal, the Israelis felt less secure, but so did Nasser. He had insisted that the British leave in order to remove the last vestige of colonialism, but he was not sure the Egyptian army was strong enough to face the Israelis. He set about to modernize his forces and, after being rebuffed by the United States, turned to the Soviet Union. In September 1955, he announced an arms deal with the Soviet bloc.

The arms deal was one of several issues that soured relations between the United States and Egypt in 1955 and 1956 and made it politically difficult for President Eisenhower to go ahead with a proposed loan for a major economic project in Egypt, a new high dam on the Nile at Aswan. In July 1956, Secretary of State John Foster Dulles abruptly withdrew support for such a loan. The news came as a surprise and shock to Nasser. Within a week he announced he was nationalizing the private international company that ran the Suez Canal. Because the company's stockholders were mainly British and French, Nasser's action most disturbed Britain and France.

The French already disliked Nasser because of the support he was giving

Figure 4.2   Sinai Peninsula and Adjacent Waterways

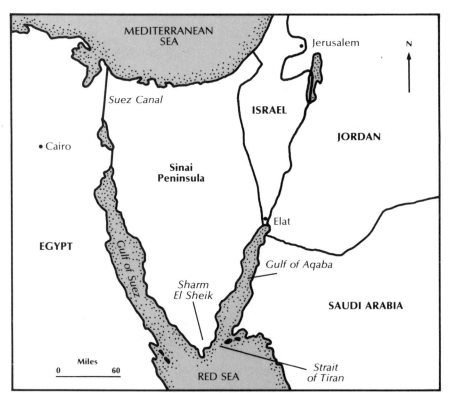

to an Arab insurrection in their territory of Algeria. Many believed that action to stop the rebellion at its source in Egypt would be more effective than sending more troops to Algeria, but they lacked the physical means to conduct operations against Egypt. When Nasser nationalized the canal company, he provided the French with both an ally for action and an excuse for acting.

The French military staff (later joined by the British) worked out a plan with Israel (later joined by Britain). Israel would attack Egypt to achieve its main objectives—elimination of terrorist bases and the opening of passages through the Strait of Tiran. France and England would secretly provide air over for Israel during this attack, but they would pretend to be surprised by it and would demand an immediate cease-fire and pullback of troops to protect the Suez Canal from damage. If Nasser did not comply (and they did not believe he would), they would land troops in the canal zone in order to protect it.

The Israeli part of the plan worked very well. On the night of October 29, 1956, Israeli forces attacked Egypt. By November 5 they had reached the canal. The British and French part failed. Because of extreme caution they did not even begin to land troops until November 6. By then, pressure from other countries for a cease-fire was irresistible. Most surprising was pressure from the United States. Britain and France had calculated that the United States would remain neutral, but they were wrong. Partly out of anger at not being informed in advance, partly to preserve Eisenhower's image as a man of peace during a presidential election, partly to avoid any recrimination that would detract from United States condemnation of the Soviet suppression of a rebellion simultaneously occurring in Hungary, the United States took the lead at the UN in condemning the invasion. The United States backed its condemnation with economic moves (such as restricting the flow of oil to Britain) designed to force capitulation.

The British and French were forced to withdraw and make way for a United Nations peacekeeping force, an operation that took only a few days. The Israelis fared slightly better, remaining in possession of the Sinai Peninsula until March 1957, when United States pressure forced them to retreat in favor of a UN force as well. The Suez Canal remained in Egyptian control. Nevertheless, the war achieved what Israel wanted. The presence of the UN force in Sinai inhibited terrorist attacks from Egyptian territory and guaranteed free passage through the Strait of Tiran. At a cost of only 189 battle deaths, Israel had achieved some important foreign policy goals.

THE 1967 WAR

The Sinai campaign brought Israel the longest period of peace in its history—from 1956 to 1967. During that time the state and economy of

Israel grew stronger, as did its military power. Outside observers considered war unlikely because the Arab armies were no match for Israel. Despite these expectations, however, in the spring of 1967 a crisis developed and turned into a war in a matter of weeks. On June 5, Israeli forces attacked Egypt; within days they had defeated Jordan and Syria as well. The prewar calculation of Israeli superiority was thus proved correct. Yet, because that calculation had not been convincing to all sides, war had occurred.

The most serious miscalculation was made by President Nasser. He had resigned himself to tolerate Israel's existence until three conditions changed: the Arabs acquired military superiority, Israel was diplomatically isolated, and the Arabs were united. Within a few weeks, in May 1967, Nasser deceived himself into thinking that these conditions had been met.[4]

Nasser's belief that the Arabs had achieved military superiority resulted from his confusing the possession of military equipment with its actual assimilation by his troops. The Soviet Union had supplied substantial amounts of equipment, but Egyptian soldiers were still far from proficient in its use. Evidence of their lack of combat readiness was soon apparent. When the Israelis overran the Sinai Peninsula in the course of the 1967 war, they did not find a single tank-repair shop. They did find plans for an Egyptian air strike on Israel similar to the strike that Israel had launched to begin the war on Egypt. But whereas the Israelis had needed only seven and one-half minutes to rearm and refuel planes between missions, the Egyptians had planned to allow from thirty to forty minutes.[5] Furthermore, the best Egyptian troops—40,000 of them—were at the southern tip of the Arabian peninsula fighting a war in Yemen, and they could not be withdrawn in time to make a difference.

Nasser's belief in Israel's diplomatic isolation was a misperception, based in part on false information, fed to him by the Soviets, that Israel was mobilizing troops on its northern frontier to attack Syria. If Israel launched such an attack, Nasser believed, no country would support it. Israel offered to allow foreign diplomats to tour its northern region to see that no such mobilization was taking place, and UN observers subsequently confirmed the Israeli claim, but Nasser persisted in his belief in Israeli aggressive designs until too late. As the focus of the crisis shifted from Syria to Egypt, Nasser persisted in his policy of tempting Israel to strike first in order to ensure its diplomatic isolation. But when war did break out, it was seen by most countries (most important, by the United States) not as Israeli aggression but as an Israeli response to provocations by Nasser. Thus, unlike in 1956, Israel did not find itself condemned by the United States and under heavy pressure to relinquish its conquests.

Even more serious for Nasser were the military consequences of allowing Israel to strike first. He even predicted that Israel would launch an air strike on June 5, the very date it occurred. But he erred in predicting a loss to Egypt of only 20 per cent of its planes; the actual loss was a crippling 60 per cent, not to mention damage to all radar stations and air fields.[6]

His final miscalculation was a belief that he had achieved Arab unity. Verbal support, amounting to war fever in the Arab countries, misled Nasser into believing that his persistent but elusive goal had been achieved. A joint command structure of the armies of Egypt, Jordan, and Syria existed on paper, suggesting that in this war, unlike the previous ones, all Arab belligerents would follow a unified and coherent strategy. But during the actual fighting, Israel again triumphed because it was able to deal with its opponents one by one, just as in the 1948 war.

Not all the miscalculations were on the Egyptian side, however. Nasser had set events in motion by ordering Egyptian troops into the Sinai Peninsula on May 14. Such a move set the stage for war, for Egypt usually held the Sinai with only a small garrison force. The move was not legally an act of aggression, because the Sinai was acknowledged Egyptian territory. Nevertheless, Nasser expected a firm Israeli reaction such as mobilization. Encountering no such reaction, Nasser proceeded on May 18 to the next step, ordering the withdrawal of the UN buffer force from Egyptian territory. This move was more serious, undoing one of the accomplishments of the 1956 war, but again Nasser provoked no threatening military reaction from the Israelis.[7] The Israeli government was divided and headed by a cautious prime minister, Levi Eshkol. Moreover, the Israelis recalled that Nasser had moved troops into the Sinai in 1960, provoking a brief war scare at that time, but nothing had come of it. Thus Israel did not feel threatened by these most recent moves.

Israel was not alone in its failure to react strongly. The United States response to Nasser's actions was very mild as well. The United States wanted very much to avoid a war in the Middle East because of the risk of involving American troops there when United States forces were strained by the war in Vietnam. Initially American diplomatic notes to Israel were much harsher, urging restraint in response to Nasser's moves.[8]

Emboldened by the caution of his opponent, Nasser pushed on. On May 22 he announced the closure of the Strait of Tiran to Israeli shipping, thereby undoing the other major accomplishment of the 1956 war. Despite the Israeli position that such an action would be treated as a *casus belli,* or action justifying war, the Israeli prime minister reacted again with a mild speech. His concluding line was not a dramatic threat but the prosaic comment that Nasser's action would "be a dangerous precedent."[9]

Nasser's belief that his three conditions had been fulfilled was reinforced by Israel's caution. Nasser, believing that time was on his side, continued to apply pressure. Egyptian troops that had been fighting in a civil war in Yemen were recalled home. An airlift of Egyptian troops into Jordan began. As the pressure for Israel to strike the first blow increased, Egypt's own military strength to withstand such a blow increased, or so Nasser believed.

But, having made war more likely by its caution and delay, Israel was now organizing itself to act. A new Cabinet was formed, including members of all Israel's political parties except the Communists. The general who had organized the 1956 Sinai campaign, Moshe Dayan, was named minister of defense. Israeli military leaders prepared to implement their plan for a first strike designed to eliminate the Egyptian air force. The strike was carried out successfully on June 5.

As in 1956, Israeli forces quickly occupied the Sinai Peninsula. But unlike in 1956, they did not subsequently withdraw. The speedy withdrawal of the UN buffer force when it was ordered out by Nasser had weakened arguments in favor of relying on such a force a second time.

In 1967, Israel fought against Jordan and Syria as well as Egypt. From Jordan the Israelis took all the territory on the west bank of the Jordan River, including parts of the city of Jerusalem that had been under Jordanian control since 1948. From Syria they captured the strategic territory of the Golan Heights, which overlooks Israeli settlements around the Sea of Galilee.

The war turned out badly for Nasser, who had set in motion the events that led to the fighting. In addition to a humiliating military defeat, Egypt lost the Sinai Peninsula and the revenues from the Suez Canal, which was blocked by Nasser when the war began and subsequently served as the cease-fire line between Israeli and Egyptian troops. For the Israelis, who struck the first blow, the war turned out well. Not only was the security of the state enhanced, as it had been by the wars of 1948 and 1956, but Israel now possessed territory that it hoped it could trade for a permanent peace settlement. War appeared to have produced results unachievable by the peaceful means of diplomacy.

THE 1973 WAR

Neither the 1948 war not the 1956 war had begun entirely at the initiative of the Arabs. In 1948 the Arabs could have chosen to accept the new state of Israel. When they decided against acceptance, the timing of the war was determined by the departure of the British and the Israeli declaration of independence. In 1956 the war clearly originated with the British, French, and Israelis. In 1967, however, despite the fact that Israel struck the first blow, the war resulted from Nasser's initiatives but failed to achieve the results he had hoped for. War for him was an extension of diplomacy by other means, although in this case the other means were as unsuccessful as diplomacy had been. In 1973 Egypt again resorted to war to achieve its goals.

President Nasser died in 1970, having failed to undo the results of the 1967 war. His successor, Anwar Sadat, had some advantages in conducting foreign policy that Nassar had lacked. Because Sadat was less flamboyant, he could dissociate himself from some of the more extreme policies of his predecessor, especially the claims to a pan-Arab state under Egyptian leadership, which threatened the stability of all the other Arab governments. Sadat's moderation won him the support of conservative Arab states such as Saudi Arabia but still did not win the support of the United States. Even Sadat's dramatic gesture of expelling all Russian advisers in 1972 did not win him American support. Nevertheless, Sadat's basic understanding of the situation was correct. Only the United States was in a position to deliver what Egypt wanted most, the restoration of the Sinai Peninsula and its accompanying economic advantages—oil from its oil fields and revenue from the Suez Canal, which could be reopened if it no longer served as a cease-fire line. As long as Israel was sure of American diplomatic and military support, Israel could dictate the terms under which the Sinai would be returned. For Sadat these terms were too high a price to pay. Only if the Americans found it in their interest to give less than total support to Israel could the deadlock be broken.

Sadat continued his diplomatic efforts into 1973, dispatching his national security adviser to consult once again with the Americans. At the same time he prepared to resort to force if his diplomacy failed. His aim was concrete and limited—the establishment of a small area under Egyptian control on the east bank of the Suez Canal. Strategically such a goal made sense because of the dilemma Israel found itself in. It could guard the canal heavily only at the great cost to its economy of maintaining a force 200 miles from its own territory. But failure to guard the canal heavily would open it to precisely the kind of move Sadat had in mind. Because the west bank of the canal was so close to the heart of Egypt, it was easy for Sadat to keep troops in a threatening posture. Furthermore, Egypt's larger population enabled it to maintain a large standing army. Israel's civilian army rapidly mobilized in time of war could match Egypt in short periods of combat, but Israel could not keep its army mobilized for any great length of time without crippling its economy.

The Egyptian military planners had learned a few lessons from the defeat in 1967. Recognizing that their soldiers had less technological proficiency than the Israelis, in 1973 they made less ambitious plans. They intended merely to cross the canal, establish themselves on a few miles of territory, and dig in. Soldiers practiced the necessary operations, such as unloading bridging equipment from trucks, again and again, day after day. The initiative and improvisation characteristic of the Israeli forces would give the Israelis little advantage in the kind of operation that the Egyptians were planning.[10]

In the spring of 1973, Egypt moved a large force into the canal area. Perhaps they were only engaging in maneuvers; perhaps they were preparing for an attack. The Israelis noticed and mobilized their army. Egypt proceeded with military maneuvers but did not attack. Israel demobilized. After a summer of further diplomacy, Egypt again moved large forces into the canal zone in the fall. Again Israel noticed but decided not to undergo the expense of mobilization. This time Egypt attacked.

The Egyptian attack was coordinated with a Syrian attack in the Golan Heights, a level of coordination the Arabs had not achieved in previous wars. Because of the coordination and the surprise, the Arab armies did quite well.

Despite the fact that the war began with an unambiguous Arab attack, the United States was slow in coming to the aid of Israel. In the mind of the American secretary of state, Henry Kissinger, Israel's overwhelming victory in 1967 had actually hindered movement toward peace. The Israelis were so confident that they felt no pressure to make concessions. The Arabs had been so humiliated that only after they had redeemed themselves in battle could they consider making peace as equals. Thus Kissinger did not want a repetition of the 1967 war.

Events outran Kissinger's policy. Working with the advantages of surprise and initiative, the Arab armies fought well. The Israelis, suffering from confusion and carelessness engendered by overconfidence, were not able to make a decisive counterattack. In the north they were able to halt the Syrian attack, but their counterattacks failed. Along the Suez Canal they could not dislodge the Egyptians.

Both sides were using munitions at a prodigious rate. The war had begun on October 5. By October 10 the Soviets began resupplying the Egyptians and Syrians. Israel began pressing the United States for new supplies. In the years since 1948, military technology had grown increasingly complex. Wars of even short duration became intense. More tanks faced each other in the Sinai than in the major tank battles of World War II. The complexity of weapons as well as the rapid rate at which they used up ammunition increased the dependence of the combatants on their suppliers. This dependency created the danger of the war's escalating by drawing in the suppliers, but it also gave the suppliers increased opportunities for influencing the outcome.

On October 14 the Israelis began to reverse the course of the war by crossing the Suez Canal to the Egyptian side, spreading out and threatening to trap the Egyptian armies already on the west side. This move would have created a military victory as spectacular as the one of 1967, precisely the outcome the Americans did not want. Because of the total dependence of Israel on the United States for supplies, the United States was able to force

Israel to agree to a cease-fire before it had entirely trapped the Egyptian armies. To the complaints of Israeli officers who felt they were being denied the victory they deserved, the minister of defense, Moshe Dayan, replied, "Shells they are firing today were not in their possession a week ago."[11]

The 1973 war ended with each side able to claim some victories. The Arab states had mounted a successful attack and, in the south, maintained a foothold in territory that had been occupied by Israel after 1967. The Israelis had recovered from the shock of surprise, held their own lines in the north, and, in the south, mounted a counterattack that put them in control of Egyptian territory on the west bank of the Suez Canal.

Kissinger's analysis was proved correct. The somewhat ambiguous results of the 1973 war paved the way for a peace treaty between Israel and Egypt signed in 1979. For Egypt the war and the resulting agreements accomplished major foreign policy objectives—a restoration of honor, a return to the Sinai Peninsula, economic gains from oil fields and the reopened Suez Canal, and the beginnings of a reduced defense burden.

For Israel, the results were less satisfactory. Recognition by one of its Arab neighbors and the conclusion of peace with it was the major gain. But Israel remained under attack from the other Arab states. The loss of the oil fields in the Sinai made Israel even more dependent on outsiders, particularly the United States, which had guaranteed to supply oil in the last resort. It is unlikely that Israel would have paid the price it did if Egypt had not gone to war.

ISRAEL AND LEBANON

In June 1982 the Middle East experienced yet another major war, this time on Israel's initiative. The war, much to the shock of some Israelis,[12] was less to repulse a clear threat to their security than to accomplish more abstract political ends. One could say that the 1956 war was not primarily defensive either; at least one could question the seriousness of the threat to Israel posed then by the terrorists operating from the Gaza Strip and the potential threat posed by the Egyptian acquisition of Russian arms. In 1982 the same two issues reappeared.

After a civil war in Jordan in 1970 between the forces of King Hussein and the forces of the various Palestinian guerrilla groups, the Palestinians were forced to relocate their political and military activities to Lebanon. The Lebanese state was too weak and divided by its own sectarian differences to impose any serious limits on their actions. As a result, the Palestinians, under the umbrella organization of the Palestinian Liberation Organization (PLO) increased in power, establishing themselves as virtual rulers in several areas of Lebanon, mounting terrorist attacks into Israel, and building up arsenals that by 1981 began to include heavy weapons—artillery, rocket launchers, and tanks. This increase in military power was accompanied by increasing international recognition, such as the invitation extended in 1974 to the head of the PLO, Yasir Arafat, to address the General Assembly of the United Nations with the same honors accorded to a head of state.

As the international stature of the PLO grew, its forays into Israel diminished, partly because of PLO policy, partly because of better Israel security, and partly because of agreements worked out by the United States. Nevertheless Israel expressed alarm at the growth in military potential as the PLO acquired long-range weapons such as rockets and artillery, which would endanger Israel if the cease-fire on its northern border ever broke down. Perhaps more alarming, although not emphasized publicly by Israeli leaders, was the growth in political power of the PLO. In Western Europe and in the United States, more groups and even governments called for some form of recognition and statehood for the Palestinians.

Since 1977 Israel had been governed (for the first time in its history) by a right-wing coalition, headed by Menachim Begin. Prominent among his cabinet ministers was Ariel Sharon, who earlier as military governor of the Gaza Strip had demonstrated his belief in the usefulness of force. Both men were committed to the annexation of the West Bank of the Jordan River— territory captured by Israel in the 1967 war—as land to which Israel had a historic claim. Both were opposed to the creation of a Palestinian state on land claimed by Israel—or anywhere if such a state were to present a military threat to Israel.

In June 1982 a gunman shot the Israeli ambassador to Britain; immediately Israeli forces in large numbers moved north into Lebanon in an obviously well-planned operation. The ineffectual Lebanese army was in no position to offer resistance. The real opponents were the forces of the PLO and the troops of Syria, who had been stationed in Lebanon since 1976 in an effort to end fighting among various factions inside Lebanon. Despite emphasis by Prime Minister Begin on the security threat to Israel posed by PLO forces in southern Lebanon, it became clear that the real target was the PLO as a political force. Israeli troops advanced to the capital, Beirut, then paused as straightforward military missions were complicated by political problems. The Syrians offered little resistance to the Israelis, withdrawing toward their own border to protect their homeland. But at the same time they did not pressure the Palestinians to surrender or evacuate. Israel could have mounted a direct military assault on Palestinian strongholds in Beirut but only at high cost to its own troops (unpopular at home) and to civilians in Beirut (unpopular abroad, especially in the United States).

The ensuing dilemma meant that instead of a war measured in days, Israel was engaged in weeks of siege warfare, attacking Beirut by airplane and artillery, while suffering small but steady losses in its own forces. The siege ended with a negotiated withdrawal of PLO forces from Beirut, ostensibly to distant Arab states such as Tunisia. Yet many of these forces quickly returned to Lebanon by way of Syria. The PLO suffered a political setback but was not eliminated as a political force. Syrian forces remained in control of much of Lebanon and to counterbalance them many Israelis remained as occupation troops.

President Sadat initiated war against Israel in 1973 with a clear political goal. From a purely military standpoint the war appeared to go badly for Egypt, with Israeli troops ending in possession of territory on both banks of the Suez Canal. Yet the diplomacy and military pressure of the following years did lead to a peace settlement, completed in 1982 by the final Israeli withdrawal from land in the Sinai captured in 1967.

The 1982 invasion of Lebanon by Israel appears to have had a similarly clear political goal. But willingness to pursue politics "by other means" (to use Clausewitz's definition of war) is no guarantee of success. The Israelis did achieve some of their goals. They forced the PLO to give up its quarters in Beirut and the quasi-sovereign status it enjoyed there. Instead of operating from one central headquarters, henceforward it would be scattered among many countries. The hold of its chairman, Yasir Arafat, over the organization was weakened, so much so that the Syrians actively encouraged rebels within the PLO to challenge his leadership. King Hussein of Jordan was able to take advantage of the PLO's weakened condition and repudiate the agreement of the Arab League made in 1974 that the PLO must be the "sole legitimate representative of the Palestinian people."

But in weakening one of its enemies, Israel had strengthened two other ones. Although during the invasion Israel had not confronted Syria directly, some Israeli forces had engaged Syrians. In these clashes, the Israelis came off well, shooting down eighty-five Syrian planes while losing only one. But Syria quickly received new (and better) equipment from the Soviet Union, becoming a more formidable opponent than before.

Most significant, the Israeli invasion unleashed a new force in its conflict with its neighbors. Many of the people in southern Lebanon were Shi'ite Muslims. In the preceding decades they had not played a direct role in the clashes along the border between Palestinians and Israelis. The prolonged Israeli occupation of their land now drew them into the conflict. Repeated attacks on the Israeli occupation forces, often taking the form of car bombs driven by suicide drivers, eventually forced the Israelis to withdraw in June of 1985, by which time their total deaths had reached 654. The PLO was no longer so strong a threat on Israel's northern border but radicalized Shi'ites, encouraged by co-religionists in Iran, were potentially more dangerous.

The inconclusive result of Israel's 1982 war sets it apart from the preceding ones. The 1948 war brought Israel into existence; the 1956 and 1967 wars strengthened its security. The major benefits from the 1973 war went to Egypt, with the reopening of the Suez Canal and recovery of oil fields in the Sinai. But that conflict also set in motion a process leading to a peace treaty between Israel and Egypt, benefiting both Egypt, by enabling it to reduce its military spending, and Israel, by reducing pressure on one of its frontiers. For Israel the first three wars, and for Egypt the 1973 wars, were the successful continuation of politics by other means.

NOTES

1. Amos Elon, *The Israelis: Founders and Sons* (New York: Holt, Rinehart and Winston, 1971), pp. 119–123.

2. Negib Azouri, *Reveil de la nation Arabe dans l'Asie Turque* (1905), in *The Israel–Arab Reader,* 2nd ed., ed. Walter Laqueur (New York: Bantam Books, 1971), p. 5.

3. "Speech to National Assembly Members, 29 May 1967," Appendix 7 in Walter Laqueur, *The Road to Jerusalem* (New York: Macmillan, 1968), pp. 316–319.

4. Nadav Safran, *Israel: The Embattled Ally* (Cambridge: Harvard University Press, 1978), pp. 397–399.

5. Nadav Safran, *From War to War* (New York: Pegasus, 1969), pp. 325–327, 353.

6. Safran, *Israel,* p. 241.

7. William B. Quandt, *Decade of Decisions: American Policy Toward the Arab–Israeli Conflict, 1967–1976* (Berkeley: University of California Press, 1977), pp. 37–43.

8. Ibid., pp. 39, 42.

9. Safran, *Israel,* p. 398.

10. Chaim Herzog, *The War of Atonement* (Boston: Little, Brown, 1975), pp. 34–35.

11. "Dayan Says U.S. Threat Forced Relief Convoys," *The New York Times,* October 31, 1973, p. 16.

12. Jacobo Timerman, *The Longest War* (New York: Random House, 1982).

Chapter 5

War in the 1970's

Cold War tensions between East and West and the threat of nuclear war have often distracted attention from the behavior of smaller states. But, as events in the Middle East illustrate, war continues to be employed as an instrument of state policy. The point is not that war is indeed useful but that states' leaders continue to think it is. Recent wars offer enough evidence to keep their belief alive. Two recent wars, one between India and Pakistan in 1971, the other between Turkey and Cyprus in 1974, are good examples of such evidence.

PAKISTAN AND THE BENGALIS

The British granted independence to their colonial possessions in India in 1947. For the most part the British had ruled directly through native princes. In 1947 each of them was given the choice of joining a new secular and democratic republic to be called India or a Muslim religious state to be called Pakistan. Most chose to join India; a few in the northeast and north-west chose Pakistan. The status of a large area in the central northern region, the state of Kashmir, was disputed because the ruler (who was Hindu) chose to join India and the population (mostly Muslim) preferred Pakistan; in the end India occupied about two-thirds, Pakistan one-third. What emerged was a Pakistan divided into two parts separated by 1,000 miles. It has been described as two wings without a bird (see Figure 5.1).[1]

The only important tie between the two parts of the country was religion; working against it were many differences. Most of the people in the eastern part of Pakistan spoke Bengali; the majority in the western part spoke Urdu. The Bengalis of East Pakistan were racially different from the peoples of West Pakistan. Bengalis were short in stature, dark in complexion, and energetic in disposition. Punjabis and related groups in West Pakistan were tall, light, and impassive. Bengalis respected traders and intellectuals. Punjabis respected warriors.

The Bengalis accused the West Pakistanis of exploitation. The capital of the country was in the western part. Most government officials came from the West. The army was made up of West Pakistanis. Yet a majority of Pakistanis (55 per cent) lived in the East. The Bengalis also pointed to economic exploitation by the West. Most of the foreign exchange of the country was

Figure 5.1   Pakistan in 1947–1971

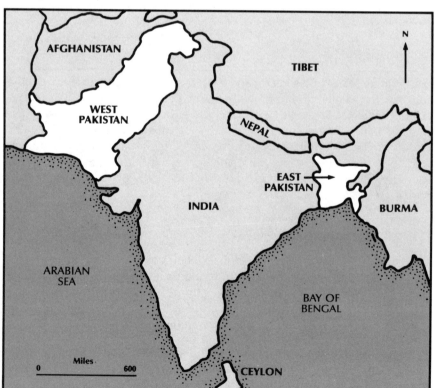

generated by jute and other agricultural products grown in East Pakistan, but the money was invested in the industrialization of the West. The result was that the West Pakistanis were more prosperous than Pakistanis in the East.

Even the religious tie was not too strong. The East had become Muslim much later, by conquest. Not all the East Pakistanis were Muslim; about 10 million (of 80 million) were Hindu. To some extent the two parts of Pakistan were held together by a common fear of India. But this fear was not so great in the East. The Bengalis were less obsessed with the Kashmir issue; they seemed more willing to seek a peaceful settlement with India. In part Bengalis felt this way because large numbers of ethnically similar Indian citizens lived across the border from East Pakistan in the Indian state of Bengal. Sharing language and culture, they found it hard to see each other as permanent enemies.

Despite these differences, the fragile union continued until 1969, when the military government of General Ayub Khan collapsed as a result of public indignation over corruption. The caretaker government that took over Pakistan from Ayub Khan scheduled new elections for December 1970. In these elections the Awami League, led by Sheikh Mujibur Rahman, won 75 per cent of the vote in East Pakistan (giving them 167 of the 169 seats allotted to East Pakistan). The Awami League drew its strength from Bengalis who felt exploited by the westerners and were asking for greater autonomy in a federal system. In reaction the federal government, situated in the West and dominated by military men recruited from the West, banned the Awami League. This led the Awami League to escalate its demands to full independence for East Pakistan. They declared the independence of a separate state, which they called "Bengal Nation" or Bangladesh.

The Pakistan government responded by arresting Sheikh Mujib, along with the rest of the Awami League leadership, in March 1971, and jailing them in West Pakistan. The Pakistan army was sent in to suppress rioting by the Bengalis and treated East Pakistan like an enemy country. Reasonable estimates of the number of people massacred range from 300,000 to 1,500,000. A team sent out by the World Bank to evaluate economic development projects for the eastern part of Pakistan reported that the devastation wrought by the Pakistani army resembled that in Europe after World War II.[2]

As might be expected, many East Pakistanis tried to escape the Pakistan army. Millions of refugees, about 90 per cent of them from the Hindu minority, crossed the border into India. About 6 million were settled in government-run camps; an estimated 4 million more were refugees outside the camps. It was this large influx of refugees that drew India into the civil conflict and led to the war. India could not very well have stopped the flow of refugees across its borders even if it had wanted to, for political as well as sheer physical reasons. Hindus in India would have opposed a policy of denying refuge to Hindus; Bengalis would have opposed denying refuge to Bengalis. But the cost to the Indian government of maintaining these refugees was enormous. The World Bank estimated that it would run at about $1.2 billion for a full year. The refugees would also use up India's food reserves, which were being accumulated for the first time as the result of India's "green revolution" in agriculture. India's prospects for economic growth were looking good as never before in its history as an independent state, and now resources and administrative talent would have to be diverted to caring for a sudden addition of 10 million people.

INDIA'S PREPARATION FOR WAR

Facing this situation, the most desirable foreign policy goal for India was to create a separate state in East Pakistan. Such a state would be able to take back the millions of refugees, relieving the economic and administrative burden they imposed on India. It would provide guarantees against continued exploitation, persecution, and massacre of the Bengalis. Such a state would have the additional benefit for India of reducing Pakistan's power and thus its ability to threaten Kashmir.

The goal of a new state of Bangladesh could be achieved in a number of ways. The Pakistani government itself could grant East Pakistan independence out of enlightened self-interest. Failing this, the Indian government could apply diplomatic pressure. If diplomatic initiatives failed, the Indians could resort to military action. War was by no means an unthinkable or irrational policy option for India. The only constraints were those imposed by the great powers and the United Nations. With proper preparation the Indians could avoid great-power interference. If the war was swift and decisive, the United Nations would not have time to act.

India began a series of diplomatic and military moves that by themselves might have persuaded the Pakistanis to allow Bangladesh its independence, but, if not, would also serve as preparations for a war against Pakistan to accomplish the same goal. India improved its ties with the Soviet Union, going so far as to sign a "friendship treaty" in August 1971. As Pakistan had ties with both the United States and China, it was logical that India should go to the other great power to counteract their influence. Then Prime Minister Indira Gandhi set off on a world tour to get countries to cut off or reduce aid to Pakistan. By presenting the case against Pakistan on the issue of the Bengalis, she could make it easier for these countries to remain neutral if not actually to support India in the event of war. Indians also encouraged rumors that China had already accepted as inevitable the breakup of the Pakistan state and was making overtures to India. True or not, they introduced an element of doubt into the calculations of other states, including Pakistan.

India also began military preparations, some of which could be interpreted as more severe forms of "diplomatic pressure," but others of which, because they were kept secret, were obviously serious preparation for war. The visible preparations included air raid drills and a call-up of doctors into the armed forces. The Indians also banned flights over Indian territory from West to East Pakistan, necessitating a long detour over the ocean for Pakistani reinforcements. At the same time, India began covert aid to guerrilla forces in East Pakistan. They supplied arms and training as well as sanctuary to a force of 6,000 or 7,000 guerrillas known as the Mukti Bahini. This support was kept hidden from foreign observers, including UN observers, and its full extent is still not clearly known. The guerrilla raids provided provocations to which the Pakistani army occasionally responded, furnishing the Indian army with excuses for "probes" and "incursions" and "protective reactions" across the border into Pakistan.

WAR BETWEEN INDIA AND PAKISTAN

The Indian main attack evidently was deliberately delayed until late fall, when preparations were completed and the winter snows had closed the Himalayan passes, preventing any Chinese assistance to the Pakistanis. On October 27, 1971, the Indians made their first crossing in force. On November 10 they occupied a salient that stuck out into India. The war itself began in December and lasted two weeks, until the cease-fire on December 17, 1971. The war was kept limited to the single goal of creating a new state in East Pakistan. Indian attacks were intended only to defeat the Pakistani army; destruction to the countryside was kept at a minimum, cities were not extensively bombed, and offensive operations were confined to East Pakistan. The Indian army, however, was prepared to take the offensive in Kashmir and West Pakistan if Pakistan decided to widen the war.

The war brought complete success for India. As a means of attaining foreign policy goals, military force had not lost its utility. Indian domestic reaction was overwhelming support; the 10,000 casualties suffered by India (including 8,000 missing or killed) was a price the population seemed willing to pay. The success came from careful preparation, both diplomatic and military, and favorable circumstances. India was better armed, getting weapons both from Russia and from its own arms industry. Pakistan suffered from a United States embargo on arms that had been imposed against both India and Pakistan after their last war in 1965 (that time over Kashmir). Pakistan was getting only limited arms from China, France, and the Soviet Union. (Soviet aid, you notice, was going to both sides. The Soviet Union was paying the price for trying to settle the war between the two sides in 1965, a position similar to the one in which the United States found itself in the Middle East after the 1973 war there.)

Pakistan fought from a disadvantageous strategic position. Forces in East Pakistan were cut off and could not be reinforced. The Indians outnumbered the Pakistanis in the East, 160,000 to 93,000. The Pakistanis also had to fight in the midst of a hostile population, including by this time as many as 50,000 Mukti Bahini.

When the fighting began, the United Nations General Assembly had condemned India by a vote of 104 to 11, with 10 abstentions.[3] But as the result of Indian success, world opinion rapidly shifted. No more resolutions were brought before the Assembly condemning India or asking it to stop. In fact, by December 19 the United States was in a lonely minority, condemned by almost all states for giving support to Pakistan, the country that was technically the victim of aggression.[4] India not only won the war but won the support of the world for its policy by doing so.

THE PROBLEM OF CYPRUS

In July 1974, fighting broke out in the island of Cyprus. The main issue was the same as that in Pakistan in 1971—mistreatment of one national group (a Turkish minority) by another (a Greek majority). The size of the Turkish minority on Cyprus made the problem difficult. About 120,000 of 640,000 inhabitants, or 18 per cent, were Turks. If the number had been smaller, say 10 per cent or less, they would not have attracted much attention and would probably have been tolerated as small minorities are elsewhere. If the number had been larger, say 35 per cent, demands for a separate state would have found more supporters. But at 18 per cent the Turks were numerous enough to cause problems, yet not numerous enough to justify a drastic solution. Furthermore, they were not concentrated in one part of the island but scattered in enclaves throughout.[5]

The Cyprus problem was complicated by three other factors. One was the proximity of Turkey, only 40 miles away; the mainland of Greece, to which the majority of Cypriots felt allegiance, was 500 miles away (see Figure 5.2). A second complication was the strategic importance of Cyprus to the countries with interests in the eastern end of the Mediterranean: Turkey; Turkey's partners in NATO (especially Britain, which has bases on Cyprus); and the traditional rival of both Turkey and NATO, Russia. Finally, the Cyprus problem was complicated by a history of animosity between Greeks and Turks on many issues other than Cyprus. One important event in this history was the massacre of Greeks by the Turks in the 1920's as the Turks set out to create a purely Turkish national state. Throughout history Greeks had been living along the edges of the Aegean Sea, but in 1923 the Turks expelled them, claiming that the eastern edge of that sea was Turkish territory. Those who did not flee soon enough were killed. This old conflict over territory appeared in new form in the 1970's when oil companies wanted to search for oil beneath the Aegean Sea. Greece claimed the right to grant exploration rights off the shore of islands inhabited by Greeks. Turkey granted exploration rights to the same area claiming that this area was part of the Turkish continental shelf. Before the war on Cyprus broke out, this quarrel had escalated so far that Turkey had sent planes to practice their bombing in the disputed waters.

The hostility between Greeks and Turks on Cyprus is part of the historic quarrel between the two peoples. Its most recent phase began in 1960, when Cyprus became an independent country. At that time, the representatives of the Greek Cypriot community agreed to give up demands for union with Greece (although most Greek Cypriots preferred it) in favor of an independent state, and the Turks agreed to give up their demands for partition of the

Figure 5.2   Cyprus

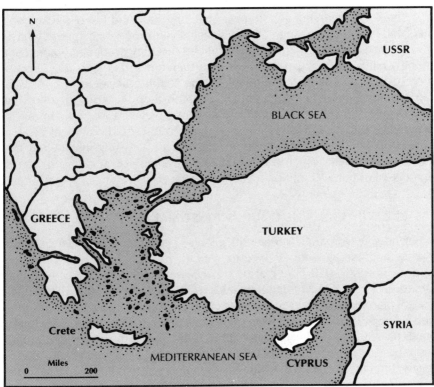

island in return for a guaranteed share of governmental powers. The arrangement lasted only three years. The Greek Cypriots claimed that the arrangement was unworkable, because the Turks, with only 18 per cent of the population, could veto any important government action. The Turkish Cypriots on the other hand claimed that the Greeks were forcing them into subordinate positions. Violent conflict broke out twice, in 1964 and in 1967, each time with Greece and Turkey threatening to go to war to help their fellow nationals.

By 1974 the situation was stalemated. Negotiations between the two communities, started after the near war in 1967, were making no progress. The Turks wanted "functional federalism," meaning that Turkish villages were to be patrolled by Turkish police, cleaned up by Turkish garbage collectors, and so on. The Greeks wanted a unitary state. There was little intermingling between the two communities. Cyprus never bothered to acquire a national anthem. Cyprus had its own flag but it was seldom used—citizens flew the flag of Greece or Turkey instead. Each community had its own school system. There was no university on Cyprus—students went to Greece or Turkey instead.

The Turks were in a subordinate position. They had lower-paying jobs and lived in poorer housing. Greek village mayors drove cars, Turkish village mayors rode bicycles.[6] The Greeks admitted that they produced 90 per cent of the wealth on Cyprus but argued that they did so because they were a more dynamic people. Some people suspected the president of Cyprus (a representative of the Greek community), Archbishop Makarios, of following a strategy of slowly strangling the Turks economically, forcing them out of productive activity and government jobs until they would no longer be able to resist Greek control. If this was his strategy, it was being frustrated by the Turkish government, which was subsidizing the Turkish community on Cyprus at a rate of about $30 million a year.

CRISIS IN 1974: THE COUP AGAINST MAKARIOS

Under the original agreements giving Cyprus its independence, both Greece and Turkey were allowed to station small contingents of troops on Cyprus. In 1974, 650 Greek army officers were with the Cypriot National Guard. In June 1974, the United States received word that this Greek contingent planned to overthrow President Makarios in a military coup, presumably because he did not advocate immediate union with Greece. The United States passed the warning on to Makarios, who replied that he did not expect such a move until he tried to expel these officers. Makarios was too optimistic. On July 15, 1974, the National Guard did carry out a coup; Makarios was lucky to escape with his life. The new military leaders named as president Nikos Giorgiades Sampson, known not only as a notorious enemy of the Turks but as a pathological killer as well. During the struggle against the British before 1960 he had boasted of how many British soldiers he had personally killed. Sampson's appointment seemed clear confirmation of what everyone already believed about the coup, that it was to prepare the way for union with Greece.

Under the treaties that gave Cyprus its independence, Greece, Turkey, and Britain (as the former colonial power) all had the right to intervene in the internal affairs of Cyprus to preserve its independence. The Turks now asked the British to help them prevent a union of Cyprus with Greece. The British were reluctant to act. They advanced a number of reasons: they wanted to avert a war between NATO allies; their bases on Cyprus depended on the good will of the Greek Cypriot majority; the thousands of British tourists and residents of Cyprus would be subject to harrassment by Greek Cypriots.

Britain did however try to avert a war by diplomacy. It requested that Greece recall the Greek officers serving with the Cypriot National Guard who had evidently been behind the coup. It also asked the Greeks to come to London for negotiations with the Turks. Greece, ruled at this time by an ultranationalist military junta, denied all responsibility for the coup. It did agree to replace its officers in Cyprus but would not send a representative to negotiate in London.

The Turks believed, not unreasonably, that the Turkish community on Cyprus was in some danger. They asked the British to cooperate with them in an intervention to guarantee the rights of the Turkish minority. When the British refused, they requested that the British at least let them use the British bases as areas in which they could land troops. When the British refused this as well, the Turks launched an amphibious invasion against the northern coast of Cyprus.

WAR BETWEEN TURKEY AND CYPRUS

Even with assistance from the Greek armed forces, the Cypriot National Guard would have been militarily inferior to the Turks. As it was, the Cypriots were fighting the Turks by themselves. Even so, the Turkish attack, beginning on July 20 and continuing until a cease-fire on July 22, was not a complete success. Turkish troops took longer to get ashore and advance than they had planned. They did not take the important airport outside Nicosia, the capital of Cyprus. In the confusion they even sank one of their own ships. When they halted, they controlled a number of Turkish Cypriot villages but 60,000 Turkish Cypriots still were in areas outside their control.

The government of Greece ordered mobilization, preparatory to an attack on Turkey, but on July 23 the ultranationalist military junta was no longer able to assert its authority. The generals who had been running the government handed power over to generals who had remained out of politics in the regular army, who then recalled the last civilian prime minister, Constantine Caramanlis, from exile. On the same day, Nikos Sampson was replaced as head of Cyprus by the civilian vice-president under Makarios, Glafkos Clerides.

The position of the Turks on Cyprus thus improved somewhat, but these changes did not fulfill all the foreign policy aims of Turkey. They still had no indication from within the Greek Cypriot government that the rights of the Turkish minority would be secure. The Turkish army began landing more troops on the northern coast of Cyprus and then broke the cease-fire by moving out from the enclave it had established there. A second cease-fire on July 30 halted their advance temporarily. An attempt to start talks at Geneva on a settlement quickly proved unsuccessful and the Turkish army moved once again, until by the time of a third and final cease-fire on August 16, it controlled 40 per cent of the territory of Cyprus (see Figure 5.3).

One of the factors that made the Cyprus problem so difficult was that the Turkish minority was not concentrated in one part of the island. When the Turkish army occupied the northern portion, it took control of a number of Greek as well as Turkish villages. Many of the Greeks fled, either out of fear of being involved in the fighting or because of a Turkish policy of expelling them. More than 180,000 Greek Cypriot refugees fled into the Greek-controlled part of the island. The Greek Cypriots in the south, however, wanted to keep the Turks in their midst from fleeing to the north. Many of them were locked up, virtual hostages, in public buildings and sports stadiums. Other Turks fled into nearby British military bases. After some hesitation, the British allowed them to be airlifted out to Turkish soil in January 1975. Many were promptly returned by the Turkish government to the northern part of Cyprus, an event that precipitated Greek Cypriot riots against the British. By February 1975, only 10,000 Turkish Cypriots were left in Greek Cypriot territory. On February 13, 1975, the Turkish Cypriot leaders proclaimed a separate state in the northern part of Cyprus, with an offer to the Greek Cypriot community to confederate with them in a single state, provided all authority was shared equally.

The Greeks rejected the Turkish offer. Despite military success and a de facto partition of the island into Greek and Turkish sections, the Turks were not able to enjoy the final satisfaction of a solution sanctioned by a treaty with the Greek Cypriots. Although the Turks were able to move unhindered to convert the northern part of Cyprus into a purely Turkish area, painting out all Greek signs, taking over Greek houses and giving them to Turks, and converting churches into mosques, they were unable to get international recognition of the changes they had brought about. The United States Congress, responding to pressure from constituents of Greek descent, cut off United States military aid in February 1975.

The United States had not found it possible to prevent this war, as it had potential wars between Turkey and Greece in 1964 and 1967; the United States also found it impossible to mediate a negotiated end to it. The major obstacle was weakness of the governments in both Turkey and Greece. The Greeks had just recalled a former prime minister, Constantine Caramanlis, to serve as acting prime minister in July 1974. Elections were set for November 1974 and no Greek politician could hope to make a conciliatory gesture toward the Turks and survive the election. Turkey also suffered from a weak government. The prime minister during the invasion, Bulent Ecevit, was a member of a minority party in a coalition government and his coalition partners did not want him to profit from the euphoria of the military success. Ecevit very much wanted to call an election, hoping for an electoral windfall,

Figure 5.3   Turkish Conquest of Cyprus in 1974

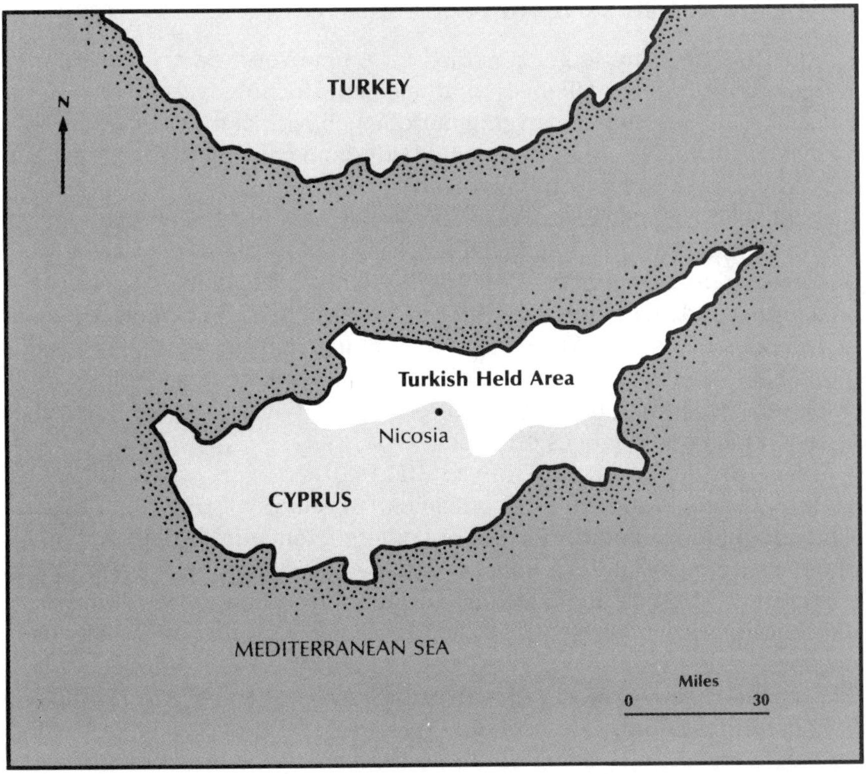

but the Turkish constitution makes it impossible for a prime minister to do so alone. Ecevit was unable to strengthen his power base at home so that he could make concessions.

Still, despite the limited achievement of objectives, it would have been hard to find a Turk who would argue that the use of military force in the summer of 1974 had not been a useful instrument of foreign policy. The Cyprus problem, which had been a serious issue for Turkey since 1960, now seemed well on the way to a permanent settlement.

The wars over Bangladesh and Cyprus in each case gave the initiating state at least part of what it wanted. Clausewitz appeared vindicated: War was useful as "a real political instrument, a continuation of political activity by other means."[7] Yet other wars in recent years have turned out less well for the initiator. From October 1978 to April 1979 Tanzania was at war with the neighboring state of Uganda; from December 1978 through January 1979 Vietnam was at war with its neighbor Cambodia. These almost simultaneous wars had many similarities.

UGANDA AND TANZANIA

In 1971 an army sergeant named Idi Amin overthrew the government of Uganda. A military takeover of an elected African government was not unusual, but the brutal and even grotesque behavior of the new leader over the next eight years was unprecedented. Idi Amin gained international notoriety from clownish but insulting behavior to other heads of state—wishing Richard Nixon a "speedy recovery from Watergate," or telling Prime Minister Golda Meir of Israel to "pull up her knickers."[8] More alarming was the well-documented massacre of hundreds of thousands of Ugandan citizens, often after torture and mutilation. Judges were seized in their courtrooms, surgeons at their operating tables. The body of one cabinet minister was found floating in the Nile; another was found stuffed into the trunk of a car. Amin himself displayed the dismembered body of one of his wives to his children as a lesson in the consequences of infidelity.[9]

As estimates of victims rose to 300,000 and more, an international outcry arose to do something to put an end to Amin's misrule. But states felt inhibited by the general principle of noninterference in the internal affairs of other sovereign states. As long as Amin's violence was confined to Urgandan citizens, no state had a clear justification for action against him.

But then Amin himself provided an excuse by ordering his troops to occupy territory belonging to his southern neighbor, Tanzania. An area of 715 square miles lay north of a river that Amin claimed was the natural boundary between the two countries. He ordered it occupied in October 1978, claiming it was being used as a base by Ugandan rebels. When he annexed it in November, Tanzania declared it would fight. In January a Tanzanian army invaded Uganda under the guise of supporting the Ugandan exiles who accompanied it. By April 1979 the Tanzanians and Ugandan exiles had proceeded so far that Amin was forced to flee the country.[10]

Despite this apparent success, the war turned out to be less than satisfactory for the Tanzanians. Internally, they found that the Ugandans who had accompanied them were unable to restore order. Even their own troops, forced to remain in the country to prevent total chaos, had little success. They finally were withdrawn in June 1981, less because they had restored stability than because they were tired of failure.

Externally, the president of Tanzania found himself under attack, especially from fellow Africans. At the summit meeting of the Organization for African Unity held in July 1979, the President of Sudan accused Tanzania of an act of aggression. The President of Nigeria, in only slightly more moderate language, expressed alarm at a "dangerous precedent."[11] The abstract principle of "humanitarian intervention," used in the past to justify warlike acts carried out not to further a state's national ambitions but simply to save lives, seemed less important to many countries than the violation of a state's sovereignty.

CAMBODIA AND VIETNAM

An equally murderous regime took power in Cambodia in 1975. The leader, Pol Pot, was unknown to the outside world; his associates and their philosophy were a total mystery. The regime immediately embarked on a policy of turning the country back to a totally rural way of life—beginning with the mass evacuation of the entire population of 2.5 million people from the capital city. Those who could not take the rigors of forced marches and a new life in primitive conditions were left to die. Those who resisted were beaten to death. Anyone discovered to have a Western education or knowledge of the outside world was marked for execution; wearing eyeglasses could be fatal. Around 25 per cent of the population, or almost 2 million out of a population of 7 million, are estimated to have died in less than four years at the hands of their own rulers.[12]

Many people in the world were as appalled by Pol Pot as they were by Idi Amin, yet again they were inhibited by the principle of nonintervention. But, as in the case of Uganda, Cambodia provided the justification for military action by its own belligerency toward a neighbor. In 1978 Cambodia began incursions into border areas disputed with Vietnam, shelling Vietnam towns and sending troops as deep as 6 miles into Vietnam. Vietnam replied with a massive military buildup along the border. Cambodia was not deterred, so the Vietnamese engaged the Cambodians in a month of sharp fighting.

Even that did not teach the Cambodians the desired lesson, and at the end of December 1978 Vietnam launched an all-out assault. The war lasted only two weeks because Pol Pot chose not to fight but to withdraw to the mountains of the west and mount a guerrilla campaign.[13]

Despite their sufferings at the hands of Pol Pot, the Cambodians could not welcome their traditional national enemies, the Vietnamese, as liberators and Vietnam was forced to occupy Cambodia with 200,000 troops. Externally Vietnam was criticized by many of its neighbors, not because they approved of Pol Pot but because they feared the growth of Vietnamese power, particulary as an ally and possible client of the Soviet Union. Neighboring Asian states sponsored a resolution in the United Nations condemning Vietnam. China took its opposition a step further by invading Vietnam, "to teach them a lesson" as the Chinese vice-premier said. The invasion, which lasted from mid-February to mid-March 1979, was not a clear success. Neutral military observers concluded that the Chinese performed poorly and suffered casualties of 20,000. But the Chinese declared themselves satisfied and withdrew their troops, claiming that they had fulfilled their aim.[14]

But if war did not serve China particularly well, neither had it served Vietnam or Tanzania before it. Both Tanzania and Vietnam achieved their initial purpose, removing an objectionable regime, yet both failed to achieve a lasting solution. And because both had resorted to war, both provoked severe international reaction.

Clausewitz's description of war as an instrument of policy appears to hold, even into the final decades of the twentieth century. The recent wars examined here can be described that way, particularly if we clear up two sources of confusion. One is the need to confine Clausewitz's description to the side that initiates war. For the side that is attacked, war is simply a matter of defense. It may find itself fighting unexpectedly or unwillingly, sometimes with disastrous consequences for other policies it wishes to pursue. War for Turkey in 1974 was a continuation of diplomacy by other means; for Cyprus it was an unexpected and hastily improvised reaction.

One must also distinguish between war as an instrument of policy and war as a *useful* instrument of policy. Wars sometimes fail to achieve their goals, just as diplomacy sometimes does. An occasional failure does not prove that war is senseless as an instrument of policy. Only if wars never produced results for states could we reject Clausewitz out of hand. Certainly stalemates like the Korean War or the wars of Tanzania and Vietnam might lead us to question Clausewitz. But wars appear to succeed frequently enough so that leaders of states, should they wish, can reasonably hold the belief that wars can be useful instruments of policy. The belief needs only occasional reinforcement for it to persist.

NOTES

1. A good summary of events in *Strategic Survey 1971*, published by the International Institute for Strategic Studies (London, 1972).

2. A graphic description of the destruction is provided by Robert Shaplen, "The Birth of Bangladesh," Parts 1 and 2, *The New Yorker*, February 12 and 19, 1972.

3. "They Called Each Other Mister," *The Economist*, December 11, 1971, p. 25.

4. Henry Tanner, "Outgrowth of War: Major Loss Is Seen for U.S. Influence," *The New York Times*, December 20, 1971, p. 1.

5. A good summary of events is in *Strategic Survey 1974*, published by the International Institute for Strategic Studies (London, 1975). An interesting background report is a survey by Ken Mackenzie, "A State, but Not a Nation," *The Economist*, July 20, 1974.

6. This, as well as other examples of life before the crisis, comes from Steven V. Roberts, "In a Cyprus Village, Amity and Antipathy," *The New York Times*, June 15, 1974, p. 2.

7. *Vom Kriege (On War)*, originally published in 1832, Chapter 1, Part 24.

8. International Commission of Jurists, *Uganda and Human Rights: Reports to the UN Commission on Human Rights* (Geneva: International Commission of Jurists, 1977), p. 8.

9. Henry Kyemba, *A State of Blood* (New York: Ace Books, 1977), p. 155.

10. *Keesing's Contemporary Archives*, August 28, 1981, p. 31049.

11. Ibid.

12. Central Intelligence Agency, National Foreign Assessment Center, *Kampuchea: A Demographic Catastrophe* (Washington, D.C.: Central Intelligence Agency), May 1980.

13. International Institute for Strategic Studies, *Strategic Survey 1979* (London: IISS, 1980), pp. 56–58.

14. Hedrick Smith, "U.S. Aides See Failure by Chinese in Vietnam and Risks of Bigger War," *The New York Times*, June 7, 1979.

Chapter 6

The Principles of International Relations

When we sit down to list the causes of all the wars we have looked at, from Prussia and Denmark in 1864 to Turkey and Cyprus in 1974, we discover not one but a multiplicity of causes. We find that World War I was caused by an arms race (which increased tensions and hostility) and by tension and hostility (which led to the arms race in the first place). We find that World War I was also caused by the failure of the major powers to appease national groups that had just grievances (the Austrians failed to allow the Serbs in Bosnia to join themselves to the neighboring state of Serbia and the Germans would not allow Alsace and Lorraine to rejoin France).

Yet when we come to World War II, we find exactly opposite causes. Hitler could get away with his aggressive moves for so long because the British and French had too little confidence in their own armed strength. In other words, it was the failure of the British and French to keep up an arms race with Germany that led to war. At the same time, Britain and France were too willing to appease Hitler when he advanced claims based on nationalism. Although World War I was caused by an arms race and lack of appeasement, World War II was brought on by appeasement and lack of an arms race.

Despite these confusing discoveries, we can still safely say some things about the cause of *all* wars. One is that wars occur because nothing exists to stop them. No world authority or world force makes war an unacceptable means of settling disputes. As a result, war has become a customary way of settling disputes. We can even go so far as to claim that war is sanctioned by the traditional principles of international politics as they have been understood for the last 300 years. We will examine some of the definitions, concepts, and practices that make up these principles and show how they permit wars to take place.

THE TRADITIONAL STATE-CENTRIC VIEW

We generally say that the present system of international politics goes back about 300 years because we often take the date 1648 as the beginning of the modern state system. In 1648 the Peace of Westphalia was signed, ending the Thirty Years' War that had involved most of the European states and caused great loss of life (perhaps as much as 30 per cent of the population in the parts of Germany where it was fought). The Thirty Years' War was a war of religion, Catholics against Protestants. The central part of Europe had been ruled (although loosely) as one unit called the Holy Roman Empire (though it had only the vaguest connection with the ancient Roman Empire). The emperor was the ruler of Austria, with power concentrated around Vienna. As years passed, the local rulers—kings and princes—became more powerful and the Holy Roman emperor could exercise less and less control. This erosion of imperial authority became clear during the Protestant Revolution of the sixteenth century when many of the kings and princes in northern Europe became Protestants in defiance of the Catholic emperor.

The Peace of Westphalia used a formula for making peace that acknowledged the end of the emperor's authority. The formula was poetic in Latin, *cuius regio eius religio*, "whose the region, his the religion," that is, the religion of a region would be determined by the religion of the ruler. This doctrine elevated the individual states of Europe above the Holy Roman emperor and the Roman Catholic Chuch and even above the private rights of the individual. The Peace of Westphalia made the state the most important political unit in the lives of the inhabitants of Europe. The year 1648 marks an important step toward transforming the state into the most important object of people's loyalties. It is remarkable how close we have remained to this principle. We think of ourselves, by and large, first as Americans (or Mexicans, or Canadians). We may quarrel with our individual tax bills but we seldom question the fundamental right of the state to tax us. Despite the objections raised during the Vietnam War to what many saw as foreign adventure unrelated to United States security, most Americans still think it shameful to refuse to die or at least risk one's life in a clear-cut case of defending the country. Few Americans hesitate to stand up and pledge their allegiance to a flag. Is there any other institution for which we would do these things? Would so many people let a church tax them, or risk their lives for a trade union, or pledge allegiance to their employer's company banner?

Before we go further, we should stop to look at a definition of the state. Occasionally the question of statehood comes up for some unconventional group—a family living on an abandoned oil rig outside territorial waters, or descendants of an aboriginal group dispossessed by colonial settlers and living on a reservation. To qualify as a state, such an entity must meet three criteria. First, it must be an association of people. Antarctica, which has no permanent human population, is not a state.

Second, these people must be politically organized. They must be capable of acting collectively. When we say, "Ohio State won the Rose Bowl," we mean more than that eleven individuals who just happened to attend Ohio State and just happened to show up on the football field that day won the game. We mean by "Ohio State" the recruiting, training, financing, emotional support, and all the other institutional contributions to the victory. Likewise, an expression such as "Sweden" is not just a metaphor for a collection of individuals. It is a term that expresses the idea that people acting together can do things that people acting individually cannot do, such as raise money by taxation and then make it available in the form of foreign aid to repair war damage in North Vietnam. A "government" is the name we give to the apparatus of decision and execution that enables an association of people to act collectively.

Third, a state is located on a definite territory. This is a very important criterion, because it excludes from treatment as states widely scattered associations of people (such as Gypsies), nomadic tribes, and guerrillas. To put it another way, a state has borders. Along with these borders goes the presumed right to exclude outsiders; there is no accepted right to emigrate to any country you please. Jurisdiction is assumed to be territorial. If I visit Mexico and commit a murder, I will be tried by the laws of Mexico, not by the laws of the United States, even though I am an American citizen.

Governments began to have a real ability to maintain borders for the first time about 1648, which is one of the reasons the Peace of Westphalia gave to states the authority it did. Developments such as gunpowder and conscript armies enabled kings to break the monopoly of force held before by independent noblemen and their knightly retainers. These developments also enabled the king to exclude outside forces, such as the armies of the emperor. Protection of subjects (whether Protestants threatened by Catholics or vice versa) was now possible.

At about the same time (1651 to be precise), an Englishman named Thomas Hobbes published a book titled *Leviathan*. This was a theoretical justification for the new state and its power. Hobbes advanced an idea that is closely associated with the idea of a state: the social contract. According to this idea, a citizen gives loyalty to the state and in return the state protects the citizen from internal disorder and foreign invasion. A citizen who does not give this loyalty has no right to protection. (This is the familiar argument used to justify military service.) The state that cannot provide order at home and protection from foreign enemies does not deserve the loyalty of its citizens (the premise of the terrorist trying to overthrow a government). It is because the state has been (at least until now) so successful in providing security to its citizens that is has been the major actor in the world system.

STATE AND NATION

The belief that states have obligations toward their citizens, as expressed in the idea of the social contract, has been reinforced by another idea, that of nationhood. The words "nation" and "state" are often used interchangeably but the concepts to which the words refer are different and we should distinguish between them. Even though 1648 marks the beginning of the modern state, states then were in at least one way very different from states today. States were then considered the property of the ruler; they could be bought, sold, traded, or used as security for loans. In the eighteenth century the Austrian ruling family mortgaged the province of Silesia to the English and Dutch in return for a loan. A major change in this attitude toward states came with the French revolution in 1789. Both in France and the countries conquered by France, many people became aware for the first time of a national identity.

A nation is somewhat harder to define than a state. It is a group of people who have some things in common, although precisely what they share may vary. Usually they have a common language, common customs, and a common tradition. To the extent that one of these is absent (for example, Jewish immigrants to Israel have spoken many languages), the other ties will be all the stronger. We say that people develop a national consciousness when they become aware of having these things in common and begin to place a positive value on them. The awareness of a common tradition in the past leads to an awareness of a common fate in the future and gives rise to the basic tenet of nationalism, that nation and state should coincide. Each nation should have its own state, each state should comprise one and only one nation.

The nation-state is only the *ideal* unit of international politics. In fact, not many components of international politics today resemble the ideal. Some states are multinational and seem likely to remain that way for some time—Canada and Switzerland, for example. Some nationalities are spread over several states, as the Koreans and the Germans are. Other participants in international politics are not states at all—organizations such as the United Nations, for example. You may notice some inconsistency in the use of terms. According to our definitions, the United Nations is not the United "Nations" at all but rather the United "States." International politics could more properly be called "interstate" politics. Nevertheless we accept terms such as "United Nations" and "international" because their usage is well established. The tendency to substitute "nation" for "state" only emphasizes that it is considered the ideal that each state should represent one and only one nation.

Let us summarize our definition of a state by returning to the group that comes forward and asks to join an association of states such as the United Nations. To gain acceptance as a state, we expect it to meet the three basic criteria of statehood: a group of people (who are most likely to be referred to as a nation), controlled by an effective government (which will claim to be acting in the best interests of the nation), in undisputed control of a clearly defined piece of territory. If the group's claim is recognized by other states, we say that the new state is recognized as sovereign.

SOVEREIGNTY

Political, social, economic, and technological developments during the seventeenth century elevated the state to the central role in international politics, signified by the Peace of Westphalia in 1648. From this basic fact of international life evolved a legal doctrine to go with it: state sovereignty.

Sovereignty was invented in 1576 by Jean Bodin. That may sound a bit strange. We normally reserve the word "invent" for mechanical devices such as the telephone, but there is no reason why the word can't be applied to intellectual concepts as well. No idea is entirely original, of course, but no mechanical device is either. For either, one person is usually given credit for successfully combining previous discoveries in a new way and then publicizing this invention. Jean Bodin was really inventing an intellectual weapon for use in the struggle between church and state. Authority in the medieval state was divided between the two—questions of marriage, divorce, and other personal matters were controlled by the church; business and political affairs were regulated by the state (although often within guidelines laid down by the church—no business on Sunday, no interest rates for loans). One consequence of the increasing power of the rulers of states was that they wanted less interference from church officials. Because all these rulers claimed to be good Christians, it was hard for them to ignore the arguments of bishops for a role in governing the lives of their citizens. Then Jean Bodin offered an argument that strengthened the king's hand.

Bodin defined sovereignty as "supreme power over citizens and sub-jects, unrestrained by law."[1] He argued that anything that can be called a state must have a sovereign somewhere—an authority that gives the laws, judges criminals, passes sentences. The important point of his argument was that there could be only one sovereign. If this power was shared it would no longer be sovereign. This argument gave the king an advantage in the quarrel with the church, because only the king had claimed total authority; the church had relied on an older argument of dual authority, a spiritual versus a temporal realm. Bodin's definition reflected the growing power of the state and gave the king arguments to use against the church.

How this internal contest between church and state developed need not concern us further. What is important is that this doctrine of sover-eignty—supreme power unrestrained by law—came to be applied to states in their external dealings as well. One of the first uses of sovereignty in the discussion of relations between states was in a book by a Dutch jurist, Hugo Grotius, On the Law of War and Peace. This is often called the first textbook on international relations. He published it in 1625, about the time that the Peace of Westphalia was laying the foundation for modern international politics. Grotius recognized that a state, if sovereign, could not be subject to legal control by another state. But his main interest was in finding a common natural law on which even sovereign states could agree. Not until the next century were the full implications of sovereignty in international relations recognized by a Swiss jurist, Emerich de Vattel. His Law of Nations, published in 1758, was the basic text on international relations at the time of the American Revolution. He wrote that states could be restrained neither by other states nor by any law.

Sovereignty in its internal and external applications might be illustrated in this way: It is universally agreed that taking human life is wrong. Legal codes only reinforce a more basic moral code on this point. Yet the sovereign (whether in the form of a king or a congress) may provide for the execution of criminals. Nothing restrains it from prescribing this form of killing, not even the moral code. In external relations, the taking of human life is treated not as a crime but as an act of valor, if done when one sovereign has declared war on another. In 1969 the Swiss courts tried a case of Arab hijackers who had killed Israeli airline passengers. The defense argued that because these Arabs were in a state of war with Israel, the killings were not murders but justifiable acts of war.[2]

In international politics today, a few states such as Monaco and Liechtenstein claim internal sovereignty only; they have given up external sovereignty by placing their foreign affairs in the hands of larger neighbors (France for Monaco, Switzerland for Liechtenstein). But the rest of the states in the world claim external as well as internal sovereignty. It follows that if all states claim to be sovereign on their own territories, there can be no single world sovereign—no world government, no world law, no restraint of any kind. The sovereign right to act unrestrained by law applies equally to the United States of America and the Caribbean state of Dominica. Dominica listed its population in 1981 as 74,859, its area as 290 square miles. Its published trade figures for its major exports (bananas, coconuts, and fruit juices) show earnings of $47 million (although it is estimated that it earns half as much again from illegal trade in marijuana). Its government budget of 4.4 million dollars enabled it to support an army of ninety-nine soldiers— a force so weak that ten mercenaries planned to embark from New Orleans and seize the government. (They were stopped—but by the American FBI, not the Dominican armed forces).[3]

Yet even a state so weak that a handful of mercenaries contemplate taking it over is nonetheless a sovereign and as such the legal equal of the United States. Both states have one vote in the United Nations. Neither can legitimately dictate policy to the other. Even more extreme is the case of the Pacific island of Nauru—8 square miles of guano (bird droppings). Despite its tiny size, the 8,000 inhabitants of Nauru claim the same sovereign rights for their country that the United States enjoys.

If the doctrine of sovereignty leads us to equate Nauru with the United States, then there is a flaw in it, or so thinkers have argued through the centuries since the doctrine first appeared. Gottfried Wilhelm Leibniz, a seventeenth-century writer, argued that external sovereignty should be judged by a state's ability to survive in peace or war, by diplomacy or strategy.[4] During the nineteenth century, sovereignty in practice came close to this meaning. Only a relatively small number of major countries were considered truly sovereign. Other parts of the world were treated as colonies or dependencies or simply unclaimed territory. Nauru was a possession of Germany.

But the twentieth century has seen a turn toward a more legalistic interpretation of sovereignty. National liberation movements, representing the populations of former colonies and dependencies, have found it useful to stress the idea of equality implicit in the doctrine of sovereignty. It is a useful symbol of independence and a tool in pressing for advantages. A small country can extend its fishing rights far beyond the traditional limits of 3 miles or 12 miles and claim that in doing so it is only exercising its sovereignty. A major state might have the military force to resist such an expansion but would hesitate to be accused of violating another state's sovereignty.

RECOGNITION

Once acquired, sovereign status is used to press for advantage. The process by which it is acquired is called *recognition*. We often come across the term, as in the statement, "For thirty years the United States did not recognize China." This does not mean that for thirty years the United States claimed that there was a vacancy on the globe at that spot. It means that the United States did not recognize the sovereignty of the regime governing China.

Recognition is a political act with legal consequences.[5] It is the official way in which one state indicates that it considers another state to exist as a responsible legal entity. By recognizing another state, a state signals that it is ready to do business with that other state, make treaties with it, extend credit, send aid, and engage in other kinds of international contact. Usually recognition is accompanied by establishment of diplomatic relations and exchange of ambassadors, although strictly speaking this step is not necessary.

Recognition is granted by a state that is already recognized. In this way it resembles the social register of high society or the exchange of Alice in *Through the Looking Glass*. Alice encounters a unicorn, who promptly exclaims, "A child! I always thought they were fabulous monsters!" Alice replies, "Do you know, I always thought unicorns were fabulous monsters, too?" The unicorn suggests diplomatically, "Well, now that we have seen each other, if you'll believe in me, I'll believe in you."[6]

Even as late as the Versailles Conference of 1919, recognition meant recognition by the great powers. With the emphasis today on sovereign equality, one state's recognition is no better than another's. There are occasional disagreements about when regimes should be recognized. In the end each state decides for itself and conducts business with only those states it does recognize. The closest we have to an international form of recognition is membership in the United Nations, but even in the UN there are states that do not recognize each other.

One problem is who does the recognizing; another is what is recognized. New states that come into existence as the result of treaties ending wars (Czechoslovakia, created by the Versailles Treaty) or because of successful civil wars (Bangladesh) require recognition. What is recognized is both the state and the political regime that controls it. When Bangladesh was created in 1971, a new regime was created at the same time and both were recognized. Sometimes, however, regimes change without any change in the territorial boundaries of the state. We are not talking here about changes in administrations (what Europeans call governments) but changes in the constitutional order. The United States has not had a change in regime since the Constitution was adopted in 1789. France, by contrast, has had a number of regimes in the same period, the most recent being the Fifth Republic. When a regime comes to power by orderly, constitutional means, the new regime is automatically recognized. When the French people approved the proposed constitution of the Fifth Republic, all the countries of the world recognized the new regime and the government headed by General Charles de Gaulle. When the regime is changed by nonconstitutional means, however, the question of recognition arises.

In January 1971, the Ugandan government of President Milton Obote was overthrown by a military officer, Idi Amin. For months Uganda's East African neighbors did not recognize this new government. Practically, this nonrecognition meant they acted as if no one was in charge of the country—they did not meet with the new ruler, sign agreements with him, exchange diplomatic notes, or engage in any business. Recognition of Amin's regime was finally signaled in October 1971 when the other countries agreed to attend a conference of the East African Common Market with representatives of the new regime. Treating them as though they were the rulers constituted recognition of the new regime.

When a new state comes into existence or when diplomatic relations have been ruptured for a long time, something more formal than common attendance at a conference is required. We sometimes refer to formal recognition as *de jure* recognition, a declaration by one state that it is extending recognition to another. When we say, "The United States did not recognize China until 1979," we mean the United States had not extended de jure recognition to China. Certainly by 1972 the United States was treating the leaders of the People's Republic of China as though they did govern China—from allowing mail to be sent to sitting on the UN Security Council with them. Treating a regime as though it is the responsible government of a state is sometimes called *de facto* recognition. Obviously de facto recognition can grow so much that the distinction between de facto and de jure no longer has much meaning.

The United States' failure to recognize the Chinese Communist regime for so long is an example of two contending theories on when recognition should be granted. One of these theories, the more traditional or orthodox one, exemplified by the practice of the British government, is that recognition is automatically accorded to the regime in power. If there are contenders for recognition, they must fight it out. The winner is recognized when it controls a governmental apparatus and at least some territory. With a government and territory, the presumption is that a regime will be able to make commitments and carry them out. Following this theory, the British recognized the Chinese Communist government in January 1950.

The other approach to recognition is a political one. It acknowledges that recognition is a political tool that can be used for helping friends and hindering enemies. The United States' refusal to recognize China is one example. The refusal of the Soviet Union to recognize the regime of Francisco Franco in Spain for all of its forty years is another. Both countries were withholding recognition to show disapproval.

The United States has been criticized for its delay in recognizing the communist regime in China. But it has also been criticized for its prompt recognition of regimes that come to power in military coups. If the United States does not recognize a secessionist movement early in its struggle, the movement may be hostile to the United States once it comes to power. But if the United States recognizes a movement that then is defeated, the state that defeated it will be hostile to the United States. Facing these conflicting demands on how to use recognition, a state is safest if it follows the British in a strictly consistent application of the doctrine of control. Another way of describing this approach is to say that if a state can be held responsible for its acts, it should be recognized. By this theory the United States should have extended de jure recognition to North Korea, because when the North Koreans seized the *Pueblo* in January 1968, the United States held North Korea responsible. On the other hand, when the Popular Front for the Liberation of Palestine hijacked a number of airliners in September 1970, the United States did not hold a Palestinian state responsible. Thus recognition of a Palestinian state is not called for, nor will it be until the Palestinian people are represented by one government in control of clearly defined territory.

NON-STATE ACTORS

Despite the failure of the Palestinians to meet the criteria for statehood, they play a part in international politics, debating in the United Nations as well as hijacking airplanes. This points out one of the inadequacies of the traditional principles of international politics: The sovereign nation-state is not the only actor in the international system. The Palestinian case does not totally invalidate the claim that the nation-state is the ideal actor because the Palestinians clearly aspire to be a state. Once they have a recognized government on a demarcated territory they will presumably claim the traditional privileges of sovereignty. But until they do, they show that groups can influence international politics without constituting themselves states.

Some of these groups are not "states-in-waiting" like the Palestinians. One important type of non-state actor is the intergovernmental organization (IGO). These run all the way from the United Nations to the Permanent International Committee on Canned Food. Often we try to force the more important IGO's into the mold of the sovereign state. We call our representatives to them "ambassadors"; we grant diplomatic immunity to their officers and premises. But it is obvious that in many important ways IGO's are different from states. Nor can we say that IGO's are equal to the sum of their parts or that positions taken by IGO's are only the sum of the positions taken by all the member states. Organizations such as the United Nations and the

European Economic Community (EEC or Common Market) are important in their own right.

The number of IGO's has grown from only a handful a century ago to more than 350 today.[7] Growth of nongovernmental organizations (NGO's) has been even more spectacular. These are sometimes called transnational organizations (although "trans-state" would be more precise) because members communicate directly with each other, bypassing their state governments. A good example of an NGO is the Roman Catholic Church, which of course is even older than the state system that evolved in 1648. Today the number of NGO's has grown to more than 4,000, including such organizations as the International Olympic Committee, the International Air Transport Association, and the Experiment in International Living.[8] Even the Roman Catholic Church is thought of today not as one but rather as a collection of nongovernmental organizations, from the Society of Jesus to the International Conference of Catholic Scouting.

As interest in non-state actors grows, scholars refine their categories to include such new institutions as multinational business corporations and transnational political groups. Today there is considerable debate among scholars about the importance of these non-state actors. One study found that about 40 per cent of the conflict in three regions of the world (the Middle East, Western Europe, and Latin America) resulted from the activities of non-state actors, but other studies play down their importance.[9]

Two facts are indisputably clear: (1) the nation-state has been for the last 300 years and continues to be today the most important unit in international politics; (2) the nation-state has never been the only participant in international politics and at present seems to be more than ever crowded by non-state actors. Still, there is much to be said for using the nation-state as the basic unit for analysis. States still control most of the armed force in the world. It is still primarily states that decide to go to war. Most of the non-state actors that resort to violence do so as part of their effort to become states; most of them could not succeed if they did not have the connivance or assistance of already established states.

Nongovernmental organizations and other transnational actors are important but much of their importance comes from the way in which they influence state governments. Multinational oil companies are important actors, but one of the most important things they try to do is to influence state behavior. Sometimes they succeed but sometimes the states are able to resist them and they fail. Transnational actors have much less influence in states such as the Soviet Union and there is no reason to think that states of this type are on the verge of extinction. Some scholars have suggested that current predictions of increasing importance for transnational actors are based on nothing more than the extrapolation of trends in recent years. They argue that these trends developed because of specific conditions that are not likely to continue in the future.[10] For our purposes it seems most sensible to focus on the state and discuss how transnational actors influence it and not vice versa.

IMPLICATIONS OF INTERNATIONAL ANARCHY

One reason why war occurs is that for the last three centuries the state system has not been well organized to prevent it. In fact the most important principle of the state system, that of sovereignty, seems to facilitate it. We can describe international politics as a system of anarchy. Because some nineteenth-century bomb-throwers called themselves anarchists, a common impression is that anarchy is the equivalent of chaos and violence. But anarchy is simply the absence of a superior authority, and clearly, in international politics, there is no authority superior to the state.

For this reason international politics differs in many ways from the kind of politics we are familiar with in our own country. All politics is a mixture of conflict and cooperation but international politics has less cooperation and more conflict than national politics. The level of distrust is higher; there is a feeling that mistakes are more likely to be irreversible.

In national politics we are used to putting the good of the whole over the good of the parts. Even when we favor a selfish interest, we try to do it in a way that denies its selfishness. The head of General Motors, about to become secretary of defense, could justify his interest in the continuing good fortune of that company by stating, "What is good for our country is good for General Motors, and vice versa."[11] But in international politics it is unusual to hear the argument that the good of the whole world is superior to the good of our part of it. Restrictive tariffs are regularly introduced to benefit our own workers, with little feeling about how these tariffs will affect workers in other countries. In 1972 the United States restricted the export of food such as soybeans to keep domestic prices down, even though this meant hardship for the Japanese who depended on American soybeans for protein. In fact a state can be criticized for not acting in a selfish way. China was criticized in the late 1950's for exporting food to win friends abroad even though there was famine in some parts of China.

The state of affairs in international politics is illustrated in a fable by an eighteenth-century political philosopher, Jean Jacques Rousseau. He describes five hunters who join to hunt a stag. They must cooperate to surround the stag. Upon killing it, they will share equally and each will receive enough to feed his family. But then one of the five breaks the ring to pursue a rabbit, which will provide enough food for his own family. The stag escapes and the other four go hungry.[12] Placing personal needs over group needs is not considered immoral in international politics. Indeed, if the hunter were treated as a state would be, he might be criticized if he failed to pursue the rabbit and thus neglected the first chance he had to feed his family, no matter how shortsighted this policy might be.

This widely shared value of national selfishness makes a virtue of the policy of isolation. The idea was expressed clearly by British Prime Minister Neville Chamberlain at the time of the Czechoslovakia crisis in 1938: "How horrible, fantastic, incredible, it is that we should be digging trenches and trying on gas-masks here because of a quarrel in a faraway country between people of whom we know nothing!"[13] Much of contemporary American political opinion finds that those who argue against American involvement in South-East Asia, Africa, or the Middle East are more moral than those who favor it. It is common to hear such issues debated not on the justice or injustice of the cause, nor for the suffering or lack of suffering that will result from our refusal to intervene, but solely on how much it will cost our country. A good example of such an argument is the widely quoted comment of John Kenneth Galbraith that we should let Vietnam "return to the obscurity it so richly deserves."

States regularly make distinctions between their own citizens and all others. According to an American newspaper correspondent in Europe, an accident was worth reporting if it involved the death of one American, five Englishmen, or ten Europeans.[14] The war in Vietnam became intolerable to many Americans not because Vietnamese weekly casualties were running in the thousands but because American weekly casualties were running in the hundreds.

Among other things, the special obligation a state feels toward its own citizens means it can never guarantee the security of others as credibly as it can that of its own. This is a fundamental weakness of all alliances and international organizations. The British guaranteed the neutrality of Belgium throughout the nineteenth century and proclaimed that this was a solemn treaty obligation, yet some doubt arose when World War I began whether the British would indeed go to war when Germany invaded Belgium; if the Germans had landed in Scotland, there would have been no question.

This primary concern with one's own affairs is reinforced by a principle derived from the doctrine of sovereignty—noninterference in the internal affairs of another country. In theory any kind of external influence may be rightfully excluded from a country by its government—foreign businesses, tourists, even radio and television broadcasts. Among the staunchest defenders of the most conservative interpretation of the principles of international politics has been the Soviet Union, which argues that satellite transmission of television programs is interference in internal affairs. All states have a point at which they react; the Soviet Union just reacts more quickly than most. Recent attempts to control the sale of nuclear materials to countries such as Brazil were rejected by Brazil on the grounds that they constituted interference in internal affairs.

The principle of noninterference is only that—a principle—generally shared as an ideal, usually but by no means always followed in practice. Another way of stating the principle of noninterference is to say that a state's borders are inviolable. The violation of a border—unauthorized entry by the forces of another state—is called "aggression." Even though it is clearly contrary to the principles of international politics, aggression occurs. When it does, the state that is the victim is on its own. There is no higher authority for it to appeal to. The German army's crossing of the French frontier in 1870, followed by Germany's annexation of Alsace and Lorraine, was recognized by all as a clear violation of France's sovereignty, yet there was no world ruler to which France could turn for redress. The implication of sovereignty, that each state has a right to pursue a policy of isolation, meant that France could not expect other European countries to come to its aid. The only redress available to France was what political philosophers used to call "self-help," or resort to violence. In the absence of world government, France had to take the law into its own hands.

The Germans in 1870 could also have argued that they were in the right. In effect France was vetoing the right of the small German states to join with Prussia in a larger nation-state. Lacking an international authority to appeal to for redress of this grievance, Prussia had to resort to self-help, taking the law into its own hands to correct this injustice. With no world tribunal to pass on the justice of these conflicting claims, one claim is as legally valid as the other.

Recourse to self-help is frequent in international politics. According to one comprehensive study, 222 wars were fought between 1648 and 1964, or one war for every one and four-tenths years of the modern nation-state system.[15] Because war has been resorted to so frequently, it has acquired some legitimacy. It is a clearly recognized relationship between states, signified at least in theory by a declaration at the beginning and a treaty at the end. Within a society, the condition of being at war may mean internal changes, such as declaring a national state of emergency or martial law. The people who have been designated to carry out warfare are identified by warpaint or, more recently, uniforms and medals. The conduct of the war itself is subject to regulation by international codes of conduct. Soldiers may not wear the uniforms of the enemy; attacks on civilians are to be avoided; some types of weapons (such as expanding or "dum-dum" bullets) are outlawed.[16]

Despite legal restrictions on certain ways of conducting war, for long periods in modern history the mere act of going to war was not considered illegal. In the twentieth century ideas began to change. In 1920 the League of Nations Covenant declared war illegal if it violated various clauses of the Covenant. But this provision still permitted war once attempts to settle disputes peacefully were exhausted. In 1928 many states signed the Pact of Paris for the Renunciation of War, but despite the pledge implied by the title, states did not abandon their weapons and the treaty remained "a moral preachment."[17] In 1945 the United Nations Charter outlawed all wars of aggression but included the loophole that states could fight in their own defense until the international organization came to their aid. Thus Iran and Iraq could go to war in 1980, each claiming it was fighting in self-defense, and, because the United Nations never acted, neither believed itself in violation of the Charter. As we approach the end of the twentieth century, changes in attitude toward war have not yet progressed to the point at which war in all its forms is clearly contrary to the principles of international politics.

No one will claim that international politics is nothing but war. But resort to war is always possible in relations between states. This shadow lurking in the background means that states are only being prudent when they take measures for defense in the event of war. But each state's defensive preparations are viewed with suspicion by other states, so that they too take up defensive measures. Ultimately states end up less secure than they were before the process of arming began. This condition has been called the "security dilemma."[18] If a state remains unarmed, it may be preyed on by an armed neighbor, but if it arms it may only provoke its neighbor to arm more.

Because states are aware of the possibility of war and because they have at least minimal armed forces to fight with, even peaceful relations between states are not free of military elements. We refer to "diplomatic relations" between states at peace with each other, but the expression "strong diplomatic pressures" may refer to very martial behavior. In 1945, the Soviet government handed a note to the Turkish government, asking for the return of some provinces then under Turkish control but controlled before 1917 by the Russian tsars. This diplomatic move was accompanied by "routine military maneuvers" by Soviet forces just across the border from the contested provinces. The Turks turned to the United States for diplomatic support. By chance, the Turkish ambassador to the United States had died of natural causes while at his post, and the United States returned the body to Turkey on a ship that just happened to be available, the battleship *Missouri*.

For 300 years the state system has been loosely organized according to certain principles, foremost among them the legal doctrine of sovereignty. The fundamental problem of world politics is that these principles work imperfectly. The principle of sovereignty is not so scrupulously respected that a state can be confident that its borders will never be violated or its political independence subverted. Yet sovereignty is regularly invoked by states when attempts are made to impose some order on international politics through a higher authority. The ideal of the sovereign nation-state is being challenged today both by attempts to control state behavior through international organizations and by the appearance of new, non-state actors. But the doctrine of sovereignty, until now at least, has been strong enough to frustrate attempts to prevent the resort to violence among states. We must conclude that one of the reasons wars occur is that the principles of international relations stand in the way of attempts to prevent them.

NOTES

1. Bodin's work, *Six Books of the Republic*, is summarized in George H. Sabine, *A History of Political Theory*, 4th ed., revised by Thomas Landon Thorson (Hinsdale, Ill.: Dryden Press, 1973), Chapter 21.
2. "Swiss Convict Three Arabs in Attack on Jet," *The New York Times*, December 23, 1969.
3. Statistics on Dominica from *The Stateman's Yearbook 1985–1986* (New York: St. Martin's Press, 1985), p. 418. On the attempted coup, see Jo Thomas, "Life Remains Unsettled in Dominica After Invasion Aborted in New Orleans," *The New York Times*, June 7, 1981, p. Y16.
4. John Herz, *International Politics in the Atomic Age* (New York: Columbia University Press, 1959), pp. 52–61.
5. Gerhard von Glahn, *Law Among Nations*, 2nd ed. (London: Macmillan, 1970), p. 91.
6. First published in 1871, Chapter 7.
7. *Yearbook of International Organization* (Munich: K. G. Saur, 1983), Vol. 1, p. 904.
8. Ibid.
9. Richard W. Mansbach, Yale H. Ferguson, Donald E. Lampert, *The Web of World Politics* (Englewood Cliffs, N.J.: Prentice-Hall, 1976), p. 281. See also Robert O. Keohane and Joseph S. Nye, Jr., *Transnational Relations and World Politics* (Cambridge: Harvard University Press, 1970).
10. Gregory Schmid, "Interdependence Has Its Limits," *Foreign Policy*, No. 21 (Winter 1975–1976), pp. 188–197; Robert W. Cox, "On Thinking About Future World Order," *World Politics*, Vol. 28, No. 2 (January 1976), pp. 189–192.
11. *Hearings Before the Committee on Armed Services, U.S. Senate, 83rd Congress, 1st Session, January 15–16, 1953*, p. 15.
12. "A Discourse on the Origin of Inequality," in Jean Jacques Rousseau, *The Social Contract and Discourses*, trans. G. D. H. Cole (New York: E. P. Dutton, 1950), p. 238.
13. Broadcast to the nation, September 27, 1938, quoted in Winston S. Churchill, *The Gathering Storm* (Boston: Houghton Mifflin, 1948), p. 315.
14. E. H. Carr, *The Twenty Years' Crisis* (London: Macmillan, 1946), p. 164.
15. Quincy Wright, *A Study of War*, 2nd ed. (Chicago: University of Chicago Press, 1965), information from tables 34–42 and Appendix C.
16. *Regulations Respecting the Laws and Customs of War on Land*, signed at The Hague, October 18, 1907, in *Treaties and Other International Agreements of the United States of America, 1776–1949*, Vol. 1 (Washington, D.C.: Department of State, 1968–1976).
17. Von Glahn, p. 521.
18. Herz, p. 231.

Chapter 7

Causes of War

We have looked at some of the generally accepted principles of international politics, especially those that have a bearing on the problem of war. One way of summarizing Chapter 6 is to say that wars occur because they have always occurred. They have become habitual ways of settling disputes.

All this is true but not very satisfying. It does not explain how war got started in the first place, or, more important, why states continue to use such destructive means to attain their ends when other means are available, at least to the imagination.

CAUSAL EXPLANATION

Poll your acquaintances on the cause of war and you will get a wide variety of answers. Advocates of a weapons freeze will tell you armaments cause war. Born-again Christians will tell you that human nature is the cause. Marxists will say the capitalist system. Before we examine any of these claims, we should take a look at the concept of causation itself.

One thing that becomes quickly obvious is that we attribute almost nothing to just one cause. We identify some thing or event as a "result" or "effect" and talk about all the conditions necessary before that effect could occur as the "causes." Any one of the conditions could be called a cause, but there are always many.

Imagine me opening a matchbook, taking out a match, and striking it on the cover—a flame appears. The flame is the effect—what is the cause? If I performed the same act on the moon, no flame would appear. So one condition is oxygen. If I struck so hard that the match head flew off, it might produce a flash but no flame. So another condition is the fuel provided by the paper match stem. And if I did not apply my energy to striking the head against the cover, no flame would appear, because the match would not be hot enough to ignite. Heat plus fuel plus oxygen are conditions that produce a flame. Take away any one and we have no fire.

Compared to human behavior, such as the transformation of a peaceful assembly into a lynch mob, simple chemical reactions such as flaming matches are easy to explain. Yet even the explanation for the appearance of the flame is more complex than we need for most purposes. Consider one variety of fire, the forest fire. Like all fires, forest fires are caused by oxygen plus fuel plus heat. Yet if our purpose is to prevent forest fires, we ignore two of the three conditions and concentrate entirely on the third.

A list prepared by the Forest Service on causes of forest fires in the United States is shown in Table 7.1. This list does not mention anything related to oxygen or fuel. Logically, of course, we could prevent forest fires by removing all oxygen—perhaps constructing huge plastic domes filled only with carbon dioxide. But because such plans are probably not feasible and certainly not economical we never even consider them. Likewise, logically, we could prevent forest fires by removing all the fuel—cutting down all the trees. Again, we don't waste time considering such a plan. We concentrate instead on the third condition—heat.

The example of forest fires provides two more insights on causation. Smokey the Bear is wrong when he says, "Only you can prevent forest fires."

Table 7.1   CAUSES OF FOREST FIRES IN THE UNITED STATES

Cause	Per cent
Incendiary	34
Lightning	21
Debris burning	16
Equipment use	8
Smoking	6
Railroads	3
Campfires	2
Children	2
Miscellaneous	8

Source: U.S. Department of Agriculture, Forest Service, Wildfire Statistics (April 1980).

The second most frequent cause of forest fires is lightning and lightning is quite beyond our capabilities to prevent. Having divided the causes of fire into three groups—oxygen, fuel, and heat—we must now subdivide one group further into conditions that result from human actions and conditions that don't.

The most common cause of forest fires is listed as "incendiary," meaning fires deliberately set, and here we must add an additional element, a purpose or intention. The exact means of applying heat—match or blowtorch—is less significant than the motivation in the minds of the persons applying the heat.

CAUSATION AND WAR

As the example of forest fires demonstrates, we can identify multiple causes for any given effect and further we can group these causes. Centuries ago the first political scientist, Aristotle, suggested grouping causes into four categories, which he called material, efficient, formal, and final.[1] If we try to explain the origin of a piece of sculpture, we can say the marble was the material cause, the sculptor was the efficient cause, the sculptor's artistic vision was the formal cause, and the money or desire for fame was the final cause. Without copying Aristotle exactly, we can still make use of his approach to help bring some sense to a discussion of the causes of war.

Some causes, such as the sculptor's marble, or the fuel and oxygen consumed in a fire, are always available (at least somewhere in the world), yet by themselves produce no further results. We can identify similar conditions that precede war, conditions that are always present yet do not always lead to war. We may label them material causes or permissive causes, because they permit war to occur. An example might be human nature.

HUMAN NATURE: KONRAD LORENZ

If you asked your acquaintances, you would probably find the theory most of them hold is that the causes of war are to be found in human nature. Perhaps the popularity of this theory is a legacy of the Christian tradition, for it has been the orthodox Christian view. Christian teachers have held that human nature is not basically good or even (by itself) capable of becoming good. One practical way in which human nature manifests itself is the inability of human beings to live in harmony with one another. According to Christian teaching, every person has inherent evil desires, sometimes called "original sin," a metaphor derived from the Biblical story of Adam's fall from grace. These desires make people want what they have no business wanting and prompt them to use violence if that is necessary to fulfill these desires.

Collective violence, carried out by states against each other, is in the Christian view only a manifestation of this basic individual nature, because states are composed of individuals. Only when the individuals change will states change.[2]

This pessimistic view of human nature is by no means confined to Christians. Hans Morgenthau, author of the first major American textbook on international politics, begins his book with the assertion, "The drives to live, to propagate, and to dominate are common to all men." He calls this "an undeniable fact of experience."[3] Many people agree with these statements, but they do so more as a result of faith than of study of scientific evidence. The Christian religion relies explicitly on faith; Morgenthau's claim does too, although he does add a footnote indicating that chickens also dominate each other. In recent years, however, this view has received scientific support from the work of biologists, especially those who specialize in the branch of biology known as "ethology" or the study of animal behavior. One of the ethologists who has done much to popularize findings in this field is Konrad Lorenz, who in 1962 published *On Aggression*.[4] Although he is not the only or the most recent writer on the subject, his views are among the best known, and for that reason we will examine them here.

Lorenz begins by arguing that human beings, like other animals, have instincts. Instincts are inherited (as opposed to learned) behavior patterns. Their presence has been convincingly demonstrated in animals; a bird raised in total isolation from other birds will still try to fly south in the autumn. Among the instincts Lorenz finds in human beings is the aggressive instinct. This means that one human being when challenged by another will react with anger and stand to fight (rather than turn and flee in terror). One bit of evidence for the argument that this behavior is inherited and not learned is that many kinds of measurable physiological changes take place when one becomes angry—among them an increase in pulse rate and blood pressure and a rise in the level of blood sugar—and these changes are the same in all human beings and indeed in all mammals.[5]

Lorenz further argues that this aggressive instinct, like everything else about the human organism, is the product of evolution. Traits that survive from generation to generation do so because they are "functional"; that is, they enhance the ability of organisms possessing them to survive. Once we accept this assumption, we can make reasonable guesses about the function (or survival value) of any trait. In the case of the aggressive instinct, it seems to serve three functions. First, it distributes members of a species evenly over territory, thus guaranteeing to each one (or at least to each strong one) enough territory to sustain life. This view is supported by the observation that the aggressive instinct manifests itself more strongly in the center of an animal's home territory and grows weaker as the animal moves away from that center.

Second, aggression makes it more likely that the strongest members of the species will breed and produce offspring. Third, it makes it more likely that parents will be able to protect their offspring while they are still young and helpless. If animals always fled rather than fought, they would desert their young whenever danger threatened.

During his observations Lorenz came to distinguish two kinds of mammals: those that are not particularly dangerous to each other physically (rabbits, for example) and those that, because they are equipped with fangs and claws, are dangerous to each other (such as wolves). Rabbits display as much aggression as wolves but there is no danger that fighting will have fatal consequences. The natural defense of the rabbit against all danger is to run away and in fights between rabbits the weaker rabbit runs away from the stronger. (However, if rabbits are confined in an unnatural way, say in cages, they will tear each other to pieces.)[6] When wolves fight, the possibility of fatalities is there, yet they rarely occur. Wolves show aggression but do not kill each other any more often than rabbits do. The reason, according to Lorenz, is that along with its aggressive instinct the wolf has evolved an inhibiting mechanism that checks the aggressive instinct at the crucial moment. The inhibiting mechanism is triggered by a movement that Lorenz calls an appeasement gesture—the losing wolf turns over on its back, exposing its throat in such a way that it would be easy for the winner to kill it. The appeasement gesture is a sign that the loser accepts an inferior status and by doing so saves its own life.

Human beings, Lorenz finds, belong in the category of animals that are harmless to each other. Like the monkeys in the zoo, they may pelt each other with rotten fruit but their natural equipment of short, blunt teeth and stubby, brittle fingernails keeps them from ever being dangerous to each other. Thus human beings have not evolved the inhibiting instinct as have the wolves; it was not necessary. Then, at some time in human development, one human picked up a rock and at that moment became as dangerous to other humans as one wolf to another. From that point progress from sharp rock to firearms was extraordinarily short (as evolutionary development goes). Human beings are now far more dangerous to each other than wolves are to each other, but they have not yet evolved the mechanism to inhibit aggression. The problem is not, as in the often quoted words of Roman playwright Plautus, that "humans are like wolves to other humans" but that humans are not wolflike enough.

We should note carefully what Lorenz is saying. The problem is not aggression; that is, that human beings fight. After all, wolves do too. The problem is that human beings fight to the death. They kill members of their species and wolves do not. It is not our lack of "humanity" but our lack of "animality" that causes our troubles. There are two sides to this feature of human nature. As victors, human beings have the ability to kill helpless victims. As losers, they have the ability not to give up even when defeated. Human beings can die for abstract causes—wolves could never fight a Battle of the Alamo.

Lorenz did not see the human situation as hopeless. Just as an inhibiting mechanism has evolved among wolves, so too could one evolve among human beings. The only difficulty—and it is a serious one—is that the evolutionary process requires a great deal of time, time measured in thousands of years.

Since Lorenz did his work, more recent students of animal behavior have found many examples of intraspecies killing, suggesting that Lorenz had too benevolent a view of "animality." Subordinate elephant seals have been observed ganging up on a dominant male. Gangs of chimpanzees have been observed killing lone males from bands other than their own. A gorilla was observed killing an older female from his own troop.[7] Many of these examples come from the so-called "higher animals," primates that resemble human beings in many ways. It is possible that another trait they share with human beings is that they too have not yet evolved mechanisms to inhibit aggression.

Even Lorenz's notion of ritualized, nonfatal combat between two males for dominance has been challenged. For some animals, at least, such duels appear to end in death. But in the debate among biologists, the core idea of Lorenz's theory still appears valid—that animals such as wolves that are losing a fight can and do signal defeat and thus inhibit the victor from killing them. The manner in which wolves fight for dominance still appears to be less destructive than the manner in which human beings do.

Even if human nature turns out to be not so different from animal nature, the ability to kill members of our own species must be considered a cause of war, in the sense that it permits wars to happen. If we could change this characteristic of human nature, we could eliminate war. Indeed, using modern techniques of behavior modification and "brainwashing," we might be able to make such changes. What is lacking is the power to force 5 billion people to submit to our treatment; that, of course, is an enormous lack. Surely if we had that much power, we could solve the problem of war much more simply. It is doubtful that techniques for changing human nature, other than drastic ones requiring total control of a person's environment, will work. Preachers and teachers have tried to change human nature by exhortation for more than 4,000 years, with little result. Obviously, if we all became good Christians, wars would cease. They would also cease if we all became good Buddhists or Taoists or just plain good. But the historical record of this approach to peace is not encouraging. The expectation of a messianic age remains a matter of faith.

"TROUBLEMAKERS": POWER GROUPS, MERCHANTS OF DEATH, WICKED STATES

Another permissive cause of war was the theme of Chapter 6: the international system. Wars occur because no sovereign exists that can stop them. If we constructed a scale of human complexity, from the individual through families, clans, nations, and alliances up to the world system, these two permissive causes would fall at opposite ends. Yet they are similar in that they are always present, not stopping war from occurring yet not by themselves enough to set one off. Both human nature and international anarchy in some sense caused the great war of 1914, yet both were present in exactly the same form in the peaceful year of 1913.

Obviously something more is needed to produce war, just as something more than marble is needed to produce a statue. Aristotle identified an agent, which he called an "efficient cause." Similarly in international politics we can identify agents that contribute to the origins of war. We might call these individuals "troublemakers." Eliminate these troublemakers, the theory goes, and you eliminate war.

An example of this approach is found in many of the histories of World War II. Most put the responsibility for the war on Adolf Hitler and his initiatives in foreign policy. Alan Bullock, author of one of the most read biographies of Hitler, entitled one of his chapters, "Hitler's War, 1939."[8]

In an attempt to apply this approach to all wars, a psychologist, Theodore Abel, wrote, "Throughout recorded human history, the initiators of war were individuals and groups who held power. . . ."[9] In his own study of twenty-five wars, he identified a power group responsible for each war. World War I he attributed to the Austrian power group, composed of the prime minister, the foreign minister, and the chief of staff. He claims that they had decided to wage war against Serbia as early as 1909 and were only waiting for an occasion, such as the one provided by the assassination of the Austrian heir to the throne.

In the 1930's many in the United States accepted the idea that a small group of arms manufacturers were responsible for United States participation in World War I. They were popularly known as "the merchants of death" and were the subject of books, magazines, and congressional hearings held by Senator Gerald Nye of North Dakota.[10] Actually Senator Nye, as an isolationist, was less interested in an answer to a scholarly problem and more interested in creating support for his policy of keeping America out of the world political crisis of the 1930's. The political impact of the Nye Committee was so great that the head of the du Pont company took his firm out of the business of manufacturing ammunition so that it would not be blamed for any subsequent wars.[11] Unfortunately for Senator Nye's theory, America got into World War II anyhow. Ironically, American business leaders were reluctant to make a full-scale conversion to war production at the beginning of World War II because they remembered that during World War I most American arms had been produced not by private industry but by federal arsenals.[12]

Sometimes the troublemaker is identified as an entire state (although "state" is often only shorthand for the leaders of a state). In 1942, Joseph Grew, former United States ambassador to Japan, stated: "Once Japan is destroyed as an aggressive force, we know of no other challenging power that can appear in the Pacific. . . . Japan is the one enemy, and the only enemy, of the peaceful peoples whose shores overlook the Pacific Ocean."[13]

Japan was destroyed as an aggressive force but the threat of war in the Pacific did not disappear. A new troublemaker was then identified. Then Vice-President Richard Nixon said in 1953, "If it were not for the Communist threat, the free world could live in peace."[14] Nixon was thinking particularly of the conventional military threat of the Sino–Soviet bloc. But even after this threat had been met by a United Nations force in Korea and by NATO in Europe, the threat to world peace reappeared in a new form, Communist-sponsored wars of liberation. In 1968, Secretary of State Dean Rusk said, "Once we remove this kind of aggression, as we are trying to do in Vietnam, the human race can perhaps look forward to peace, to the solutions of lesser problems, and to the benefits deriving from the conquests of science."[15]

CRITIQUE OF TROUBLEMAKERS AS THE CAUSE OF WAR

The regularity with which one troublemaker is eliminated only to be replaced by another should make us suspicious. These claims to have found the cause of war appear to be less analyses of the cause of all war than rationalizations for fighting in particular ones. "Help us fight just one last war," these polemicists seem to say, "and then we will have peace."

In fact none of these theories applies very broadly; once we move away from the one or two wars they were originally applied to, they no longer fit. If World War II can be attributed to an individual such as Hitler, then we cannot very well claim that all wars are started by merchants of death. Eliminating the private manufacture of armaments, which was the remedy proposed after World War I, is then no guarantee that war will be eliminated. But we cannot identify an individual such as Hitler to blame for every war. World War I was distinguished by its lack of individual villains. In the recent wars in Bangladesh and Cyprus, it is difficult to identify individuals or groups who were responsible for starting them. On the other hand, in these wars it is easy to identify political and social issues, such as the persecution of ethnic minorities, that led to the conflict. The wars in Bangladesh and Cyprus seem to have been genuinely popular in the countries that initiated them. No power-hungry premier dragged reluctant Indians or Turks into wars against their will.

These exceptions suggest another problem with the individual troublemaker theory. A leader cannot be effective without followers. Hitler may have made decisions that led to World War II, but if others had not implemented these decisions, nothing would have happened. If Adolf Hitler were to reappear today, he would be ignored as a political crackpot if not subjected to psychiatric care.

These obvious deficiencies with troublemaker theories have led scholars to hunt for more general explanations that will cover all wars. They have looked for patterns that seem likely either to generate grievances or to lead states to warlike ways of resolving grievances. A number of these theories have won wide followings at one time or another.

One of the most important nineteenth-century theorists was Karl Marx. Despite the connotations of political activism that the name "Marxist" has today, Karl Marx himself spent most of his time in the library, not on the barricades. His theories, in spite of the practical uses to which they have been put, were scholarly attempts to take into account all the evidence. For Marx, war was caused mainly by the feudal class, a class whose prime function was fighting. War was common in the Middle Ages, when the feudal class, represented by knights on horseback, was dominant. But Marx expected war to die out with feudalism. Remnants of the feudal class survived the bourgeois revolution in England and France, most of them in the officer corps of the army, but Marx expected them gradually to lose their influence. Capitalism, Marx thought, was essentially peaceful. It transcended national boundaries and worked to create a single world state. War was bad for business. This view is not that of many people who call themselves "Marxists" today but it is clearly evident in Marx's writings.[16]

Marx was soon proved wrong. Prussia, which was a capitalist society, fought a number of wars in the nineteenth century. Worse for Marx's theory, Prussia seemed to become more, not less, militaristic as its economy developed. When the most advanced capitalist societies of the day (England, Germany, and France) went to war in 1914, it was clear that Marx's views needed correction. One of the best known updatings of Marx was provided by a Russian follower, Lenin, and because today many political activists come to Marx by way of Lenin they accept the Leninist version as "Marxist." In a way Marx and Lenin were similar. They both saw wars as caused by a specific economic class. But Lenin identified a different culprit, the capitalist class, and particularly the new type of capitalist who had appeared in the later stages of capitalism, the finance capitalist or banker. We have looked at Lenin's theory when examining explanations for World War I.[17] Though not fundamentally different from Senator Gerald Nye's "merchants of death" theory, it is more complex, blaming not just a handful of private manufacturers of arms but a whole network of bankers, industrialists, and government officials. A good way of seeing whether you have grasped someone's theory on what causes war is to ask, "What would have to be eliminated from social and political life in order to eliminate war?" The remedy proposed by Lenin was more radical than that of Nye—not just prohibiting arms manufacturing by private individuals but completely reordering society to eliminate any private ownership of property. Only when capitalism is replaced by socialism, Lenin argued, will war be eliminated.

Lenin's theory has not held up much better than Marx's. In 1917, followers of Marx and Lenin took over the government of Russia; in 1949 followers of Marx and Lenin took over the government of China. In 1969 the two governments engaged in warlike behavior against each other. Neither society had private ownership of industrial enterprises. Neither had a class of finance capitalists. Yet large armies faced each other across the Ussuri River, shots were exchanged and soldiers killed.

One of Lenin's contemporaries was American President Woodrow Wilson. Wilson's analysis was in some ways not very different from Lenin's. Lenin identified a class—finance capitalists—and the states they controlled as the cause of war. Wilson also identified a class—the small ruling class of undemocratic countries unanswerable to the public at large. The states controlled by such small groups are called autocracies. Wilson contrasted autocracies unfavorably with democracies. The common people are the ones who have to fight wars and these common people, Wilson believed, would not voluntarily send their sons off to fight, particularly in wars of conquest. Furthermore, democracies would put an end to secret diplomacy and secret treaties and thus to the suspicions that had a part in starting World War I. The connection of autocracy with war is indicated by two slogans used during World War I: "The War To End All Wars" and "The War To Make the World Safe for Democracy." The two slogans were logically connected. Once the states of the world were democratic, wars would end.

Subsequent events make us skeptical of the claim that increased popular participation reduces the likelihood of war. Even while President Wilson was promoting his views there was some evidence that should have given him pause. The United States, by no means the most autocratic country in the world at the time, had occupied the Philippines in 1899 and 1900 despite fierce opposition from the inhabitants. The resistance was so fierce that United States Army "pacification" programs resulted in the massacre of hundreds of Filipinos. It is hard to see how this could have been interpreted as anything but a war of conquest being conducted by a democracy.

Some forest fires are started by accident, some on purpose. Wars, by contrast, are always begun for a purpose (or almost always—a purely accidental war, especially in the computer age, is at least conceivable). Aristotle referred to purpose as the "final cause." We might find it more in keeping with modern usage to refer to issues.

NATIONALISM: MAZZINI

Looking for some common theme in the seven wars described in earlier chapters, we are struck by the frequency with which issues of nationalism play a part in the origin of wars. The wars of Bismarck were fought to create a national state. In 1914 the Austrians went to war with Serbia because of Serbian nationalist claims; France went to war eagerly to reclaim the provinces of Alsace and Lorraine. In the 1930's, Hitler based many of his claims on the right of Germans to live together in one state. The wars in Korea, the Middle East, Bangladesh, and Cyprus had strong national components.

One of the earliest theorists on the role of nationalism in international politics was an Italian, Giuseppe Mazzini.[18] In the middle of the nineteenth century he argued for national independence for the Italians, not just for the benefit of Italians but as a way of promoting international peace. If each nation had its own state, free from control by foreigners, there would be peace. The many conflicts that arise from national differences would be eliminated. Subjects would accept willingly demands from a government of their fellow nationals that they would resist coming from outsiders.

Mazzini's views are discussed today mainly in classes on the history of political thought, not in contemporary political debate. Perhaps it is because his ideas are so widely accepted that there is no need for discussion. The underlying premise of contemporary anticolonialism and national liberation movements is the one put forward by Mazzini. It is seen as "only natural" for people to want to be ruled by members of their own nation, no matter how incompetent or tyrannical, and not by colonialists. General Idi Amin may have murdered 200,000 Ugandans, but no Ugandan suggested that the remedy was a return to British colonial rule.

Still, the Mazzinian theory is not totally satisfying. First, one can ask, where does the process of granting national self-rule end? The Nigerians may have asked for an end to British colonial rule in 1960 in the name of national liberation, but within seven years one of the major tribal groupings of the Nigerian nation, the Ibos, were proclaiming the right to secede and form a smaller state that they wanted to call Biafra. Had the Ibos succeeded, there was no guarantee that even smaller tribes among the Ibos, such as the Ibibio and the Ijaw, would not have asked for similar national liberation.

Second, some national problems have not led to war. The Germans are divided again today as they were in the time of Bismarck: In addition to the states of East and West Germany and Austria, there are German-speaking populations in Switzerland, Italy, and other parts of Europe. We would expect the national resentment to be even stronger than in 1870 because people generally feel more strongly about something they have enjoyed and been deprived of than they do about something they have never enjoyed. Yet the division of Germany has not been a cause of war in the past forty years and it does not now seem likely that it will be. Nor do all multinational states become sources of conflict. In Switzerland, three distinct national groups have lived together for several hundred years in a state distinguished by its total freedom from any kind of war.

There is a third difficulty in attributing all wars to national quarrels. The major threat to peace today, as measured by the amount of money spent for armaments, is not from a national dispute but from the tensions between the Soviet Union and the United States. Unsatisfied desires for national liberation or persecution of national minorities have almost nothing to do with this conflict.

Nationalism is often the basis for a group's feelings that it is being wronged or that it has a grievance. Other types of grievances may also provide issues for wars: violations of territory or national honor, for example. But states can also desire war not because they feel in the wrong but simply because they desire what someone else has. We might call such desires "greed." Of course one's interpretation may depend on one's vested interest. What looked to Poland and Czechoslovakia like Germany's greed toward their countries in the 1930's was presented to the world by Hitler as rectification of grievances against the German people.

This examination of causes is meant to be illustrative, not exhaustive. The alert reader will amplify and elaborate on the list. Several more need brief mention.

Wars occur because states' leaders have at their disposal instruments of violence—armaments and armed forces. Without arms there could be no war. One might imagine some unpleasantness if Canadians threw rocks at Americans visiting Niagara Falls but we would hardly label it war.

Wars occur because states' leaders choose not to use alternative means to settle their grievances or satisfy their greed. Without the decision to resort to war there would be no war. At times almost no alternatives exist—the position the world found itself in in 1914 when there was no League of Nations or United Nations. At other times alternatives exist but states believe that they will not work, or will not produce the result desired.

Wars occur because states' leaders believe there is a reasonable prospect of victory. There are far more issues about which states could fight than there are actual wars. The nationalist feelings of people in both North and South Korea were strong before 1950 and remained strong after 1953. Both sides remained armed, and neither could agree on peaceful means of settling their dispute. But neither could see a reasonable prospect of victory and war on the Korean Peninsula came to an end.

Finally, wars occur because one or more states choose to use force and the victim or victims choose to resist. In 1914 German troops sought to march through Belgium on their way to France and the Belgians put up armed resistance. In 1940 German troops sought to occupy Denmark and the Danes decided not to resist. Wars would not occur if the victims of aggression cooperated with the aggressors.

One could approach the problem of war by eliminating any of its many causes—just as one could with forest fires. But as with forest fires, some causes seem easier for us to deal with than do others. Over decades some approaches to peace have developed that seek to eliminate one or another of the many causes of war. These approaches have dealt with the causes that seemed most amenable to human control, at least within a time span short enough to yield results we could live to benefit from. Transforming human nature would undoubtedly work, yet limiting international anarchy, controlling armaments, influencing leaders' decision to go to war, and eliminating grievances seem to hold more promise.

NOTES

1. Aristotle, *Physics*, Book 2, Chapter 3. One source is Richard McKeon, ed., *The Basic Works of Aristotle* (New York: Random House, 1941), pp. 240–241.

2. Literature distributed on college campuses in 1972 and 1973 by the Campus Crusade for Christ shows that among some Christians at least this view is still widely held.

3. *Politics Among Nations*, 4th ed. (New York: Alfred A. Knopf, 1967), p. 31.

4. The English translation was published in New York by Harcourt, Brace & World in 1966. For a more recent survey on the topic see Peter A. Corning, "The Biological Bases of Behavior and Some Implications for Political Science," *World Politics*, Vol. 23, No. 3 (April 1971), pp. 321–370.

5. Anthony Storr, in his *Human Aggression* (New York: Bantam Books, 1970) refers to the work of W. B. Cannon, *Bodily Changes in Pain, Hunger, Fear and Rage*, first published in 1915.

6. Lorenz gives this and other illustrations in *King Solomon's Ring* (London: Methuen, 1961), pp. 181–185.

7. Natalie Angier, "Mother Nature's Murderers," *Discover*, (October 1983), pp. 79–82.

8. *Hitler: A Study in Tyranny*, rev. ed. (New York: Harper & Row, 1962), Chapter 9.

9. "The Element of Decision in the Pattern of War," *American Sociological Review*, Vol. 6, No. 6 (December 1941), pp. 853–859.

10. For example, H. C. Engelbrecht and F. C. Hanighen, *Merchants of Death* (New York: Dodd, Mead, 1934).

11. Bernard Brodie, *War and Politics* (New York: Macmillan, 1973), p. 289.

12. Richard J. Barnet, *Roots of War* (New York: Atheneum, 1972), p. 36.

13. Published as *Report from Tokyo* (New York: Simon & Schuster, 1942), pp. 69–70.

14. *The New York Times,* November 19, 1953, quoted by Kenneth N. Waltz in *Man, the State, and War* (New York: Columbia University Press, 1959), p. 157.

15. Quoted by Gary Porter in *The Viet-Nam Reader,* ed. Marcus G. Raskin and Bernard B. Fall (New York: Random House Vintage Books, 1965), p. 324.

16. See, for example, Part I of the *Communist Manifesto.* This point on Marx's theory is made by Adam Ulam in *Expansion and Coexistence* (New York: Frederick A. Praeger, 1968), p. 14.

17. Ibid., page 26.

18. Mazzini's views are presented by Waltz, p. 143.

PART II

APPROACHES TO PEACE

Chapter 8

World Government

World government is the most obvious solution to the problem of war. Our own national government controls fighting between groups with conflicting interests: white supremacists versus black militants, farm laborers versus farm owners, even feuding Appalachian families such as the fabled Hatfields versus the McCoys. Why not then a world government to control fighting on a world scale?

World government is more difficult to discuss than other approaches to peace because we lack actual cases to study. There have been historical examples of disarmament agreements, peacekeeping forces, and other proposed methods of bringing peace, but never a world state. The closest approximation to a world state was the ancient Roman Empire with its *pax Romana*. Most of our discussion therefore will be theoretical. We can draw analogies from experiences in the past and in the present, but they will be nothing more than analogies; that is, comparisons of situations that are alike in only some respects.

WORLD GOVERNMENT THEORY

Historical experience of world government may be lacking, but plans for it are not. Even as the modern state system was beginning to take form, writers were putting forth plans for transcending it. The Italian Dante, known for his long poem *The Divine Comedy*, advocated a universal kingdom including all the states of Europe. In his book *De Monarchia*, which appeared in 1313, Dante uses a style of argument that may seem strange to a modern reader. Nevertheless, his fundamental argument for world government survives unchanged among modern advocates: Peace is impossible without a single supreme authority that can settle quarrels among those beneath it. Only universal empire will bring universal peace.[1]

Modern advocates of world government do not often refer to *De Monarchia* when arguing their case, but they start with the same fundamental assumption. Today, however, in addition to many competing sovereign states, we must come to terms with nuclear weapons, intercontinental missiles, and global economic interdependence. Consequently, the most carefully worked-out proposals for world government consist of many components: a world legislature, a world police force, abolition of existing armies, machinery for peaceful settlement of disputes, and rule of law. Disarmament, peaceful settlement, and law can be advanced as approaches to peace on their own, and we will examine them later in separate chapters. In this chapter we will concentrate on the fundamental problems of a world government and look in detail at its most distinctive feature, a world police force.

Wars occur, we have seen, because no higher authority exists to prevent them. We call this condition international anarchy. If a world state existed, it would provide that missing higher authority and thus bring an end to anarchy. By disarming existing states, it not only would take away the means of fighting, but it would also take away the governments that decide to build armies in the first place. The present system, with authority widely scattered, would be replaced by one in which authority would be concentrated in one center. Resort to war as a means of settling disputes would no more be allowed than is resort to duels in domestic society. The private use of violence is known as taking the law into one's own hands, and it is universally condemned. Under our national government the Hatfields are not allowed to take revenge on the McCoys. Under a world government the Greeks would not be allowed to carry on their feud with the Turks in the Aegean Sea.

This description of world government relies on analogy. We must remember that analogies don't prove anything; they only illustrate. By drawing an analogy to domestic society, we haven't proved that a world state would prevent war or even that a world state would be possible. At most, we've given a vivid picture of what we are talking about. Argument by analogy is listed as a fallacy in textbooks on logic. We must be especially wary of this fallacy in thinking about something such as world government, which has never existed in reality.

We are all familiar with our own domestic society. If you have a quarrel with your neighbor about where your property line runs, you don't settle the quarrel by invading your neighbor's property with an armor-plated lawn-mower; you go to court. Domestic disputes are settled, ideally and most often in practice as well, without force or threat of force. In international politics, that is not always the case. If a national oil shortage develops, the president may drop hints about landing the Marines to take over another country's oil fields. Domestic political problems are supposed to be handled differently. Motorists waiting in line for gasoline don't talk about seizing the corner gas station.

One problem with this analogy is that it is not a very complete description of how domestic politics works. Some kinds of violence are in fact beyond the control of national governments. If you're a little short of cash one month and walk into your local bank to demand all the cash in the drawer, it won't be long before the local police come around to pick you up. But if firefighters go out on strike in direct violation of a law forbidding strikes by city employees, the mayor does not always send a constable around to arrest the head of the firefighters' union. Government leaders realize that using force, no matter how legitimate, would only make the firefighters more determined and possibly win them sympathy from other groups. In most cities strikes by public employees are illegal, but that has not prevented them.

Government leaders may decide that they cannot satisfy the grievances of some group; instead of negotiating they try to employ force. But the use of force fails. In Northern Ireland the government decided that giving in to the demands of the Irish Republican Army (IRA) would be unacceptable to the Protestant majority of Northern Ireland, but the use of force has failed to suppress the IRA. There is no question that the British government legally governs the territory of Northern Ireland. It meets all the normal criteria — governmental machinery in place, recognition by the inhabitants as well as foreign countries that it is the government, collection of taxes, issuance of authoritative laws. But it cannot maintain order.

When people talk about the ability of world government to control aggression, the analogy they usually use is the police versus the lone bank robber. But the analogy with the firefighters' union or the IRA would be more appropriate. Individual criminal acts are easy to deal with, organized political acts much harder. The threat to peace in the world comes not from individuals but from organized groups such as revisionist states, military factions, and revolutionary parties.[2]

The argument for world government is that war will be eliminated when the whole world is run like a single nation. But in fact many international conflicts arise from the failures of national governments to keep the peace.[3] The government in Pakistan could not control the Bengalis in East Pakistan, either by meeting their demands or by suppressing them. The failure of governmental power within the state of Pakistan led to international war with India. If the prescription "government" doesn't always work at the national level, why should we be certain that it will work at the international level?

Another problem with analogies is that we naturally draw them from our own experience. Americans think world government will be like American government, that violators of world law will be punished as violators of domestic laws are. But United States experience is not necessarily typical. When the Supreme Court of the United States ruled that Richard Nixon had to turn over tapes of his White House conversations to the special prosecutor, he did so even though the tapes damaged him irreparably. When a court in India ruled that Prime Minister Indira Gandhi had to relinquish her office because she had violated campaign laws, she refused and threw the opposition leaders into jail. Why should we think that a violator of world law would follow the United States model (and resign like Nixon) instead of the Indian model (and counterattack like Gandhi)?

Argument by analogy is one fallacy. A second fallacy to watch for is peace by definition.[4] Someone using this fallacy makes peace part of the definition of the proposal that is supposed to achieve peace. For example, someone might argue that diplomacy is the best approach to peace and define diplomacy as "negotiations instead of war." Well, we say, what about the Cyprus conflict of 1974? Diplomacy wasn't able to prevent that war. "Oh, no," replies the advocate of diplomacy, "the negotiations before fighting broke out were not really a substitute for war, so they weren't really diplomacy." In other words, success in preventing war is built right into the definition of diplomacy. If that's what someone insists diplomacy must mean, of course it will prevent war.

We should begin to suspect attempts to to achieve peace by definition when we encounter forceful adjectives attached to proposals. For example, followers of the Baha'i religion believe in world government and describe how a "world tribunal will adjudicate and deliver its compulsory and final verdict in all and any disputes that may arise between the various elements constituting this universal system."[5] Simply adding the words "compulsory" and "final" does not make the argument more convincing.

When we are defining world government, we must take care not to do so in a way that produces peace by definition. Government is often said to be "legitimate monopoly of armed force." But this definition should not blind us to the frequent existence of armed force, even though illegitimate, that rivals the government monopoly. An obvious case of such rivalry is a civil war.

If we use "government" in the commonly accepted way, we can say that during the nineteenth century the states of the United States formed a single government but the states making up Europe did not; Europe was in a condition of international anarchy. But because of the American Civil War, deaths from military action in the United States in the nineteenth century nearly equaled military deaths in the European countries.[6] Clearly government alone is no guarantee of peace and order. In Quincy Wright's list of 278 wars fought from 1480 to 1941, seventy-eight of them (28 per cent) were civil wars.[7] It seems likely that a world state would continue to have wars, though they might be called rebellions or insurrections.

ARGUMENTS IN FAVOR OF WORLD GOVERNMENT

Some defenders of world government may use fallacious arguments, but that doesn't make the idea itself wrong. Critics of world government sometimes employ a fallacy themselves, the fallacy of perfectionism. They argue that unless a system functions perfectly it is of no use at all. However, many systems function imperfectly yet are useful. Some people cheat with their checkbooks. They write checks when they have no money in their accounts or when they don't even have an account. But this misuse does not make checks useless devices. Merchants find the honest use of checks worthwhile enough to put up with occasional abuse. Only if the system were grossly abused would it make sense to do without it.

Even though world government would have flaws, it wouldn't need to function perfectly to be an improvement over what we have now. Wars in the form of rebellions or insurrections might indeed occur, but we could expect that there would be fewer of these civil wars. In Quincy Wright's list only 28 per cent of all wars were civil wars. One could hypothesize that under a world government civil wars would continue to occur only one-third as frequently as international wars. Thus, even if world government did not eliminate war, it might reduce it by two-thirds. These figures do not constitute conclusive proof, of course, but they do give what lawyers call a *prima facie* case; that is, upon first looking at them they seem to argue in favor of world government and not against it.

It is true that the United States, despite a central government, experienced a severe war in the nineteenth century. But without such a government, war between the states might have come sooner and been fought repeatedly, and total military casualties might have been far greater than those in Europe.

Nor is the analogy with domestic politics totally worthless. One thousand years ago the area known today as France consisted of separate states — Burgundy, Lorraine, Normandy, and many others — usually at war with each other. Over a period of five centuries, the separate provinces were brought together in a unified state. Two facts about this unification could discourage advocates of world government. One is that it took many years. Another is that these years were full of wars fought to resist unification. Both of these are drawbacks for those who want instant peace. But, on the positive side, we can say that a unitary state was finally created, that war between the formerly sovereign units disappeared, and that reversion to anarchy has become less and less likely.

The development of peace and order within France was helped by the creative role of the state. War between Burgundy and Provence is unlikely today, not just because the central authority in Paris prevents it but also because a French state fosters a sense of community between Burgundy and Provence. Children in school learn the same history; radio and television broadcast the same news and entertainment; a single code of laws makes it easy for people in one region to travel, change jobs, or engage in business in another region.

Even if we have reservations about world government, we should not underestimate how important a central authority can be in prohibiting violence. International politics differs from other kinds of politics because large-scale murder (which we call war) is still legitimate. This type of murder is not totally unregulated. Ordinarily, individuals are not entitled to cross the border with Mexico and gun down people at will. But if a few conditions are fulfilled — making a declaration of war, joining the armed forces, and being ordered to attack — they could receive medals for gunning down Mexicans. This kind of behavior is approved at no other level of politics. World government would abolish legalized mass killing. Deaths would still occur, just as they do when a state's police force resorts to violence. Such deaths would no longer be considered a normal way of doing business, however, and we would not make especially violent police officers into folk heroes.

World government would thus contribute to an enlargement of people's moral horizons. At one time morality extended only as far as one's family; it was considered moral to cheat, rob, or kill outsiders in the defense of family interests. Gradually moral horizons were extended to the village and region and tribe. Killing members of one's own tribe was considered murder, but killing members of other tribes was not. In many tribal languages, the word for "human being" was often the same as the name of the tribe. Members of other tribes were by definition not human beings, and killing them was no more murder than was killing a wolf. Today our moral horizons have extended as far as our own nation-state. The bombardier who released the atomic bomb on Hiroshima would likely have had grave scruples about releasing it on Milwaukee.[8] Advocates of world government are asking us to take one last step and extend our moral horizons to encompass all human beings.

ADVOCATES OF WORLD GOVERNMENT

Interest in world government waxes and wanes. It wanes when national states seem to be doing well, providing security and prosperity for their citizens. When they do not provide these things, interest in replacing them with larger units begins to grow. The thirteen American colonies federated after a period of revolution. The countries of Europe began to move toward a European community after the disruptions of World War II. Even in the United States interest in a world government grew after World War II. Some polls at that time showed almost two-thirds of the respondents willing to support at least the abstract principle of a world body able to settle disputes between states and enforce its decisions.[9]

Such sentiment was cultivated by writers such as Norman Cousins, for years editor of the *Saturday Review.* You can read his arguments in editorials appearing in that magazine or in his influential book *In Place of Folly.*[10] According to Cousins, there is no alternative to world government. In the past we could afford to hesitate, bicker, and procrastinate because the consequences of failure were not the total destruction of humanity. No more, Cousins argues, in what might be labeled the *in extremis* position. The situation has changed so radically because of nuclear weapons and their delivery systems that equally radical departures in thinking are required. We face the possibility that all human life will be destroyed within a few days as the result of actions by a handful of military leaders. In this extreme situation all the old hesitations about taking radical steps are no longer valid.

Cousins and others with similar views clearly were writing under the impact of the then-new atomic weapon. Today it is easy for us to say that these fears were exaggerated. World government was not instituted, but the world did not come to an end. We were not in the extreme situation Cousins thought we were in. Perhaps his problem was that he was neither a scientist nor a military expert and lacked the competence to judge the new weapons. However, before we dismiss the in extremis argument, we should look at the version of it offered by Herman Kahn, a thinker with a background very different from Cousins'. Kahn made his reputation with his book *On Thermonuclear War.*[11] In it he looked in great detail and with great detachment at the consequences of nuclear weapons that Cousins warned about. What would happen in atomic war? Would all humanity be destroyed? Would the survivors envy the dead?

Kahn outraged many people by his answer. No, the survivors would not envy the dead. Thermonuclear war would be bad but not nearly so bad as many people expected. Kahn himself had a background in physics, and he used techniques of analysis developed at the Rand Corporation. These credentials did not impress some people, to whom he became a symbol of bloodthirsty irrationality. A reviewer in *Scientific American* asked, "Is there really a Herman Kahn," or is this a "staff hoax in poor taste"?[12]

Although Kahn warned against exaggerating the effects of nuclear war, he never advocated nuclear war — a distinction that was lost on some people because of their emotional reaction to his book. In fact, Kahn devoted much effort to devising ways to keep the initial stages of an international crisis from escalating to all-out war. His writings deal only with short-run measures to prevent escalation. In the long run, he wrote, the only plausible alternative is some variant of world government.[13]

Kahn, like Cousins, uses the in extremis argument. Suppose, he suggested, a few missiles are launched accidentally. Faced with the awesome prospect of escalation to total destruction, the United States and the Soviet Union might quickly conclude that deterrence and anarchy are no way to run the world and sign an agreement in a matter of days. Whatever theoretical proposal was available might be implemented almost overnight.

PRACTICAL DETAILS OF THE WORLD STATE

If world opinion suddenly shifts in favor of world government, what kind of blueprint do we want to have waiting? We should be clear that we are talking about a *government,* not a technocracy or rule by nonpolitical experts. A plan for world government is not like a plan for an automated telephone switchboard. It cannot operate without human judgment and political decisions. The constitution of a world state may read, "Arms are prohibited; violaters will be automatically punished," but words alone tell very little about what a world government will be like in practice. The Soviet Union has a constitution with written guarantees of civil liberties; the United Kingdom, in contrast, has no written constitution at all. Clearly anyone who relies on words alone to guarantee the protection of civil liberties could be seriously deceived.

Obviously a police force cannot be employed against a violator without a decision to do so. Someone must tell the police to arrest conspirators arming in secret, and the decision to arrest depends on other decisions. An official must decide to "see" a violation in the first place. Support a constable on duty at midnight in Bliggens City stops a car for weaving over the center line on Main Street and discovers that the car is driven by W. W. Bliggens, Chairman of the Board of Bliggens Textile Mills. Does the constable see a case of drunken driving and make the required arrest, or does he see a motorist fatigued by a hard day's work and in obvious need of a lift home? Blacks in the United States have charged that standards of law and order differ within the black and white communities. Murders in which both attacker and victim are black have been tolerated in a way that other murders have not been. Law enforcement officers, it is claimed, do not "see" crimes committed by blacks against blacks. Similarly some forms of world government could lead to toleration of certain kinds of collective violence — acts that did not threaten the interests of the world rulers, acts that were allowed because the world rulers were intimidated by the perpetrators. We have no right to be more naive about world government than we are about our own.

The question of "seeing" a violation is only one matter to be resolved. There are many others. Suppose a violation is clearly identified. How much force is to be employed against it? If an alleged violator promises to stop before enforcement has begun, is punishment then called for? Matters of judgment always come up. Who will make these judgments? Questions about who will run a world state, how they will be selected, and how they will be held accountable are very important.

Governments may range from very loose associations to very tightly controlled totalitarian states. The distinguishing characteristic is the amount of behavior they control. The government that governs least may control very little behavior; it may do little more than catch thieves and repel invaders. A totalitarian government strives for total control, over leisure activities, family life, and private thoughts. Again we must avoid the pitfall of analogy. When Americans use the term "government," they naturally think first of the United States government and focus on two of its prominent features — its democracy and its federalism.

"Democracy" is an elastic term, and we need define it only loosely. *Democracy* is a form of government in which fairly large numbers of people participate in decision-making and even larger numbers are consulted before the decisions are made. At the opposite pole is *autocracy,* a system in which decisions are made by a very few and the decisions are not challenged. Whatever one's reservations about the present American system, one will probably admit that all decision-making is not concentrated in the hands of a very few. The president, members of Congress, and most other officials agree that something must be done to conserve energy, but no one official or group can decree that its solution be implemented.

Not all governments operate under such restraints. Although no government is entirely free of restraint, some are a lot freer than others. When the revolutionary government took over in South Vietnam, it decided to stop crime on the streets by shooting thieves and looters and letting their bodies lie at the scene of the crime. Some Americans have proposed the same solution, but they have little chance of implementing it because too many groups would oppose it.

Americans generally agree that they pay a price for these restraints, the price of relative inefficiency. The United States has responded very slowly to a shortage of energy because so many groups need to be consulted. In contrast, the revolutionary Cambodian government in 1975 decided to reduce dependence on imported oil quickly by destroying motor vehicles and then just as quickly did so.

This line of thought suggests that a world government, if it were to be efficient, might be less democratic than the government we are used to. It might consult fewer people and pay less heed to objections to policies. The kind of opposition to registering firearms expressed by some Americans could not be tolerated on a world scale if a world government were to achieve the goal of preventing war. If a world government did have the power to compel people to surrender firearms (stop and think how much power the United States government would have to use just to have firearms registered), what else would it be able to do? Perhaps control the content of books, newspapers, and television programs? After all, this sort of regulation could be justified as helping to prevent war because books, newspapers, and television shape attitudes toward war and peace.

The firearms example is enlightening in another way. It is difficult to imagine the registration, much less the abolition, of private firearms in the United States, yet opinion polls have repeatedly demonstrated that only a minority of Americans opposes such control.[14] But this minority is well organized and politically active. The majority is confronting not isolated individuals but political groups. As we pointed out earlier, it is the political group that gives government the most trouble. We do not anticipate that a world government will encounter problems from solitary lawbreakers building atom bombs in their hobby rooms. Trouble will come from organized groups — the IRA, the PLO, or whatever may be active. Considering recent history, we do not have much reason for confidence that world government will be able to control them. In a few countries terrorists are controlled, but these countries can hardly be used as an argument in favor of world government, for they have enormous repressive forces. Neither Paraguay nor the Soviet Union has terrorists blowing up buildings, but most of us would not like to live there.

Most of us would oppose a government with extensive repressive power, preferring to take our chances with the present risk of war instead. For this reason most of the serious proposals for world government advanced in the West envisage the relatively weak control associated with the central government in a federal state. The federalism of the United States is often used as an example.

Unfortunately for the advocates of a weak world government, American federalism looks more attractive in its historical version than in its present-day form. Almost universal complaints about big government have not stopped the enormous growth of central government in recent decades. Behavior is now regulated in a way never imagined by the writers of the Constitution. Government has a say in what kinds of workers are employed, how packages are labeled, and even where children are sent to school. This development is not unique to the United States. Governments around the world are growing bigger, not smaller.

Unsuccessful attempts to limit the scope of national governments have not discouraged proponents of a world federal system with limited powers. The best known of these proposals is described in *World Peace Through World Law,* by Grenville Clark and Louis Sohn.[15] The Clark and Sohn proposal is so modest that it hardly deserves the name "world government." Governmental authority would extend only to preventing war. In conformity with this limited aim, Clark and Sohn propose not to create a new organization but merely to revise the existing United Nations organization. The major parts of the revamped United Nations would be a General Assembly, an Executive Council, an Inspection Commission, and a World Police Force.

1. The General Assembly. Today the General Assembly of the United Nations has only limited advisory powers. Under the revision it would have no more power except in one area — maintaining peace. Because it would have real legislative powers for this purpose, Clark and Sohn propose a new voting system, weighted according to population. But they propose that the weighting be done by steps. The four largest countries would have thirty representatives each; the eight next-largest countries would have fifteen representatives each; and so on. The four largest countries are China, India, the USSR, and the United States. A system of direct proportionality would mean that China, with three or four times the population of the United States, would have three or four times the representation. The system proposed by Clark and Sohn makes America's representation equal to China's (and also makes that of major communist countries equal to that of major noncommunist ones).

2. Executive Council. This body would be essentially the same as the Security Council of the United Nations, having the power to intervene and prevent war. However, in the current Security Council each of the five major states has the power to block action by voting against it. Clark and Sohn wish to eliminate this veto power. A qualified majority (twelve votes out of a total seventeen) would still be required for action. These twelve votes would have to include a majority of the four biggest countries, but a country could no longer prevent action against itself.

3. Inspection Commission. This commission, along with its staff, the Inspection Service, is entirely new. It would supervise disarmament. Because states, by agreeing to the Clark–Sohn plan, would be agreeing to disarm, the Inspection Commission would have to do no persuading. Its function

would be to see that disarmament is carried out. During the first two years, it would take an arms census, counting the weapons each country has; over the next ten years it would supervise the reduction of the weapons at a rate of 10 per cent a year.

4. World Police Force. This is another addition to the existing system. The World Police Force would enforce disarmament and prevent attacks by any remaining armed forces. In a disarmed world, the municipal police force of a large state could threaten a small neighbor. A small Caribbean island, for example, might hesitate to host a convention of American sheriffs if they came armed. The World Police Force would be large enough to reassure any small country. It would consist of a regular force of about half a million and reserves up to twice that number. The police would be recruited from many countries and would be stationed around the world.

Clark and Sohn put forth many other specific proposals. They have considered many issues and provided many answers. If we do not now have a world government, the reason is not because no thinking has been done about it. What is needed is not further elaboration of schemes but the approval of states.

Clark and Sohn suggest ratification by five-sixths of the countries of the world (provided that these countries constitute five-sixths of the world's population) before the plan goes into effect. Approval of that magnitude — 83.3 per cent — would reduce fear that the system would never work. The question is how to get that much approval. Perhaps Herman Kahn's prognostication is the best: After a big scare resulting from a close brush with war, people will suddenly find themselves ready to change their thinking; then the Clark–Sohn proposals, being the best at hand, will be adopted in a few days.

RESISTANCE TO WORLD GOVERNMENT

Proponents of world government do not rely solely on catastrophe to implement their plans. Traditionally they have used analogy not only to explain how world government would prevent war but also to show how it would come about. And again the analogy is frequently drawn from the United States. In 1783 the thirteen colonies were separate, sovereign states, loosely bound by the Articles of Confederation. By 1787 they had agreed to form a strong federal union and central government. The motto they chose, E pluribus unum, "out of many, one," summarizes what happened. One historian of these years entitled his book The Great Rehearsal, suggesting that other parts of the world might later follow the American example.[16]

Opponents of world government likewise have traditional arguments.

Their basic argument is that the American situation was unique. Those thirteen colonies had just completed a revolutionary war; the shift of political loyalties from small units to a larger one occurs only when other political and social habits are changing as well; in other words, in a revolutionary situation.[17] The revolutionary war was fought against a common enemy under one commander, who went on to become head of the new state. This cooperation in waging a war was facilitated by many things the colonists already had in common — language, culture, political tradition. It was not accidental that the part of North America where a different language was spoken, Quebec, was not included in the new state, or that those who did not share the political values of the revolution were often forced to emigrate to Canada. Whatever petty jealousies separated the thirteen colonies, there were no traditional barriers to movement or trade, certainly nothing comparable to what years of independent sovereign existence had created in Europe.

No one should deny, of course, that a union of small units is possible. The United States was formed of small units; so too was modern Switzerland. But we should not ignore the enormous barriers that vested interests normally put in the way of amalgamation. A so-called Greater New York joining the parts of New Jersey, Pennsylvania, Connecticut, and New York State that are economically and in other ways tied to New York City is a rational solution to many of New York's problems, but such a solution is not likely because of set patterns and vested interests.

Similarly countries resist amalgamation. In fact, such resistance is given the highest priority in a state's policy and is termed "national security." It is a basic policy of Pakistan to resist amalgamation with India, of Mexico to resist amalgamation with the United States, and so on. Four reasons are usually given.

1. People are attached to their culture, language, and traditions. They fear that these will be changed by amalgamation. The Protestants in Northern Ireland, for example, fear the effects of incorporation into an Irish state that is mostly Catholic.

2. People fear disruption of their economic system. Although all Koreans would like to live in one country, the difference between North Korea's state-controlled economy and South Korea's free-enterprise economy is a major reason the halves have not yet reunited.

3. People fear that a large political unit will be less responsive to their wishes. The Norwegians rejected membership in the European Communities in September 1972, in part out of fear that this loose union of states could eventually acquire too much authority and their own control over that authority would be diluted.

4. People who benefit from existing arrangements, such as those with jobs in government, fear they will lose income or power. It might be logical to have a single prairie state called Dakota, but we would expect any such proposal to be resisted by the existing governments in North Dakota and South Dakota.

Resistance to amalgamation appears to be very ingrained. This is clear if we look at a situation in which the four factors just listed do not apply, or at least do not apply with the force they normally have. Canada and the United States share a language (although both have a sizable minority speaking another language — French in one case, Spanish in the other). Canadians and Americans have a common political tradition. The economies of Canada and the United States work according to the same principles. The fourth factor, vested interests, is present, but both countries have a federal system, which would minimize the disruptions caused by any kind of union.

In spite of these similarities, these two neighbors have trouble taking even small steps toward political union. At the extreme western end of the United States–Canada boundary is the peninsula of Point Roberts, an area of the United States that can be reached on land only by traveling through Canada. A joint Canadian–United States commission tries to deal with special problems that this enclave causes, such as the need to bus children through Canada to get them to school in the United States. In 1973 the Point Roberts Board presented a modest proposal to make the enclave the headquarters of an international park that would encompass much of the surrounding waters. The proposal was greeted with fury by the local residents. One called the Americans on the board "Benedict Arnolds." A sexton at the Point Roberts cemetery said he would gladly dig two graves free if the two major American proponents of the plan would drop dead.[18] If good neighbors sharing an unarmed border with a common language, tradition, culture, and economy react so strongly to the mildest proposal for cooperation, how will traditional enemies react to proposed amalgamation?

CONSENSUS VERSUS COERCION

Behavior in the Point Roberts case illustrates a basic proposition about government: It depends on subjective feelings as well as on objective institutions. If many people are opposed to cooperation with a group they view as outsiders, then objective factors such as a common language make little difference. The subjective element in government is termed *shared values,* or *consensus.* All successful states depend at least in part on consensus. States also use force or coercion, but the amount of coercion depends on the amount of consensus — the greater the consensus, the less coercion is needed. This is why small, homogeneous, well-integrated states like Denmark and Costa Rica have both small police forces and low crime rates. They enjoy a wide consensus. On the other hand, in countries where different groups hold very different values — South Africa or Chile — larger repressive forces are needed.

It seems clear that in the world today there is little consensus on values important to a community. Differences are wide on such issues as the way to organize an economy and distribute wealth, the right to hold religious beliefs different from those of others, and the morality of divorce, birth control, and abortion. Any attempt to create a world state without consensus to build on will have to rely on coercion — in fact, a great deal of coercion. A world state that would include the Irish Republican Army and the British, the Palestinians and the Israelis, and the Greeks and the Turks would require a great deal of centralized power just to stay in existence.

This dependence on coercion undermines the claim that a world state would be limited. If the central authority could prevent the United States from having a cache of arms, could it not also prevent the United States from having a cache of surplus grain? Grain could be taken away from productive countries as a legitimate way to prevent war, on the argument that starvation is a cause of violence. Drastic changes in diet might follow. Would Americans accept world government if it meant an end to backyard barbeques? Or the central authority might decree that cattle in India should be slaughtered to save the grain they would otherwise consume. Fears of such action would provoke widespread resistance in India. Resistance to this kind of governmental control would generate new conflict, possibly more than the world has right now.

The need to rely on coercion when consensus is absent is supported by the little historical evidence about world government that we have. The closest humanity has ever come to a world state was the Roman Empire. It brought together the formerly separate states bordering the Mediterranean. Although there were areas of civilization elsewhere in the world, they had such little contact with the Mediterranean that in the minds of the Romans they did not exist. For all practical purposes, the Roman Empire did what world states are supposed to do. It abolished individual sovereignties and replaced them with a centralized authority.

The Roman Empire was created by force. Order was maintained by the famous Roman legions. The phrase *pax Romana*, the peace of Rome, stands for peace maintained by force. The peace was constantly tested by wars in the form of revolts against Roman rule, similar to national liberation movements today, and the revolts were brutally suppressed. The defeat of the Jewish Zealots, with the destruction of the Temple and the dispersal of the inhabitants of Judea, is the best known.

A WORLD POLICE FORCE

The need for coercion in any world government that might come into existence in the foreseeable future means that we must pay special attention to the World Police Force proposed by Clark and Sohn. Where would this force of up to half a million young people come from? Obviously they would have to come from many countries to keep the force from being too lenient with any one country. Therefore most members would need the intellectual ability to learn a second language, yet be willing to take orders, live a regimented barracks life, and put their lives at risk. In an age when military service in all countries is increasingly unpopular, why would talented young people join? One author suggests high salaries and an appeal to idealism.[19] Perhaps such incentives would work, but the force would serve mainly garrison duty in enclaves scattered around the world. Garrison duty has always been considered tedious and has no obvious attraction for idealists. For the Allied Control Commission in charge of enforcing the disarmament of Germany after World War I, such duty led to laxness and unwillingness to investigate complaints. A study of the UN peacekeeping force on Cyprus found that the overriding feature of peacekeeping duty was "tedium and monotony."[20]

What about occasions when enforcement action must be taken? The kind of idealism called for is a new one — willingness to act against one's own country. One wonders if those willing to do this would make the best soldiers.[21] Traditionally military duty has not been incompatible with other attachments; sacrificing for one's country did not mean going against one's family. The same qualities that made Robert E. Lee an admired soldier led him to leave the United States Army and fight along with the rebellious forces in his own section of the country. In a future state, it is hard to imagine a Bengali contingent on a World Police Force willing to use force against armed Bengalis trying to save themselves from extermination by Punjabis.

The attraction of high salaries is not clear either. One could hardly enjoy them while on garrison duty. Moreover, if the police force took part in unpopular acts, its members might have difficulty finding a place back home to enjoy their savings after retirement. The historical record is not encouraging. Going off to die for a patriotic cause has produced better soldiers than going off for monetary reward. Mercenary armies were possible only when the alternative was unbearable poverty, and even then they did not fare well against idealistic armies.

The source of high salaries is another problem. Police forces are not just men and women; they are also supplies, bases, and the finances to run them. The financial burden might be less than the present arms burden, but it would not be negligible any more than the police force is a negligible item in the budget of New York City. In the development of modern nation-states, monarchs started out with their own power base — royal lands and royal retainers. Louis XI of France relied on the area around Paris known as the Ile de France; the kings of Prussia relied on the Mark of Brandenburg. Proponents of a World Police Force, by contrast, propose that the force be dependent on charity. It is not difficult to imagine cases in which this would cause grave difficulties.

Suppose, in a disarmed world, Mexico gets massive United States investment to develop oil fields near the United States border but then refuses to share their output with the United States. A force consisting of Texas Rangers and oil company security guards moves into Mexico to take over the oil fields. The World Police Force is sent in against them, but the United States, in self-righteous anger, cuts off its share of financing for the force and stops delivery of equipment such as helicopters that would be vital to enforcement action. It is easy to see that the success of a World Police Force will depend on its possessing an independent power base.

But once it gets such a power base, how can a police force be controlled by anyone for any purpose? How could demands for incredibly large salaries be resisted? How could protests against even the grossest violations of neutrality be effective? Even if the force did not become corrupt, it would have to be strong enough to prevent change, and a system that prevents change is for all practical purposes a tyranny.

One of the dangers of a name such as "World Police Force" is that again we draw an analogy to our own experience. We think of President Truman dismissing General MacArthur, with General MacArthur quietly fading away. We don't think of the more typical case, in which the attempt to dismiss the head of the armed forces leads to the overthrow of the government. The latter possibility is far more likely. In recent years about two-thirds of the countries in the world have experienced military coups. America's experience with a totally housebroken military is unusual and misleading as a model of what a world army would be like. Instead of politicians controlling their police, it is more likely that the police would control politics.

World government is a frontal attack on the problem of state sovereignty. Advocates of world government identify state sovereignty as a major cause of war. They wish to deprive the individual states of both the ability and the excuse to use force in their own behalf to settle disputes. Under world government, force would be centralized under one authority. But much of the case for world government rests on an analogy with domestic society, and analogies though helpful in illustrating proposals are not convincing proof. The differences between domestic society and the international society are large — one of the most important being that people within states (at least within stable ones) have a lot more in common with each other than they have with outsiders. In the absence of consensus, great amounts of power would be needed to institute and maintain a world government. But concentrating all this power in one place would create a temptation to seize it. For this reason, too much reliance on force to solve the problem of war among states raises serious doubts about world government.

Even if you might find an enforced peace, a pax Romana, preferable to present international anarchy, the power to bring it about does not seem available in the world today. The Roman legions, however undemocratic, could govern an empire. Modern political leaders have difficulty governing New York City, not to mention Cyprus, Northern Ireland, or Lebanon. Those who wish to resist authority have many more weapons at their disposal than the Jewish Zealots did. From cars you can siphon gasoline to make Molotov cocktails; from construction sites you can steal dynamite to make bombs; and from nuclear reactors you can make off with enough plutonium to build a nuclear device. In the face of such developments, the amount of power needed to create and administer a world state simply is not available.

Devices such as police forces are called *external constraints*. If people obey a law without an external constraint, we say that they have internalized the law. We mentioned briefly that a consensus that would serve as a foundation for world government does not yet exist. But we still have to consider the question of whether a limited consensus exists that would enable us to regulate conduct among states according to law. Regulating state behavior through the internalized constraint of international law is our next subject.

NOTES

1. For a discussion of Dante's style of argument and conclusion, see George H. Sabine and Thomas L. Thorson, *A History of Political Theory,* 4th ed. (Hinsdale, Ill.: Dryden Press, 1973), pp. 243–248.

2. Inis L. Claude, Jr., discusses this point at length in his excellent chapters on world government in *Power and International Relations* (New York: Random House, 1962), especially pp. 243–255.

3. Inis L. Claude, Jr., *Swords into Plowshares,* 4th ed. (New York: Random House, 1971), p. 424.

4. Claude, *Power and International Relations,* p. 218; he calls it "solution by definition."

5. Shoghi Effendi, *The World Order of Bah'u'llah,* rev. ed. (Wilmette, Ill.: Baha'i Publishing Trust, 1955), pp. 203–204.

6. Consult J. David Singer and Melvin Small, *The Wages of War,* 1816–1965 (New York: John Wiley, 1972) for statistics on war. Using the list of European wars on page 297 and the battle deaths for these wars on pages 60–75, one arrives at a total of 648, 180 battle deaths for Europe in the nineteenth century, excluding the period of the Napoleonic Wars. The American Civil War caused about 630,000 deaths in battle.

7. Quincy Wright, *A Study of War,* 2nd ed. (Chicago: University of Chicago Press, 1965), p. 651.

8. This point was made by Kenneth Boulding in *The World Community*, ed. Quincy Wright (Chicago: University of Chicago Press, 1948), pp. 101–102.

9. *Newsweek*, October 14, 1946, pp. 44–45.

10. Norman Cousins, *In Place of Folly* (New York: Harper, 1961).

11. Herman Kahn, *On Thermonuclear War* (Princeton, N.J.: Princeton University Press, 1959).

12. James R. Newman, "Books: Six Discussions of Thermonuclear War," *Scientific American*, Vol. 204, No. 3 (March 1961), p. 197.

13. Herman Kahn, "The Arms Race and World Order," in *The Revolution in World Politics*, ed. Morton A. Kaplan (New York: John Wiley, 1962).

14. For example, see the *Gallup Report*, No. 187 (Princeton, N.J.: The Gallup Poll, April 1981), p. 14; see also *The New York Times*, June 20, 1983, p. Y9.

15. Grenville Clark and Louis Sohn, *World Peace Through World Law* (Cambridge: Harvard University Press, 1958). See especially the Introduction.

16. Carl Van Doren, *The Great Rehearsal* (New York: Viking Press, 1948).

17. Karl W. Deutsch et al., *Political Community and the North Atlantic Area* (Princeton, N.J.: Princeton University Press, 1957), p. 48.

18. *Bellingham* (Washington) *Herald*, December 4, 1973.

19. See the discussion very much in the vein of Clark and Sohn by Arthur Larson, "Arms Control Through World Law," in *Arms Control, Disarmament, and National Security*, ed. Donald G. Brennan (New York: George Braziller, 1961), pp. 423–436.

20. Charles C. Moskos, Jr., *Peace Soldiers* (Chicago: University of Chicago Press, 1976), p. 84.

21. This point has been made by a number of commentators, among them Thomas C. Schelling in "Strategy: A World Force in Operation," in *International Military Forces*, ed. Lincoln P. Bloomfield (Boston: Little, Brown, 1964), p. 230.

Chapter 9

International Law

If might made right, we would expect legislators and judges to come from the ranks of professional wrestlers. But in our society might doesn't necessarily make right. On the contrary, the comparatively small, weak wife of a professional football player is able to take her husband to court for mistreating her. In our country, we have the rule of law, and this rule contrasts sharply with the anarchy of international politics. If law can prevent serious disorder within a state, can it also prevent violence between states?

WHAT LAW IS

We make a distinction between *is* and *ought* statements. "Eating a dozen green apples at one sitting is bad for your digestion" is an *is* statement, or *description*. "You should not steal green apples from Mr. McGuffy's tree" is an *ought* statement, or *prescription*. We normally think of law as a prescription backed up by a state-imposed sanction, or penalty: "You shouldn't steal apples, and if you do you will be fined ten dollars."

There are many kinds of prescription — folkways, mores, ethical imperatives, laws. A *folkway* may prescribe some aspect of daily conduct. Penalties for ignoring folkways are often no more severe than mild disapproval. Rules governing the proper kind of footwear for formal occasions might be called folkways. Before Piere Elliott Trudeau became prime minister of Canada, he was known for violating this folkway by wearing sandals in the House of Commons. The sanctions against him were not serious — raised eyebrows, a few jokes, nothing more. *Mores* prescribe more important behavior. The rule "women and children first" reflects values widely held in our society. The male captain of a sinking ship who shoved aside women and children so that he could use the only lifeboat would live the rest of his life in disgrace. *Ethical imperatives* such as "It is wrong to steal even if you're sure you won't get caught" are enforced by conscience. Finally, *laws* are enforced by penalties imposed by governments.

Obviously, laws do not require a continuously visible threat of sanction to be effective. Compliance is usually automatic; people have internalized the prescriptions. Most drivers stop at stop signs even when no police car is behind them. The police need pay attention to only the few who do run stop signs. Laws that have not been internalized, such as prohibitions on the use of alcohol or marijuana, are not effective despite the best efforts of police. Still, at the back of every law is a sanction imposed by government. It is the sanction that makes law different from other kinds of prescription.

With no equivalent of a sovereign or a police force in international politics, it is hard to imagine what kind of sanctions could back up prescriptions on interstate behavior. And who would apply sanctions even if they did exist? Yet we do talk about international law, and when we do we are talking about something real. There are indeed prescriptions about how states should behave. States know what they are and follow them. They are *ought* statements, not *is* statements, and states usually do what these laws say they ought to do even if it is not always in their immediate interest. These prescriptions are occasionally violated, but that only proves they are significant. A law prohibiting what people have no desire to do would not be a very significant law.

EXAMPLES OF INTERNATIONAL LAW

International law regulates several kinds of activity. Diplomacy is one. One of the oldest rules of international law observed today came out of the Congress of Vienna in 1815, which met to make peace in Europe after the Napoleonic Wars. One minor difficulty at the Vienna Congress was deciding which representatives were most important. Some countries called their delegates ambassador; others called theirs minister plenipotentiary, envoy, or nuncio. Confusion about rank disrupted the formal receptions and balls, which were as important a part of the Vienna Congress as the bargaining sessions. To put each other at ease, the delegates agreed on an order of precedence, which continues to this day. Highest in rank is ambassador, followed by minister, minister resident, and chargé d'affaires. Thus assigning a minister instead of an ambassador to a country — as the United States did to Hungary after the 1956 revolution — is a sign of less than cordial relations.

In 1818, at the Congress of Aix-la-Chapelle, the diplomats solved another issue of precedence: the matter of which country would be given the highest honors. At a banquet, seats at the table vary in importance, depending on how close they are to the host. Diplomats from major countries had been known to walk out of banquets because they weren't given the seats they thought their countries deserved. The clever solution was to rank countries according to the individual ambassador's seniority. The person who had been accredited to a country longest would be first in rank. If he or she retired, the representative of another country (the one who had been there next longest) would fill the place. This sytem continues to this day, with the ranking ambassador known as the dean of the diplomatic corps. A number of ceremonial duties are connected with the post of dean, and a capable person who is filling it is usually left in place by the sending country for many years. The ambassador from Nicaragua to the United States served for almost 36 years, for 21 of them as dean. The original problem of which country is most powerful and prestigious has been solved, we might say, in a diplomatic way.

A universally known prescription is "Don't shoot an envoy who comes under a white flag." The age-old practice of immunity for diplomats has been codified in a convention drawn up in Vienna in 1961. It lays down basic rules for diplomacy. One is that ambassadors and other embassy officials are immune from criminal prosecution. If they commit crimes, they may be expelled, but they cannot be hauled into court, even as witnesses. Another rule is that embassy premises are immune from search; they may not be entered even in wartime without permission. At the same time the embassy may not be used in a manner inconsistent with diplomatic practices. If you rob a bank while you are traveling abroad, don't head for the nearest embassy; the staff will turn you right over to the police. Another rule is that embassies must have the freedom to communicate in secret with their home country. Usually they do so through the diplomatic bag or pouch, which is immune to search by customs officials. By mutual consent, communication may also be carried out by radio transmission.

All states acknowledge these international laws protecting diplomats. Most of the time, states respect these laws, despite strong temptations to violate them. The diplomatic bag is often suspected of being used for purposes other than communication with the home country. It has been strongly hinted that the United States diplomatic bag was used to smuggle manuscripts of Aleksandr Solzhenitsyn out of the Soviet Union, yet Soviet authorities did not violate the law by searching the bag.[1] The British suspected some Arab countries, particularly Libya, of using their bag to smuggle arms for terrorists, yet the British did not violate international law by searching Libya's diplomatic bag.[2] In fact, the only recent case of violating the diplomatic bag occurred when the prerevolutionary government of Cambodia searched the Chinese diplomatic bag for counterfeit currency that the Chinese were smuggling in to undermine the Cambodian economy, and it was Cambodia, not China, that was universally condemned.[3] There is often an advantage to be gained by doing something prohibited such as searching the diplomatic bag. When states refrain, it is because they do not wish to break the law.

A second kind of law deals with intercourse among nations. It has long been agreed that sovereignty gives a government the right to require all foreigners to stop at the border and submit to inspection before entering a country. In the days of ship travel this search presented little problem; officials could inspect a ship before the passengers disembarked at dock. But with the invention of the airplane a new problem arose. Sovereignty extends upward into a country's airspace. How do you stop an airplane as it enters your airspace and ask it to submit to inspection? In Paris in 1919 and then at Chicago in 1944, procedures were worked out by which aircraft could at times enter another country's airspace without having to wait for specific permission. The frequent entry into other countries' airspace by international airlines is regulated by a series of bilateral treaties between the countries involved.

The complex of international laws dealing with air travel is termed "the regime of the air." Likewise there are regimes of the sea and outer space. The regime of the sea includes the provision for freedom of the high seas. Although states have not been able to agree precisely how far from shore the high seas begin, without question they include all waters more than 200 miles from land. Any state may sail in the high seas or fly aircraft over them. This right was reaffirmed in the Convention on the High Seas drawn up at Geneva in 1958. In recent years the states of the world have been negotiating to restrict economic exploitation of the high seas, by regulating the hunting of whales and by licensing enterprises to mine the deep sea bed. These negotiations have not yet produced a new set of laws and in any case do not restrict the legal right to freedom to navigate the high seas.

A third kind of international law deals with war. Some laws regulate warfare itself. The rules of land warfare, agreed on in conferences at The Hague in 1899 and 1907, are intended to limit violence in war. One rule requires combatants to wear a distinctive uniform or emblem, recognizable at a distance, and to carry arms openly. The purpose is to demarcate clearly those fighting from those not, to minimize the shooting of civilians by mistake. Another rule of warfare, adopted by the 1907 Hague Conference, is the requirement that wars first be declared before fighting commences, to enable noncombatants to get out of the way.

One of the best-known rules on war is the 1929 Geneva Convention on Prisoners of War. They may not be made to do war-related work for the enemy; they must be fed at the same level of nutrition as the captor's troops; they need only tell their name, birth date, rank, and serial number. The Convention was revised at Geneva in 1949 to include wars other than declared ones, such as a war in which one side is a rebel movement not yet internationally recognized as a government. An additional Convention in 1949 provided for the protection of civilians in time of war.

Other international law deals with kinds of weapons. One outlawed weapon is poison gas. The Hague Conference of 1899 issued the Hague Gas Declaration, making it illegal to fire projectiles with noxious gases. This law was ignored in World War I, and as a result many of the treaties with the defeated countries had special disarmament provisions prohibiting gas. In 1925, at Geneva, the major states declared that if they were not already bound by one of these treaties, they would be now. This statement, known as the Geneva Gas Protocol of 1925, outlaws "the use in war of asphyxiating, poisonous or other gases." Compliance with the Geneva Protocol has been better than with its predecessor the Hague Gas Declaration. Poison gas was not used by major combatants against each other during World War II. There were several reported cases of use by the Japanese against the Chinese in 1941 and 1942, but Japan had not signed the Geneva Protocol.

The laws regulating warfare have continued to expand in recent years. A series of treaties regulate aspects of arms competition. The first to be signed was the Antarctica Treaty of 1959. It provides that there will be no military activity and no nuclear activity in Antarctica. Facilities built there by one country will be open for inspection by others. A similar treaty was signed in 1967 to regulate outer space. It prohibits nuclear weapons in orbit or on celestial bodies. Space installations will be open on a reciprocal basis.

Other treaties of this type are the:

Partial Test Ban Treaty of 1963, outlawing nuclear tests in the atmosphere, above the atmosphere, or under water

Non-Proliferation Treaty of 1968, prohibiting countries already having nuclear weapons from giving them away and countries not in possession of such weapons from acquiring them

Seabed Treaty of 1971, prohibiting military emplacements on the ocean floor

Biological Weapons Treaty of 1972, outlawing the use or production of germ weapons

Other attempts to regulate warfare have failed. In 1936, a convention was signed at London regulating submarine warfare; it provided that merchant ships should not be sunk without warning and without making provision for survivors. As you can see from late-night movies on television, the London Convention on Submarine Warfare was not observed during World War II. Recent treaties on arms control may not stand up well over time. Not all states have agreed to all of them.

Unsuccessful treaties, however, cannot detract from the substantial body of successful international law. It is clear that when we talk about international law, we are talking about something real. Even without a world police force, some regulation of behavior among states is possible.

SOURCES OF LAW

Law is not just another name for something we do anyway. Much observance of law is habitual, but something special attaches to law and makes it more than just habit. The prescriptions known as law include an authoritative element. Part of this authority comes from the way in which law originates. Law has clearly recognized sources. In domestic society the most obvious of these sources are the decrees of the sovereign power — the king or queen in early modern times, the parliament or congress today. But monarchs and legislatures are not the only sources of law. The customary division of government into law-making and law-adjudicating branches should not mislead us. Judicial decisions can also be sources of law. The Supreme Court decision of 1954 in *Brown* v. *Board of Education* made segregated schools as illegal as a statute of Congress would have done.

Another source of law recognized in our society is custom. If you own a vacant lot and don't fence it, people may begin to use it as a short cut between a public road and their own property. If you take no steps to stop this trespass and it continues long enough, you may then lose your right to fence off the lot. In this case customary usage gradually acquires the force of law.

These cases demonstrate the need for community assent to a source of law. Judicial decisions are binding because people accept them as binding. Custom is binding because people accept it as binding. A source of law that was once viewed as binding, but in our society is no longer so viewed, is the Bible. Even though some people still accept Biblical prescriptions, our society as a whole does not consider the Bible a source of law.

In international politics, three sources of law are generally recognized. One is, as in our own society, custom. A good illustration of custom is the case known as the *Paquette Habana*. In 1900 the United States Supreme Court ruled that even though the United States had been at war with Spain in 1898 and had blockaded its possession Cuba, it was illegal for the United States to have captured Cuban fishing boats as prizes of war because ancient usage exempted coastal fishing vessels from capture.[4]

A second source of international law is "general principles of law recognized among civilized nations."[5] In practice this means teachings of legal scholars and previous decisions of judicial bodies (such as courts of arbitration). But court decisions are not as important in international law as they are in our society because the principle of *stare decisis*, "precedent must be followed," is not always accepted.

The third and most important source of international law is the treaty. Sometimes it is bilateral; sometimes it includes additional parties as guarantors; and sometimes it is open-ended, intended to be signed by as many states as possible. It may be called a convention, a protocol, or an agreement. Whatever the name, a treaty is like a contract. It must be agreed to voluntarily, and it is valid only for those who agree to it. For this reason we say that much of international law is consensual: It must have the consent of a state before the law applies to the state. For years France and China refused to adhere to the Partial Test Ban Treaty of 1963, and for them the treaty was not valid law.

The examples of international laws regulating diplomacy, the regimes of sea and air, warfare, and arms control were in the form of treaties. Let's take one of them, the Non-Proliferation Treaty of 1968, to illustrate how a treaty becomes binding law. There are three steps. First is the *signature*, which means nothing more than agreement on wording. This is not unimportant, of course, because signing a treaty typically follows months of negotiations in which the wording was the main issue. But signature alone does not bind a state. The Geneva Gas Protocol of 1925 was signed by the United States; in fact, the United States was responsible for the original draft. But the next two steps by which a treaty becomes a law were not taken for fifty years; thus the United States in all that time was not legally bound by the agreement.

The next stage is *ratification*, which means the treaty is accepted as binding by the state. Each state has its own procedures for ratifying treaties. The constitution of the Fifth Republic of France provides that the French president alone will ratify treaties; the president therefore could sign a treaty and, by the next stroke of the pen, ratify it. Technically, this is done by signing another document called the article of ratification.

In the United States we commonly say that the Senate ratifies treaties, but this is not precisely correct. The Senate gives its approval for ratification, but the president does the actual ratifying. Normally, approval by the Senate is tantamount to ratification. Because the executive branch had to sign the treaty to bring it to the Senate in the first place, one would not expect the president to refuse to ratify it.

In the case of the Geneva Gas Protocol, it was the Senate that blocked the ratification; the president wanted the treaty very much. The Non-Proliferation Treaty was one case in which the distinction between approval of ratification and ratification was important. The Senate approved ratification on March 13, 1969, but the treaty was not ratified by the president until November 24, 1969. It was even considered possible that the president would not ratify it at all. Part of the reason for the delay was that between the signing and the ratifying a new president was elected. President Johnson's Administration negotiated and signed the treaty, but President Nixon was not enthusiastic about it. He waited to sign it until his staff completed an overall assessment of relations with the USSR.

Even after ratification a treaty does not go into effect until states exchange articles of ratification or (more commonly) until the treaty is deposited. This third step, *deposition*, means that the treaty is stored in designated archives from which it can be retrieved for examination if a question arises about its exact wording. Even then the treaty may have a provision that it will not enter into force until a specified time has elapsed or a set number of states have ratified it. One article of the Non-Proliferation Treaty specified that forty countries plus the United States, the United Kingdom, and the Soviet Union had to sign it before it took effect. It finally became binding law on March 5, 1970, when the three countries in whose capitals it was originally signed — the United States, the United Kingdom, and the USSR — by agreement all deposited it at once. Each of these three countries was designated to provide archives for an authentic copy of the treaty.

Deposition is usually accompanied by publication. A treaty is more likely to be respected by those it affects if its contents are widely known. But sometimes treaties are secret, and these treaties are just as valid as published ones.

REASONS FOR OBSERVING TREATIES

We have shown what international law is and how it comes into being, but we still have to show why it is obeyed. All laws, domestic as well as international, are obeyed for many reasons. Because the definition of law includes the idea of sanctions or punishment, it is natural to think first of obedience out of fear of punishment. But this is not the only reason or even the most important. Much law is obeyed because we think it rational to do so. Take the law that says you should drive your car on the right side of the road. This is a prescription, not a description of what people would do in any case (British visitors to the United States might prefer to drive on the left side, as they do back home). Imagine what would happen if there were no law: Each time you saw a car approaching, you would have to stop, get out, and negotiate with the driver about which side to pass on. Traffic law makes life a lot easier for drivers by providing predictability, and therefore it is rational to obey it.

Law provides predictability in many areas. A check written today will be honored by the bank tomorrow; a rental agreement signed this month will still apply six months from now. Such predictability makes much of social and economic life possible, and we have little hesitation about obeying most of these laws.

Driving on the right side of the road is an obvious case in which it is rational to obey the law. But what about a case in which obedience is not so obviously rational, such as not cheating on an examination? Is honesty the best policy, or is cheating?

There are a number of possible situations:

1. I alone cheat; everyone else is honest.
2. I and a few others cheat; no one else does.
3. Nobody cheats.
4. Quite a few cheat, including me.
5. Everyone cheats.
6. Almost everyone cheats, but not me.
7. Everyone cheats but me.

These situations are listed in the rational (although not ethical) order of preference. I do best when the number of cheaters is so small (either case 1 or case 2) that the risk of detection by the proctors is minimal. The reason for ranking 4 and 5 lower is that the risk of discovery and penalization becomes too great. Better to pick 3, which avoids the risk. As a practical matter it may be impossible to act on the basis of case 1 or case 2. If everyone else in the class has a copy of this list, the minute it becomes obvious that I am cheating, they will start cheating too. For this reason it may, practically speaking, be most rational to act on case 3. You could say, "All things considered, honesty is often the best policy."[6]

The same logic applies to many international laws. There may be a rational advantage to breaking them ("cheating") if you are the only one doing it; but if the chances are great that your violation will be followed by others' violations, you obey the law. Thus one reason for obedience is rational self-interest.

Another reason becomes clear when we compare the fate of two laws regulating weapons, the Geneva Gas Protocol of 1925 and the London Convention on Submarine Warfare of 1936. During World War II, almost all sides observed the gas prohibition, mostly because each side had gas shells and bombs ready to use in retaliation if the other side initiated the use of gas. Because of mutual deterrence, gas was not used; international law simply reflected this underlying condition. But with submarines the conditions were very different. In the Atlantic the Germans had no surface fleet to speak of; they had only submarines. The Allies were heavily dependent on surface ships. The situation was asymmetrical. Obeying the London Convention by giving advance warning would have put German submarines at great risk. Therefore the Germans sank surface vessels without warning. In the Pacific the situation was reversed. There the Japanese had the surface ships and the Americans the submarines. Again there was no mutual deterrence because the situation was asymmetrical, and this time the Americans broke the London Convention.

We have then a second reason for obeying law: sanctions. That is, breaking a law will result in some kind of penalty for the lawbreaker. A major sanction in international politics is retaliation. The practice of retaliation has been so common that it is considered legal, if it is conducted within guidelines: Peaceful efforts should be made first; a reprisal should be proportional to the offense; and retaliation should cease when the violation does. In its simplest form, this means that if one side breaks a treaty, the other side no longer feels itself bound by the treaty. When Germany used poison gas against the French and British in World War I, the French and British declared themselves no longer bound by the Hague Gas Declaration and used gas against the Germans.

Other cases of sanctions are more complex. In 1960 Cuba nationalized all large industrial and commercial enterprises, including those owned by Americans. The United States protested that this was a violation of international law because the Cuban government did not offer adequate and prompt compensation. There were no sizable Cuban investments in the United States to seize in retaliation, so the United States embargoed exports to Cuba. Was that form of retaliation proportionate to the offense? That kind of question is difficult to decide.

Other costs are incurred by a country breaking a treaty, and these may be considered forms of punishment. Other countries will think twice before signing another agreement with a lawbreaker. Even friendly states may be less inclined to show trust or support. One may even come under pressure from domestic sources (if one's governmental system is the kind that allows domestic criticism).

DIFFICULTIES WITH INTERNATIONAL LAW

International society lacks an authority capable of imposing sanctions on lawbreakers. Although several types of courts with impartial judges exist, they lack the ability to impose penalties and the police force to carry them out. Sanctions in international law must be imposed by the aggrieved party, not by a third party. Such self-help raises difficult questions.

A frequent question, which occurs in domestic society as well, is, "Was the law actually violated?" When American investments abroad are nationalized, the law is broken only if compensation is not prompt and adequate. It is not always easy to tell whether such compensation has been made. When Peru nationalized the International Petroleum Company in 1969, it offered compensation but first subtracted from it the $690 million it said the company owed in back taxes. Standard Oil of New Jersey (which owned International Petroleum) resisted this interpretation, and the Peruvians resisted the American claim for more compensation. Neither side said it was disregarding international law, but the dispute could not be settled.

Then one must decide whether a response to a violation is appropriate. In 1914, during revolutionary upheaval in Mexico, some American soldiers were temporarily jailed by one of the factions. The United States demanded both their release and an apology. It got the release but did not get the apology, so United States troops seized and held the Mexican city of Veracruz until the apology was given. It is hard to imagine a domestic system of law in which a neutral judge would allow such a severe sanction for such a trivial offense.

Assuming that a violation is unambiguous and a proportionate sanction can be found, such a sanction may turn out to be ineffective. Retaliation seems to work best if the situation is perfectly symmetrical. The law protecting diplomats is usually respected, even when war breaks out, because each country's diplomats serve as hostages to the other country. When the situation is not symmetrical, it is often difficult to find an effective sanction. The United States embargoed trade with Cuba, but Cuba did not pay the $2 billion of claims against it, perhaps because by the time the embargo was imposed annual trade with Cuba amounted to only $14 million.[7] Other countries have nationalized foreign investments and no embargo has been applied, sometimes in the belief that an embargo would have no effect, sometimes because the embargo would hurt the country applying it more than it would hurt the alleged culprit. Sometimes no sanction is available short of military action. If the violator is militarily stronger than the aggrieved country, then this kind of sanction is ruled out. The application of military sanctions more often reflects relative military power than relative legal merit. The United States could safely seize Veracruz, but when the United States refused in 1911 to abide by a decision of an arbitration court ordering it to return 600 acres of land to Mexico, the Mexicans did not seize El Paso to enforce the law.

International law must rely more than domestic law on internalization of norms, or self-restraint. But self-restraint is a weak restraint. If an issue is not considered vital to national security, law will often be effective. The bulk of valid international law deals with matters such as currency transfers, rules for navigation at sea, and public health measures. But even with nonvital interests, the law runs into occasional difficulty as the problems with compensation for nationalized investments illustrate. In questions of vital interest, self-restraint is no restraint at all.

One area of international law that has been deeply eroded in this century is the law protecting neutral states in time of war. Warring states claim that vital interests require them to violate neutral countries' rights. The Germans began sinking neutral ships carrying goods to Britain during World War I, on the very sound argument that those goods were giving Britain the ability to carry on the war. In 1939 the British planned to put mines in the neutral waters of Norway to prevent Swedish iron ore from reaching Germany. Churchill defended this plan by saying, "The letter of the law must not in supreme emergency obstruct those who are charged with its preservation and enforcement."[8] Similarly former Secretary of State Dean Acheson argued that the propriety of United States actions against Cuba during the 1962 missile crisis was not a legal issue. He argued, "The power, position, and prestige of the United States had been challenged by another state; and law simply does not deal with such questions of ultimate power. . . . No law can destroy the state creating the law. The survival of states is not a matter of law."[9] If the leaders of states noted for their respect for law can argue in this way, who cannot?

International law is often disregarded in the name of self-defense. This sometimes happens in domestic society as well: Specific kinds of normally illegal behavior, even killing, are considered justifiable if done in self-defense. But in domestic law, cases of self-defense are considered exceptional, and someone wishing to use self-defense as an excuse must show that a variety of special conditions were met. In international law, by contrast, self-defense is neither unusual nor hard to justify. In fact, the right to plead self-defense is built into the structure of treaties. We assume that when a state signs a treaty, it does so in good faith. We expect the state to abide by the provisions of the treaty. Pacta sunt servanda, "treaties are to be observed," is the legal name we give to this principle. But with each treaty is a clause, understood if not always written out, known as *rebus sic stantibus,* "if things remain the same." That is, the treaty is valid only for as long as the conditions under which it was ratified continue.

For example, the United States and the Soviet Union agreed in 1963 not to test nuclear weapons in space. But suppose a country that did not sign the treaty (such as China) develops a stunning new nuclear weapon for use in space. The USSR (or the United States or even both) might then argue that conditions had changed and, invoking Article IV of the treaty that "extraordinary events" had "jeopardized the supreme interest of its country," withdraw from the treaty. We may agree that some sort of escape clause is reasonable; contracts in domestic law often have them. But this escape clause is so elastic that almost any act can be justified by it.

In 1919 the Germans signed the Versailles Treaty and promised to disarm. But they did so only because they were weak, isolated, and occupied after a defeat in war. Fifteen years later conditions had changed, and the Germans began to rearm. To the charge that they were violating law, the Germans could reply, rebus sic stantibus.[10]

For a while, in the late nineteenth and early twentieth centuries, such clauses were not actually written into treaties, and some scholars argued that the doctrine was obsolete. But recently states have gone back to making the clause explicit. You can see from the wording how big a loophole it provides. Here is Article X from the Non-Proliferation Treaty:

> Each Party shall in exercising its national sovereignty have the right to withdraw from the Treaty if it decides that extraordinary events, related to the subject matter of this Treaty, have jeopardized the supreme interests of its country.[11]

Notice who does the deciding. Each country is judge in its own case, and no other country has the right, legally, to stop it. The only safeguard in this treaty is a requirement to give three months' notice before withdrawing.

The idea of rebus sic stantibus appears to contradict the argument that law provides predictability; in fact the two are related. By predictability we mean that things will work tomorrow the way they work today. Law extends the present into the future. It is by nature conservative, for it freezes the status quo. But what if some group doesn't like the status quo? If they can bring about a change in the status quo and then in the accompanying law, there is no problem. But if there is no mechanism for changing the law, then it is only realistic to expect such a group to disregard the law if they are at all able to.

Suppose the law says, "Colored people will sit at the back of the bus." This law reflects a relationship in society: white superiority and black inferiority. But what if conditions change? What if whites are no longer so sure of their superiority and blacks don't accept inferiority? Using the metaphor of law as frozen political relationships, we might say that the old law must be unfrozen. In a system that functions well, the time required to thaw it will be kept to a minimum. There will be recognized ways of unfreezing the old law and bringing it into line with the new relationship. The city council will pass a new ordinance, and the signs in the buses will come down.

International politics lacks the institutionalized ways of changing laws that we have in domestic society. The only recourse for a state that believes it is suffering under a particular treaty obligation is to go to the other parties of the treaty and ask them to change it. But often there is no incentive for other states to agree to a change. Thus, the gap between the law (reflecting past political conditions) and new political conditions can be very great.

The fate of the Versailles Treaty illustrates such a gap. The treaty reflected the political conditions of 1919 — Germany defeated and France victorious. In subsequent years the relationship changed, but there was no way for Germany to get its increasing power translated into a new treaty. In fact, as German power grew, the French clung more stubbornly to the provisions of the Versailles Treaty, giving the Germans little choice but to break the treaty.

From this argument you can deduce that law will be stronger in a system in which relationships are changing slowly if at all. In such a conservative system, law will grow in extent and in force. We see such growth of law in the international politics of the nineteenth century. The nineteenth-century system was conservative, and international law flourished. One example from this period will show how close international law came to working in the same way as domestic law does. In 1899 a revolutionary government took over in Venezuela and refused to pay debts that its predecessor government owed to Britain, Germany, and Italy. This was a clear violation of law, which states that new states or regimes are responsible for obligations incurred by the states or regimes they succeed. When the new Venezuelan government refused to comply with the law, British, German, and Italian gunboats blockaded Venezuelan ports until the government did obey, in the same way a loan company would reclaim a car if payments were not made on it.

TWO REVOLUTIONS AND THEIR EFFECTS

An enforcement action such as the blockade of Venezuelan ports would be impossible in the world today. We live no longer in the conservative system of the nineteenth century but in a revolutionary time. Two revolutions are going on simultaneously, making it difficult to arrive at an effective system of international law. We might call them the "anticolonial" and the "technological" revolutions. We will discuss the anticolonial revolution first.

Most Third World countries are former colonies and do not want to be bound by rules drawn up by their former masters. It seems clear to them that the international law of the nineteenth century reflected European superiority and Asian, African, and Latin American inferiority.

In 1961 India used military force to occupy and annex an enclave on its coast that had for 450 years been the Portuguese colony of Goa. Portugal claimed that the invasion was a clear violation of international law. If the crossing of a frontier by 40,000 troops — without provocation, with no calls for liberation from the inhabitants, and with no previous attempt to negotiate — was not aggression, what was? But the Indians argued, with the support of the majority in the United Nations General Assembly, that any international law that could be twisted to such conclusions was unacceptable. The Indian delegate dismissed the existing body of international law with a sentence: "If any narrow-minded, legalistic considerations — considerations arising from international law as written by European law writers — should arise, those writers were, after all, brought up in the atmosphere of colonialism."[12] The new version of international law, argued by the Indians, was that because there could be no legitimacy in colonial possession, aggression in this case was not aggression.

Because of the anticolonial revolution, some of the oldest doctrines in international law are under attack. In November 1979, Iranian revolutionaries seized the United States embassy in Teheran and held diplomatic personnel hostage with the connivance if not the approval of the Iranian government. Such a flagrant violation of one of the oldest international laws was justified as an attack on American imperialism and espionage. Despite the obvious self-interest of all governments in guaranteeing the immunity of their own diplomats, the violation of international law by Iran was not universally condemned in the Third World. The governments of Pakistan and Libya failed to live up to their obligations to protect embassy premises and allowed mobs sympathetic to the Iranian cause to burn American embassies in their capitals. There were even people in the academic field willing to defend the Iranian violation of international law. They referred to "the onesidedness of the old international law" that among other things extended protection only to diplomats but not to resistance fighters.[13] According to this line of reasoning, if a system of law has any flaws, then even individual parts of it lack validity. The implication is that as long as fundamental disagreements exist among states, even legal agreements limited to such traditional practices as protecting diplomats should not be considered binding.

The doctrine of the freedom of the high seas is also under attack. The countries of the west coast of South America — Chile, Peru, and Ecuador — were among the first to claim a zone of economic control 200 miles out into the ocean and to patrol it to keep out fishing boats from states that once dominated the region economically. Their argument was that because the cultivable land between the Pacific Ocean and the Andes Mountains was so limited, they needed exclusive access to the fisheries to feed their people. They would no longer allow these fisheries to be exploited by distant countries that were already rich and well fed. Freedom of the high seas, they claimed, was only an excuse for developed countries with large fishing fleets to exploit resources needed by underdeveloped countries. Even Hugo Grotius in 1625, argued a Chilean diplomat, supported the freedom of the high seas not simply as an intellectual concept but to defend the trading interests of the Dutch East India Company.[14]

The second revolution in the world today is in technology, and we can use the law of the sea again to see how these changes undermine international law. For centuries it was generally agreed that sovereignty extended out to sea in "territorial" waters to a distance of 3 miles. Not that countries would not have been happy to claim more, but 3 miles was as far as the military technology of the time would allow them to patrol. Territorial waters were in effect determined by technology. A decision on territorial waters made by a Dutch jurists in 1737 is known as the "cannon-shot rule" because the range of cannon was about 3 miles.

Because of changes in technology there is now almost no limit to how far out a state can patrol. But with the technological limits removed, states have found it difficult to agree on a new guideline for the extent of territorial waters. Conferences in 1958, 1960, 1974, and 1975 failed to come up with any agreement at all. States were claiming anywhere from 3 miles to 200 miles. Countries (such as Japan and Great Britain) with extensive ocean-going fishing fleets argued for narrow territorial waters. Countries (such as Burma and Iceland) that wanted to protect their own fishing industries from foreign fishing fleets argued for wider territorial waters. Unlike the Dutch in 1737, states could no longer let technology answer the question. In 1982, the Third United Nations Conference on the Law of the Sea finally produced a treaty that, among many other provisions, defined territorial waters as 12 miles. Even then, not all states — most prominent among them the United States — signed it.

WORLD PEACE THROUGH WORLD LAW?

Proposals for replacing the rule of force with the rule of law run the danger of trying to achieve peace by definition. Of course rule of law will bring peace, if rule means "effective settlement of disputes." By the same logic rule of poets or rule of political scientists would also bring peace, but only because the desired end is already built into the definition of the means.

Unlike the hypothetical world state, international law already exists.

We can see that it does not provide an effective restraint on the behavior of states in the crucial area of war and peace. We must reject the argument that law has not yet been tried so that one can know whether it would prevent war or not. It has been tried, and it has not prevented war.

The problem is not in any technical deficiency in the law itself — failure to word treaties in ironclad language, for example — but in the refusal of states to accept law when vital interests are at stake. The confusion that we sometimes find on this point is evident in a statement made by American Secretary of State Christian Herter. He proposed "to create certain universally accepted rules of law which, if followed, would prevent all nations from attacking other nations."[15] Mr. Herter's statement is confused. One cannot create universally accepted rules of law. Either one discovers which norms are already accepted and codifies them, or one prescribes norms and then tries to create acceptance for them.

International law today follows mainly the first alternative. For the most part it is a codification of what states would do anyway. Poison gas was not a militarily decisive weapon. Because gas required so much protective equipment for the side that used it, the material was awkward to train with, to transport to and store in the battle area, and to employ in battle. Without much incentive to use gas in the first place, states found it easy to agree on outlawing it. Submarines, on the other hand, proved useful and have not been outlawed.

This is not to say that law can make no contribution at all to controlling international violence. It is useful for states to acknowledge that they agree on the few things they do. It is useful to set off areas of agreement from areas of disagreement. It is useful to conclude agreements in the relatively calm atmosphere of peacetime; during war, agreement may be desired but hard to achieve. Despite the violence of World War II, the Geneva Convention on Prisoners of War was largely observed by the Germans and the Americans in relation to each other. It was easier to observe it because the agreement had been ratified before the war began. Had no such agreement existed, it is easy to see how midwar negotiations on treating prisoners could have gotten bogged down on issues such as the rights of the prisoners to have Coca-Cola or a lager beer, with each side accusing the other of trying to write the rules to its own advantage.

We have some reason to believe that neither side in World War II originally intended to engage in large-scale bombing of civilian targets.[16] But the desires of the two sides were not reinforced by a treaty as they were in the case of poison gas. It is at least possible that a convention limiting aerial bombardment to, for example, the zone of military operations could have prevented escalation into massive raids of the type that destroyed Dresden.

International law can be useful in cases in which basic agreement among states seems to exist and can be strengthened by being made more explicit. But often there is no basic agreement. It is one thing to rule out a weapon considered marginally effective by military experts; it is something very different to renounce a technique considered basic to self-defense.

Advocates of world law seek not to create accepted laws but to win acceptance for laws already created. One way to win acceptance would be enlightened self-interest. The same motivation would lead all students to be honest on examinations. But this incentive has not been effective over past centuries, and it is hard to imagine what kind of radical change would suddenly make it effective now. Another possibility is to change the nature of international law. But doing away altogether with the consensual basis of international law and replacing it with the kind of law we have in domestic society is another way of saying world government. In a state, people are bound by laws even if they do not explicitly agree to them, provided the laws are arrived at by the proper procedures. But these laws have the sanction of the state behind them. The more controversial the law and the more powerful the group resisting it, the more force is needed to impose the sanction.

We are back where we ended Chapter 8, with a fear of too much concentration of force. Law without such a force is ineffectual; law backed up by such force is frightening. This dilemma has led some thinkers to take an entirely different approach to the problem of preventing war. Instead of concentrating power in one center, they recommend distributing it among many centers, so that no one can threaten the others. This distribution is often called the balance of power, and we will look at it as an alternative to world government and world law.

NOTES

1. David K. Shipler, *The New York Times*, December 14, 1978.
2. "When the Diplomatic Bag Goes Off in the Streets of London," *The Economist*, August 26, 1978, p. 17.
3. Henry Kamm, "Cambodia Scans Diplomatic Mail," *The New York Times*, February 23, 1970, p. 1, 11.
4. An excellent textbook describing this case among others is Gerhard von Glahn, *Law Among Nations*, 3rd ed. (New York: Macmillan, 1976).
5. This is part of the Statute of the International Court of Justice (see Chapter 17). The Statute lists teachings of scholars as a separate source, but it seems to me only an operational definition of general principles. How else could we know what they are?
6. This is a modified version of material presented by Herman Kahn in *On Escalation* (Baltimore: Penguin Books, 1968), p. 19.
7. *The Economist*, August 27, 1977, p. 38.
8. Winston S. Churchill, *The Gathering Storm* (Boston: Houghton Mifflin, 1948), p. 547.

9. Dean Acheson, *Proceedings of the American Society of International Law* (Washington, D.C., 1963), pp. 13–15.

10. This argument is developed by E. H. Carr in *The Twenty Years' Crisis* (London: Macmillan, 1961), Chapter 11.

11. *United States Treaties and Other International Agreements* (Washington, D.C.: U.S. Government Printing Office, 1971), Vol. 21, Part 1, p. 483.

12. Quoted by Rupert Emerson, "The New Higher Law of Anticolonialsm," in *The Relevance of International Law*, ed. Karl W. Deutsch and Stanley Hoffman (Garden City, N.Y.: Doubleday, 1971), p. 224.

13. Statement of concerned scholars at Lisbon Conference of World Order Models Project, July 13–20, 1980, in *Macroscope*, No. 8 (Fall 1980), p. 12.

14. Robert L. Friedheim, "The 'Satisfied' and 'Dissatisfied' States Negotiate International Law," *World Politics*, Vol. 18, No. 1 (October 1965), pp. 20–41.

15. Christian Herter, speech to the National Press Club, Washington, D.C., February 18, 1960, in *Vital Speeches*, Vol. 26, No. 1 (March 15, 1960), p. 327.

16. See George Quester, *Deterrence Before Hiroshima* (New York: John Wiley, 1966).

Chapter 10

Balance of Power

For extended periods in history, international politics has operated in a way that is at the opposite pole from world government. Instead of one sovereign authority, there have been many sovereign states, each jealously guarding its autonomy. Power, instead of being concentrated in a central police force, has been distributed among all the states, and each state has kept total control of its own army. This absence of central authority and centralized force has been considered desirable. Leaders have tried to keep power distributed among many states in such a way that each state would be too weak to threaten any of the others. In theory, if any state did try to increase its power enough to pose a threat, all the other states would unite to stop it. In reality, however, states united only when the need arose. To draw an analogy with the Wild West, there was no world police force, only a world posse.

THE BALANCE OF POWER AS INTERNATIONAL SYSTEM

The policy followed in these periods was generally called the *balance of power*. This term has been applied to so many situations and policies (one author has counted eight usages)[1] that it is not useful without an accompanying definition. Here the expression refers to a proposal to prevent or limit war by distributing power among many states. The proposal rests on the assumption that as long as power is not abolished (as it might be, for example, under a proposal for peace by disarmament), then it must be met by countervailing power. It is not safe for a state to rely on only the good will of powerful neighbors; only matching power can provide adequate protection in all circumstances. Or, to put it differently, this proposal depends on mutual deterrence. Any potential aggressor is deterred by the potential combined power of all the other states in the system.

But here confusion sets in. If this is all balance of power means, many arrangements could be called by that name. A bipolar system of the type we had during the Cold War years would fit the definition. After all, was not the United States just trying to keep the balance with the USSR (and vice versa)? An accelerating arms race would also fit. Yet these situations are clearly different from the classic balance of power systems that operated in the eighteenth and nineteenth centuries.

A balance of power system differs from other approaches to peace not by its goal of deterrence but by its means of achieving deterrence. The emphasis in the eighteenth and nineteenth centuries was on matching a rival's power not by building up one's own armed forces but by forming a coalition of one or more other states also threatened by the growing power of the rival. Deterrence was achieved by alliances, not by arms races, and that is what sets this proposal off from the international system of today. In historical balance of power systems there was no increase in the power of a single state or even in the system as a whole; rather, power was rearranged to counter aggression. Most of the time states pursued independent policies, not bound to each other by permanent alliances. Only when one state threatened the independence of another did a group begin to coalesce to oppose the belligerent. If the aggressor state was smart, it quit right then. If not, it faced a war in which it was outnumbered. If not deterred from pursuing its disruptive aims, it was defeated by preponderance. But once the war is over, the alliance of victors broke up, and the newly defeated aggressor was returned to its former place and size, ready to serve as an ally if some other country threatened the system.

For the political leaders of the time, the primary reason for maintaining a balance of power system was to prevent not war but *hegemony,* the domination of the entire system by one powerful state. As we shall see, willingness to go to war was an essential part of the policy. Nevertheless, we may consider the balance of power as a possible approach to peace. For one thing, if it works as it is supposed to, it does prevent all war by deterrence. Participants in a balance of power system are willing to go to war but hope their willingness will make war unnecessary. For another, even if such a system does not deter all war, the resulting wars could be shorter and less destructive than those that would occur under any other kind of system. Small wars fought to regulate the balance might be the closest to peace the world can come. We need not endorse such small wars in order to find them preferable to the destructive violence of World War I and World War II.

Here are two examples of how the principles of the balance of power were applied to concrete political situations. In March 1936, Winston Churchill was urging that England take the lead in organizing an "armed League of all Nations," led by England and France, to take action against Nazi Germany. This policy was not popular in England at the time (Churchill was widely considered a warmonger), and to win adherents Churchill used this version of history:

> For four hundred years the foreign policy of England has been to oppose the strongest, most aggressive, most dominating Power on the Continent. . . . We always took the harder course, joined with the less strong Powers, made a combination among them, and thus defeated and frustrated the Continental military tyrant whoever he was, whatever nation he led.[2]

In the past, the strongest power had been France under Louis XIV or Napoleon. In 1936, it was Germany under Hitler, but that didn't really matter, argued Churchill. England's policy should be to oppose *any* country that tried to dominate the continent of Europe. Concentration of power was dangerous in any hands. Safety for England lay in the distribution of power among several countries.

To cite a second example, in 1972 the socialist government of Ceylon initiated a dramatic change in its relationship with the United States. Attacks on "United States imperialism" in the local press and demonstrations in front of the United States embassy stopped. The prime minister, Sirimavo Bandaranaike, dropped from her official rhetoric a proposal that the Indian Ocean be declared a peace zone. For the first time in years, United States warships began making rest stops in Ceylon. The explanation for all this is that Ceylon believed power relationships had shifted because of India's victory over Pakistan in late 1971. India was supported by the Soviet Union in that war, and Ceylon was uneasy at this concentration of power. Ceylon therefore moved to improve its relations with a rival of the Soviet Union, going so far as to accept United States military aid. At the same time, Ceylon did not abandon its internal policy of socialism and continued to maintain good relations with China.[3]

Although this way of arranging international relations is usually termed the "balance of power," it would be more precise to call it a *multistate, shifting alliance system*. The system rests on the assumption that a state's own interests are served by having a number of other states around. If power is to be distributed (as opposed to being centralized in a world government), then it is best distributed uniformly. If a state wants to preserve its own independence, it must support the independence of others.

Ideally, the system should operate according to a set of informal but widely understood principles or rules:

1. Be suspicious of an increase in power by another country—any country. Be concerned with capabilities, not intentions. (Realistically, state leaders do pay attention to intentions. Winston Churchill had to admit in his anti-German speech in 1936 that France still had a bigger army than did Germany. But he pointed out that the German army was growing rapidly.)

2. Always ally with the weaker side. Ignore considerations such as friendship or morality. (As Churchill said, "If Hitler invaded Hell, I would make at least a favorable reference to the Devil in the House of Commons."[4])

3. Support a state or group of states only until it is out of danger. Remember that no alliance is permanent.

4. Show moderation toward the aggressor after it is defeated. Because no alliance is permanent, today's enemy may be tomorrow's ally.

THE SYSTEM IN OPERATION, 1740–1763

In discussing the balance of power system (unlike world government), we have some historical cases to examine. One of these is the European system of the eighteenth century.[5] The major actors are depicted in Figure 10.1. At the center are the two great land powers, France and Austria. Russia was also a great land power but was less actively involved, as its geographic position suggests. Great Britain was also less actively involved in the affairs of central Europe because it concentrated its strength in a navy. Small powers occupied the center of Europe. Three are important for us: Saxony, Bavaria, and Hanover (which was tied to England because the English had recently acquired a king from there when their own dynastic line ran out). Finally, a bit smaller than the great powers, but bigger than the small powers, was Prussia, ruled by the remarkable Frederick II, known as Frederick the Great.

The system was stable because the two big powers, France and Austria, took opposite sides and the other states aligned themselves according to the danger they perceived. In 1740, however, Frederick the Great attempted to move Prussia up from a second-rate power to a great power. He thought he saw his chance because the ruler of Austria had died without leaving any sons. But he did leave an able daughter, Maria Theresa, who became a capable ruler (and a mother as well — she had sixteen children). Frederick attempted to detach the northern part of the Austrian kingdom, the region of Silesia. He thought he might get away with it because as a woman Maria

Theresa would not be a warrior and because as a woman her claim to succeed her father as ruler of all the Austrian territory was in some doubt. Silesia was desirable for its strategic position and its rich iron ore and flourishing linen industry. Adding Silesia to Prussia would greatly increase the latter's strength.

With the passage of time our views of historical figures mellow, but in the eighteenth century Frederick was considered an aggressor. His policies were as disruptive as those of Napoleon and Hitler would be later. He ordered his generals to prepare an invasion and then told his lawyers to provide a legal excuse for his aggression.

Because Prussia was not considered a major power at this time, its invasion of Silesia served mainly to activate old alliances. Because Prussia was attacking Austria, Austria's traditional rival France was happy to join the war on Prussia's side. On the other side, some of the smaller German states, more alarmed about Prussia because it was their close neighbor, joined with

Figure 10.1   Europe in 1740

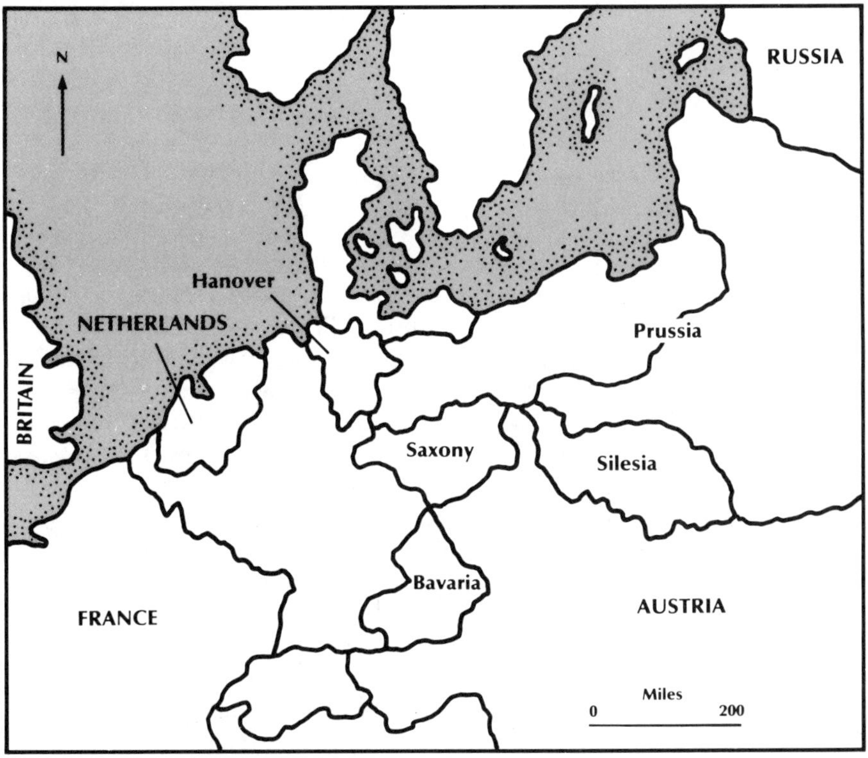

Austria. England, as a rival to France, did too. Thus the lineup in the war for Silesia (1740–1743) looked like this (the more powerful states are in upper-case letters):

FRANCE   AUSTRIA
Prussia   ENGLAND
Saxony   Hanover
Bavaria

Frederick II acquired the nickname "the Great" because of his military skill, and he demonstrated it in this war. By 1742 he had forced Austria to conclude a separate peace, giving him most of Silesia. France and Austria kept on fighting for another year, demonstrating that at this time Prussia was not the greatest problem in their minds.

The reason that Austria was not primarily worried about Prussia is that Austria expected to be able to reconquer Silesia later. But Frederick expected Austria to try this and decided to take the offensive. In 1744 he launched a preventive war to retain Silesia. Again France joined with him to get at its traditional rival Austria, and again Austria was joined by England. But one of the smaller German states shifted allegiance this time. Saxony, close enough to Prussia to share a border, already feared what other European countries would later come to fear, that Prussian power was growing too large. As a result, the lineup in the second war for Silesia (1744–1745) looked like this:

FRANCE   AUSTRIA
Prussia   ENGLAND
Bavaria   Hanover
            Saxony

Saxony's change of sides was not enough to make a difference. Again Frederick won battles, and again Austria and Prussia signed a peace treaty (in 1745) before the war between Austria and France was over. By this treaty Prussia got to keep Silesia and dropped out of the war. Austria and France kept on fighting. France had been winning, but in 1746 Russia, which up to this time had stayed out of the alliances, now joined with Austria to restore the balance. The war ended in 1748 with an agreement to restore conditions as they were before the war began.

The event that happened next distinguishes the balance of power system. Prussia was no longer considered a middle-level power but was viewed as a major power and a threat to the order of Europe as it was then. Austria and Russia remained allies, along with England, Hanover, and Saxony. But Austria was able to add France to its side, thereby confronting Frederick with an unbeatable coalition. This reversal of alliances, called the "Great Diplomatic Revolution of 1756," was brought about by the Austrian foreign minister. His task was made easier because each of the three major countries was ruled by a woman, Austria by Maria Theresa, Russia by Empress Elizabeth, and France, it was said, by the mistress of the king. Moreover, Frederick was given to uncomplimentary remarks about women. He commissioned as a sculpture for the top of the Brandenburg Gate in Berlin a chariot depicting Prussia drawn by the figures of three women.

Confronted with overwhelming power, Frederick should have capitulated and given back Silesia immediately. But in practice the balance of power did not work so smoothly. England had been fighting France in America (leading up to the French and Indian War), and now that France had joined the coalition that England used to belong to, England felt it had to withdraw from that coalition. Besides, its hands were full in North America, and so it signed a treaty of neutrality with Frederick. In 1756, Frederick took advantage of the fighting between France and England in North America to launch another preventive war. In Europe, it is known as the Seven Years' War (1756–1763); in America, the French and Indian War. By whatever name, it was the third war fought over Silesia. This time the sides lined up like this:

PRUSSIA	AUSTRIA
Hanover	RUSSIA
(English money)	FRANCE
	Saxony

Again Frederick won battles, but this time Austria could afford to take losses. By 1760 the tide of the war had turned, and Frederick's capital city of Berlin was burned. The new English king stopped subsidies to Frederick and his cause looked lost. The balance of power seemed to be working to control aggressors.

Then in 1762 occurred one of those accidents that make international politics so unpredictable. Empress Elizabeth of Russia died and was succeeded by her nephew Peter III. Peter III was a great admirer of Frederick the Great and took Russia out of the war against Prussia. This defection gave Frederick new energy, and he went on to defeat Austria. A treaty in 1763 ended the third war by ratifying the previous treaties. In other words, Prussia got to keep Silesia and the increase in its power that went with it.

Because these events are often cited in discussions of the balance of power, it is useful to take a moment to examine them. Two things stand out. First, the system involved a lot of war. The wars were not the ideological crusades we have seen in the twentieth century. There was no talk of "de-Fredericking" Prussia as the United States "de-Nazified" Germany after World War II. Nor did the wars kill large numbers of civilians, although they did kill large numbers of soldiers. Second, the system did not work as it was supposed to. With all the attention on the Great Diplomatic Revolution of 1756, it is easy to forget that this new alignment did not deter Prussia; nor, when deterrence failed, did it produce an unbeatable coalition in war. Frederick the Great committed aggression and got away with it. That is the plain lesson of the eighteenth century.

Ideally, a balance of power system operates according to the four rules previously cited. But even when followed, as we have just seen, those rules did not always produce the desired results. The failure of the system to stop Frederick the Great does not prove the system worthless, however. Frederick succeeded by luck, and he knew it. He controlled his ambitions after his third victory. The coalition against him was powerful enough to deter further expansion.

Assessing any proposal that rests on deterrence is difficult, because there is no way of determining when it works. The absence of aggression could mean either of two things: all potential aggressors are deterred, or no state has any aggressive designs. We can guess that there were other rulers like Frederick and that those rulers were deterred by the balance of power, but we can never be sure. We can, however, evaluate how costly the system was when it failed. It failed to deter Frederick, and the cost was three limited but still relatively destructive wars.

In addition to the negative mechanism of deterrence, the traditional balance of power system worked in a more active way to control violence. Leaders acted according to a fifth rule, which we may add to the four already listed:

5. Settle nonessential quarrels in peripheral areas in a way that does not disturb the central balance.

In Figure 10.1, the large area between Prussia and Russia was officially the Kingdom of Poland. It had too little power to play a significant part in international politics. Instead it was a source of temptation to the neighboring countries, Austria as well as Russia and Prussia. To prevent Poland from becoming another Silesia, over which three more wars could be fought, the major powers agreed to divide Poland among themselves. The partition was done in three stages, in 1772, 1793, and 1795. At each stage each of the three big countries took another slice. By 1795 nothing was left of Poland; it ceased to exist as a country. An attempted uprising by the Poles in 1794 had been easily suppressed by the cooperative efforts of the big countries and only paved the way for the country's final division.

Partition was one device used to preserve the balance. Neutralization was another. A century later, in the international system created by Bismarck, colonial disputes in Africa threatened to lead to war between European countries. One focus of conflict was the Congo River Basin. When Henry Stanley began exploring it for King Leopold of Belgium, the French hurried to send in an explorer of their own. Then the British tried to secure a foothold by backing up the Portuguese in an old claim that had never been followed up by occupation. Competition for this area, considered a rich source of trade, could have led to war. Instead Bismarck convened a conference on problems in Africa at Berlin in 1884. One result of the conference was to declare the Congo Basin neutral and open to navigation by all countries, thereby taking it out of the European power struggle.

BALANCE OF POWER AND THE CONTROL OF INTERNATIONAL VIOLENCE

Seen from the twentieth century, the balance of power systems of the eighteenth and nineteenth centuries have some attraction. There were wars, but they were less destructive than the major wars of the twentieth century. They were fought for limited objectives, not for universal goals such as converting whole populations to a superior way of life. Major states were assured of survival even if defeated in war. They were not subjected to division into parts and reform of their social system, as happened to Germany in 1945. In the balance of power system, each state had an interest in preserving all the other states.

But on closer examination, it is not clear that the balance of power system actually had all those advantages. Let us take the points one by one. One scholar, Michael Haas, did a careful study of systems with many states (multipolar or balance of power) and systems with only two states (bipolar).[6] He concluded that in multipolar systems wars were on the whole shorter but more numerous than in a bipolar system, and in multipolar systems wars were relatively more violent and involved more countries.

Wars waged to preserve the balance of power system were fought for limited objectives (to restore the balance, not to create something new), but new wars kept occurring because not all states shared the limited objectives. The system would not keep a Frederick the Great from appearing on the scene, trying to expand his power, and at times succeeding. But even if the system had contained him, the wars necessary to do it would illustrate the basic point that the balance of power system depends on war as an essential instrument to keep functioning. It must fight limited wars to avoid unlimited ones. In the end, balance of power systems of the eighteenth and nineteenth centuries failed to avoid big wars too. The eighteenth-century system ended in the ideological wars of the French revolution and the expansionist wars of Napoleon. The nineteenth-century system ended in World War I.

It is true that major states had a reasonable chance of survival under the balance of power system, but minor states did not fare so well. They were neutralized or even partitioned against their will. Each state had an interest in preserving a multistate system, but the exact identity of the states making up the system might change over time.

A RETURN TO THE BALANCE OF POWER?

With all these arguments against the balance of power system, you may wonder why we bother to mention it. The reason is that serious thought has been given to a return to such a system.

> We must remember the only time in the history of the world that we have had any extended period of peace is when there has been a balance of power.
> I think it will be a safer world and a better world if we have a strong, healthy United States, Europe, Soviet Union, China, Japan, each balancing the other, not playing one against the other, an even balance.[7]

These were the words of President Nixon in 1972. They were echoed in 1978 by President Carter's national security advisor, Zbigniew Brzezinski:

> The accommodation with China opens up the possibility of a genuine framework for wide-ranging international cooperation involving the United States and Europe, the United States and Japan, the United States and China, and I would also hope, eventually, the United States and the Soviet Union.[8]

In part these statements reflect undeniable changes in the world. The unquestioned dominance of the superpowers is passing. Two European countries and China have nuclear weapons; Japan could acquire them in a short time if it decided to. The industrial and economic potential that is readily translated into military power is available to these countries. We do not think of China as an underdeveloped country any more. Japan is a rival of the United States in many areas. The resources of a united Europe would likewise rival those of the United States. If these trends continue, we will be facing in the next twenty years a world with five major powers. Would international politics then return to what the world experienced before in such multistate systems, the practice of balance of power policies?

Writers on the balance of power have listed conditions needed before such a system can function.[9] Let us look at some of them.

1. Minimum Number of States. Because the system's essence is in shifting alliances, three is the logical minimum. With two there can be no shift. Even three may be too few, because presumably two states could always ally against and defeat the third. (George Orwell does create such a three-state balance of power system in *1984*, but then *1984* is fiction.) A practical

minimum would be five or six, which is in fact the number of major states active in the systems of the eighteenth and nineteenth centuries.

2. Equality of Power. When we speak of five or six states, we assume that these states are roughly equal in power. Power is defined as the ability to win war. If two states are equal in power, then the outcome of a war between them is not obvious beforehand.

3. Commensurability of Power. What this phrase means is that power can be measured by some common standard, so that the power of one state can be compared with that of another. In the eighteenth and nineteenth centuries, power was directly related to territory and its accompanying population and resources. Acquisition of territory (such as Silesia by Frederick the Great) was alarming because it meant an increase of power. A case in which power is not commensurable is that of David and Goliath. By traditional measures David was weak, but his secret weapon — the slingshot — upset traditional calculations.

4. Stability of Power. Even if power is commensurable, and when measured found roughly equal, the system would not work if power could be immeasurably increased overnight by some secret weapon. As long as there is no hope of a technological breakthrough, increasing allies is the only way to increase power. But if some invention could instantly revolutionize warfare (imagine what a helicopter gunship would have done in the eighteenth century), then an overwhelming coalition need not necessarily cause a country to refrain from aggression. There is always the chance that a country could succeed even if it acted alone.

5. Usefulness of War. In the eighteenth and nineteenth centuries, the technology of warfare — basically foot soldiers armed with rifles and short-range artillery — made a balance of power system possible. On the one hand, war was a serious enough business to work as a threat; the consequences of having states at war with you were potentially disastrous. On the other hand, war was not so destructive that it scared states from even making the threat to use it. War was a credible instrument of policy. It cost something to wage war, but the cost was bearable.

6. Shared Values. In previous balance of power systems, diplomats, generals, and cabinet ministers in all countries all had the same values; most important were suspicion and amorality. Each country's leaders paid close attention to the activities of all other states and assumed the worst when they saw any change in relative power. Each state was capable of either allying with or allying against any other state; bonds of friendship or shared ideology did not rule out specific combinations of states. In 1756, France was able to put aside years of rivalry with Austria to form an alliance against Prussia. In 1893, France, the only republican government in Europe, was able to ally with Russia, which was by far the most autocratic.

THE BALANCE OF POWER IN THE CONTEMPORARY WORLD

We can now answer the question about how applicable the traditional balance of power is to the present world. On the first point, the number of actors needed, the condition is met. The ideas advanced by Nixon and Brzezinski were often called "a pentagonal balance of power" because they involved five actors.

Whether these five actors meet the second condition, rough equality of power, is debatable. The United States and the Soviet Union clearly are major powers, capable of what is often called "projecting power"; that is, sending forces and supplies to areas far from their own borders. But China is strictly a regional power, and Japan and Europe have not yet achieved even that status. Europe is still far from political unity and can hardly be considered a unified actor. Japan has not yet shown an inclination to act in world affairs. (Japan has not even made a serious bid for a symbolically important seat as a permanent membership on the Security Council of the United Nations.) Both Europe and Japan are militarily dependent on the United States; they have thousands of American troops stationed in their countries (over 350,000 in Europe, 50,000 in Japan). The oil crisis of the 1970's demonstrated how dependent they were on outside sources for their energy. One critic remarked at the time that it would make more sense to talk of a new pentagonal balance consisting of America, Russia, China, Kuwait, and Abu Dhabi.[10] Even with the precipitant decline in oil prices in the 1980's, Europeans were reluctant to take firm action against terrorism for fear of jeopardizing their supply of oil.

The dependence of Europe and Japan on outside sources of energy shows how difficult it is to measure power today. Economically Japan is certainly a power. In resources, Middle Eastern states have more power. China is not especially powerful either in its industrial economy or in its resources, but it has developed modern nuclear weapons. How are nuclear weapons to be compared? How many submarines with small but accurate warheads equal how many mammoth ICBM's? In traditional balance of power systems, power was the ability to take and hold territory, or defense. Nuclear power is used for the very different purpose of deterrence. The theory of limited deterrence states that when a specific number of deliverable weapons has been attained, a country has deterrent capability; adding to its weapons does not improve its deterrent capability. Under this theory, adding allies, even those with nuclear weapons, would make no improvement in a country's strength.

Even without nuclear weapons, the modern technology of warfare might make a traditional balance of power system impossible. In the traditional system, the defense could not be very effective or the system would not work because the threat of going to war would not be credible. The system depended on the threat of war, and if war were not a useful instrument of policy because defense was perfect, the whole idea of stopping an aggressor by offensive action would evaporate. Two countries that came close to having perfect geographic defenses—the Swiss protected by mountains and the Americans protected by oceans—did not have to participate in the balance of power systems of the eighteenth and nineteenth centuries.

In the traditional system, the offense could not be too good either. A quick and decisive offensive campaign would be over before the balance could go into operation and build a coalition to stop it. The aggressor would then have created a fait accompli, and the other countries would face the very difficult task of undoing it. In the mid-twentieth century, wars are measured in days—the 1971 Indian campaign against Pakistan, the 1974 Turkish campaign against the Greek Cypriots. A balance of power system would be too sluggish to prevent such preemptive moves, and the costs of undoing them would be too great.

The balance of power system assumed that countries would grow strong enough to threaten others only by conquering territory and population. But we have become accustomed to the rapid growth of state power for entirely internal reasons — the discovery of a new technology or the increased importance of a natural resource. The balance of power mechanism provides little help in cases such as these. A Soviet advantage in intercontinental missile technology cannot be offset by adding millions of poorly equipped Chinese soldiers to our side. Declaring war against a country because of a purely domestic development (such as a new weapon system) is not called for by the rules of a balance of power system, yet ignoring such events would violate a basic tenet not to let one country grow too powerful.

An essential characteristic of the balance of power system was the freedom to maneuver and change alignment, regardless of ideology and friendship. After twenty years of Cold War rivalry it is with relief that we foresee a system in which relations between states are something other than total enmity or total friendship. But we should not exaggerate how far the world has moved toward this freedom to shift alignment. President Nixon was received by Chairman Mao Zedung, but it is still hard to imagine a Soviet leader being received in Beijing. Temporary accommodation with a capitalist rival doomed to extinction is one thing; reconciliation with a heretic is much more difficult. After all, during the early modern period in European history it was possible for Catholic Christian monarchs to combine with the Muslim Turks while persecuting their own Protestant Christian minorities.

We might also ask how easy it will be for Europe and Japan, whose economies are so dependent on trade, to join an alliance against major trade

partners.[11] The devaluation of the dollar and the United States import surcharge of 1971 were more severe blows to the Japanese economy than the
oil embargo of 1973 was. A Japanese move against the United States in some
future balancing maneuver could provoke the United States into retaliation
against Japan more drastic than a mere 10 per cent import surcharge. Would
the Japanese risk losing a market for all those Toyotas and Sonys in order to
preserve an equilibrium of power in some distant part of the world?

Another characteristic of policy-makers in the balance of power system
was constant vigilance and suspicion of every other country's moves. The
opposite characteristic, a desire to withdraw from world affairs, has appeared
more frequently in recent years. One manifestation was the United States
policy in the eastern Mediterranean in 1974, when we did not apply the
pressure to Turkey that we had in 1964 and 1967 to head off a Turkish
invasion of Cyprus. Paradoxically, one of the features that makes a return to
the balance of power system seem attractive to Americans is the apparent
reduction it makes in one country's responsibility for maintaining world order.
With five major countries, the burden falls less on any one. But it is hard to
imagine popular support for the United States doing even its proportionate
share. Many Americans think of war as a crusade or a crime: Either you fight
for a morally justified cause, or you shouldn't be involved at all. Using force
for a goal such as preserving an equilibrium of power in the world would
not be well received, particularly if it meant supporting a traditionally hostile
country against a former ally. The lesson many Americans seem to have
learned from Vietnam was, "If you are going to fight at all, fight to win." This
belief would make it difficult for American policy-makers to engage in the
limited use of violence that was essential to the balance of power system.

Another factor makes us less likely to intervene in world conflicts than
we were in the past. Most of us share the basic premise of nationalism, that
members of the same national group should share the same state. This has
meant that we are not alarmed by conflict meant to consolidate a national
group into a state. Such conflict is thought to be entirely understandable.
When critics of the United States involvement in Vietnam said, "Ho Chi
Minh is really a nationalist," they were making an effective argument. Not
many Americans took seriously the idea that the North Vietnamese, after
taking over South Vietnam, would move on to the Hawaiian Islands or even
Malaysia. Nationalism seemed to put a definite limit on their expansion.
Americans were not directly threatened by North Vietnamese moves. By
contrast, the Austrians were threatened by Frederick the Great's move into
Silesia in 1740, because national considerations were not important in those
days and there was no readily perceived limit to his desires. Times had
changed by the 1930's. Many people did not feel alarmed by the policy of
Hitler when he annexed German-speaking Austria and German-speaking

Sudetenland. It was only when he moved to incorporate the obviously non-German populations of Czechoslovakia and Poland that the rest of the world became convinced he had to be stopped.

In the past, quarrels between the smaller states were often ignored to preserve the major power balance. But to ignore them today would be to abdicate responsibility for world order. The number of independent sovereign states approaches 170. With the dispersion of modern weapons (and potentially nuclear ones), quarrels among even the smallest of them can affect the entire world. The old balance of power system would occasionally sacrifice the interests of small countries such as Poland to maintain the great power equilibrium. But today Korea, Vietnam, and other countries have demonstrated that they do not so easily accept partition, and military technology enables them to make it difficult for the great powers to impose such solutions.

There is another reason why countries other than the big five might not welcome a new pentagonal balance of power. Diminished American interest in some areas of the world would be accompanied by increased interest on the part of one of the other powers.[12] The Pacific area is now dominated by the United States. Under a new balance of power Japan would be the country primarily interested in this region. Because of traditional hostility, Korea might dislike looking to Japan as protector against China. Whatever the difficulties of guarantees from the United States, Korea and Taiwan still find us preferable to a country that formerly occupied them as a colonizer and is geographically much closer than the United States.

It seems clear that the balance of power would not function in the last part of the twentieth century as it did in the eighteenth and nineteenth centuries, and we have seen that it did not function all that well even then. Frederick the Great got away with his aggression, despite three wars to stop him. The powers that partitioned Poland were able to suppress the Polish revolution in protest but then were not able to suppress the French revolution, which plunged Europe into two decades of war. The nineteenth-century balance of power could not avoid the catastrophe of World War I; indeed one could argue that it was responsible for that war. Each side recognized that a temporary equilibrium existed (it was for this reason that the war was stalemated for so long), but each feared that equilibrium was slipping and the balance turning against it.

Yet the basic ideas of a balance of power system remain attractive: Keep power distributed among a number of states. Keep a close watch on other states to make sure they do not grow excessively strong. If a state does begin to increase its strength at the expense of others, meet it by a coalition that, although temporary, is overpowering.

Many people believe that a world with five or more states of equivalent power would be a more secure place to live in than a world dominated by a single state or one divided between two superpowers. But return to a balance of power system in the near future seems unlikely because many of the basic conditions (at least five states of equivalent power, technological stability) cannot be met.

The multistate world after the end of World War I still met conditions for a balance of power system. The idea of a balance of power was still attractive enough so that the system then instituted — collective security — did not so much abolish the balance of power system as make its rules more explicit and its coverage more nearly universal.

NOTES

1. Ernst B. Haas, "The Balance of Power: Prescription, Concept, or Propaganda?" *World Politics,* Vol. 5, No. 4 (July 1953), pp. 442–477.

2. Winston S. Churchill, *The Gathering Storm* (Boston: Houghton Mifflin, 1948), pp. 207–208.

3. James P. Sterba, "Ceylon Warming Toward the U.S.," *The New York Times,* April 10, 1972.

4. Winston S. Churchill, *The Grand Alliance* (Boston: Houghton Mifflin, 1950), p. 370.

5. There are many histories of this period. For one that is readily accessible and serves as a good introduction, see Walter L. Dorn, *Competition for Empire,* 1740–1763 (New York: Harper, 1940), especially Chapters 1, 4, 7, and 8.

6. Michael Haas, "International Subsystems: Stability and Polarity," *American Political Science Review,* Vol. 64, No. 1 (March 1970), pp. 98–121.

7. Interview with the staff of *Time,* January 3, 1972, p. 15.

8. James Reston, "The World According to Brzezinski," *The New York Times Magazine,* December 31, 1978, p. 9.

9. For a somewhat lengthier list and accompanying discussion, see Inis L. Claude, Jr., *Power and International Relations* (New York: Random House, 1962), Chapters 2 and 3.

10. Walter Laqueur, "Detente: What's Left of It?" *The New York Times Magazine,* December 16, 1973, p. 100.

11. For a discussion of this and other points, see Stanley Hoffmann, "Weighing Balance of Power," *Foreign Affairs,* Vol. 50, No. 4 (July 1972), pp. 618–643.

12. Ibid., p. 638.

Chapter 11

Collective
Security

World government and the balance of power system are in many ways opposites. World government means one central authority, a permanent standing world police force, and clearly defined conditions under which this force will go into action. A balance of power system has many sovereign authorities, each controlling its own army, combining only when they feel like it to control aggression. To most people world government now seems unattainable. Balance of power systems have existed but are not trustworthy ways to prevent war. Some people have proposed something in between the two, whereby states would give up some but not all of their authority. This proposal is known as "collective security."

WHAT COLLECTIVE SECURITY IS

You must take care with the phrase "collective security." It is a technical term, with a specific meaning, but it is often loosely used or even misused. Part of the trouble is that it looks as though you should be able to figure out the meaning just by looking at the words. Another part of the trouble comes from deliberate misuse by people trying to win acceptance for other schemes that have nothing to do with collective security but look more attractive packaged under that label. Things such as military aid and peacetime alliances have been given this label to win acceptance from a reluctant American public.

Collective security, in its technical meaning, is a system of states that join together, usually by signing a treaty, and make an explicit commitment to do two things: (1) they renounce the use of force to settle disputes with each other, and (2) they promise to use force against any of their number who break rule 1. Notice that collective security shares with the balance of power the principle "meet force with opposing force," or "gang up on the aggressor." The aggressor should be deterred by the prospect of an overwhelming coalition. If deterrence fails, then the aggressor will be defeated by military action undertaken by this coalition.

Collective security applies to only what goes on inside the system; its purpose is to keep peace among its members, not to protect them against outsiders. For this reason, we cannot properly call NATO a collective security system. It is not the main purpose of NATO to defend Iceland from aggression by England (which *would* be collective security because they are both members of NATO), but to defend both Iceland and England against aggression by non-NATO countries.

NATO, the Warsaw Pact, and similar organizations might more properly be called collective defense organizations or simply alliances. Competing alliances are specifically ruled out between any members of a collective security system. In such a system a state has no need to designate a few other states as especially trustworthy in case of need. According to collective security *all* other states in the system will automatically become allies in case of aggression. Alliances at any other time would only arouse suspicion.

Collective security makes it possible for states to renounce the use of force by assuring them that they will not be helpless if another state illegally uses force against them. At the same time, it requires that all states participate in sanctions against an aggressor. A policy of neutrality or isolation is not allowed.

Thus in two ways collective security is a move from the unrestricted state sovereignty of the balance of power to the abolition of state sovereignty of world government. It *forbids* its members to resort to force to settle disputes and it *requires* them to use force to punish any member state that does. In these two ways it infringes on the traditional rights of sovereign states. But in all other respects states remain independent and sovereign. They are free to pursue other national interests, to enrich themselves, to compete for trade, and to run their domestic affairs as they see fit.

THE ADVANTAGES OF COLLECTIVE SECURITY

A collective security system offers advantages over the balance of power system. It offers security to all states in the system, not just the big ones.

Because it does guarantee protection for all states, all have an incentive to join it. No state knows when it might be a victim of aggression and need the backing of all the others.

Collective security also avoids the biggest weakness of a balance of power system — its uncertainty. The balance operated haphazardly because it was never clear when states should move to shift alliances. They preferred to wait and see if a small addition of territory would make any difference in the overall balance. If it made no difference, they would not act. Frederick the Great thought he had at least a chance of getting away with a small grab of territory from Austria. Collective security, by its explicit commitments to all states in the form of a treaty, eliminates doubt about what will happen to any state that resorts to force for any reason whatsoever: It will be met by opposition from all the other states. The balance of power system allowed one state to make a move and then if other states did not like it they could fight a "war of adjustment." Because aggression will be countered immediately, there will be no need for subsequent wars of adjustment in collective security.

Another advantage of collective security is its simplicity. Use of force in interstate relations is simply outlawed. Disputes between states will undoubtedly continue to arise but states will have to find peaceful ways of resolving them. The principle of collective security has nothing to do with the reasons for using force, the background of the quarrel, or the probable consequences of defeat for one side or the other. All these calculations were very important in a balance of power system, as each great power tried to calculate the possible effects of a given war on the equilibrium of the entire system. In Frederick the Great's first war for Silesia, France was not opposed to Prussia's use of force because the most important outcome would be a reduction of power for Austria, which was already too big in France's eyes. In collective security there is no need for these calculations; all countries act against the one that first resorts to force.

A collective security system is set up by a treaty or other agreement that identifies the members and describes the conditions under which it goes into operation. A typical formulation for the aggression that triggers a collective response is "violation of territorial integrity and political independence," although an agreement could be more limited than that. For example, in March 1935, Britain proposed a regional pact to prevent aerial warfare. According to this proposal (which in the end was not agreed to), Britain, France, Germany, Italy, and Belgium would all agree that an unprovoked air attack by one on any other would trigger automatic massive retaliation against the violator by all the other countries.

This British plan lacked a feature that probably would have been added if it had come anywhere close to adoption — an organization to supervise it. Collective security systems need some kind of machinery to identify violations and coordinate efforts for defense: The most elaborate system of this kind was the League of Nations, which was set up after World War I. It was the first global organization whose primary task was preventing war. Its effective life ran from 1920 to 1936 and provides us with a case study of collective security in practice.

AN ATTEMPT TO IMPLEMENT COLLECTIVE SECURITY: THE LEAGUE OF NATIONS

In many ways the League of Nations was only a logical extension of practices that had developed before World War I. Conference diplomacy, by which all countries' delegates met in a public assembly instead of in secret bilateral talks, had been used at the Hague Conferences in 1899 and 1907 to draw up rules for warfare. An international civil service, with bureaucrats owing loyalty to the world community rather than to a single country, was already running organizations such as the Universal Postal Union and the International Labor Organization. Even the essential feature of the League, the surrender of sovereignty in questions of war and peace, had been at least foreshadowed by the many alliances that committed states to go to war to aid others in specified circumstances. What made the League different was its universality. It was theoretically open to all states that would accept its obligations. In practice some states were rejected, in the beginning at least, on the argument that their governments were not democratic and therefore not subject to the effects of outraged public opinion if they chose to disregard collective security obligations. Germany was not yet considered rehabilitated in the eyes of the victors and was not allowed to join the League until 1926. Russia did not join until 1934. The majority of countries in Asia and Africa were not admitted because most were some kind of colonial dependents of European powers; even Ethiopia had a hard time getting accepted because the ruler was not able to govern his country effectively enough to abolish slavery. A major omission was the United States, not because it wasn't welcome but because the United States refused to approve ratification.

The founders of the League designed it according to what they thought were the lessons of World War I. Chief among these was the failure of the balance of power to prevent war. Instead of allowing themselves flexibility to realign against an aggressor, the great powers had let themselves be locked into two competing blocs. The remedy was collective security, which would rule out any alliance bloc until aggression was committed, at which time the aggressor would be automatically confronted by all other states. This principle of collective security was embodied in Article 16 of the Covenant of the League of Nations:

> Article 16. 1. Should any Member of the League resort to war in disregard of its covenants . . . it shall, *ipso facto,* be deemed to have committed an act of war against other Members of the League.

The Latin phrase *ipso facto* means "by that fact"; in other words, the resort to force is considered an act of war no matter what the explanation.

Another lesson of World War I was that secret diplomacy and secret treaties made every country uncertain about what would happen if any country did use force. Therefore founders of the League spoke of "open covenants openly arrived at." Any business that needed discussing could be discussed openly in the Assembly of the League of Nations. There was no need for secret treaties because a state could have only one alliance obligation in any case, to its collective security partners.

Another apparent lesson of World War I was the decisive importance of economic power. It was evident that the British and French had finally won the war when the Americans joined not because the Americans were superior fighters but because they were backed by industrial might. The Covenant therefore stressed economic sanctions against an aggressor. Article 16 goes on to state that if a country resorts to force, other members of the League would

> . . . undertake immediately to subject it to the severance of all trade or financial relations . . . and the prevention of all financial, commercial or personal intercourse between the nationals of the Covenant-breaking State and the nationals of any other State, whether a Member of the League or not.

It would take time to coordinate other sanctions, such as military ones, but in the meantime economic sanctions would be taking effect. It was widely expected that those alone would be enough to make an aggressor stop.

The first decade of the League passed without a decisive test of collective security. Some minor disputes were settled inside the League and some were ignored or settled outside the League.[1] But the League was not confronted with a major international crisis that would test the theory and practice of collective security until the Manchurian crisis of 1931 (see Figure 11.1). Manchuria at this time, although nominally still part of China, was being exploited (in the economic sense) by its more powerful neighbors, chief of which was Japan. Japan already occupied the neighboring territory of Korea and had leases on factories, mines, and railroads in Manchuria. The military party in Japan wanted to occupy all of Manchuria outright, annex it, exclude the growing number of Chinese emigrating from the southern part of China, and develop its industrial potential for Japan's benefit. This expansionist faction was well represented among the Japanese troops stationed in Manchuria to guard Japanese investments.

On September 18, 1931, a minor explosion occurred on a railroad line administered by the Japanese. Japanese troops stationed in the railroad zone blamed Chinese troops and immediately staged a suspiciously well-planned takeover of Chinese arsenals and garrisons in the area. Civilians in the Japanese government tried to control the military party while explaining to the world that this was only a local incident. At first the world was unaware of what was happening, because communications from such a distant area were slow and not very accurate and because the Japanese diplomats at the League headquarters in Geneva were themselves opposed to imperial expansion. But on October 8, 1931, a hopelessly outclassed Chinese garrison decided to resist anyway, and the Japanese in angry retaliation bombed the city of Chinchow. Events in Manchuria had become impossible for the League to ignore. In response to Chinese protests, the League passed resolutions requesting that the Japanese withdraw, but the Japanese ignored them, continuing to expand their control until, on February 18, 1932, they set up a

Figure 11.1   Manchuria in 1931

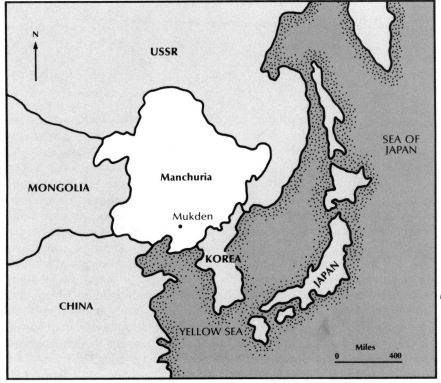

puppet state to govern all of Manchuria, ostensibly a national liberation movement but obviously controlled by the Japanese.

The League reacted cautiously. It appointed a Commission of Inquiry in December 1931, which made a thorough investigation and issued a report of 100,000 words that was adopted by the League on February 24, 1933; that is, seventeen months after the Japanese troops began their takeover. For all its length, the report's conclusions were quite simple. It concluded that "without any declaration of war, a large part of Chinese territory has been forcibly seized and occupied by Japanese troops."[2] It would seem that China had been the victim of aggression and the League would come to China's aid. But, no, the League decided that because Japan had not declared war, Article 16 did not apply. All the League did was accept a suggestion by the commission that changes in territory made by armed force would not be recognized. In other words, the only penalty applied to Japan would be that the postage stamps and currency of the puppet state would not be accepted by other countries. This moral condemnation of the Japanese merely angered them without in any way making them change their behavior. The next month they announced their withdrawal from the League.

The Manchurian crisis revealed a basic feature of the League's collective security system. Theoretically all states would participate in sanctions against an aggressor. In practice, some state would have to bear a bigger burden than others. Japan was an island nation in the Pacific, "Far East" in European eyes. Enforcing an embargo (or stronger action) would require considerable power. Of the League members, only Britain had the kind of power — naval power — that could be projected into this region, and British leaders agreed that an expedition in Asia would distract attention and divert energy from Europe, where the real danger to their security would come from. The United States, also a naval power and with more direct interests in this area, was not a member of the League, and the isolationist mood that had kept it from joining the League continued strong. The only other state capable of acting in this area was Russia, but it was not yet a League member and was in any case preoccupied with domestic disorder brought on by the forced collectivization of the peasantry. Russia chose instead to pursue an appeasement policy with Japan, granting de facto recognition to the puppet state in March 1935. Manchuria was in Japan's sphere of influence and no major power chose to challenge it.

The next major crisis to confront the League came from Latin America. Conflict between Bolivia and Paraguay over 100,000 square miles of an uninhabited river basin known as the Chaco turned into full-scale war in 1932 (see Figure 11.2). The League tried to impose sanctions in the form of an arms embargo but it did not succeed in stopping shipments of arms until August 1934. Rapid action by the United States Congress at this time suddenly made an arms embargo possible. American opinion had been aroused by advertisements of United States armaments companies in a Bolivian newspaper and Congress unanimously gave the president power to prohibit sales of arms and munitions to Bolivia and Paraguay. By this time the two countries were coming to realize that neither of them could win in any case, and in June 1935 they allowed other American states to work out a peace. As in the case of Manchuria, the dispute occurred in the sphere of influence of one power and only if that power chose to act was the League able to act. The United States was not the aggressor, as Japan was, but the inability of outsiders to intrude in a great power's sphere of influence was similar.

The third major crisis that the League confronted was too much for it and led to its collapse. The crisis involved Abyssinia or, as it is called today, Ethiopia (see Figure 11.3). Italy, which already controlled a colony in the neighboring territory of Eritrea, had wanted for decades to extend its control to Ethiopia, one of the few remaining territories in Africa not controlled by

Figure 11.2   The Gran Chaco

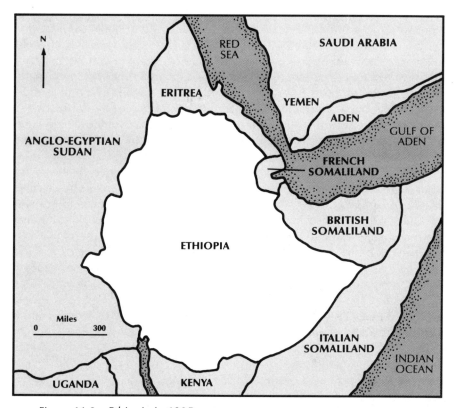

Figure 11.3   Ethiopia in 1935

Europeans. The Italians had tried at the end of the nineteenth century but failed, suffering a humiliating defeat at the battle of Adowa in 1896. Now Mussolini wanted to avenge that defeat and demonstrate the new Italian renaissance under fascism. Italy's ambitions were no different from France's and Britain's when they had earlier occupied territory in Africa; they just came too late in history. Ethiopia was not "unoccupied" territory but a member of the League of Nations.

But Italy was not ashamed to be pursuing nineteenth-century aims in the twentieth century and made no effort to hide its intentions. Preparations for invasion in the neighboring colony of Eritrea were obvious. Italy employed thousands of laborers to build roads, docks, and airfields there. Natives of Eritrea were mobilized for military training. Reserves in Italy were called up. In December 1934, Italian troops clashed with Ethiopians. According to the Italians this was a border dispute, although the Italians were 50 miles inside Ethiopia. In January 1935, Emperor Haile Selassie of Ethiopia appealed to the League for support. But because Italy had committed no overt aggression there were no grounds for action under the doctrine of collective security. In October 1935, the Italian invasion began. The League, within a week, found that Italy had resorted to war and ten days later voted to apply sanctions against Italy. These were to include an embargo on arms, loans, bank credits, and all imports from Italy. But the League could not bring itself to embargo the one commodity essential to Italy's invasion, oil. Furthermore, the League did not insist on closure of the Suez Canal, which would have cut Italy's supply line. There was no discussion at all of military action against Italy in defense of Ethiopia.

This failure to take decisive steps against Italy, it turned out, was the result of a secret agreement between the two major powers in the League, Britain and France. British Foreign Minister Hoare and French Premier Laval not only had agreed to apply only limited sanctions to Italy but had also worked out a solution to the crisis whereby Italy could keep control of about half of Ethiopia under the pretext of administering it for the League. Even when the Hoare–Laval plan was leaked to the public in December 1935, it did not generate enough outrage to force the League to take sterner measures against Italy. The limited sanctions that had been applied were not severe enough to make Italy stop. In fact, they had the unintended effect of uniting the majority of the Italian people behind Mussolini for the first time since he took office. Italy went on to win the war against Ethiopia, using airplanes and poison gas among other modern weapons. Emperor Haile Selassie fled the country and appeared before the League in May 1936, as a living reproach to its cowardice and passivity. But in July 1936, the League acknowledged its bankruptcy by lifting even the limited sanctions against Italy; later it even recognized Italian sovereignty over Ethiopia.

REASONS FOR THE FAILURE OF THE LEAGUE

The Ethiopian crisis marked the death of collective security as practiced by the League of Nations. The League's failures in this crisis illustrate some of its structural weaknesses. The great powers gave lip service to the new idea of collective security but secretly they still believed in the old idea of the balance of power. Britain and France did not want to push Italy too hard because they thought they might need Italy as an ally against Germany. Of course we know with the benefit of hindsight that Italy and Germany fought on the same side in World War II, but it was not obvious to observers in 1935 that that was going to happen. The issue of German Tyrol under Italian rule was widely believed to be an insurmountable obstacle to German–Italian cooperation. The secret desire to maintain a balance against a specific opponent (in this case, Germany) was also responsible for inaction in the Manchurian crisis. Preparing a defense against Germany in Europe was more important to Britain and France than the abstract principle of opposing aggression no matter where it occurred.

The behavior of the smaller members of the League was no more virtuous. Those states in favor of applying sanctions against Italy in the Ethiopian crisis were mostly countries close to Italy that feared an expansion of its power — Czechoslovakia, Rumania, Yugoslavia, Greece, and Turkey. But other countries in this area supported Italy, not because they thought Italy was in the right but for reasons of self-interest. Austria shared with Italy a fear of Germany. Albania was a client state dependent on Italy. Other states in more distant parts of the world (Scandinavia, Latin America) showed little direct interest in the crisis.

Perhaps the attitude of the smaller members would have been less important if all the major states had been members. But Japan had by this time quit the League as a result of the Manchurian crisis and Germany had left the League over the issue of rearmament. (In any case Germany felt it would benefit no matter how the Ethiopian crisis was resolved: Either Italy would be defeated and a potential rival cut down, enabling Hitler to get back Tyrol, or the Western democracies would demonstrate their impotence and Germany could make gains elsewhere.) But the most serious omission was the absence of the United States. Even if oil products had been included in the League embargo, the United States would have been glad to send its oil to Italy to make up what they were denied. League members probably would not have risked interference with United States ships to enforce an embargo.

The ability of one country to undermine effectively the embargo of all the others reveals the weakness of the belief in the automatic success of economic sanctions. In the absence of unanimous support for an embargo, some kind of force must be used to make it work. An embargo must be turned into a blockade, which means reliance on naval power. Only a navy could deny supplies to Italy, and at this time only Britain had a navy capable of doing the job. But the British admiralty was justifiably worried about the consequences of modern military technology on naval power. In 1924 a United States general, Billy Mitchell, had demonstrated the vulnerability of ships to air attack by sinking old battleships off Cape Hatteras, and the British did not want their navy to confirm these experimental results in actual combat.

THE PROBLEMS OF COLLECTIVE SECURITY

The failure of the League of Nations can be seen as the result of the historical situation it found itself in, particularly the failure of the United States to join and the harsh Versailles peace settlement that encouraged the

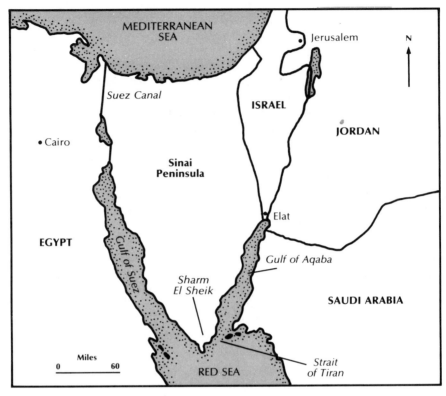

Figure 11.4   The Strait of Tiran

rise of Hitler. But in many ways the League reflected fundamental difficulties with any collective security system.

One problem is the defining of "aggression." A collective security system needs explicit, unambiguous criteria on which to act. This is one way in which it contrasts with the balance of power, for under balance of power suspicion about another side's intentions was enough to justify a preventive war. But the need for legal definition leads collective security to concentrate on overt acts, such as sending troops over a frontier. Thus when Haile Selassie became alarmed at Italian preparations for invasion in January 1935, he could not get the League to act, not only because members were reluctant to oppose Italy (although they were) but also because Italy had yet done anything to violate the League of Nations Covenant. Likewise, the best way to have headed off World War II would have been to do something about German rearmament beginning in 1935. But this would have been interfering in the internal affairs of a sovereign state. One result was that when the wars did break out they were much bigger and the aggressor was much harder to defeat.

It appears impossible to arrive at an unambiguous definition of aggression. The classic formulation of "violation of territorial integrity and political independence" is not always adequate. Consider the Middle East in May 1967 (see Figure 11.4). Egypt closed the Strait of Tiran to ships going to the Israeli port of Elat, thereby cutting off Israel's trade (including oil) from Asia. Israel then attacked Egypt. Which country was the aggressor? Egypt was blockading an Israeli port and a blockade has traditionally been considered an act of war. By this criterion Egypt started the war. But Egypt claimed it was merely excluding ships from its territorial waters, and this was not an act of war. The states of the world disagree on the legal issue. The Strait of Tiran is a place where ships must pass through the territorial waters of a state (Egypt) to get from one international body of water (the Red Sea) to another (the Gulf of Aqaba). The "right of innocent passage" through such waters was guaranteed by a convention on the law of the sea drawn up at Geneva in 1958. That convention has been accepted by some countries but not by Egypt.

Or take another case. In 1956 a popular movement in Hungary called for expelling the Russians. After withdrawing their troops for a few days, the Russians then invaded with new troops and crushed the rebellion. Was this aggression, or was it simply a Russian response to a legitimate request by the Hungarian government for assistance in putting down an insurrection?

The United Nations, after years of trying to define aggression, issued a definition in 1974 covering many kinds of behavior — invasion, bombardment of territory, blockade of ports, attack on the armed forces of another state, and sending terrorists into another state. But the usefulness of the definition is badly weakened by two loopholes. One is that "acts enumerated above are not exhaustive and the Security Council may determine that other acts constitute aggression under the provision of the Charter."[3] In other words, aggression is whatever the Security Council says it is. Given the right political alignment Egypt could find support for Gamal Abdel Nasser's statement that the very existence of the state of Israel is an act of aggression.

The first loophole expands the definition of aggression; the second contracts it. It states that "nothing in this definition could in any way prejudice the right to self-determination, freedom and independence of peoples forcibly deprived of that right, particularly peoples under colonial and racist regimes or other forms of alien domination; nor the right of these peoples to struggle to that end and to seek and receive support, in accordance with the principles of the Charter." In other words, when Indian troops crossed the frontier into Goa in 1961 it was not aggression because people forcibly deprived of the right of self-determination were seeking and receiving support in their struggle to that end. In the changed composition of the United Nations today, we might find the North Korean attack of June 1950 no longer considered aggression but support for self-determination.

A second problem with collective security is the requirement that all states participate in actions against an aggressor. It doesn't much matter if one or two minor states refuse to join in enforcement action, but participation by major states is essential. If power is not evenly distributed among the members of a collective security system, then refusal by even one or two of the major powers to cooperate may doom any attempt at enforcement. In practice it may be difficult to get all states to participate in action against an aggressor. A state will be reluctant to act against another state that is a very powerful neighbor, a longstanding friend or ally, or the perceived victim of a dispute. Albania would not oppose its powerful protector Italy in 1935, the Soviet Union would not condemn its ideological ally North Korea in 1950, and many states would not blame Israel for initiating hostilities in 1967.

Furthermore, states will be reluctant to make sacrifices for quarrels that seem remote. In September 1948, Indian troops invaded the state of Hyderabad to force it to join the Republic of India (see Figure 11.5). Hyderabad appealed to the United Nations but its appeal was ignored. No member of the UN felt threatened because no member saw itself as another candidate for incorporation into the new Indian state. Hyderabad had been part of the British colonial possession of India and was totally surrounded by states that had joined the new Republic of India. No other state was in a similar position.

The United Nations did come to the defense of South Korea in 1950. At first glance it appears to be collective security in action, with states from many parts of the world coming to the aid of a small, remote country under attack. But in fact the North Korean invasion aroused the United States not so much because of concern for the abstract principle of collective security (after all, the United States had not reacted to the Indian invasion of Hyderabad two years earlier) as because of interest in neighboring Japan, which was then under American occupation. European countries supported action in Korea because they saw an analogy with Germany, where the Communist half of a divided country was also preparing for reunification by force. They believed that by showing resolve in Korea they might deter a Communist attack in Europe.

The theoretical requirement of collective security that all states take part in actions against an aggressor is often justified by the claim that "peace is indivisible." That is, peace in each country is threatened by war anywhere. Conflict in distant parts of the world cannot be walled off and ignored. The indivisibility of the peace is often contrasted favorably with the appeasement policy of Britain before World War II, when Chamberlain argued against helping Czechoslovakia because the Sudetenland crisis was a "quarrel in a faraway country between people of whom we know nothing."[4] The British of course found themselves shortly thereafter at war, and Chamberlain's statement has been ridiculed ever since.

Traumatic as the Munich experience was for Europeans and Americans, it may be an error to make too much of this single example. In fact not all small disputes lead to larger ones. India's annexation of Goa in 1961 was not a prelude to Indian world conquest. Whatever the justice of the settlement, to either the Portuguese, who were deprived of their territory by armed force, or the native Goans, who were never consulted on their preferences but seemed in fact to prefer Portuguese rule, that conflict did not bring the world to the brink of war.

In recent years the belief in the "indivisible peace" has taken the form of the Domino Theory, and lately the Domino Theory has been under attack. It is hard to find someone who would argue that a Communist victory in

Figure 11.5   Hyderabad in 1947

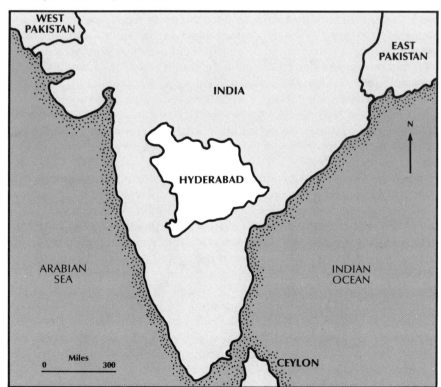

Vietnam is going to lead to a Communist victory in New Zealand. One might even ask whether the solution offered by the balance of power system wasn't better: Instead of trying to prevent all conflicts, isolate them when they occur in remote parts of the world. The South Americans fought a number of destructive wars in the nineteenth and twentieth centuries (the Chaco War, the War of the Pacific, the War of La Plata) but these are almost unknown to North Americans because the conflicts were isolated by the Monroe Doctrine, which kept Europeans out, and did not become world wars. They were nobody's "Vietnams."

Another difficulty with collective security is that it naturally reacts slowly to a crisis. First it must be determined who is at fault. War is a serious matter and states must be sure of the facts before they engage in belligerent acts against aggressors. It is easy to criticize the League for its ponderous efforts in the Manchurian crisis, but communications were poor and information spotty. Even the Japanese government was not sure of what was happening. Critics always have the benefit of hindsight.

Because action may be taken only when actual acts of aggression occur, no advance planning is possible merely on the basis of suspicion. This means that an aggressor has an enormous advantage. An aggressor can plan for months or even years, carry through a move with lightning speed, and then present the world with a fait accompli. The collective security organization then has the unpleasant choice of accepting the results of aggression or mounting a massive campaign that will cause destruction all out of proportion to the violation. In the era of nuclear weapons, the aggressor can carry out an operation with conventional weapons but then use nuclear deterrence to prevent attempts to undo the results. In such circumstances it is tempting for the rest of the world to redefine aggression to exclude such acts and let the results stand.

Recent wars in the Middle East in 1967, the Indian subcontinent in 1971, and the eastern Mediterranean in 1974 all illustrate this problem. Israel, India, and Turkey each carried out rapid military operations, which were completed before the world could react. The task of reversing the results of these operations was so massive that the results were allowed to stand. One or more countries continued to protest against the results of these quick operations, but no one expected countries of the world to combine in military operations to undo them. You can argue (as I will later) that the UN is not a true collective security organization, so its members had no legal obligation to act in any of these three cases. But even if there had been such an organization, you can see the difficulties its members would have confronted when faced with such faits accomplis, and this was true even though none of these states at the time had nuclear forces.

Finally, like so many plans, collective security preserves the status quo and so works to the advantage of states that benefit most from the status quo. An ironclad collective security agreement has been compared to a poker game interrupted in the middle when one player is far ahead. Gambling is suddenly declared illegal but the player who is ahead is allowed to keep his or her winnings.

As long as the principle of noninterference in internal affairs is observed, groups such as the Bengalis will have to suffer whatever a dominant ethnic group subjects them to. Going to their aid would be interference in internal affairs and thus aggression. For this reason, the UN definition of aggression, even with its enormous loopholes, is more realistic than a rigid one would be, for it reflects the need to have ways of changing the status quo. But the problem with such elastic definitions is that they provide no assurance to any state that it will receive support if another state uses force against it. The same African states that opposed the use of force to aid the Ibo people of Nigeria in their war to set up an independent state in 1967 encouraged the use of force against the Portuguese colonies in Mozambique and Angola. Winning support as a victim of aggression is more the result of having enough political supporters than of any objective conditions such as having enemy troops cross your frontier.

All the problems of collective security are more acute in the present international system. An ideological commitment to Marxism by some governments makes it even more difficult to agree on a definition of aggression. Marxism is seen by its adherents not just as one belief system among many but as scientific truth; no compromise is possible. It claims to understand the workings of history and any action that furthers the march of history, even violent action, is considered good in the ethical system of a Marxist. The Chinese Communists, upon entering the United Nations, announced that they were not opposed to all war. "There are two categories of war," the Chinese delegate said, "just and unjust. We support just wars and oppose unjust wars."[5] "Just wars" is the name that countries have always given to those wars that support their foreign policy aims. With such a hopelessly subjective standard, agreement on a definition of aggression seems as far away as ever.

Modern weapons technology makes discussion of enforcement action seem futile. Action against an aggressor with conventional weapons might be countered by nuclear weapons, and a world organization would be reluctant to undertake the nuclear destruction of a country no matter what its offense.

In addition to its problems with ideological divisions and nuclear weapons, the present international system is unstable because of the large number of dissatisfied states and the minimal agreement on legitimacy. Even the question of a country's boundaries at sea — is it 3 miles? is it 12 miles? —

has not been decided. Collective security would have deficiencies in any situation; in the present one collective security is almost certainly unworkable on a global scale.

REGIONAL COLLECTIVE SECURITY

Both theory and practice suggest that collective security will not work on the global level. But it might have a chance in more limited areas, where differences between states are not so great. Some people have advocated more emphasis on organizations that limit their membership to states in a geographic region of the world. We call this approach to peace *regional collective security.*

Like all collective security systems, a regional one would try to preserve peace only among its members. It would create an island of peace in a world where great power rivalry, ideological struggles, and competition for resources might continue to cause conflict elsewhere. In this way regionalism reverses a basic tenet of supporters of the League of Nations that peace was indivisible, because the idea rests on the assumption that one region of the world can be sealed off from the rest of the world.[6]

Regional organizations, by this argument, will have more success in maintaining peace among their numbers because these members are more likely to have common interests. They may have similar resources (such as oil or coffee) or similar problems (such as tribal divisions). These similarities will enable them to understand regional disputes better and come up with appropriate solutions, and such solutions are more likely to be heeded, coming from sympathetic sources.

In many parts of the world numerous state boundaries are the result of artificial divisions between imperialist powers. Syria and Jordan are separate countries mainly because France administered one and Britain the other. A world organization is too big and unwieldly to deal with problems arising from such divisions; individual states by themselves cannot handle them either. Only at the regional level can realistic solutions be found, argue the regionalists. Also, confining the business of maintaining peace to the regional level provides a good excuse for excluding major powers. Even Asian states fearful of their Communist neighbors might not want outside assistance if they would have to pay the price of massive destruction that Vietnam did.

Although no regional organizations exist strictly for collective security, a number have the potential and have taken some actions in the name of preserving peace. Typical of these is the Organization of African Unity (OAU). It was founded in 1963 and is open to all independent states on the continent of Africa. Outsiders are exluded from membership, and its primary goal is solving problems within the region, not providing protection for members against external enemies. Other organizations in this category are the Arab League, formed in 1945 and gradually increasing its membership as more Arab states become independent, and the Organization of American States (OAS), formed in 1948.

How regional organizations might work to maintain peace is illustrated by a conflict between two former British possessions in the Middle East, Iraq and Kuwait (see Figure 11.6). Iraq became independent in 1936, but the British retained Kuwait as a protectorate until 1961. As independence for Kuwait approached, the Iraqis laid claim to it as a former province. Kuwait, unwilling to be absorbed, asked the British to station troops. After several meetings the Arab League decided to admit Kuwait as a member, thereby giving increased legitimacy to its claim to exist as a sovereign, independent state. Iraq alone resisted. Meanwhile the Arabs, eager to be rid of a British military presence, sent troops of their own to replace the British in Kuwait. A force of 3,300 from five Arab countries backed up the Arab League's

Figure 11.6   Iraq and Kuwait

decision to recognize Kuwait's sovereignty by giving it protection against Iraq. Iraq finally gave up its opposition in 1963.

Part of the reason regionalism was viewed optimistically was that it conformed nicely with a widespread desire in the United States to reduce American responsibility in other parts of the world. If regional organizations worked better anyhow, then we could do what we wanted and be virtuous at the same time. President Nixon expressed this view in his State of the World message of 1971: "It is no longer possible to . . . argue that security or development around the globe is primarily America's concern. The defense and progress of other countries must be first their responsibility and second a regional responsibility."[7]

Events during the decade following Nixon's speech struck severe blows to the hopes of regionalism. The most important regional organizations suffered major setbacks in their attempts to keep peace. The organization that many considered the most promising, the OAU, suffered the most. The African continent experienced many serious conflicts, several of them coming to their own violent conclusions with the OAU standing helplessly by.

The most serious conflict is the ongoing quarrel between Somalia and Ethiopia; over the last decade it has claimed perhaps 50,000 lives. Somalia claims that the Ogaden desert region, inhabited mostly by Somali nomads, was seized forcibly by Ethiopia in 1897 (see Figure 11.7). Ethiopia claims that it is merely trying to control its sovereign territory. At the 1977 conference of heads of states of OAU members, the two states exchanged bitter accusations over fighting in the Ogaden. The OAU was able to do nothing more than refer the conflict to a special committee. The OAU was not able to stop Ethiopia from settling the dispute, at least for a number of years, by a massive attack on Somali troops. The Ethiopians won a decisive victory with the help of Cuban troops and Soviet equipment. The conflict was thus settled by the very means regionalism is supposed to supplant, outside military assistance.

Another failure of the OAU was to solve the conflict between Zaïre and its southern neighbor Angola. President Mobutu of Zaïre claimed in 1978 that the province of Shaba was being invaded by forces from Angola. The level of violence was much lower than in the Ogaden war, but again the OAU had little do with its resolution. An outside intervention force, organized primarily by France and consisting largely of French and Belgian troops, restored the sovereignty of Zaïre in Shaba Province.

Likewise the OAU was unable to prevent an attack on Tanzania by its northern neighbor Uganda in fall of 1978, nor a much larger retaliatory attack by Tanzania in the spring of 1979. And conflict between Morocco and Algeria over the status of the former Spanish colony of Sahara continued

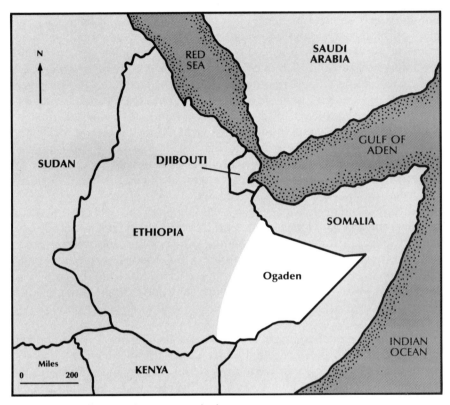

Figure 11.7   Ogaden Region of Ethiopia

into the 1980's despite repeated efforts at OAU summit meetings to bring the sides to negotiate.

By 1982 the OAU was moribund. Instead of the organization's working to prevent or control conflict, conflicts now paralyzed the OAU. Twice in 1982 the OAU scheduled a meeting of its heads of state and twice they failed to meet. A meeting in August aborted over the issue of the former Spanish Sahara. About half of the OAU membership recognized the Polisario guerrila movement as the "Sahrawi Arab Democratic Republic." The other half continued to recognize Morocco's control of the territory and refused to attend a meeting at which the rival group was represented.

Another meeting scheduled for November 1982 failed over the same issue and the additional one of Chad. In late 1980, Libya had sent 14,000 troops to help one faction in a civil war in Chad. After a year of indecisive fighting, the Libyans pulled out, replaced by an OAU peacekeeping force.

But the peacekeeping force failed — only three of the six African countries that had promised to send troops did so, and even they required subsidies from outside powers such as France and the United States. By April 1982 the force had run out of money and in June the commander ordered it withdrawn, citing the failure of the Chadians to accept the OAU proposals for political settlement. With the outside force gone, the civil war continued.

But Libya continued to give diplomatic support to one faction. The support included using its position as host to the OAU summit meeting to grant a seat to the faction it favored. Because of Libya's behavior, enough states stayed away to prevent a quorum. The weakness of the OAU went far beyond its ability to settle conflicts. It was so divided it could not even convene meetings.

The OAU did resume meeting in 1983, although still with quarrels about both membership and leadership, but did nothing to move the various conflicts in Africa toward solutions. After the failure of the OAU to bring peace to Chad, the forces in the northern part of the country were increasingly under the control of Libya. The forces in the south turned to the French for support, following the pattern set earlier in Zaïre and Ethiopia. After regional forces had demonstrated their weakness, the victim of aggression turned to an outside power.

Another regional organization, the Arab League, suffered a similar failure in the conflict between South Yemen and North Yemen. Attempts at mediation by Syria and Iraq were unsuccessful in bringing stability. To the dismay of regionalists, stability was finally restored when the United States sent arms to North Yemen, helping to balance the arms that South Yemen was receiving from the Soviet Union.

The only modest success for a regional organization in recent years was the effort to contain the 1979 civil war in Nicaragua. Although the OAS did little to limit the violence of the war itself, which caused over 20,000 deaths, it did inhibit the Nicaraguan government from retaliating against its unarmed neighbor Costa Rica for providing sanctuary for guerrillas.

Yet in the subsequent violence in Central America, the OAS played almost no role at all. El Salvador fought a civil war, charging that the insurgents were armed by neighboring Nicaragua. Nicaragua in turn charged that forces based in Honduras were conducting operations designed to overthrow its government. Such initiatives as were put forward to settle these conflicts came from individual countries, such as Mexico and Venezuela. Regional organizations were hardly even mentioned.

Following this series of disappointments, it is difficult to accept the claim that regional organization can succeed where global organizations have failed. Likewise, the hope expressed in the Nixon Doctrine has proved illusory. The problems of agreeing on what constitutes aggression, organizing a timely response, and getting states to participate in collective action when it is not clearly in their self-interest have been too serious for collective security to overcome. Modern weapons of mass destruction and contemporary ideological divisions have made these problems even more serious than in the days of the League of Nations. Ever since the failure of the League in the 1930's, states have been convinced that they must look first to their own power as a source of security — in other words, to armaments.

NOTES

1. The standard history of the League is F. P. Walters, *A History of the League of Nations*, 2 vols. (London: Oxford University Press, 1952).

2. Westel W. Willoughby, *The Sino–Japanese Controversy and the League of Nations* (Baltimore: Johns Hopkins Press, 1935).

3. *The New York Times*, April 13, 1974. The abbreviated version of the text is in the accompanying news story.

4. Winston S. Churchill, *The Gathering Storm* (Boston: Houghton Mifflin, 1948), p. 315.

5. Robert Alden, "China, at the UN, Backs 'Just Wars,'" *The New York Times*, October 4, 1972.

6. Joseph S. Nye, *Peace in Parts* (Boston: Little, Brown, 1971), pp. 3, 129.

7. *U.S. Foreign Policy for the 1970's: Building for Peace: A Report to the Congress by Richard Nixon* (Washington, D.C.: U.S. Government Printing Office, February 25, 1971), p. 14.

Chapter 12

Armaments

If we go by what states *do* rather than by what they *say*, then the most widely accepted theory on how to prevent war is to arm. Almost every state spends much more for arms than for its contributions to the United Nations and regional organizations. Iceland and Costa Rica are the only countries with no budget for regular armed forces, but even so Iceland had enough force in the form of coast guard vessels to keep British fishing boats out of waters over which it claimed jurisdiction.[1] Even Sweden and Switzerland, countries with a traditional, explicit policy of neutrality, spend substantial amounts for arms.

"IF YOU WANT PEACE, PREPARE FOR WAR"

All states today refer to these expenditures as "defense spending" and, for the most part, even a cynic wouldn't question that designation. Most arms are not for conquest; they genuinely reflect states' judgments about how best to preserve their security. "Peace Is Our Profession" was the slogan chosen by the United States Strategic Air Command, and it was more than a public relations gimmick. The slogan has a venerable ancestor in Latin, *si vis pacem para bellum*, "If you want peace, prepare for war." It is an idea that seems to make sense. Certainly we see examples of it in everyday life.

Police officers on duty are not mugged nearly so often as fragile old women on their way home from cashing their Social Security checks.

But how much preparation for war is needed to secure peace? The ideal would be enough arms to prevent any conceivable enemy from even trying to test your strength. Sir John Fisher, the head of the British navy before World War I, was given to colorful language:

> My sole objective is PEACE in doing all this! Because if you rub it in both at home and abroad that you are ready for instant war with every unit of your strength in the first line and intend to be "first in" and hit your enemy in the belly and kick him when he's down and boil your prisoners in oil (if you take any!) and torture his women and children, then people will keep clear of you.[2]

Many decades have passed since Lord Fisher wrote that, and contemporary writers generally bring up the arms race only to condemn it. But let us pause to ask the questions: Could military expenditure prevent war? Might not all these governments be correct when they spend large amounts for weapons? Could not a sincere proponent of world peace advocate, under some circumstances, *increased* spending for military forces?

We should seriously consider the possibility that these arguments might be correct. Most of the time most states are not at war with each other, and most of the time most have armaments. Is there a connection? Advocates of military spending like to point to the period before World War II, when Western European countries did ignore defense spending and allowed Hitler to achieve the superiority in new weapons that led to the swift German victories in 1939 and 1940. The French planes being built to match the Luftwaffe were still on the assembly lines when the Germans overran the French factories.

We often hear of the dangers of an arms race, but a situation in which only *one* country is arming seems even more dangerous. Even if it were our country alone that had weapons, we might doubt that this was the best road to peace. The distinction between defensive uses and other uses (such as conquest) might gradually be erased. There are some psychological experiments showing that if people have a weapon they tend to use it, even if its use doesn't make a lot of sense.[3] Resort to arms by a country with superior weapons might present itself as the simple solution to a foreign policy problem, even if leaders realized it was not the best solution. Or a state might use its weapons to justify both to the leaders and to the taxpayers why it had spent all the money to acquire them. (This was one reason the atomic bomb was dropped on Japan, even though it had been built in a secret race with Germany.)

We find then no serious advocate of unilateral armament — that is, armament by one country to the point of superiority. But in the world today there is no danger that one country alone would arm and others not try to keep up. Realistically, if we are talking about si vis pacem para bellum, we mean an armaments race.

Do arms races prevent war? If we use a very narrow definition, we may end up with a biased selection of cases. Lewis F. Richardson, a Quaker who used mathematics to study arms races, wrote, "There have been only three great arms-races. The first two of them ended in wars in 1914 and 1939; the third is still going on."[4] It is easy to see his answer to the question, "Do arms races causes war?" but we may suspect that Richardson already knew what his answer would be before he selected his definition.

On the other hand, a broad definition is equally useless. If we equate arms races with *any* acquisition of armaments by states, then obviously arms races do not prevent but instead cause war; without weapons, no state could fight what we call a war. But with such a broad definition we are really saying, "Armaments cause war," which is as helpful as the statement, "Combustible materials cause fire" would be in a fire marshal's investigation.

We need a definition that will enable us to identify the times when states are not simply arming but are arming *in competition*. Following the suggestions of one scholar, we might confine our use of the label "arms race" to those occasions when two or more countries see themselves as rivals and increase or improve their armaments at a rapid rate, making these increases or improvements with attention to the armaments possessed by their rivals.[5] Agreeing on a definition of "at a rapid rate" would pose some problems, but not serious ones; public health officers are able to make similar judgments about how rapidly a disease must spread to be called an epidemic. A more serious problem is that we might try to measure an arms race by increases in military spending, yet be misled by the results. In the 1860's the British replaced their wooden ships with ironclad ships in response to French innovations; yet the British spent less on their navy in those years than they had in preceding ones, despite the fact they were in an arms race with France.[6]

Even when arms budgets are increasing, the published data are not always reliable, and only limited data are available. Items that are included (such as basic research) change from time to time. The unit of measurement — usually the fiscal year — may be too long to provide frequent enough observations to measure change.[7] With all these problems, it is not surprising that there is no universally accepted list of arms races. Most lists would include the British–German naval race from 1898 to 1914 and the French–German army race from 1911 to 1914, but there is disagreement about the present relationship between the United States and the Soviet Union. According to some critics, for years the United States was increasing neither the quantity nor the quality of its strategic weapons and in fact was allowing its military spending in this category to drop. It was not an arms race, they say, but at best an "arms crawl."[8] Despite these objections, we will include the present United States–Soviet rivalry in our list of arms races and look now at what generalizations we can safely make about such races.

QUANTITATIVE ARMS RACES: THE PRE–WORLD WAR I RACE AND WORST-CASE ESTIMATION

We can divide arms races into two types: quantitative and technological. In quantitative races the basic weapons remain the same, and countries compete to see which can acquire the most of them.[9] An example of a quantitative arms race occurred between France and Germany before World War I. The principal weapon was the foot soldier armed with a rifle. Both the French and the Germans started with armies as prescribed in their constitutions — a minimum of 1 per cent of the population. In 1912, after several crises in the Mediterranean area, the German general staff asked for an increase. They estimated that their army would grow in this way:[10]

1912	595,000
1913	694,000
1914	761,000

The French followed events in Germany very closely. They knew the Germans were going to increase the size of their army, but they weren't sure by how much. What mattered from the military point of view was not the number of soldiers in uniform but the number of effectives — soldiers who actually fired their rifles in combat. It wasn't always easy to tell by looking at tables of organization how many effectives the Germans had. Should the French count cooks, telegraph operators, tuba players in military bands? Only the German general staff's secret plans would tell exactly how many men could be thrown into combat. To be on the safe side, the French military did its own estimating and came up with a figure of 870,000 for the German army, more than 100,000 above the Germans' own figure.

France wanted to expand its army. Having a smaller population to draw from than Germany (39 million as opposed to 65 million Germans), it extended the term of military service to three years, giving the army an effective increase of 160,000 troops. The French estimated the size of their army by 1914 would be 736,000. But the German general staff was just as prudent as the French military leaders; and when they counted the number of French soldiers, they arrived at the figure of 882,500. Let's look at these estimates:

German estimates	
French strength in 1914	882,500
German strength in 1914	761,000
French superiority	121,500 or 16%
French estimates	
German strength in 1914	870,000
French strength in 1914	736,000
German superiority	134,000 or 18%
Actual strength	
German strength in 1914	761,000 (German estimate)
French strength in 1914	736,000 (French estimate)
German superiority	25,000 or 3%

The process of assuming the greatest possible strength for an opponent is called *worst-case estimation*. Each side is only being prudent, but the worst-case estimates by both sides speed up an arms race.

Another factor in the 1914 arms race was that each country had allies. Austria had about 450,000 troops, and the French added that number to the German total. France was allied to Russia, which had a large population and a large army. In 1906 the Russian army numbered 1,500,000 troops. It was being reorganized and expanded with French help and was expected to number 2,000,000 troops by 1917[11] When the Germans compared themselves with the Russians, they felt as the French had felt when they compared themselves with the Germans: They could never catch up. Their rival had too large a population to draw from. The worst-case estimation and the German fear that the Russian army would soon be too large to fight figured prominently in the deliberation of German leaders in the summer of 1914.[12]

TECHNOLOGICAL ARMS RACE:
SALT I AND THE INTERIM AGREEMENT

A technological (or qualitative) race differs from a quantitative arms race in that each side tries to introduce new and superior weapons. The emphasis is not on *more* but on *better*. Technological competition first became important during the Industrial Revolution of the mid-nineteenth century. Before that, weapons had remained pretty much the same for long periods. The sailing ship of 1850 was not fundamentally different from that of 1650; the naval gun on that ship was not much different from the gun of 1560.[13] It is hard to imagine a major weapon today remaining in use for 200 years; the arms race we are familiar with is clearly technological.

Technological races differ in some important ways from quantitative ones. In quantitative races, one country would get ahead and stay ahead because of superior resources or greater willingness to make sacrifices. The German army was larger than the French army because there were 20 million more Germans to recruit it from. The British navy stayed larger than any other because of the British conviction that a superior navy was vital to their security. Before the age of rapid technological change, states found it difficult to change their relative power position by internal efforts and so turned to external sources of power in the form of allies. As technology grew more important, the search for allies (the balance of power system) became less important.

In technological races there is always the chance that a new discovery, a technological breakthrough, will suddenly render all existing weapons obsolete and wipe out whatever advantage the leading power might have. In effect, the new discovery starts the race all over again with the states equal. One technological breakthrough was a new type of battleship, capable of high speed and of mounting all big guns. The first one, launched by the British in 1906, was the *Dreadnought,* whose name was later applied to similar battleships. Because the *Dreadnought* could destroy any existing battleship, the navies of the world (including the British navy) suddenly found they had a lot of obsolete ships on their hands. Before 1906, the British had sixty-three battleships, the Germans twenty-six. Overnight this British margin of superiority had been wiped out. If the Germans began to build *Dreadnoughts* at the same rate as the British did, the naval power of the two countries would be nearly equal. (Sir John Fisher, who was responsible for the building of the *Dreadnought,* was criticized for introducing a ship that rendered the British navy obsolete. His defense was that the Germans were about to build a similar ship in any case.)[14]

Another characteristic of a technological race is the difficulty of figuring out who is ahead. This is a recurring problem in the present race. In 1972, when the United States concluded an agreement on limiting arms with the Soviet Union, Senator Henry Jackson made this statement: "The Soviets are granted numerical superiority in every area: land-based missiles (1,618 to 1,054); modern submarines (up to 62 for them and 44 for us); missile delivery capability (4 to 5 times as much for them)."[15] There was no question about the accuracy of Senator Jackson's facts. But defenders of the agreement pointed out that there were qualitative differences between the weapons of the United States and those of the USSR.

Senator Jackson referred to two kinds of superiority. His first point was Soviet superiority in numbers of land-based missiles and submarine-based missiles, or launchers. His opponents said that the number of launchers didn't matter as much as the number of different targets, or aiming points, at which the launchers could direct warheads. The United States, at the time the agreement was signed in July 1972, had fifty-four Titan missiles and 1,000 Minuteman missiles, but 200 of the Minutemen were equipped to launch more than one warhead. Not only that, these warheads were MIRV's (multiple independently targetable reentry vehicles); each of them could be directed to an entirely separate target, just as if it had its own separate launcher. The same is true of submarines. Of the forty-one that the United States had at the time, ten had missiles of a type called Poseidon, which were also MIRVed. If, instead of counting launchers, we count aiming points, we get these figures for 1972:[16]

United States	Soviet Union
3,550	2,090

One must allow for another difference between United States and Soviet weapons. In 1972 all Soviet submarines were based in the Soviet Union, whereas some United States submarines were based in Scotland and Spain. The overall effect was that Soviet submarines had to spend more time getting to stations in the oceans from which they could launch their missiles. United States submarines could spend roughly 60 per cent of their time on station, Soviet submarines only 40 per cent. If we make appropriate corrections in our calculations of aiming points to allow for this discrepancy, the comparative figures are:[17]

United States	Soviet Union
2,710	1,750

Senator Jackson's third point was missile delivery capability, or throw-weight — the amount of explosive power a missile can deliver to a target. In 1972 the largest Soviet missile, the SS-9, could deliver about 25 megatons; the MIRVed United States Minuteman missile had three warheads of 200 kilotons each — in other words, only about one-hundredth the power of an SS-9. But Jackson's opponents pointed out that explosive power or throw-weight didn't matter as much as accuracy. A 1-megaton warhead that could hit within a quarter mile of its target could do just as much damage as a 5-megaton warhead that could hit within half a mile. In other words, with these weapons at these ranges, improving the accuracy by 440 yards enables you to cut the explosive power to one-fifth. It was generally believed at the time of the SALT I agreement that United States weapons were more accurate than Soviet ones.[18]

At the stage reached in 1972, the United States appeared to be ahead in the technological race, at least by many measures. But Senator Jackson had a valid point: Once the USSR acquired the technology to multiply the number of reentry vehicles per launcher and improve their accuracy, superiority in number of launchers would give the Soviets overall superiority. By

1979, when the SALT II treaty was signed, the predictions of critics from the beginning of the decade were coming true and generating great pressure for the United States to develop a new military technology, the land-based mobile missile.

ARMS RACES AS ACTION–REACTION

The kind of technology available can affect arms races, either accelerating or slowing them. A race that keeps escalating is said to be "self-aggravating"; one that eventually slows down is known as a "damped" race. What is crucial is the relative cost and effectiveness of offense as compared with defense. When offensive weapons are cheaper or more effective than defensive ones, races are self-aggravating; when defensive weapons are cheaper or more effective, races are damped. In conventional twentieth-century land warfare, we use a rule of thumb that the attacking side needs 3-to-1 superiority to be successful. A country that intends only to defend itself need build up an army only a third (or slightly more) the size of a potential attacker. The attacker need not fear this buildup, because the defense forces would not be large enough to be used for a successful attack.

On the other hand, if the weapons give a great advantage to the attacker, the race could become self-aggravating. The MIRV is such a weapon. Imagine two rival countries, each with one-hundred missiles and each missile with ten MIRV's. That is a total of 1,000 warheads or aiming points. If one side decides to shoot first and wipe out its rival's missiles, it has only one-hundred targets to shoot at. It can aim two, three, four, or more warheads per enemy missile and still have hundreds left over to threaten enemy cities, once the enemy's missile force is wiped out. Such a race would quickly accelerate as each side tried to acquire more missiles than its rival had warheads.[19]

Such a race would assume that each country builds its weapons in response to the acquisition of weapons by the other. This is known as the *action–reaction phenomenon*. Some people claim that it fuels the arms race today, particularly because of two factors. One is that with present weapons defense has no clear advantage over offense. In fact, MIRV's, as we have just seen, given an advantage to the side that fires first, and MIRV's are becoming more common. The other factor is worst-case estimation. The claim is made that the United States Department of Defense "invariably exaggerated the Soviet claim to obtain public and congressional support for weapons that will undermine the Soviet deterrent."[20]

Here is how the action–reaction phenomenon works. In the 1960's United States intelligence sources noticed a line of radars being built along the western edge of the Soviet Union. Because the line ran through the Baltic city of Tallinn, it was called the Tallinn Line. This was interpreted as the first stage of an anti-ballistic missile system (ABM), presumably to counter the submarine-launched Polaris missiles. Anticipating this development before the Soviets had even demonstrated that their Tallinn Line would work, the United States took steps to overcome it, substituting a new, bigger submarine-launched missile, the Poseidon, for the Polaris. With bigger missiles American submarines could move farther out into the oceans and launch their missiles from other directions, avoiding the defenses of the Tallinn Line.

In the mid-1970's there was still debate about what the Tallinn Line really was, but it never did develop into an ABM system. In fact, the best guess is that it was a Soviet anti-aircraft system, built in anticipation of the United States deployment of a new bomber, the B-70. The United States never built that bomber, but the Soviets went ahead with their preparations, assuming the worst, that the United States would build it. Meanwhile, United States planners, also assuming the worst (that the Tallinn Line was an ABM system) went ahead with their planning. When the error was discovered, the United States did not say, "Oh, we made a mistake," and tear out the more powerful Poseidon missiles. The United States said, in effect, "As long as we have these improved missiles, we might as well keep them." This gave Soviet planners something new to react to.[21]

It seems safe to say that arms races could be fueled by this action–reaction dynamic, and our example suggests that at least parts of recent Soviet and American expenditures illustrate such a dynamic. But that does not answer the question of whether action–reaction provides a good explanation for all arms races. One noted strategic writer, Albert Wohlstetter, argued that it does not.[22] First, he argued, it was not true that the United States invariably overestimated the number of ICBM's (intercontinental ballistic missiles) the Soviet Union would deploy. On the contrary, he found that the United States from 1962 to 1971 (the years he studied) was much more likely to underestimate what the Soviets were doing. Of the fifty-one predictions made by the secretary of defense in his annual statements, only nine overestimated what the Soviets actually did. In the other forty-two cases, the Soviets actually built more weapons than our highest estimates had predicted.[23]

Second, Wohlstetter argued that United States reaction to Soviet buildups was not invariably to build more. In at least one case the size of the Soviet buildup led the United States to decide not to react. One of Secretary of Defense McNamara's arguments against building an ABM was that the large size of the Russian ICBM force and their potential for expansion made it futile.[24] Wohlstetter argued that the pattern of underreaction to Soviet advances was reflected in a *declining* expenditure for strategic arms. Making an adjustment in his figures to allow for inflation, he showed that United States spending on strategic weapons went from a high of $19 billion in the early 1960's to $6.77 billion in the early 1970's, a reduction of two-thirds.[25] Notice that these figures refer to spending only for strategic weapons such as missiles, not for items such as increased pay for a volunteer army (which now takes up 55 per cent of the defense budget).

Third, Wohlstetter argued that weapons were not getting more and more destructive. It is difficult to compare weapons of different sizes. Very small weapons are not as effective as large ones, but when weapons get very large, they do proportionately less damage. A 10-megaton bomb thoroughly pulverizes the ground under it but doesn't do as much total damage to a large city as would four 1-megaton bombs scattered over it. For this reason Wohlstetter used a measure called "equivalent megatonnage," which calculates how large an area weapons can destroy (rather than how many aiming points there are, which would exaggerate the effect of small warheads, or how much explosive power they have, which would exaggerate the effect of large ones). He found, by a measure of equivalent megatonnage, that the destructive power of weapons available to the United States had declined by 1971 to about half of what it was in the early 1960's.[26]

A later study by two political scientists, covering a slightly longer period — 1952 through 1976 — reached the same conclusion. "We conclude," they wrote, "that no arms race was waged, that the two nations were scarcely competing."[27] Recent requests for increases in the defense budget by the Reagan Administration may lead us into a competition that future researchers will identify as an arms race. However, the important point is not what label best fits the present situation but what these studies tell us about the nature of arms races.

OTHER SOURCES OF ARMS RACES

In short, these authors reject the action–reaction explanation of the arms race as a "closed cycle of tightly coupled interaction between US and Soviet processes of decision to acquire weapons."[28] They reach the same conclusion about the present race that other analysts have reached about arms races in general: Arms are purchased for many reasons. The action–reaction hypothesis assumes that states base their decisions solely on the belief si vis pacem para bellum, or that buildups occur only for the purpose of deterrence. But this is not always so. Any arms buildup is the result of a number of factors. Perhaps one or two motives predominate, but other considerations are usually present as well.[29]

Arms have been purchased primarily to increase the diplomatic weight of a country. This seems to have been the main reason for Germany's decision to build a fleet in 1898. In the late nineteenth century, a fleet was a symbol of world influence, reflecting industrial as well as military power and influencing policy in distant parts. (In 1902 German ships participated in the blockade of Venezuelan ports to force that country to pay debts owed to German citizens.) Possibly some Germans believed that Germany needed security on the sea as well as on land. Most German military thinkers, however, agreed that Germany was a land power and its major enemies were also land powers. Therefore a fleet was not needed for national security. The British seem to have misinterpreted German intentions (understandably, because the Germans with all their anti-British talk made their intentions obscure). The British considered naval superiority vital to Britain's well-being, both to defend its island territory and to keep its sea lanes open. For Germany, the British thought, a fleet serves no defensive purpose; it is a waste of money unless they really intend to attack us.

The rather vague goal of increasing diplomatic weight seems to be motivating many states today to try to acquire their own nuclear weapons. In 1975 an Argentine legislator introduced a bill calling on the Argentine government to build its own nuclear bomb. He argued that "recent events have demonstrated that nations gain increasing recognition in the international arena in accordance with their power" and cited China as a state that had been ignored by major powers until it exploded its own nuclear weapons.[30] Whatever the intellectual merits of such arguments, if such legislation succeeded, it would certainly stimulate Argentina's neighbors, Brazil and Chile, to consider acquiring nuclear weapons.

Another reason states build weapons is sometimes called the "ripening plum argument." Just as we pick ripe fruit whether we are hungry or not, so states order new technologies whether they need them or not. To return to the case of the Poseidon submarine missile: Although intended to overcome a possible Soviet ABM system with its greater range, it also had greater accuracy, which could threaten to destroy Soviet missiles in their silos and thus make it possible for the United States to consider striking first in a nuclear war. This greater accuracy was not needed to fulfill the basic mission of Poseidon, which was simply to deter a Soviet strike, but, as one expert testified, "The technology is available — why not use it?"[31]

Domestic politics also affect decisions about weapons. There are always profits to be made by building weapons and careers to be advanced by deploying them. Domestic politics stimulated the German–British naval race. The kaiser himself took the kind of interest in ships that an adolescent might take in high-performance automobiles. Admiral Tirpitz, head of the German navy, was eager to have his branch of the service get a larger share of the budget. A pressure group, the Navy League, helped the German navy get the government to increase spending on ships.

One political scientist, James Kurth, advanced a more sophisticated version of this argument in what he calls "the follow-on imperative." According to Kurth, the production lines for modern weapons are viewed by government planners as a rational resource. It takes years to assemble the thousands of scientists, engineers, and skilled workers needed to run Boeing or Lockheed; it takes more time for the team to learn to work together efficiently. If these companies were closed even temporarily, for lack of contracts, it would take years to reassemble them. Therefore, according to Kurth's argument, a new contract is awarded to a firm whenever a previous contract is about to run out. The new contract is structurally similar to the old one (missiles replacing missiles, for example) and is awarded not to the firm best qualified but to the one with empty production lines. According to Kurth's research, the follow-on imperative explains eleven out of twelve decisions to build major weapons from 1960 to 1972.[32]

But domestic politics, whether in the form of a military–industrial complex or a follow-on imperative, is not a total explanation for arms races. Not all pleas from vested interests are heeded. The United States has canceled some weapons (the B-70 bomber and the B-1A bomber) and has agreed to terminate others (the ABM system), despite military and industrial interest in continuing them.[33] Nor should we neglect the ability of domestic pressure groups to prevent a government from spending on armaments. The British and French governments in the 1940's were slow to engage in an arms race with the Germans because of widespread pacifism among their citizens. Disillusionment with military spending in the wake of the Vietnam War generated pressures that contributed to President Carter's decision to cancel the B-1 bomber in 1977.

ARMS RACES AND WAR

States may engage in arms races for reasons that have little to do with the objective of preventing war, but it is the effectiveness of these arms races in preventing war that is of primary interest to us. Unfortunately it is difficult to answer the question, "Do arms races make war less or more likely?" because no definitive study on arms races has been carried out. At best we have only fragmentary or preliminary findings.[34] One scholar claims (but without much evidence) that of eighty-four wars ending between 1820 and 1929, only ten were preceded by arms races that someone has asserted were a cause.[35] This suggests that arms races are not the only cause (or even a frequent cause) of wars.

On the other hand, an investigation of serious international disputes between major powers from 1815 to 1965 found that in twenty-eight cases in which the dispute was accompanied by an arms race, war resulted twenty-three times; in seventy-one cases in which disputes were not accompanied by arms races, war resulted only three times.[36] This research suggests that arms races are more likely to promote war than to inhibit it. Yet we are not justified in claiming that arms races invariably cause war, for Samuel Huntington lists six cases in the last hundred years when arms races ended by peaceful agreement instead of war.[37]

Huntington goes on to offer an interesting thesis on the relation of arms races to war. Using the distinction between quantitative races and technological ones, he argues that because quantitative races put progressively greater strains on society, they are more likely to come to a definite end, either in a peace agreement or in war. With more and more soldiers drafted into the army and more and more resources diverted into manufacturing weapons, the time comes when a state's leaders say, "It can't go on like this anymore." A quantitative race that ended in a peace agreement was the race between Chile and Argentina, which began in 1890 and ended with a treaty in 1902. A quantitative race that ended in war was the race preceding World War I.

The qualitative race, Huntington argues, is different. It puts less pressure on society. Scientists and engineers work on new forms of weapons, but not many of their inventions actually go into production. Those that are produced are not produced for long, because soon a new weapon comes along and the process starts all over. Each state can hope that luck will give it the technological breakthrough needed to put it ahead, even if only temporarily. The result is that technological races tend to go on and on. No great pressure is felt to bring them to a definitive end, either by fighting or by agreement.[38]

Huntington's ideas must be regarded as hypotheses rather than as accepted theories; he offers little systematic proof. Because he does not give a precise definition of "technological race," it is hard to know which races fit that category. Even with qualitative change, a state needs a specific quantity of weapons before it gains the upper hand. Still, Huntington's ideas offer a plausible explanation of events in recent years. The United States–Soviet race has been primarily technological, and it has gone on without great pressure for either war or agreement.

COSTS AND HAZARDS OF THE ARMS RACE

Even if the record of past races does not clearly indicate that the present technological arms race will inevitably lead to war, the race has a number of other undesirable aspects. One of these is cost. A great many resources are being diverted into weapons that at best will never be used, at worst will be used for destruction. Metal used for refrigerators and stoves keeps your beer cold and your pizza warm; metal used for missiles and warheads sits in underground silos and brings you no enjoyment at all. Many people think that the world does not have such an abundance of metals or of artifacts made of them that we can afford to make things from which we get no enjoyment. As far back as 1953, President Eisenhower pointed out trade-offs that could be made: The dollars spent for a bomber could buy thirty schools or two fully equipped hospitals or electric power plants for two moderately large cities.[39] Some years later a former secretary of defense, Robert McNamara, suggested that high levels of military expenditure actually erode security by reducing resources available for other vital government services. He estimated that in 1979 the world was spending $30 billion a year for research and development of weapons, more than the combined total for research and development in the fields of energy, food, health, and education.[40]

Although Samuel Huntington argued that technological arms races do not put great strains on societies, he wrote his article in 1958. Recent developments suggest his judgment may no longer be valid. By 1971 even the conservative Senate Armed Services Committee was beginning to warn about the escalating cost of weapons. As an example they cited air-to-air combat. For years the basic weapon had been a .50-caliber machine gun, a burst of which cost about twenty dollars. By the 1970's machine guns were replaced by the air-to-air missiles, which then cost $300,000 per round.[41] The more modern Phoenix missiles cost about $1 million apiece.[42]

Costs have escalated faster than overall inflation for all major weapons. The basic aircraft used in the Vietnam War, the F-4 Phantom, was replaced in the 1970's by the F-14 Tomcat. One analysis of the full cost of the F-14 was $28 million per plane — seven times more than the Phantom.[43] Thus, even though military spending increased dramatically under President Reagan, the Air Force actually was able to afford fewer planes than it bought during the Carter Administration.[44] One aerospace executive pointed out that at present rates of increase, by "the year 2054, the entire defense budget will purchase just one tactical aircraft. This aircraft will have to be shared between the Air Force and Navy, three and a half days each per week."[45]

Another problem is that arms races strengthen some domestic constituencies. They strengthen these elements in society by diverting large amounts of resources to them, which in turn gives those elements a bigger voice in decision-making. A military establishment that receives progressively larger shares of the budget is going to have more and more political influence. It will be harder to cut military spending because more people will be thrown out of work. More funds are available to finance pressure groups and lobbies. This problem may be even more acute in the Soviet Union because of the organization of Soviet forces. In the United States, missile forces are distributed among the Army, Air Force, and Navy, and these strategic forces make up only part of the total of the budget for each service. The total abolition of missiles by a disarmament agreement would mean some loss of personnel and budget for these services, but it would not mean their elimination. In the Soviet Union, by contrast, missiles are under a separate branch of the armed forces, the Strategic Rocket Forces, equivalent to the United States Navy or Air Force. We can assume that the Strategic Rocket Forces would strenuously resist any attempt to abolish missiles, for their abolition would mean the end of that branch of the armed forces.

A hazard of the arms race is that, with increasing numbers of weapons, there is an increasing chance that one might be used accidentally. All sorts of guarantees can be built into a military system to ensure that it reacts slowly to a crisis. We call such guarantees the "stiff trigger." But stiff-trigger forces are vulnerable to surprise attack. The remarkable success of the Japanese at Pearl Harbor has not been forgotten by Americans, who repeatedly refer to a possible "Nuclear Pearl Harbor."[46] This sensitivity has led some people to advocate a policy of launching missiles when warning of an attack is received, so that our missiles are not all destroyed on the ground. But a policy of launch on warning would be very prone to accident. Leaders find themselves in a dilemma. The stiffer the trigger, the more vulnerable the force is to surprise attack. The more sensitive trigger, the more likely it is to go off accidentally.

President Nixon said, "The adversaries in the world are not in conflict because they are armed. They are armed because they are in conflict and have not yet learned peaceful ways to resolve their conflicting national interests."[47] Others have argued that it is the arms race that poisons relations between states and that we must work on it first. No matter how the question is answered, there is agreement that, at the least, armaments add another element to rivalries between states. Once two states have armed against each other, they have one more issue to settle. Arms races may not cause tensions, but neither do they seem to alleviate them.

NOTES

1. Iceland and Costa Rica are the only two traditional states of significant size with no military budget. A number of new microstates also report no military spending. See *World Military Expenditures and Arms Transfers, 1968–1977* (Washington, D.C.: U.S. Arms Control and Disarmament Agency, October 1979).

2. Quoted by Leonard Wainstein in "The Dreadnought Gap," *United States Naval Institute Proceedings* (September 1966), reprinted in Robert J. Art and Kenneth Waltz, *The Use of Force* (Boston: Little, Brown, 1971), p. 168.

3. See the experiment described by Morton Deutsch and Robert M. Krauss, "Studies of Interpersonal Bargaining," *The Journal of Conflict Resolution,* Vol. 6, No. 1 (March 1962), pp. 52–76.

4. Lewis F. Richardson, "Could an Arms Race End Without Fighting?" *Nature,* Vol. 168 (September 29, 1951), pp. 567–568.

5. Colin S. Gray, "The Arms Race Phenomenon," *World Politics,* Vol. 24, No. 1 (October 1971), p. 40.

6. Samuel P. Huntington, "Arms Races: Prerequisites and Results," in *Public Policy,* ed. Carl Friedrich and Seymour Harris (Cambridge: Harvard University, Graduate School of Public Administration, 1958), p. 76.

7. Bruce M. Russet, *What Price Vigilance?* (New Haven: Yale University Press, 1970), pp. 8–9.

8. Albert Wohlstetter, "Racing Forward? or Ambling Back?" *Survey,* Vol. 22, Nos. 3 and 4 (Summer–Autumn 1976), pp. 163–217.

9. Huntington, p. 65.

10. Bernadotte E. Schmitt, *The Coming of the War, 1914,* Vol. 1 (New York: Charles Scribner's Sons, 1930), p. 54 fn.

11. Fritz Fischer, *Germany's Aims in the First World War* (New York: W. W. Norton, 1967), p. 36.

12. Barbara Tuchman, *The Guns of August* (New York: Dell, 1962), pp. 43–44.

13. Huntington, p. 48.

14. Arthur J. Marder, *From Dreadnought to Scapa Flow,* Vol. 1: *The Road to War, 1904–1914* (London: Oxford University Press, 1961), p. 57.

15. Press release from the office of Senator Henry J. Jackson, "On Understanding Attached to SALT Agreements," June 14, 1972.

16. International Institute of Strategic Studies, *The Military Balance, 1972–1973,* Appendix I, "SALT and the Strategic Balance" (London, 1972), pp. 83–86.

17. Ibid.

18. International Institute of Strategic Studies, *Strategic Survey, 1969* (London, 1970), pp. 30–33.

19. Malcolm W. Hoag, "On Stability in Deterrent Races," in *The Revolution in World Politics,* ed. Morton A. Kaplan (New York: John Wiley, 1962), pp. 338–410.

20. Remarks by Jeremy J. Stone at the Congressional Conference on the Military Budget and National Priorities, Washington, D.C., March 28–29, 1969, quoted in *American Militarism, 1970,* ed. Erwin Knoll and Judith Nies McFadden (New York: Viking Press, 1969), p. 71.

21. George Rathjens, "The Dynamics of the Arms Race," *Scientific American,* Vol. 220, No. 4 (April 1969), pp. 15–25.

22. Albert Wohlstetter, "Is There a Strategic Arms Race?" *Foreign Policy,* No. 15 (Summer 1974), pp. 3–20; Albert Wohlstetter, "Rivals, But No 'Race,' " *Foreign Policy,* No. 16 (Fall 1974), pp. 48–81.

23. Wohlstetter, "Is There a Strategic Arms Race?" p. 16.

24. Ibid., p. 9.

25. Wohlstetter, "Rivals, But No 'Race,' " p. 62.

26. Ibid., p. 61.

27. A. F. K. Organski and Jacek Kugler, *The War Ledger* (Chicago: University of Chicago Press, 1980), p. 192.

28. Ibid., p. 80.

29. Colin Gray, "The Urge to Compete: Rationales for Arms Racing," *World Politics,* Vol. 26, No. 2 (January 1974), pp. 207–233.

30. Jonathan Kandell, "Argentines Assay Their Atom Potential," *The New York Times,* April 2, 1975, p. 2.

31. Charles Schultze in testimony before the Subcommittee on Economy in Government of the Joint Economic Committee, "The Military Budget and National Economic Priorities (Part I)," 91st Cong., 1st sess., June 1969, p. 51.

32. James Kurth, "Aerospace Production Lines and American Defense Spending," in *Testing the Theory of the Military Industrial Complex,* ed. Steven Rosen (Lexington, Mass.: Lexington Books, 1973), pp. 135–156.

33. Wohlstetter, "Rivals, But No 'Race,' " p. 73.

34. This point is emphasized in the writings of Colin Gray. See the two articles cited in notes 5 and 28.

35. Michael Nicholson, *Conflict Analysis* (New York: Barnes & Noble, 1971), pp. 133–136.

36. Michael D. Wallace, "Arms Races and Escalation," *The Journal of Conflict Resolution,* Vol. 23, No. 1 (March 1979), p. 15.

37. Huntington, pp. 64–65.

38. Ibid., p. 76.

39. Stephen Ambrose, *Eisenhower: The President* (New York: Simon & Schuster, 1984), p. 95. The calculations were made by Paul Nitze, now a key official in the Reagan Administration. See Greg Herken *Counsels of War* (New York: Alfred A. Knopf, 1985), pp. 103–104.

40. Speech in Chicago, quoted in *The New York Times,* May 23, 1979.

41. John W. Finney, "Senate Unit Says Costlier Weapons May Cut Defense," *The New York Times,* September 9, 1971.

42. James Fallows, *National Defense* (New York: Random House, 1981), p. 99.

43. Drew Middleton, "Rising Plane Costs Stir Air-Tactics Debate," *The New York Times,* December 1, 1974.

44. Testimony by Franklin C. Spinney to President's Blue Ribbon Commission on Defense Management, *The New York Times,* December 13, 1985, p. Y11.

45. Quoted by Fallows, p. 38.

46. For example, James Buckley, Column in *The New York Times,* July 23, 1971.

47. Commencement address at the Air Force Academy, quoted in *The New York Times,* June 5, 1969.

Chapter 13

The Balance of Terror

The assumption behind armaments as an approach to peace is *si vis pacem para bellum,* "If you want peace, prepare for war." Potential aggressors will then not start wars because they would fear losing. Another approach to peace is to make war so horrible that states fear not simply losing a war but getting into one in the first place no matter how it turns out. Alfred Nobel, the inventor of dynamite, made this argument in the last century. In 1892 he told a leading organizer of disarmament conferences: "Perhaps my factories will put an end to war even sooner than your Congresses; on the day that two army corps may mutually annihilate each other in a second, probably all civilized nations will recoil with horror and disband their troops."[1] Alfred Nobel was speaking long before the advent of nuclear weapons. Such weapons make his arguments even more compelling.

THE NATURE OF NUCLEAR WEAPONS

We usually fix the beginning of the atomic age at July 16, 1945, when the first bomb was exploded at a test site near Alamogordo, New Mexico. There had been revolutionary innovations in military technology in the past, from gunpowder to the airplane. With each new development it took time before the effects of the new weapons were recognized and taken into account in strategic planning. Atomic weapons were assimilated more quickly. Within a few weeks after the first test, they were used for all the world to see, with apparently decisive effects. Thinking and planning immediately began to take account of them.

The bomb exploded on July 16, 1945, was technically a *fission* weapon. It depended for its explosive force on a rapid chain reaction set off by splitting heavy elements, either a naturally occurring radioactive isotope of uranium (U-235) or an artificial element (plutonium) that is made by placing normal uranium in a reactor with an excess of neutrons. The theory of how to produce an atomic explosion was already clear in 1938 from work done by German scientists. The difficult part was producing enough fuel, either enriched uranium (U-235) or plutonium, to produce a bomb. It is estimated that, by the closing years of World War II, 10 per cent of the electrical capacity of the United States was going to produce material for the atomic bombs.[2]

The bombs were so powerful that a new measure of explosive power was needed to describe them. The standard used was the equivalent of 1 ton of TNT, the stuff of which World War II bombs were made. The big bombs of World War II, known as *blockbusters,* contained about a ton of TNT. In the 1970's the biggest TNT bomb was 7.5 tons, so large it had to be rolled out the door of a cargo plane. The atomic bombs were measured in terms of *thousands* of tons of TNT. The basic unit of measurement was called a *kiloton,* equal to 1,000 tons of TNT. The test bomb at Alamogordo had a force of 19,000 tons of TNT, or 19 kilotons; the Hiroshima bomb, 14 kilotons; the Nagasaki bomb, 20 kilotons.[3]

Powerful as these bombs were, they were nowhere close to the most powerful explosive that scientists could think of. The fission or splitting of heavy atoms releases only a fraction of the energy released by another process, the *fusion* or combining of light atoms. This process, similar to what goes on inside the sun, is clean. Unlike fission it produces no long-lasting radioactive particles. The major obstacle to achieving a fusion reaction is that starting it requires very high temperatures. The fusion bomb, originally called the "hydrogen bomb" because of the light elements used in it, is now usually referred to as a "thermonuclear weapon," because of the high temperatures needed to begin the fusion. So far, the only way we have to achieve these high temperatures is by a fission reaction. In other words, the fusion bomb needs an atomic bomb as a trigger, and this trigger will produce long-lasting radiation, called "fallout," even if the fusion reaction itself does not.

The first thermonuclear device tested by the United States, on November 1, 1952, vaporized the small Pacific island on which it was detonated and left in its place a crater 1 mile across. The great increase in power of this weapon over the atomic bomb called for still another measure of explosive power — the equivalent of 1 *million* tons of TNT, or 1 megaton. The test explosion of November 1952 had a force of 20 million tons of TNT, or

20 megatons. The biggest bomb ever tested was exploded by the Russians in 1961; it had a force of 58 megatons.

THE DIFFERENCE THAT NUCLEAR WEAPONS MADE

Politicians and commentators are tireless in telling us that nuclear weapons radically changed international politics. Undeniably they did, but it is important to be clear about exactly how they did it. The idea that first comes to mind is their destructive power. Without minimizing this destructive capacity, however, we must point out that the destruction caused by the atomic bombs was not so much greater than that of TNT weapons. Many people were killed by the atomic bombs — 70,000 at Hiroshima, 35,000 at Nagasaki — but these attacks were not the most destructive air raids of World War II. The raid on Tokyo of May 1945 killed 84,000 with TNT bombs and fire bombs. It would have taken at least 400 atomic bombs to equal the amount of damage that TNT bombs did to Germany during World War II and between 800 and 1,200 atomic bombs to do as much damage to the Soviet Union as German forces did during World War II.[4] Granted that 400 bombs are far fewer than the number of TNT bombs actually dropped, it is at the same time a long way from saying that one atomic bomb equals all the bombs dropped during World War II.

It was the introduction of the fusion bomb in 1952 that brought a truly horrifying level of destruction. we think of a normal fusion bomb as being about 1 megaton. The radius of destruction of such a bomb is great; near misses are the same as direct hits. A 1-megaton bomb would destroy brick structures out to a distance of 3.5 miles; it would ignite most fabrics and paper out to 6 miles; it would cause second-degree burns out to 11 miles.[5] You can visualize this by picking a spot 11 miles from your home. If a 1-megaton thermonuclear bomb went off over your home and you were standing out in the open at that spot 11 miles away, you would suffer painful burns on your exposed skin.

But still, we must guard against exaggerating the power of these weapons. Because we express their power in terms of TNT, we can be misled by too close an analogy with TNT. Suppose we are trying to visualize a 20-megaton bomb (a large weapon, but one that can be carried by a single intercontinental missile). By "20 megatons" we mean the equivalent of 20 million tons of TNT. The average railroad boxcar holds 80,000 pounds of goods, or 40 tons. It would take 500,000 boxcars to hold the 20 million tons of TNT. Each boxcar is 40 feet long, so we would have a train 20 million feet long, or 3,788 miles. The rail distance from Los Angeles to New York is 3,082 miles. Thus we can say that a 20-megaton bomb would be more powerful than the TNT in a train stretching from one end of the country to the other.

Vivid as it is, this metaphor is misleading. In fact the damage from one 20-megaton bomb would be nowhere nearly equivalent to the damage our hypothetical freight train could do. A thermonuclear bomb would overdestroy a very small area: It would expend most of its energy in pulverizing and vaporizing the few thousand square feet directly beneath it. The amount of damage would rapidly diminish farther from the center of the explosion. Furthermore, because the explosive force is exerted in all directions (that is, the explosion is spherical), a lot of the power goes up and out into the atmosphere. That characteristic mushroom cloud represents wasted energy. For this reason, even though the bomb dropped on Hiroshima was one thousand times as big as a World War II blockbuster, the area it destroyed was only one hundred times as great.

Having all this power packed into one bomb is not as destructive as having it spread out, say among twenty bombs of 1 megaton each. Another important point is that having bombs of any size stored in a bunker is not the same as having useful military weapons. Without effective delivery systems, these nuclear bombs are useless. This important fact is often obscured by the misleading term "overkill." People who use the word seem to mean something like this: The world has 3.5 billion people. If you add up the megatonnage of all the strategic nuclear weapons the United States has, you get a total of perhaps 35,000 megatons. Therefore, we have the equivalent of 10 tons of TNT for every man, woman, and child in the world. Because 1 ton of TNT is more than enough to kill, we supposedly have an overkill capacity.

This sounds impressive, until you consider that in World War I the world had 1.8 billion people and the battling armies were equipped with at least 9 billion rifle bullets, or an overkill of five bullets for every man, woman, and child in the world. Put this way, overkill does not seem so useful a concept. Many steps intervene between the weapon stored in the arsenal (whether a bullet or a nuclear bomb) and actual destruction. The weapon must be loaded and fired. It must travel with enough power and accuracy to hit its target. It must penetrate active and passive defenses. It must not be wasted by hitting a target already destroyed. At any of these points a weapon can fail, and that is just as true of intercontinental ballistic missiles as of rifle bullets. Adding more missiles to a country's strategic arsenal is not necessarily more wasteful than adding an extra clip of rifle bullets to an infantry soldier's ammunition belt.

This is not to say that nuclear weapon make no difference at all. They certainly do, but the difference lies in areas other than sheer destructive power. One important difference is the speed with which the destruction can be accomplished. Even if it would have taken 400 atomic bombs to equal the destruction inflicted on Germany in World War II, atomic weapons would have greatly speeded up the work. The conventional bombing of Germany went on for five years; the 400 atomic bombs could conceivably have been dropped in one night.

The overkill capacity in rifle bullets would have enabled the French to kill all the inhabitants of Germany once the German army quit fighting in 1918. As far as that goes, they could have killed them all with just one bayonet. But that would have taken a long time. It would have required deliberate planning. With nuclear weapons the population of Germany could be exterminated in a few minutes, even by accident, without any personal involvement by those doing the exterminating.[6]

We use the phrase "psychological distance" to describe our way of engaging in morally repugnant acts without feeling personally involved. Killing a rabbit with our natural weapons — teeth and fingernails — would be difficult for most people. Using a rifle makes it a lot easier because we can emotionally separate the squeezing of the trigger finger from the death of the rabbit. When the victim fades into total invisibility, killing becomes even easier. During the Vietnam War, helicopter pilots described strafing runs as shooting at little cloth dummies on the ground below. Yet a B-52 pilot, who normally bombed at a height so great that the plane was not visible from the ground, was horrified when he accompanied a friend on a helicopter gunship. "How can you stand to do this?" he asked. "You can actually see the people you are shooting!" Nuclear weapons, launched by an electronic signal given hundreds of miles from the missile silo and carried thousands of miles by intercontinental missiles, provide the ultimate in psychological distance.[7]

It is common to say that nuclear weapons add a new dimension to the strength of states, greatly increasing their power. In fact the overall effect is the opposite, making states as a group weaker, not stronger. States today are less able to do one of the important things that states are supposed to do: provide security for their inhabitants. The reason is that nuclear weapons give a great advantage to the offensive side.

It is sometimes said that for every offensive weapon, a defensive weapon is eventually developed. Actually, defensive weapons have never been very good. Defense was possible because offensive weapons weren't too good either. Armor could be penetrated by arrows, but arrows weren't always fatal even when they did penetrate. In 1940, during the Battle of Britain, the Royal Air Force defeated the German Luftwaffe by destroying only about 10 per cent of the German planes in each raid. Because TNT bombs were not that destructive against cities, an attrition rate of 10 per cent was enough to provide effective defense. Against nuclear weapons, however, an attrition rate of even 95 per cent would be useless. Because defensive weapons can do so little, nuclear war cannot be kept away from cities and civilians. No longer would the outcome of a battlefield struggle among military specialists determine the fate of cities and civilians. The cities and civilians are available as targets for military operations from the inception of the war.

DETERRENCE

One result is that strategy today is not adequately described by the words "defense" and "offense." Strategic thinkers have had to develop new terms. A major distinction employed today is between "defense" and "deterrence." A practical example will show how they differ in meaning. Suppose I want to protect a sum of money. One way of doing it would be to make it physically impossible for someone else to take it. I could put it in a safe, or I could stand over it with a pitchfork and jab at anyone who came near. The physical denial of some value to an opponent is what strategists mean by defense. Another way of protecting my money would be to stand over it with a cup of hot coffee in my hand, threatening to throw the coffee on anyone trying to take the money. In this case I am not making it physically impossible to take the money (the hot coffee would hurt but not disable); instead, I am trying to influence the mental calculations of a potential thief. If I am successful, then I have established a psychological relationship that strategists call deterrence.

Defense is *physical*. It goes into operation when war breaks out. For example, tanks move to the frontier, making it physically impossible for the enemy to advance. Deterrence is *psychological,* useful before war breaks out. It keeps the enemy from moving in the first place. In fact, once war has broken out, deterrence has failed, and defense must take over.

In April 1969, the North Koreans shot down a United States electronic intelligence plane flying off their coast. President Nixon wanted to protect planes on similar missions in the future. What deterrent measure could he have taken and what defensive measure? Keeping in mind that deterrence is psychological (working on the other side's mind), you might say that a deterrent measure would be some kind of warning, such as, "If you shoot down another plane, we will bomb Wonsan Harbor." If you remember that defense is a physical measure, you might suggest sending along fighter planes as escorts that can physically interpose themselves between intelligence planes and attacking North Korean fighters.

Measures designed for defense can also deter. The pitchfork that I wave over my pile of money, although a physical measure itself, will probably discourage anyone from trying to steal the bills. Fighter escorts for intelligence planes have a deterrent effect, often making it unnecessary for them to actually defend the planes they are escorting. This combination of defense and deterrence has been the rule throughout military history. Only recently have these two functions begun to separate. That is another important difference between the nuclear age and the non-nuclear age. Today we invest great sums in weapons that are designed for deterrence only; they have no value at all for defense. This condition is unlike anything we have had in the past.

In the past, a strong tank force might have had a deterrent effect, but if deterrence failed and an invasion began, that same tank force could defend the country. An ICBM force with nuclear warheads of megaton strength has only deterrent value; it can provide no defense. If war breaks out and an enemy attacks, will any American lives be saved if missiles are fired back? The answer is no. If war breaks out, deterrence has failed, and the sole reason for the existence of the missiles disappears.

If our missiles could in some way destroy enemy missiles on the ground before they were launched, that of course would be defense. When the enemy launches a massive attack and no targets are left, our missiles would lose their purpose. Or if we expect a war to last for years, then the destruction of the enemy's industrial capacity might physically impair the enemy's ability to attack us. But the kind of war in which we expect these missiles to be launched is the kind we expect to last at most a few days.

Once the capabilities and limitations of nuclear weapons became clear, it became necessary to work out new strategic doctrines; that is, guidelines on how to use the weapons. In the past, military strategy was straightforward. Weapons deterred enemy aggression before war broke out and defended against that aggression if deterrence failed. Today one has to choose which of the two goals one wishes to emphasize and build weapons accordingly.

MINIMUM DETERRENCE

When both sides possess enormous means of destruction, the traditional fear of losing a war is joined by a second fear, that of ever getting into a war in the first place. Norman Cousins articulated this idea in 1961: "Nations no longer declare war or wage war, they declare or wage mutual suicide."[8] This unpleasant state of affairs has come to be known as the *balance of terror.*

With time, however, some people began to see positive aspects in such a balance. The balance of terror is maintained by deterrent weapons. If they fail to deter war, they are of no further use; they cannot be used for defense. Because they are not needed to fight enemy weapons, there is no need for superiority or even equality in numbers of weapons. All a strategist has to do is calculate the minimum level of force needed to deter.

Secretary of Defense McNamara suggested that the United States need only be able to inflict "unacceptable damage" on the Soviet Union to keep it from starting a war. Perhaps the Soviets themselves would find it hard to say exactly what theoretical level of damage they would find unacceptable, but McNamara estimated it conservatively at from 20 to 25 per cent of the population and 50 per cent of industrial capacity. In other words, any Soviet leaders mad enough to risk 25 per cent of the Soviet population would be so mad that no further amount of damage could deter them, not 30 per cent or 35 per cent or whatever was attainable.

McNamara had his experts calculate the number of weapons needed to inflict various levels of damage on the Soviet Union (see Table 13.1). They found that with only 400 warheads the United States could be sure of destroying 30 per cent of the Soviet population and 76 per cent of its industrial capacity. Because the United States already had warheads far in excess of this number (by the 1960's, well over 10,000), no more were needed. A buildup in Soviet arms did not need to be matched by adding more United States arms. If the Soviets persisted in adding more, it was only a waste of money. Once they had obtained the ability to inflict unacceptable damage on us, extra weapons did them no more good than they did us.

McNamara made it clear that the ability to inflict unacceptable damage has to be assured. If exactly 400 warheads were needed to inflict predicted levels of damage, then the United States would need more than 400 weapons in its arsenal to allow for failures in launching, weapons off course, and possible Soviet defensive measures. We even allowed for the number of weapons that could be destroyed if the Soviet Union fired first in an effort to wipe out as many of our weapons as it could. McNamara's doctrine of assured destruction called for adequate numbers of weapons landing on Soviet targets even after a disarming first strike.

McNamara's doctrine of assured destruction is one example of a type

Table 13.1   WARHEADS AND CALCULATED LEVELS OF DAMAGE

1-megaton warhead (or equivalent) delivered to target	Percentage of population killed	Percentage of industry destroyed
100	15	59
200	21	72
400	30	76
800	39	77
1,200	44	77
1,600	47	77

Source: Data from U.S Congress, House, Committee on Armed Services, Hearings on Military Posture, 90th Cong., 2nd sess., April 3–27, 1968, p. 8507.

of strategic theory known as "finite deterrence." All such theories share the assumption that once a given level of deterrent weapons is reached, no more are necessary. Theorists differ on what the level should be. Secretary McNamara set it at from 20 to 30 per cent of population and 50 per cent of industry. McGeorge Bundy, former national security adviser, implied that it could be set much lower when he stated, "One bomb on a city would be a catastrophe without precedent."[9]

The theory implies that more than the minimum is actually bad, because excessive levels might suggest to the other side that we are not interested simply in deterring war. They might believe we are building toward a disarming first strike. This belief would impel them to engage in more building of their own and so fuel an arms race. Advocates of finite deterrence believe that the disarming first strike is an unattainable goal in any case and building arsenals with this aim, in addition to risking a war, wastes money.

MAD AND ITS CRITICS

Advocates of finite deterrence prefer that both sides follow the same policy. They believe in *mutual assured destruction,* which their opponents have shortened to MAD. Proponents of MAD admit that some of the corollaries of their basic premise do contradict our customary ways of thinking and require some reflection before they seem acceptable. What is mad, though, is not the doctrine but the situation into which nuclear weapons have forced us.

One corollary is that any weapon that would make it rational to contemplate striking first is a bad weapon. This includes many defensive weapons, for example, an effective defense against ICBM's. Such a system, if possessed by only one side, would allow the possessor to attack an opponent, secure in its impunity from retaliation. Because deterrence would be undermined, proponents of MAD opposed the ABM system. For similar reasons they oppose improved civil defense systems. Logically such defense systems would not make it rational to fire first if both sides possessed them, but advocates of MAD fear that one side might gain some kind of temporary advantage from the installation of a system and be tempted to use its temporary invulnerability to strike first.

Another corollary is that weapons intended to destroy other weapons are bad, but weapons intended to destroy people are good. The essence of finite deterrence is that populations must be exposed to retaliatory attack — in effect, held hostage. To make them hostages, weapons (such as missiles) must be aimed at them. Because cities are large and undefended targets, the missiles need not be very big or very accurate. The sorts of missiles the United States carries on its submarines are quite good for attacking cities even though they are small and inaccurate. On the other hand, any missile that is very large or very accurate could be used in an attempt to disarm the opponent by striking first, whatever the declared intentions of a state, and for this reason such weapons are opposed by advocates of mutual assured deterrence.

This corollary provides another reason for proponents of finite deterence to oppose defense systems. If a perfect defense against strategic weapons existed, war would continue as in the past at lower levels of violence, and the unique contribution of nuclear weapons to keep the peace at the relatively low cost of maintaining a limited number of missiles would be lost.

Finite deterrence is not without its critics. They raise a number of disturbing points. For one thing, they point out, finite deterrence reduces the usefulness of military force to just one purpose — the prevention of an all-out attack on the United States. But in fact such an attack is among the least likely possibilities in the world today. The Soviet Union would not gain from the wanton destruction of American cities and has never expressed any interest in such a goal. Far more likely are threats to vital interests, such as oil fields in the North Sea, or piecemeal attacks, such as a takeover of West Berlin. Finite deterrence could not credibly prevent such attacks. A country that relied solely on finite deterrence would be at the mercy of another country with conventional superiority.

Some critics even question whether finite deterrence would prevent a direct attack on the United States. If the Soviet Union continued to build more missiles once the United States had stopped at a minimum number, it would soon have superior numbers; in fact this condition existed already in the 1970's. If they chose to strike first, they would target some of their weapons at ours, leaving others in reserve. They would not destroy all our weapons, but we would not have very many left. On the other hand, because their attack was directed at our weapons and not at our population, most of our cities would be intact. The president would then have a dreadful choice. Because we would not have enough missiles left to destroy their remaining missiles, we would have to aim our missiles at Soviet cities. But this would do us no good and would in fact only guarantee that the Soviets would use their remaining missiles to attack our cities. In such a situation the president might decide not to retaliate at all.

It is significant that among those who first raised this doubt were leaders who would have had to make the decision, particularly President Nixon and his secretary of defense, James Schlesinger. What bothers the critics of minimum deterrence is that all this reasoning could be done in advance by a Soviet planner who, if willing to take risks, might try a disarming first strike in the belief that the president would not act. It is not the certainty of any such paralysis but the mere possibility that bothers the critics.

Critics of MAD also point out that relying solely on minimum deterrence, especially if the minimum is set low, makes a deterrent vulnerable to sudden upset by a technological breakthrough. The United States, for example, could dismantle part of its strategic forces triad of bombers and land-based missiles and rely exclusively on missile-carrying submarines. With sixteen missiles apiece and ten MIRVed warheads per missile, only three submarines could carry the 400-plus minimum postulated by McNamara in 1968. A sudden breakthrough in anti-submarine warfare, however, could jeopardize the United States deterrent force overnight.

Because the nature of the strategic balance has changed since 1968, when McNamara prepared his table, the objections to mutual assured deterrence are not academic. Increased numbers of Soviet warheads, improved accuracies for them, and continued high yields mean that the Soviet Union has acquired a progressively greater ability to destroy United States weapons. The ability of our deterrent to survive is not as assured as it was in the 1960's. Some of our weapons would undoubtedly survive, but the damage they could inflict in retaliation might fall below the minimum set by McNamara.

DAMAGE LIMITATION

The ultimate argument of the defenders of MAD is implied in the question, "What strategy would you put in its place?" Many critics suggest a doctrine of damage limitation. Such a doctrine would require several new strategic capabilities. One would be active defenses, such as ABM's, which would limit if not totally eliminate damage to our society if deterrence should fail. Active defenses would be supplemented by passive measures, such as blast and fallout shelters, industrial dispersal and hardening, and evacuation plans. Finally, the doctrine calls for offensive weapons with warheads accurate enough so they could be used to destroy enemy weapons without causing heavy casualities to civilians. Then wars could be fought the way wars have been fought in the past, with the main targets being enemy weapons (counterforce targeting), not enemy civilians (countercity or countervalue targeting).[10]

Advocates of damage limitation argue that their proposals would actually strengthen deterrence by making our force seem more credible. No one would seriously believe we would use a handful of missiles to destroy a few Soviet cities if the inevitable consequences would be the total destruction of all major United States cities. With some measures to protect some of our population, as well as the means to eliminate many of the Soviet weapons before they could strike, our retaliatory threat would become at least credible.

Such a capability avoids the problem of the inherent uselessness of minimum deterrence to respond to low levels of provocation. With accurate weapons and civil defense, we would have some hope of keeping a war limited. Thus the range options would be expanded, from the no use/all-out war options of finite deterrence to the no use/limited war/all-out war options. This possibility, even if never exploited, would help prevent a rival from exploiting conventional superiority. The sudden takeover of West Berlin by a tank army would probably go unopposed if the only response available was all-out war. If, however, we had the choice of eliminating some military bases and air fields in European Russia with small, accurate weapons that caused little damage to civilians, we might respond with such limited attacks. More important, the very knowledge that we *might* respond would deter such an attack in the first place.

Advocates of MAD in their turn criticize damage limitation. Their most important point is that the doctrine is unrealistic because damage could never be kept within acceptable limits. Active defenses, critics argue, would never be totally effective. An ABM system would have to work perfectly twenty-four hours a day, every day of the year. Even one ICBM warhead eluding an ABM system would cause unprecedented damage. Similarly critics claim that civil defense would not make much difference. Plans to evacuate cities would cause much greater congestion than American cities now experience on holiday weekends. Such evacuation could not be sustained for any length of time without serious deficiencies in food or dramatic drops in industrial production.[11] Furthermore, critics argue, limited uses of strategic weapons, even if aimed only at other weapons, would still cause very high civilian casualties. When Secretary of Defense James Schlesinger first presented the theory of limited strategic war, he estimated that a Soviet attack on the United States weapons would produce 800,000 casualties. Congress asked the Office of Technology Assessment to check his figures and was given a revised estimate of 18,300,000, a figure that Schlesinger then accepted.[12] With so many casualties, critics argue, a war could not be considered "limited."

One of the major problems with an approach to peace such as the balance of terror is that we can never know whether it is effective. There has been no nuclear war between the major powers over the past thirty-five years. Is that because we deterred each other or because neither side would have gone to war in any case? Even if we assume that deterrence prevented war, what level of force is necessary to maintain that deterrence? The fundamental problem with finite deterrence is that we can never determine what the minimum is, short of going below it and getting into a war.

Other approaches to peace, such as the balance of power and arms races, attempt to deal with the problem of force by using deterrence; unlike them, the balance of terror depends solely on deterrence. If deterrence fails, the approach fails totally. Unlike the balance of power and arms races, the forces acquired for finite deterrence do nothing to limit damage or deny gains to the enemy.

Furthermore, even if the balance of terror works perfectly, it does not eliminate the risk of conflict. It just moves the conflict down to a lower level. Countries stalemated at the nuclear level may feel free to pursue their policies with conventional arms as they did in the past. A country would still need the weapons it had in the past because the threat of total nuclear devastation would not seem credible against small acts of aggression.

A policy of finite deterrence would help reduce some of the costs of an arms race but would not eliminate the hazards. Weapons designed to destroy large numbers of civilians in wartime are just as capable of doing so in peacetime. If the number of such weapons is small, the importance that each weapon survive a disarming first strike is much greater, thereby increasing the state of readiness in which they must be held. But such readiness only increases the likelihood of accident. Even in the relatively calm period from 1945 to 1976 there were at least 125 accidents with nuclear weapons. The United States alone had 27 accidents classified as major in this period — from the loss of nuclear bombs from airplanes to missiles blowing up on launch pads.[13]

NUCLEAR WINTER

A new element in the debate was the gradual recognition of the potentially disastrous effects of nuclear war on climate. This realization came less from a new scientific discovery than a pulling together of existing knowledge.[14] The argument is that the nuclear explosions during a war will set massive fires, in forests and particularly in cities. These fires will produce smoke and soot, which the intense heat will drive up into the stratosphere. Once the soot gets up that high, natural forces such as rain will not quickly drive it down, and we can expect it to stay there, drifting around the earth for a year or more, blotting out the sun. As a result, for months the earth will experience a sudden and profound cooling, with temperatures in summer dropping an average of 25° C (equivalent to a drop from 75° F to 32° F), the normal difference between winter and summer.[15] In other words, even summer will be like winter — a "nuclear winter" — and crops will fail, animals will die, rivers and lakes will freeze. The northern hemisphere, if not the entire planet, will be in danger of returning to prehistoric population levels and economies.

The argument rests on many uncertainties: How much fuel is there to burn in cities? How much soot will it generate? How high will the soot go?

How long will it remain? Differences in assumptions can make big differences in outcomes. Carl Sagan writes of a threshold of between 500 and 2000 explosions that will trigger a nuclear winter.[16] Because of the uncertainties, other scientists resist Sagan's notion and prefer to speak of increased probabilities. But there is consensus that at some level a catastrophe will occur.

For Sagan the implication is that we must reduce total warheads held by all sides to 500, which is his conservative estimate of the threshold number. Each major power, then possessing at most 250 warheads, would have no choice but to follow a strategy of finite deterrence. Even without disarmament down to the levels Sagan suggests, the prospect of a nuclear winter appears to force states to choose finite deterrence; even if all states tried to limit damage to themselves by aiming their weapons only at enemy weapons and avoiding each other's cities, when the threshold number of explosions had occurred, nuclear winter would follow. According to this reasoning, damage limitation is not possible and reliance on the threat of retaliation against cities is the only option.

But the prospect of a nuclear winter does nothing to make the strategy of finite deterrence more credible. Why would a state retaliate at all, especially if a first strike by an enemy had already moved the total number of explosions close to the threshold number? Attacks against cities, as called for by finite deterrence, are the ones that produce the most smoke and soot. Thus any retaliation at all, because it would make climatic catastrophe likely, would be tantamount to suicide. It is no more credible to threaten suicide by climatic catastrophe than by reciprocal destruction of cities.

The possibility of a nuclear winter appears to weaken the case for a damage limitation strategy. But a proponent of that strategy, Albert Wohlstetter, has argued vigorously that the nuclear winter studies are based on implausible assumptions. No country, he argues, would be so stupid as to use the kind of weapons (big and inaccurate) and aim them at the type of targets (cities and industry) that these studies assume.[17] The studies assume that attackers will not even try to reduce unnecessary or collateral damage and thus deal with a case so unlikely as to be almost irrelevant. Wohlstetter tries to show how the prospect of nuclear winter gives support to the strategy of damage limitation. In his view, nuclear winter can and probably will be avoided if nuclear weapons are targeted at limited numbers of military targets (as damage limitation prescribes) and not at cities (as finite deterrence prescribes). Wohlstetter's opponents would not be likely to concede the degree of rationality on the part of leaders and of tight control over the use of nuclear weapons during a war that he postulates. But his argument shows how nuclear winter can be appropriated to support any of several strategies.

STRATEGIC DEFENSE INITIATIVE: A WAY OUT?

In March of 1983 President Reagan proposed what he later came to call the Strategic Defense Initiative (SDI) — that "we embark on a program to counter the awesome Soviet missile threat with measures that are defensive." He was, he said, ordering "a comprehensive and intensive effort to define a long-term research and development program to begin to achieve our ultimate goal of eliminating the threat posed by strategic nuclear missiles."[18] This idea was not new. It had been voiced in the late 1960's in defense of the ABM program. The argument was: As long as we are going to spend such large sums on security, why not spend the money to save more American lives instead of killing more Russians? During that earlier debate, a proponent of the ABM had quoted a statement made in 1967 by Soviet Premier Kosygin: "Maybe an anti-missile system is more expensive than an offensive system, but it is designed not to kill people but to preserve human lives."[19]

Reagan's speech was followed by more detailed administration expositions of high-technology weaponry. Lasers orbiting on satellites would burn holes in enemy missiles during the minutes when they were being launched. Those missiles not destroyed during the boost phase would be attacked by other devices as they traveled through space toward their targets. As the remaining warheads reentered the atmosphere, still other devices would knock them out. Some proposals postulated seven layers in all, creating something like a protective astrodome over the United States. Reagan's political opponents gave it the name "Star Wars."[20]

The consensus in the scientific community was that the technology for such a "leakproof" defense system was not available, and would not be for a long time.[21] Someone commented that President Reagan's asking for space-based lasers was as if President Rutherford B. Hayes had asked for an air force. (Hayes became president in 1877; the Wright brothers first flew in 1903.)

But the ease with which the more extravagant claims for the SDI are refuted should not preclude a careful analysis of more modest ones. Some defensive technology has been developed to the point that it could be deployed — particularly a successor to ABM called LOADS (low-altitude defense system), a missile system that would defend hardened targets such as missile silos. Because missile silos are located away from cities, LOADS could be used at low altitudes without danger to the population from exploding warheads. In fact, the interceptor warheads might employ new technology that would make them so accurate that they would not have to be nuclear. Even if they were, they would explode in the air, not on the ground, and therefore would not generate the large amounts of dust or smoke that would cause significant nuclear fallout or set off a nuclear winter.

LOADS would also meet the criterion that a defense must cost less than efforts by the offense to overcome it; in the case of defense against ballistic missiles, this might take the form of building enough missiles to overwhelm it. If the cost of an additional defensive missile is greater than the cost of an additional offensive missile, we say that the defense suffers from an unfavorable cost-exchange ratio and an enemy of equal financial strength can drive the defender into bankruptcy. Advocates of LOADS argue that although the system is expensive, if it is mobile and if the ICBMs it defends are also mobile, a potential enemy would need to add so many extra missiles that the cost-exchange ratio would favor the defense.[22]

The BMD component might make the SDI attractive to believers in finite deterrence by assuring the survival of the minimum numbers of retaliatory missiles that the strategy requires. Not everyone today believes that such survival is assured. As missiles have become increasingly accurate, they have become more capable of wiping out a rival's missiles in a first strike. Therefore, finite deterrence resting on a limited number of missiles becomes less secure as missiles become more vulnerable. One way to overcome such vulnerability is to launch the missiles on first detection of incoming warheads, so that when the warheads arrive they hit only empty holes in the ground. The possibility of "launch on warning" by mistake — responding not to a real attack but to only a malfunction in the warning system — makes such an option too risky in the minds of most defense analysts.[23]

Another way to overcome vulnerability and preserve the retaliatory capability that finite deterrence requires is to build more missiles, put more warheads on existing missiles, and build new means of launching warheads such as cruise missiles — in other words, to engage in a competition in offensive nuclear arms. The rationale for building more missiles is that then, even if the other side strikes first, some retaliatory weapons survive. But such a response undermines one of the advantages of finite deterrence: that it keeps costs limited. With more weapons in existence the problems of controlling them to prevent unauthorized or accidental launches increase. And an increase in numbers blurs the distinction between merely ensuring a retaliatory capability and preparing to launch a first strike. Thus, according to proponents of the SDI, finite deterrence has not kept nuclear capabilities limited. As long as we continue to build new weapons, they argue, it is preferable to build defensive ones.[24]

Building more and more weapons to guarantee the survival of one's own deterrent makes the other side nervous — after all, these weapons could be used to strike first. Defenders of the SDI argue that a defensive program, by contrast, could not be used in a first strike against the other side. Critics of SDI disagree and point out that in some circumstances defenses might make a first strike more likely. A country with defenses around its cities — a "near-leakproof astrodome" — could try to eliminate most enemy missiles with a first strike and then use its defense system to stop the few remaining missiles fired in retaliation. Supporters of missile defense systems have usually argued that no government would ever think that either its first-strike capability or defensive shield was so good that it would attempt such a risky venture.[25]

Within a short time after President Reagan's speech, the debate on the SDI had assumed the characteristics of a religious controversy. Defenders of the program made claims unsupported by evidence. Opponents refused to see anything of value in any part of the plan whatever. One's position on the issue, indeed one's very choice of a label for it — Star Wars or the SDI — was often a function more of one's political affiliations than of reasoned analysis.

We should pause for a moment to look beyond the immediate issues of how big the budget appropriation for the SDI should be this year or which president proposed it. By the time of Reagan's speech, the intellectual debate between assured destruction and damage limitation had exhausted itself. Neither side could develop a convincing case in favor of its preferred strategy; the strongest arguments were those pointing out the flaws of the opposed strategy. Unilateral nuclear disarmament, an alternative, had few supporters. The proposal to emphasize defensive weapons raised the possibility of a way out.

Opponents of the SDI raise objections that have to be taken seriously. The feasibility of much of the new defensive technology has not been demonstrated yet. Even if practicable, an attempt to create an effective defense system would make no sense if it bankrupted the country it was supposed to defend. If successful, defensive measures could under some circumstances appear to be part of a plan to strike first and thus could cause apprehension on the other side.

But if part of a carefully thought-out plan that included a concurrent reduction in offensive weapons and perhaps a negotiated agreement with the Soviet Union to avoid any obvious unilateral advantage, a move to an emphasis on defense might be feasible. The most likely alternative appears to be perpetuation of the balance of terror, a system in which rival countries hold each other's population hostage decade after decade, provided there is never a technical malfunction or lapse in rationality on the part of their leaders. Even a convincing case that the SDI was fatally flawed would in no way increase the effectiveness of a perpetual balance of terror in preventing war.[26]

NOTES

1. Bertha von Suttner, *Memoirs,* Vol. I (New York: Garland, 1972), p. 437; originally published in 1910.

2. Robert M. Lawrence and Joel Larus, eds., *Nuclear Proliferation: Phase II* (Lawrence, KS.: University Press of Kansas for the National Security Education Program, 1974), p. 49.

3. The size of the Hiroshima explosion is often but incorrectly given as 20 kilotons. See Bernard Brodie, *War and Politics* (New York: Macmillan, 1973), p. 53 fn.

4. P. M. S. Blackett, "Is the Atomic Bomb an Absolute Weapon?" *Scientific American,* Vol. 180, No. 3 (March 1949), p. 15.

5. Samuel Glasstone, ed., *The Effects of Nuclear Weapons,* rev. ed., prepared by United States Department of Defense for the Atomic Energy Commission (Washington, D.C.: U.S. Government Printing Office, 1964).

6. Thomas C. Schelling, *Arms and Influence* (New Haven: Yale University Press, 1966), Chapter 1.

7. Konrad Lorenz, *On Aggression,* trans. Marjorie Kerr Wilson (New York: Bantam Books, 1967), p. 234; Frank Harvey, *Air War — Vietnam* (New York: Bantam Books, 1967), p. 2. The incident of the B-52 pilot was related by a student in a political science class at Western Washington State College in 1969.

8. Norman Cousins, *In Place of Folly* (New York: Harper, 1961), pp. 107–108.

9. McGeorge Bundy, "To Cap the Volcano" *Foreign Affairs,* Vol. 48, No. 1 (October 1969), p. 10.

10. Among advocates of such views are Paul Nitze, "Assuring Strategic Stability in an Era of Détente," *Foreign Affairs,* Vol. 54, No. 2 (January 1976), pp. 207–232; and T. K. Jones and W. Scott Thompson, "Central War and Civil Defense," *Orbis,* Vol. 22, No. 3 (Fall 1978), pp. 681–712.

11. U.S. Congress, Joint Committee on Defense Production, *Civil Preparedness Review,* Part II, 95th Cong., 1st sess., April 1977.

12. Sidney D. Drell and Frank von Hippel, "Limited Nuclear War," *Scientific American,* Vol. 235, No. 5 (November 1976), pp. 27–37.

13. Stockholm International Peace Research Institute, *World Armaments and Disarmament: SIPRI Yearbook, 1977* (Cambridge: MIT Press, 1977), p. 52.

14. R. P. Turco, et al., "Nucler Winter: Global Consequences of Multiple Nuclear Explosions," *Science* (December 23, 1983), pp. 1283–1292.

15. Conway Leovy, "The Effects on the Atmosphere of a Major Nuclear Exchange," paper presented at the 18th meeting of the Pacific Northwest Colloquium on International Security, University of Washington, January 11, 1985.

16. Carl Sagan, "Nuclear War and Climatic Catastrophe," *Foreign Affairs,* Vol. 62, No. 2 (Winter 1983–1984), p. 275.

17. Albert Wohlstetter, "Between a Free World and None," *Foreign Affairs,* Vol. 63, No. 5 (Summer 1985), pp. 962–994.

18. Speech, March 23, 1983, *Vital Speeches,* (April 15, 1983), pp. 389–390.

19. Donald G. Brennan, "The Case for Missile Defense," *Foreign Affairs,* Vol. 47, No. 3 (April 1969), p. 445.

20. A favorable account of such a system is given by Robert Jastrow in *How to Make Nuclear Weapons Obsolete* (Boston: Little, Brown, 1985). A detailed criticism of such a system is given by the Union of Concerned Scientists in *The Fallacy of Star Wars* (New York: Vintage, 1984).

21. Ashton D. Carter, *Directed Energy Missile Defense in Space* (Washington: Office of Technology Assessment, April 1984), p. 81.

22. Ibid.

23. Richard Garwin, "Launch Under Attack to Redress Minuteman Vulnerability?," *International Security,* Vol. 4, No. 3 (Winter 1979–1980), pp. 117–139.

24. Keith B. Payne and Colin S. Gray, "Nuclear Policy and the Defensive Transition," *Foreign Affairs,* Vol. 62, No. 4 (Spring 1984), p. 839.

25. Ibid., p. 827.

26. An early challenge to faith in the durability of deterrence was presented in Fred Charles Iklé, "Can Nuclear Deterrence Last Out the Century?," *Foreign Affairs,* Vol. 51, No. 2 (January 1973), pp. 267–285. The questions he raised have not been answered.

Chapter 14

Arms Control

Any attempt to maintain peace by building weapons, either in a traditional arms race or in an effort to maintain a balance of terror, entails hazards. We could eliminate some of these hazards while leaving intact the basic idea of peace by mutual deterrence if we regulated the acquisition, maintenance, and use of armaments so that the decision to use them stayed under the control of a state's top decision-makers. Such an approach to peace is known as *arms control*. The definition does not specify eliminating weapons or even limiting their numbers. Eliminating a particularly destabilizing type of weapon, of course, could be a form of arms control, but in another situation arms control might call for building more weapons. Later in the chapter, we will explain why this could happen. But first let us define arms control in a different way.

Arms control as an approach to peace was first put forward in the early 1960's with the paradoxical definition that it was a form of military cooperation among enemies or potential enemies.[1] It may seem puzzling to suggest that enemies cooperate militarily but even the bitterest enemies have some interests in common and it is on the basis of these shared interests that cooperation can occur. Consider two belligerent countries, each secretly preparing to wage unremitting war against the other, a hated enemy. No matter how aggressive the leaders of each state are, each wants the war to begin when he or she gives the order and not earlier because of accident or because some low-ranking officer jumps the gun. Even bitter enemies have a common interest in preventing actions that start unintended wars.

Another shared interest is that each of these aggressive leaders wants to protect his or her own population from being destroyed by the state's own weapons — as might be the case if germ warfare were used. And should war actually break out and then start to go badly, each leader would like to be able to signal that he or she was serious about bringing it to an end.

Arms control as conceived in the early 1960's thus focused not on the political causes of conflict but on the potentially harmful consequences of having weapons. This emphasis led to several concrete achievements and made the label "arms control" politically appealing to military leaders because it did not appear to weaken deterrence through strength, and to the general population because it seemed to be doing something about the growing numbers and destructiveness of weapons. As a result of its political utility, the label came to be applied to a wide variety of activities, including some that would in the past have been called "disarmament." Both SALT I and SALT II were essentially quantitative limits on arms and the essence of proposals in START was reductions in arms. In some instances, of course, disarmament can serve the purposes of arms control, but "arms control" was applied to so many proposals more for political expediency than for analytic clarity. We will here limit use of the term to its earlier, more limited meaning.

ACCIDENTAL AND UNAUTHORIZED ATTACKS: THE HOT LINE, RECONNAISSANCE

No one, not even a reckless aggressor, wants an all-out nuclear war to start because of a technical accident. Perhaps a mouse chews the insulation from a wire and the short circuit launches a missile. It's not entirely a science-fiction writer's fantasy. Nikita Khrushchev indicated that a Soviet ICBM was accidentally fired toward Alaska and had to be destroyed. The United States has not revealed whether that stray missile showed up on its warning network, but on one occasion a flock of geese showed up and for a while was interpreted as a Soviet attack.[2]

Another type of unwanted trigger for all-out war is an unauthorized attack by, for example, a mad colonel who steals a plane and a bomb and takes off to start a war all by himself. A third type of trigger is a catalyst, a third country that starts a war between two others without becoming involved itself. In the early 1960's, people used the example of the Chinese, who had an atomic bomb but no modern means of delivery, smuggling the bomb into New York Harbor on a freighter. They would explode it, preferably at a time of tension between the United States and the USSR. The United States would assume that the Russians had begun an attack. We would launch our bombers and missiles against the Russians; the Russians would retaliate with any forces that survived; and China would emerge as the strongest country in the world. No one takes this scenario seriously any longer, but with smaller countries such as India developing nuclear devices, the possibility of catalytic war is still a worry. In time of tension in the Middle East, would we stop to ascertain who was responsible for a nuclear explosion that destroyed one of our aircraft carriers, or would we assume that the Russians were responsible and feel the need to launch an all-out attack before they could destroy more of our forces?

A number of arms control measures are designed to prevent war resulting from accidental or unauthorized or catalytic use of weapons. Some measures improve command and control systems. An electronic lock, called the permissive action link (PAL), makes it impossible for one person acting alone to prepare a nuclear device for detonation. The United States developed the system after one of our bombers accidentally crashed in South Carolina in 1961 while carrying thermonuclear bombs and five of the six switches on the system we were using at that time were activated by the crash. We felt our system needed improvement. We found that the Russian system apparently had more problems than ours. The Russians couldn't trust themselves enough to put their missiles on full alert during the Cuban missile crisis in 1962. We passed on to them information on how to protect their weapons from unauthorized use.[3] You could call this giving the Russians our secrets — military cooperation with our potential opponents — but it is in our interest to avoid wars started by mad Russian colonels or by mad American colonels.

Avoiding accidents is important, but it is not the accident itself so much as the reaction to it that could set off a full-scale nuclear war. One way of keeping the leaders in each country from pushing the panic button is to eliminate the kinds of weapons that might make them panicky. Liquid-fueled missiles, sitting unprotected on the surface of the earth, are that kind of weapon. The Russians put such a missile, a type we called SS-4, into Cuba in 1962. Because a missile such as this would have been so easy to destroy if the United States struck first, American planners assumed the Russians, if they were rational, could use them only if *they* fired first. Knowing how vulnerable the missiles were, the Russians would have been tempted to fire them immediately if they had even suspected we were getting ready to strike at them. Fortunately the crisis was resolved before either side acted in accord with this complicated logic. Vulnerable missiles such as the SS-4 have now been replaced by storable-liquid or solid-fueled missiles protected in concrete silos underground. These newer missiles are more expensive, and both sides have many more of them, but we feel more secure now (especially now that *both* sides have them) than we did in the early 1960's.

But types of weapons continue to be a problem in the debate on the anti-ballistic missile. If an ABM system really works, and a nation's population is entirely protected, then that nation could start a war and wipe out its opponents without risking its own population. The possibility that this might happen is small, but the destruction such a war would cause is so great we must at least think about that possibility. Arms control advocates argue that any weapon that makes it rational to strike first in war is bad. The ABM is such a weapon; therefore, they argue, we should severely restrict it. And that is what the first major treaty resulting from the Strategic Arms Limitation Talks (SALT) did. The ABM Treaty of May 1972 limits each country to two missile sites with only 100 missiles for each site, not enough to provide a meaningful defense for a country's population.[4]

Another way of keeping leaders from starting wars as the result of accidents or unauthorized attacks is to increase the amount of information available to them when they make their decisions. An example of this technique is found in a story from World War II. Neither the Germans nor the Americans wanted to use poison gas, but each produced a stockpile of poison gas to have ready for retaliation in case the other side used it first. During the Allied invasion of Italy at Anzio, a German shell hit an American ammunition dump that had some of these poison gas shells stockpiled for retaliatory use. The gas that was released began drifting toward German lines. The American commander made a great effort to get a warning to his German opponent that poison gas was coming his way, that the German troops should take precautions, and that it certainly was not a deliberate attack. His efforts were successful, and the accident at Anzio did not lead to all-out use of poison gas in World War II.[5]

Today the best-known technique for increasing information available to the Russian and American leaders is the Hot Line. "Hot" means that the line is always open. The Hot Line is not a telephone (American presidents have not as a rule been fluent in Russian, or vice versa) but a set of Teletype machines, one printing in the Cyrillic alphabet, one in the Latin alphabet. Originally connected by land and sea cable, they now are linked by communications satellites, which are more secure and less subject to disruption. (On one occasion a Finnish farmer is said to have cut the Hot Line cable beneath his field as he was plowing.)[6]

The Hot Line was established by an agreement signed in June 1963, six months after the Cuban missile crisis had revealed how unsatisfactory traditional diplomatic means of sending notes were. Messages from foreign office to ambassador to foreign office were taking more than six hours in an era when missiles could cover the same distance in forty minutes. Since its installation, the Hot Line has been used a number of times. Its most significant use as an arms control measure was during the 1967 war in the Middle East.

On the third day of that war, an Israeli torpedo boat tore a large hole in an American intelligence-gathering ship, the *Liberty*. A message to the *Liberty* from the Pentagon to pull back from the coast of Israel had been misrouted and ended up in the Philippines. Both the Israelis and the United States Navy assumed the ship had withdrawn. The attack was a surprise to both. The United States, upon learning that an American ship had been attacked, wanted to send a task force to investigate. But, conscious that the Russians were closely shadowing the movements of the American fleet, particularly after Egyptian charges of United States assistance to the Israelis, we first signaled the Russians by the Hot Line that our ships would be moving close to the area where the war was being waged and that the purpose of this move was to rescue one of our ships that had been attacked.[7]

In September 1971, the United States and the Soviet Union signed an Agreement on Nuclear Accidents, which strengthens the Hot Line by obligating each country to use it in the event of accidents or the discovery of unidentified objects on early warning systems. It also obligates each country to give advance notice to the other of missile tests that will extend beyond its own territory in the direction of the other.[8]

The Hot Line is not foolproof. There is no guarantee that what is coming over the Hot Line is true. Certainly any plans for a first strike would include use of the Hot Line to lull the other side into believing it was only a test of a salvo of missiles. But it is important that the other side learn about an accident as quickly as possible, and learn about it from the side that is responsible. A warning that might enable defensive measures to be taken will help allay suspicions.

Another technique that can increase information available to the decision-maker is espionage. Espionage is information-gathering that the other side objects to. When it occurs (or, more precisely, when it is discovered), it usually increases tension. In 1960, a high-flying American spy plane, the U-2, was shot down over the Soviet Union just as a summit conference in Paris was about to begin. The Russians used the incident as a reason for canceling the summit. However, a good case can be made *for* such information gathering.

During the 1950's, the United States strategic force consisted of the bombers of the Strategic Air Command. Bombers are comparatively fragile. Fighter aircraft can shoot them down with machine guns. The vast increase of explosive power in nuclear weapons meant that even warheads striking at some distance from an airfield could put the bombers stationed there out of commission. In the late 1950's the USSR began developing an ICBM. American planners began to worry that, if the Russians built enough of them, a surprise attack might eliminate most of our bombers. The problem was that we didn't know how many of the ICBM's the USSR had deployed, and we had no way of finding out. We did know that they had tested them. In

October 1957 they used one of these rockets to launch the first artificial earth satellite, the Sputnik. Khrushchev boasted that Russian factories were turning out rockets on assembly lines.

The United States had developed an airplane, the U-2, which could fly over the Soviet Union at an altitude of 14 miles and take photographs that could be studied for signs of missile deployment. These flights were violations of the Soviets' sovereignty, and they protested, though privately, because they didn't want to publicize the fact that they couldn't stop the flights. But even though the United States was willing to risk running these flights, the intelligence they gathered wasn't very satisfactory. The U-2 had to be launched from countries near the USSR, such as Pakistan and Norway, and these countries were apprehensive about Soviet reaction if something should go wrong. The flights therefore could not be frequent.

Only thirty were made, and as each covered only a small portion of European USSR, we never could be sure if we had spotted all the Soviet ICBM's.[9] The result was that the military services took a prudent approach and estimated that the Russians had a large number of missiles, enough to cause a missile gap between their strength and ours. The services urged the United States to build missiles that would be less vulnerable than bombers to a Russian surprise attack. The extent of the missile gap became a foreign policy issue in the 1960 presidential election, and the Kennedy Administration, immediately upon taking office, speeded up the production of United States missiles.[10]

Then the United States began using a new means of ascertaining Soviet capabilities: reconnaissance or spy satellites. These have many advantages over the U-2. They can be launched from the United States, eliminating dependence on allies. In the first decades of their use, they traveled too high above the earth to be shot down, and because they travel far above the atmosphere they do not violate the air space of other countries. They make repeated orbits, as many as one every ninety minutes, and thus have an improved chance of finding clear weather over their targets. Those in operation in the 1980's are technological monsters, as long as a six-story building and capable of staying aloft two years or more. They are coordinated with weather observation satellites, which tell them when to photograph. They can change their altitudes and orbits to get the best pictures and use a variety of films to produce stereo or multispectral photographs. Photo interpreters claim a satellite once photographed a man on a street in a northern Russian town reading *Pravda*; they knew it was *Pravda* because they could read the name on the masthead.[11]

The first United States reconnaissance satellite was launched at the very end of 1960. In the early 1960's, for lack of information, the United States needlessly accelerated the arms race by building many missiles to catch up with a Soviet force that did not exist. It was an honest mistake, but it was a mistake nevertheless. When the Russians did begin building large numbers of missiles, they could claim that *they* were trying to close the missile gap. By the early 1970's, when the spy satellites were supplying us with detailed information (reportedly they could pick out objects less than 12 inches wide), we were totally confident about entering into arms limitation agreements with the USSR — not only because we knew how many missiles they had but also because we were sure we would know if they cheated.[12]

Photographic reconnaissance by satellites is no longer considered espionage (even though the information they acquire is much better than that collected by the U-2 flights), for now we have the Soviets' agreement on it. A provision included in both SALT I and SALT II (including the fully ratified ABM Treaty of 1972) states that each party shall use "national technical means of verification." That phrase is understood to include, among other methods, photographic or imagery satellites.

EXCESSIVE COLLATERAL DAMAGE AND THRESHOLDS

So far we have been talking about military cooperation between potential opponents for just one purpose: to prevent all-out war from beginning in specified ways. But arms control can extend *into* a war, even if one should break out. A shared interest among opponents (not just potential opponents but those actually fighting each other) is to make the fighting less unpleasant. One way is to eliminate weapons that may cause excessive collateral damage, that is, harm to bystanders or the environment that serves no military purpose. Biological agents would be of this type — for example, bacteria that cause diseases such as the plague or anthrax. They would affect not only enemy troops but civilians, perhaps one's own troops and perhaps even people in the home territory of the country that first used them. Chemical agents such as poison gas and herbicides also cause excessive collateral damage.[13]

Weapons such as these present a problem. Most experts agree that all-out use of the most deadly of them would serve no useful military purpose. But the limited use of some of them, such as tear gas, might be very useful in some circumstances. If a guerrilla band used a group of women and children as a defensive shield behind which they launched an attack, who would not agree that it would be better to use tear gas than machine-gun fire?

Still, arms control advocates argue against *any* use of gas, even non-lethal gas. They call their argument "maintaining the threshold."[14] A *threshold* is a clear dividing line between one weapon and another, or between one way of using weapons and another. Gas is very different from high explosives, and thus there is a clear threshold between them. A .38-caliber bullet is not very different from a .45-caliber bullet, and thus no threshold separates them. A threshold helps prevent violence from escalating by accident. In the confusion of combat, an attack with nonlethal gas might be mistaken for an attack by lethal gas. If many of the troops being gassed were already suffering from respiratory infection, the attack might result in many fatalities. The commander of the troops who were gassed might then order what he thought was retaliation, but with lethal gas. "No gas" is unambiguously distinct from "gas"; "a little nonlethal gas" is not so unambiguously distinct from "a lot of nonlethal gas" or "a little lethal gas."

For this reason, stockpiling poison gas in ammunition dumps near the battlefield, as the Americans did at Anzio, was very risky. The German policy during World War II, by contrast, is an example of arms control: "The transport of German gases or any chemical warfare agent or spraying containers filled with agents, gas candles or gas munitions or airplane gas bombs to any points beyond the borders of the German Reich, or their storage at any such point . . . was strictly prohibited."[15]

A case in which the United States did take a step that could be described as maintaining a threshold was the announcement in May 1974 that the United States would unilaterally renounce the development of miniaturized nuclear weapons — those with an explosive power of less than 1 kiloton, which could be used interchangeably with conventional weapons on the battlefield for tactical operations such as knocking out tanks.[16] By denying ourselves even the possibility of using nuclear weapons in tactical operations, we keep the decision to use them (if we ever do use nuclear weapons) more firmly in the hands of the top leaders.

Another form of nuclear weapons poses much more difficult problems for arms control. This is the enhanced-radiation warhead, also called the neutron bomb. Most of the destructive power of such a weapon is in the form of prompt radiation — radiation from fast-moving neutrons that quickly lose their force — as opposed to either explosive power or lingering radiation in the form of fallout. Because the prompt radiation would be directed mainly at enemy soldiers, it would not cause excessive collateral damage to nearby civilian structures (or to distant civilian targets in the form of fallout), and thus it fulfills one of the aims of arms control. On the other hand, precisely because of this effect it would tempt political and military leaders to use it, and thus it lowers the nuclear threshold. A leader who might be terrified of unleashing a cataclysmic war with blast and fallout threatening the entire world might employ an enhanced-radiation weapon, thereby taking the first step up the so-called escalation ladder. Thus although the weapon might be desirable according to one line of reasoning, it is undesirable from another.[17]

WAR TERMINATION AND COST REDUCTION

Arms control, besides preventing wars from starting and controlling the violence if they do, can serve a third purpose. It can make ending wars easier. Wars are not always easy to end. The side that wishes to de-escalate a conflict or withdraw at least partially may find that this action only encourages the other side to press harder and perhaps to increase its demands. In international politics there was an example during the Korean War. The original, stated purpose of the United States was to restore the territorial integrity of South Korea, but after the startling success of the amphibious landing at Inchon and the retreat of the North Korean troops, we changed our policy to reunification of the entire Korean peninsula.

One arms control measure that might facilitate war termination is to help the enemy retain its command and control structure. The United States did not eliminate the Japanese emperor at the close of World War II, and the emperor was able to call on Japanese soldiers to surrender. If he had not been there to do so, Japanese survivors in jungles around the Pacific would not have been just an occasional news curiosity but a major security problem.[18] More recently, the ABM Treaty of May 1972 states that one of the two ABM sites that is permitted should be around the "National Command Authority," that is, the capital. Even without this treaty provision, one can doubt the wisdom of trying to destroy the Kremlin or the Pentagon as part of the first blow in a war. After the Germans destroyed the French government with their stunning military victory in the Franco–Prussian War of 1870, they had to spend six months looking around for someone who could surrender (see Chapter 1).

Finally, we come to a purpose that people often advance for arms control: to reduce the costs of the arms race. Sometimes this happens. The ABM Treaty saved the United States what the government very conservatively estimated to be $40 billion. But saving money is more often an accidental than an intentional result of arms control. In some cases it may not be an area in which interests overlap. A very rich country competing against a poor country has no interest in reducing costs because the ability to meet these costs is one of its advantages.

In other cases, an arms control measure might actually increase costs. One of the proposals discussed in the early 1980's was a new, small ICBM with a single warhead, referred to as "Midgetman." Unlike the latest version of the Minuteman with three MIRV's or its proposed successor MX with as many as ten MIRV's, Midgetman would reduce the advantages of going first and thus make a preemptive strike less likely. A program to install large numbers of Midgetmen would be expensive, yet contribute to arms control.

DIFFICULTIES WITH ARMS CONTROL

Advocates of arms control do not claim that it can prevent all wars, and we cannot fairly criticize the approach for something that was never claimed. Still, we should realize that arms control cannot prevent a war that results from a rational calculation. In December 1971, India went to war according to a carefully prepared plan in order to accomplish specific foreign policy objectives, most important of which was the return to Pakistan of millions of Bengali refugees who were straining the Indian economy. It is hard to think of an arms control measure that could have prevented the India–Pakistan War of 1971.[19]

A more serious criticism is that arms control may not even be able to achieve the limited objectives it does have. The basic and mutual distrust that characterizes all states in the international condition of anarchy and makes complete disarmament seem impossible affects even the comparatively modest measures of arms control (see Chapter 7). Herman Kahn offers a vivid parable.[20] Suppose, he writes, two men are fighting a duel to the death with blowtorches, and they are fighting inside a dynamite factory. Then surely an arms control measure would be having the lights on. But, Kahn continues, it is not at all clear that this could be negotiated. Each would distrust the other. "Exactly which lights are to be left on?" "Does the other guy have sunglasses that will give him a temporary advantage the instant the lights go on?" And so an eminently rational agreement might never be reached.

One might think that the 1968 treaty prohibiting the spread of nuclear weapons was eminently rational. Yet France and China have refused to sign it, and perhaps in response India, among others, has also refused.[21]

One of the premises of arms control, as we have seen, is that increasing the information available to decision-makers often provides more stability and less uncontrolled outbreak of war. But more knowledge is not always better. During World War II the Germans achieved a technological breakthrough and acquired a weapon no one else had. That weapon was a gas that could attack the body anywhere through the skin and paralyze the nervous system. Because no one else had it, no one had a defense against it. But the Germans never used their nerve gas, because they did not know they were the only ones who had it. The disarmament provisions of the Versailles Treaty had delayed their research for ten years, and they assumed that countries such as the United States had nerve gas and even more deadly types.[22] Not knowledge, but ignorance restricted the violence in this case.

A reconnaissance satellite puts to rest doubts about missile gaps and helps prevent overreaction to ill-defined threats. But those same satellites also provide excellent information for targeting. The same satellites that told us the Soviets were far behind us in numbers of ICBM's deployed also told us exactly where those few ICBM's were. Perhaps that is what scared the Russians into trying to put their SS-4's into Cuba in the fall of 1962 in an effort to close their own missile gap.[23]

Advocates of arms control tell us not to count on saving money.[24] Nevertheless, saving money is often advanced as a reason for arms control. We might look at the cost of one small item: The electronic locks of a permissive action link for one nuclear warhead cost about $50,000.[25] Assuming that each of our 6,000 nuclear warheads in Europe is so protected, we are spending $300 million just to control one part of one system in our arsenal.[26]

A FAREWELL TO ARMS CONTROL? SALT II

Theoretical problems with arms control have been reinforced by recent historical experience suggesting practical difficulties as well. During the 1960's and early 1970's newly articulated concepts were applied to contemporary problems, and arms control agreements blossomed — the Hot Line (1963), the Non-Proliferation Treaty (1968), the ABM Treaty (1972), and several others. But the promise of the Interim Agreement that accompanied the ABM Treaty has not been fulfilled. Since then the agreements that have been reached are minor — agreements on biological weapons, the seabed, accidents at sea. Others that were negotiated were not passed on for ratification — a treaty limiting underground nuclear tests to under 150 kilotons, a treaty regulating peaceful nuclear explosions. In other cases, negotiations did not produce results — talks on mutual and balanced forced reductions in Europe, limitations on great power activity in the Indian Ocean, restrictions on weapons designed to shoot down reconnaissance satellites.

The SALT II Treaty, signed in 1979, made clear the impasse that arms control had reached. In the late 1970's the major defense issue confronting the United States was the coming vulnerability of its land-based ICBM force to Soviet counterforce weapons. The problem was created by the Soviet shift to MIRVed warheads, a technology not limited by SALT I. The MIRV is a weapon that aggravates arms races because it is inherently destabilizing. One country's MIRVed ICBM's present few targets to the enemy, yet provide many weapons with which to hit the enemy's ICBM's. To illustrate, ten ICBM's with eight MIRV's on each present only ten targets if the other side strikes first, yet they provide eighty chances to wipe out enemy ICBM's if your side fires first. Thus the MIRV violates a basic tenet of arms control by making it rational to think about striking first.

Many experts, including Henry Kissinger, think that the failure to control MIRV technology was the biggest weakness of SALT I. SALT II likewise fails to put any meaningful limit on the deployment of MIRV's. The large numbers of launchers permitted the Soviets (820), plus the average number of MIRV's per launcher (around seven), plus the explosive power of each MIRV (over 500 kilotons), have produced general agreement among United States officials that when the Soviet Union reaches the limits permitted by SALT II it could eliminate all but a few United States land-based missiles if it chose to strike first.[27] There is no reason to think the Soviet leaders would make that choice, but that is not the point. The point is that SALT II did not increase stability by eliminating a weapon that would make it rational under some circumstances to think about striking first.

Because of these weaknesses in the SALT II treaty, the United States Senate was reluctant to give its approval for ratification. Following the Soviet invasion of Afghanistan in 1979, President Carter withdrew the treaty, in effect giving up on ratification. The Soviet Union, which had been waiting for United States ratification, did not ratify SALT II either, although both countries promised to act as if it were in force. But by the mid-1980's both sides were funding weapons programs that at least came close to violating the provisions of the 1979 SALT II treaty.

SALT II failed in large part because of a fundamental flaw present from the beginning of the arms limitation talks. The Soviets and the Americans operated according to different strategic doctrines. At the heart of the American doctrine (at least the one accepted by most arms controllers) was some variant of finite deterrence — that after a certain number of weapons have been built, more are useless. The view was expressed by Henry Kissinger in his explosive response to a critical question: "What in the name of God is strategic superiority? What is the significance of it, politically, militarily, operationally, at these levels of numbers? What do you do with it?"[28] The Soviet Union, on the other hand, continued to increase its force of big, accurate, multiple-warhead missiles, to a level far in excess of even the most extravagant definition of finite deterrence. The size of the Soviet force made sense only if the Soviet Union intended to make a first strike against American missiles, not if they wanted only the ability to make a retaliatory strike against American cities. And Soviet leaders said as much — that their missiles were "designed to annihilate the means of the enemy's nuclear attack,"[29] a purpose that can be accomplished only by going first. Thus SALT II could not reduce the threat of Soviet weapons to the United States retaliatory capability, because such a threat was central to Soviet strategy.

SALT II failed in addition because opponents of the agreement convinced many people that the Soviets were taking actions to make monitoring of any agreement very difficult. It was widely publicized that the Soviets had developed weapons capable of shooting down or blinding satellites; according to some accounts, the Russians had actually tested such weapons on American satellites.[30] Efforts to negotiate a prohibition on such weapons were unsuccessful. In addition to satellites, the United States was using electronic monitoring stations to observe Soviet weapons tests. After signing the treaty in 1979, the Soviets began to conceal or "encrypt" the electronic information broadcast from sensors on their rockets during such tests. Many Americans thought such encryption went beyond the limited degree of concealment that the treaty permitted.[31]

But more important difficulties with verification arose not from Soviet behavior but from changes in military technology. The basic weapons systems of the 1960's — the land-based ICBM's — were easy to detect. They reposed in large, concrete-lined holes in the ground (silos) that took two or three years to build. The construction process was difficult to conceal and, once the silos were constructed, they could not be moved. Each silo could be used only once, so one silo was the equivalent of one missile. Weapons coming into use today do not lend themselves so easily to surveillance. Some ICBM's are mobile. Some can be fired such that they do not destroy the silo, thus making possible reloading — so one silo no longer equals one missile.

Entirely new types of weapons have been introduced. One weapon that attracted a lot of attention in the 1970's was the cruise missile, which is essentially a pilotless airplane. Like an airplane, it is continuously powered. It is supported by wings and therefore flies relatively slowly and well within the earth's atmosphere. Because of new types of fuel and engines, its range is potentially intercontinental. Because of modern, high-technology sensors and computers, it can correct deviations from course in midflight, even without a pilot, and can hit its target with extreme accuracy — perhaps to within 10 feet. With such accuracy, it can theoretically destroy many targets with conventional (that is, TNT) explosives and does not necessarily need a nuclear warhead.[32]

The cruise missile troubles arms control negotiators; it is hard to decide whether it is a stabilizing or destabilizing weapon. One problem is that the same missile can be made to fly anywhere from a few hundred miles to intercontinental range, making it useful as either a battlefield weapon or a strategic one. Furthermore, it is impossible to tell from observing its external configuration or even tests what its range is. So a rival country must assume that all enemy cruise missiles could threaten its homeland, even though some in fact might be designated for battlefield use. This "dual use" feature makes the cruise missile quite unlike an ICBM, which can have only the purpose of threatening the other's homeland.

Another problem is that cruise missiles would be easy to hide, and so verification of numbers would be impossible. Unlike ICBM's in fixed launchers (or even the relatively large mobile ICBM's), cruise missiles could be kept in sheds, under railroad cars, even in college dormitories — any place big enough to conceal a weapon 2 feet in diameter and only about 20 feet long.

Moreover, because they do not require any special launching facilities, cruise missiles could be fired almost as soon as they were taken from their hiding places.

On the other hand, cruise missiles have some stabilizing features. The fact that they are so easily concealed means they would not tempt the other side to strike first — without knowledge of the location of the targets, such a strike would be futile. Cruise missiles travel much more slowly than ICBM's do; to attain intercontinental range, they would have to fly under the speed of sound. This is another obstacle to using them for a first strike. They would provide hours of warning time and, to do any good, would be launched in such numbers that the warning would be unambiguous. Because they are so accurate, they would cause very little collateral damage; if armed with TNT, they would not even cause fallout, thus fulfilling another objective of arms control. And because they are relatively inexpensive they would meet the objective of saving money.[33]

The cruise missile illustrates how developing technology upsets old solutions and creates new problems for approaches to peace — in this case, for arms control. Even without these new complicating factors, arms control does not solve the basic problem raised by armaments. States still have weapons, even if they are controlled, and if states have them, they can use them. As one critic says, arms control is to the power market what antitrust legislation is to the economic market; it does not affect the basic nature of the system, it just makes the system work more smoothly.[34] In fact, it may increase the probability of war by lulling us into a false sense of security. If we believe that our arms are safely controlled, we may slacken our efforts to work for disarmament or for whatever other solution will bring an end to the problem of war.

NOTES

1. This definition comes from an important early work on the subject, Thomas C. Schelling and Morton Halperin, *Strategy and Arms Control* (New York: Twentieth Century Fund, 1961), p. 2.

2. For some of these accidents, see Edward Klein and Robert Littell, "Shh! Let's Tell the Russians," *Newsweek*, May 5, 1969, pp. 46–47. Geese on the radar screen are mentioned by Oskar Morgenstern, *The Question of National Defense* (New York: Random House, 1959), p. 65.

3. See Klein and Littell; and, Lewis A. Dunn, *Controlling the Bomb* (New Haven: Yale University Press, 1982), pp. 22–23, 184 n. 45.

4. The treaty was amended by a protocol signed in Moscow in 1974 limiting the number of sites in each country to one with one hundred missiles. A good source for the texts of treaties is *Keesing's Contemporary Archives*, published in London every two weeks.

5. The incident is reported by Lord Ritchie-Calder in the Introduction to Steven Rose, ed., *CBW: Chemical and Biological Warfare* (Boston: Beacon Press, 1968). No mention of it is made, however, in the official United States Army history of Anzio, Martin Blumensen, *The*

United States Army in World War II: Salerno to Cassino (Washington, D.C.: Office of the Chief of Military History, 1969).

6. *The New York Times,* July 21, 1968; see also Richard Hudson, "Molink Is Always Ready," *The New York Times Magazine,* August 26, 1973.

7. Lyndon Johnson recounts this event in his memoirs, *The Vantage Point* (New York: Holt, Rinehart and Winston, 1971), p. 301.

8. *The New York Times,* October 1, 1971.

9. Charles J. V. Murphy, "Khrushchev's Paper Bear," *Fortune,* Vol. 70, No. 6 (December 1964), pp. 114, 224–230.

10. For an account of the missile gap, see George H. Quester, *Nuclear Diplomacy* (New York: Dunellen, 1970), Chapter 4.

11. Jeffrey Richelson, *The U.S. Intelligence Community* (Cambridge: Ballinger, 1985), pp. 114–115; Drew Middleton, "Satellites Main Source of Photo Data for U.S.," *The New York Times,* September 11, 1983, p. Y6.

12. For a fascinating description of satellites, see Ted Greenwood, "Reconnaissance and Arms Control," *Scientific American,* Vol. 228, No. 2 (February 1973), pp. 14–25.

13. For a description of some of these agents, see Seymour Hersh, *Chemical and Biological Warfare* (Indianapolis: Bobbs-Merrill, 1968).

14. A good statement of this argument is in Thomas Schelling, "Bargaining, Communication and Limited War," *The Journal of Conflict Resolution,* Vol. 1, No. 1 (March 1957), pp. 19–36.

15. Frederic J. Brown, *Chemical Warfare* (Princeton: Princeton University Press, 1968), p. 244 n.

16. *The New York Times,* May 24, 1974.

17. Fred M. Kaplan, "Enhanced-Radiation Weapons," *Scientific American,* Vol. 238, No. 5 (May 1978), pp. 44–51.

18. Actually, this reason was not a major factor considered by American decision-makers. See Herbert Feis, *The Atomic Bomb and the End of World War II* (Princeton: Princeton University Press, 1966).

19. For an account of this war, see International Institute of Strategic Studies, *Strategic Survey, 1971* (London, 1972).

20. Herman Kahn, *On Escalation,* rev. ed. (Baltimore: Penguin Books, 1968), p. 16 n.

21. On the Non-Proliferation Treaty, see Michael J. Sullivan, "Indian Attitudes on International Atomic Energy Controls," *Pacific Affairs,* Vol. 43, No. 3 (Fall 1970), pp. 353–369.

22. Brown, pp. 232–233.

23. For an argument along this line, see J. David Singer, "Disarmament: The Domestic and Global Context," in *The New Era in American Foreign Policy,* ed. John H. Gilbert (New York: St. Martin's Press, 1973).

24. Thomas C. Schelling, "Arms Control Will Not Cut Defense Costs," *Harvard Business Review* (March–April 1961).

25. Thomas B. Cochran et al., *Nuclear Weapons Databook* (Cambridge: Ballinger, 1984), Vol. 1, p. 30.

26. In 1983 the Defense Department told Congress in a secret report (leaked to the press) that it had 5,845 nuclear warheads in Europe. See Richard Halloran, "Report to Congress Provides Figures for Nuclear Arsenal," *The New York Times,* November 15, 1983, p. Y7.

27. Colin S. Gray, "The Strategic Forces Triad," *Foreign Affairs,* Vol. 56, No. 4 (July 1978), pp. 771–789.

28. Press Conference of July 3, 1974, cited by Lawrence Freedom, *The Evolution of Nuclear Strategy* (New York: St. Martin's Press, 1981), p. 363.

29. A. A. Grechko, *On Guard for Peace and the Building of Communism* (Moscow 1971), p. 41, cited by Freeman Dyson, *Weapons and Hope* (New York: Harper & Row, 1984), p. 230.

30. "War's Fourth Dimension," *Newsweek,* November 29, 1976, pp. 46–48.

31. For a discussion of encryption, see Strobe Talbot, *Endgame* (New York: Harper & Row, 1979), Chapter 11.

32. Kosta Tsipis, "Cruise Missiles," *Scientific American*, Vol. 236, No. 2 (February 1977), pp. 20–29.

33. Thomas Schelling, "What Went Wrong with Arms Control?" *Foreign Affairs*, Vol. 64, No. 2 (Winter 1985–1986), pp. 228–229.

34. From a paper by Johan Galtung delivered at the National Meeting of the International Studies Association, March 1972, quoted by Walter C. Clemens, *The Superpowers and Arms Control* (Lexington, MA: Lexington Books, 1973), p. 163.

Chapter 15

Disarmament

What seems to be one of the simplest proposals for preventing war turns out on closer examination to be one of the most complex. Defining *disarmament* is not hard; it means the reduction or elimination of weapons. As a means of preventing war it is logically unassailable. Without the means to fight, you cannot have a war, any more than you can have highway accidents without vehicles. The problem comes when you try to describe precisely what weapons you want states to eliminate.

WAYS TO DISARM

Suppose that governments say they are willing to disarm. What should we recommend? There are at least seven distinct possibilities.

1. Total Disarmament. This would mean the elimination of all weapons (a "weapon" being defined as any device that could be used to kill or injure). A critic could argue that because you can strangle someone with a shoelace, shoelaces must be prohibited. Such a criticism is a frivolous version of a much more serious objection, that many devices common in modern industrial societies can be used as weapons. Dynamite, for example, has many commercial uses — in logging, mining, and construction. But chemically it is the same substance that is packed into bombs and artillery shells. Com-

mercial jetliners are widely used to transport people, messages, and goods. But if you load a Boeing 727 with a coal mine's supply of dynamite, you have a bomber more potent than any used in World War II. Total disarmament would mean the elimination of these and many other components of modern industrial life, in effect forcing all humanity into a primitive and frugal existence.

Even if we got rid of all weapons and all potential weapons, we could not do away with the knowledge of how to build them. Even if we could get rid of nuclear weapons, we would have to perform lobotomies on all people with advanced degrees in physics to be sure that in times of international crisis someone would not start up their production. The study of physics, engineering, and any other science would have to be strictly prohibited.

Of course we would find no support for any proposal that would lead to the eradication of the pursuit of knowledge or of modern industrial technology built on this knowledge. We would probably not even find support for the elimination of hunting rifles. And with firearms still in private possession there would be a demand for equipping law enforcement officers with firearms as well.

2. Disarmament to the Lowest Point Consistent with Domestic Safety. No government leader has ever advocated disarmament that eliminated even the domestic police force. The most radical proposal seriously advanced was Point Four of Woodrow Wilson's Fourteen Points, "that national armaments will be reduced to the lowest point consistent with domestic safety." But even this proposal was too radical for states to consider. One reason is the great disparity in size among states. A minimal police force for a large state such as Germany could threaten the security of one of its tiny neighbors such as Luxembourg and would probably make its more sizable neighbor Belgium nervous. Another reason is that states have widely varied opinions about how much domestic safety they need. England in the last century and a half has had a tradition of police armed with no more than a nightstick. France, by contrast, has had a paramilitary force, the Republican Security Companies, living in barracks, equipped with armored vehicles, and carrying firearms including light machine guns. The French government maintains its Republican Security Companies as a riot control force, but in a totally disarmed world they would serve as an effective invading army against an England defended only by London bobbies and village constables.

3. Disarmament to the Lowest Point Consistent with National Safety. President Wilson's Point Four was reworded at the Versailles Conference, so that Article 8 of the Versailles Treaty read, "The maintenance of peace requires the reduction of national armaments to the lowest point consistent with national safety." By changing "domestic safety" to "national safety," a much wider latitude was permitted to states. Regular armies would be allowed,

although only for self-defense. This goal has two problems, an old one and a new one. The old one is the question of how much of a force is needed for legitimate self-defense. Almost any force could be justified by that language. Do we set a basic number of 100,000 troops for each country? By those standards Luxembourg would be armed to the teeth. Do some states get larger forces because of special problems such as terrain? Poland, being flat, would need more than Switzerland with its mountains. But don't we then have to account for intentions? In recent European history the Swiss have seemed more trustworthy than the Poles.

As if these old problems weren't staggering enough, we have new ones related to modern weapons. Nuclear weapons delivered by planes and missiles cannot be categorized as either offensive or defensive. We have had to develop the entirely new category of "deterrent." But an intercontinental missile with a nuclear warhead could be used in a disarming first strike as well. *How* the weapon will be used depends entirely on the intentions of a state's leaders, and those intentions could change from one minute to the next. The bare minimum needed to retaliate in a second strike could also be all that is needed to launch a crippling first strike.

4. Qualitative Disarmament. Because of difficulties with the general concept of national defense, proponents of disarmament have often turned to more technical discussions of types of weapons. They try to identify some weapons as offensive and eliminate them. This was attempted at the unsuccessful Geneva Disarmament Conference of 1932, which found it impossible to separate offensive from defensive weapons because modern weapons can be used for both offense and defense. Recently the United States tried to make the same distinction and failed. When the United States occupation of South Korea ended in 1949, the United States took along with its withdrawing forces its tanks and airplanes, to keep South Korea from mounting an offensive against the North. But, as the South Koreans discovered in June 1950, without tanks and airplanes a country cannot conduct a successful defense either. Even something so obviously defensive as fortification (which cannot be moved into an enemy's country) can be part of an overall offensive plan. In 1939, Germany built a defensive line along its border with France to keep France from coming to the aid of its East European allies when Germany attacked them.

The most promising area for qualitative disarmament is obnoxious weapons. The only true disarmament agreement (that is, one calling for the actual destruction of weapons) that has been reached since World War II has been the 1972 treaty outlawing biological weapons. By this treaty countries have agreed not only not to use such weapons in war but also to destroy existing cultures of various diseases that could be loaded into shells and bombs. This agreement could become the first of a series that would include poison gas (only the use, not possession, of which is now prohibited) and napalm.

The most obvious candidate for qualitative disarmament is the nuclear weapon, because more than anything else it has made international politics a serious concern for so many people. In the early 1960's the "ban the bomb" movement was active, contributing the superimposed semaphore signals for *N* and *D* (standing for nuclear disarmament), which have become the emblem of the peace movement. But peace activists have turned their attention away from the issue of immediate nuclear disarmament. Seymour Melman, one of the most influential writers in the peace movement, has proposed a variation of minimum deterrence: reducing nuclear warheads to the number necessary to destroy all United States and Russian cities of more than 100,000 (150 cities in the United States, 175 in the USSR). Melman claims that leaders "who would not be deterred from nuclear military initiative by the prospect of destruction of these 150 cities would be too insane to be deterred by anything."[1] He is undoubtedly correct, but he is implicitly accepting the continued existence of nuclear weapons.

5. Quantitative Disarmament. Instead of seeking to eliminate one type of weapon, as the qualitative approach recommends, states could agree to cut back numbers of one or more types of weapons, or they could agree to preserve a ratio of forces. This attention to numbers of weapons, or quantitative approach, was used successfully in 1922 at the Washington Naval Conference. The five major naval powers agreed to reduce the number of battleships each had and to preserve the same ratio when they built new ships to replace old ones. The ratio was 5:5:3:1.67:1.67. The United States and Britain had the largest number; Japan was in the middle; and France and Italy had the smallest number.

The agreement, though successful, had two undesirable effects. One was to channel competition into nonregulated fields. The following years saw the states turn to building submarines and cruisers instead of battleships. The other effect was to preserve the status quo. Japan, relegated to a secondary place (only three battleships for every five the United States had), was unhappy and in 1934 demanded that the ratio be changed to allow Japan to build more battleships. When the other powers refused, Japan gave notice that it would refuse to renew the pact.

6. Budgetary Limitation. Frustrated by the difficulties of either qualitative or quantitative limitations on weapons, states have from time to time turned to an indirect approach: limiting the amount of money states can spend on weapons. At the Hague Conference of 1899, Russia proposed a five-year freeze on all military budgets. The Germans were quick to object. Russia, they pointed out, already had superiority in numbers of soldiers. Russia could use the money saved from military budgets to build more rail-

roads, which, although technically nonmilitary, could be used to transport Russian soldiers more quickly to the front in the event of war.[2]

At the Geneva Disarmament Conference of 1932 the issue of budgetary limitation again came up. In preparation for the conference, a commission compiled statistics on military spending around the world. But the conference never got to make use of them. Again, it was Germany that objected, although this time for different reasons. German armaments already were limited in quantity by the Versailles Treaty; Germany hoped to make up for numerical inferiority in improved quality, which would require more expenditure.[3]

The Soviet foreign minister, Andrei Gromyko, brought up budgetary limitation at the 1973 session of the United Nations. He proposed that the major states of the world cut their military budgets by 10 per cent and that 10 per cent of these savings be donated to developing countries.[4] The proposal seems no more likely to be adopted today than in 1899 or 1932. There is no agreement on what constitutes the defense budget, even within our own country.

For example, the cost of the ABM system submitted to Congress by the Nixon Administration in 1969 did not include one crucial item — the nuclear warheads for those ABM's. Later, some members of Congress discovered that nuclear weapons were under the jurisdiction of the Atomic Energy Commission (AEC) and that money for them was included in the AEC budget.[5] In the Soviet Union, the problem is even more difficult. Soviet practice is to keep all kinds of statistics secret — military spending, agricultural production, even airplane accidents. We assume (but have never been told) that Soviet nuclear weapons are funded under the budget category of "Medium Machine Building."

To verify a country's claims of what its military expenditures are would require extensive interference in its internal affairs — auditors looking at books, inspectors checking to see that production matched what the books said (one could always keep two sets of books), and many other controls. Even in the relatively open society of the United States, Congress sometimes has been slow to discover that parts of the executive branch have been violating financial limitations Congress has tried to place on it.[6]

7. Regional Disarmament. Finding general disarmament too difficult, states have occasionally tried regional disarmament. Some agreements of this type are in effect right now. They affect Antarctica, outer space, and the seabed. These were easy cases. Very little armament was going on anyway in those areas, and they were not inhabited by people who could claim they needed arms for self-defense. There have been proposals to extend the concept of disarmament by geographic area to other regions — the Indian subcontinent, Latin America, central Europe, Africa. None of them has yet shown

any success, though some Latin American states have taken a first step in this direction.

In February 1975, eight Latin American countries signed the Ayacucho Pact, agreeing to limit their acquisition of offensive weapons. But since the signing of the pact there has been no follow-up meeting. Peru, which initiated the agreement, continued to order weapons, including armored personnel carriers, tanks, and submarines. Within three years, Argentina had doubled its military budget. Neither the similarities among these countries nor their common interest in insulating their region from outside pressures was strong enough to overcome the traditional problems in implementing a disarmament agreement.[7]

A HISTORY OF DISARMAMENT AGREEMENTS: FROM RUSH–BAGOT TO GENERAL AND COMPLETE DISARMAMENT

Disarmament proposals are relatively recent additions to the history of the search for peace. Only in recent times have weapons become so specialized that they are clearly distinguishable from the tools of everyday life. The Bible talks of beating swords into plowshares and plowshares back into swords.[8] In Biblical times rearmament could be accomplished overnight. The complexity of modern weapons makes this no longer possible. The disarmament movement came into being only after the Industrial Revolution had created weapons whose complexity gave rise to talk about abolishing weapons.

The late nineteenth century saw a number of organized attempts to get states to reduce their arms, culminating in the conferences at The Hague in 1899 and 1907.[9] The Hague Conferences did provide for laws regulating the conduct of war but did not achieve any reduction or elimination of arms. What is often described as the only successful disarmament agreement of the nineteenth century goes back much earlier. This was the Rush–Bagot Agreement of 1817 between the United States and Britain.

The Rush–Bagot Agreement provided for disarmament on the Great Lakes. Each country agreed to have only three ships, of equal size and armament. Contrary to what many schoolbooks say, the agreement was violated repeatedly. The worst violations occurred in the late 1830's, when the British sent armed ships into the Great Lakes to mount retaliatory raids against American sanctuaries for guerrilla parties who were raiding Canada. Land fortifications were maintained until 1871, when the United States signed a treaty with Britain settling claims arising from the Civil War. Only then was disarmament extended gradually and without formal agreement to the long land border. Not until the twentieth century, when the possibility of war between Canada and the United States finally disappeared from the minds of policy-planners, did violation cease.

The Rush–Bagot Agreement is sometimes cited to prove that disarmament agreement leads to peaceful relations between states. A close examination of the historical record seems to support the opposite view: Only when there are already peaceful relations among states is a disarmament agreement workable. An agreement may exist on paper, such as the Rush–Bagot Agreement did, but it is in danger of violation at any crisis.[10]

The period after World War I saw two kinds of disarmament. One was the disarmament forced on the losing countries by the winners. This was justified as the first step toward general disarmament by all European states. But as the years passed it became clear that the victors did not intend to disarm down to the levels they had imposed on Germany. As a result, the Germans began to insist on the right to arm up to their level. In the end, disarmament only exacerbated the tensions that brought about World War II.

The other kind of disarmament was voluntary, and it met with some success, at least in the beginning. One consequence of World War I was that the United States developed its military potential. Despite the fact that the United States was an ally of Britain's, the British looked upon increased United States naval power as they did upon increases by any country: with grave suspicion. Partly because of this budding conflict, a naval conference was convened in Washington in 1922. It resulted in the agreement mentioned earlier on reducing the number of battleships.

It is hard to decide what lesson to draw from the 1922 agreement. Some have argued that it proves disarmament possible.[11] Others have used it to illustrate the point that disarmament can be limited to a region or to a type of weapon but cannot be both general (applying to all countries) and complete (covering all weapons).[12] The most pessimistic observers have mentioned that the battleship was already considered obsolescent by the time the conference convened and the participants had no plans to build more ships in any case.[13] By this interpretation, the Washington Naval Treaty did contribute something: At least states did not hang onto outdated weapons just because all other states did. But that contribution was minute.

Even this type of modest contribution was no longer possible by the time of the Geneva Disarmament Conference of 1932. The Geneva Conference was the long-delayed fulfillment of the promise of the Versailles Settlement that German disarmament would be the first step toward general disarmament. By the time the conference convened, it was too late for that. The conference failed for both technical and political reasons. Technically, it proved impossible to agree on the questions raised by new weapons. How were tanks and airplanes to be treated? As offensive weapons or as defensive ones? Politically, the conflict between France and Germany was too severe. Germany insisted on equality of armaments with France; France insisted on security from attack by Germany. Any slim hope of compromise was ended by the accession to power of the Nazis in January 1933.

The period after World War II again saw two kinds of disarmament, forced and voluntary. Germany and Japan were forcibly disarmed in consequence of their losing the war. But events in international politics led to very different outcomes this time. The United States' perception of a Soviet threat led it to take the initiative in urging rearmament of both these countries within less than ten years. The most dramatic shift in policy was toward Japan. As part of the American occupation, the Japanese had been given a new constitution that was in effect dictated by the head of the occupation, General Douglas MacArthur. MacArthur had insisted on including Article IX, that "the Japanese people forever renounce war as a sovereign right of the nation and the threat or use of force as a means of settling international disputes." To accomplish this, the article states, "land, sea, and air forces, as well as other war potential, will never be maintained." But in 1950 all four United States occupation divisions in Japan were transferred to fight in Korea, and General MacArthur insisted that the Japanese form a National Police Reserve Force of 75,000 men, equipped with tanks, mortars, and machine guns. In 1954 this became the Self-Defense Force. Today, with 250,000 men, it is larger than the defense forces of most other states.[14]

Voluntary attempts to reduce or abolish arms have met with failure since World War II. Most attention in the early years was focused on atomic weapons. A number of plans were advanced, but none was ever accepted even as a talking point. The failure of disarmament is ironically best represented by the stated public positions of the United States and the Soviet Union on the question of disarmament. Both claim that their policy is aimed at the most thorough disarmament imaginable. In a joint report submitted to the United Nations General Assembly in 1961, they both called for general and complete disarmament ("general" meaning all kinds of weapons). Precisely what the United States meant was outlined in a draft treaty presented to a UN disarmament committee in 1962: elimination of all weapons of mass destruction (nuclear, chemical, and biological); elimination of all non-nuclear forces except (1) those needed for internal security, and (2) agreed personnel for a UN peace force.[15] The Soviet draft treaty proposed similar goals.

The very comprehensiveness of this goal is often taken as proof of the insincerity of both the United States and USSR. Not able to achieve the slightest progress on limited disarmament, both countries expressed their policy in the most extravagant terms possible. (When the draft treaties on general and complete disarmament were submitted to the UN, the United States and USSR had not yet agreed on even a limited nuclear test ban.) Each country seemed to be acting on the principle that if you expect no agreement, you might as well extract maximum propaganda value from your proposals.

OBSTACLES TO DISARMAMENT

Much of the post–World War II negotiation between the United States and the USSR has stumbled over the issue of inspection to ensure compliance with agreements. The inspection issue has been a troublesome one since people first proposed disarmament. States arm because they distrust each other. Once they begin to disarm, this distrust continues, at least until some evidence to the contrary has been accumulated. Any state that distrusted its rivals enough to arm against them will distrust them enough to require more than their word that they are disarming.

Inspection for disarmament is exceedingly difficult. It requires something almost impossible to provide: positive evidence of nonactivity. Positive evidence of activity is a lot easier to acquire. The part of disarmament that calls for destroying existing weapons is fairly easy. You build a big bonfire, invite your enemies in, and throw your bombers on it. The hard part is to prove that no new weapons are being built, or that no existing weapons were hidden to escape the original census that indicated how many each country had. You could have a number of sources of information — tourists, military attachés, airplane flights once a month — and still find nothing. That would not prove that hidden arsenals did not exist, only that you hadn't found any. The problem is more troubling today because of the destructive power modern weapons have. It would not matter if a country hid a couple of dozen tanks under haystacks. They would not be a big threat. A couple of dozen ICBM's with megaton warheads would be an entirely different matter.

We can expect that noncompliance with a disarmament agreement will be accompanied by deception to make discovery more difficult. When the Germans were secretly rearming after World War I, they used a number of devices. One was to build ammunition factories in Russia in return for some of the output. Another was to develop sport flying clubs and commercial airline pilot schools to train young men for the then-forbidden air force.

One of the most ingenious (and discouraging) examples of deception occurred during the Italian war against Ethiopia in 1935 and 1936. The Italians, contrary to international law, were using poison gas. Foreign journalists discovered what the Italians were doing and photographed victims of the gas attacks. The Italian military censor, instead of forbidding the dispatch of all photographs, substituted pictures showing leprosy victims. The world press printed the substituted pictures with the original captions stating that the pictures showed gas victims. Prominent medical authorities came forward to state that the people shown in the photographs were not gas victims at all but suffered from leprosy. Not only was the truth about what the Italians were doing obscured but subsequent reports were treated with skepticism.[16]

A similar problem developed for the Czechs in 1938, when Hitler began making threats over the issue of the Sudeten Germans. The alarmed Czechs accused the Germans of mobilizing against them. At that time, the accusation was false, and Hitler seized the opportunity to invite French and British representatives to tour the border area. They found no signs of mobilization, and as a result French and British faith in the judgment and even in the motives of the Czechs was weakened. It became harder for the Czechs to argue their case in the following months, although we now know that Hitler had his general staff prepare plans for an invasion of Czechoslovakia in 1937.[17]

With all the opportunities the violator has for manipulating inspectors, it is easy to see why inspection has been a stumbling block. The issue has been an even more solid obstacle with the Soviet Union because of Soviet secrecy in all things. Exchanges between foreign visitors and Soviet citizens are discouraged. Travel abroad is just about impossible for Soviet citizens. Radio broadcasts from abroad are sometimes jammed. American space flights were televised live from the beginning, but for a long time Soviet flights were not announced until after they were successfully under way. This asymmetry in freedom of information has made any inspection proposal seem to the Russians a serious encroachment on their security. Topographic maps of the kind available at an American stationery store are treated in Russia like military documents. Even school atlases seem to be made deliberately inaccurate, as though they otherwise might be of some value to foreign military planners.[18] When President Eisenhower in 1955 proposed "open skies," allowing Soviet planes to make regular inspection flights over the United States and American planes to make similar flights over the USSR, the Russians felt the flights would add little to their knowledge of the United States but would add a great deal to Americans' knowledge of the USSR. They rejected the proposal.

Inspection is such a difficult issue that negotiations have not often moved beyond it; but when they do, they are confronted by a second obstacle — enforcement. What if inspection reveals a violation? Until now, the only remedy has been to imitate the violator. In 1922 the Washington Naval Conference imposed limitations on battleships. In 1934 the Japanese informed the other parties of the treaty that if Japan were not allowed equality, Japan would withdraw from the treaty. In the absence of a world government and world police force, no penalty could be applied to Japan short of going to war. States could respond only by building additional ships of their own.

In the event of total disarmament, a violation would lead to rearmament by rivals, and however unstable an arms race may be, a rearmament race would be even more unstable. The technological arms race today is full of uncertainties about what weapons can be built, how well they will work, and what countermeasures the enemy might have. But in a rearmament race, states would know how to reproduce the weapons they had earlier destroyed, and the first state to rebuild those weapons would be tempted to use them before other states could catch up.

Another aspect of the enforcement question is the refusal of some countries to go along with a disarmament agreement. One solution would be to include them by force, going to war if necessary to disarm them. If the countries that refuse to agree are major powers, this course might be ruled out as unwise. Both France and China have refused to agree to the partial test ban on nuclear weapons. No attempt has been made to force them into compliance. If French or Chinese testing programs ever seem to threaten the security of countries adhering to the Partial Test Ban Treaty, they will surely break the treaty and resume testing themselves.

The Chinese and the French argue that arms control agreements such as the limited test ban freeze the status quo and thus are unfair to the less developed countries. An Indian diplomat called the Non-Proliferation Treaty of 1968 an agreement on prohibition by two alcoholics.[19] India not only refused to sign it but went ahead and developed its own nuclear explosive device, which it exploded in 1974. Disarmament proposals in the nineteenth century ran into the same difficulty. Prussia, which wanted most to change the status quo in the 1870's, resisted the appeals of various disarmament groups the most vigorously.[20] But even if these nineteenth-century plans had been adopted, they would have permitted colonial wars under the excuse of "internal order."[21]

The entrance of former colonial possessions into world politics has compounded the problem of arriving at disarmament agreements because all these countries do not put the avoidance of war at the top of their priorities. Che Guevara said in 1962, "We must proceed along the path of liberation, even if that costs millions of atomic victims."[22] Horrifying as that statement is to Americans — who not long ago celebrated the two centuries that have passed since they resorted to arms for liberation — it is a reminder that disarmament proposals that freeze the status quo will not find universal acceptance.

Because an inferior side is reluctant to make its inferiority permanent, we might expect disarmament to be easiest when two sides approach equality. Unfortunately even this does not always work. The distrust that permeates international relations sometimes makes agreement impossible under the best of circumstances. In 1907 the British were leading in the *Dreadnought* competition, having demonstrated their resolve not to let the Germans or anyone else threaten their naval supremacy. Having made their point, the British offered to cut back on *Dreadnoughts* if other countries would follow. For the Germans this cutback would have been a sensible move because Germany was basically a land power, facing its principal danger from enemies on the continent. But the proponents of the German navy seized on this British initiative to argue their case more fervently. "The British economy must be hurting," they cried. "Now is the time to push harder."[23] Equality or near equality can be as much a spur to increased effort as an incentive to agree.

A greater gap separated the Americans from the rest of the world in 1945, when they alone had atomic weapons. It was thus natural that they viewed their proposal to submit this weapon to international control as a generous move. The United States plan, drawn up by Dean Acheson and David Lilienthal but often called the "Baruch Plan" after the man who submitted it, called for establishing an international authority with the right to inspect production facilities around the world. After this authority was in operation, the United States would destroy its atomic weapons. The Russians rejected the Baruch Plan and offered a counterproposal: The United States would destroy its atomic weapons first, and then inspection would be permitted.[24] In each case the proposal was framed in such a way that the other side would have to make the first move in giving up whatever gave it an advantage.

This pattern has been repeated often enough to lead some observers to conclude that disarmament proposals are more often than not simply moves in the armament game.[25] Eisenhower's "open skies" proposal is one example. The Soviet and United States draft treaties on general and complete disarmament are another. Although the final goals were basically the same, the Soviet draft emphasized as a first step eliminating overseas bases (which only the United States had), and the United States draft emphasized inspection (secrecy was what the Russians had). The problem is often illustrated by a modern animal fable. The members of the animal kingdom gathered for a disarmament conference. The eagle asked for the abolition of fangs. The lion asked for the abolition of beaks and tusks. The elephant asked for the abolition of talons and teeth. Finally, the bear, in tones of sweet reasonableness, asked for the abolition of *all* weapons. Quarrels, he said, should be settled by hugging.[26]

UNILATERAL INITIATIVES

These remarks on disarmament have been pessimistic, but the record since World War II justifies pessimism. There have been the barest number of actual agreements to disarm. Biological weapons is the only clear case.

Neutralizing Antarctica, outer space, and the seabed might also be counted, although none was armed to start with. A great many disarmament plans have been put forward, but most of them have been designed more to enhance the power of the state presenting them than to move both sides toward genuine reduction of force. With the high level of distrust that separates countries, the proposal of a rival is carefully scrutinized for traps, and traps are always found, whether intentional or not.

Obviously, if we all waited for a proposal that all sides found both acceptable and foolproof, we would wait a long time. This has prompted some people to recommend that a state, instead of waiting for a multilateral agreement that might never come, take a unilateral initiative in moving toward disarmament. In the 1960's, a vocal and active group in Britain proposed that Britain be the first state to take the step of abolishing nuclear weapons. Part of their argument was that precisely because Britain was no longer a first-class power, it could afford this step — because it didn't have much to lose.[27]

Americans have on the whole been more cautious in what they propose. A widely discussed proposal asks not for total unilateral disarmament, but merely for a unilateral initiative on the road to disarmament. It is not surprising, in view of the pessimism of professional strategists and politicians, that the proposal came from someone outside this field — a psychologist named Charles Osgood. He articulated a proposal that he called GRIT, which stands for graduated reciprocation in tension-reduction.[28]

CHARLES OSGOOD'S GRIT

In several ways GRIT reflected Osgood's expertise as a psychologist. Osgood believed that positive reinforcement is more effective than negative reinforcement, or, as we often say, that carrots work better than sticks. GRIT emphasized rewards for moves that reduce tension instead of punishment for moves that increase it. Another psychological side is the importance the proposal gave to worst-case estimation as a cause of the arms race. Osgood believed that it is because we fear and distrust the other side that we put the most unfavorable interpretation on anything they do. Each move, even a disarmament proposal, is seen solely as an effort by the other side to increase their strength. On the whole, Osgood saw the arms race as a psychological problem, similar to a mental illness such as paranoia, not as a rational solution to a collective problem.[29]

Osgood began his proposal with a surprising statement: States should retain nuclear weapons until last. Even though Osgood thought that fear of those weapons justified risk taking, he believed that at the beginning of the disarmament process each state should retain the capacity to inflict unacceptable nuclear retaliation. In other words, he believed in minimum deterrence. He carefully qualified this by emphasizing that the United States would retain only second-strike weapons and that ultimately we would get rid of even these. But in the meantime these weapons would provide a secure base from which to take limited risks.

We would not give up all strategic nuclear weapons. Neither would we eliminate all other weapons. We would instead announce that we were taking one step to disarm, such as destroying all units of one type of aircraft (say, B-52's) and not replacing them with something better. Because this would be a limited step, affecting only one part of our arsenal, it would not jeopardize our security. We would invite inspection and verification of this move by foreign observers, particularly our major rivals. We would also invite reciprocation on their part. We would suggest that our rivals destroy all of one type of their aircraft. Our own action, however, would be entirely independent of their response. We would go ahead and do what we had announced, even if they did not reciprocate. We would give them no reason to think we were trying to trick them.

Because a single gesture might be explained away by the other side, we would follow it with others. Our initiatives would be diversified, affecting different types of weapons or different areas of the world, so as not to jeopardize our overall strategic position. We could announce that we were stopping production of nuclear weapons, or that we were reducing the number of troops stationed overseas, or that our missile-firing submarines would normally be stationed outside the range of the Soviet Union.

How far we would go with these initiatives would in the end depend on how much reciprocation they were met with. If the Russians responded with large steps of their own, we would be justified in taking greater risks; if they did nothing, we would continue our initiatives until we had clearly demonstrated our sincerity, but not to the point of endangering our security. If the Russians responded by encroaching on an area from which we were disengaging by threatening a country from which we removed troops, we would resist. Osgood recommended that we respond vigorously to demonstrate that we are taking initiatives not because we are "going soft" but because we think it is the most rational way to reduce tension. He praised President Kennedy's policy in Cuba in 1962, in opposing the Russian introduction of missiles there, because it demonstrated our resolve. But even while we were resisting encroachment in one area, we would be continuing our initiatives in other, unrelated areas.

Osgood first published his proposal more than twenty years ago. When he was writing, there was talk of war over Berlin. President Kennedy called up reserves in the summer of 1961. Premier Khrushchev would periodically refer to the power of the Soviet rockets. By any measure there was international tension in the early 1960's. Since then, a number of things have changed in the world. Many of Osgood's specific proposals for initiatives have been implemented (although not always because of American initiatives). Trade restrictions with China have been lifted, and China is a member of the UN with a permanent seat on the Security Council. The United States and the Soviet Union have worked out some tension-reducing agreements — to avoid collisions at sea between ships of our respective navies, to give warning of missile tests — and major negotiations on strategic arms and conventional arms in Europe are going on. During much of the 1970's, at least, Osgood's goal of reducing international tension was achieved.

But reduced tension has not been enough to ensure success in negotiations. The general expectation of war is lower, but disarmament does not seem much closer. Could unilateral initiatives now be used to begin actual disarmament?

One problem is that reciprocation is not the only possible response to a unilateral disarmament initiative. Another response might be to accelerate arming. On occasion this has happened. One unilateral restraint by the United States was the decision by Secretary McNamara to limit the number of land-based ICBM's to 1,000, even though we had the capacity to keep on building to much higher numbers. The United States reached this level in 1967 and held it from then on. The USSR reached 1,000 missiles in 1967 but kept right on building. Some experts have argued that it was precisely this unilateral restraint that encouraged the Soviet Union to try for superiority.[30]

Nor are the Soviets the only offenders. The United States responded in a similar way to a unilateral restraint by the Soviets. Khrushchev was rapidly reducing the number of Soviet ground forces in Europe until 1961. This cutback encouraged American planners to try to build up NATO forces because they saw that for the first time since World War II it was possible to catch up with the Russians.[31] Each time, a unilateral move had an effect opposite from the one Osgood hoped for.

Osgood might have replied that these were not explicitly announced initiatives as part of an overall plan, and that is true. But would one side's awareness of the theory the other side is acting on make a difference? It might, but some experimental evidence suggests it might not.

Researchers at the Massachusetts Institute of Technology constructed an experiment in which the purpose was to transmit a message by a mechanical device.[32] The message was five units long and had to be inserted one unit at a time into a communication channel. Once the message was fully inserted, it was transmitted at once by the device, and the player received a payoff. There were two players, each trying to insert his message into the channel from opposite ends, alternating turns. The channel could hold a total of six units. After each player had three turns, the channel would be full and neither could proceed. They got payoffs only for messages transmitted, so it did them no good to sit there stalemated. One would have to withdraw units and let the other transmit. Once a message was transmitted, the channel was cleared and the other player could proceed. The players had fifteen turns, so each could hope to win some payoff if they took turns using the channel.

The subjects in the experiment were male college students. Each was told he would be playing with another student, although he would not be able to see the other player. In fact, each was playing against a computer. The computer was playing a pacifist strategy, letting the other player win the first time but seeking to win the second time. The experiment included another feature. Once a player had transmitted the first message, he was given the power to eject the other player's message units by force from the communication channel. Once the pacifist player had allowed the other player to win the first round, the pacifist would have to depend entirely on the good will of the other player to transmit messages himself.

A total of 143 students participated in the experiment. Each was asked which strategy he planned to follow. They replied:

Dominate	75
Share equally	66
Settle for less	2
	143

After the first four trials, they were asked again about their strategies. This time they said:

Dominate	125 (including 71 of the original dominators, 54 of others)
Cooperate	18 (including 4 of the original dominators)[33]

In other words, playing against a pacifist increased the number of dominators.

The subjects were shown questionnaires that supposedly had been given to their imaginary opponent. In them he was portrayed as an ethically motivated pacifist. The subjects reported that they perceived their opponent correctly — more moral, wiser, more peaceful, and more honest — but that did not make them less willing to dominate. It even changed some and made them more willing to dominate.

The experiment had other aspects, and the article describing it is well worth reading.[34] Readers should be cautious about drawing conclusions, however, because the subjects were all young men at a competitive institution. All were products of the same culture and did not have the tradition of mistrust, the vested interests, or the political constraints that would be found among heads of state. The experiment does suggest that a pacifist strategy is no guarantee of success, at least not of immediate success, and those advocating one should be prepared for this reaction.

Experiments with small groups such as the one just described can never provide satisfactory evidence for propositions about international politics, although it is from such experiments that Osgood and other psychologists draw evidence for *their* beliefs (for example, that positive reinforcement is more effective than negative reinforcement). American college students (or whoever makes up the experimental group) are different in so many ways from the leaders of rival states that there is little justification for transferring the results of such an experiment to international politics. How American students react to pacifists may not be at all how Russian generals would react.

A crucial aspect of Osgood's plan, as in any plan for peace, is the theory of the cause of war that underlies it. Osgood put most emphasis on misunderstanding. He believed that if we clear up the misconceptions we have of each other, we will clear up the conflict. Palestinians and Israelis, however, are in conflict not because they misunderstand each other. They are in conflict because their interests clash: They both want to live on the same piece of land. Thirty years ago the conflict in central Europe was caused not by misperception but by Hitler's plan to dominate neighboring states and their resistance to that domination.

There are elements of misperception in the present Soviet–American rivalry, but these are not the only elements of the rivalry. A firm believer in the doctrine of Marx and Lenin would not argue that the conflict is caused by American misperception of Soviet intentions. "Wars are caused by imperialists," a Marxist would argue. "If you want to get rid of wars, get rid of imperialists." Arguments and even demonstrations of peaceful intent by these imperialists would not impress a firm Marxist. The Marxist argument would go like this: "Violence is the result of maladjustment in your capitalist society. Your society is basically unjust and in the end will be brought down by its own internal contradictions. You may make gestures of appeasement to buy time, but we socialists must always be aware that as your society begins to collapse, you might try something desperate."

Have recent Soviet leaders been committed Marxist-Leninists? Scholars who study the Soviet Union have found evidence of ideological influence in both statements and foreign policy behavior.[35] In the realm of military policy also their thinking seems to derive from Marx. In the words of one scholar, summarizing the works of others, "The object of Soviet policy is to further the movement of the correlation of forces towards socialism, not to maintain a balance of power between socialism and capitalism."[36] Nor do they express alarm at violence as a means of bringing about change, claiming that "it is impossible to ban civil and national liberation wars."[37]

Before undertaking unilateral initiatives, we should have a reasonable understanding of how they would be received and what the most likely reaction to them would be. A key element of this understanding is the theory of conflict that the other side is operating on. If both sides agree that they have distorted images of each other, then unilateral steps to correct these misperceptions can lead to lasting peace. But if at least one side persists in a dogmatic interpretation of politics, war, and the nature of its rivals, unilateral initiatives may bring about results opposite to those intended.

THE EVOLUTION OF COOPERATION

A recent set of experiments has provided some evidence that rivals, such as two countries engaged in competitive armament, may still learn to cooperate.[38] The experiments involved not people but computer programs. They were all designed to play a game commonly used in simulations called "Prisoner's Dilemma." The name derives from a supposed bargain a jailor once made separately with each of two male prisoners held for jointly committing a crime. To each the jailor said, "If you confess before your accomplice does, I'll give you one thousand dollars (your accomplice will hang); if you confess at the same time as your accomplice does, you'll both go to jail; if neither of you confesses, you'll both go free." The prisoner understood that the same bargain would be offered to the other, so if he failed to confess but his accomplice did, he would hang and his accomplice would get the reward.

The game is intriguing because a rational decision by each prisoner leads to an irrational choice for both. The first prisoner calculates: "What if the other prisoner holds out? Then if I confess, I get one-thousand dollars. If I hold out, I go free." Clearly $1,000 is better than just going free, so in this case, confessing is better. Then the first prisoner calculates: "What if the other prisoner confesses? Then if I confess I go to jail. If I hold out, I hang." Clearly going to jail is better than hanging, so in this case as well, confessing is better. No matter what the other prisoner does, confessing is better. The other prisoner calculates the same way, both confess and both go to jail — which is clearly less desirable than both going free. Thus apparently faultless reasoning leads to an apparently faulty conclusion.

Without interfering with the game's logic, the payoffs in Prisoner's Dilemma can be reduced to numerical point values, with 5 replacing $1,000, 3 replacing freedom, 1 replacing jail, and 0 replacing hanging. Replacing the drastic penalty of hanging with a point value means the game can be played more than once, and when it can, the logic changes too. If the numbers (5, 3, and so on) represent dollars, the goal of repeated games is to win as much as possible, and one can do that by cooperating with the other player (what was called "holding out" in the original game) more easily than by defecting from the other player (what was called "confessing"). Even an occasional defection (which might yield 5 points; to the opponent, 0 for that round) would not be a good strategy in the long run, because the opponent could retaliate and both scores would stay low.

Using repeated plays of Prisoner's Dilemma (about 200 games between each pair of opponents), Robert Axelrod organized a tourney conducted on a computer. Each entrant submitted a program telling the computer how to play. Points were awarded on a numerical system and the winner was the person whose program had the most points after it had played all rivals. Some astonishing and entirely unforseen results emerged: One strategy was the undisputed winner. It won the preliminary round, it won the next round, and then, even after competitors knew the winning plan and had time to design strategies against it, it won the final round, against 62 competing strategies. Furthermore, it was the simplest of all the strategies submitted, requiring just five lines of computer code. The winning strategy was: Cooperate on the first move, then for each subsequent move do exactly what the other player did on the preceding move.

The strategy was submitted by an expert on game theory, Anatol Rapoport, and was called "Tit for Tat." Although it had a quality known as being "nice" — that is, it never sought advantage by being the first to defect — it was not a pacifist strategy. Tit for Tat called for instant retaliation — if the other player defected on one move, the player using Tit for Tat defected on the very next move, without fail. More charitable strategies entered in the tourney did not do well, because some "nasty" strategies were able to exploit them. Failing to retaliate instantly — for example, in a strategy with the self-explanatory title "A Tit for Two Tats," tempted opponents to exploit the strategy by repeated defections.

The tourney is described in Robert Axelrod's book *The Evolution of Cooperation.*[39] The book reports many other discoveries as well, and has stimulated research to see how well the strategy applies to various real-life situations.[40] The book suggests that enemies can learn to cooperate under certain conditions; but following the correct strategy is a very important condition. Prescriptions such as "turn the other cheek" or "do unto others as you would have them do unto you" do not stand up as well as the simple rule, "first be nice, then reciprocate."

The findings of Axelrod and others have not yet been translated into concrete proposals or actual disarmament initiatives. Even if they were, there is no reason to think that they would be immediately successful. One feature of the simulation using Prisoner's Dilemma was that games went on for many, many moves. What the findings do suggest is that perhaps Charles Osgood's proposal had merit and that persistence will eventually pay off. Until then, it is likely that disarmament proposals will be viewed with great suspicion (similar to what the prisoners felt toward each other when the jailor made his original offer), that disarmament proposals will in fact be moves to improve a state's position in the arms race, and that states' leaders will persist in their belief that the best guarantee of peace is to be prepared for war.

The approaches to peace we have looked at so far are ways to control force. World government is designed to centralize force. Balance of power is designed to disperse it. Collective security makes the principles of the balance of power more explicit and more universal: Those who advocate armament as the best approach to peace would like to see force retained by individual states. Advocates of arms control agree but try to eliminate the worst hazards of the arms race. Advocates of disarmament would like to see force abolished altogether. Having found no totally satisfying solution to the problem of war in any of these approaches, let us turn our attention from ways of controlling force to ways of solving the disagreements that in the end cause force to be employed among states.

NOTES

1. Theodore Shabad, "An American Asks Cut in Arms Race," The New York Times, October 31, 1971.

2. Merze Tate, The Disarmament Illusion (New York: Macmillan, 1942), pp. 66–67.

3. Francis P. Walters, A History of the League of Nations, Vol. 1 (London: Oxford University Press, 1952), p. 440.

4. "U.N. Bids the Big Five Cut Arms Budgets to Aid Poor Nations," The New York Times, December 8, 1973.

5. John Finney, "Safeguard's Cost was Understated," The New York Times, May 6, 1969.

6. Peter Grose, "$3.4 Billion Surplus Arms Given to Allies in 19 Years," The New York Times, March 30, 1970.

7. David Binder, "Eight Latin Nations Declare Intention to Limit Arms," The New York Times, December 13, 1974; Marvine Howe, "A Big Latin Arms Pact That May Signify Little," The New York Times, February 16, 1975; Allan Riding, "Mexicans Proposing Cuts in Latin Arms," The New York Times, December 27, 1978.

8. The better-known passage is in Isaiah 2:4; it is reversed in Joel 3:10.

9. These conferences are described in Tate.

10. James Eayrs, "Arms Control on the Great Lakes," Disarmament and Arms Control, Vol. 2, No. 4 (Autumn 1964), pp. 372–404; Trevor N. Dupey and Gay M. Hammerman, eds., A Documentary History of Arms Control and Disarmament (New York: R. R. Bowker, 1973), p. 39.

11. Philip Noel-Baker, The Arms Race (New York: Oceana Publications, 1958), p. 86.

12. Hedley Bull, "Disarmament and the International System" (a review of The Arms Race by Philip Noel-Baker), Australian Journal of Politics and History, Vol. 1 (May 1959).

13. Hedley Bull, Strategic Arms Limitation: The Precedent of the Washington and London Naval Treaties, Occasional Paper, Center for Policy Study (Chicago, 1971), p. 31.

14. Robert Shaplen, "From MacArthur to Miki," The New Yorker, August 4, 1975, p. 72.

15. A Documentary History, pp. 494ff.

16. Angelo del Boca, The Ethiopian War, 1935–1941 (Chicago: University of Chicago Press, 1965), pp. 80–81.

17. Alan Bullock, *Hitler,* rev. ed. (New York: Harper & Row, 1962), p.447.

18. *The New York Times,* January 18, 1970.

19. Mr Trivedi, delegate of India to Geneva, quoted in *The Economist,* February 19, 1966, p. 687.

20. Tate, p. 21.

21. Ibid., p. 121.

22. *Verde Olivo,* October 6, 1968, quoted by Hugh Thomas, *Cuba* (New York: Harper & Row, 1971), p. 1470.

23. Tate, p. 353.

24. See the summary in Bull, "Disarmament and the International System."

25. For example, John W. Spanier and Joseph L. Nogee, *The Politics of Disarmament: A Study in Soviet–American Gamesmanship* (New York: Frederick A. Praeger, 1962).

26. This fable has been attributed both to Salvadore de Madariga and to Winston Churchill.

27. A leading publicist for this movement was Bertrand Russell.

28. Charles Osgood, *An Alternative to War or Surrender* (Urbana: University of Illinois Press, 1962), especially Chapter 5.

29. The idea is also developed by another psychologist, Jerome Frank, in *Sanity and Survival* (New York: Random House, 1967).

30. Colin S. Gray, "The Arms Race Phenomenon," *World Politics,* Vol. 24, No. 1 (October 1971), pp. 63–64.

31. Alain C. Enthoven and K. Wayne Smith, *How Much Is Enough?* (New York: Harper & Row, 1971); Bernard Brodie, *War and Politics* (New York: Macmillan, 1973), p. 401.

32. Gerald H. Shure, Robert J. Meeker, and Earle A Hansford, "The Effectiveness of Pacifist Strategies in Bargaining Games," *Journal of Conflict Resolution,* Vol. 9, No. 1 (March 1965), pp. 106–117.

33. Ibid., p. 112.

34. Ibid.

35. Robert Conquest, "A New Russia? A New World?" *Foreign Affairs,* Vol. 53, No. 3 (April 1975), pp. 486–487.

36. David Holloway, *The Soviet Union and the Arms Race* (New Haven: Yale University Press, 1983), p. 82.

37. Aleksandr Bovin, *Kommunist,* No. 10 (July 1980), p. 79, quoted by Dimitri Simes, "Deterrence and Coercion in Soviet Policy," *International Security,* Vol. 5, No. 3 (Winter 1980–1981), pp. 94–95.

38. Robert Axelrod, *The Evolution of Cooperation* (New York: Basic Books, 1984).

39. Ibid.

40. For example, the entire issue of *World Politics,* Vol. 38, No. 1 (October 1985).

Chapter 16

Diplomacy

Balance of power, collective security, and disarmament all deal with the *instrument* of war, not with the *reasons* states have for fighting in the first place. If we could eliminate the quarrels that lead to war, we would wipe out war as surely as if we had total disarmament. Few times in history have the objectives that a war was fought for been worth the price that was paid. Suppose the French government in 1914 had been confronted with this simple proposition: "If you will take 1,363,000 of your strongest and healthiest young men, stand them against walls, and shoot them, you will be allowed to put the provinces of Alsace and Lorraine back under your administration." No government would have dared accept such an exchange, yet in the end, that is the price France paid in World War 1 for exactly that gain.

One of the problems in World War I was that no country was sure of the war aims of the others. Consequently, each imagined the worst and so fought more stubbornly. Clarification of aims would have alleviated if not eliminated much of the suffering that war caused.

The process of talking over differences, clarifying aims, and exploring adjustments short of fighting is called *diplomacy*. It has many aspects. The one we want to concentrate on might be defined as the art of resolving disputes between states by highly skilled communication among the trained representatives of governments. The emphasis in diplomacy is on communication; everything connected with diplomacy — special representatives, high training, and formal procedures — is designed to enhance such communication.

THE STRUCTURE OF DIPLOMACY

There are two parts to diplomacy — the apparatus that conducts it and the forms that it follows. The apparatus consists of two parts — officials inside one's own country and officials overseas. We usually reserve the name "diplomat" for the ambassadorial staff serving abroad, but its counterparts at home are also part of the diplomatic service. The branch of the government responsible for sending representatives to other states is typically called the "foreign ministry," although for historical reasons it is called the Department of External Affairs in Canada, Foreign Office in Great Britain, and the State Department in the United States. Most of the important officials in diplomacy are members of a professional service (called the Foreign Service in the United States), similar to the officer corps of an army. They are selected on a competitive basis, given special training, and promoted through the ranks. Members of the Foreign Service serve both at foreign posts and at home.

Officials in the State Department are essential to diplomacy, but attention is usually focused on embassy officials posted abroad. The most important of these is the ambassador, who is the official personal representative from one head of state to another. The idea that an ambassador is a personal representative goes back to monarchic times, when all kings considered themselves brothers and sent representatives more as a family obligation than as a government service. The notion that a diplomat is a personal representative is still taken seriously. Ambassadors must present their credentials in person to the head of state, and when a head of state is changed, the ambassadors must be reaccredited.

An ambassador must actually reside in the country to which he or she is accredited. But the ambassador and the ambassadorial staff have special privileges and immunities in their host country, such as freedom from taxes, from prosecution for criminal offenses, and even from "insults to diplomatic dignity." (One practical meaning of that phrase is that suitable housing must be made available.) The embassy itself must have freedom from search and seizure, and it must have the right to secret communication with the home country. All this is designed to facilitate communication among states. In time of crisis it is not necessary to go looking for ways to get messages to another state. One merely summons the ambassador. On more than one occasion ambassadors have been summoned in the middle of the night.

Below the ambassador come a number of other embassy officials — counsellors, secretaries, and attachés. If the embassy is very large, as it often is for a major country, these ranks are further divided into first counsellor, second counsellor, first secretary, second secretary, and so on. When the ambassador is absent from the country, one of these high-ranking officials will be appointed chargé d'affaires, to run the embassy until the ambassador returns. Attachés are embassy personnel with technical specialties, often drawn from outside the ranks of the Foreign Service. There can be agricultural attachés, aviation attachés, cultural attachés, military attachés, and others depending on the kinds of business conducted between the two states involved. California citrus growers want to protect their groves from insects found in Asian citrus groves; an American agricultural attaché in Japan can help with the negotiation of necessary safeguards for importing Japanese produce to the United States.

Another type of diplomatic official, dealing exclusively with administrative matters, is the consul. Although each country has only one embassy in any other country, it may have a number of consulates, located in the cities that do most business with that country. West Coast port cities frequently have consulates from Asian countries. Cities in the northern United States frequently have Canadian consulates. It is to a consulate that you go for visas or for help on shipping and business regulation. If you are abroad, the consulates of your own country can provide help with legal matters — marriage, taxes, and sometimes even trouble with the local police.

The number of embassy personnel can be quite high; United States embassies in Germany and Italy have had from 400 to 500 officials in recent years. (When the Khomeini regime took over in Iran, President Carter ordered 1,100 United States diplomatic personnel home — and there were still sixty-three left to take as hostages.) Such countries are assigned not just a military attaché but an army attaché, an air force attaché, a naval attaché, and corresponding staffs. The number of officials is sometimes criticized as excessive, but there is often a justification for each one. An example of how they might be useful comes from the 1967 War in the Middle East.

On June 8, Israeli jets spotted an unidentified vessel 15 miles off their coast. According to one version, they then approached both the United States military attaché and the Soviet military attaché, asking each whether the ship was from either of their countries. When told it was not, they assumed it was a hostile ship. An error was made, as it turned out, because the ship belonged to the United States. Some sources now argue that the story was no more than a fiction to cover a deliberate attack.[1] But the story remains an example of how diplomats *could* be useful.

MODERN TECHNOLOGY AND DIPLOMACY

The large size (and the large expense) of embassies and the increasing number of them, as the number of countries in the world increases, have led people to ask whether all this apparatus is necessary. Norway has considered abolishing all embassies. In their place it would create teams of experts who would fly to other countries when a matter arose in which Norway's interests needed representing. All other contacts with states would be maintained through the UN.[2]

The assumption that underlies this proposal is that in the modern world the traditional diplomat is obsolete. The modern world is too complex for one representative to deal with, no matter how well trained. If the American ambassador to Japan wants to negotiate an agreement to prevent the spread of citrus grove pests, he or she must rely on agricultural experts. If the ambassador wants to negotiate monetary matters, he or she must rely on financial experts. Furthermore, with improved transportation and communications, it is easy to fly in the relevant experts, even the secretary of state. The days are long past when travel time to a diplomatic post was measured in weeks and consequently the ambassador was the authoritative voice of the United States abroad.

In the conduct of a state's foreign policy, the ambassador is often bypassed. During the long American engagement in Vietnam, there were times when the United States ambassador in Saigon appeared to be little more than a briefing officer for visiting officials from Washington. When the president wanted more information, he did not call home the ambassador; he sent out members of his cabinet. In 1986, when the United States was pressuring Ferdinand Marcos of the Philippines to leave office after a dishonest election, Marcos did not trust messages transmitted by the United States ambassador. He thought these messages originated with low-level bureaucrats in the State Department. Despite the presence in Manila of the ambassador, defined as "the personal representative of one head of state to another," Marcos chose instead to telephone in the middle of the night a United States Senator in Washington known to be a personal friend of President Reagan. Only when receiving a message from this unofficial representative to "cut and cut cleanly" did he decide to leave office.[3]

Professional diplomats are bypassed only at a cost, however. When the trained ambassador is neglected, so too are the virtues we associate with diplomats: first-hand knowledge of a country, discretion in communications, caution in making commitments or public statements. When the conduct of foreign policy is in the hands of untrained politicians, mistakes and embarrassment are more likely.

Presidents at the beginning of their term are likely to complicate American foreign policy. In 1969, President Nixon made a tour of Asia. Speaking about the United States possession of Guam, he proclaimed the Nixon Doctrine, that Asians would be left to take care of their own affairs. "Peace in Asia cannot come from the United States," he said. "It must come from Asia."

Yet shortly afterward, in Thailand, he seemed to reverse himself: "The United States will stand proudly with Thailand against those who might threaten it from abroad or from within."[4] Foreign observers were understandably puzzled. Which was the *real* United States policy? It is typical for politicians to promise different things for different audiences — high grain prices to farmers, low bread prices to homemakers. This is understood, even expected, and because few campaign promises are taken seriously, little harm is done. But diplomats pride themselves on precision. Contradictory statements breed confusion and make foreign relations difficult.

President Ford made a similar error at the beginning of his presidency. In response to a question at a news conference following the fall of Saigon, he reaffirmed American commitments to Asian countries, naming South Korea, Indonesia, the Philippines, and Taiwan. Yet ever since President Nixon's visit to China the United States had worked assiduously to convey the impression that the Taiwan issue was different from all the others. President Ford's spontaneous remark, like President Nixon's spontaneous remark in Thailand, required weeks of "clarification" and "amplification."[5]

At the beginning of his term of office, President Carter welcomed Israeli Prime Minister Yitzhak Rabin to the United States and spoke of United States support for "defensible borders" for Israel. Through years of usage in Mideast diplomacy, "defensible borders" has become a shorthand expression for the Israeli policy of not returning all the territory it occupied in the 1967 war. Evidently without realizing what he was doing, President Carter was committing the United States to a policy position he did not intend. The next week President Carter referred to the United States goal of a "homeland" for Palestinians, using another shorthand expression, this time one meaning Palestinian control of all disputed territory, with no room for a state of Israel. Both statements created confusion and alarm in Arab states and Israel, effects that would have been averted if the president had left diplomacy in the hands of professional diplomats.[6]

The growth of electronic communications has meant greater public attention to foreign policy. Satellite reports on television have made available to millions of Americans the sort of information about foreign countries once available only to officials of the State Department. Greater public involvement in diplomacy restricts the freedom of the diplomat; what were once almost purely foreign policy questions become domestic questions as well. The hostile demonstrators in front of the United States embassy in Teheran in 1979 made it impossible for President Carter to pursue quiet accommodation, even if he had been so inclined. The one outstanding success of recent diplomacy, the 1979 peace treaty between Egypt and Israel, was possible in part because of the unusual step of excluding the press from the negotiations at Camp David in September 1978. Politicians in Israel, Egypt, and the United States, unable to learn of offers and concessions as they were made, were unable to voice opposition piecemeal. When the final balanced package was announced, opposition was more difficult.

Increased public attention to foreign affairs creates a temptation for political leaders to sacrifice foreign policy for domestic advantage. Someone in the government opposed to Kissinger's pro-Pakistan policy in the 1971 war between India and Pakistan leaked secret memoranda to the press, making relations with India even worse. Israeli leaders in 1975, desperate to win domestic support for concessions to Egypt in the Sinai, leaked secret United States commitments to them. Someone in the State Department who favored the Greeks in the Cyprus dispute leaked a confidential memorandum suggesting how aid might be used to improve United States relations with the Turks.[7] The cumulative effect of such leaks is the inhibition of free discussion or even free thought inside the government. No one will suggest for discussion any policy that might later prove to be unpopular. The foreign policy interests of the country become secondary to protecting one's own career.

DUTIES OF DIPLOMATS

Contemporary conditions make life more difficult for the diplomat, yet it is not clear that the traditional services of the diplomat can be provided by anyone else. Let us turn to the list of duties of diplomats as defined by the Vienna Convention of 1961 to see exactly what diplomats should do.[8]

The first duty of a diplomat is to represent his or her state. This means doing such things as attending the celebration of other states' national holidays or expressing condolences upon the death of other states' high officials. This is a symbolic function and leads to some symbolic behavior. For a long time West Germany did not recognize East Germany. Yet West German ambassadors would find themselves in countries where the East Germans had trade missions or consulates. The West German ambassador would be careful to leave parties whenever East Germans arrived, thereby making a symbolic contribution to the claim that only one Germany existed. Another case: When the Soviet defense minister began to insult the United States during a May Day speech, the American ambassador left the platform.

A diplomat is also charged with promoting friendly relations between the sending country and the receiving country. The ambassador is the chief interpreter of his or her country's policy abroad. When you think about it, where else can you go to find out another country's side of a story? Why does Ecuador seize American tuna boats? Our news agencies are staffed by Americans, and even if they strive for objectivity they cannot always attain it. In such a case you can write to the Ecuadorian embassy. Probably you will receive copious amounts of information supporting the Ecuadorian side of the controversy.

With increased popular participation in government, states have made an effort to promote friendly relations not just with the members of the governing elite but with the broad masses of population. In 1953, the United States Information Agency (for several years called the International Communications Agency) was set up as a separate agency, although working with the State Department, to make information about America available abroad. Among other things, it runs libraries in foreign cities, making available books and periodicals on America, education programs, films, and speakers. Other countries provide similar services.

One of the most important duties of diplomats is ascertaining conditions in the host state. The periodic reports (known as diplomatic cables) sent back from embassies are an important source of information for the government, even though they now compete with both foreign correspondents and intelligence reports. These cables cover all aspects of relations with another country. They may cover purely domestic developments. For example, it is the job of ambassadors in Washington to predict for their home governments who is most likely to win an American election. A candidate for president will be received more warmly on a foreign fact-finding tour if his or her chances of winning are evaluated by the ambassador as very high.

In recent years this function of diplomats has been a source of friction with unstable or revolutionary countries. During the cultural revolution in China, the Red Guards showed great sensitivity to foreign diplomats who tried to read the wall newspapers that recorded their debates. After the overthrow of the shah, Iranian militants accused the United States embassy of being a "nest of espionage." Yet when diplomats attempt to ascertain political conditions within a host state — including possible strife and discontent — they are only doing their job.

Of course a diplomat is not entitled to all information. States may keep secrets, and diplomats are restricted to legitimate methods for learning them. The tension between a state's attempts to keep secrets and a diplomat's attempts to discover them is most acute in the case of the military attaché. The military attaché is part of the ambassadorial staff and, because of special interest and expertise in military affairs, is most likely to be interested in what the host state is most likely to consider secret — types or numbers of weapons, states of readiness of armed forces, new weapons under development. Some channels of information, such as items in the newspapers, are obviously open even to a military attaché. Other kinds of information are clearly prohibited. Between what is clearly allowed and what is clearly prohibited is a gray area. Photographs of a military air field may be forbidden. But what about a snapshot of friends at a picnic that just happens to include in the background a plane taking off from an air field? Occasionally an attaché is caught in this gray area and is expelled. Such expulsion is usually accompanied by the simultaneous expulsion of a military attaché by the sending state (that is, when the Poles expel a Canadian military attaché, the Canadians expel a Polish one), often making it impossible for outsiders to determine who got caught spying and who is only the victim of retaliation.

It is useful for one state to obtain from its diplomats specific bits of information. In addition, diplomats convey a general impression, the climate of relations. It could be argued that if, during most of the 1960's and late 1970's, the president of the United States had picked up his red telephone and ordered an all-out attack on the Soviet Union, nothing would have happened, at least not for a long time. The order would most probably not have been believed. "What is this — some kind of joke?" would have been the first response. Attempts would have been made to verify first the order and then the president's sanity. The climate of relations between the United States and the Soviet Union during the past decades was not compatible with nuclear attack. Even so simple a matter as the number of Americans in the USSR at any time (diplomats, tourists, musicians, business representatives) would have made an attack difficult. By contrast, when the Germans were preparing to attack the Russians in 1941, they gradually recalled as many Germans as they could. Workers on loan to Russian shipyards were sent home on vacation and never returned. Diplomats were recalled and never replaced. When the German attack came in June 1941, only a handful of Germans were left in Moscow.[9] The mere presence of diplomatic personnel is reassuring; their departure, cause for alarm.

When there are no diplomatic relations at all, one state may have very distorted views of another's policies. It is generally agreed that the United States exaggerated the threat of China in the 1960's, in part because we were accepting a Soviet version of what the Chinese were saying. Lacking official representatives of our own in China, we found it difficult to disprove Russian charges such as the one that the Chinese would welcome a nuclear war.

Ascertaining conditions is a duty of a diplomat that ranks in importance with another duty, protecting a state's interest. This protection includes the interest of a state's citizens. Some of the forms this takes are well known: efforts to promote trade, protests against the seizure of property, responsibility for evacuating Americans in the event of hostilities. Protection also extends to simple matters. A man in my town had once been hospitalized in Morocco. When a local hospital wanted his records, they found the Moroccan hospital unresponsive. They then applied to the State Department, which through a consul in Morocco was able to facilitate transferral of the records.

The duty of the diplomat that is probably of least importance today is negotiation. Increasingly, the resident ambassador has been bypassed in major negotiations between two countries. But this does not mean a downgrading of diplomacy as a means of resolving disputes. Officials of the State Department are as much diplomats (in our meaning of the term) as are ambassadors. When the secretary of state negotiates, a diplomat is at work. And even on those occasions when the secretary of state comes from a background devoid of training in diplomacy, his or her deputies and assistants are from the Foreign Service.

DIPLOMATIC PROCEDURE

Diplomats are quick to point out that there is no substitute for personal contact, even in the day of transoceanic television. Even allowing for their bias on the subject, we may grant that they have a point, as a story from World War II illustrates. By June 1945 it was clear that the Japanese were defeated. Confidential reports from the general staff to the Japanese cabinet indicated that their industry could no longer produce even ammunition. But Japanese leaders were reluctant to surrender because they thought doing so would mean the removal and perhaps even execution of the emperor. Some Americans in the State Department were aware that this was the main obstacle to a Japanese surrender, but they were hampered both by promises to the Russians of unconditional surrender and by domestic propaganda against the Japanese. At the Potsdam Conference at the end of July 1945, the Allies drew up a declaration hinting, without actually coming out and saying it, that the emperor might be retained even after surrender. The Japanese received this declaration by radio because, in accordance with normal practice, diplomatic relations had been broken when the war began. Some members of the Japanese cabinet wished to study the declaration and see whether there was some way they could use it to justify a surrender. Before this study took place, they wished to reserve comment on the declaration. But the word used by the Japanese premier to describe this wish to reserve comment was *mokusatsu*, which is best translated "to treat with silent contempt." One of the premier's advisers later commented:

> To interpret *mokusatsu* as "ignore" was a great mistake. Really, we meant "no comment." During the war, the Japanese people were urged not to use the English language — to forget English. Therefore, I could not recall the English term "no comment." I thought that the Japanese expression which was most close to "no comment" was *mokusatsu*.[10]

The Japanese reply to the declaration was communicated, again by radio, and the Americans interpreted it as a rejection of their offer. The president then ordered the chief of the air force to drop the atomic bomb at the first opportunity.

But imagine this exchange taking place not through radio waves but face to face. The Japanese foreign minister says, "We wish to treat your offer with silent contempt." The face of the American ambassador clouds over, his jaw drops, he begins to turn away in sorrow. The Japanese foreign minister says, "Wait, perhaps you misunderstand. If you comprehend what I am saying you would not have that look on your face. Let me rephrase it. Perhaps 'no comment' is the phrase I want." The American ambassador smiles with relief and rushes to the embassy to cable Washington to hold off any vigorous military moves.

Perhaps the historical case was not so simple. The quotation comes from a man who had a great deal of self-interest in his interpretation of events. There is in fact reason to believe that the Japanese cabinet would ultimately have rejected the Potsdam Declaration in any case. But by seeing a concrete illustration of how personal contact could make a crucial difference, we can see why political leaders continue to affirm the importance of diplomacy. Henry Kissinger, after discussing his contacts over the years with Soviet Ambassador Dobrynin, describes the role of the professional diplomat as "crucial in crises when judgments affecting matters of life and death depend on a subtle and rapid understanding of intangibles."[11]

Diplomats, when performing their official duties, follow codified procedure known as *diplomatic protocol*. Much of the behavior this regulates is ceremonial — spelling out, for example, who greets an official arriving at the airport. Because contemporary American society has become so informal, such details may strike us as comical, but they are still taken seriously by many people. Protocol prescribes that a departing head of government be seen off at the airport by the ambassador of the country he or she is going to visit. When the head of the Indian government left for the United States in 1970, the American ambassador was not present at the airport. His excuse was that the switchboard operator had failed to wake him on time. One member of the Indian Parliament, in a fitting gesture, made him a present of a musical alarm clock.[12]

A more important purpose of protocol is to allow governments great precision in their communication with each other. A government may decide to deliver a formal *Note,* a less formal *Note Verbal,* or an even less formal *Aide-Memoir.* By its choice of means, a government indicates how serious it considers a matter. In 1968 the United States sent two destroyers into the Black Sea. According to the Montreux Convention of 1936, which regulates traffic into the Black Sea, ships from states not bordering the Black Sea may enter it only if their guns are less than 203 millimeters (8 inches). The destroyers had guns of only 127 millimeters but one had missile-launchers of 305 millimeters. The Russians issued a protest to Turkey, which, as the country controlling the straits into the Black Sea, was given the responsibility by the Montreux Convention for enforcing the convention's terms. The Russians delivered their protest in a Note, which was addressed to the foreign minister and signed by the ambassador. The Turks replied with the less formal Note Verbal or "oral note," which despite its name is written but addressed more impersonally to the foreign ministry and never signed. The Turks not only rejected the Russian claim but indicated by this means that they did not wish to treat the question as a serious matter.[13]

Although protocol permits precision, it does not guarantee it. Defenders of traditional diplomacy, such as Harold Nicolson, neglect an important part of diplomacy: lying. Indeed, a famous definition describes a diplomat as an honest man sent abroad to lie for his country.[14] Often, a diplomat tries to be at least ambiguous or equivocal if not downright deceptive. China, in the years after the Communist accession to power, frequently used the phrase "not stand idly by" to suggest support for various threatened neighbors such as Korea or Vietnam. But the precise nature of the commitment of China to these neighbors was never made clear, which was in fact China's intention.

In 1950, when China used diplomatic channels to send a warning to the United States not to cross the 38th parallel and carry the Korean War into North Korea, the major problem for the United States was not lack of clarity. The United States knew the meaning of the words conveyed by intermediaries from the Chinese. The major problem was the truth of the words. Did China truly intend to enter the war if United States troops crossed the 38th parallel, or were they only bluffing? Even the presence of a Chinese diplomatic mission in Washington staffed by the most highly trained diplomats would not have solved the problem.[15]

The language of diplomatic notes is extremely formal, but this formality serves a useful purpose. Here is an example from the height of the Cold War. In April 1950, the Soviet Union shot down a United States Navy plane over the Baltic Sea. The United States delivered a written note of protest, part of which read:

> The Ambassador of the United States has been instructed to protest in the most solemn manner against this violation of international law and of the most elementary rules of peaceful conduct between nations. . . . The United States Government confidently expects that, when its investigation is completed, the Soviet Government will express its regret for the unlawful behavior of its aviators, will see to it that those responsible for this action are promptly and severely punished, and will, in accordance with established custom among peace loving nations, pay appropriate indemnity for the unprovoked destruction of American lives and property.[16]

Notice the characteristics of diplomatic language. The ambassador does not take personal responsibility; rather he "has been instructed to protest." Nor does he blame the foreign minister to whom he is protesting; rather it is "those responsible for this action." The Soviet Union is given time to make up its mind how to respond; this is described as time to complete "its investigation." Finally, the United States is telling the Soviet Union what its demands are: expression of regret, disclaimer of responsibility (which is what punishment of "those responsible" means), and indemnity.

THE VALUE OF DIPLOMACY

The 1950 incident, while providing an example of diplomatic formality and correctness even under provocation, is not a case in which diplomacy succeeded. The Soviet Union did not comply with United States demands. The Cold War did not abate. Although the number of incidents of this sort did not escalate, that may have been as much the result of American attempts to avoid them as of diplomatic warnings.

A better illustration of the value of diplomacy occurred almost twenty years later. On June 30, 1968, Soviet fighters forced down on Soviet territory in the Kurile Islands a United States plane taking soldiers to Vietnam (see Figure 16.1). The next day, July 1, was scheduled for signing the Non-Proliferation Treaty. We have some reason to think that the plane incident was an effort by someone in the Soviet military forces opposed to arms control to provoke an incident with the United States that would lead to cancellation of the ceremony. A few days before, Foreign Minister Andrei Gromyko had referred to such opponents: "To the good-for-nothing theoreticians who try to tell us . . . that disarmament is an illusion, we reply: by taking such a stand you fall into step with the most dyed-in-the-wool imperialist reaction."[17]

But the United States government did not let itself be drawn into a crisis. It immediately got in touch with Soviet officials to clarify the incident. Secretary of State Dean Rusk telephoned Soviet Ambassador Anatoly Dobrynin. United States Ambassador to the Soviet Union Llewellyn Thompson discussed the matter with Soviet Premier Kosygin the next day during the signing ceremonies for the Non-Proliferation Treaty, which went ahead as planned. The United States expressed regret over a violation of Soviet airspace, even though the radar records of the Japanese Air Self-Defense Force indicated that the plane was first approached by other aircraft and only then changed course. The next day, July 2, the plane and passengers were released, to continue on to Vietnam. Neither the Soviet press nor the official *Department of State Bulletin* reported the incident. Diplomacy had turned a possible conflagration into cold and scattered ashes.[18]

Here is a second example of a dispute solved by diplomacy. In November 1969 the foreign ministers of Italy and Austria (meeting in a neutral third country, Denmark) signed a 120-point agreement on South Tyrol, putting to

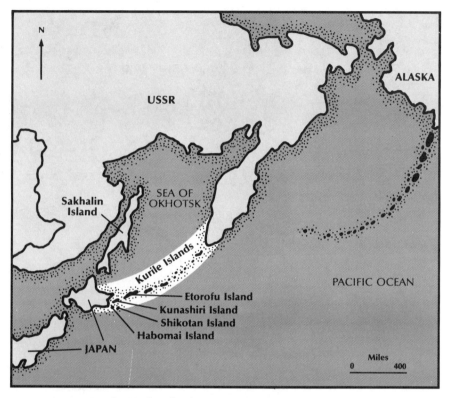

Figure 16.1   The Kurile Islands

an end a dispute going back fifty years. South Tyrol (see Figure 16.2), though it had a German-speaking majority, was transferred to Italy as part of the spoils of World War I. For decades the Italians had tried to assimilate the province, but even in 1969 the German-speaking population still outnumbered the Italian-speaking, 230,000 to 130,000. In the mid-1960's terrorists based in the northern part of Tyrol, on the Austrian side of the border, began attacks on border guards and customs houses to call attention to their demands for greater autonomy if not return to Austria. The Italians warned the Austrians that they would close the border if the attacks were not stopped. Negotiations between diplomats of the two countries finally led to the 1969 agreement. The Italians promised greater autonomy for the region of South Tyrol (although nothing close to the unification with Austria that the extremists wanted). They also promised the Austrians that they would support the Austrian request to associate with the Common Market. These concessions enabled the Austrians to overcome domestic opposition and to crack down on terrorists operating out of Austria.[19]

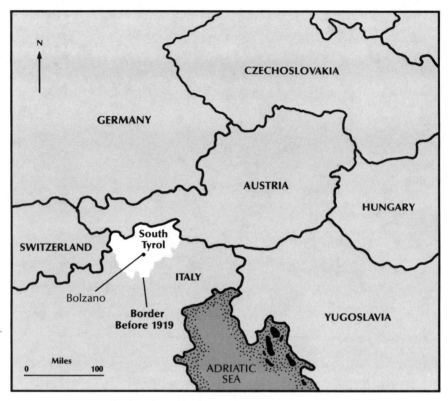

Figure 16.2   The South Tyrol

The first example, the settlement of the Kurile incident of 1968, illustrates how diplomacy can avert conflict. The two countries involved were quick to communicate to each other what the issue was, how seriously they viewed it, and what they intended to do about it. Presumably the United States received assurance that this was an "unauthorized" act and those responsible would be punished. Presumably the Russians made it clear that such acts were not part of Soviet policy and would not stop the signing of arms control agreements. A more violent response, perhaps even escalating to war, was averted. Diplomacy is also helpful to governments that want to avoid a conflict being forced on them by domestic pressure. Austrian government leaders in 1969 ranked many foreign policy objectives higher than the recovery of South Tyrol, but a strong nationalist minority that could awaken widespread sympathy made it difficult for them to avoid the issue. The Italians, aware of the pressures the Austrians were subjected to, were able to offer some small concessions to their German-speaking minority, enabling the Austrian government to claim that it had won some gains and justifying their actions against national extremists. Furthermore, by offering a concession in an unrelated area — support for association with the Common Market, to which Italy belonged and which Austria wanted to join — the Italians enabled the Austrian government to turn attention away from the nationalist issue. Good diplomacy can make it easier for a government to take a course of action that it knows is for the best even if it is unpopular.

THE NEW DIPLOMACY AND ITS PROBLEMS

Diplomats operate, but wars still occur. Negotiations between Greeks and Turks over Cyprus in 1974 could not prevent war from breaking out. This is not because diplomats weren't doing their job but because there are limits to what even the best diplomats can do.

Some writers have blamed conditions of the modern world for the inability of diplomacy to resolve more disputes.[20] They contrast the "new diplomacy" of the twentieth century unfavorably with the "old diplomacy" of the nineteenth century and earlier. In the nineteenth century diplomats spoke the same language, both literally and figuratively. Not only were they all fluent in French; they also came from the same social class, attended the same schools, and lived in the same style, no matter which country they represented. The result was a shared set of values: discretion, face-saving, compromise, above all avoidance of personal rudeness. A diplomat never called another a liar; the proper locution was "Your Excellency appears to be misinformed." This was a far cry from the Russian coal miner calling for attention by pounding his shoe on the table at the UN.

And yet, we may ask, is this objection so serious? Khrushchev, the Russian coal miner, has been replaced by more polished leaders. Henry Kissinger was able to negotiate with the North Vietnamese and the Chinese despite their public attacks on the United States. Anwar Sadat and Menachem Begin were able to overcome decades of invective against each other and agree on a peace treaty within eighteen months. On the other hand, even the stiff formality of the nineteenth century was not successful in avoiding all war. The wars for German unification were as serious as wars in the modern world and were not averted because Prussians, Austrians, and French all spoke French. Henry Kissinger has pointed out that resident diplomats, who acquire a "feel for the complexities of other capitals and leaders," may be all the more necessary today precisely because political leaders do not come from similar backgrounds and communicate within the same cultural framework.[21]

Another criticism of the new diplomacy is the loss of confidentiality. A keystone of the new diplomacy, as promoted by President Woodrow Wilson, was "open covenants openly arrived at." President Wilson himself found this impossible to put into practice. He negotiated crucial parts of the Versailles Treaty behind closed doors with the French and British prime ministers while Marine guards patrolled the corridors.[22] But in recent years technological and political changes have brought us closer to Wilson's ideal. Reporters pursue important diplomatic figures, making secret contact with other diplomats difficult. Television crews on motorcycles waited outside Henry Kissinger's residence in Paris to record any meeting with North Vietnamese diplomats. Since the invention of the Xerographic copying machine, it is difficult to preserve the secrecy of documents; in only a short time they can be reproduced in massive quantities.

An even more serious obstacle to confidentiality comes from politicians. Members of Congress increasingly demand to learn the details of negotiations. The diplomat must heed these demands. Failure to inform Congress ensures that blame for failure will rest solely with the executive branch. It may also lead to failure to provide the necessary appropriations to make good on promises. But the need to explain and justify in public decisions made during private negotiations places a constraint on the negotiators. Politicians are interested more in domestic opinion than in reaching an agreement with a foreign country. They may see more political advantage in crying, "Sellout!"

The attempts of American diplomats to negotiate an end to the war with the Japanese in 1945 met with protests from Congress. Senator Richard Russell of Georgia, upon reading the Potsdam Declaration in the newspaper, telegraphed a protest to the White House. He wrote that Americans "believe that we should continue to strike the Japanese until they are brought groveling to their knees. We should cease our appeals to Japan to sue for peace. The next plea for peace should come from an utterly destroyed Tokyo."[23] Public pressure of this sort appears to have weighed more heavily on the president than the advice of professional diplomats, such as Joseph Grew, who were urging that we induce the Japanese to surrender not by dropping the atomic bomb but by promising that we would allow them to retain their emperor.

Similarly, the Cyprus dispute was intractable in 1974, even following a clear-cut Turkish military victory, because neither Turkey nor Greece had a government strong enough to make a concession. Each was afraid that the charge of sellout would be enough to topple it. The diplomats could have devised a solution; the politicians would have been afraid to implement it.

Democratic leaders are presumed to be the representatives of their people, and it is seen as undemocratic for representatives not to tell these people what they have been doing on their behalf. Furthermore, promises made in negotiation often require extensive domestic support for their fulfillment. Henry Kissinger's negotiations with Middle Eastern countries involved extensive promises of aid, but this money could not come out of his own pocket. Knowledge by foreign countries that Congress might not make good on such promises undermines the secretary of state's effectiveness. Yet when Congress comes to consider the issue, it brings its own priorities. Proposals to deal with the Cyprus problem were viewed differently by the secretary of state and the Congress, because many members of Congress had vocal constituents of Greek origin but few had constituents of Turkish origin. The argument by the secretary of state that one-sided measures (such as cutting off aid to Turkey) by themselves would not resolve the dispute was less persuasive to representatives seeking reelection than the votes of Greek Americans.

Increased popular participation in politics is a characteristic not only of the United States but of the entire world. This has meant that some solutions to disputes available to diplomats in the nineteenth century are no longer available in the twentieth century. One traditional solution was neutralizing an area. After Belgium declared its independence from France in 1830, there was concern among European countries about how the new country would affect the balance of power. This concern was alleviated by declaring it neutral — permanently out of the balance of power. Another traditional solution was partition. European countries avoided war in Africa by simply dividing up the continent, ignoring in the process any political units or ethnic boundaries already established. Where partition was not applied, spheres of influence often were. The United States, by the Monroe Doctrine, reserved for itself special rights in the western hemisphere. Russia, Britain, and other European countries did the same in parts of China.

Increased participation in politics makes such solutions difficult to the point of impossibility. The people living in these countries do not want to submit to partition, foreign influences, or even neutralization. The wars in Korea in 1950 and in Vietnam from 1946 to 1975 were fundamentally wars in opposition to partition. Cuba's foreign policy under Castro is a repudiation of the Monroe Doctrine. Even pledges of neutralization are seen as conflicting with the sovereign rights of a nation. Austria, bound to neutrality by the peace treaty of 1955, has declared its right to join the Common Market, even though the Soviet Union has claimed this move would violate Austrian neutrality.

The role of diplomats is changing in other ways. Domestic constituents are increasingly important in foreign policy. The president embargoes grain sales to Russia because of the invasion of Afghanistan and farmers protest. The United States tries to maintain normal relations with South Africa and protesters harass South African diplomats. More ambassadors accredited to the US government in Washington show up on Capitol Hill, the Japanese to lobby against bills aimed at forcing them to open their markets to American goods, the Turks to make the case for more aid.[24] Under these new conditions, diplomats are beginning to see part of their job as mollifying subnational groups or even mediating among them. Diplomats are losing their unique status as agents of a unified and coherent state and are becoming instead political operators.[25]

But we should not spend too much time lamenting the passing of the old aristocratic world. In 1661 France came close to declaring war on Spain because the Spanish ambassador's coach had cut in front of the French ambassador's coach in London.[26] Then and now, diplomats have always had obstacles in the way of preventing war. Diplomats encounter the greatest difficulty when neither side has any desire to concede. Some wars are not the result of failure in communication; the sides may understand all too well exactly what is at stake.

In 1967 the United States urged restraint on Israel, to give diplomacy time to work. We had little reason to think it would. Nasser believed he had the upper hand militarily and had no reason to compromise. Even when the Israelis had demonstrated their military superiority in their attack on June 5, he could not accept it, believing instead that the attack had been made with British and American help. If an actual demonstration of military power is not effective, it is hard to see how the words of diplomats would be.

Sometimes people advocate diplomacy on the grounds that "if we're talking, we're not fighting."[27] This is a strange argument. No factory manager would say, "We should bargain with the union, because if they're talking, they're not striking." Strikes go on during negotiations and so do wars. The Vietnam negotiations finally were brought to a conclusion after the bombing of North Vietnamese cities. Critics have argued that this bombing was unnecessary, but they can hardly argue that it was incompatible with diplomacy. The agreement was signed shortly thereafter. Fighting can enhance bargaining power, so we might expect, on some occasions at least, diplomacy to be accompanied by an increase in conflict. This is more likely to be true of negotiations to end fighting in progress than of those to head fighting off, and it may not be true even then. But clearly negotiations do not make war disappear.

LIMITATIONS OF DIPLOMACY

Advocates of diplomacy as an approach to peace assume an underlying harmony of interests among states. Even when states differ in philosophy and national characteristics, they can still find overlapping interests. Iran, whatever the character of the regime in power, has oil; the United States, whatever policies it may be following, has grain. Both countries would benefit from trade with each other, even though domestic politicians in each may temporarily obscure that basic interest in appeals to passion. Professional diplomats try to emphasize common interests and reduce the importance of passion in the relations among states. To the extent that political leaders heed them, diplomats make relations among states more rational.[28]

If states' interests are fundamentally in harmony, then reasoned discussion will serve to make this harmony more apparent. The more states communicate with each other, the more rational their policies toward each other will become. Over the centuries, diplomacy has developed into a highly formal system of communication. But the importance of the traditional practitioners of this art, the professional diplomats, in preventing war has been diminished by the modern technology of transportation and communication and by increased popular participation in policy-making. The cool reason of the diplomatic elite is being replaced by the more emotional demands of the less well informed masses.

Without question the world of diplomats on many occasions has helped prevent small incidents from becoming the occasion for war. On the other hand, there have been enough cases to demonstrate that diplomacy alone is not enough to prevent war. Perhaps the assumption of a basic harmony of interests is mistaken; perhaps political leaders are not yet rational enough to recognize such basic harmony. Whatever the reason, historical experience should not make us optimistic about the ability of diplomats alone to prevent all wars.

But unlike some proposals for achieving peace, one could not argue that diplomacy in some ways makes the world more dangerous. World government or balance of power systems may increase violence in the world; arms races increase violence if they fail to deter war. Increased reliance on diplomacy may not bring peace, but it is unlikely to increase the risk of war.

In one particular way, diplomatic contact needs to be increased. Because of the symbolic function of a diplomat, it has been customary to break diplomatic relations in time of war. The ambassadors go home and embassies are turned over to the custody of third states. This also happens in crises short of war. The United States broke relations with Cuba in 1961 over the expropriation of American investments. Such behavior reduces communication at the time it is needed most. It demonstrates that two states are not always the best judges of their own interests or able to conduct business with each other in a rational fashion. Sometimes neutral outsiders, third parties, can provide valuable assistance. This assistance can take various forms: mediation, arbitration, adjudication. A number of means and institutions are designed for these purposes, and we will look at them next.

NOTES

1. Joseph Goulden, *Truth is the First Casualty* (Chicago: Rand McNally, 1969), p. 103; see also James Bamford, *The Puzzle Palace* (New York: Penguin, 1983, pp. 279–293.

2. C. L. Sulzberger, "Sent to Lie Abroad No More," *The New York Times*, January 28, 1972.

3. Bernard Gwertzman, "For Marcos, a Restless Night of Calls to U.S.," *The New York Times*, February 26, 1986, p. Y8.

4. *Newsweek*, August 4, 1969, p. 38; *Newsweek*, August 11, 1969, p. 17.

5. News conference on May 6, 1975; transcript reprinted in *The New York Times*, May 7, 1975.

6. Nadav Safran, *Israel: The Embattled Ally* (Cambridge: Harvard University Press, 1978), pp. 567–568.

7. Leslie H. Gelb, "Senate Unit Charges U.S. with Using Cyprus Relief to Help Turkey," *The New York Times*, October 14, 1974, p. 3.

8. United Nations, *Conference on Diplomatic Intercourse and Immunities, Vienna, March 2–April 14, 1961*, 2 vols. (Geneva, 1962).

9. Barton Whaley, *Codeword BARBAROSSA* (Cambridge: MIT Press, 1973), pp. 110–111.

10. Len Giovannitti and Fred Freed, *The Decision to Drop the Bomb* (New York: Coward-McCann, 1965), p. 231.

11. Henry Kissinger, *White House Years* (Boston: Little, Brown, 1979), p. 139.

12. *The New York Times*, October 23, 1970; *The New York Times*, October 25, 1970.

13. *The New York Times*, December 7, 1968; Charles W. Thayer *Diplomat* (New York: Harper & Brothers, 1959), p. 99.

14. Henry Wotton, 1651, "An ambassador is an honest man sent to lie abroad for the commonwealth."

15. This point is developed in detail in Robert Jervis, *The Logic of Images in International Relations* (Princeton: Princeton University Press, 1970), pp. 24–25.,

16. *Department of State Bulletin*, Vol. 22, No. 565 (May 1, 1950), pp. 667–668.

17. John Newhouse, *Cold Dawn: The Story of SALT* (New York: Holt, Rinehart and Winston, 1973), p. 104 (quoting from *Pravda*).

18. *The New York Times*, July 1–3, 1968.

19. *The New York Times*, December 1, 1969.

20. Hans J. Morgenthau, in "The Decline of Diplomacy," *Politics Among Nations*, 4th ed. (New York: Alfred A. Knopf, 1967), pp. 525–531; Harold Nicolson, *Diplomacy*, 3rd ed. (London: Oxford University Press, 1963).

21. Kissinger, p. 139.

22. Nicolson, p. 43.

23. Paul Kecskemeti, *Strategic Surrender* (New York: Atheneum, 1964), p. 165.

24. Steven V. Robert, "Foreign Policy: Lot of Table Thumping Going On," *The New York Times*, May 29, 1985, p. Y10.

25. Gilbert R. Winham, "Practitioners' Views of International Negotiation," *World Politics*, Vol. 32, No. 1 (October 1979) pp. 111–135.

26. Nicolson, p. 99.

27. Vice-Admiral J. Victor Smith to *Pueblo* court of inquiry, *Christian Science Monitor*, March 13, 1969, p. 3.

28. Hedley Bull, *The Anarchical Society* (New York: Columbia University Press, 1977), pp. 170–183.

Chapter 17

Third Parties

Diplomacy cannot always prevent war. If there are no diplomatic relations between states, then diplomats have no opportunity to exercise their skills. Sometimes domestic forces keep states from maintaining diplomatic contact. The United States initially broke off relations with the new Communist Chinese regime in 1949 for the legitimate reason that the Communists were refusing to respect the diplomatic immunity of American diplomats. But long after the dispute had occurred the United States was inhibited from renewing diplomatic ties by powerful domestic pressures from the "China Lobby." As President Eisenhower and Vice-President Nixon left office in 1960, they both warned incoming President Kennedy that although they would support the new administration on most foreign policy issues, they would publicly oppose any conciliatory moves toward China.[1] Similarly in the Middle East the governments of Arab states have encountered strong opposition in establishing diplomatic relations with Israel.

At other times, diplomatic contact may be present but the communication between two states can be seriously distorted by the stress of crisis. Communication among states during the weeks of crisis preceding World War I has been intensively studied by scholars from Stanford University. They conclude that during periods of high tension between states the communication channels are overloaded, with the result that messages become shorter, with less detail and less discussion of alternatives. Decision-makers tend to "suture off" part of the communications apparatus, relying on fewer and fewer sources of information. Along with this they show a tendency to make decisions on the basis of feelings and emotions rather than rational calculations.[2] This distortion of communication is the result of crisis. But even when there is no crisis, religious and national feelings distort communication. It is difficult for a Turk to react dispassionately to a report that Greek Cypriots are murdering Turkish Cypriots, or for Arabs to examine critically a report that Israelis are desecrating Moslem holy places.

Communication often breaks down so thoroughly that it is impossible even to agree on the facts of a case. Border disputes typically involve different interpretations of matters that should be factual. Another case that is often a dispute over facts is the accusation by one country that another is arming against it. In 1967 Egypt accused Israel of mobilizing forces on its northern border for an attack on Syria. Lacking diplomatic representatives in Israel, it was difficult for the Egyptians to verify this act or for the Israelis to prove to them that these fears were unfounded.

Even when communication among states is not greatly distorted, diplomacy may reach an impasse because each side has its prestige committed to a publicly stated position. Compromise is then difficult because the original contest is replaced by one over prestige. All disputes have two aspects: the dispute itself and the bigger question of what the solution to the dispute is going to reveal about the relative power of the disputants. When the child asks the baby-sitter for permission to watch one-half hour more of television, the question is primarily a test of power. Baby-sitters, like states, hesitate to give in because they know that one request will be followed by many more. But if both sides are determined not to appear to be appeasers, even reasonable compromises are ruled out.

THE VALUE OF THIRD PARTIES

Third parties can help alleviate these difficulties. For one thing, they can facilitate communication. One common form of this is what we call providing *good offices*. Good offices are the services of a neutral agent, trusted by both sides, who transmits messages. Children have to provide good offices when parents aren't speaking to each other and mother says, "You tell your father that his dinner is ready." Back in 1968, before airplane hijackings had become commonplace, a Palestinian group, the Popular Front for the Liberation of Palestine (PFLP), hijacked an Israeli airliner as it flew over Italy and diverted it to Algeria. The Algerians, embarrassed by this unexpected landing, held onto the plane, crew, and passengers, not knowing what to do with them. Israel, having no diplomatic relations with Algeria, went to Secretary General of the United Nations U Thant and asked him to use his good offices to arrange for return of the plane, crew, and passengers.

The Algerians hesitated and two weeks later the International Association of Airline Pilots threatened a boycott of Algeria unless the crew was released. Now it was Algeria that turned to the secretary general for his good offices.

Neutral third parties can also facilitate settlement by a method known as *inquiry*, or establishing the facts of the case. When tension is high, such a simple step is often difficult for rivals. In 1974 a clash on the border between Iran and Iraq resulted in the death of sixty-five soldiers. The United Nations secretary general appointed a Mexican diplomat to help the two countries find a solution. One of his first findings was that the two countries were using entirely different maps of the border.[3]

Another contribution to peaceful settlement that can be provided by third parties is to delay any action until tempers have cooled down a bit. This contribution was described by a former American ambassador to the UN in this way:

> I see some things that you cannot solve, now. Maybe in 10 years you can, but you can't do it now, and the best thing you can do is to sort of spin it out and drag it along and temporize and pettifog, and that way they don't shoot each other, and that is that much clear gain.[4]

If you suspect that diplomats are trying to bore countries to the point at which they accept a solution, you might be right. There are cases in which inaction and delay seem to have contributed to a solution. After World War II both Italy and Yugoslavia claimed Trieste and the area around it (See Figure 17.1). As part of the possessions of Mussolini's Italy it was occupied by the victors of World War II. Because Italian and Yugoslav populations were interspersed, no solution was acceptable to both sides. Diplomatic protests were accompanied by violent demonstrations, reaching their climax in September 1947, when only a United States roadblock stopped invading Yugoslav troops. The issue was put before the United Nations but no country moved to impose a solution. Periodic resorts to violence continued, with riots in 1948, 1952, and 1953, but by 1955 tempers had calmed down enough for the countries involved to sign an agreement providing for a compromise settlement. Final agreement was not reached until 1975.

The Trieste case illustrates another contribution of third parties: providing a neutral place for disputants to meet. The discussions leading to the 1955 agreement on Trieste were held in London. Not only did this avoid suggestions of inequality between the two sides (for the Yugoslavs to negotiate in Italy would indicate Yugoslav subservience to Italy, and vice versa) but it also helped shield the diplomats from inquiring reporters and noisy demonstrators from one side or the other. The United States ambassador to Austria, Llewellyn E. Thompson, was sent to London to facilitate the Trieste talks. To keep his purpose secret, he pretended that he was going to London to buy clothes. He was ordered to London the day his youngest child was born; when the agreement was finally signed, his fictitious wardrobe had assumed incredible proportions and his daughter was eight months old. But, in the early phases, neither the Italian nor Yugoslav press had an inkling that the volatile Trieste issue was under discussion, a fact to which Thompson later attributed much of the success of the conference.[5]

MEDIATION: CYPRUS, INDO-CHINA, THE MIDDLE EAST

Of course a third party may go considerably further in helping to settle a dispute. Two recognized methods are mediation and conciliation. In *mediation*, the third party not only carries messages but also adds to them suggestions for settlement. In *conciliation*, a person or commission studies

Figure 17.1   Trieste

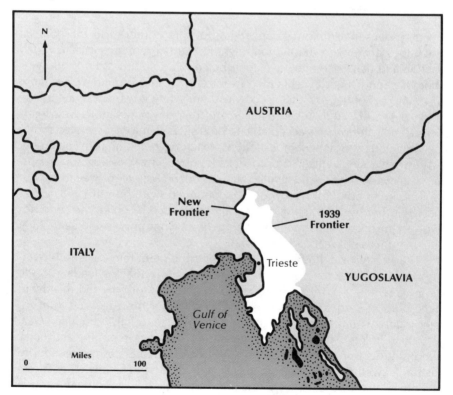

the problem and issues a report. Both methods are nonbinding; their success depends on the basic desire of each side to reach a settlement.

The record of these methods is mixed, as the recent history of the Middle East shows. The United Nations appointed Count Bernadotte as official mediator between Israel and the Arabs in spring of 1948, but he failed to head off war. During the fighting, his proposals were considered so favorable to the Arabs that he was assassinated by Zionist extremists. His successor, Ralph Bunche, fared much better and won the Nobel Peace Prize for arranging the armistices that ended the war. Following the 1967 war, the UN mediator Gunnar Jarring failed to move the sides toward settlement. After the 1973 war, Henry Kissinger, acting for the United States, arranged a cease-fire in 1973 and disengagements in 1974 and 1975.

An episode from the 1974 "shuttle diplomacy" of Kissinger illustrates the way in which mediators can facilitate settlement. The Israelis had made a proposal that Kissinger thought the Syrians would find so unacceptable that they would break off negotiations. They proposed that they withdraw their troops to allow the UN to set up a buffer zone, but only from territory they had recently captured from Syria. In the next stage of his shuttle, Kissinger did not give the Syrians the details of the Israeli plan; he concentrated instead on the concept of a buffer zone. After winning adherence to this concept from both sides, he was then able to get agreement on the location of the zone as part of "working out the details."[6]

Mediation makes it possible for a state with prestige committed to a publicly stated position to back down. The value of a third party was demonstrated in the Cyprus dispute of 1967. Cyprus has been a perennial problem because of its strategic location and its ethnic diversity. Slightly more than 80 percent of the population are Greeks, and most of them would prefer union with Greece; slightly less than 20 per cent are Turks and would prefer partition of the island. In 1967 the central government of Cyprus, which was dominated by the Greek Cypriots, attempted to extend governmental control into Turkish villages. The Turks resisted, firing on Greek Cypriot police patrols. The violence quickly escalated. Thousands of troops from the Greek mainland were sent to reinforce the Greek Cypriot National Guard, far in excess of the 950 troops permitted by treaty. Demonstrations in Turkish cities by students and young men called for war with Greece; the Turkish government mobilized an invasion force and invasion fleet.

Several organizations sent mediators to the area — the United Nations, NATO, and the United States government. The most effective of them was the one sent by President Johnson, Cyrus Vance. He made half a dozen trips between the Greek and Turkish capitals, as well as several trips to the Cypriot capital, and got an agreement. Although it was never announced publicly, the Turks demobilized their invasion force, the Greeks recalled their troops, the National Guard was downgraded, and the UN peacekeeping force already on Cyprus was expanded. Neither side really wanted war. The Greeks, in the assessment of experts, would have lost any war with Turkey. The Turks wished to avoid a conflict with the United States, which might mean loss of United States aid and support. But both governments were under domestic pressure not to give in. It helped them to be able to say that they were acceding to American wishes. Furthermore, because the suggestions for concessions came from Cyrus Vance, neither side could interpret the other's move as a sign of weakness. Vance provided each of them a ladder to climb down, while keeping the other side from kicking the ladder over.[7]

Unfortunately not all mediation attempts end with success. Even Cyrus Vance's efforts on Cyprus in 1967 did not achieve a permanent solution. The invasion averted in 1967 took place in 1974, over the same issue. Unlike the case of Trieste, delay did not make a solution easier.

Two other conflicts have also seen mediation efforts fail to cool off violence. Vietnam was the major conflict of the 1960's; the Middle East was the major conflict of the 1970's. In each case mediation played a part in a settlement, but in each case the settlement failed. The war in Vietnam between the forces of Ho Chi Minh, at that time called the Viet Minh, and the French was brought to an end by the Geneva Conference of 1954. At that conference the British, the Russians, and the Chinese all mediated between the French and the Viet Minh.[8] As a result of the conference, the French withdrew from all of Indo-China, but the Viet Minh got control of only the northern half of the country. Article Seven of the Final Declaration of the Geneva Conference called for elections in all of Vietnam within two years, provided "all necessary conditions obtain." But the declaration is totally ambiguous on this point. It doesn't say what kind of elections. A vote on whether to reunify? A vote for a government for the entire country? And the meaning of the qualification "all necessary conditions" is never spelled out. One commentator described his meeting a member of the delegation to the 1954 Geneva Conference six years later and commenting on the vagueness of Article Seven, whereupon the Frenchman seized his hand and said, "'Thank you for the compliment, for such was our intention; we stayed up all night phrasing and rephrasing Article Seven.'"[9] The diplomats provided a formula that could be interpreted in different ways by different parties, enabling each side to describe the conference as a victory. The diplomats of course knew what they were doing; they were not solving the problem, they were buying time, hoping that the problem would solve itself. In Vietnam it did not.

In the Middle East the war in 1967 came to an end after only six days but it was not until six months later that the Security Council endorsed Resolution 242, which was to provide a basis for solving the conflict. The six-month delay was devoted to an attempt by third parties to word a resolution in a way that both sides could accept. The mediation was successful to the extent that wording was agreed on. Israel on the one hand and Egypt and Jordan on the other accepted Resolution 242, as did the various Security Council members, but only because it cold be read in different ways. The Arabs stressed Israeli withdrawal from conquered territory; the Israelis stressed "secure and recognized boundaries." As in Vietnam, the time gained by this measure did not lead to peace; by 1970 Egypt and Israel were fighting the War of Attrition and by 1973 a full-scale war.

ARBITRATION: THE RANN OF CUTCH, THE *ALABAMA* CLAIMS

It is debatable whether clarity or vagueness is more conducive to settling disputes. Those who prefer clarity advocate arbitration and adjudication. *Arbitration* is settlement by a third party, where each side agrees in advance to accept the decision of the third party. Unlike mediation, where the third party merely makes suggestions, arbitration gives the final say to the arbitrator. Arbitration has been used to settle hundreds of international disputes in the nineteenth century, thousands in the twentieth century. Almost all have been minor or peripheral but occasionally a major one has been settled in this way. One case is a dispute between India and Pakistan. There were armed clashes between India and Pakistan in the spring of 1965 in the Rann of Cutch. A rann is a salt marsh; this one is 35,000 square miles. The boundary had been undefined since the former British possession was partitioned into the two states, India and Pakistan, in 1947. Following these clashes Britain mediated the dispute and got India and Pakistan to agree to arbitration. An arbitration panel of three members was set up, one member nominated by India, one by Pakistan, and one by the secretary general of the UN. The panel made its award in February 1968: 350 square miles to Pakistan, the rest to India, with the 275-mile border to be demarcated by stone pillars. The decision appears to be unfair to Pakistan, but in fact the 350 square miles they received was the highest ground in the Rann, suitable for grazing. The territory awarded to India, though not useful for grazing, was of course much larger and the Indian government could also suggest that gas and oil might be found beneath it. The award was implemented by June 1969.[10] India and Pakistan did subsequently go to war but not over the Rann of Cutch. The question of the border in this area appears to have been solved.

International arbitration became popular in the nineteenth century with the success of the procedure in resolving a dispute between the United States and Great Britain in 1872. This case, known as the *Alabama* claims, grew out of the American Civil War. The United States claimed that warships (one of them a cruiser named the *Alabama*) that had been bought illegally in the neutral country of Britain by Confederate agents had damaged United States interests. By the Washington Treaty of 1871 both countries agreed to arbitration. The next year the arbitration panel awarded $15.5 million to the United States. The British accepted this decision and possible hostilities between the two countries were averted.

The success of the *Alabama* claims case led to a number of proposals for applying arbitration to all cases of international conflict. The Hague Conference of 1899 set up the "Permanent Court of International Arbitration," although it was not a court at all but rather a list of names from which states could choose arbitrators. It was not extensively used, however. Undaunted, President William H. Taft in 1909 proposed setting up an international tribunal to settle international disputes, in the beginning among the United States, Great Britain, and France, and later among all states. President Taft indicated in speeches to the public that he thought this would be the first step toward a world court that would eventually solve the problem of war, eliminate the burden of armament, and bring international harmony.[11]

ADJUDICATION: THE "LOBSTER WAR,"
THE CORFU CHANNEL

Settling disputes in already existing courts is called *adjudication* and differs somewhat from arbitration. In arbitrating disputes, the arbitrators have some freedom in making their award. They can compromise, make concessions to both sides, and in general make their award as much on the basis of its acceptability as on the basis of fairness. Adjudication, on the other hand, is thought of as depending on the legal rights and wrongs of the case, which President Taft called "a clean judgment of the facts and the law on its merits."[12] Under adjudication the likelihood is greater that one party will come out a clear winner and the other a clear loser, because the judges are deciding on the legal merits of the case, not the acceptability of their judgment.

Progress toward a world court was interrupted by World War I, but in 1920 a Permanent Court of International Justice was set up under the League of Nations. In 1946 its official name was changed to the International Court of Justice; it is commonly called the World Court. With the demise of the League of Nations, its affiliation was transferred to the United Nations. Any member of the United Nations is automatically a party to it. It consists of fifteen judges, sitting in The Hague. It provides what President Taft advocated, a way for states to settle disputes peacefully.

Consider this war that did *not* take place between France and Brazil in 1963. The two states were quarreling over lobsters. The Geneva Convention of 1958 on the Continental Shelf gives states the rights on anything of value on or under their continental shelves (such as oysters or oil) out to the limits of exploitability or to where the water is about 200 meters (650 feet) deep. In 1962 France began sending lobster boats to South American waters, over the continental shelf of Brazil. The Brazilians ordered the French to move out to deeper waters, leaving the continental shelf to smaller Brazilian vessels. The French rejected this demand and sent a destroyer to accompany the lobster boats. Brazil then put its navy on the alert. By this time (April 1963), both states were asking themselves if they really wanted to go to war over lobsters. Deciding that they didn't, they agreed to send the dispute to adjudication. France claimed that lobsters are like fish — they swim about; therefore they are not part of the continental shelf. Brazil claimed that lobsters are like oysters — they cling to the bottom; therefore they are part of the continental shelf. The court had an essentially zoological question on its hands — are lobsters swimmers or crawlers?

It sounds like the story of the "Lobster War" would be a perfect illustration of the value of international adjudication. Sad to say for the advocates of the World Court, it is not. The dispute was settled without violence, but not by adjudication. Agreement was worked out in private by diplomats from the two countries and ratified by an exchange of letters between presidents in December 1964. Both the negotiations and the content of the letters were kept secret, so that it is difficult to say more about them. The agreement by the two countries to send the dispute for adjudication seems to have been a diplomatic ploy. At first Brazil wanted the dispute adjudicated but France did not. Then there was a legal dispute about which procedure was appropriate under a treaty between the two countries signed in 1909. Finally France submitted the dispute not the World Court but to the International Bureau of the Permanent Court of Arbitration in The Hague. Before that body could act, the dispute was settled by diplomacy.[13]

The "Lobster War" is thus a case where the World Court could have been used but was not. In this way it is typical of international disputes, which rarely wind up before the World Court. From 1945 to 1975, according to a detailed study by one scholar, there were 310 significant conflicts between states.[14] In approximately the same period only 26 disputes were brought before the World Court (along with an additional 14 requests for advisory opinions). Of the 26, 7 went unsettled and 8 were settled independently of the Court; in only 11 cases was the Court partially or entirely responsible for the settlement.[15]

The major reason for the poor record of the World Court is clear from an examination of one of the first cases to come before it, the Corfu Channel case (see Figure 17.2). It resulted from an incident in October 1946, when British destroyers were heavily damaged by mines in the waters of the channel between the island of Corfu (owned by Greece) and Albania. The British claimed that at the very least the Albanians knew that the mines were there, even if they hadn't put them there, and had failed to give warning. The case was brought before the Court in May 1947; judgment was rendered in April 1949. (Like all other courts, the World Court moves slowly.) The Court found that Albania was guilty of failing to notify the world in general and the approaching British naval units in particular of the minefield in an international channel. The Court then awarded damages to Great Britain for the damage to the ships and the loss of life of forty-four sailors. All this was strictly in accordance with prescribed procedures. Expert testimony backed up the decision of the Court. The law on the matter was very clear. But Albania disregarded the decision. No compensation was ever paid.[16]

The Court had no means of enforcing its judgment. In domestic political systems, a court calls on members of the executive branch — sheriffs or marshalls — to see that its decisions are carried out. The World Court is part of a much less well developed political system. The Court has no agents of its own to enforce its judgments. At best, the losing party can invoke article

Figure 17.2   Corfu Channel

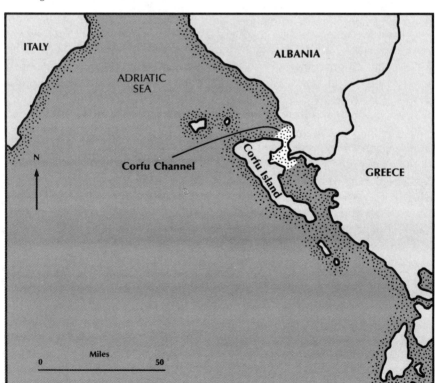

94 of the United Nations Charter, which states: "If any party to a case fails to perform the obligations incumbant upon it under a Judgment rendered by the Court, the other Party may have recourse to the Security Council, which may, if it deems necessary make recommendations or decide upon measures to be taken to give effect to the judgment." Repeated use of the word "may" indicates that even in theory the Council offers no ironclad guarantee of implementing a Court's decision. In practice, the Security Council has had a case referred to it only once. (We will look at the weaknesses of the Security Council in the next chapter.)

The lack of a dependable enforcement mechanism is one weakness of the Court. Another weakness was also revealed by the Corfu Channel case. The Court consists of fifteen members, each from a different country. In this case, because there was a British judge but no Albanian, Albania was allowed to pick an additional judge for the case. (It picked a judge from Czechoslovakia, a country that presumably would be sympathetic.) The final vote of the court was eleven to five against Albania. Those voting in the minority were the Soviet Union, Poland, Czechoslovakia, Egypt, and Brazil. Three of these dissenters were Communist, as was Albania, and a fourth, Egypt had an interest in upholding the principle of control of international channels by neighboring states because of a similar situation in the Middle East, where Egypt bordered on the Strait of Tiran. On the other hand, the judges who voted for Britain came from "free world" states. In other words, there did not seem to be much difference between the way a judge on the Court voted and the way the foreign minister of the same country would vote in a strictly political conference, where there was no pretense of judicial impartiality. From this it is a short step to predicting how a case will be decided, by examining the foreign policies of the states represented on the Court. That is, in fact, a good guide to how the World Court has decided. But knowing in advance how the Court will decide, the side what will lose has no incentive to submit its case. We often guess what the decision of the United States Supreme Court will be but these guesses sometimes turn out to be wrong; the Nixon Administration was surprised by decisions of a supposedly "conservative" Supreme Court on more than one occasion. But it is this unpredictability that makes the Supreme Court effective. It reinforces the belief that the Supreme Court does decide issues on their merits and not the political preferences of the judges. The World Court enjoys no such confidence.

As a contrast to the Corfu Channel case we might look at one of the eight cases successfully resolved by the World Court, the Arbitral Awards case, which settled a border dispute between Nicaragua and Honduras. These two countries engaged in limited hostilities in 1957 before agreeing to a suggestion by the Organization of American States (OAS) to submit it to the World Court in 1958. Both accepted the decision of the Court when it was issued in 1960. But these two states are exceptional. They are among only eight states in the world that accept the jurisdiction of the Court without reservation. The dispute involved neither ideological differences nor professional vital interests. Both states were under pressure from their neighbors in the OAS to accept the decision. In no way did the dispute begin to match the complexity and intractability of the issues that trouble the Middle East or have led to conflict between East and West.

The inability of the World Court to settle disputes with ideological components is evident from the record of states that have used the Court. In the three decades following its creation in 1945, thirty-four states appeared before it; of them, half (seventeen) were either Western European or English-speaking democracies. Only eight states appeared more than once, and almost all of them (seven) also were Western European or English-speaking democracies. By contrast, no Communist state has ever initiated a case. In fact, Czechoslovakia, Hungary, and the Soviet Union have all refused to submit to the Court's jurisdiction, and cases in which they were involved were discontinued without settlement.[17]

AN EVALUATION: EL CHAMIZAL, SPANISH SAHARA

One political scientist, K. J. Holsti, has made a systematic attempt to compare various forms of settlement.[18] He first identified seventy-seven conflicts over a forty-year period (1919–1939 and 1945–1965, excluding the years of World War I and World War II). He defined "conflict" as limited to serious disputes between states where force or threat of force was used. After finding seven disputes of this type, he identified 131 attempts to settle them (obviously, more than one attempt was made to solve some of the conflicts). Table 17.1 shows what Holsti found about these various forms of settlement. Notice that none of these methods was successful as much as half of the time; the best rate of success achieved was only 47 per cent. Of course even

Table 17.1   SUCCESS IN SETTLING DISPUTES

Method used	Number of times used	Percentage of success
Mediation	9	22
International tribunal	11	45
Multilateral conference	16	44
Bilateral negotiations	47	47
International organization	48	37

Source: Compiled from K. J. Holsti, "Resolving International Conflicts," *Journal of Conflict Resolution*, Vol. 10, No. 3 (September 1966), pp. 285–289.

that rate of success justifies the efforts of diplomats and third parties. We probably would be willing to undergo an operation for terminal cancer even if the success rate was only 47 per cent. But the findings suggest that as practiced today diplomacy and third-party settlement do not guarantee an end to war.

A major obstacle to any peaceful settlement is the still universally accepted principle of sovereignty. Sovereignty means supreme power, unrestrained by anything, and, as Albania demonstrated in the Corfu Channel case, that means unrestrained by a decision of the World Court. A dramatic illustration of the pervasiveness of sovereignty comes from the United States. For a long time the boundary between the United States and Mexico has been the Rio Grande. In 1864 a flood on the river in the neighborhood of El Paso led to a relocation of the river bed, with the result that 630 acres that had been on the Mexican side of the river were now on the American side. This piece of land is known as the Chamizal Tract. Almost half a century passed before the United States and Mexico agreed to resolve the dispute by arbitration. An arbitration commission consisting of one United States citizen, one Mexican, and one Canadian was set up in 1910. In 1911 it awarded the tract to Mexico. Even though arbitration means that states bind themselves in advance to the decision of the arbitrators, when the decision was announced, the United States refused to accept it; not until 1967 was the land returned to Mexico. Yet the president of the United States at this time was William H. Taft, the same one who was trying to introduce treaties that would require arbitration of disputes between states. Speaking in 1914 to the New York Peace Society in favor of his plan, President Taft said:

> But the query is made: "How will judgments of such a court be enforced; what will be the sanction of their execution?" I am very little concerned about that. After we have gotten the cases into court and decided and the judgments embodied in a solemn declaration of a court thus established, few nations will care to face the condemnation of international public opinion and disobey the judgment.[19]

One wonders what other states he had in mind by that phrase "few nations."

Outright defiance of judicial or arbitral decisions is an extreme manifestation of sovereignty. It is more common for states to place restrictions on techniques of peaceful settlement before submitting to them. The United States agreed in 1946 to the compulsory jurisdiction of the World Court for international disputes, but it did so only with a reservation. When the Senate was debating acceptance of compulsory jurisdiction, Senator Tom Connally of Texas attached an amendment stating that "this declaration shall not apply to . . . disputes with regard to matters which are essentially within the domestic jurisdiction of the United States of America as determined by the United

States of America. . . ."[20] The Connally Reservation shielded the United States from many potential cases. In 1984, however, the government of Nicaragua brought before the World Court a complaint that the United States was violating its sovereignty by such acts as mining Nicaraguan harbors in support of guerrillas opposed to Nicaragua's Sandinista regime. The United States first argued that the Court did not have jurisdiction in a "political dispute." When the Court ruled that it did, the United States then said it would no longer take part in the case and finally, in October of 1985, withdrew from the compulsory jurisdiction of the Court.[21]

The United States was not alone in applying a reservation to its acceptance of the Court's jurisdiction. Canada declared in 1974 that it would not be bound by the World Court in matters relating to its marine environment — hence, a possible dispute arising from a United States supertanker carrying oil along the British Columbia coast from Alaska would not go to the Court.[22] Nor was the United States alone in retracting its acceptance of compulsory jurisdiction. France did the same in 1974, after the Court refused to accept its argument in a dispute with Australia and New Zealand that French nuclear tests on French possessions in the Pacific were domestic matters outside the jurisdiction of the Court.[23] At the time when the United States withdrew from compulsory jurisdiction, out of 160 parties to the Statute of the International Court of Justice, only forty-four accepted its compulsory jurisdiction.[24]

Even in the unlikely event that states would willingly renounce their sovereignty and allow a World Court to settle quarrels between them, and in the equally unlikely event that a truly neutral, widely respected Court could be set up, there is reason to doubt that the problem of war would be solved. One feature of adjudication that its advocates point to is what President Taft called its "clear judgment of the facts and the law on the merits." But such judgments may not be the wisest solutions or the most just. A decision based on law can only be as just as the law and, as we have seen, much of international law today derives from the imperialist age of the nineteenth century and is perceived by many countries as anything but just. Courts can only restate established rights and duties. But sometimes it is a change in these rights and duties that is called for. Sometimes a state may resort to the law precisely to avoid a more just solution. In the mid-twentieth century most people accept the right of self-determination — that people living in an area should decide themselves to which state they want to belong and what form of government they want to have. Yet King Hassan of Morocco in 1974 tried to take his dispute with Spain over the Spanish colony of Spanish Sahara to the World Court to head off a referendum by Spain that would have given the inhabitants of Spanish Sahara self-determination. He seems to have calculated that the inhabitants might not have voted to join

Morocco, as he wished, but that with the right political combination on the World Court he could obtain a ruling that Spanish Sahara legally belonged to Morocco, regardless of what its inhabitants wanted.

Third parties can make a contribution to settling disputes without war. They can help ascertain the facts of a case. Mediators can restore broken communication and reduce distortion in messages. All these services cut down the number of wars that might otherwise start from misunderstanding. When parties to a dispute recognize that it is not in their best interest to fight, arbitration panels and courts can provide face-saving ways of accepting compromise. The rate of compliance with judgments in disputes that do get submitted for arbitration and adjudication is fairly high. The problem is that not all disputes get submitted and, because of sovereignty, it is difficult to force a state to agree to allow a third party to intervene. The difficulty of getting such agreement, however, is a little less when the third party is an international organization to which the disputing states belong. Within the context of third-party settlement we turn to the major international organization of our time, the United Nations.

NOTES

1. Morton Halperin, *Bureaucratic Politics and Foreign Policy* (Washington, D.C.: Brookings Institution, 1974), pp. 73–74.

2. Robert North et al., *Content Analysis* (Evanston, Ill.: Northwestern University Press, 1963); Ole R. Holsti, "The 1914 Case," *American Political Science Review*, Vol. 49, No 2 (June 1965), pp. 365–378.

3. Kathleen Teltsch, "Iraq and Iran Agree to Discuss Border Under U.N. Auspices," *The New York Times*, May 22, 1974.

4. Henry Cabot Lodge, Jr., testimony before Charter Review Hearing, quoted by Inis L. Claude, Jr., *Swords into Plowshares*, 4th ed. (New York: Random House, 1971), p. 238.

5. Charles W. Thayer, *Diplomat* (New York: Harper & Brothers, 1959), pp. 96–97.

6. William B. Quandt, *Decade of Decisions* (Berkeley: University of California Press, 1977), p. 233.

7. *The Economist*, December 9, 1967.

8. Philippe Devillers and Jean Lacouture, *End of a War* (New York: Frederick A. Praeger, 1969), for example, pp. 292–293.

9. Douglas Pike, *War, Peace, and the Viet Cong* (Cambridge: MIT Press, 1969), p. 160.

10. Thomas J. Hamilton, "Court Awards Pakistanis Portions of Rann of Cutch," *The New York Times*, February 20, 1968; Qutubuddin Aziz, "India and Pakistan Complete Rann of Kutch Demarcation," *Christian Science Monitor*, June 11, 1969.

11. William H. Taft, *The United States and Peace* (New York: Charles Scribner's Sons, 1914).

12. Ibid., p. 169.

13. *Keesing's Contemporary Archives*, June 15–22, 1963, p. 19, 474.

14. Robert Lyle Butterworth, *Managing Interstate Conflict, 1945–74* (Pittsburgh: Center for International Studies, University of Pittsburgh, 1976).

15. John King Gamble and Dana Fischer, *The International Court of Justice: Analysis of a Failure* (Lexington, Mass: Lexington Books, 1976), pp. 110–111.

16. Gerhard von Glahn, *Law Among Nations*, 2nd ed. (London: Macmillan, 1970), pp. 292–295.

17. Gamble and Fischer.

18. K. J. Holsti, "Resolving International Conflicts," *The Journal of Conflict Resolution*, Vol. 10, No. 3 (September 1966), pp. 272–296; with some additions in K. J. Holsti, *International Politics*, 2nd ed. (Englewood Cliffs, N.J.: Prentice-Hall, 1972), p. 476.

19. Taft, pp. 179–180.

20. *Department of State Bulletin*, Vol. 15, No. 375 (September 8, 1946), p. 453.

21. Text of Nicaragua's complaint, *The New York Times*, April 11, 1984, p. Y8.

22. International Legal Materials, Vol. 9, No. 3 (May 1970), pp. 598–599.

23. *The Economist*, May 22, 1973, p. 33.

24. *U.S. Decision to Withdraw from the International Court of Justice. Hearing* before the Subcommittee on Human Rights and International Organizations of the Committee on Foreign Affairs, House of Representatives, 99th Congress, 1st Session, 30 October 1985; printed statement by Abraham Sofaer, p. 22.

Chapter 18

The United Nations

The United Nations comes readily to mind in a discussion of international politics and peace. But categorizing it as a specific approach to peace is difficult. In fact, the UN Charter incorporates elements of a number of approaches. As the institution has evolved since the Charter was adopted in 1945, its major contribution to world peace fits most closely with third-party settlement. Although its prominence as an institution merits it a separate chapter, it is primarily as an extension of third-party settlement that we will look at it.

THE UN AND STATE SOVEREIGNTY: CHARTER PROVISIONS

The United Nations is like the inkblots of a Rorschach test — people see in it mostly a reflection of their own fears and desires. Extreme conservatives display bumper stickers saying, "Get the US out of the UN and the UN out of the US," because they see the UN as limiting our sovereignty. Advocates of world government welcomed the founding of the UN as the first step toward a world state. Students of history see the UN as the logical successor to the League of Nations, designed to avoid the weaknesses of the League. Cynics, looking at its dismal record, dismiss it as the "debating society on the East River."

There is some basis to all of these views. Let us first consider the claim that the UN infringes on the sovereignty of its members. We must define more carefully what we mean by the "United Nations." We would be more accurate if we thought of it as a system with seven main parts. In Chapter 17 we looked at one of these, the International Court of Justice. Because of the reservations that states have attached to their adherence to the Court, that is one part of the UN that does not seriously infringe on a state's sovereignty. Four other components are not considered threats to sovereignty, either: the Secretariat (including the Secretary General); the Trusteeship Council; the Economic and Social Council; and the functional agencies (such as the World Health Organization). But these bodies are not what we normally think of when we hear the term "United Nations"; we usually think first of the remaining two components, the General Assembly and the Security Council. It is the General Assembly that gets most attention in the newspapers these days, but the Security Council is, according to the UN Charter, most concerned with issues of war and peace. Article 24 of the Charter states that the Security Council has "primary responsibility for the maintenance of international peace and security." To meet its responsibility, the Security Council has been given the most far-reaching authority in the United Nations system.

Article 39 of the Charter states that the Security Council "shall determine the existence of any threat to the peace, breach of the peace, or act of aggression and shall make recommendations, or decide what measure shall be taken . . . to maintain or restore international peace and security." That is a very comprehensive mandate. There is no need to wait for overt acts of aggression, such as tanks crossing borders; a "threat to peace" is enough. Article 41 authorizes the Security Council to call on members to apply non-violent sanctions against offenders. Article 42 authorizes the Security Council to call for military operations against offenders. And Article 43 calls on member states to make available to the Security Council military forces for such operations.

On paper at least, the UN clearly limits the sovereignty of its members in two ways: It decides when they are to employ armed force, thereby taking away from states their traditional power to decide when to declare war; and it has the power to send troops against a sovereign state for some violation of international peace or threat to peace, even though the state in question might view this as a purely internal matter. The election of an extreme nationalist leader to head of state (another Hitler) might be considered by other states a "threat to peace" and be used to justify international action to nullify such an election. Nothing in the UN Charter rules out such a possibility.

But what is written down on paper is not always what is done in practice. Articles 42 and 43 of the UN Charter are universally recognized as dead letters. They never have been employed and no one expects them to be employed. A good illustration of what has happened to this whole section of the Charter is the fate of the Military Staff Committee, which according to Article 46 is to prepare the UN military force called for in Article 43. For years the Military Staff Committee met at regular intervals, on alternate Thursdays, in a basement conference room at UN headquarters in New York. Military attachés from the United States, the United Kingdom, France, the USSR, and China would assemble for a business meeting that lasted five minutes, including translation. The only item of business was to fix the time for the next meeting, which was always set at Thursday in two weeks. The only time meetings were longer was when one member was being assigned to new duties by his or her government; on those occasions the others gave speeches praising his or her contributions to the work of the committee.[1] This committee is as far as the UN has gone in implementing the military enforcement provisions of the Charter.

Those who saw the UN as a first step toward world government were clearly mistaken. The unity among the victors of World War II did not last long; such unity rarely does. If the UN was to survive, it had to make only minimal demands on its members. The nation-state is still the sovereign unit of international politics. The name taken for the organization, the United Nations, reveals who has the real power in the world. States have joined the UN because they believe it will further their national interests. They may put up with some small inconveniences that membership in it causes, but if UN action seems to harm an important national interest, they will simply withdraw from it. One state has already done so. Indonesia protested the creation of the state of Malaysia in South-East Asia. Malaysia included not only the former British colonies of Malaya and Singapore but also some territory claimed by Indonesia. In early 1965 President Sukarno of Indonesia took his country out of the UN rather than share membership with a country that he claimed had no right to exist. (President Sukarno was overthrown shortly thereafter and Indonesia then returned to the UN.)

THE UN AND COLLECTIVE SECURITY

The UN does not even go so far as to outlaw all war. Article 51 states that "nothing in the present Charter shall impair the inherent right of individual or collective self-defense if an armed attack occurs against a Member of the United Nations, until the Security Council has taken the measures necessary to maintain international peace and security." The difficulty of determining when an action is self-defense makes the qualification of this article next to useless. In 1971 there was a war between India and Pakistan. Pakistan claimed that it was defending itself against all-out attack from India. India claimed that it was engaged in "protective reaction" against attacks from Pakistan. Because violence between the two countries had escalated gradually, it was difficult for a neutral outsider to determine exactly when aggressive action began.

This article also qualifies the right of self-defense by limiting it to the period before the Security Council can act. But the Security Council often does not act, indeed cannot act, and for this reason the UN cannot be called a collective security organization. The essence of collective security is "all for one." If one state is attacked, all the others must come to the victim's aid. It is especially important that the major states participate in collective security; their absence was a major reason for the failure of the League of Nations. Yet the United Nations Charter provides an explicit escape clause for major states. This is the "unanimity rule," more commonly called "the veto." The Security Council was set up with eleven members. Five of them were permanent members, and these five were actual or potential great powers — United States, USSR, Britain, France, and China. (It was not such a bad selection. These were the first five countries to acquire nuclear weapons.) The other six members of the Security Council were elected for two-year terms. Action by the Security Council on matters affecting peace and security (including the employment of military force) required a vote of seven out of eleven, but that seven had to include "the concurring votes of the permanent members." In other words, unanimity by the five major powers was required; any one of them, by refusing to give its concurrence, could in effect veto any proposal. (The membership of the Security Council was enlarged in 1965 to include ten nonpermanent members. Now nine votes are required for action, but the unanimity rule still holds.)

This was not an oversight. It was a deliberate plan to keep the organization from destroying itself on the opposition of the major states. There is little point in trying to mount collective action against a state that is threatening peace if the major states are not giving that action their support. The League of Nations discovered this in Manchuria, the Chaco, and Ethiopia. There is also no point in trying to mount collective action against a major state. Even before the power of nuclear weapons was evident, states were aware that such an attempt could end only in a major war. The unanimity principle acts as a fuse for the UN machinery — when too great a load is placed on the machine, the fuse blows out and keeps the overload from destroying the machine. The UN, like the League of Nations before it, has failed to solve some major international conflicts; unlike the League, the UN was not itself destroyed by this failure.

THE UN AND THE KOREAN WAR

For a brief time in 1950, it looked as though the UN might transform itself into a collective security organization after all, regardless of the wishes of its founders or even of all its members. The occasion was the North Korean attack on South Korea. The United States had said that it did not consider South Korea within its defensive perimeter and that seemed to mean that the United States would not resist a North Korean attack, inside the UN or out. But then United States leaders acted contrary to their own publicly stated policy and decided to use military force against North Korea. Following the decision to deploy American forces, the United States went to the UN for an endorsement of this action. At this time the Russians were boycotting meetings of the Security Council to protest against its failure to allow the newly victorious Chinese Communists to take the Chinese seat, so that the Russians were not present to veto the United States move in Korea. (By this time, the unanimity rule had come to be interpreted to mean "no negative vote by a permanent member of the Security Council." In other words, action could be taken if a permanent member was absent or abstained.)

The Russians quickly abandoned their boycott and returned to their place on the Security Council. They could not retract UN support already given but they could prevent any further Security Council action. In September 1950 a successful American landing at Inchon turned the war around. For the first time the Americans saw the possibility not just of driving the North Koreans back across the 38th parallel but of actually defeating them altogether so that Korea could be reunited under South Korean leadership. Russian presence in the Security Council guaranteed that such a change in goal for the UN forces in Korea would be vetoed, and the United States devised what it called the "Uniting for Peace" resolution. This was passed by the General Assembly on November 3, 1950. It stated that if the Security Council failed to act because of the great power veto, the item could then be transferred to the General Assembly. The General Assembly could not *require* action (as the Security Council could, under the Charter) but by a two-thirds majority it could *recommend* collective action. (Participation in the Korean effort was voluntary in any case, even though the Security Council had approved it — only sixteen countries of the membership of sixty were contributing to the UN force.) The Uniting for Peace resolution reveals its American parentage by its obvious parallels to the American constitutional system for overriding presidential vetoes. Unfortunately other parts of the UN system are not at all analogous to the American system. If the unanimity rule was the fuse to protect the UN, then the Uniting for Peace resolution was the penny in the fuse box. It kept the organization functioning despite the opposition of one of its most powerful members and increased the risk of total breakdown.

The Korean action was the closest the UN got to collective security. In succeeding years it began backing away, for two reasons. One was the acquisition of nuclear weapons by the USSR — not just a single atomic "device" such as had been tested in 1949 but quantities of usable weapons of the thermonuclear type. If collective security seemed a risky proposition in 1945, it seemed downright foolish in 1955. The other development was the beginning of a shift in the composition of the UN. In 1950 the UN consisted of so many dependable United States allies that critics could justifiably speak of an "automatic majority" for the United States. Getting an item transferred to the General Assembly was a guarantee that the United States position would prevail. Then in 1955 the membership of the UN began to grow. Of sixteen countries admitted that year, six were members of neither the United States nor the Soviet bloc. This shift continued, as Table 18.1 shows. In this table I do not try to summarize actual voting behavior in the UN; some countries formally allied with the United States often voted against the United States. But the trend is clear. The UN has greatly increased in size and most of the new members are not allied with either of the great powers. Many of these new members call themselves "nonaligned" and have formed a bloc of their own, with its own priorities. Cold War issues and even fundamental questions of war and peace are of less interest to these states than colonialism and the distribution of the world's resources. The willingness of the Soviet Union and its allies to support these states on many of these issues has meant that, if anything, the General Assembly is more likely to produce a two-thirds majority opposed to United States interests.

THE UN AND PREVENTION OF WAR

If you accept the argument that the UN was never intended to be a collective security organization, you are less likely to be disappointed by its failures to maintain international peace and security. It has not prevented wars because it is not capable of doing so without going beyond the guidelines that its members have agreed to. Attempts to use it to prevent war would mean not success but massive defections.

Table 18.1 UNITED NATIONS MEMBERSHIP

Year	Total UN membership	US and allies	Communist bloc	Others
1945	51	34	5	12
1950	60	37	5	18
1955	76	39	9	28
1960	100	40	9	51
1965	118	41	11	66
1970	132	42	11	79
1975	141	42	13	86
1980	152	35	12	105

The inability of the UN to prevent war was evident in 1967 in the Middle East. It seemed to be the ideal place for the organization to be effective. Two previous wars in the area, in 1948–1949 and in 1956, had been ended by UN cease-fires; a UN Truce Supervisory Organization was still in operation from the 1948–1949 war; a UN Emergency Force (UNEF) of several thousand men was patrolling an area that Israel had evacuated after the 1956 war. United Nations attention was focused on the Middle East when the crisis began in May 1967. The Security Council considered the issue; the secretary general urged caution. Then the Egyptians ordered the expulsion of the UNEF. It left in a matter of hours and Egypt moved troops into the Sinai area vacated by it. President Nasser stated privately that his intention was to provoke Israel into an attack, in order to put the blame for starting the war on Israel.[2] Israel did what Nasser wanted, although with greater success than he had predicted.

The UN in general, and the secretary general (as the one responsible for UNEF) in particular, have been criticized for this rapid withdrawal. Yet the UN had no alternative. The UNEF was stationed on only the Egyptian side of the armistice line; Israel had refused to allow UNEF on its soil. The conditions under which such UN forces were dispatched clearly included the provision that they would not violate the host state's sovereignty, that they were present only with the host state's permission, and that they could be removed at any time. In any case, Egypt had already arranged through diplomacy with India and Yugoslavia for withdrawing their contingents of UNEF and, with their departure, the smaller remaining contingents had no wish to remain. An international force could have prevented the war in 1967 but one operating under the conditions imposed by UN members on the UNEF could not.

The war in 1971 between India and Pakistan also illustrates the fundamental inability of the UN to prevent war. The crisis between the two countries began building up in February 1971, long before full-scale war broke out in December. Yet no country would even put the matter on the agenda of the Security Council. Perhaps this refusal came from recognition of how futile such a move would be — with one permanent member (the USSR) backing India and another permanent member (China) backing Pakistan, any proposal not acceptable to both would have been vetoed. Faced with this potential Council deadlock, Secretary General U Thant tried quiet diplomacy, but three months of secret negotiations were fruitless. Even the secretary general's suggestion for a modest force of one-hundred civilian observers on the border was not accepted.[3] Pakistan for its part claimed that there was no threat to peace, because events inside East Pakistan were a purely internal matter. India was already giving military aid to the rebels and planning large-scale military action and wanted no UN interference.

In some ways a greater tragedy was the failure of the UN to do anything about the civil war in Nigeria. In 1967 one tribal group, the Ibos, attempted to set up their own state in the southeastern third of the country, which they named Biafra. From then until early 1969 they fought a war with the central Nigerian government that caused about 2 million deaths. Compared with the Vietnam War, which drew much more attention, this was a vastly more destructive conflict. Yet no effort was made in the UN to stop it. Unlike the Vietnam War, the Middle East conflict, or even the India–Pakistan dispute, this was in no way a Cold War issue. The major powers had no stakes in the conflict. Yet the UN was unable to act. Too many members feared secessionist movements in their own countries. Any move that would have given legitimacy to the secessionist movement of Biafra, even engaging in negotiations with them, might have encouraged movement elsewhere. When a large number of the UN's members are reluctant to act, the UN can do nothing.

The inability of the United Nations to prevent war is built into its very structure. Thus we should not be surprised to see the pattern of inaction established in past decades repeated again and again. In more recent years the regimes of Pol Pot in Cambodia and Idi Amin in Uganda murdered large numbers of their own citizens (perhaps one-quarter of the entire population in the case of Cambodia), yet as in the case of the Nigerian civil war the UN did not act. Each of these murderous regimes was eventually removed by war waged by a neighboring state, yet as in the case of the India–Pakistan War the UN did not act. China, on its own, launched an attack on Vietnam in early 1979, partly in response to the Vietnamese war against Cambodia. The United Nations Security Council did no more than debate the attack for two weeks; in the end no resolution was even brought to a vote.

The failure of the UN to act on obvious questions of international peace has been accompanied by an all-too-great willingness to act on other issues. Action is the wrong word, because what the UN does is pass resolutions that have no chance of being implemented. These are usually directed against one or more of the major powers. They may be supported by large majorities in the General Assembly, but all these votes may represent very little in the way of total and economic strength. As critics of the UN like to point out, one could put together in the General Assembly a two-thirds majority of states whose total contribution to the UN budget is only 2.75 per cent of the total budget. Because dues are assessed according to a country's ability to pay, budget contribution is a fair if rough estimate of a state's power. Another way of illustrating the same point is to consider that a two-thirds majority can consist of states whose combined total population is only 10 per cent that of the world's; again, such a vote is hardly a reflection of actual power.

Many of these resolutions, far from aiming at the pacific settlement of disputes, are meant to increase tension. The countries sponsoring the resolutions are using the UN as a tool of their foreign policy; they want to bring pressure on their enemies and force a capitulation instead of seeking a compromise solution. It is generally agreed that the United States was not wise to attempt to use the UN in this way in the first decade of the organization's existence (keeping China out of the UN while condemning it for aggression in Korea), and it does not seem wise for others to do so today.

An example of a resolution used for combat rather than conciliation is one from 1968 on the status of Gibraltar. Gibraltar is an enclave on the tip of the Iberian Peninsula, controlled by the British since the Treaty of Utrecht of 1713. The Spanish would like to incorporate this area in their own country but the inhabitants of Gibraltar, not of Spanish descent themselves, show no desire to be joined forcibly to Spain. In September 1967, the British held a plebiscite in Gibraltar: 12,762 voted to remain a British colony; only forty-four voted against it. Nevertheless, in December 1968, the UN General Assembly passed a resolution requesting the "administering power to terminate the colonial situation in Gibraltar no later than 1 October 1969."[4] This resolution was supported by sixty-seven countries and reveals a fundamental fact about voting in the UN: It is no different from voting anywhere else. Spain put together a coalition of Communist, Arab, and African states, promising in return its vote on other issues. Many of the Arab states did not care one way or the other about Gibraltar but were glad to have the Spanish vote on questions relating to Israel. The Communists and the Africans seem to have been glad for a chance to embarrass the British. Certainly states were not voting on the basis of some abstract principles of justice. United Nations votes do not represent some higher "world interest." They are the results of horse-trading among individual states.

Many of the African states were willing to support Spain on the Gibraltar issue because of their resentment of the British on the issue of Rhodesia. Rhodesia had declared its independence from Britain in 1965 rather than accept British plans for increasing black African representation in its government. The same coalition of states that in December 1968 condemned the British for not ending the colonial situation in Gibraltar had condemned the British in November 1968 for its "failure and refusal" to use force to *restore* the colonial situation in Rhodesia and then compel the white minority to accept majority rule.[5]

The judgment that the United Nations serves more often to heighten tension than to abate it is reinforced by the observation that states with fundamentally friendly relations do not turn to the UN for help in settling disputes. The United States settled disputes with Mexico on water from the Colorado River and with Canada on fishing rights entirely outside the United Nations system. Even with Cuba, the United States was able to negotiate an agreement on extraditing airplane hijackers outside the UN. Only when states do not seriously expect agreement do they turn to the United Nations — as illustrated by Cuban resolutions asking for an end to "colonialism" in Puerto Rico.[6]

United Nations resolutions reflect not a world community but the sum of selfish interests of the states that can put together a majority. These states may claim to be acting on principle, but when their interests change, the principle they claim to espouse changes. In October 1973, when Egypt attacked Israel, the Arab oil-producing states imposed an embargo of oil products on states that did not support the Arab side. Yet three years earlier, the UN had passed a resolution proposed by Third World countries declaring that "no state may use or encourage the use of economic, political or any other type of measures to coerce another State in order to obtain from it the subordination of the exercise of its sovereign rights and to secure from it advantages of any kind."[7] States threatened with the loss of oil were reluctant to point out the inconsistency between the oil embargo and this resolution, but the Russians and Chinese went so far as to praise the Arab states for using oil as a political weapon.

Recently states have seized on the weapon of expulsion from the UN as a way to punish their enemies. Targets of campaigns for expulsion have been Taiwan, Cambodia, South Africa, and Israel. Although no state has been formally expelled, the same effect has been achieved by the refusal to recognize the credentials of a state's delegates. This device was used in 1981 to exclude South Africa from a special session of the General Assembly on Namibia, a former German colony under South African control and whose future South Africa considered a matter of vital national interest. However much emotional satisfaction a state may derive from seeing an enemy banished by a majority of the General Assembly, it is hard to see how this behavior increases the possibilities for world peace. Expulsion both reduces the likelihood that the expelled state will comply with UN requests and cuts down on the communication that is the prime purpose of diplomacy.

CONTRIBUTIONS OF THE UN TO PEACE

It is clear that the United Nations, as it is now constituted and as it now functions, is not a world government. It is not even a collective security organization. In some cases it is more likely to increase than decrease international conflicts. But this is not to say that it is totally without value. The UN's contributions to peace are similar to those of third parties in disputes. Its advantages are that it is permanently available and, in some cases, more dependably neutral than other third parties.

One thing a third party can do is provide good offices, and the UN has done this. The secretary general, officially the head of the Secretariat and in practice spokesman for the entire organization, has frequently been called on to provide good offices. A notable success for Secretary General Dag Hammarskjöld came when eleven American fliers, held in Chinese prisons after coming down on Chinese territory during the Korean War, were released by the Chinese. The United States, having no diplomatic relations with China, asked the secretary general to use his good offices to secure their release. Hammarskjöld was an exceedingly discreet diplomat and never took credit for the release of the fliers, but their release followed a trip of his to Peking and it took place on the occasion of his birthday.[8]

Another contribution the UN makes to peaceful relations between states is providing a neutral place where diplomats can meet. A survey in 1960 of randomly selected delegates revealed that 86 per cent believed they had more contact with other diplomats at the UN than at a post in a national capital. Moreover, 91 per cent said that they had more contact with delegates from unfriendly countries. Some reported that they had been instructed to stay away from the foreign ministry when posted to an unfriendly country. A visit by the Ethiopian ambassador to the Foreign Ministry of Somalia (when those two countries were quarreling over the boundary between them) might have given rise to speculation about secret deals or concessions by one country or the other. The UN headquarters in New York provides greater anonymity. If tentative contact toward an unfriendly country is fruitless, it can always be denied.[9]

The UN can also be used as a fact-finding body, although not much use has been made of this potential. The immediate cause of the Middle East war of 1967 was a report that Egypt received that Israel was mobilizing troops against Syria. Israel denied this and invited the Russian ambassador to inspect the area himself. He declined but the UN Truce Supervisory Organization reported that the charges were unfounded. Unfortunately events were out of control by that time and the finding came too late to prevent the war.[10]

Another area in which the UN has been employed without complete success is truce supervision and observation. A UN Truce Supervisory Organization has kept a record of violations in the Middle East since the 1949 armistices but that has not prevented additional wars. In 1958 the UN was called into Lebanon during a civil war. The Lebanese Christians charged that the Lebanese Muslims were getting arms from across the border in Syria (which at that time was joined to Egypt in the United Arab Republic). Anthony Nutting, a pro-Arab British diplomat who was friendly with President Nasser, revealed in his biography of Nasser that weapons were indeed being smuggled and the UN teams were unable to discover them. He wrote:

A team of United Nations observers, led by representatives of India, Norway and Ecuador, was sent to Lebanon to investigate these complaints. But since they were unable to operate at night when the main traffic in arms from Syria took place, the observers reported to Hammarskjöld that they had found no evidence of any large-scale gun-running.[11]

The UN has also supplied mediators, again not always with success. In the Arab–Israeli conflict, the UN has appointed a number of mediators, with mixed results. Count Folke Bernadotte was appointed at the time the first war broke out in 1948. He was assassinated by Jewish extremists in September but even in the period before that his efforts were of no avail. The Israelis noticed that his peace proposals always reflected the actual military situation and so broke several cease-fires to improve their military situation before returning to bargain with him.[12] United Nations efforts also failed after the 1967 war. Gunnar Jarring, Swedish ambassador to the Soviet Union, was appointed mediator in the same Security Council resolution that was to lay a basis for settlement. Despite praise from all sides for the professional competence with which he handled his job, he had no success.

Secretary General Hammarskjöld had some limited success in working out arrangements between Israel and Egypt to de-escalate violence along the border in 1956. But the greatest success for a UN mediator was the series of armistice agreements ending the 1948–1949 war, mediated by a deputy to the secretary general, Ralph Bunche. Under what became known as the "Rhodes formula," Bunche met with Arab and Israeli delegations in a hotel on the Greek island of Rhodes. Because the Arabs did not recognize Israel, Bunche had to carry messages from one floor of the hotel to another. His efforts resulted in signed agreements that are the closest to recognized international frontiers that Israel has come.

We have compiled quite a list of contributions the UN can make to world peace. But notice something about every item on this list. Each contribution could be (and often is) made equally effectively by some other agency. Take "good offices." They can be provided by any neutral party. In the chapter on third parties we used as an example the 1968 hijacking of an Israeli airliner to Algeria. First Israel and then Algeria requested the UN secretary general to use his good offices to secure the release of the plane, passengers, and crew. Although the hostages were eventually let go, the release was arranged through the good offices not of the UN but of Italy, in whose airspace the Palestinian guerrilla group had initially hijacked the plane. In 1985, in a well-publicized hijacking of a TWA airliner, the passengers of which eventually were held hostage in Beirut by Shi'ite Muslims, the UN secretary general had to ask if he could be of help. But both sides virtually ignored him and it was the International Committee of the Red Cross that played the major role in arranging a settlement.[13]

The UN may provide a better meeting place for diplomats than national capitals, on the whole, but before the UN existed the capital of a major power (Paris or London or Washington) provided neutral meeting places for diplomats; even with the UN in New York City these other cities still function as "diplomatic capitals," where ambassadors from quarreling countries can meet unobtrusively to sound each other out. Fact finding and truce observation can also be performed by other groups, as in one of the minor diplomatic exchanges during the Cuban missile crisis of 1962. The United States asked that the UN verify that Soviet missiles had indeed been removed from Cuba; the Russians suggested representatives of the International Committee of the Red Cross instead. (In the end, no group verified the removal of missiles.)[14] Finally, mediators have as often come from outside the UN as within. United Nations officials Ralph Bunche and Dag Hammarskjöld had successes in the Middle East but so too did United States officials Cyrus Vance and Henry Kissinger.

In one way the UN is unique, and that is as a world forum for speechmaking. If the UN were to disappear, such activity would diminish. It is not clear that speeches always further the cause of peace. You could make a good case that often it does the opposite. One may doubt that the Israelis were made more willing to make concessions to Arabs after repeatedly hearing themselves compared to Nazis. Those who argue that virulent rhetoric is a substitute for war would have to argue that the Czechs should have been reassured by Hitler's rhetorical attacks on them in 1938 — shortly before he took over their country.[15]

Still, there have been occasions when the purely rhetorical function of the UN may have made a contribution to peace. In 1956 the Hungarians rose in revolt against Russian control of their country. The Russians, judging a pro-Russian government in Hungary to be of vital interest, sent large numbers of troops into Hungary to put down the revolt. The Republicans, who then controlled the executive branch in the United States, had for years been talking about liberating Eastern Europe. The Hungarian revolt provided an excuse. But by this time the Republicans wished to avoid an armed confrontation with the Russians, especially with President Eisenhower seeking reelection that year on the theme of peace and prosperity. Instead of sending troops to Hungary, the United States sent debaters to the UN, where they roundly condemned the Russians. The Russians ignored the UN but great publicity was given to its debates in the United States, conveying the impression to the American people that their government was doing something to aid the cause of the Hungarians.

The UN provided the same service for the Russians in 1967. Israel attacked Egypt and destroyed most of its aircraft, which had been supplied by the USSR; it overran the Egyptian armies, which had been equipped and trained by the Russians. Thus Russian prestige was called into question by the war. But instead of committing troops to aid the Egyptians, they chose to go to the UN and attack the Israelis verbally. The UN, as a world forum, provides a way of meeting obligations to give support without going to war.

UN PEACEKEEPING FORCES: UNEF, ONUC, UNFICYP

One of the UN's activities has grown in importance in recent years so much that we would be justified in saying it is now the major UN contribution to world peace. Its beginnings are in the truce supervisory organizations of the UN's first years. Today it is the most visible of the UN's activities on questions of war and peace. It is known as UN peacekeeping or, after a speech by Secretary General Hammarskjöld in 1961, "preventive diplomacy." Peacekeeping, it should be emphasized, is a technical term with a precise meaning. It is not the same as collective security or enforcement of Security Council decisions or settling disputes. It means only using UN troops to physically separate two sides after an armed conflict.

At first glance the dispatch of UN troops to a crisis area may seem to be collective security. The similarity seems to have confused George McGovern, who said in a 1972 campaign statement on the UN, "We need to strengthen the peacekeeping forces until they truly can keep the peace whenever war threatens and whenever conflict begins."[16] But peacekeeping operations, as now conducted by the UN, are in important ways the opposite of traditional collective security. Collective security emphasizes drawing in all states against the aggressor; in practice this means relying primarily on the major powers. But a main purpose of peacekeeping is to keep the major powers out. This fundamental justification for UN operations was outlined by Secretary General Hammarskjöld in a report in 1961. He said that the preceding years had demonstrated that the UN could not be effective in areas of big power rivalry. The UN did not act on Cold War issues such as the status of Berlin and no one expected it to. But there were, Hammarskjöld said, many conflicts in the world not directly related to big power rivalry. He recommended that the UN work to localize these disputes; he recommended keeping the big powers out by bringing the little powers in. If an external force was needed to restore order, it should come from the small powers, under the direction of the UN, rather than from a big power. It was called "preventive diplomacy" because it would prevent small conflicts from being drawn into the great power rivalry. Of course what Hammarskjöld had in mind went beyond what we normally think of as diplomacy. Armed soldiers were an essential component.

The UN made use of military personnel as early as 1948 in the Middle East but the members of the original Truce Supervisory Organization were guards from UN headquarters. Not until 1956 did we get the first UN deployment of force of the kind we now refer to as peacekeeping. That force, known as UNEF, for United Nations Emergency Force, consisted of regular soldiers made available to the UN by their governments. It was set up in a great hurry, without months of committee work and endless debate, in response to the Suez war of 1956. At the end of October Israel invaded Egypt and then France and England sent troops into the Suez Canal zone in order, they said, to protect the canal during the fighting. In fact, the invasion had been arranged ahead of time by the three states to give the French and British an excuse to reclaim the canal, which Nasser had nationalized in July. The British and French were counting on the passive acceptance of their move by the United States. They didn't get it and found themselves under diplomatic attack by Americans as well as by the Soviets and Third World countries. Because of extreme caution, their military operations were not going well either and the British were soon looking for a face-saving way to retreat. Lester Pearson of Canada then proposed a solution that satisfied everyone.

Pearson recommended creating a UN military force to replace the British and French and provide whatever protection the Suez Canal might need. (By this time, the Egyptians had already sunk block ships (worthless hulks) and closed the canal, depriving the British and French of a major excuse for intervening.) The British were happy to have an excuse for an otherwise humiliating retreat; the French were not happy but had no choice once the British accepted the UN cease-fire. The United States was happy to see its NATO allies terminate an unpopular adventure. The Egyptians were happy to be rid of the British and French and have some protection against further Israeli advances.

Dag Hammarskjöld acted with great dispatch and put together a force of 6,000, drawn from twenty-five countries. To keep Americans and Russians out, as well as French and British, the UN specified that no permanent members of the Security Council could participate. The members of UNEF came from middle-level powers such as Finland, Canada, Brazil, and India. The UNEF, created on November 6, began arriving November 15; by December 22 it had completely replaced the French and British forces. At the beginning of the next year Hammarskjöld negotiated an agreement with the Israelis for a withdrawal from the Sinai in return for stationing UNEF between Egypt and Israel.

The success of UNEF encouraged the UN to apply the solution of a peacekeeping force to a crisis in 1960. At the end of June 1960, Belgium granted independence to its colony of the Congo, but before the end of July it was clear that the new government could not maintain order. One province seceded, the army mutinied, and Europeans who had stayed in the Congo came under attack. The Belgians were planning to use force to rescue their nationals. The Russians accused them of using this as a front behind which they would restore colonial control. The Russians in turn were accused of taking sides in the Congolese civil war for their own purposes. In the midst of accusation and counteraccusation, the UN voted for a force known as ONUC (from its French title: *Opération des Nations Unies — Congo*). It was justified as an effort to keep outside powers from interfering in the domestic affairs of the country. In fact, ONUC had to interfere in domestic affairs in order to restore order. The force grew very large — 20,000 — and very costly. At its maximum it cost $120 million a year, larger than the UN's regular budget. At one time or another almost every country found something to complain about in ONUC but in the end a central government was restored without interference by the major powers.

A third important peacekeeping force was the one of 6,500 sent to Cyprus in 1964 to patrol the lines between the hostile Greek and Turkish communities. This force, known as the UN force in Cyprus, UNFICYP, was still in place when the war broke out in the Middle East in 1973. When a cease-fire there was arranged, the UN Security Council authorized the secretary general to raise a peacekeeping force to administer it. A contingent of 645 troops from Cyprus was immediately transferred to become the basis for the fourth peacekeeping force, the United Nations Emergency Force in the Sinai Peninsula. A short time later a second group, known as the UN Disengagement Observer Force, was sent to the Golan Heights. Together they eventually numbered about 6,000.

A close look at these cases will clarify exactly what a peacekeeping force is. Notice that it does not bring about agreement between two sides that are fighting; rather, it assists in implementing agreements already reached. In the Middle East and in Cyprus, cease-fires had already been arranged and then the peacekeeping force was dispatched. A cease-fire, particularly in its first hours, is not always very firm. The presence of a neutral party patrolling a buffer zone between two enemy forces will not prevent one or the other from resuming hostilities but it will complicate efforts to mount a surprise attack. Either one side gives a warning to the peacekeeping force (and thus to the other side) or it doesn't, and then has a lot of apologies to make to the Austrians and Finns and Canadians whose soldiers it has killed.

A peacekeeping force can investigate reported violations of the cease-fire and prevent accidents from escalating into renewed fighting. The effect of an unexplained gunshot can be disastrous when two tense armies face each other. In July 1975, Air France sent its new plane, the Concorde, on a test flight over the Mediterranean. Because it travels faster than sound, it creates a sonic boom. When it passed south of Beirut, gunmen in two hostile Lebanese communities started shooting at each other, each thinking the other had taken a shot at them.[17] Peacekeeping forces can avert that kind of accident. In addition to investigating and reporting to both sides on the origins of such unexplained noise, a peacekeeping force by its physical presence inhibits each side from resorting too quickly to violence, each knowing that if it does, the peacekeepers will be the first to be hit.

Finally, peacekeeping forces can provide local police functions, including such simple matters as directing traffic in frontier areas. In the Congo the demands on the ONUC grew to such proportions that for a while the UN was running the country.

Notice that these activities are not the kind of enforcement of Security Council directives envisaged by Articles 41 and 42 of the Charter. Nor are they attempts to bring two sides together in pacific settlement. The peacekeeping forces make no efforts to settle the conflict or even to bring the two sides together for talks. In both the Middle East and Cyprus there have been mediation efforts by the UN, but these came not from UNEF or UNFICYP but from a separate agency.

LIMITATIONS OF PEACEKEEPING

Let us return to George McGovern's hope that peacekeeping forces can be strengthened until "they truly can keep the peace whenever war threatens and whenever conflict begins." Peacekeeping, as it is practiced now, operates under such stringent conditions that not much expansion is possible. Dag Hammarskjöld, in elaborating the "preventive diplomacy" role of the UN, laid down conditions that he thought were essential for UN peacekeeping. The basic one is that a force cannot be stationed on the territory of a state without that state's consent. Far from being able to send a force in whenever conflict breaks out, the UN must wait for a request from the state or states involved. This condition implies that the state also has the right to revoke its invitation and expel a force at any time, although beginning in 1973 the Security Council authorized forces for minimum periods of six months. The authorization must be renewed every six months, and if a state decides to exercise its sovereignty and deny entry to a peacekeeping force, the United Nations will comply.

Another condition is that troops in the force must be neutral — in two senses. They must not be directly involved in big power rivalries and they must not be involved in the dispute at hand. Typically this requirement excludes permanent members of the Security Council (although in Cyprus, because British forces were already stationed at bases on the island, they were included in UNFICYP). It also implies that each party to a dispute gets a veto over the contingents that make up the peacekeeping force.

Furthermore, the UN force does not become a party to the dispute in any way. Finally, the UN force never initiates the use of armed force. This rule had to be modified somewhat in the Congo, to permit the UN to disarm some of the rebel forces, but in other cases of peacekeeping the rule has been followed. The UN forces rely on their blue UN flag and blue helmets, not on the light weapons they carry, to protect themselves.

It was Hammarskjöld's view that only if these conditions were imposed would a majority of states, and particularly the big powers, support peace-keeping forces. He was probably right but the practical effect is that only certain disputes lend themselves to the services of a peacekeeping force. These must be disputes in which neither party by itself is capable of imposing a settlement; if one country is strong enough (and determined enough) it will presumably have its way. Unless the conflict was stalemated there would be no incentive to call in the UN. Thus the India–Pakistan dispute of 1971 was settled purely by India's military superiority. Another kind of dispute that precludes use of a UN force involves a major power or even one in an area considered vital by a major power. We can confidently say that the UN will not be called in to patrol the border between Czechoslovakia and the USSR if tensions should again rise to the level they reached in 1968.

The deployment of a UN force depends on a decision by the appropriate international body. Which body is appropriate has been a subject of contro-versy. The position of some states — most notably the Soviet Union but also France — has been that only the Security Council can authorize and control peacekeeping forces. Back in 1956, when the first such force was being proposed, essentially for use against France and Britain, the presence of both countries on the Security Council guaranteed a veto. Under the Uniting for Peace Resolution the matter was transferred to the General Assembly. Thus it was the General Assembly that authorized the first major UN peacekeeping force, the UNEF. The Russians had objections but were willing to go along because Egypt favored such a force. At the beginning of the next dispute, over the Congo, the Soviet Union at first was willing to back UNEF because it interpreted the force as an anti-Belgian, therefore anti-imperialist, move. But when ONUC did not perform as the Soviet Union had expected, it withdrew support, especially in the vital area of financing. Because ONUC was so expensive, this withdrawal created a crisis for the UN organization. In 1964, when the UN decided to send a force to Cyprus, contributions to it were voluntary and the force itself was modest in size and scope of activity. It was only after the 1973 war in the Middle East, when a force was dis-patched to the buffer zones created there, that the Soviet Union's condition of authorization by the Security Council was met. But by this time agreement in the Security Council was complicated by a new factor: Communist Chinese membership on the Security Council. China had a veto and China favored continued war by the Arabs. In the end, when the war began to go badly for the Arabs, China did not veto the peacekeeping force, choosing instead to abstain. But in future conflict it may be harder to deploy a UN force, because the interests of China and the Soviet Union and the United States (not to mention Britain and France) are more likely than not to diverge.

Even if a peacekeeping force is authorized, troops must be forthcoming and so must financing. The General Assembly can only recommend action, and even the Security Council is unlikely to go beyond a polite request for troops. Until now, the United States has financed a large part of these forces (25 per cent of those in the Sinai, for example), and some of the middle-level powers have been willing to supply troops. The Scandinavian countries, along with Canada and Austria, have made notable contributions, their soldiers volunteering for hazardous duty at a time when young men in other countries generally enjoy freedom from military service. But these are volunteers, and there is no guarantee that they will be available in all situations.

Recent events have raised doubts about even the limited functions of peacekeeping forces. The newest force, the United Nations Interim Force in Lebanon, UNIFIL, has been in many ways the least successful. It was created in March 1978, after a Palestinian raid into Israel from Lebanon provoked an Israeli retaliatory attack and occupation of territory in southern Lebanon. UNIFIL was created with different intentions on the part of its supporters. The Arab states expected it to stop Israeli interference in southern Lebanon; the Israelis expected it to stop Palestinian attacks into Israel. It did neither very well and, unlike previous UN peacekeeping forces, suffered considerable casualties from repeated clashes with armed bands. When large Israeli forces swept into Lebanon in June 1982, UNIFIL was unable to even slow them down. At the conclusion of the fighting, PLO forces agreed to evacuate Beirut, but their withdrawal was protected not by the UN force but rather an ad hoc force composed of French, Italian, and American troops.

The UN was replaced as the peacekeeper on Israel's southern border as well, following the conclusion of a peace treaty between Egypt and Israel in March 1979. Because the Soviet Union opposed the treaty, it threatened to veto any attempt to allow the UN peacekeeping force already in the Sinai to supervise Israeli withdrawal under the treaty. Instead of being authorized for another six-month period in July 1979, the UNEF was allowed to lapse. The peace treaty was implemented nonetheless, supervised by American technicians already in the Sinai to run an electronic watch station, by a small force of Truce Supervisory personnel remaining from the 1948 war (and directly under the control of the secretary general), and by the Israelis and Egyptians themselves.

At the final withdrawal of Israeli forces from Egyptian territory in April 1982, peacekeeping duties were taken over by a force of 2,500 soldiers, organized entirely outside of the United Nations. This ability of states to achieve workable arrangements outside of the UN makes clear just how limited the UN's contribution to peace is. Although helpful, UN forces are not indispensable. In this area as in others, were the UN to disappear, substitutes to perform its functions would be found.

The potential of the United Nations to help as a third party in resolving disputes remains. But the potential is increasingly ignored. Even Secretary General Javier Pérez de Cuéllar noted in his first annual report the "erosion of the authority and status" of the organization and warned, "We are perilously near to a new international anarchy."[18] In the long list of violent conflicts between states in the preceding year — the Falkland Islands, Lebanon, Iraq and Iran, Afghanistan, South-East Asia, Africa, and Central America — the secretary general admitted his organization played no significant role at all.

In 1985 the United Nations celebrated its fortieth anniversary. The General Assembly passed 259 resolutions during its annual session, but time ran out before it considered such issues as the war between Iran and Iraq or conflict in Central America. The only action taken by the UN on the most serious conflicts facing the world during its anniversary year was to put them on the agenda for the coming year.[19]

As is the case with many human institutions, the United Nations is unlikely to be disbanded just because it no longer serves a useful purpose. But neither are the repeated demonstrations of its ineffectiveness likely to encourage states with grievances to turn to it for solutions.

NOTES

1. *The New York Times*, January 19, 1969.
2. Nadav Safran, *From War to War* (New York: Pegasus, 1969), pp. 300–301; see also Nasser's speech at Cairo University, July 23, 1967, in *The Israel–Arab Reader*, rev. ed., ed. Walter Laqueur (New York: Bantam, 1971), especially p. 203.
3. Kathleen Teltsch, "Effort to Get U.N. Presence in Pakistan Deadlocked," *The New York Times*, October 14, 1971.
4. United Nations, General Assembly, Official Records, Twenty-Third Session, Supplement No. 18 (A/7218), "Resolutions Adopted by the General Assembly During Its Twenty-Third Session," p. 64.
5. Ibid., p. 58.
6. Abraham Yeselson and Anthony Gaglione, *A Dangerous Place: The United Nations as a Weapon in World Politics* (New York: Grossman, 1974), pp. 193–195.
7. United Nations, General Assembly, Official Records, Twenty-Fifth Session, Supplement No. 28 (A/8028), "Resolutions Adopted by the General Assembly During Its Twenty-Fifth Session," p. 123.
8. Kathleen Teltsch, *Crosscurrents at Turtle Bay* (Chicago: Quadrangle Books, 1970), pp. 52–53.

9. C. F. Alger, "Personal Contact in International Exchanges," in *International Behavior*, ed. H. C. Kelman (New York: Holt, Rinehart and Winston, 1965), p. 527.
10. Safran, p. 274.
11. Anthony Nutting, *Nasser* (New York: E. P. Dutton, 1972), p. 233.
12. Safran, p. 32.

13. *The New York Times*, June 22, 1985, p. Y4.

14. *The New York Times*, November 3, 1962, p. 7.

15. Yeselson and Gaglione, pp. 166–167.

16. Douglas E. Kneeland, "Senator Proposes a Greater Reliance on United Nations to Keep the Peace," *The New York Times*, October 29, 1972.

17. *The New York Times*, July 19, 1975, p. 2.

18. Javier Pérez de Cuéllar, "Report on the Work of the Organization," *UN Chronicle*, Vol. 19, No. 9 (October 1982), p. 12.

19. Elaine Sciolino, "259 Edicts and Many Festivities Later, U.N. Ends Historic Session," *The New York Times*, December 22, 1985, p. Y4.

Chapter 19

Functionalism

One part of the United Nations system, the Specialized Agencies, is usually relegated to last place in discussions of the UN. These agencies (also called "functional" agencies, because each deals with practical activities or functions) include the World Health Organization (WHO), the Food and Agriculture Organization (FAO), and the International Atomic Energy Agency (IAEA). Concentrating first on the Security Council and the General Assembly, many an author will mention, almost as an afterthought, that these agencies are also associated with the UN, to solve technical problems such as malaria, food shortages, and control of atomic energy. But for people who call themselves "functionalists," these specialized agencies are the most important part of the UN. It is they, and not the Security Council and General Assembly, that will bring world peace, the functionalists believe.

This theory requires some elaboration. It does not seem to be the stated purpose of these agencies to solve disputes among states. Take the World Health Organization. Article 1 of its Constitution states, "The object of the WHO shall be the attainment by all peoples of the highest possible levels of health." It then goes on to list some specific tasks: control of communicable diseases (such as smallpox and malaria), improvement of maternal and child care, and environmental health (through pure drinking water and sewage disposal). The membership of the WHO is practically the same as the membership of the UN. Its members come together for a yearly assembly; the rest of the time its affairs are run by an executive board. But at its yearly assemblies it does not discuss world peace or abolishing war; it discusses world health. In 1967 the WHO assembly embarked on a ten-year campaign to eradicate smallpox. It mobilized 2,000 epidemic experts from fifty countries, plus hundreds of thousands of local public health workers. The Soviet Union supplied large amounts of vaccine; the United States contributed many of the medical experts. At one point China gave up some funds due to it from the WHO so they could be spent to check a recently discovered epidemic of smallpox in India. The cooperative effort by countries that are often rivals succeeded. In 1968, smallpox was still found in thirty-two countries and caused thousands of deaths. By 1975 the number of cases was down to only 125, in two countries, and in October 1977 the last case of the disease was identified and treated. After more than two years of searching for further cases in remote regions of the world, the WHO at its assembly in May 1980 declared the disease eradicated.

FUNCTIONALISM'S THREE-PRONGED ATTACK

It is heartening to learn of such successes in health, but their connection with world peace needs some explanation. Functionalists see this kind of activity as promoting peace in three ways.[1] First, it solves basic human problems and so reduces the tensions that lead to war. Hunger is a basic human problem in many parts of the world. Functional organizations develop new strains of wheat and rice, which enable countries to feed their populations by producing more food instead of by going to war. (Notice the assumption of the functionalists: War is caused, in part at least, by human misery.)

Second, activities such as the WHO's attack on smallpox subvert the sovereignty of the nation-state. Subversion is not an activity that governments approve of, at least not when they are the governments being subverted. But with widespread agreement that the sovereignty of many separate states is a major obstacle to world peace, attempts to erode that sovereignty are welcomed by many advocates of world peace. Most often they are not so blunt as to call it subversion; they might refer to "limitations on unbridled sovereignty" instead. To illustrate why functionalism is subversive, let us look at smallpox eradication. One of the last states to have a number of cases was Bangladesh and the WHO was concentrating much of its effort there. The vaccine and many of the health workers working to eradicate smallpox were not coming from the sovereign state of Bangladesh but from the world as a whole, so that the citizens of Bangladesh would feel less cause to give undivided loyalty to Bangladesh. If the world community (in the form of the WHO) assisted them when they needed help, citizens of Bangladesh might be inclined to offer assistance to others in the world when it is needed elsewhere. They might be less inclined to support policies of their own government hostile toward countries that contributed to helping them.

Functional activities go even beyond that. They create within a country, even within a government, groups whose interests are closely tied with international interests. The minister of health is charged, among other things, with controlling communicable diseases. If the best way for him or her to fulfill this responsibility is by making use of the WHO, then the minister becomes an advocate of world cooperation. A village doctor needs smallpox vaccine to carry out his or her duties. If that vaccine comes from the WHO, then the village doctor has a vested interest in seeing that the WHO continues to function inside that country. Functional activities thus give some people inside a country vested interests in international activity.

We sometimes use the expression "social contract" as an imaginative way of saying that people are loyal to government because government provides benefits for them. Functionalism undermines the "social contract" of the nation-state. We need not be blindly loyal to our country's government because the government is not the only source of benefits. Little by little, the national "social contract" is replaced by an international one — if it is international organizations that provide benefits, it is to them we feel loyalty. (Notice the assumption of the functionalists that underlies this second aspect of their proposals: Wars are caused, at least in part, because the world is broken into separate sovereign units, and these units create vested interests in keeping states apart instead of cooperating.)

The third way in which functional activities promote peace is to bring together people from different countries in face-to-face contact. Foreigners seem less "foreign" and more human when they are living right in your midst. It is harder to accept generalizations about other national groups ("all Germans are militarists," "all Americans are greedy") when German and American doctors are living in your village or town, vaccinating your neighbors against smallpox, and offering living proof that all the generalizations are wrong. (Notice, finally, the assumption underlying this aspect of functionalism: War is caused, in part, by one country's distorted image of another.)

Functionalism is a very attractive theory. It is difficult to voice opposition to activities such as wiping out smallpox, increasing grain production, and sending students to study abroad. We should be doing these things anyway, for their own sake, and if we get world peace as a bonus, so much the better. A state might resist direct attempts to limit its authority, say by setting up a world police force; it would be more difficult for a state to turn down an offer of international assistance in introducing new, more productive strains of rice. But in the long run, say the functionalists, these techniques will be just as destructive of national sovereignty as any world police force.

Another attractive feature of functionalism is that it appears to involve a lot less effort than many other plans for world peace. The rapid pace of technological change is doing a lot of the work for us. Writings by people associated with the World Order Models Project have emphasized this feature. A book devoted entirely to this theme is *World Without Borders* by Lester R. Brown.[2] One example from the book will illustrate his argument. Brown discusses the impact of communications satellites, which make possible direct communication between any two points on earth. Before they went into operation, direct communication between Argentina and Chile was next to impossible, even though they had a 1,000-mile border in common; the Andes Mountains (which delineate that border) were an insuperable barrier to telephone lines. Now these two countries lease fifty-six satellite circuits and can enjoy direct telephone contact and even simultaneous television broadcasts.[3] National differences will not disappear overnight, but the national boundaries between the two countries will become less firm and contacts between people will depend less on permission of the governments.

ROBBERS' CAVE AND MIDDLE EAST WATER

Of course we can't say yet where technological changes and technical cooperation will lead. But perhaps we can get an idea by looking at the evidence we do have — historical and experimental. The historical evidence comes from a widely held view of how ancient civilizations began. This theory, advanced by Karl Wittfogel, might be called the "hydraulic theory" of society: Civilization developed along large rivers such as the Nile and the Yellow River because flood control and irrigation projects require central planning and collective action. This gave rise to a specific type of political system, which Wittfogel calls "oriental despotism." If Wittfogel's theory is correct, then it supports the functionalists' claim that technical cooperation gives rise to political cooperation. World cooperation today, the functionalists believe, would create something very different from oriental despotism, but the connection between technical activity and political structure would be the same.[4]

Experimental confirmation of the functionalist theses comes from the "Robbers' Cave" experiment, named after a boys' summer camp in Oklahoma. At this camp, the boys were arbitrarily divided into two groups, then rivalry between the two was promoted by such means as competitive sports. With rivalry well entrenched, the counsellors tried to maneuver the groups into cooperative activities. The water supply was cut and cooperation from both groups was necessary to restore it. A desirable movie was available only if both groups pooled their treasuries. Throughout the summer the counsellors interviewed the boys to find the amount of trust they showed toward members of the other group. They found that after the two groups were forced to cooperate there was more trust and less hostility.[5]

It is hard to say how valid it is to apply experimental evidence of this kind to international relations. You are more likely to find it convincing proof that functionalism could work if you are already favorably disposed toward functionalist proposals. If you are skeptical of functionalist claims, you will find it easy to list reasons why the Robbers' Cave was not at all like international relations. All the participants were from the same society — white, middle-class, Protestant Americans. They were all young (eleven years old). Their groups had been in existence for a very short time. The stakes in their rivalry were trivial. And the counsellors were always in control and in the end could always make binding decisions. Nevertheless, I cite it because it is one of the few bits of evidence we have. There are no comparable experiments on the international level.

But there have been a number of proposals that, if enacted, would do what the Robbers' Cave experiment was trying to do. Consider this plan proposed by President Eisenhower to bring peace to the Middle East. After the war in 1956, and again in 1967, he proposed that an international corporation build three large nuclear power plants in the Middle East, to be operated under the International Atomic Energy Agency. They were to do two things — generate 1.4 million kilowatts of electricity and produce 1 billion gallons of fresh water every day. The power and water thus produced would be made available to Israel, Jordan, Egypt, and Syria. In the words of President Eisenhower, this "would bring a more abundant life to some millions of people and reduce the tensions from which wars are generated."[6]

A CRITIQUE OF FUNCTIONALISM

The Eisenhower plan was never accepted by the Middle Eastern countries, but if it had been, would it have achieved the results Eisenhower expected? Let us look first at his assumption that misery is a cause of war, so that by alleviating misery you eliminate war. You will remember that this was the assumption underlying the first prong of the three-pronged functionalist attack on war. One of the first systematic attempts to examine the relationship between economic conditions and violence was made in the mid-nineteenth century by a French sociologist, Alexis de Tocqueville. In 1856, in a book called *The Old Regime and the French Revolution*, Tocqueville made a startling discovery. The years preceding the outbreak of revolutionary violence in France in 1789 had not brought a falling standard of living but rather increasing prosperity. This prosperity, however, did not lead to greater contentment. On the contrary, Tocqueville wrote, "It is a singular fact that this steadily increasing prosperity, far from tranquilizing the population, everywhere promoted a spirit of unrest." Further confirming this idea, he discovered, "those parts of France in which the improvement in the standard of living was most pronounced were the chief centers of the revolutionary movement."[7]

Since Tocqueville first pointed out that the evidence does not support the common-sense view that misery causes violence, the relationship between economic conditions and violence has become a major subject for research. Scholars have produced a number of theories but have not arrived at any agreement, beyond agreeing that the common-sense view is wrong. That which is true within a society seems also to be true between societies. War is not likely to occur when people are most miserable. Life in Germany was very difficult during the great inflation of 1923, when even a wheelbarrowfull of paper money would buy little. But it was not in 1923 that Germany went to war; that came in 1914, after a period of steady economic growth at a rate unparalleled by any other country. In 1914 the Germans were enjoying the highest standard of living they had ever experienced. Again, it was not in the depths of the great depression in 1932 and 1933 that Germany went to war, but in 1939, when conditions had improved.

There is a lot of evidence to support the claim that prosperity will not prevent violence. This is not to say that we should not try to alleviate human misery and improve living standards around the world. But we should be clear that the best reason for doing so is moral obligation and not political expediency.

The failure of Eisenhower's Middle East plan even to win acceptance reveals another weakness of functionalist theory: Governments will resist subversion. Governments will say "no" to plans that would provide them with economic benefits if they feel their own power is threatened. This was clearly shown in a case where the government was not even in power yet. Algerian nationalists began a war for independence from France in 1954. By 1958 they were doing so well that the regime of the Fourth Republic could no longer survive and was replaced by the Fifth Republic under Charles de Gaulle. General de Gaulle, in an effort to end the Algerian rebellion, went to the Algerian city of Constantine in 1958 and offered the Algerian nationalists increased prosperity if they would stop fighting. French technicians, he said, would develop newly found deposits of natural gas and oil in the Sahara and the economic benefits would be shared with the Algerians, raising their standard of living. The Algerian nationalists rejected the offer. The standard of living in Algeria went down after Algeria became independent in 1962 but it would have been hard to find an Algerian to argue that prosperity was preferable to national sovereignty.

Unfortunately for functionalists, there are many more cases demonstrating that states frequently put political goals ahead of economic ones. East Africa is periodically troubled by plagues of locusts, as destructive today as they were in Biblical times. They appear in swarms that cover from 10 to 40 square miles; each square mile of locusts devours 14 tons of vegetation a day. To control them seven states in East Africa cooperate in the Desert Locust Control Organization. They maintain aircraft to locate swarms, a radio network for tracking them, and planes and trucks for spraying. In 1978 locust swarms threatened severe destruction to crops and grazing land because the program had failed. War between two member states, Ethiopia and Somalia, prevented cooperation. Even though all countries stood to suffer, this war for nationalist objectives had priority over preventing famine. Such cases call into question a basic fundamentalist tenet, that technical cooperation leads to political cooperation. In East Africa, political conflict destroyed technical cooperation.[8]

Again we encounter one of the chief villains in our story, state sovereignty. State governments will invoke this principle to justify breaking off cooperation if they feel a vital interest is threatened and the state alone is judge of its vital interests. In a head-on contest between sovereignty and functionalism, sovereignty wins. Here is an actual case. Cholera is a highly contagious disease. In centuries past it was fatal to millions of people. Today it can be controlled, but an essential part of control is quarantine. The WHO requires countries discovering cases of cholera to report them so that restrictions can be imposed on the area where it is found. But these restrictions damage a country's economy; the state has difficulty exporting food products, attracting tourists, even maintaining normal business contacts. In 1970 the West African country of Guinea had 2,000 cases of cholera but refused to report them, calling them "summer diarrhea" instead. Finally, the WHO, on its own, reported that there was cholera in Guinea. Guinea's reaction was a threat to quit the WHO.[9] Instead of producing international cooperation, the incident created tension. If pushed too far, a state can always invoke the principle of sovereignty and refuse to accept international help by calling it interference in domestic affairs.

States do of course often accept international assistance. The smallpox campaign, despite some resistance, was successful in the end. But the chances of a program's being welcomed seem to be inversely proportional to the degree that it threatens a country's sovereignty: The more subversive the program, the less likely it is to be accepted. The Universal Postal Union is one of the oldest international organizations, founded in 1875. It arranges for the delivery of foreign mail and equalizes the costs of delivery between countries. But in its hundred years of existence it has not created a political superstructure. The hydraulic civilizations of the past may have required a centralized political structure to work, as Karl Wittfogel theorized; the same has not been true of postal services.[10]

There was one more way in which Eisenhower's Middle East plan was supposed to promote peace — by facilitating personal contact between Arabs and Israelis. Engineers from each of the countries, under the supervision of the International Atomic Energy Agency, would have had some task in the operation of the plants. We must be careful to avoid proof by definition. If we postulate lack of personal contact as one element of hostility, then the minute we have put citizens from hostile states side by side we have reduced hostilities. The question is whether this initial contact produces any wider effects.

It is clear that at times hostile states can cooperate on limited measures to meet a common threat. What is less clear is that such limited cooperation will spill over into other areas. The United States, the Soviet Union, and China all played a major part in the eradication of smallpox, but relations among them seemed worse by the time the campaign ended. The states bordering the Mediterranean faced a common threat from the pollution of that sea. Meeting in Barcelona in 1976, they signed a convention prohibiting the dumping of harmful substances, including crude oil, mercury, and DDT. Despite serious conflicts in the region, the convention was signed by Greece, Turkey, and Cyprus, and by Israel, Egypt, Syria, and Libya. The states have continued to cooperate in follow-up meetings held several times a year under the auspices of the United Nations Environmental Program. Yet this limited cooperation did not even extend so far as to promote cooperation in another functional organization. At the 1979 meeting of the WHO assembly, the Arab states (with the sole exception of Egypt) tried to suspend Israel's rights as a member of the WHO.

It would be discouraging enough to learn that limited technical cooperation has no spillover effect, but there is evidence to suggest that such cooperation may even have harmful effects. Researchers have looked at what happens to people's attitudes when they come in contact with people from other countries. Some of the findings seem to support the hopes of the functionalists. There is support for the proposition that as a result of foreign contact people acquire a more differentiated view of other societies — that is, they see the societies as complex and the people as individuals. But some of the research suggests that personal contact will not have a particularly powerful effect in eliminating misunderstandings that may lead to war. Studying the effect of foreign travel, one researcher concluded that people who travel abroad become more committed to their own country and its policies. An American who may be critical of America upon leaving the country becomes more pro-American and identifies more closely with American policies as the result of being abroad. The same is true in reverse for foreign visitors to America.[11] This research finding does not invalidate the entire functionalist premise but it does suggest that the result of personal contact will not be immediate acceptance of opposing points of view.

More evidence against the functionalist position comes from studies conducted in Israel. Researchers there studying Arab workers in Israel found that despite years of working side by side with Israelis, the Arabs showed no significant decrease in hostility. Researchers questioned Arabs who had worked alongside Israelis for at least a year, showing them pictures and asking them to provide captions. A typical example was a picture showing Israelis bringing electric power lines to an Arab village. All Arab comments were negative, stressing Israel's political and economic motives and not the economic benefits to the villagers. Furthermore, the research found the highest incidence of negative attitudes among Arabs who had worked in Israeli industry for the longest periods.[12]

Finally, we turn to the claim that technological change is doing the functionalists' work for them, creating a global society whether governments are in favor of it or not. Without question technology is changing world politics, but the changes are not necessarily all in the direction of more cooperation. Technology can create new conflicts, as the following example shows.

Because the number of frequencies at which radio stations can broadcast is limited, some regulation is needed; the alternative would be so much interference that no one could be heard. Within the United States, regulation is the responsibility of the Federal Communications Commission. In international politics, regulation is done through a functional agency, the International Telecommunications Union (ITU). The ITU sponsors conferences every twenty years to discuss the allocation of frequencies. A major problem at the World Administrative Radio Conference of 1979 was the assignment of short-wave bands.

At the preceding conference in 1959 there were only 300 short-wave transmitters; by 1979 there were 1,500, and many of the new ones were in developing countries that had not been members of the ITU in 1959. The ITU, like the United Nations, operates on the principle of one state, one vote. Because 90 per cent of the short-wave frequencies were used by only 10 per cent of all countries, the developing countries could argue that fairness required redistribution of the assignments. But such a straightforward political solution ignores the disparities in population size, geographic extent, and sheer technical ability to make use of the reserved bands.[13]

In addition, many of the developing countries use short-wave radio for what are called "fixed services" — business and military communication that is handled by telephone services in more advanced countries. Using short wave for fixed services, for which alternatives are available, deprives others of the same short-wave frequencies for use in broadcasting, for which no alternatives are available. The problem is further complicated by the desire of many governments to prevent broadcasts into their countries that might undermine their monopolies on news. Reducing the short-wave frequencies available to advanced countries would enhance political control. What were formerly technical issues have become political ones. Instead of the area of political conflict being narrowed as technical cooperation grows, technology is bringing new areas of conflict.

Functionalist proposals are worthy of support. No one is going to argue in favor of smallpox. But to expect these activities to lead to world peace may be expecting too much. As they begin to encroach on deeply held values, they encounter more and more resistance. The WHO has had success with its malaria and smallpox campaigns; it has not been able to do anything about population control because of conflicting political, moral, and religious views on that question. Sovereignty is a value deeply held by many people in many countries today. Many wars have been waged in the twentieth century to achieve it or preserve it. And sovereignty is invoked to resist roundabout attempts to subvert the nation-state as much as to resist direct attacks. The advocates of world government have correctly identified the major obstacle to world peace: division of the world into sovereign nation-states. The solution they propose, a head-on assault on the principle of sovereignty, in the end may be no more difficult than any other.

NOTES

1. David Mitrany is generally considered the leading exponent of this point of view. See his *A Working Peace System* (Chicago: Quadrangle Books, 1966). A more readable introduction is found in Inis L. Claude, Jr., *Swords into Plowshares*, 4th ed. (New York: Random House, 1971), Chapter 17.

2. Lester R. Brown, *World Without Borders* (New York: Vintage Books, 1973).

3. Ibid., p. 266.

4. Karl A. Wittfogel, *Oriental Despotism* (New Haven: Yale University Press, 1957).

5. M. Sherif et al., *Intergroup Conflict and Cooperation* (Norman, Okla.: University Book Exchange, 1961).

6. John W. Finney, "G.O.P. Pushes Plan on Mideast Water," *The New York Times*, October 20, 1967.

7. Alexis de Tocqueville, *The Old Regime and the French Revolution* (Garden City, N.Y.: Doubleday Anchor Books, 1955), p. 175.

8. "The Year of the Locust," *The Economist*, June 17, 1978.

9. *The Economist*, September 12, 1970, p. 34.

10. This point is made by George H. Quester, *The Continuing Problem of International Politics* (Hinsdale, Ill.: Dryden Press, 1974), p. 11.

11. Ithiel de Sola Pool, "Effects of Cross-National Contact on National and International Images," in *International Behavior*, ed. Herbert C. Kelman (New York: Holt, Rinehart and Winston), 1965.

12. "Israeli Jobs Failing to Win Arabs," *The New York Times*, November 1, 1977; Yehuda Amir et al., "Contact Between Israelis and Arabs and Its Effects," mimeographed (Tel Aviv: Bar-Ilan University, n.d.), p. 17.

13. "Scramble for the Waves," *The Economist*, September 1, 1979, p. 37.

PART III

SOURCES
OF CONFLICT IN THE
CONTEMPORARY
WORLD

Chapter 20

The Soviet Union

In his first public speech after taking office, Secretary of State Alexander Haig declared: "A major focus of American policy must be the Soviet Union, not because of ideological preoccupation but simply because Moscow is the greatest source of international insecurity today. Let us be plain about it: Soviet promotion of violence as the instrument of change constitutes the greatest danger to the world."[1] Coming from such an important source, it is a view we ought to consider seriously. At the same time, we ought not accept it simply because of its source but look at the evidence and try to assess its validity ourselves.

There are several kinds of evidence available to us, none so conclusive that we can be absolutely sure but a few good enough so we can come to an independent judgment. We can look at what Soviet leaders themselves say they intend to do — what we call declaratory policy. We can look at what the Soviet Union actually does — its foreign policies. And we can look at the capabilities it has created — the military forces and other resources that can be used as instruments of foreign policy.

DECLARATORY POLICY: MARXISM–LENINISM

Soviet leaders regularly refer to themselves as Marxists–Leninists, although outsiders debate how seriously to take this claim. After all, popes during the

Renaissance claimed to be following Jesus' teachings while living in sump-
tuous palaces, fathering children, and poisoning their rivals. But Karl Marx
died only one-hundred years ago and we might reasonably expect many of
his ideas to survive unchanged.

A fundamental idea, borrowed by Marx from his predecessor Hegel and
accepted by successors such as Lenin, was the idea of contradictions. Society
as it exists in the world today contains forces that are inherently incompatible
— contradictions. Thus, social life is not by nature harmonious but rather
full of conflict. As Stalin put it in 1927, "He who thinks that one can conduct
in the countryside a policy that will please everybody, the rich as well as
the poor, is not a Marxist but an idiot, because, comrades, such a policy
does not exist in the nature of things."[2] The most important contradiction is
the one resulting from different relationships to property — the contradiction
between those who have property and those who do not. This contradiction
can be resolved only by abolishing the right to private property, but, because
property owners (capitalists) will resist to the bitter end, only the violence
of a revolution can resolve the contradiction.

Even after the revolution, the new socialist society that has abolished
private property lives in tension with those societies in which private property still exists. Thus Soviet leaders continue to declare, "The Communist
Party of the Soviet Union always held and now holds that the class struggle
between the two systems — the capitalist and the socialist — will continue.
It cannot be otherwise, because the world outlook and class aims of socialism and capitalism are opposed and irreconcilable."[3]

The social systems based on private property were in Marx's view morally wrong because they inevitably meant exploitation of those without property by those with it. Building on Marx, Lenin said that such exploitation
also occurred at the international level, between capitalist states and colonies. Only with the abolition of capitalist states will exploitation end. Thus
the international struggle between the Soviet Union and its major rival, the
United States, is seen as a moral one.

Even if we recognize this moral imperative in Soviet thinking, we still
need to determine how the struggle is to be carried out. Undoubtedly the
Soviet Union would like the world to change, but is it accurate to say the
Soviet Union promotes violence as the instrument of change?

Soviet leaders express a belief in the utility of military force. "Unquestionably military force plays a great role in the relations among states," one
official wrote.[4] "The lessons of history teach us that imperialists heed only
force," the Soviet minister of defense said in 1974.[5] Such views echo Russian
political history, reinforced by Marxist doctrine.

According to Marx, the resolution of the contradiction between the
major social classes was possible only by violent conflict. When Lenin wrote

that the class struggle had been translated to the international level, it followed that violent conflict between states was likewise inevitable. War was the international equivalent of revolution and both were historically inevitable.

The doctrine of the inevitability of war began to change after the death of Stalin in 1953. First, one of Stalin's several successors, Georgi Malenkov, suggested that war was no longer inevitable. Malenkov lost the struggle for succession, and some of the ideas he espoused (such as more emphasis on consumer goods) were discredited, but by 1961 the man who had triumphed over Malenkov and others, Nikita Khrushchev, was making the same argument: War is no longer "fatalistically inevitable." He even suggested that war might be banished from the life of society.[6]

Although Brezhnev succeeded in deposing Khrushchev in 1964 with the backing of the military, perhaps because Khrushchev was not spending enough on them, Khrushchev's ideas on war were never repudiated. By the end of Brezhnev's tenure even the chief of the general staff was writing, "In terms of the ferocity and the scale of potential destruction it [nuclear war] could be compared with no wars of the past. The very nature of modern weapons is such that, if they are put into play, the future of all mankind would be at stake."[7]

DECLARATORY POLICY: PEACEFUL COEXISTENCE

In place of emphasis on the inevitability of war, we find emphasis on "peaceful coexistence." The phrase goes back to Lenin and the early years of the Soviet regime, when it was clear that the revolution begun in Russia in 1917 would not sweep through all the industrialized countries of the world and that the new revolutionary regime would have to accommodate itself to the realities of international politics. The phrase itself disappeared for a while — Stalin said in 1927 that "the period of 'peaceful coexistence' is receding into the past"[8] — to be brought back by Khrushchev and Brezhnev. The policy was formally affirmed by an agreement signed in Moscow in 1972 by Secretary Brezhnev and President Nixon on "principles of relations," which were called "peaceful coexistence" in the Soviet press (although the United States preferred the term *détente*).

Yet the Soviet leadership made clear to its own people from the beginning of détente the limitations of such a policy. Peaceful coexistence, said the official party journal in 1974, "does not imply the preservation of the social and political status quo." Indeed, it does not "clash with the oppressed peoples' right to fight for their liberation following whatever method they consider necessary — armed or non-armed struggle."[9] Soviet leaders continue to be quite open about this policy. The official party journal claimed in 1980, "It is impossible to ban civil and national liberation wars. It is impossible in general to ban revolution as a way of changing the political and social order."[10]

The Soviet Union applauds such revolutions, even supports them with arms and advisers. At the same time, they do not see themselves as causing such revolutions. When President Reagan told a press conference that Soviet leaders themselves said that "their goal must be the promotion of world revolution,"[11] the Soviet press agency replied, "In Washington they cannot grasp the nature of the changes going on in the world. These changes are generated by people's struggle for independence and economic and social progress. These processes are not dependent on the power of the United States or the Soviet Union. They have an objective nature."[12]

Soviet declaratory policy thus provides some evidence to support Secretary Haig's contention. Certainly, as Brezhnev said, "We are not pacifists. We are not for peace at any price, and we are not, of course, for any freezing of socio-political processes taking place inside countries."[13]

SOVIET FOREIGN POLICY

A practical consequence of Soviet ideology is that the Soviet Union gives assistance to revolutions and national liberation wars — or at least some of them, for here the record becomes confusing. The Soviet Union does indeed sometimes act to promote violent change in the world, and it justifies its behavior by its ideology. Thus, when the Soviet Union gave massive assistance to one faction in the Angolan civil war in 1975, Secretary Brezhnev defended it with these words:

> Some bourgeois leaders affect surprise over the solidarity of Soviet Communists, the Soviet people, with the struggle of other peoples for freedom and progress. . . . We make no secret of the fact that we see detente as the way to create more favorable conditions for peaceful socialist and Communist construction.[14]

And after Brezhnev's death in 1982, the successor regime reaffirmed its intention to "fulfill up to the end its internationalist duty" in Afghanistan.[15]

Yet the Soviet Union does not always act with vigor in situations in which it might aid "the struggle of other peoples." Beginning in 1955, the Soviet Union supplied arms, training, and diplomatic assistance to Egypt. When the Egyptians lost many of these arms first in the 1956 war and again in the 1967 war, the Soviet Union resupplied them. When Israel sought to end the War of Attrition by deep-penetration bombing raids close to Cairo, the Soviet Union sent its own fighters and pilots to counter the Israelis. Yet abruptly in July 1972 President Sadat ordered all bases and equipment put under exclusive Egyptian control and ordered about 10,000 Soviet advisers out of the country. The Soviets complied. In 1977 President Siad Barre of Somalia ordered out all 6,000 Soviet advisers in his country and again they complied. The meek reaction of the Soviets could be read in many ways, but it was hard to see it as pursuing a relentless drive to expand its influence, by violence as necessary.

In 1973 the Marxist government of Salvador Allende in Chile was overthrown by a military coup, following months of instability caused at least in part by economic warfare against Chile by the United States. In 1975 the Communist Party of Portugal attempted a coup against the government that had been set up after Portugal's dictatorial regime had been overthrown in 1974. Yet in neither Chile nor Portugal did the Soviet Union act to aid its friends.

It was commonly thought that the Soviet Union was not capable of providing useful support to such distant areas. Thus it came as a big shock when the Soviet Union did go to the aid of friends in an area far out of its traditional sphere of influence, southern Africa. In the wake of the Portuguese revolution of 1974, the Portuguese colony of Angola was given its independence before any agreement could be reached on what regime would take the place of the Portuguese. Disagreement among three factions led to a civil war, inconclusive at first, then resolved quite suddenly in 1975 when the Soviet Union mounted a massive airlift of modern weapons and about 10,000 Cuban troops to help one of the factions.

Assistance to Angola was followed by assistance to another African country a few years later. In 1977 the Soviet Union airlifted about $2 billion of arms, 3,000 of its own military advisers, and 20,000 Cuban troops to Ethiopia to help the Ethiopians defeat the Somalis in their war over the Ogaden region. Both of these moves were unprecedented. Never before had the Soviet Union involved itself so directly in military adventures so far from its own frontiers, in matters apparently unrelated to any direct national interest of its own.

Then in December 1979 the Soviet Union moved large numbers of Soviet troops into Afghanistan, supposedly to assist a pro-Soviet government. Almost simultaneously they arrested and executed the head of the government who had supposedly invited them in and installed an Afghan who had been living in Czechoslovakia. The Soviet move shocked many people in the world, including the president of the United States, who declared that Soviet aggression in Afghanistan "has made a more dramatic change in my own opinion of what the Soviets' ultimate goals are than anything they've done in the previous time I've been in office."[16]

Yet following their bold move into Afghanistan, the Soviet Union appeared to enter a period of caution. Other opportunities for intervention in Africa appeared, but successes in Angola and Ethiopia were not followed by further

Soviet moves. They stayed out of the war between various factions in Chad and out of the struggle for succession in the Spanish colony of Sahara. They reduced their earlier involvement in the war to end white rule in Rhodesia and did not obstruct the settlement of that conflict by British mediation.

Even in conflicts closer to their own border they displayed caution. In 1982 the Israeli invasion of Lebanon threatened two groups closely identified with the Soviet Union: the Syrian leadership (which had been careful not to join other Arab states in condemning the invasion of Afghanistan) and the PLO. Yet the Soviet Union offered no significant material assistance, even while American equipment in the hands of the Israelis was triumphing over Soviet equipment in the hands of the Syrians. (The Israelis shot down 79 Syrian planes, the Syrians shot down one Israeli plane.) Soviet behavior was far different from 1970, when they sent planes and pilots to Egypt to defend against Israeli attack, or even from the 1960's, when Khrushchev supported Arab states with speeches and press statements.

The quiescence in Soviet foreign policy of the late 1970's and early 1980's seemed such a contrast to the activism of the mid-1970's that Western commentators were tempted to attribute it first to the "softness and indecision of the aging Brezhnev,"[17] then to the clearly temporary nature of the brief Andropov and Chernenko regimes, and finally to the priorities of Gorbachev first to consolidate his power and then to concentrate on domestic reform. Whatever the cause, the extended period of apparent Soviet caution makes the Soviet record in foreign policy an inconclusive piece of evidence in assessing the Soviet threat to world peace.

MILITARY CAPABILITY

In addition to considering what Soviet leaders say they intend to do, we must look at what means they have to carry out their policies. Declaratory policy could change very rapidly; capabilities change more slowly. Governments in Western Europe, China, and the United States must contemplate at least the possibility of direct attack with the most destructive weapons available. Even should such an attack never be launched, a powerful military capability could be used to gain political leverage. Thus analysts spend much time considering the military balance between the two superpowers. The debate is complex, not only because of military secrecy and uncertainties about the actual performance of untried weapons but also because of disagreement about what elements need to be included in drawing up a balance. For example, should French and British nuclear forces be counted alongside the American? Disagreement on the answer has been a major stumbling block in United States–Soviet negotiations on arms reductions.

Table 20.1   UNITED STATES–SOVIET STRATEGIC BALANCE

	United States		Soviet Union	
Weapons	1972	1985	1972	1985
ICBM	1,054	1,018	1,527	1,398
SLBM	656	616	500	979
Long-range bomber	390	180	140	170

Source: International Institute for Strategic Studies, The Military Balance 1985–1986 (London: IISS, 1985), p. 180; The Military Balance 1981–1982 (London: IISS, 1981), pp. 106–107.

Even a consideration of only a few of the basic issues will illustrate the problem of assessing Soviet capabilities.

A comparison of Soviet with U.S. forces is called net assessment. Because net assessment compares only types of equipment — numbers of missiles, numbers of warheads, and so on — it deals with only the "static balance" and does not take into account other factors that might well be more important in an actual war — which side went first, whether the attack was a surprise, or what other countries were involved. But even realizing the limitations of studying the static balance, we can learn something from it (see Table 20.1).

In 1972 the first strategic arms limitations agreements were signed. Ten years later, the figures show no dramatic change. Some older weapons were dropped in all categories by the United States and in the category of ICBMs alone by the Soviet Union. The Soviet addition of SLBM's (submarine-launched ballistic missiles) represents a relatively small increase in strength because of Soviet difficulties in getting and keeping submarines on station and because of the comparatively smaller number of warheads that each carries.

Yet real change did occur in this period. Both sides increased the number of warheads (and therefore the number of targets they could hit), as Table 20.2 shows.

The great increase in warheads resulted from the shift to multiple warheads (MIRV's) on most missiles. At the same time, not shown on Table 20.2, warheads on both sides increased in accuracy. But while the United States

Table 20.2   UNITED STATES–SOVIET STRATEGIC WARHEADS

Year	United States	Soviet Union
1972	3,550	2,090
1982	9,628	7,300
1985	10,174	9,987

Source: International Institute for Strategic Studies, The Military Balance 1985–1986 (London: IISS, 1985), p. 180; The Military Balance 1981–1982 (London: IISS, 1981), pp. 106–107; The Military Balance 1972–1973 (London: IISS, 1972), pp. 83–86.

initially accompanied this increase in number and accuracy with a decrease in explosive yield (initially down to only 40 kilotons in the case of SLBM's), the Soviet Union continued to deploy warheads with relatively large yields. A new Soviet missile, known in the West as the SS-18, was deployed in two versions — one with MIRV's of 2 megatons each, one with a single warhead of from 10 to 25 megatons. By contrast, the US Minuteman III had MIRV's of only 170 kilotons when first introduced, less than one-tenth as big as the smaller Soviet warhead and only one-hundredth as big as the larger one. (Later versions of these US weapons had somewhat bigger warheads — up to 100 kilotons for SLBM's and 340 kilotons for ICBM's, but these were justified in large measure as a response to the Soviet weapons.)

Small warheads, no matter how plentiful or accurate, do not pose a serious threat to the hardened concrete silos in which ICBM's are kept. But the large-yield warheads of the type the Russians deployed do. If the Soviets followed an assured-destruction policy, such as that advocated in the United States in 1972 at the time of the SALT I agreement, such a force would be unnecessary, indeed a waste of resources. If the force's only purpose is to strike back at cities in retaliation, the 40-kiloton warheads are enough.

Because the Soviets were not building the kind of force the United States was, some people concluded the Soviets were not following the same strategy we were. Rather, they were pursuing a first-strike strategy.

Yet the head of the Soviet Union, Leonid Brezhnev, proclaimed that these were not Soviet intentions. He stated in 1977, "The allegations that the Soviet Union is going beyond what is sufficient for defense, that it is striving for superiority in armaments in the aim of delivering a 'first strike,' are absurd and utterly unfounded."[18]

The apparent contradiction between military capability and declared policy can be resolved by more careful study of Soviet military doctrine. There is indeed a difference between Soviet and American views of how to use nuclear weapons. But this difference does not mean that the Soviets do not take deterrence as their primary mission, or that they are planning to strike first. The key difference is the Soviet belief that the only effective way to deter a nuclear war is to prepare to fight it and win it. One analyst calls this "deterrence through denial," which he contrasts with American "deterrence through retaliation."[19]

According to this view, Americans believe that fear of punishment inflicted on civilians and industry will be sufficient to deter a war. Soviet military leaders believe that only the prospect of actually losing the war will deter a potential aggressor. To this end they hope to destroy as many American missiles as possible, thus limiting damage to their own country. This capability is complemented by plans for civil defense (blast shelters, fallout shelters, evacuation), and, according to some sources, research into systems that will defend against incoming warheads, such as upgraded anti-aircraft missiles and radars, lasers, and particle beams.[20]

A major destabilizing element in this Soviet doctrine is that it is difficult for other countries (such as the United States) to distinguish between "deterrence through denial" and first-strike capability. Indeed a capability to deny an enemy any gains in the event of war would not only be a perfect deterrent; it would also be the equivalent to a perfect first-strike capability. Should Soviet leaders ever want to change to the latter strategy and strike first, they would have the capability at hand.

CONVENTIONAL AND THEATER CAPABILITY

Non-nuclear forces today are referred to as "conventional forces." One of the most important components is military personnel — the number of men (and in the case of the United States, of women) in uniform (see Table 20.3).

The year 1973 is the first year after United States withdrawal from Vietnam. In the following ten years United States forces declined by 136,000; in the same period Soviet forces increased by 280,000. And at the same time the Soviet Union was investing in increased firepower, mobility, and logistic support for its troops. We used to say that Western technology compensated for Soviet numbers. Over the last two decades, the numerical balance has moved steadily in favor of the Soviet Union and its allies, while the technological superiority that gave the United States the edge has largely been lost. Soviet tactical aircraft today, for example, match those of the West in numbers, and, except for the relatively few latest American models, in quality as well.

In the late 1970's the Soviet Union began introducing new weapons, called *theater nuclear weapons*, capable of striking targets in Europe. A medium-range bomber, known in the West as Backfire, and an intermediate-range missile with multiple warheads, known as the SS-20, gave the Soviet Union superiority over NATO weapons in the same category. Thus, the Soviets had moved a long way toward their goal of being able to prevail at any level of combat. According to this goal, at no matter what level hostilities

Table 20.3   UNITED STATES–SOVIET MILITARY PERSONNEL

Year	United States	Soviet Union
1973	2,252,900	3,425,000
1985	2,151,568	5,300,000

Source: International Institute for Strategic Studies, *The Military Balance 1985–1986* (London: IISS, 1985), pp. 6, 21; *The Military Balance 1973–1974* (London: IISS, 1973), pp. 2, 5.

were initiated — from conventionally armed ground forces up to nuclear missiles — Soviet forces would predominate over Western forces because of superior numbers and quality.[21]

If this was the motivation for the continuing Soviet investment in conventional forces, exploiting this superiority was not an easy matter. The invasion of Afghanistan in 1979 tied down Soviet troops; first 85,000 and, as years went by without a clear victory, up to 110,000. Such a force was far short of the more than 5,300,000 troops in the Soviet armed forces (or even of the 500,000 troops that the United States had at one time deployed in Vietnam). For reasons that remained a mystery to outsiders, the Soviet leaders preferred a prolonged struggle to the deployment of more troops.

A possible reason for this caution was the concern of Soviet leaders about other threats along its borders. The border with China alone stretches about 4,000 miles, the longest land frontier in the world. In Europe Soviet troops faced not only the forces of NATO but also potentially rebellious allies. In Poland in the early 1980's a great surge in popularity and power on the part of the trade union movement Solidarity tied down Soviet troops in Europe. From the time Solidarity was recognized by the Polish government in August 1980 to the time martial law was imposed in December 1981, Soviet troops were engaged in military maneuvers in neighboring areas as a reminder of who held ultimate power in that area of Europe. Calculations of the balance of forces in Europe had to be redone; not only could Polish forces not automatically be counted as firm allies of the Soviets, but also additional Soviet troops might be needed to restrain the Poles. But Soviet military strength in Europe guaranteed that the Polish crisis would be resolved the way the Soviet Union desired. It also guaranteed that Western countries would give no more than token assistance to a free trade union movement in East Europe.

A review of the evidence turns up enough support for several conclusions in addition to the alarmist views expressed by Secretary Haig. The Soviet Union has pursued its objective with military means, direct and indirect, in many parts of the world. But it has not always succeeded (as in Afghanistan), and it has not always acted with the vigor it was capable of (as in Lebanon).

What the evidence does suggest is that the Soviet Union is different from many other countries in the world, particularly our own. According to its own declaratory policy, it is not satisfied with the status quo and is unlikely to accept a "live and let live" philosophy. It has built a military capability different from ours, according to a military doctrine different from ours. The potential for conflict — if not from directly opposing goals, then from misunderstanding — is great.

NOTES

1. *The New York Times*, April 25, 1981, p. 1.

2. Adam Ulam, *Stalin* (New York: Viking Press, 1974), p. 300.

3. Leonid Brezhnev, December 21, 1972, quoted by Leon Goure in *War Survival in Soviet Strategy* (Coral Gables, Fla.: Center for Advanced International Studies, 1976), p. 25.

4. G. F. Voronstov, 1976, quoted by Michael J. Deane, in Donald C. Daniel, ed. *International Perceptions of the Superpower Military Balance* (New York: Praeger, 1978), pp. 78–79.

5. Marshall Grechko, January 1974, quoted by Goure, p. 37.

6. Frederic S. Burin, "The Communist Doctrine of the Inevitability of War," *American Political Science Review*, Vol. 57, No. 2 (June 1963), p. 345.

7. Marshall Nikolai Ogarkov, quoted by Dimitri Simes, "Moscow and War," *The New York Times*, November 8, 1981.

8. Alvin Z. Rubinstein, ed., *The Foreign Policy of the Soviet Union,* 2nd ed. (New York: Random House, 1966), p. 107.

9. *Party Life*, February 1974, quoted by Foy Kohler, testimony before the Subcommittee on Europe of the Committee on Foreign Affairs, House of Representatives, 93rd Congress, 2nd sess., May 15, 1974, p. 87.

10. Aleksandr Bovin, *Kommunist*, July 1980, quoted by Dimitri Simes, "Deterrence and Coercion in Soviet Policy," *International Security*, Vol. 5, No. 3 (Winter 1980–1981), pp. 94–95.

11. *The New York Times*, January 30, 1981, p. 3.

12. *The New York Times*, January 31, 1983, p. 3.

13. Kohler testimony, p. 86.

14. Leonid Brezhnev, 1976, quoted in *The New York Times Magazine*, January 27, 1980, p. 45.

15. Michael Tatu, "U.S.–Soviet Relations: A Turning Point?" *Foreign Affairs*, Vol. 61, No. 3 (America and the World 1982), p. 603.

16. Robert G. Kaiser, "U.S.–Soviet Relations: Goodby to Detente," *Foreign Affairs*, Vol. 59, No. 3 (America and the World 1980), p. 510.

17. Dimitri K. Simes, "How to Affect Moscow," *The New York Times*, July 4, 1982.

18. *Pravda*, January 19, 1977, quoted by Raymond Garthoff, "Mutual Deterrence and Strategic Arms Limitation in Soviet Policy," *International Security*, Vol. 3, No. 1 (Summer 1978), p. 139–140.

19. Dennis Ross, "Rethinking Soviet Strategic Policy," *Journal of Strategic Studies* (May 1978), pp. 3–30.

20. Richard Pipes, "Why the Soviet Union Thinks It Could Fight and Win a Nuclear War," *Commentary*, Vol. 64, No. 1 (July 1977), pp. 21–34; George J. Keegan, "New Assessment Put on Soviet Threat," *Aviation Week and Space Technology* (March 28, 1977), pp. 38–43, 46–48.

21. John Erickson, "The Soviet Military Effort in the 1970's," *R.U.S.I. and Brassey's Defense Yearbook 1976/1977* (Boulder, Colo.: Westview Press, 1976), p. 96.

Chapter 21

The United States

"In the present situation, the main danger to peace comes from the policy of the U.S. Government," declared a member of the West German parliament in 1981.[1] He was speaking at a rally opposing the introduction of new nuclear weapons into Western Europe. Such a context favors overstatement, yet his claim nicely balances that of Secretary of State Haig citing the Soviet Union as the major threat to peace. We can approach this claim as we did Secretary Haig's, looking at the evidence and seeing what conclusions it will support. As we did with the Soviet Union, we can look at what the United States says and how it acts. In addition, because our political system is more accessible to study, we can look at some of the means by which decisions are made.

UNITED STATES DECLARATORY POLICY: HUMAN RIGHTS

For years it was customary for Americans to refer to their friends and allies without self-consciousness as the "Free World." The specific content of freedom was often left undefined and thus came to mean different things to different people. For entrepreneurs, it referred to free enterprise or capitalism, with its opportunity to amass personal property with the guarantee it would be protected by the state. For others, freedom was defined in social and particularly religious terms: Americans could choose how they wanted to live, whereas citizens in Communist countries led regimented lives.

None of these definitions offered much guidance in foreign policy. Freedom for many Americans was summarized in the phrase "no government interference," and that phrase is a prescription for inaction. Concern with world affairs would only interfere with the pursuit of private goals; only the most obvious threats to such private pursuits could justify interest in foreign policy.

In the years after World War II, the Soviet Union seemed to pose such a threat, and the need to defend freedom became the justification for economic and military steps to contain Soviet expansion. Yet in practice containment led to specific policies that many Americans found distasteful, particularly the buildup of military power and the support of repressive regimes whose internal policies in no way resembled the American image of freedom. It seemed to many Americans that "Free World" was too vague a term if it could be applied to dictators who came to power by military coups and ruled by torture and summary execution.

The Administration of Jimmy Carter tried to turn American ideals into more specific policy prescriptions through its focus on human rights. For Americans these rights were above all the civil liberties enumerated by the first ten amendments to the United States Constitution, and particularly freedom from arbitrary arrest and detention, from torture, and from summary execution.

It was the declared policy of the Carter Administration to promote human rights, primarily by punishing regimes that violated them. The declared policy was clear enough but in applying it the Carter Administration ran into problems. President Carter asked Congress to deny assistance to military regimes in Latin America, such as Argentina, where over 6,000 people had disappeared without a trace during a government campaign to eliminate urban guerrillas. Congress responded by adding countries of its own to the list of those to be denied aid (including indirect aid via international organizations to which the United States contributed). Whereas Carter had identified right-wing regimes in countries that traditionally had been allied with or cooperated with us, Congress targeted leftist regimes in hostile countries — Cuba, Angola, Vietnam. Whereas the president focused on specific abuses such as torturing prisoners, Congress referred to political and economic systems it called "repressive".

In another attempt to implement his policy, President Carter attacked the Soviet Union for its treatment of its dissidents. Yet he never mentioned Chinese treatment of political prisoners such as the "Gang of Four." Thus, while the policy was stated in universal terms, the list of states targeted for punishment seemed arbitrary, depending on the caprices of American politics.

Although the Carter Administration did speak out on behalf of dissidents in the Soviet Union, it found that withholding economic assistance was more effective than merely lecturing regimes on their behavior. Thus in effect the human rights policy became one limited to those regimes over which we had some leverage. Because we gave aid only to our friends, it was only our friends we could punish by withholding it. Countries to which we gave no assistance — Cambodia, Vietnam, the Soviet Union — were beyond our influence. The application of the policy did not depend on the severity of the violation but on the relationship between the violator and the United States. Iran was a target, Cambodia was not.

The human rights policy ran into further difficulties because it was hard to specify in any objective way what a "right" was. Rights are essentially what people collectively decide they are. If American Plains Indians customarily stopped feeding sick and elderly people in times of food shortages, as a way of preserving the rest of the tribe, a European would make no impression by arguing about the "rights" of the aged. And if a European such as Archduke Franz Ferdinand found it sporting to shoot hundreds of wild animals on a "hunt," an American Indian would have made no impression arguing about the "rights" of the animals. Human rights was little more than a label for the policies a particular state wished to emphasize. For the United States, values related to personal integrity were most important. For many other states in the world, values such as health care and employment were more important. The Universal Declaration on Human Rights, passed by the United Nations in 1948, mentions all of these. States defended themselves against charges that they were violating human rights by pointing to other rights violated by their accusers. Typically, the United States accused other countries of violating political rights, while they in turn accused the United States of neglecting economic rights.

The human rights policy of the United States became a source of vast confusion. For countries suffering from cutoffs of aid, it appeared to be a justification for selective meddling in internal affairs. Argentines could argue that the United States was not threatened, as they were, by an urban guerrilla movement and thus were in no position to sit in judgment. For impoverished countries needing economic assistance, human rights appeared to be a sham. Cubans, whom the United States tried to punish by cutting contributions made via the United Nations, could argue that the United States was hypocritical in stressing only political rights and ignoring economic rights. For countries where our policy was limited to verbal protests, the human rights policy was both a sign of American impotence and a source of annoyance. United States' protests over Soviet treatment of dissidents did little to improve the latter's lot, yet created much tension with the Soviet leadership.

In return for increased tension, the Carter Administration got little. Countries such as Argentina and Guatemala refused United States aid and continued their policies as before. One of the few cases where the United States did succeed in bringing about change was Iran. "It was President

Carter who made the world conscious of human rights and gave us courage to demand ours," said one mullah in 1978.[2] Yet ironically within months the Iranians found themselves governed by an even more repressive regime.

In the years after World War II, a school of theorists of international relations known as "realists" argued that by setting one's goals too high and acting too idealistically, one frequently made matters worse. According to realist logic, the human rights policy, for all its idealism, increased tension and conflict in the world.

UNITED STATES DECLARATORY POLICY: THE REAGAN DOCTRINE

If the promotion of human rights was the hallmark of the Carter Administration, promotion of armed rebellion against Communist regimes was the hallmark of the Reagan Administration. Support for anti-Communist insurgents was the only foreign policy theme in President Reagan's second inaugural address. Conflicts involving such insurgents were put on the agenda of the 1985 Geneva Summit Conference at the insistence of the United States, to balance the Soviet attack on American research into space weapons.

Covert assistance to Afghans resisting the Soviet invasion had begun under the Carter Administration. The program was continued, expanded, and eventually openly acknowledged by the Reagan Administration. The opponents of the Sandinista government in Nicaragua were given assistance that soon became "covert" in name only. Public support and perhaps true covert assistance was supplied to the UNITA movement of Jonas Savimbi in Angola fighting a government supported by Soviet supplies and Cuban troops. The active support of these policies by President Reagan himself, including repeated interventions with Congress to win votes for the appropriation of funds, led the press to call this policy "the Reagan Doctrine."

The policy provoked opposition in the United States, particularly from some of the strongest supporters of Carter's human rights policies. These critics pointed out that the Afghan insurgents were doctrinaire or even fanatical Muslims, not too different from the ones ruling the neighboring country of Iran. They pointed out that no one was entirely sure of the policies Savimbi would follow should he win power in Angola. His movement was receiving most of its support from the government of South Africa and American support would mean our policy was paralleling South Africa's. But the most criticism was directed at opponents of the Sandinistas, who had been labeled "counterrevolutionaries" by the Nicaraguan government and were happy to be called by the shortened form, "contras." Congress itself uncovered considerable evidence that the contras were engaged in rape, torture, and indiscriminate killing of civilians without noticeable progress in weakening the regime they were fighting (see Chapter 24, Terrorism).

From one perspective, the Reagan Doctrine was the opposite of the Carter policy of human rights. But from another, it was not so different. Both policies arose from a similar American impulse — the urge to interfere in the internal affairs of other countries and set things right. Woodrow Wilson had expressed this impulse three-quarters of a century ago, justifying his interference in Latin America: "I am going to teach the South American Republics to elect good men!"[3] For Carter, the urge to interfere expressed itself in the relatively benign form of lectures to others on how to behave, followed, on occasion, by the withholding of aid. For Reagan, it expressed itself in inciting and arming for combat.

Some writers believe that the urge to interfere arises from the simple fact of great power status. The leading powers of the world, from Athens and Rome in the ancient world to Britain in the late nineteenth and early twentieth centuries, have taken an interest in affairs outside their borders, usually in the name of preserving "world order."[4] Other analysts think the United States' urge to interfere is more specifically tied to the rivalry with the Soviet Union. According to a style of reasoning common during the period of the Cold War, most local conflicts are interpreted in America in the light of world power rivalry. If one side to a conflict shows sympathy to the Soviet Union, we are then urged to support the other side.[5] For example, one of the key factors inducing many members of Congress to vote in support of at least "nonlethal" aid to the contras was the fact that the leading figure of the junta ruling Nicaragua, Daniel Ortega, made a visit to Moscow. He signed no treaty, he received no arms, he firmly disavowed any intention of allowing a Soviet military presence in his country. But the mere fact of his visit was enough to convince many members of Congress to vote to fund a movement that aimed to depose him. Finally, there are some people who see this impulse to interfere as arising not so much from America's world status or great power rivalry as from its history and culture.

UNITED STATES DECLARATORY POLICY: A SENSE OF MISSION

The United States has traditionally thought of itself as unique. The motto on the dollar bill, *novus ordo seclorum*, "a new order of the ages," expresses this American sense of mission. One can see this thinking behind the human rights policy. Other states pursued national interests; the United States declared itself acting on behalf of humanity. Various other practices by the United States, out of keeping with accepted international behavior, reflect this sense of uniqueness.

The United States has traditionally been open to immigrants, particularly those identified as political or religious refugees. From time to time immigration has been restricted when it appears to pose the economic threat of cheap labor (Asians in the nineteenth century, East European Jews in the early twentieth), but, compared with other states, the United States is still unusually receptive to immigrants. In recent years the United States has admitted large numbers of South-East Asians, Cubans, and Haitians. (States such as Japan accepted no South-East Asian "boat people" and at one point China was turning away even ethnic Chinese expelled from Vietnam.)

United States laws are unusually solicitous of aliens. President Carter, angered by the violent anti-shah demonstrations on the part of Iranian students in the United States, found it almost impossible to deport the rioters. The courts had ruled that the same guarantees applying to citizens applied to aliens. The United States Supreme Court ruled in 1971 that not only were noncitizens entitled to welfare, but that aliens as a class were a "prime example of a 'discrete and insular' minority" for whom "heightened judicial solicitude is appropriate."[6]

A lenient policy toward immigrants has worked to prevent serious conflict in at least one area. The United States, one of the world's richest countries, shares a 2,000-mile border with Mexico, a relatively poor and very rapidly growing county. Mexico does not rank among the poorest of states, because of industrialization and more recently increased production of oil, but the crisis caused by the 1983 drop of oil prices reveals the potential weakness of the Mexican economy. The number of Mexicans illegally in the United States is estimated in the millions. Yet a massive effort to deport them, comparable to Nigeria's expulsion of almost 2 million foreign workers when oil prices fell in 1983, is politically unthinkable, not least because for many people it would violate American ideals.

But the United States' view of itself as unique has taken other forms annoying to other states. During the time Iran held American diplomats hostage, the United States froze Iranian assets, not just in United States banks (which was perfectly legal) but in European branches of American banks (which was not). Only the delicate nature of the negotiations with Iran and the flagrant violation of international law that the hostage-taking represented kept the Europeans from protesting more loudly against this United States violation of their sovereignty. Then in 1982 the United States sought to punish the Soviet Union for its role in the imposition of martial law in Poland. In June the president imposed an embargo of goods intended for a Soviet natural-gas pipeline, not only coming from companies in the United States (and therefore governed by American laws) but from subsidiaries of American companies abroad and from foreign companies working under American license. European governments expressed shock at this attempt to apply American law extraterritorially, or, in other words, to violate their sovereignty.[7]

Americans' sense of mission, in the minds of some critics, led them into policies that were disruptive of world order. Countries such as Britain and France were much quicker to accept realities by recognizing Red China or trading with Cuba. The United States, in its self-appointed role as leader of the Free World, was much slower to accept change.

But perhaps criticism of American idealism is tinged with envy. America's strength gives it opportunities that smaller states do not have. Perhaps it is America's strength as much as America's idealism that appears to constitute a threat to peace.

UNITED STATES CAPABILITIES: MILITARY POWER

An observer trying to deduce United States intentions from military capabilities would encounter a few clear facts and much confusion. One fact is that the United States defense budget is very large. But a heated debate rages about how it compares with the Soviet budget. In the 1960's and early 1970's, the United States defense budget was generally thought to be larger. Then in the mid-1970's some analysts convinced United States policy-makers that Soviet defense spending was much greater than thought, not only for the present but for preceding years as well. They claimed this fact had been overlooked because of faulty methods of estimation. Other analysts replied that the gap was mostly a result of counting methods and only proved that the Soviet Union was more inefficient in using its resources.[8] But whatever the merits of the various arguments, it is undeniable that in absolute terms the United States spends vast amounts to maintain a very large military establishment.

The writer James Fallows has pointed out that United States defense spending from 1954 to 1980 remained remarkably constant at about $125 billion a year (measured in constant 1980 dollars), varying no more than $10 billion a year from that average. But as the gross national product (GNP) and government spending grew, the proportion going to defense dropped from 45 per cent to 26 per cent of the federal budget and from about 8.5 per cent to 5 per cent of the GNP.[9] This relative drop, combined with claims of higher Soviet spending, led succeeding administrations to ask for increases. President Carter, in his last budget presentation, asked for an increase from $157.6 billion in 1981 to $293.3 billion in 1986. President Reagan, in his first independent request, asked for $182.8 billion in 1982, to grow to $356.0 by 1987 — by which time it would constitute 35 per cent of the federal budget and 7.4 per cent of the GNP.[10] Although the most optimistic goal was not met, from fiscal year 1980 to fiscal year 1985 defense spending rose a total of 85 per cent in current dollars (50 per cent, accounting for inflation).[11]

Plans for the increases were justified by references to Soviet increases in the 1970's, called "a build-up without precedent in history."[12] Yet as one respected scholar, Bernard Brodie, pointed out, from 1970 to 1980 the United States built and deployed more ICBM's than the Soviet Union — 550 to 330. The United States retired its older models when new ones replaced them, whereas the Soviet Union did not, thereby giving the Soviets larger numbers but of lesser quality. Soviet warheads were bigger but only because the United States deliberately decided to make smaller ones. Smaller warheads could be launched from solid-fueled missiles, which would have higher readiness than Soviet liquid-fueled missiles. Though smaller, American warheads were more accurate, at least in the 1970's. And "small" was a relative term — the weapon dropped on Hiroshima was 14 kilotons; the first Minuteman II warhead was 170 kilotons. Brodie concluded, "Since we are looking so hard for the reasons for the Soviet build-up, one possibility that ought to be considered is that it was simply triggered by ours, and that it continues to be stimulated by a desire to catch up."[13]

In fact, should Soviet leaders look, they could find evidence that the United States was seeking superiority. The Republican Party platform of 1980 gave as one of the party's goals "to achieve overall military technological superiority over the Soviet Union."[14] People familiar with American politics know that platforms are not always to be taken literally and in fact Ronald Reagan dropped his explicit call for superiority even before taking office. Yet Reagan Administration officials continued to call for a "margin of safety," which implies something more than equality.[15] They advocated other programs giving the United States advantage. The Navy pressed for a 600-ship fleet that would provide clear superiority at sea. Despite the willingness President Reagan professed in the 1984 presidential candidate debates to share "Star Wars" technology with the Soviet Union, many proponents justified the SDI program on the grounds that it took advantage of superior United States technology. Soviet objections to "the militarization of space" were explained by these proponents as deriving from Soviet fear of not being able to match United States achievements.

From a study of American military capabilities one could draw conclusions similar to those drawn from a study of Soviet capabilities. Although officials (or many of them) sought a rough equality or parity with the other side, the phenomenon of worst-case estimation led to programs that would produce superiority. Even while some officials seemed to advocate parity, others pushed for superiority in special areas. Perhaps such superiority would never be attained, for technological or political reasons, but the mere statement of such goals was enough to alarm the other side. Even a modest "margin of safety", if achieved, might tempt leaders in the future to exploit the advantages it offered. And even if it did not, such a margin would surely provoke the Soviet Union in efforts to catch up, thereby perpetuating the arms race.

UNITED STATES POLICY: COVERT ACTION

President Truman's address to Congress in 1947 marked the appearance of "globalism" as a major theme in American foreign policy. Truman had announced that the United States would "free peoples" everywhere. Unlike the rejection of President Wilson's global interests and the return to isolation after World War I, Americans followed President Truman's lead and accepted the fact that what happened in other countries affected their security.

In pursuing its goal, the United States employed traditional instruments of foreign policy, such as alliances (NATO) and economic assistance (the Marshall Plan). But these traditional instruments did not seem adequate. The twentieth century had seen the rise of "informal penetration" — attempts to influence events inside another country by going around the legitimate government and appealing directly to the people. Adolf Hitler used the technique in 1938 by getting ethnic Germans living in the Sudetenland to agitate against the Czech government. After World War II the Soviet Union used Communist parties in Western Europe to influence the policies of those countries. Soviet actions alarmed American officials such as George Kennan, who sought means to engage in similar actions — bypassing sovereign governments and directly influencing the population. Neither the State Department nor the armed forces wanted such a mission and so the job was assigned to the newly created Central Intelligence Agency (CIA).

Acts of informal penetration, known as "covert action", began in 1948 with secret subsidies to political parties in Western Europe, to balance the subsidies going to communist parties from the Soviet Union. Other funds were used to set up radio stations to broadcast into East Europe and the Soviet Union. The success of these programs created an institutional structure that then sought new operations to justify its continued existence, a process aided by the outbreak of war in Korea in 1950. The personnel of the section of the CIA in charge of covert operations went from 302 in 1949 to almost 6,000 in 1952, the budget from $4.7 million to $82 million.[16]

One of the best-documented cases of covert action occurred in Guatemala in 1954. In 1951, elections in that country brought to power a social reformer named Jacobo Arbenz Guzmán. He was not a Communist or even by most standards very radical. Guatemala, like many countries in the Third World, was one of extremes; Guatemalans were either very poor or very rich. Any attempt to help the poor had to come at the expense of the rich. Arbenz's major efforts were to build up a trade union movement and to distribute land from the largest estates to those who were landless. One target of land reform was an American firm, the United Fruit Company. The Arbenz government wanted to appropriate 234,000 acres that the company owned but was not cultivating. Because the company had declared the value of these acres at $627,572 for tax purposes, that is what the Arbenz government offered as compensation. The United Fruit Company demanded $15,854,849 instead.[17]

The CIA then approached a former Guatemalan colonel who was living in exile because he had tried and failed to take over the government in 1950. With CIA support he raised a small army and invaded from the neighboring country of Honduras in June 1954, supported by planes flown by American pilots. CIA radio transmitters gave the impression that large guerrilla forces were operating in the hills. In fact, the invaders numbered only about 160 and penetrated only 6 miles into the country. But Arbenz lost his nerve and resigned. The colonel supported by the CIA took over. The claims against the United Fruit Company were revoked. In fact, the government even revoked the tax on interest and dividends to foreign investors.

The move against Guatemala was portrayed in the United States as defensive, to stop the spread of Communism in the western hemisphere. Although the argument was widely accepted at the time, the evidence does not seem convincing today. Although President Arbenz got support from the Communists, they were only a small group in Guatemala, with just four seats out of fifty-four in the legislature. The Guatemalan Communists themselves seemed to have been largely ignored by the Soviet Union. There is no evidence they were controlled from Moscow. The specific event that provoked the action in 1954 was a shipment of arms to Guatemala from Czechoslovakia. But this was only one shipment of obsolete weapons, many unusable, and it came from Czechoslovakia because Arbenz was unable to buy arms elsewhere as a consequence of the United States policy of keeping European allies from selling to them. Far from being a threat to the Panama Canal (which was in any case over 1,000 miles away), these weapons were mostly small arms, intended for the armed forces, which were not radical and in the end refused to support Arbenz in the crisis.[18]

Subsequently the CIA was accused of attempting to overthrow other governments — Syria, 1957; Indonesia, 1958; the Congo, 1960; Cuba, 1961; Cambodia, 1970; and Chile in both 1970 and 1973.[19] The amount of evidence to support these accusations varies, but in the case of Chile, the president's National Security Adviser (and later Secretary of State) Henry Kissinger stated openly in his memoirs that it was United States policy to "encourage a military move to produce a new election."[20] Kissinger was also quoted as saying, "I don't see why we need to stand by and watch a country go Communist due to the irresponsibility of its own people."[21] And in 1974, after the government of Salvador Allende had been overthrown by the Chilean armed forces, President Ford declared, "Our Government, like other governments, does take certain action in the intelligence fields to help implement foreign policy and protect national security. . . . I think this is in the best interest of the people of Chile, and certainly in our own best interest."[22]

Public exposure of CIA activity led to restrictions under President Carter. During his Administration the CIA's budget was cut 40 per cent, the number of personnel 50 per cent. Personnel assigned to covert operations were reduced from 2,000 to fewer than 200.[23] But with the advent of the Reagan Administration, the CIA began to grow again, enjoying its biggest buildup since the early 1950's; in 1983 alone its budget increased 25 percent, in large part to help implement the "Reagan Doctrine."[24]

From the perspective of countries such as Nicaragua and Angola, the United States could easily appear to be a major source of instability in the world. The reply of people speaking for the administration was that the United States was only reacting to instability created by others. In the words of the head of the CIA, William Casey, "The Soviet Union has been extraordinarily successful in extending its influence worldwide by destabilizing established governments and installing and supporting new ones which follow its line. . . . This is a process we work hard to spot and measure and help friendly governments avoid."[25] However one answers the question of who was initially responsible, the evidence is overwhelming that the United States government too was following a policy of "destabilizing established governments."

UNITED STATES POLICY: INCONSISTENCIES

Even as President Reagan was ordering the CIA to help insurgents against Soviet-supported governments, the United States Congress was trying to thwart that policy. In response to the first open request for money for what was formerly "covert" action, Congress attached an amendment to the bill specifically prohibiting use of funds for military activity to overthrow the government of Nicaragua. Earlier the Nixon Administration had applied economic pressure to bring down the Allende regime in Chile, yet after the military coup of 1973 Congress passed laws severely restricting aid to the successor regime. Such inconsistency raises the question of which policy truly represents "the United States" — the policy of the president or the policy of the Congress?

One must always make allowances when referring to social groups as though they were single actors. We engage in a process called "reification" when we speak of "the United States" as though it were a tangible object. Reification is a useful intellectual tool, because groups can make decisions and carry them out, just as individual persons do. Yet sometimes reification must be carefully qualified. It is somewhat more accurate to refer to "Japanese policy," because of the homogeneity of Japanese society and its emphasis on consensus, or to "Soviet policy," because of the strong, centralized Soviet Government, than it is to refer to "American policy."

American policy suffers from inconsistency in part because of America's form of government. Even back in 1830, the visiting French sociologist Alexis de Tocqueville observed, "As for myself, I do not hesitate to say that it is especially in the conduct of their foreign relations that democracies appear to me decidedly inferior to other governments. . . . A democracy can only with great difficulty regulate the details of an important undertaking, persevere in a fixed design, and work out its execution in spite of serious obstacles. It cannot combine its measures with secrecy or await their consequences with patience."[26]

One trait of American democracy, as Tocqueville intimates, is openness. Because American government is open and other governments, particularly the Soviet, are not, comparisons and assessment of claims are often difficult. In the controversy over defense spending, United States figures are available to all, whereas Soviet figures are a mystery. Perhaps the Soviet Union is greatly outspending the United States and constitutes a danger to world stability. Or perhaps, as many people thought during the 1970's, the United States spends more than any other country on defense. There is no way to be sure.

The American legislative process requires the government to reveal details of new weapons at an early stage. Thus the enhanced-radiation warhead and the cruise missile were topics of debate long before they were deployed. In contrast, Soviet weapons become known only when they are deployed or are paraded through Red Square. People making comparisons are tempted to compare existing Soviet systems with proposed American systems. Not all proposed weapons are built, so the asymmetry in information inflates United States strength.[27]

Publicity about the covert operations of the CIA occurred through Congressional hearings and investigative reporting using the Freedom of Information Act. Other democratic countries, such as Britain, keep much tighter control on their secrets. American openness focuses attention on covert activities by the United States, whereas such policies may in fact be widespread. For example, a book by a CIA official about his role in the overthrow of the government in Iran in 1953 makes only the barest mention of the role of British intelligence, yet given the history and circumstances of Iran, it is possible that the British played a larger role than the United States.[28]

One might dispute the significance of openness in singling America out for special condemnation. But other traits of American democracy are undisputed sources of annoyance to other countries. One trait is the division of authority among several branches of government. Because presidents do not automatically have a majority in the legislature, they cannot guarantee passage of their proposals. Thus when President Carter promised at an economic summit meeting in Germany in 1978 that the United States would cut oil consumption, unlike other leaders there he could not deliver on his promise.

Division of authority also makes the United States slow to react to changes in the world. In the months following the Middle East war of 1973, the embargo and cutback of oil by Arab producers revealed how dependent the United States had become on foreign oil. Yet by 1979 dependence had increased, from about 25 per cent of all oil consumed to 50 per cent. Furthermore, United States' consumption of oil increased by the same number of barrels that the Europeans through government policies were able to save, thereby keeping demand for oil constant and guaranteeing that the price would remain high.[29] In 1977 President Carter boldly announced an energy policy to reduce dependence on foreign sources, which he called "the moral equivalent of war." A watered-down, much-compromised version was signed into law on November 9, 1978 — one year, six months, and nineteen days after Carter had submitted it. In subsequent years the United States did reduce consumption and imports, but the great amount of time it took, particularly compared with other industrialized states, does not encourage optimism about meeting future challenges.

Conflicts between the executive and judicial branches have also undermined foreign policy. The United States negotiated an agreement with Mexico whereby American prisoners in Mexican jails could finish their sentences in United States jails. The agreement specified that the original sentencing by Mexican courts could not be questioned, yet when prisoners were returned to the United States, courts did allow prisoners to appeal their sentences.[30]

The United States, like all other states, has national interests that it pursues in world politics. These interests lead it to disapprove of certain changes in the world — Soviet occupation of Afghanistan, martial law in Poland, anti-American regimes in Chile or Nicaragua. What constitutes a threat to peace is not what goals a state pursues but what policies it chooses to attain these goals.

Over the past decades, the United States has not used its vast military power to oppose every change it disapproved of. It did not send the Marines to depose Allende in Chile in 1970. It did not go to the aid of the shah against Islamic rebels in 1978. It did not send troops to help the Somoza government fight the Sandinista guerrillas in 1978.

Several different explanations exist for these instances of inaction. Perhaps United States leaders believed that they lacked the power to act, much as they wanted to. Or perhaps they believed that any move against a foreign government had to be carefully prepared (according to this view, Allende was not overthrown until 1973 because it took time to make preparations). Or perhaps United States leaders were genuinely willing to accept change in the world, so long as direct security interests were not threatened (although elections can bring to power another set of leaders).

Most Americans believe that the United States has less power today to influence events in the world than it did in the years immediately following World War II. But opinion is divided on how we should react to that diminished influence. Some people advocate accepting it and learning to live with changes we don't always approve of. They would like America to act "like an ordinary country," accepting limits on its power. Other people regret the loss of American power and advocate efforts to recover our lost strength. Some of these advocates of a strong America view anything less as an abdication of responsibility.

The proper role of America in the world is a subject more fit for political debate than for academic analysis. Yet it is important to remember that for all the changes in the world, the United States is still enormously powerful.

At the close of her trip to Wonderland, while attending the trial of the Knave of Hearts, Alice grows back to her normal height. The King reads from his book: "Rule Forty-two. All persons more than a mile high to leave the court." Everybody looks at Alice. "*I'm* not a mile high," says Alice. "You are," says the King. "Nearly two miles high," says the Queen.

From the perspective of many countries, the United States is a mile high. Whether from the zeal of idealism or the mere possession of power, the United States is seen as disruptive and at least a potential threat to peace in many situations. Perhaps such charges are unavoidable. Only with the greatest care and consistency in formulating and conducting foreign policy can we hope to avoid others' invoking Rule Forty-two, and perhaps, as Alice found, even care and consistency may not be enough.

NOTES

1. Manfred Coppik, Frankfurt, May 16, 1981, reported in *The New York Times*, May 18, 1981, p. 5.

2. Mullah Mohammed Hojatti, Babul, Iran, reported in *The New York Times*, December 9, 1978, p. 3.

3. Harley Notter, *The Origins of the Foreign Policy of Woodrow Wilson* (Baltimore: The Johns Hopkins Press, 1937), p. 274.

4. Robert Gilpin, *War and Change in World Politics* (Cambridge: Cambridge University Press, 1981), for example, pp. 168 ff.

5. Norman Podhoretz, "The Neo-Conservative Anguish Over Reagan's Foreign Policy," *The New York Times Magazine*, May 2, 1982, p. 32.

6. Graham v. Richardson, 403 U.S. 372 (1971).

7. Michel Tatu, "U.S.–Soviet Relations: A Turning Point," *Foreign Affairs*, Vol. 61, No. 3 (America and the World 1983), p. 599.

8. William T. Lee, *Understanding the Soviet Military Threat* (New York: National Strategy Information Center, 1977); Franklyn D. Holzman, "Soviet Military Spending," *International Security*, Vol. 6, No. 4 (Spring 1982), pp. 78–101.

9. James Fallows, *National Defense* (New York: Random House, 1981), p. 4.

10. Caspar W. Weinberger, *Annual Report to the Congress, Fiscal Year 1983,* February 8, 1982, pp. 1–4.

11. Richard Stubbing, "The Defense Program: Buildup or Binge?" *Foreign Affairs*, Vol. 63, No. 4 (Spring 1985), p. 848.

12. Committee on the Present Danger, quoted by Bernard Brodie, "The Development of Nuclear Strategy," *International Security*, Vol. 2, No. 4a (Spring 1978), p. 75.

13. Brodie, pp. 74–75.

14. *Congressional Quarterly Weekly Report,* "1980 Republican Platform Text," Vol. 38, No. 29 (July 19, 1980), p. 2049.

15. Robert E. Osgood, "The Revitalization of Containment" *Foreign Affairs*, Vol. 60, No. 3 (America and the World 1981), p. 475.

16. U.S. Congress, Senate, Select Committee to Study Governmental Operations with Respect to Intelligence Activities, *Staff Reports*, Book IV (Washington, D.C., 1976), pp. 31–32.

17. Stephen Schlesinger and Stephen Kinzer, *Bitter Fruit* (Garden City, NY: Doubleday, 1983), p. 76.

18. Ibid.; also Richard D. Immerman, *The CIA in Guatemala* (Austin: University of Texas Press, 1982).

19. Thomas Powers, *The Man Who Kept the Secrets* (New York: Alfred A. Knopf, 1979).

20. Henry Kissinger, *White House Years* (Boston: Little, Brown, 1979), p. 674.

21. Attributed to several different sources in Robert C. Johansen, *The National Interest and the Human Interest* (Princeton: Princeton University Press, 1980), p. 260.

22. "Transcript of President's News Conference," *The New York Times*, September 17, 1974, p. 22.

23. Ibid.

24. Philip Taubman, "Casey and His C.I.A. On the Rebound," *The New York Times Magazine*, January 16, 1983, p. 21.

25. Quoted by Taubman, p. 35.

26. Alexis de Tocqueville, *Democracy in America,* trans. Henry Reeve and Francis Bowen (New York: Alfred A. Knopf, 1980), Vol. 1, pp. 234–235.

27. Edward N. Luttwak, "Perceptions of Military Force and U.S. Defense Policy," *Survival*, Vol. 19, No. 1 (January–February 1977), pp. 6–7.

28. Kermit Roosevelt, *Countercoup* (New York: McGraw-Hill, 1979).

29. Clyde H. Farnsworth, "Lag in Oil Conservation Troubles Aides of West's Energy Agency," *The New York Times*, November 2, 1976.

30. Alfred Stepan, "The United States and Latin America: Vital Interests and the Instruments of Power," *Foreign Affairs*, Vol. 58, No. 3 (America and the World 1979), pp. 667–668.

Chapter 22

China, Japan, Europe

Because so many of the major elements that make up international politics remain constant, it is possible to study the subject in a systematic way. For several decades, the United States and the Soviet Union have been major powers in the world. China, Japan, and the countries of Western Europe have persisted as important actors, though clearly of the second rank. But despite many constant features, individual elements can change in ways that make prediction difficult. Events in Europe, Japan, and especially China illustrate this difficulty.

CHINA AS A THREAT TO WORLD PEACE

At a press conference in 1967 Secretary of State Dean Rusk was asked what American security interests justified United States fighting in Vietnam. In his answer Rusk did not refer to Vietnam at all but to China:

> Within the next decade or two there will be a billion Chinese on the mainland, armed with nuclear weapons, with no certainty about what their attitude toward the rest of Asia will be. Now the free nations of Asia will make up at least a billion people. They don't want China to overrun them on the basis of a doctrine of world revolution.[1]

373

In February 1979 China did indeed go to war against one of its Asian neighbors, its first major military move since Dean Rusk's statement. Everything about the war was at variance with American expectations ten years earlier. The enemy China was warring against was Vietnam. Despite the size of its military establishment, China did not do very well against the Vietnamese. After temporarily holding some border areas, China justified its withdrawal by claiming it had only intended to teach Vietnam a lesson. Yet the lesson cost China more than it did Vietnam. Despite its unspectacular military performance, at no time did China attempt to use or even threaten to use its nuclear arsenal.

Finally, the war did not cause great alarm or send waves of apprehension through the world, certainly nothing comparable to the Soviet invasion of Afghanistan at the end of 1979. The United Nations Security Council did not even attempt to vote on a resolution of condemnation (although of course any attempt would have been vetoed), nor was the matter transferred to the General Assembly. The Soviet Union did not provoke incidents along its border with China, despite a treaty of friendship and cooperation with Vietnam. The comparatively mild reaction of the world to China's aggression is evidence that China today is not perceived as a major threat to peace.

Much of the change in perceptions about China is a result of changes in China itself. The "doctrine of world revolution" that Secretary Rusk referred to has been muted to the point of inaudibility. In 1965, Lin Biao, the Chinese minister of defense, published an article entitled, "Long Live the Victory of the People's War," a document described by Rusk as a blueprint for aggression. People's war, according to Lin, was the kind of struggle that had brought the Communists to power in China in 1949 and was what the Viet Cong were conducting in South Vietnam. Lin seemed to be calling for more of these struggles all over the world. "The struggles waged by the different peoples against U.S. imperialism," he wrote, "reinforce each other and merge into a torrential worldwide tide of opposition to U.S. imperialism."[2]

Such rhetoric had not been heard from China since the early 1970's. In fact, China's attack on Vietnam in 1979 occurred upon the return to China of Vice Premier Deng Xiaoping from a well-publicized tour of the United States. Chinese declaratory policy today is devoted to urging Turkey to stay in NATO and encouraging European countries and Japan to spend more on military defense.

Before China was admitted to the United Nations in 1971, a major argument among opponents of Chinese membership was that China, in promoting world revolution, would obstruct what little good the United Nations did. In the intervening years, China has not used its power as a permanent member of the Security Council to veto measures in areas not of direct concern to it. China did not veto the UN's cease-fire proposal for the Mideast war of 1973, nor did it prevent the renewal of peacekeeping forces there. Although China welcomed the Egyptian attack on Israel in 1973, it also welcomed President Sadat's peace initiative.

The Chinese applauded the Arab use of oil as a political weapon in 1973. But this stand is consistent with China's attempt to identify itself with the poor and developing countries of the world. In 1975 Premier Deng declared, "China is a developing socialist country belonging to the third world."[3]

Paradoxically it was the revolutionary policy of Mao Zedung that ended up making China less of a threat to peace. One of Mao's successors referred to the decade preceding Mao's death in 1976 as "the ten lost years."[4] During the period known as the "great proletarian cultural revolution," Mao attempted to overcome the stifling effects of bureaucracy and recreate the revolutionary fervor of the early years of the communist movement by urging young people, organized as Red Guards, to attack authority and destroy institutions. The resulting convulsions severely reduced China's economic output. Correct political views were valued more highly than expert knowledge. Scientists were put to work in the fields to improve their political attitudes. Universities shut down. Managers and party leaders were subject to humiliation by Red Guards. As a consequence, Premier Hua confessed in 1979 that over a quarter of China's state enterprises were operating at a loss.

The cultural revolution weakened Chinese military potential as well. Military spending dropped during the first years of the cultural revolution and remained at low levels until the death of Mao. Research and development of new military technology were halted as the emphasis shifted to "people's war," or guerrilla war. As central authority crumbled under the attack of the Red Guards, the army was diverted from defense to the more basic task of holding the country together.

Mao's encouragement of the cultural revolution was all the more surprising in light of the threat China felt from the Soviet Union. In early 1966 the Soviet Union began transferring well-trained and well-equipped troops from Eastern Europe to its border with China, raising the number of its divisions in the Far East from twelve in 1964 to over forty in 1970. In 1968 Soviet troops moved into Czechoslovakia to remove a regime that, while calling itself Communist, showed too much independence from Moscow. The parallels between Czechoslovakia and their own country must have made the Chinese uncomfortable. Then in 1969 Soviet military attachés in cities such as Tokyo and Canberra approached United States officials at diplomatic receptions and struck up seemingly casual conversations on the theme, "Wouldn't it be a good idea if Chinese nuclear capabilities were destroyed before they got too far along?" Similar approaches were made to the State Department in Washington.[5] The Russians evidently were asking the United States to watch passively as they launched an attack on Chinese nuclear fabrication plants and test sites and on Chinese strategic weapons (about seventy-five missiles and about 150 medium-range bombers).

The United States repulsed the Soviet request to stand idly by. This American response facilitated improved relations between China and the United States but did little to improve China's strategically vulnerable position. Despite the size of its military establishment, militarily China is decidedly inferior to the Soviet Union. Some of its military equipment dates back to the Korean War. Shells from its anti-tank weapons would bounce off modern Soviet tanks. Its aircraft could not stay in the sky more than a few hours against modern Soviet planes. Even its large army of 3 million troops could do little because they lack means of transportation; during the 1979 war with Vietnam they traveled by foot.[6]

Concern about a Soviet threat has led to the development of Chinese policies that parallel American policies. During the war in Angola in 1975, the Chinese gave military aid to one of the groups fighting against the Soviet-backed faction. After the Soviet invasion of Afghanistan in 1979, the Chinese provided assistance to Pakistan, with at least some reportedly going to Afghan guerrillas. In 1978, concern over an expanded Soviet presence in Asia led China to sign a treaty of peace and friendship with Japan, a country denounced for its revived militarism as recently as Nixon's visit to China in 1972.

CHINA'S PROSPECTS

China's military weakness presents a serious problem for the United States and its allies. A war between China and the Soviet Union resulting in a Soviet victory is not in their interest. A China so weak that it has no hopes of defending itself might be an invitation to attack. Yet a direct attempt to improve China's military capability would undoubtedly anger the Soviets and be taken as an unfriendly act.

The West is also inhibited by the magnitude of the task. It was estimated in 1979 that bringing the Chinese army up to modern standards would cost $10 billion a year for four to six years, or a total of $41 to $63 billion, a burden that China could not afford by itself.[7] China's needs were staggering — up to 8,600 tanks, up to 24,800 trucks. Nor is it clear that the Chinese would be able to assimilate modern equipment within a few years. Even the sale by the United States to China of a Boeing 707 airplane — hardly the most modern of airliners — was a major technological jump for the Chinese.

Despite its expressions of alarm about Soviet intentions, China did not always give the impression that it considered its defense a pressing concern. In the program inaugurated after the death of Mao and called "the four modernizations," defense modernization ranked fourth. Defense spending actually declined, from $13 billion in 1979 to under $10 billion in 1981.[8] The official defense budget figures for 1985, calculated at the official exchange rate, amounted to only a little over $8 billion.[9] These figures are not strictly comparable to Western defense budgets, because they exclude pay and allowances for troops, but they indicate the downward trend in Chinese military spending, which is shown in other ways as well. The People's Liberation Army has been cut by at least 800,000. A former tank factory now makes sewing machines. In fact, it is estimated that half of the previous defense plants now make civilian goods.[10]

Yet China has recently indicated that its military capabilities will expand, not *more* quickly than the civilian economy but at least *as* quickly.[11] Its nuclear program, interrupted by the cultural revolution, has resumed. In 1980 China tested its first ICBM at intercontinental range; in 1981 it put several satellites in orbit from one launcher, using the same technique used for multiple warheads; in 1982 it fired its first missile from a submarine.

Regardless of what outside assistance China gets, it will be a long time before it ranks as a major military power. Its arsenal of several hundred nuclear weapons is small compared to the almost 10,000 ready-to-deliver weapons possessed by both the United States and the Soviet Union. All but a handful of its operational missiles are of the medium-range, liquid-fueled type. Its bombers are obsolete. All but three of its submarines are diesel powered. Even China's conventional threat to its neighbors in Asia is limited, as its unimpressive performance against the Vietnamese demonstrated. Yet as the war with Vietnam also demonstrated, China is willing to defend its interest with force, even at cost to itself. Because of its large population, underdeveloped economy, and limited military capacity, China is not likely to undertake aggressive foreign policy initiatives. But it is likely to continue its policy of showing great sensitivity to events near its frontiers and responding to perceived threats.

JAPAN: A RESURGENCE OF POWER?

At one time or another all the major powers in the Pacific have viewed Japan as a threat to peace. In 1942 an American diplomat declared that "Japan is the one enemy, and the only enemy, of the peaceful peoples whose shores overlook the Pacific Ocean."[12] The United States has since come to view Japan as an ally, but for a long time the Chinese remained suspicious of Japanese intentions. In the Shanghai communiqué that ended President Nixon's first visit to China in 1972, the Chinese denounced "the revival and outward expansion of Japanese militarism."[13] Since then, the Chinese have changed their minds about the Japanese, signing a treaty of peace and friendship with them in 1978. This reconciliation has disturbed the Russians, who fear a possible combination of American, Chinese, and Japanese power against them.

Without question Japan is an important country. Its power is almost entirely in the economic realm, but the process by which it has acquired this economic power raises questions about possible political and military policies it might some day pursue.

Although not exceptionally large in area (about the size of California) or in population (about half that of the United States), Japan has the second-largest gross national product (GNP) in the world. Its economic performance has been the most spectacular the world has ever seen. From 1950 to 1980 Japan's GNP increased by more than 1,300 per cent; in the late 1960's its economy was growing at over 12 per cent a year, more than twice as fast as other countries.

But because Japan is poor in natural resources, its economy is highly vulnerable. It must import raw materials, fuel, and food to sustain its high standard of living. And to pay for these imports it must export manufactured goods. It has been argued that the Japanese economy experienced such impressive growth during the 1960's because in that period the prices of imported primary products were comparatively low. One demonstration of this price advantage is that in the 1960's imports into Japan accounted for only 8 to 10 per cent of Japan's GNP even though they made up about 75 per cent of all Japanese imports.[14] Japan's dependence on products from abroad is nowhere so crucial as in energy supplies. Japan gets about 70 per cent of its energy from oil and over 99 per cent of that oil must be imported, most of it from the Middle East.[15]

Because of this vulnerability, some analysts argue, the Japanese would be deeply affected by changes in international politics, such as a sharp rise in the price of primary products or a total cutoff of oil supplies. The shock to Japan's economy would bring the collapse of the Japanese social and political structure. In such a situation the Japanese might choose to use military force to ensure access to oil and other primary products. If the government in power did not take adequate steps and allowed a collapse to occur, a regime similar to the militarist one of the 1930's might emerge from the resulting chaos.

Events in the Middle East in 1973 made this argument seem much less a fantasy. Japanese diplomatic efforts to show more sympathy toward the Arab states kept the oil embargo from applying to Japan, but the overall cutback in oil production affected all countries, as did the sharp rise in prices. In 1972 Japan paid $4 billion for imported oil; in 1974, its bill was closer to $20 billion.[16] Yet in the following years Japan was able to contain the effects of higher prices by making its already efficient economy even more efficient. Between 1970 and 1973 each 1 per cent of growth in the economy cost 1.4 per cent growth in the use of energy. Between 1975 and 1977 this was brought down so that a 1 per cent growth in the economy cost only 0.6 per cent growth in the use of energy. Japanese households and industry use only 65 per cent as much energy as the other wealthy industrial countries. And Japan was able to keep its inflation rate down to around 4 per cent by increasing productivity per worker at a rate of from 8 to 12 per cent a year, while increasing wages only 6 per cent a year. (In the United States at the same time, productivity was increasing less than 1 per cent, while wages were increasing from 8 to 9 per cent a year.)[17]

The second major round of oil price increases in 1979 and 1980 meant that the Japanese bill for oil imports tripled, from about $20 billion in 1978 to over $60 billion. Yet the Japanese pursued foreign trade with such vigor that they achieved large trade surpluses (in 1981, $15 billion with the United States, $12 billion with Europe), enabling them to pay for their oil. As the price of oil declined, Japan found itself in 1982 with a $21 billion trade surplus. In that year, while the economies of the other Organization for Economic Cooperation and Development (OECD) countries were shrinking (that of the United States by 1.8 per cent), Japan's grew by 2.4 per cent. But in solving the problem of high oil prices at the expense of others, Japan created resentment among other OECD states. As one analyst put it, "While the Japanese concede the world has a major trade problem, . . . much of that world argues it has basically a Japan problem.[18]

The first great jump in oil prices in 1974 was accompanied by another event that increased the anxiety of the Japanese. The prime minister of Japan, on a visit to the countries of Asia with whom the Japanese do most of their trading, was confronted by rioters in Jakarta, Indonesia. For years the Japanese have avoided any attempt to play a political role, concentrating instead on commercial relations. (President Charles de Gaulle of France went so far as to refer to a Japanese foreign minister as a "transistor salesman.")[19] But now the Japanese discovered that avoiding politics did not make them immune from resentment and criticism by their less powerful neighbors. If the attitudes expressed by the Jakarta rioters reappear, the Japanese could see the disappearance of many of the markets on which their prosperity depends.

Another problem of the Japanese is an increased attempt by various countries to regulate use of the sea. Proposals to extend countries' jurisdictions out to 200 miles would profoundly affect a sea power such as Japan. (In one conference the South Koreans admitted that one of their major motivations in pressing for such a zone was to exclude Japanese fishing vessels.)[20] Environmental legislation could also make it more difficult for the Japanese to obtain needed raw materials. The most convenient route for oil coming to Japan from the Middle East is through the Strait of Malacca, but fear of oil spills has made the adjacent states of Malaysia and Indonesia consider closing the strait to supertankers.

Finally, political tensions in the Pacific area have increased. In the wake of the war between China and Vietnam in 1979, all the states of South-East Asia increased their military spending. Relations between Japan and the Soviet Union remain poor, partly because the Soviets refuse to return the four Kurile Islands they took from Japan after World War II, partly because in the 1978 treaty they signed with China, the Japanese agreed to an "anti-hegemony clause," which the Russians see as directed against them.

JAPANESE MILITARY CAPABILITY AND INTENTIONS

Japan has coupled its aggressive pursuit of economic prosperity with a policy of minimal efforts at national defense. It would be difficult for Japan to respond to a sudden emergency with military force because its military capability is so limited. This weakness is not only deliberate government policy but also a consequence of the Japanese constitution. During the postwar occupation of Japan by American troops, the American commander General Douglas MacArthur virtually dictated the new constitution to the Japanese. He said he wanted "to insure that Japan would not again become a menace to the United States or to the peace and security of the world," and he included in the 1947 constitution an article that renounces "war as a sovereign right of the nation and the threat or use of force in settling international disputes."[21]

However, the North Korean attack on South Korea in 1950 led the United States to reassess its views on the most likely sources of conflict in Asia and MacArthur to reverse his policy toward Japan. With all four American occupation divisions transferred to Korea, MacArthur ordered the Japanese government to create a National Police Reserve Force of 75,000 men. In 1954 this was renamed the Self-Defense Force. Today it numbers about 250,000 and is divided into branches — the Ground Self-Defense Force, the Maritime Self-Defense Force, and the Air Self-Defense Force. Its equipment includes tanks, destroyers, and fighter-bombers. Although by a 1976 Cabinet decision the government agreed to keep defense spending below 1 per cent of the gross national product (compared with over 7 per cent for the United States), because of the large size of its GNP Japan's spending for military purposes in absolute figures is eighth highest in the world.[22] The Japanese argue that these forces would never be used for any purpose but defending the homeland. They do not have strategic delivery systems, such as missiles and bombers, nor do they have nuclear weapons. Yet the level of Japanese technology is so high that they could probably acquire nuclear weapons within six months of a decision to build them.[23]

Despite its potential, the declared policy of Japan avoids any emphasis on military force. Even the shock of higher oil prices did not lead to serious consideration of expanding Japan's military power. One reason the Japanese have dispensed with complete rearmament is their defense alliance with the United States. The peace treaty with Japan in 1951, followed by a security treaty in 1960, gave the United States the right to maintain bases in Japan and to use these bases to maintain peace and security in Asia. In 1985 there were 52,400 United States militarily personnel in Japan, at 120 installations, including 12 major bases.[24] The United States has also specifically extended a nuclear umbrella over Japan, promising to defend it in the event of a nuclear threat.[25]

Despite initial left-wing opposition to the security treaty, the Japanese as a whole have found it a favorable arrangement. It has enabled them to avoid high military spending; yet has provided them with security. It has also enabled them to avoid the suspicions that would inevitably accompany their acquisition of nuclear weapons. (Japan's small and crowded land area makes it such a vulnerable target in a nuclear war that only by striking a decisive first blow could Japan hope to survive.) Other countries in Asia, including the Chinese, have indicated they favor the continuation of American military bases in Japan, preferring them to full-scale Japanese rearmament.[26]

Even if the United States were to withdraw its protection from Japan, there are major obstacles to a resurgence of Japanese military might. One of these is the attitude of many Japanese themselves. Newspapers commented in 1974, when former Japanese Prime Minister Sato received the Nobel Peace Prize, that the prize should have gone to the Japanese as a whole. Yet slowly Japanese attitudes have been changing. The percentage of the population believing that defense forces are necessary grew from 73 per cent in 1972 to 86 per cent in 1978. Those favoring the strengthening of defense forces grew from between 11 and 15 per cent in 1972 to between 22 and 23 per cent in 1978. These higher levels of support have persisted into the 1980's.[27]

The Japanese have been particularly opposed to nuclear weapons, demonstrating even against nuclear-powered ships that have visited their ports. Many have referred to Japan's "nuclear allergy", the result of being the only people in the world to experience a nuclear attack. But today the nuclear allergy may be wearing off. As long ago as 1969 a public opinion poll found that 45 per cent favored the acquisition by Japan of nuclear weapons under certain circumstances.[28]

Even if psychological obstacles are no longer so great, there are convincing strategic arguments against Japan's acquiring nuclear weapons. Japan itself is far too vulnerable to such weapons. One large thermonuclear bomb, directed at the right target area, could destroy 11 per cent of the Japanese population. To cause equivalent damage to China, Japan would need a minimum of 1,000 bombs.[29] The major population centers of the Soviet Union are so distant that such destruction is not conceivable from any feasible potential Japanese force. Another strategic argument is that it would be self-defeating for the Japanese to rely on military force to obtain material such as oil. If the entire country is dependent on foreign oil, then the military forces would be too, and cutting off supplies to them would be much easier to justify than cutting off oil to an unarmed and nonbelligerent Japan.

Although the military option looks unpromising, diplomatic options are available. Japan occupies a strategic position between China and Russia. Each of them seems afraid that Japan will combine with the other, which gives the Japanese some diplomatic leverage. Until now, the obstacles to close Japanese relations with either power have been too great. For the Soviet Union, the major obstacle has been the final disposition of the Kurile Islands. For China, the primary difficulty has been that the Communist Chinese expected the Japanese to sever relations with the Nationalist Chinese on Taiwan. Following the signing of a treaty in 1978, relations between China and Japan improved markedly. Japan soon became the biggest source of investment in China and its major inspiration for development.[30] Yet because of its poverty, China has little to offer Japan by way of return. The development of potential oil fields has been slow. China's own military weakness keeps it from being able to provide Japan with any benefits from a close alliance.

Japan's ties with the United States are still close; the United States remains a major trading partner. In 1985 about 37 per cent of all Japanese exports went to the United States; in the same year about 20 per cent of all Japanese imports came from the United States.[31] For the United States, Japan is not quite so important a partner. In 1984, about 11 per cent of all American exports went to Japan and about 18 per cent of all American imports came from Japan.[32] Nor has the United States–Japanese relationship always been free of trouble. In 1971 the United States without warning imposed a 10 per cent surcharge on all imports. In 1973 the United States imposed a sudden embargo on the export of soybeans (a major source of protein for the Japanese). Oil sales from the Alaskan North Slope fields have been banned to all foreign states, despite the fact that both Japan and the United States would profit from the proximity of Alaska to Japanese markets. The hostility aroused by the Japanese trade surplus in the mid-1980's was a further reminder that the interests of the two countries are not always identical.

In 1979 Japan's Self-Defense Forces prepared a five-year plan for the improvement of its forces. The plan called for an increase in personnel of about 2 per cent and in spending on equipment of about 18 per cent. But the increases were planned for strictly defensive programs — interceptor aircraft, three-dimensional radar, anti-submarine aircraft. There were no requests for forces that could deliver strategic weapons or project power beyond Japan's own territory.[33] Nothing contradicted the policy set down in a defense policy paper in 1970: "Japan will become a big power in terms of economy, but never will it be so in terms of military strength."[34]

Despite this expression of Japanese wishes, American officials have been trying to push Japan into spending more on defense. At a time when Japan was running an overall trade surplus of over $20 billion and the United States an overall trade deficit of over $40 billion (about $20 billion in its account with Japan alone), it was hard for Americans to overlook the great difference in defense spending. Japan, with about half the GNP of the United States, was spending $11 billion; the United States $208 billion. Yet United States forces, some of them stationed in Japan, provided security for Japan. President Carter's secretary of defense hinted that if Japan did not increase defense spending, United States–Japanese relations in other areas would be adversely affected. President Reagan's secretary of defense pressed the same theme. In response, Prime Minister Zenko Suzuki in May 1981 pledged to take over defense of air and sea lanes out to 1,000 miles from Japan. The pledge, made to pacify the Americans, was not followed by any immediate increase in capability to carry it out, yet it provoked strong reactions from the Philippines and Indonesia, two countries with memories of Japanese military expansion in the past.[35]

This departure from unobtrusive diplomacy and minimal defense policies was more a response to pressure from a major trading partner than to any perceived threat to Japanese security. The reaction it provoked confirmed the fears of those Japanese reluctant to abandon a policy that had served them so well. Nor can a Japanese government ignore opinion at home. Despite greater acceptance of some level of defense spending, a 1982 Gallup poll found that, whereas 71 per cent of American and 35 per cent of West German respondents were willing to fight for their country, only 22 per cent of the Japanese were.[36] Until such attitudes change and demand a change in military equipment to match, a major Japanese military role is unlikely.

EUROPE AND THE BEGINNING OF INTEGRATION

Some United States officials have speculated on a return to the balance of power system and count among the participants in such a system the United States, the Soviet Union, China, Japan, and Western Europe. Having examined the first four in this list, we turn now to the remaining one.

We have two problems to consider. First, unlike the other powers, Western Europe is not a single sovereign state. Some of its constituent states, however, are moving toward such an entity, and we will examine how far they have moved in that direction. Second, Europe has been the origin of a number of major wars in the twentieth century. Both World War I and World War II could in some sense be considered European civil wars. We want to consider whether war could again break out because of European rivalries.

The second question was answered by the president of France in May 1975, when he announced that the anniversary of the defeat of Germany in World War II would no longer be celebrated as a holiday in France. The organization of Europe, he said, had put an end to wars on the continent.[37]

The grievances to which recent European wars have been attributed have not all disappeared. One major cause of war in the last century was the desire of German nationalists to create a single German state. Yet today the German Empire founded by Bismarck is divided between two German states, with further portions of its former territory controlled by Poland and Russia. Likewise the basis for economic rivalry among European states remains. The same amount of territory now holds much larger populations, without the colonial empires to provide resources or absorb immigrants.

Nevertheless, in Europe in the past thirty years the movement has been toward cooperation, not conflict. In fact, the movement toward European integration has proceeded so far that one can seriously talk about the eventual disappearance of the separate nation-states that for three centuries were responsible for so many wars.

The movement toward European integration that seems to have abolished war in Europe was in large part created by the most recent and terrible of these wars. As a result of World War II, a number of Europeans found that they had more in common than they had realized. This was especially true of the members of the prewar Christian parties. These parties, which had existed in all the continental countries, had been conservative in orientation, acting mainly to protect the narrowly defined interests of the Catholic Church, such as the right to run Church schools. The temporary ascendancy of the enemies of the Church — the Nazis in Germany (and after 1940 in France), the Fascists in Italy — put them in the opposition. Some of the more thoughtful leaders drew several conclusions from their experience. One was the need to be concerned with broader social issues, such as more equal distribution of wealth. Another conclusion, important in countries such as Germany with sizable Protestant populations, was the need to transcend the narrow Catholic interests that had characterized the prewar parties. The movement that emerged from this wartime experience was known as Christian Democracy. Although loosely organized at the international level, it led to the creation of important parties in each of the major countries — the Christian Democratic Union in Germany, the Christian Democracy in Italy, and the Popular Republican Movement (MRP) in France — each led by men committed to European cooperation. Two of these leaders, Konrad Adenauer in Germany and Alcide de Gasperi in Italy, became prime ministers in their countries and one, Robert Schuman in France, served as foreign minister.

The Christian Democratic movement was only part of a more general change in attitude on the part of many Europeans. There was a common reaction to nationalism. Extreme nationalism had been at the heart of both Nazism and fascism, and these two movements not only had been discredited by defeat but were blamed for the desolate condition Europeans found themselves in at the end of the war.

The change in attitude resulting from the war was reinforced by external pressures. Some of these came from the Soviet Union, which was absorbing the East European countries one by one into its sphere of influence. In the part of Germany under Soviet occupation, the popular Socialist party was forced to merge with the unpopular Communist party in order to make the Communists more respectable. In Czechoslovakia a coalition government in which a number of parties were represented came to an end when the Communists expelled by force all the other parties. Party leaders in Western Europe feared that the same thing might happen to them if they were weak and divided in the face of Soviet pressures.

Another external force was the United States, which encouraged a movement toward a "United States of Europe." The motivation behind this seems to have been mainly idealistic, founded on an analogy with the Americans' own experience. Americans do not seem to have given much thought to the possibility that such a United States of Europe would eventually be a formidable rival. The United States was able to add a material incentive to its promptings in the form of economic aid for European recovery. Commonly called "the Marshall Plan" after Secretary of State George Marshall, who proposed it in 1947, this aid was essential if the Europeans were to recover from the destruction of six years of war. The aid was not granted on a strictly bilateral basis but was coordinated through an organization, the Organization for European Economic Cooperation (OEEC). The OEEC became one of the first of the organizations responsible for "the organization of Europe" that the president of France referred to in his 1975 speech.

THE EUROPE OF THE SIX: ECSC, EURATOM, EEC

Progress toward a United States of Europe has been neither as uniform nor as rapid as the optimists hoped for. But compare the past forty years to the preceding 300 years and the progress has been remarkable indeed. The first steps toward European integration were taken by six countries in the area of heavy industry. In May 1950, French Foreign Minister Robert Schuman proposed a European Coal and Steel Community (ECSC), a proposal that was accepted and went into effect in 1952. Members of the ECSC set up a High Authority of nine members (two each from the larger states, one each from the smaller ones). By a simple majority this High Authority was empowered to make binding decisions in its area of competence, the production and marketing of coal and steel and related products. It could set production levels, fix price ceilings, or prohibit marketing cartels, and could (and did) levy fines against companies that violated its regulations. Companies within the member states could not use an appeal to sovereignty as a reason for disregarding its rules. In its area of competence, the ECSC was truly "supranational."[38]

The High Authority did not operate without some oversight. Its actions were subject to review by a court (composed of judges from the member states), a council (composed of the foreign ministers of the member states), and an assembly (composed of delegates from the parliaments of the member states). But in each of these bodies the principle of majority rule prevailed. No absolute veto was granted to each state as had been the practice in international bodies in the past. (Bodies such as the League of Nations had been set up with the intention of ruling out vetoes by individual states, but in practice they respected the wishes of member states. The ECSC was different: Its members really did relinquish their sovereignty.)

The ECSC came into existence because it was supported by a number of groups, even though each was supporting the community for its own reasons. The functionalists supported it as the first step toward total European integration. The French nationalists saw it as a way to restrain German industrial might (which many of them believed had been responsible for Hitler's rise to power). The German industrialists supported ECSC because it appeared to them to be the only way they could end the controls imposed by the occupation forces of the victors of World War II and get their industry going again.

The ECSC was not as inclusive as Schuman had hoped. Only France, Germany, Italy, Belgium, Netherlands, and Luxembourg were members. The British refused requests to join, out of a traditional distrust for permanent ties with continental countries and out of fear that it would jeopardize British ties with the Commonwealth countries. European neutral countries such as Switzerland and Sweden were reluctant to join and European countries still ruled by dictators such as Portugal and Spain were not invited.

The success of the European Coal and Steel Community led to the creation of two additional communities among the same six countries. These were agreed to in 1955 and put into effect in January 1958. One of these was the European Atomic Energy Community (Euratom), the main concern of which was helping its member states forestall an energy shortage by using nuclear reactors to generate power. Euratom provided among other things common safety standards, shared research facilities, and community control of fissionable materials. The other new community was commonly called the Common Market; its formal title was the European Economic Community (EEC). By the EEC treaty the six countries agreed to establish a customs union over a period of twelve years, reducing to zero their tariffs on goods produced in the community and adjusting the tariffs on goods produced outside until they were all at the same level. The EEC also included provisions to encourage economic cooperation among its members in other ways. It facilitated the free movement of laborers from one country to another by allowing them to transfer social security benefits earned in one country to another.

Both Euratom and EEC were patterned on the ECSC. Each consisted of a higher authority (called a "commission" in the new communities), controlled by a court, a council, and an assembly. In 1967 the structures of all three communities were merged into one. A single Commission in Brussels administers all three, controlled by a single court, a council of foreign ministers, and an assembly now called the "European Parliament."

THE ENLARGEMENT OF THE EUROPEAN COMMUNITY

European prosperity grew in the 1960's. Although this was part of a worldwide increase in prosperity and probably not entirely due to European cooperation, it worked to the benefit of the European communities. The EEC goal of abolishing internal tariffs was reached eighteen months ahead of schedule, and supporters of European integration began to talk of more ambitious projects.

An important milestone in the development of Europe was the enlargement of the European Community beyond the original six members. The success of the Community, along with the deterioration of Britain's position in the world, led the British to reconsider their refusal to join, and in the 1960's they made several requests for membership. After several rebuffs, most coming from French President Charles de Gaulle, Britain, Ireland, and Denmark were accepted as members in January 1973. Membership was also extended to the Norwegians, but they rejected it in a referendum in September 1972.

It was not clear that the enlargement of the Community strengthened it. More members brought greater diversity — more official languages, more national problems, more economic differences. British membership caused problems with the Community's Common Agricultural Polity (CAP), a program for subsidizing prices of farm products well above world market levels. The British found they were paying large amounts into CAP, yet British farmers were receiving little benefit. The disparity led to disenchantment with the Community and even to threats by the British to pull out.

Further proposals for enlargement extended membership to Greece (beginning in 1981) and Spain and Portugal (beginning in 1986). Full membership by these countries, closer in some ways to the less developed countries of the Third World than to the industrialized democracies of northern Europe, will dilute economic coherence even further. They will also bring with them new political problems, particularly Greece's continuing tension with Turkey.

Increased heterogeneity in membership will slow even more what little progress has been made toward further integration. A tentative first step toward a common European currency was taken in March 1979 with the establishment of a European Monetary System, designed to help countries manage short-term fluctuations in the values of their currencies. Yet even this step, modest as it was, did not include all nine members: Britain remained outside. Increasing financial and monetary problems in all countries of the world make a common currency seem very remote.

Another small step toward further integration was the direct election to the all-European Parliament held in June 1979. Over 60 per cent of all the eligible voters in the nine countries voted. But the Parliament's powers remain very limited — little beyond removing members of the Commission in Belgium by a two-thirds vote and rejecting the budget. In contrast to these small steps toward formal unity, Europe showed very little unity in the substance of its approach to the major problems of the late 1970's and early 1980's. It did not develop a unified position on a Palestinian state or the revolution in Iran or the Soviet invasion of Afghanistan. A common set of policies in foreign affairs, not to mention agreement on the use of military force to back them up, is very far off indeed.

Yet, measured against European history from the wars of Bismarck to World War II, the achievement has been remarkable. War or even the vaguest threat of force has been effectively ruled out as a means of settling disputes between the members of the European Community. The chain of wars resulting from the French–German rivalry has come to an end. In part it was the very destructiveness of those wars that created the conditions for recent cooperation. If that is the price that must be paid, then we should not be too optimistic in expecting similar integration movements to develop in other parts of the world. Yet the European experience does suggest that war need not be a permanent part of the relations among states.

NOTES

1. Quoted by Richard J. Barnet in *Roots of War* (New York: Atheneum, 1972), p. 132.
2. Published by the Foreign Broadcast Information Service (Washington, D.C.: U.S. Government Printing Office, 1966), p. 32.

3. *Peking Review*, Vol. 24 (June 13, 1975), p. 9.

4. Harrison E. Salisbury, "China's Leaders View Last 10 Years as 'Lost,'" *The New York Times*, November 5, 1977, p. 3.

5. Joseph Alsop, "Thoughts Out of China. Part 1: Go Versus No-Go," *The New York Times* Magazine, March 11, 1973, pp. 31, 100–108; Henry Kissinger, *White House Years* (Boston: Little, Brown, 1979), pp. 183–184.

6. Drew Middleton, "China Given Little Chance of Success in a Full-Scale War with Soviet Union," *The New York Times*, October 7, 1975; Lucian Pye, "Dilemmas for America in China's Modernization," *International Security*, Vol. 4, No. 1 (Summer 1979), p. 8.

7. Pye.

8. *The New York Times*, May 6, 1982.

9. International Institute for Strategic Studies, *The Military Balance 1985–1986* (London: IISS, 1985), p. 112.

10. David M. Lampton, "Misreading China," *Foreign Policy*, No. 45 (Winter 1981–1982), p. 104–105.

11. *The Economist*, March 12, 1983, pp. 46–47.

12. Joseph Grew, *Report from Tokyo* (New York: Simon & Schuster, 1942), pp. 69–70.

13. Peter G. Mueller and Douglas A. Ross, *China and Japan — Emerging Global Powers* (New York: Praeger, 1975), p. 97.

14. Donald C. Hellmann, "The United States and Japan," in *Conflict in World Politics*, ed. Steven L. Spiegel and Kenneth N. Waltz (Cambridge: Winthrop, 1971), p. 362.

15. Mueller and Ross, p. 178.

16. Ibid., p. 175.

17. Norman Macrae, "Must Japan Slow?" *The Economist*, February 23, 1980, pp. 37–38.

18. Robert Keatley, "East Asia: The Recession Arrives," *Foreign Affairs*, Vol. 61, No. 3 (America and the World 1982), p. 694.

19. T. C. Rhee, "Japan: 'Same Bed, Different Dreams,'" *Interplay*, Vol. 3, No. 11 (August 1970), p. 4.

20. Morton A. Kaplan and Nicholas deB. Katzenbach, *The Political Foundations of International Law* (New York: John Wiley, 1961), pp. 149–151.

21. Hellmann, pp. 359–360.

22. Calculated from U.S. Arms Control and Disarmament Agency, *World Military Expenditures and Arms Transfers, 1970–1979* (Washington, D.C.: United States Government Printing Office, 1982).

23. Keyes Beech, "Japan — The Ultimate Domino?" *Saturday Review, reprinted in At Issue*, 2nd ed., ed. Steven L. Spiegel (New York: St. Martin's Press), p. 220.

24. *The Military Balance 1985–1986*, p. 14.

25. During President Ford's trip to Japan in 1975, he said the United States would defend Japan against non-nuclear as well as nuclear attack. *The Economist*, August 16, 1975, p. 43.

26. Vernon V. Aspaturian, "Moscow's Options in a Changing World," *Problems of Communism*, Vol. 21, No. 4 (July–August 1972), pp. 18–19.

27. *Nihon no Mamori* [The Defense of Japan] (Tokyo: Defense Agency, 1983) (in Japanese), pp. 16, 17.

28. Hellmann, p. 372.

29. Kunio Muraoka, "Japanese Security and the United States," *Adelphi Paper*, No. 95 (London: International Institute of Strategic Studies, February 1973), p. 24.

30. Robert A. Scalapino, "Asia at the End of the 1970s," *Foreign Affairs*, Vol. 58, No. 3 (1980), p. 705.

31. *Monthly Statistics of Japan*, No. 298 (April 1986) (Tokyo: Statistics Bureau), pp. 75, 79.

32. *The Economist*, September 14, 1985, p. 72.

33. "Rearming, Slowly," *The Economist*, July 28, 1979.

34. Mueller and Ross, p. 102.

35. *The Economist*, May 16, 1981, p. 70; *The New York Times*, October 14, 1982, p. Y3.

36. "Survey Finds Work Rated High in U.S.," *The New York Times*, May 19, 1982, p. A23.

37. Flora Lewis, "Giscard Ending of V-E Day Stirs a Wide Controversy," *The New York Times*, May 10, 1975.

38. See Harold K. Jacobson and Robert S. Jordan, "Economic and Political Integration: From the Schuman Plan to the European Communities," in *Problems in International Relations*, 3rd ed., ed. Andrew Gyorgy et al. (Englewood Cliffs,N.J.: Prentice-Hall, 19760); Roy F. Willis, *France, Germany and the New Europe, 1945–1967*, rev. ed. (London: Oxford University Press, 1968).

Chapter 23

The Third World

The concept of sovereignty, as developed in Europe in the seventeenth and eighteenth centuries, was until recently applied only to the most powerful states, most of which were located in Europe. The rest of the world, lacking sovereignty, could therefore legitimately be "discovered" and then "claimed" by these powerful states and added to their own territory. It was only with the League of Nations in the 1920's and 1930's that some inroads were made on the traditional view that the non-Western world was territory in which the inhabitants had no legitimate claims of their own. The League provided for what it called "mandates" in some areas of the world. Although the effect on the inhabitants of mandated territories was not very different from colonial rule, the presumption was that the major power in charge of the mandate would not rule indefinitely but only as long as it took to prepare the people for self-government. This system provided some hope for the future, but it did little to change the day-to-day realities. In 1935, 70 per cent of the world's population was still under the control of Western governments.[1]

RISE TO PROMINENCE

It was only with the foundation and growth of the United Nations that a significant number of non-Western states began to play an important role in world politics. The UN Charter mentions as a basic principle the self-determination of peoples. Although in its first years the membership of the UN was confined to just about the same countries that had composed the League of Nations, this balance began to change as former colonies acquired their independence. The year 1960 marks an important turning point. In that year sixteen newly independent African states were admitted as members of the UN. The number of such states has continued to grow, and at present they make up more than half of the states of the world.

The term often used to describe these new states is a remnant of Cold War thinking. In the bipolar conception developed in the 1950's, states belonged to the world of the United States and its allies or to the world of the Soviet Union and its allies. The remaining countries were said to make up the *Third World*.

DEFINITION OF "THIRD WORLD"

People use the name "Third World" as though it referred to a coherent group of states — much in the way "the Soviet bloc" refers to centrally planned economies ruled by Marxist–Leninist parties with close ties to the Soviet Union. But Third World is a label lacking precision. Both Sweden and Switzerland were neutral states, yet they were not considered Third World countries. The Third World countries were said to be located in Asia, Africa, and Latin America, but that area includes Taiwan, Israel, and South Africa, which were not considered part of the Third World. Most Third World states were poor and struggling with problems of economic development, yet so were Greece and Turkey, both members of NATO. In short, Third World is a residual category, where we put what is left over.

Efforts to define Third World positively — as the membership of some group — are more useful. In political terms, the most significant such group is the Non-Aligned Nations. President Sukarno of Indonesia called the first conference of states wishing to avoid involvement with the major powers at Bandung in 1955. Six years later, Sukarno, along with Nehru of India, Nasser of Egypt, and Tito of Yugoslavia, turned it into a permanent organization, with twenty-five members. The movement grew to almost one-hundred members, with yearly meetings of foreign ministers and summit conferences of heads of state every three years.

Yet divisions within the movement began to appear in 1975, when it added to its membership North Korea and North Vietnam, states that were by any reasonable definition not non-aligned but members of the Soviet bloc. Internal divisions appeared in 1978 as some of the original members tried to resist attempts by Cuba, Angola, and Vietnam — all of whom had pacts with the Soviet Union — to take consistently pro-Soviet positions on foreign policy issues. A summit conference in Havana in 1979 was dominated by

Castro, with only minor concessions to the more traditional aims represented by Tito, the last of the original founders to attend. The final declaration of the Havana Conference included numerous attacks on the United States — for example, for its colonialism of Puerto Rico — but none on the Soviet Union. The unity of the movement and the influence of Castro as its chairperson received a sharp setback, however, in early 1980, when half of the membership in a United Nations vote condemned the Soviet Union for its invasion of Afghanistan.

The disunity of the Non-Aligned Nations illustrated a basic feature of the concept of the Third World. Despite the desire by many members of these states to think of themselves as a unified group, they are beset by serious differences. Even if alliances with major powers are discounted, the political differences among these states are very great. Saudi Arabia, which has a conservative monarchy, is a member; so is its radical neighbor South Yemen. In fact the only ideology they share is that of nationalism, but because nationalism stresses the particular state, it tends to divide and not to unite.

The emphasis in the 1950's and 1960's was on defining the Third World politically. Recent years have seen more emphasis on economic condition as a defining characteristic. Thus, the twenty-four wealthy states known as "industrially developed market economies" are members of the Organization for Economic Cooperation and Development (OECD). States modeled on the Marxist-Leninist ideal of a "centrally planned economy" are members of the Council for Mutual Economic Assistance (CMEA). The remaining states are members of the Group of 77, a somewhat misleading name that was taken from the actual number at the time of its formation in 1964 but which today comprises well over one-hundred states. Because the most prominent OECD countries are in the northern hemisphere — United States, Japan, Western Europe — and many of the Group of 77 are in the southern, they are sometimes referred to as the North and the South. (The CMEA has tried to attract little attention, claiming that whatever poverty exists in the poor countries is the result of imperialism and so they share no responsibility.)

An economic definition of the Third World is not particularly helpful. At the one extreme are countries with suddenly very high incomes per capita because of oil wealth — Saudi Arabia, Kuwait, United Arab Emirates. At the other extreme are countries so poor they are often put in a separate category of "Fourth World." Over 1 billion people live in countries where the per capita income is under $220 a year. These are countries with no natural resources and a growth rate of under 1 per cent a year — enough to add only two dollars to each person's yearly income.

In between the oil-rich and the low-income are the "newly industrialized" countries — South Korea, Brazil, India, Mexico. In some ways these countries are much closer to the OECD countries than they are to other members of the Group of 77. They have no interest inn the cancellation of debts, for example, because much of the high growth rate they have achieved (an average in 1979 and 1980 of 5.5 per cent) results from international loans. Defaulting on loans or having them cancelled would deprive them of loans in the future to sustain their growth rate.

The differences among countries generally considered Third World — whether defined politically or economically — are so great that we cannot reasonably speak of the Third World as a unified actor in international politics.

THIRD WORLD INFLUENCE ON WAR AND PEACE

The participation in international politics by over one-hundred new states in Asia, Africa, and Latin America poses two obstacles to peace. On the one hand, it has vitiated some of the traditional approaches to peace. On the other, it has been the source of many new conflicts.

We have already seen the effects of the Third World in preceding chapters. The extent and force of international law have been seriously restricted by the anti-colonial revolution promoted by and working to the benefit of these states. Legal principles of long standing, such as freedom of the high seas or immunity for diplomats, are disregarded in the name of anti-imperialism. Likewise the focus of international organizations such as the United Nations has been shifted away from issues of war and peace toward support first of liberation from colonial rule and then economic development.

The gap between the Third World's new aspirations and traditional ways of conducting international relations is a source of conflict. It widened particularly in the 1960's and 1970's, as people's attitudes in one group of states — above all our own, but also many of the states of Western Europe — were moving in one direction while the people's attitudes in the Third World were moving in another. Many of the states in the Third World had been part of larger, multinational political units, usually colonial empires. As these empires ended they were replaced by more numerous, smaller states.

At the same time, many people in long-established states were calling for a broadening of horizons beyond the nation, for seeing problems in global terms, for viewing ourselves as travelers on "Spaceship Earth." Among many young people patriotism came to be seen as old-fashioned. Proposals to reinstitute the draft were greeted by students holding signs proclaiming, "Nothing is worth dying for." National barriers seemed less important to Europeans, as more states joined the European Community.

These trends were not mirrored in the Third World. The opposite was more likely to be the case. States jealously defended their sovereignty. Young people seemed to find many issues worth dying for, as they joined armies to liberate unredeemed territory (Somalis in the 1970's), to aid other members of their national group (Turks in 1974), or expel foreigners from their land (Iranians in the 1980's). While the United States worried about the proper way to deal with an increase in illegal aliens, the government of Nigeria one day simply announced the forcible expulsion of all foreigners without work permits. According to the Nigerian government's own estimate, 2 million aliens were deported.

Many states have tried to remove foreign influences in a process called *indigenization*. Joseph Mobutu changed the name of his country from the "Congo" to what he saw as the more native name "Zaïre," then changed his own name to Mobutu Sesu Seko. In Libya and Iran street signs in English or even ones using the Latin alphabet have been removed, leaving only signs in Arabic script.

Sometimes attempts by international organizations to implement policies were vigorously resisted in the name of sovereignty. Out of sensitivity to the charge that they were not managing their affairs as well as they had been under colonial rule, states tried to cover up health problems, even if the latter were not the result of government policy. Most African states denied for a long time that they had any cases of acquired immune deficiency syndrome (AIDS), despite an international obligation to report all cases to the World Health Organization; exercising their sovereignty they routinely denied visas to reporters investigating AIDS. Ethiopia expelled foreign doctors who reported cases of cholera after the government had denied that such cases existed.[2] Many other states objected to the austerity measures demanded by the International Monetary Fund (IMF) as a condition for loans to support collapsing economies; blame for the resulting rise in cost of living was placed on the IMF, not their own countries' mistaken policies, and governments were tempted to repudiate the IMF rather than face down rioters.[3]

We have seen repeatedly how sovereignty is a major obstacle to peace. The increase in the number of states enamored of it and glorifying it multiplies the obstacles to international agreement and cooperation.

SOURCES OF CONFLICT WITHIN
THE THIRD WORLD

The Third World is an important source of conflict quite apart from great power interests. One study has put the total deaths from 1945 to 1967 resulting from violence within and among these countries at 7,480,000.[4] If we add to that the deaths from only two of the conflicts that have occurred since 1967 — the Nigerian civil war (2 million deaths) and the Pakistan civil war (500,000 deaths) — we already exceed the number of battle deaths of World War I. With violence of such magnitude, the disputes are worth looking at for their own sake, but in addition they frequently have repercussions in international politics. After looking at the origin of many of these disputes, we shall see why their effects spread so far.

Conflict in the Third World has been attributed to a number of factors — the desire to acquire modern industrial technology, resentment at higher standards of living in economically developed countries, colonial exploitation in the past, and racial discrimination in the present. Important as these may be, they are overshadowed by another source of conflict: national sentiment.

The word "nation" is often inappropriately used (as in the name the United Nations), and so it is necessary to first define carefully what we mean. By *nation* we mean a distinct ethnic group that is clearly set off from its neighbors by such features as a separate language, separate customs, and separate traditions. One important feature of a nation is that you have no control over which one you belong to — you are born into it. Nationality is sometimes called a "primordial tie," a primary bond as opposed to second-order ties or associations. You can choose to join the Audobon Society or the Democratic Party or the Free Will Baptist Church; you can also choose to quit these associations if you desire. The element of choice is absent from a primordial tie.[5]

Conflict resulting from nationalist and other primordial ties is not limited to the Third World. Canada's problems with Quebec and Britain's problems with Northern Ireland are conflicts that have their origin in primordial ties. But it is in the Third World that the problems are most severe. For in the Third World the conditions that facilitated secondary or associational ties are becoming weaker and the conditions that activate primordial ties are becoming stronger. The British Empire, like other colonial empires, was an association. Although membership in it was not always strictly voluntary, no group was excluded because of a primordial trait. Nigerians and Indians alike were free to embrace Anglican or Catholic Christianity, learn English, study at Oxford, and participate in whatever other privileges were extended to British subjects. But Nigeria and India were themselves composed of many ethnic groups. These groups united to free themselves of British rule, but once the British left, the primordial ties reasserted themselves. In Nigeria 250 different languages are spoken; in India the number is 1,652. With the British imposing English on the entire country, it was possible to have a uniform school system and a common government language. With the departure of the British, the question of what language would be used for instruction and government business became a hotly contested political issue.

It is precisely those developments to which we refer as modernizing and progressive — such things as increased industrialization, improved means of communication, and higher standards of education — that increase the importance of primordial ties. This is so because all these developments mix together people from different groups who previously had no contact with each other. By increasing contact you increase the possibilities for conflict. We might take the case of Nigeria. Suppose several Ibo-speakers from the east take advantage of a new highway to travel north to the part of Nigeria inhabited by Hausa-speakers. Perhaps they open a shop there to sell products newly imported from Europe or Japan, such as sewing machines. The Ibos are likely to be Christians and offend the Muslim Hausas by raising and eating pigs (which are forbidden to Muslims). The language of trade between Ibos and Hausas may be English but among themselves the Ibos use their own language, which arouses suspicions among the Hausas that the Ibos are saying things about them, making fun of them, plotting to cheat them. This example is not a hypothetical one. It was precisely such movement by the Ibos and such hostility that it aroused that it led to a massacre of 50,000 Ibos in northern Nigeria in 1966. Another 1 million Ibos were driven out. They fled back to the east and demanded their own state as the only sure source of protection, an event that led to a bloody and ultimately unsuccessful civil war.

It was precisely the modern developments such as better roads and imported sewing machines that generated this conflict. In the past diverse ethnic groups had little contact with each other. Colonial rule by the British set in motion the process by which the groups came in contact, although the British also were able to prevent tensions from erupting into violence. When the British departed, the process continued, now without any effective central control.

PRIMORDIAL TIES AS A SOURCE OF CONFLICT

The experience of the Ibos in Nigeria illustrates what many people have come to believe, that security for an ethnic group can be found only when that group controls its own state. With thousands of ethnic groups in the world and only about 150 states, it is clear that not all groups control their own states. The most obvious problem is that one state may include many ethnic groups.

But this is not the only problem. In some places states' borders cut right through the territory inhabited by an ethnic group. Sometimes the group so divided is only one of many; this is the case in many African countries where the boundaries were drawn by European colonial powers with no concern for local inhabitants. In other cases the group divided by a state boundary makes up the entire population of each political unit — in other words, a single nation is divided into several states. It was this condition that led to the German wars of unification in the nineteenth century. A century later the division of Vietnam and Korea caused wars for the same reason.

Even though these few cases have been the source of international conflict, they are far outnumbered by the cases in which one state embraces
many nations. Only fourteen states (or fewer, if you treat Germany, Vietnam,
and Korea each as one), about 10 per cent of the world's states, are homogeneous in ethnic makeup. In another 40 per cent, one ethnic group is
dominant, making up 75 per cent or more of the population. But, as Cyprus
showed, this is no guarantee of peace; although the Greeks made up more
than 80 per cent of the population, the Turks were not willing to submit to
rule by them. The problems are even more acute in those states in which no
one group makes up even as much as half the population. Almost 30 per
cent of the states of the world fall into this category. Nigeria is one example;
India and Pakistan are others.

The conflicts generated by ethnic questions within such states are a
threat to international peace because they frequently spread beyond the
borders of a single country. There are a number of reasons why this happens.
When one nation is divided among several states, the issue is by definition
international. When one ethnic group finds itself divided between two states,
efforts by the group to ignore the border may provoke international disputes.
This has been the case when Somali nomads ignored the borders between
Somalia and the neighboring countries of Ethiopia and Kenya that cut across
their traditional grazing land.

Another reason why conflict spreads is that ethnic ties are valued so
highly in the world today that actions taken to support members of one's
own ethnic group are considered justification for violating the basic principle
of noninterference in the internal affairs of a sovereign state. India felt justified in entering Pakistan's civil war in 1971 because the massacre of Bengalis in Pakistan could not be tolerated by the Bengalis in India. The internal
governance of Rhodesia and South Africa is a major concern to black African
states; support for guerrillas seeking to overthrow regimes in these countries
is not seen as illegitimate. The conflict over Israel has been escalated into a
world conflict by primordial ties: Countries as distant as Morocco send troops
to fight because of solidarity with other Arabs. American Jews translate their
solidarity with Israel into active pressure on the United States government
for greater commitment to Israel.

NATIONALISM AND WAR

In states that have been established for a long time, primordial ties are
often weaker. Many Latin American states have been independent for over
a century and in their populations nationalism is the primary emotion. (In
states only recently independent, however, ethnic ties are still major factors.
Guyana, a British colony until 1966, is split between groups originating in

Africa and ones from the East Indies.) Conflicts between states in Latin America have been made more difficult to solve by intense nationalist feelings and in some cases have led to war. In 1969 El Salvador and Honduras fought over a disputed border. Argentina and Chile have gone as far as mobilizing troops over disputed islands in the sea south of Argentina. Argentina, to most people's surprise, landed troops on islands claimed by them in 1982. The British, who ruled the islands under the name of the Falklands, underestimated the intensity of nationalist feeling that led the Argentines to challenge a superior military power.

The war in the Falklands illustrates how conflicts in the Third World may draw in other powers. The British felt directly challenged because of political claims for British protection by the people living on the Falklands, most of whom were of British origin. (Had the islands been uninhabited, the British would have turned them over to the Argentines years ago.) Sometimes outside powers are drawn in in less direct ways. Third World states may actively seek the support of major powers in their quarrels. India actively solicited the support of the Soviet Union in its quarrel with Pakistan. Pakistan in turn sought support from both China and the United States. Thus the war between India and Pakistan in 1971 over an essentially ethnic issue became a potential confrontation between the major powers.

The conflict between India and Pakistan also appears to have been the major motivation for first India and then Pakistan to try to acquire nuclear weapons. In 1974 India exploded a nuclear device that it termed "peaceful." In the absence of any clear-cut need for such a device or any subsequent use of nuclear technology for peaceful purposes, the impression remains strong that India was interested mainly in demonstrating its potential to acquire nuclear weapons. Pakistan's prime minister certainly perceived such an intent, because he declared, "We will eat leaves and grass, even go hungry, but we will have to get one."[6] By April 1979 Pakistan's program was so advanced that the United States government cut off all aid to Pakistan under the provisions of a law requiring such termination to countries acquiring nuclear weapons.[7]

NUCLEAR PROLIFERATION

The Indian explosion of a nuclear device in 1974 was important for three reasons. It was the first acquisition of nuclear capability by a country in over a decade (China's had been the most recent, in 1964). It was the first by a country not generally considered a great power (all other acknowledged nuclear states were permanent members of the Security Council). And it was the first nuclear device built with fuel diverted from power reactors. This last feature was the most alarming. A standard 1,000-megawatt thermal power reactor of current design produces over 200 kilograms of spent fuel a year, enough to make forty small nuclear explosives. With over 200 such reactors operating in more than forty-two countries, the potential for the spread of nuclear weapons to more countries is very great.[8]

Reaction to the Indian explosion illustrates again the essential lack of cohesion in the Third World. Although most of the Third World states adhered to the Non-Proliferation Treaty of 1968 (and thereby made it possible in the first place), when India exploded its nuclear device in 1974, Pakistan was the only member of the Third World to criticize India in the subsequent United Nations General Assembly. Some of these states may have been contemplating nuclear programs of their own; there is evidence that Iraq and Argentina were. Others may have been reluctant to criticize so prominent a member of the Non-Aligned Movement; they may even have enjoyed the technological triumph of what was once called a "backward nation."

But these feelings of solidarity among members of the Non-Aligned Movement have generated anxieties in states not accepted by the Non-Aligned Movement and not fitting comfortably into any grouping. Such states are sometimes called "pariah" or outcast states and many of them are considered the most likely to acquire nuclear weapons of their own — for example Israel, South Africa, Taiwan, South Korea. Although not normally considered Third World states, these states are geographically in the middle of the Third World and have Third World states for neighbors.

The proliferation of nuclear weapons to Third World states makes the Third World an even more serious source of international conflict. The use of such weapons in local or regional quarrels would quickly turn such quarrels into world crises. In another round of war between India and Pakistan or between Israel and its Arab neighbors, one can imagine the losing side resorting to nuclear weapons in desperation. Had Argentina possessed nuclear weapons when it was fighting Britain for the Falkland Islands, it might have been tempted to use them to save its position or even as an emotional reaction to the British sinking of one of their ships.

In response to evidence that Pakistan was building nuclear weapons, the United States suspended military aid; India, feeling more directly threatened, considered stronger measures. In 1982 United States intelligence officials suspected that India was developing a plan for a preemptive air strike to destroy the Pakistani facilities.[9] Israel carried out such a strike against Iraq in 1981, and although that strike did not escalate into war, an Indian strike against Pakistan could have. The Israelis struck against a small program, still far from completion, and evidently were completely successful. An only partially successful strike against an extensive program might provoke the target state to retaliate with whatever nuclear weapons remained.

Some analysts have speculated that some of Pakistan's weapons could find their way into the hands of Libya's President Muammar Qaddafi, perhaps in return for his financial support. Some of Qaddafi's public statements suggest he would be more willing to use such weapons against his avowed enemies, particularly Israel, than many other leaders would be. Or Qaddafi might transfer such weapons to a terrorist group, putting that group beyond the control of any state.[10]

We might recall the arguments of those who advocate a balance of terror. According to this line of thought, the possession of nuclear weapons by Third World states might make war less likely just as nuclear weapons have restrained the United States–Soviet rivalry. The argument has some merit but is not completely comforting. The United States and the Soviet Union have ample arsenals, not just a few weapons they would be tempted to use or lose. They have had years to consider carefully the implications of such weapons and to devise doctrines that try to deal with the complexities. They have invested in control devices to prevent unauthorized use. Neither the United States nor the Soviet Union is plagued by the problem common to most Third World states — military coups or takeovers by rival factions within the military.

The internal problems of Third World states are the most common cause of conflict in the world today. Tension between the superpowers occupies the attention of many people, but the actual fighting and dying occurs in countries such as Cambodia, Iraq, and Chad. In the older states, the conflicts generated by primordial ties have been largely settled. This has been the result not of superior wisdom or inherent virtue but simply of the relatively long time these countries have had to work on the problem. In some cases the problem was solved by the creation of separate states. Norway and Sweden became separate countries in 1905, for example. In other cases ethnic minorities were subdued by military conquest, as happened in the English wars against the Welsh and the Scots. In 1945 the Poles adopted an equally drastic measure against the Germans, expelling 10 million Germans from the territory they claimed as the Polish state. But even in the older states, not all conflicts over ethnic issues have been settled. The British have been struggling with the Irish for hundreds of years, and it appears that they will continue to do so for many more. With such struggles just beginning in many parts of the Third World, we can expect conflict there to continue for a long time to come.

NOTES

1. Grover Clark, *A Place in the Sun* (1936), cited by Harold Isaacs, *Idols of the Tribe* (New York: Harper & Row, 1975), p. 6.

2. Lawrence K. Altman, "In Africa, Problems Change But the Frustrations Go On," *The New York Times*, December 10, 1985, p. Y18.

3. It is generally accepted that the government of Sudan was overthrown in 1985 because it tried to implement austerity measures demanded by the IMF.

4. Robert D. Crane, "Postwar Ethnic Cultural Conflicts" (1968), cited by Isaacs, p. 7.

5. There is some disagreement about terms. "Primordial" is used in approximately this way by Clifford Geertz, "The Integrative Revolution: Primordial Sentiments and Civil Politics in the New States," in *Old Societies and New States*, ed. Clifford Geertz (New York: Free Press, 1963), especially pp. 109–119. See also the definition by Walker Connor, "The Politics of Ethnonationalism," *Journal of International Affairs*, Vol. 27, No. 1 (1973), p. 2 n.

6. Donna S. Kramer (Congressional Research Service), *Nuclear Energy: The Threat of Pakistan Going Nuclear*, Issue Brief No. IB 79093, October 23, 1979.

7. U.S. Senate, Committee on Governmental Affairs, Subcommittee on Energy, Nuclear Proliferation, and Federal Services, *Nuclear Proliferation: The Situation in Pakistan and India: Hearings*, 96th Congress, 1st sess., May 1, 1979.

8. Walter Marshall, "On Plutonium Fears," *The New York Times*, April 18, 1978, p. 33.

9. Leonard S. Spector, *Nuclear Proliferation Today* (New York: Vintage, 1985), p. 48.

10. Steve Weissman and Herbert Krosney, *The Islamic Bomb* (New York: Times Books, 1981).

Chapter 24

Non-State Actors

In each of the preceding chapters we looked at potential threats to world peace from states or groups of states. But states are not the only participants in world politics today. A lot of attention is focused on organizations that transcend the boundaries of states. The subject of countless books and articles today is the "transnational organization." "Transnational" is a relatively new word, coined as a contrast to "international." "International" refers to organizations in which the members are the recognized governments of sovereign states, "transnational" to organizations with members or operations in more than one state in which state governments do not directly participate. The International Olympic Committee is one example of a transnational organization; General Motors (GM) is another.

The International Olympic Committee belongs in one subcategory of transnational organizations, the nonprofit organizations. A 1971 study counted 1,899 such transnational nonprofit organizations; on the average they had members from twenty-five countries.[1] The numbers suggest that some significant development is taking place in the world, but closer inspection shows that we should not exaggerate the importance of this trend. The average organization of this kind had a budget of only $629,000 and a staff of only nine.[2] From such limited resources we can presumably expect only limited influence on world events.

THE MULTINATIONAL ENTERPRISE: GROWTH AND INFLUENCE

In the 1970's, many people became alarmed at the growing power of one form of non-state actor, the corporation doing business in more than one country. Such businesses, called *transnational corporations* (by the United Nations) or *multinational enterprises* (by many scholars) or *multinational corporations* (by most Americans), had been in existence since the 1930's; they were primarily concerned with extracting basic raw materials (known as "primary products"). What alarmed people in the 1970's was their explosive growth and their expansion into direct investment, manufacturing, and service.

It was common to read comparisons such as these: In 1973 the annual sales of General Motors were greater than the combined gross national products of Switzerland, Pakistan, and South Africa; or, Goodyear Tire's annual sales were greater than the GNP of Saudi Arabia.[3] A widespread attitude was expressed by Gary Hart in 1975, at that time the junior senator from Colorado but later a major candidate for the presidency: "Giant multinational corporations — chartered in this country, but owing allegiance to no flag — run roughshod over our foreign policy and dominate our economy through control of vast quantities of raw materials and productive facilities."[4]

In analyzing such statements, it is helpful to distinguish between the multinational enterprises (MNE's) themselves and the economic activity they engage in. Without question, MNE's remain important; one study found that in 1981 total sales of the 500 largest MNE's represented 20 per cent of the total gross domestic product of the world (excluding the Communist countries).[5] In 1980 the value of the stock of direct foreign investment by MNE's was $512 billion, about eight times greater than it was in 1960.[6]

By 1980, only 20 per cent of the activity of MNE's involved primary products (for example, extracting oil in Saudi Arabia and selling it abroad). About 30 per cent involved import substitution (that is, manufacturing in a country a category of goods that until that time had been imported) and about 20 per cent involved services (such as insurance or banking). The remaining 20 per cent was what economists call "rationalized investment"; that is, taking advantage of ways to cut costs, such as setting up a plant in a country where people expect to work for lower wages.[7] (As a result of this last factor, by 1980 about half of the cotton textiles and almost all of the television sets sold in the United States were produced by affiliates of MNE's in Latin America or South East Asia.)[8]

The explosive growth of multinational enterprises was facilitated by new technology. The ease of air travel and the even greater ease of telecommunications enabled central headquarters to maintain constant contact with even the most detailed developments on the other side of the world. The incentive to use these facilities and move abroad came from pressures making it difficult for a business in one country to export its products to others. A country in Latin America might be short on foreign exchange, or have various tariffs to protect local industry, or want to provide employment for its own citizens. In such a situation, it made more sense for, say, a German automobile manufacturer to set up a plant in Brazil than for it to try to export Volkswagens made in Germany.

CRITICISM OF MULTINATIONAL ENTERPRISES

Complaints against multinational corporations varied, depending on whether they came from a country that was primarily a *source* (where MNE's had their headquarters) or a *host* (where they did most of their business). In addition to economic exploitation, host countries feared political manipulation, either by a corporation itself or by a government acting through a corporation. In one well-publicized case, the United States–based International Telephone and Telegraph (ITT), which at that time controlled various businesses in Chile such as the telephone company, offered hundreds of thousands of dollars to help opponents of the socialist candidate Salvador Allende in the 1970 Chilean elections. When Allende was elected nonetheless, a member of the ITT board of directors, John McCone (himself a former head of the Central Intelligence Agency), approached the CIA with an offer of $1 million to assist any CIA plan for stopping Allende (the money was refused).[9] In a less well known case, the Exxon corporation gave $86,000 to the Italian Communist Party between 1971 and 1975, part of a total of $50 million that American businesses gave to various Italian politicians to make the latter friendlier to specific business projects.[10]

MNE source countries were somewhat slower to perceive a threat from transnational economic activity. The generally high level of prosperity after World War II resulted in expanding economies and rising standards of living in all these countries. Under such conditions, the diversion of production overseas was not a serious matter. Some American academicians even wrote with satisfaction about how the United States was passing from a producer economy to a service economy. They seemed pleased that fewer and fewer Americans were raising food on farms or assembling cars in factories. More recently, however, higher levels of unemployment and slower economic growth have changed attitudes. The much touted "postindustrial society" is now widely seen as one in which more and more Americans work for low wages serving fast food or selling imported shoes, if they are not filling out welfare applications. The movement of jobs from New Jersey to Taiwan is no longer hidden in the statistics of an overall increase in the number of jobs in the American economy.[11] The belief that "high technology" would compensate for such losses was shattered when a major manufacturer of video games moved from California to Hong Kong and Taiwan, at a time when United States unemployment was over 10 per cent.[12]

When we examine the charge that MNE's are responsible for the loss of American jobs, we would do well to remember our distinction between the MNE as an institution and the economic activity it engages in. The search for cheaper ways of doing business is fundamental to any economic growth. Earlier in this century it led shoe and textile manufacturers to leave New England and relocate in the South where costs were lower. Such relocation directly hurt one group (workers in New England), directly benefited another (workers in the South), and indirectly benefited the country as a whole by enabling more people to buy more shoes and towels because the prices stayed low.

The same logic applies to relocation overseas. The source country loses jobs, but the workers in the new host country are now able to afford exports from some enterprise in which the source country still has an advantage, such as highly skilled workers. Of course this cold economic logic is no more comforting to Southern textile workers who watch their jobs go to Taiwan and Singapore than it was to the New England workers who earlier watched their jobs go to South Carolina and Georgia. New jobs stimulated by trade with newly developing countries may come slowly, if at all. But considered in the light of economic theory, the multinational enterprise is not uniquely evil; it is only one more instrument in the universal economic process of searching for more efficient ways of doing business.

THE MULTINATIONAL ENTERPRISE VERSUS THE STATE

Of more concern to a student of international politics is the charge made by Senator Hart that MNE's dominate economies and ride roughshod over foreign policy. A review of recent data will help us evaluate this claim. Although there are about 10,000 enterprises that can be considered multinational, only about 5 per cent (or 500 of them) account for 80 per cent of total production. Of these 500, 242 have their headquarters in the United States. Measured by the value of stock issued by the biggest MNE's, in 1980 the United States was still the biggest source country, but its share declined from 1967 (48.3 per cent) to 1980 (42.2 per cent). Britain, Germany, Japan, France, and Sweden were also source countries for major MNE's, and even the less developed countries (LDC's) or the newly industrialized countries (NIC's) such as Brazil, South Korea, and India had MNE's. In fact, in the 1970's, Indian MNE's invested more outside India than foreign MNE's did inside India.[13]

Competition among MNE's, particularly those with headquarters in different countries, enhanced the power of individual states to resist the MNE's. Thus, in order to establish themselves, Japanese corporations were willing to settle for minority shares in their subsidiaries abroad, giving the host governments a bargaining lever with corporations based in other states. At one time corporations could insist that a country accept an entire package of capital investment, technology, and marketing agreements. By the late 1970's states were insisting on the right to choose — capital from one source, technology from another, management from a third, depending on where they could get each least expensively. Argentina was able to require that at least 85 per cent of top-level personnel be Argentinians. Australia required that capital come from abroad. Mexico permitted complete foreign ownership only if the firm exported all of its output.[14]

The ability of India to curtail the activities of MNE's within its own borders shows that the worst fears of critics in the 1970's — that MNE's would ride roughshod over states — did not materialize. India required that by 1977 at least 60 per cent of the control of foreign companies operating in India be in the hands of local shareholders. Because Coca Cola feared such an arrangement would lead to the loss of the secret formula for its flagship beverage, the corporation decided to end its operations in India.[15] In this struggle between a state and an MNE, the state won. Nor was this an isolated example. In 1985 Mexico was able to extract very favorable terms, including setting up a development center for local industry, from the giant International Business Machines (IBM).[16] Brazil was able to exclude foreign computer makers entirely from any further participation in its domestic market.[17]

As it became clear in the late 1970's that MNE's were not able to ride roughshod over states, attitudes toward them began to change, and by the 1980's even states formerly hostile to the idea began to seek investment by MNE's. Vietnam was the winner of a war that it described as anti-imperialist; many critics in the United States had described it as a war by the United States to make the world safe for MNE's. Ten years after the end of that war, Vietnam was applying to the United Nations Center on Transnational Corporations and inviting a delegation of fifty top executives of large American corporations as the beginning of an attempt to attract investment.[18]

Some writers go as far as to suggest that major economic strains in the 1980's were in part the result of too little direct foreign investment by MNE's. Between 1968 and 1970, the share of capital going to LDC's by means of MNE's was 22.1 per cent of the total; bank lending accounted for 17.4 per cent. With the increase of money in the hands of banks following the oil price increases, the percentage of capital from MNE's dropped to 13.9 per cent during the period from 1978 to 1980, while bank lending rose to 26.3

per cent. But investors, unlike bankers, don't expect to be repaid on a fixed schedule. They share the risk, and if an economy does not perform well, they share the loss.[19] Thus more activity by MNE's might have spared the world the agony of the Third World debt crisis. The MNE's, seen as a villain in the 1970's, has emerged in the 1980's as a benign, even helpful instrument of international cooperation and stability.

PRODUCERS' CARTELS

On the heels of the concern about the newly powerful multinational corporations came the discovery that the traditional institution of the sovereign government of a state still had a lot of power, especially in combination with those of other states. In other words, *intergovernmental organizations* were just as powerful as *transnational corporations*. One area in which states could cooperate was in the marketing of crucial raw materials. Agreements by states to control such resources collectively are known as *producers' cartels*. The best known of these is the Organization of Petroleum Exporting Countries (OPEC), founded in 1960 but not achieving real power until 1973. Then it began to play an influential role in the world as the price of a barrel of crude oil rose to more than four times its original level, from roughly three dollars to roughly twelve dollars. OPEC demonstrated its power again in 1979 when oil prices tripled, this time to a level of roughly forty dollars a barrel.

The success of OPEC led to much speculation about the formation of cartels for other products, such as copper, tin, bauxite, coffee, and even bananas. Some writers were skeptical, suggesting that only special conditions permitted an organization such as OPEC to succeed:[20]

1. The product involved must be an essential one, for which no good substitute is available (at least in the short run). This means that people will continue to buy it even if the price goes up. In the language of economists, the product must be *price-inelastic*.

2. The members of the cartel must have adequate financial reserves to withstand a temporary boycott by consumers. The Arab oil producers had tried in 1967 to withhold oil from Western supporters of Israel, on the occasion of the Six Day War, but failed. Within two weeks the major Arab producer, Saudi Arabia, was almost bankrupt and had to resume selling its oil to survive. By contrast, by the time of the 1973 war in the Middle East, the major oil producers had adequate financial reserves.

3. Some issue must induce the various producers to cooperate. In 1973, as in the abortive attempt in 1967, the issue was the war in the Middle East.

4. There must be some collusion between major marketing corpora-

tions and producers. The oil companies were happy to cooperate with the oil-producing countries, because higher prices for oil meant higher profits for them. In the case of cartels for other products, the marketing corporations have not always cooperated — for example, the chocolate companies were active opponents of the ultimately unsuccessful cartel formed to control the price of cocoa.

On the other hand, there were those who argued that the success of OPEC would be contagious and cartels would control the prices of many other products. They thought cartels would be successful because:[21]

1. Many products are relatively price-inelastic.

2. Multiple cartels would be even more effective than a single one, such as OPEC, because they could make substitution more difficult. For example, copper wire is used to conduct electricity. If the price of copper goes up, consumers can switch to aluminum wire. But if both copper ore and bauxite (from which aluminum is extracted) are controlled by cartels, consumers will not be able to defeat the copper cartel by switching to the other product.

3. The issue of financial reserves raised by the skeptics may have been exaggerated, even in the case of OPEC. Not all OPEC countries had reserves. One wealthy country could support weaker members of a cartel. Or one successful cartel, such as OPEC, could lend its support to the struggling members of a new cartel.

4. The importance of political catalysts also may have been exaggerated. Venezuela was one of the founders of OPEC back in 1960, and by 1973 Nigeria was a major member, yet neither had direct concern with the issues in the Middle East. In any case, the success of one cartel, such as OPEC, could serve as a powerful incentive bringing other states into other cartels.

5. Marketing corporations did not show willingness to block cartels. Although worldwide distribution and marketing of OPEC's output was in the hands of the major oil companies, these companies did not lose profits. On the contrary, their profits rose as the price of oil rose. Other marketing corporations could see that cooperation served their self-interest.

The debate between these two schools was serious in the 1970's. By the early 1980's, it became clear that the skeptics were correct. Producers' cartels had not multiplied. A union of copper-producing countries (known by the French acronym CIPEC) failed to achieve price increases and a union of banana exporters (known by the Spanish acronym of UPEB) failed even to win adherence by all the major countries.

Then even OPEC began to reveal serious flaws in the cartel system. In 1983 the organization for the first time voted to lower its prices. The reasons were exactly what classical economists would have predicted: Demand was falling and supplies were rising. The higher prices brought about by OPEC led consumers both to consume less (say, driving their cars less) and to invest in conservation measures (for example, cars that got more miles per gallon). From 1973 to 1985, the amount of oil consumed per unit of GNP in the industrial countries had fallen by 33 per cent, with further gains in efficiency possible.[22] At the same time the higher prices made it worthwhile to exploit less accessible (and thus more expensive) sources of oil. As a result, the production of oil from non-OPEC sources (outside the Communist world) climbed from 17.4 million barrels per day in 1973 to 26.2 million barrels per day in 1985.[23] OPEC at first tried to keep prices up by getting its own members to restrain production, but it abandoned this policy in late 1985. Within a month the price of one barrel of oil dropped to below twenty dollars, its level before its last price hike in 1979.

The failure of OPEC revealed an important truth. OPEC was no more than it claimed to be, an association of sovereign states. Adherence to its decisions was always voluntary. One economist, after studying the history of cartels, concluded that when total production by a cartel falls below 75 per cent of total capacity, pressures build up among members to undercut each other.[24] In 1983, OPEC production was 14 million barrels a day, out of a possible 32 million, and some members were producing more than they had promised their associates. Nigeria was heavily in debt and needed to continue sales of oil, even if that meant surreptitiously cutting prices to sell it. Iran needed money to finance its war against Iraq (incidentally, a fellow OPEC member). Thus the selfish interests of sovereign states triumphed over the collective good of limiting production and keeping prices high.

With the benefit of hindsight, analysts began to write that OPEC did not cause higher oil prices but merely took advantage of economic and political conditions.[25] According to this argument, oil was underpriced in the early 1970's, in the sense that the selling price of a barrel was less than the cost of finding a replacement barrel. A price rise was called for by market forces. The 1973 war in the Middle East enabled OPEC to raise prices considerably above market levels for a while. The revolution in Iran, accompanied by fears of a drop in production in the Persian Gulf, permitted another large price rise. But by 1981 economic forces had begun to push prices down. Large quantities of oil were reaching the market from British and Norwegian wells in the North Sea and American wells on Alaska's North Slope. The cartel was not powerful enough to resist.

There is no reason to think that the glut in oil or any other product is permanent. Market forces will again begin to work; prices will drop, encouraging people to use the products and thus gradually increasing demand. As demand begins to put pressure on supply, cartels may renew some of their strength. Indeed, even as OPEC and its spinoffs in copper, bauxite, and tin were foundering, the price of coffee was rising to new levels, managed by the International Coffee Agreement. But such fluctuations in price are seen as responses to market forces, not as the result of political decisions by a handful of governments acting as a cartel. Cartels merely take advantage of the market. Were producers' cartels alone in control, prices would never go down, only up, and this has manifestly not happened.

A return to the alarmist days of the 1970's, when even the US secretary of state dropped hints about military takeover of oilfields as a remedy to the power of cartels, is unlikely. Producers' cartels are recognized as being far more fragile than many people thought when they first appeared. The division of the world into unions of consumers fighting cartels of producers over artificially scarce resources is an unlikely source of international conflict.

INTERNATIONAL TERRORISM

Another non-state actor that has attracted attention in recent years is the terrorist organization. Some groups usually characterized as terrorist are well known — the Irish Republican Army (IRA) and the Palestine Liberation Organization (PLO). Many of these organizations, however, would object to the label "terrorist," and it would be more precise to speak of them as non-state actors who occasionally use terrorist tactics. But because terrorism more than any other trait brings them to international attention, we will make that the focus of this discussion.

Terrorism, like nuclear war and conventional war, is a form of violence for a political purpose. But unlike these other forms of violence, its purpose is almost entirely psychological. It is directed at those watching, not at those who are its victims. The PLO hijacks an airliner not because it wishes to harm the particular passengers on that plane but because it wants to focus world attention on its cause. Because of its nature and purpose, terrorism can be engaged in by very small numbers. It is almost the only way a small group or even an individual can become an internationally significant actor. Furthermore, because nuclear warfare is too frightening to contemplate and because conventional warfare is expensive, terrorism is one of the few tactics available to groups unable to achieve their goals by diplomatic means. Even the traditional actors in international politics, the states, may be tempted to employ terrorism, using terrorist groups as surrogates whose actions they can deny any responsibility for, while benefiting from them.

Terrorism has become a problem in international politics for several reasons. The victims of terrorist attacks are often diplomats or foreign nationals, such as executives of multinational corporations. The kidnapping of a diplomat often creates tension between the host state, which may wish to resist the terrorists' demands, and the state that sent the diplomat, which wants above all else to have the diplomat released safely. The kidnapping of citizens while abroad deprives states of one of their traditional functions, that of providing security for citizens. Security in such conditions ceases to be a purely national problem and must be addressed internationally.

When terrorist acts involve several different jurisdictions, terrorism becomes an international problem. In one well-known incident in 1976, an airliner belonging to France, carrying passengers from many countries, was hijacked by Palestinians while flying from Athens to Paris. It was diverted first to Libya and then to Uganda. Because the government of Uganda did nothing to facilitate the freeing of the aircraft and its passengers, the Israelis mounted a raid against the Ugandan airport at Entebbe. Traditional legal concepts such as sovereignty are inadequate to sort out the various claims in such situations.

Although much public attention is currently being given to the potential devastation of nuclear war and the actual destruction of conventional wars in places such as Afghanistan and Iran and Iraq, it is fair to say even more is given to terrorism. In the early 1980's, one international relations scholar felt confident enough to write, "The principal security problem of this decade is low-intensity warfare, especially terrorism."[26] Events in following years appeared to confirm his prediction.

We must pause to define the word *terrorism*. One reason is that without a careful definition the statement just cited is made true simply by declaring every threat to security an act of "terrorism." A more important reason is that "terrorist" is a convenient label to attach to someone you dislike; if you get others to accept the label, you have won a substantial victory in the struggle by getting others to adopt your value system.[27] A widely circulated cartoon in the early 1980's showed two identically equipped guerrilla fighters, one in El Salvador, the other in Nicaragua. The cartoon identified one as a "terrorist," the other a "freedom fighter." The point was to make fun of the political rhetoric that made the definition depend wholly on whether a guerrilla was on our side or theirs.[28] In the rhetorical struggle the term was expanded to apply to governments as well. Thus, raids by Israel in retaliation for what it called "terrorist attacks" were routinely labeled "state terrorism" by Israel's enemies.

Some of the most careful — and nonpartisan — studies of terrorism have been conducted at the Rand Corporation under the direction of Brian Jenkins, and the definition that he offered is free of the political bias of many others. Terrorism, according to Jenkins, is an act or threat of violence calculated to create an atmosphere of fear and alarm. These acts or threats must be ones that would normally be considered criminal, both under domestic law (murder, kidnapping, arson) and under the laws of war (attacking civilians, taking hostages, harming captives).[29] They are usually carried out by organized groups who not only take credit for what they do but seek the widest possible publicity. Indeed the purpose of terrorist acts is not the physical damage they cause but the psychological terror they create. In the words of one official charged with combating terrorism: "You don't do terrorism to kill people. You do it to create an echo that makes you larger than life. No echo, no success."[30]

According to this definition, there could be acts of state terrorism. In the mid-1970's, Argentina was ruled by military juntas who, in the course of their war against terrorism, arrested without warrants and executed without trial over 6,000 people merely suspected of opposing the government. In 1985 the new, democratically elected government of Argentina put on trial the leaders of the former military governments, charging them with "terrorist acts." In the words of the prosecutor, "In their disregard for life and property and their conviction that the ends justified the means, the juntas behaved like common criminals or terrorists, and thus deserve to be punished accordingly. If it was a war, then the juntas have violated the terms of the Geneva convention, and are as guilty as the Nazis of crimes against humanity."[31]

The case of Argentina illustrates two points. One is that states can, by Jenkins' definition, commit terrorist acts, although such acts must be clearly criminal and not merely the exercise of a state's powers to maintain domestic order. The other point is that "terrorist" is a label best applied to acts, not persons or groups. The Argentine government may at one time have been responsible for terrorist acts but it would not have helped one's understanding to call Argentina a "terrorist organization." A person, group, or even state may commit a terrorist act, but it does not follow that every subsequent act committed is automatically terrorist. It would help to clarify debate if we replaced "terrorist group" with "groups willing to commit terrorist acts."

INCIDENCE OF INTERNATIONAL TERRORISM

It is difficult to obtain statistics on current levels of terrorism. Different sources disagree on what constitutes a terrorist act and give different numbers for the incidence of terrorism. There is general agreement that the trend is up. According to the statistics of the United States government, between 1975 and 1985 there were more than 5,000 international terrorist incidents. In 1984 there were 600, an increase of about 20 per cent over the average of the preceding six years.[32] Furthermore, attacks have become more lethal and more likely to involve innocent bystanders, both because bloodier attacks buy more media exposure and because government facilities have become more protected (making unprotected civilians more attractive as targets).[33]

In absolute numbers, the victims of terrorism during that decade were not many. In the worst year, 1983, 720 died, one-third of them in a single bombing of the United States Marine barracks in Beirut.[34] That number is somewhat below the number of victims annually of airline crashes and far below the annual deaths on United States highways (around 50,000 a year). But the number of victims is not the most important index. Because the purpose of terrorist attacks is not physical damage but "an atmosphere of fear and alarm," another measure might be more useful — for example, hours of television coverage devoted to hijackings and hostage-takings. By such measures the threat from terrorism might seem much greater.

Terrorist tactics are used by two or perhaps three kinds of groups. First are nationalist groups with aspirations to statehood. Their activities are directed toward the state or states that thwart their aspirations. Prominent examples are the ETA, a Basque organization that seeks some measure of autonomy of Spain; the IRA, which seeks unification of the British territory of Northern Ireland with the Irish Republic; and various Palestinian groups, many of them affiliated with the PLO.

A second kind of group is the politically motivated domestic opposition group, which seeks a radical transformation of a domestic regime, such as the Red Brigades in Italy or the Baader–Meinhof Gang in Germany. Such groups tend to confine their activities to their own country, although they may cooperate with other groups, including nationalist groups of the first kind, in procuring weapons, training, and support for operations. Such cooperation gave rise to speculation about an international network of terrorists, reflected in the claim by Attorney General Edwin Meese that Nicaragua had become a "country club" for terrorists, offering refuge to members of the PLO, ETA, IRA, Baader–Meinhof Gang, and Red Brigades.[35] Little beyond opportunistic cooperation has been documented; groups lend help to each other but no evidence of central planning or coordinating bodies has been uncovered.

This is not to say that groups are not aware of each other. A newspaper columnist visited headquarters of the political front for the IRA in the Catholic part of Belfast and found the emblems and posters of self-styled radical groups — Palestinians, Armenians, and others; she then crossed town to the equivalent Protestant group and found there posters from the "contras" in Nicaragua, UNITA in Angola, and other groups that have found support among conservatives in the United States.[36] If anything, what is emerging is not one but two "terrorist networks." But this second group of "conservative terrorists" has shown no more coherence than the first. An attempt by a conservative American politician to bring four anti-Soviet groups together in

June 1985 into what he wanted to call a "Democratic International" produced very little in the way of concrete results.[37] The case for a "terrorist network" as a unitary non-state actor in world politics remains unproved.

The claim is also made that there is a third kind of group using terrorist tactics, the state-sponsored group. Such groups would not be actors in their own right but mere extensions of that traditional actor, the state. An analyst must be careful to distinguish between terrorism that is *sponsored* by a state in the pursuit of specific foreign policy goals and terrorism that is *supported* or perhaps merely tolerated by a state. Terrorists of necessity engage in physical acts such as recruiting, training, and equipping themselves before attacks and seeking hiding places after attacks, and these physical acts must take place in some physical location. Undoubtedly at times these activities are known to the governments of states where they are taking place. But the crucial question is: Would these terrorists seek to act on their own in any case, even without state encouragement, or would terrorism disappear if governments stopped sponsoring it?

Three such groups have been identified as instances of state-sponsored terrorism. First, there were claims of groups sponsored by the Soviet Union, a major theme in the first years of the Reagan Administration.[38] But experts in the field were able to find little evidence to support the claims of politicians.[39] Then during the American involvement in the civil war in Lebanon, from 1982 to 1984, accusations of state-sponsored terrorism were made again, this time blaming Iran or Syria for supporting radical Muslim groups, sometimes known as "Islamic Jihad" (Holy War). The evidence produced to support the claim was circumstantial — for example, that the groups could not have acquired the weapons they used (such as high-technology explosives) without state aid.[40] Direct evidence, such as a statement by a terrorist or a government official, seems almost impossible to obtain. The responsibility for assassinations carried out decades ago, such as that in Sarajevo in 1914, has often not been determined until archives were opened and private papers made available. It is unlikely we will soon discover if a state was behind recent events in the Middle East.

Attention then turned to Libya. Diplomats and foreign ministries agreed that Libya had in the past decade used its embassies abroad as sanctuaries from which to mount assassinations against Libyan opponents of the Qaddafi regime. In one case a London policewoman was killed by a shot fired from the Libyan embassy from a weapon presumably smuggled in in the diplomatic pouch. But such actions, while clearly state-sponsored, were directed against domestic opponents and thus not clear cases of state-sponsored terrorism for foreign policy goals.

It was only after the United States Navy challenged Qaddafi's claim to control the entire Gulf of Sidra, and in the process sank several Libyan naval vessels, that evidence emerged of Libya's use of terrorism for foreign policy goals. The United States released evidence to its European allies showing that Libya had ordered its embassy in East Berlin to arrange the bombing of a discotheque in West Berlin frequented by United States soldiers. This bombing was then used by the United States to justify a retaliatory air raid on Libya.

Yet other allegations remained difficult to prove. Several cases were uncovered by British and French police of terrorists who had received weapons from the staffs of embassies, but the precise degree of state direction was hard to ascertain. Likewise, known terrorists sought asylum in various countries, but the harboring of such terrorists may prove nothing more than a general approval of the aims of the group carrying out an attack. Or it may not prove even that. The fact that Ireland (or even the United States) will not extradite persons wanted by the British government for terrorist acts in Northern Ireland does not prove that the violence in Northern Ireland is state-sponsored terrorism.

Finally, the charge of state-sponsored terrorism was laid to the United States for its support of guerrillas (the "contras") seeking to overthrow the government of Nicaragua. In this last case, the goals of the United States were clearly acknowledged when President Reagan said in a news conference that he wanted to remove "the present structure" of the government of Nicaragua.[41] The appropriation of millions of dollars to finance the contras was openly debated in Congress. And the use by the contras of such criminal means as torture and killing of unarmed civilians was uncovered in an investigation by the House Select Committee on Intelligence.[42] The investigation was prompted by the publication of a ninety-page manual, "Psychological Operations in Guerrilla War," produced by the CIA for the contras, discussing such activities as "neutralizing" Nicaraguan officials by hiring criminals to kill them and coercing Nicaraguan civilians into carrying out rebel assignments. (This last case was the easiest for American opponents of state-supported terrorism to deal with, by putting pressure on Congress to withdraw all support for such groups.)

INTERNATIONAL ACTION AGAINST TERRORISM

International efforts to deal with international terrorism have been slow and ineffective. The United Nations has had difficulty even passing resolutions condemning various terrorist acts — ineffective as such resolutions are. After four years of effort, the UN did pass a convention against the taking of hostages. In the words of a UN diplomat, "to do this . . . in four years' time . . . is indeed remarkable."[43] Many people would find it remarkable, although not in the laudatory sense that this UN diplomat meant it. If it takes the UN four years merely to acknowledge that an act recognized as criminal in all

domestic legal systems was also criminal in international politics, the hope
of effective action from such a body is slim indeed.

Nor were states able to cooperate outside the United Nations. Unless
the incidents are directed at it, a state usually finds terrorist incidents only
annoying.[44] If a state is free of terrorist incidents, it has little incentive to
join the "fight against terrorism," especially if such an action draws the wrath
of terrorists. Typically a state has more to fear from acts of hostile terrorists
than from the disapproving opinion of friendly states.[45]

States can agree on the general principle of opposing "terrorism" but
have differing national perceptions of what terrorism is. Thus, when the
Italian liner *Achille Lauro* was hijacked by a Palestinian group in 1985, the
organizer of the hijacking passed successively through the hands of the Egyptians, Italians, and Yugoslavs, ultimately being flown away to freedom despite
clear evidence implicating him in the episode. For the Egyptians, the major
terrorist threat came from Muslim fundamentalists, the group that had assassinated Anwar Sadat for not defending the cause of the Palestinians vigorously enough. For the Italians, the terrorist threat came from the internal Red
Brigades, not from Palestinians with whom the Italian government had been
cultivating good relations. For the Yugoslavs, the terrorist threat came from
domestic ethnic groups with nationalist aspirations, such as the Croats and
Albanians; they pointed out, when asked about their failure to extradite the
Palestinian mastermind of the *Achille Lauro* hijacking, that the United States
had not complied with a request that had been made more than thirty years
earlier for the extradition of a Croat separatist wanted for war crimes.[46]

Ending international terrorism would require widespread international
cooperation, and such cooperation is not likely. States are no more likely to
create serious domestic problems for themselves to solve a less pressing
global problem in this area than they are in such areas as international
monetary systems or acid rain. Egypt will continue to worry more about
Islamic fundamentalists and Italy will continue to worry more about Red
Brigades; neither wants to add another terrorist group to its enemies.

Despite stress on the international nature of terrorism, it is really the
old-fashioned state-centric system, with each state jealously guarding its
sovereignty, that makes terrorism possible. Only because terrorists can flee
to states where they will be immune from prosecution do they survive. And
only because the states that suffer from terrorism are willing to respect the
sovereignty of other states can havens for terrorists exist. Thomas Jefferson
was able to dispatch the United States Navy to deal with pirates along the
shores of Tripoli. Ronald Reagan is commander in chief of a far more powerful Navy, yet is severely limited by universal respect for the sovereignty of
all states, including the one whose capital is now in Tripoli.

The demands of one or more groups now using terrorist tactics might be satisfied and such groups might turn away from terrorism. One can foresee a day of reconciliation between Basque separatists and the government of Spain or even among the British, the Protestants of Northern Ireland, and the Irish nationalists. But new issues will arise and new groups, educated to the value of terrorism and tutored in its tactics, will appear. The competition for media time will encourage ever more spectacular acts, employing ever more destructive military technology — chemical weapons, biological agents, radioactive materials, or nuclear explosives. Nor can one have much faith that terrorists will exercise self-restraint. The architect of many of the early Palestinian terrorist actions was asked, "Does it matter to you that the Middle East crisis might develop into a world war?" "Not really," he replied, "The world has forgotten Palestine. Now it must pay attention to our struggle."[47] The world did pay attention, and the leader of the Palestinians was invited to address the General Assembly of the United Nations in 1974. Others paid attention to the successful use of terrorist tactics. The lesson will not be forgotten in our time.

NOTES

1. Kjell Skjelsbaek, "The Growth of International Nongovernmental Organization in the Twentieth Century," in Robert O. Keohane and Joseph S. Nye, Jr., eds., *Transnational Relations and World Politics* (Cambridge: Harvard University Press, 1971), pp. 75–76.

2. Ibid., p. 77.

3. Richard J. Barnet and Ronald E. Müller, *Global Reach: The Power of the Multinational Corporations* (New York: Simon & Schuster, 1974), p. 15.

4. "Free Lunch is Over," *The New York Times*, April 21, 1975.

5. John M. Stopford and John H. Dunning, *Multinationals: Company Performance and Global Trends* (London: Macmillan, 1983), p. 53.

6. Ibid., p. 5.

7. Ibid., p. 31.

8. Ibid., p. 18.

9. Thomas Powers, *The Man Who Kept the Secrets* (New York: Alfred A. Knopf, 1979), p. 227.

10. Robert M. Smith, "Big Business and the Plans to Make It Behave . . ." *The New York Times*, February 1, 1976, p. E3.

11. Barnet and Müller, pp. 303–333.

12. Atari Inc., reported in *The New York Times*, March 19, 1983.

13. Ibid., pp. 5–6.

14. Samuel P. Huntington, "Transnational Organizations in World Politics," *World Politics*, Vol. 25, No. 3 (April 1973), p. 340.

15. Richard J. Barnet, "The World's Resources," *The New Yorker*, April 7, 1980, p. 48.

16. David E. Sanger, "I.B.M. Concessions to Mexico," *The New York Times*, July 25, 1985, p. Y31.

17. Alan Riding, "Brazil Curbs Computer Competition," *The New York Times*, October 8, 1984, p. Y21.

18. Barbara Crossette, "Vietnam Crusades Against Markets," *The New York Times*, October 21, 1985, p. Y26.

19. Pedro-Pablo Kuczynski, "Latin American Debt: Act Two," *Foreign Affairs*, Vol. 62, No. 1 (Fall 1983), p. 36.

20. Stephen D. Krasner, "Oil Is the Exception," *Foreign Policy*, No. 14 (Spring 1974), pp. 68–84.

21. C. Fred Bergsten, "The Threat is Real," *Foreign Policy*, No. 14 (Spring 1974), pp. 84–90.

22. *Secretary of Energy: Annual Report to Congress* (United States Department of Energy, 1984), p. 10.

23. Leonard Silk, "Confronting New Oil Fears," *The New York Times*, January 29, 1986, p. Y34.

24. Henry L. Wojtyla, quoted by Thomas L. Friedman, "The Future of OPEC," *The New York Times*, July 7, 1981, p. Y24.

25. The argument was made by some people even without benefit of hindsight; for example, V. H. Oppenheim, "Why Oil Prices Go Up," *Foreign Policy*, No. 25 (Winter 1976–1977), pp. 24–57.

26. Robert H. Kupperman, "Coping With Terrorism," *The New York Times*, March 18, 1981, p. 23.

27. Brian Jenkins, "Statements About Terrorism," *Annals of the American Academy of Political and Social Science*, Vol. 463 (September 1982), p. 12.

28. *Editorials on File*, Vol. 14, No. 8 (April 16–30, 1983), p. 428.

29. Jenkins, "Statements," pp. 12–13; Bonnie Cordes, et al., *Trends in International Terrorism, 1982 and 1983* (Santa Monica: RAND, 1984), p. 1.

30. Thomas L. Friedman, "New Syrian Ties Found in Suicide Terror War," *The New York Times*, February 16, 1986, p. Y10, quoting an Israeli official.

31. *The Economist*, September 28, 1985, p. 38.

32. United States Department of State, Bureau of Public Affairs, "International Terrorism," *Gist*, August 1985.

33. Cordes, et al., pp. 7–8.

34. Ibid.

35. Speech to jurists in Washington D.C., September 14, 1985, reported in *The New York Times*, September 15, 1985, p. Y3.

36. Flora Lewis, "Which Terrorists to Punish?" *The New York Times*, November 15, 1985, p. Y27.

37. Lewis E. Lehrman, acting for "Citizens for America," organized a conference in Angola attended by representatives from Angola, Afghanistan, Laos, and Nicaragua. See Alan Cowell, "4 Rebel Units Sign Anti–Soviet Pact," *The New York Times*, June 6, 1985, p. A16.

38. See statements by Secretary of State Alexander Haig at his first press conference, January 28, 1981, *The New York Times*, January 29, 1981, p. A10.

39. Harry Rositzke, "If There Were No K.G.B. . . . ," *The New York Times*, July 20, 1981, p. A17.

40. Thomas L. Friedman, "State-Sponsored Terrorism Called a Threat to U.S.," *The New York Times*, December 30, 1983, pp. Y1, 6–7.

41. Press conference of February 21, 1985, transcript in *The New York Times*, February 22, 1985, p. A14.

42. Joel Brinkley, "Nicaraguan Rebels Accused of Atrocities," *The New York Times*, December 27, 1984, p. 1.

43. John W. McDonald, Jr., "The United Nations Convention Against the Taking of Hostages," *Terrorism*, Vol. 6, No. 4 (1963), p. 446.

44. Jenkins, "Statements," p. 17.

45. Flora Lewis, "Response to Terrorism," *The New York Times*, June 24, 1985, p. Y21.

46. David Binder, "Yugoslavs of Two Minds on Battling Terrorism," *The New York Times*, December 19, 1985, p. Y4.

47. George Habash, Popular Front for the Liberation of Palestine, interviewed by Lee Griggs, "A Voice of Extremism," *Time*, June 13, 1969, p. 42.

Chapter 25

Economic Issues

For most Americans the prospects of involvement in war have faded. In 1973 the draft was abolished, acknowledging this new perception. But economic issues have grown more important, in the United States and in other advanced industrialized democracies. The major economic recession the United States entered in the early 1980's was part of a world recession. Jimmy Carter's defeat in 1980 was attributed largely to economic issues, as were the defeats of James Callaghan in Britain in 1979, Giscard d'Estaing in France in 1981, and Helmut Schmidt in Germany in 1982. Economic issues were not only a major source of concern, but also a rich source of international conflict.

TRADE WARS

By the 1980's it had become commonplace to recite figures illustrating the importance of world trade to the United States economy. One out of every six United States manufacturing jobs depends on markets abroad. One out of every three acres of United States farmland produces for export. One out of every three dollars of United States corporate profits derives from international activity.[1]

Of course the importance of world trade is not new for many of our trading partners; Germany derives 25 per cent of its gross national product from exports, the Netherlands 46 per cent.[2] But for the United States such importance is new. In 1960, exports equaled 5.7 per cent of the GNP, imports equaled 4.6 per cent. Adding exports and imports together, you can see that 10.3 per cent of the GNP was affected by international trade. Ten per cent is significant but not crucial. Had world trade dried up, an adjustment to life without bananas or coffee would have been unpleasant but manageable.[3]

But by 1980, exports had grown to 12.9 per cent of the GNP, imports to 12.0 per cent. Added together, they show that now almost a quarter of the GNP was affected by world trade. No longer was world trade a matter of luxury; it was essential to economic stability.[4]

By itself, increased participation in world trade causes no problems, as the thriving economies of Germany and Japan in the 1960's and 1970's demonstrated. But for the United States the rise to importance coincided with another trend, the end to growth in the overall volume of world trade. From 1963 to 1973, world trade grew at an average annual rate of 8.5 per cent. From 1974 to 1980, the growth rate declined to an annual average of 4.5 per cent. In 1981, it did not grow at all.[5] In the mid-1980's, world trade began to grow again, but at only half the rate of the boom years before 1973.[6]

When a market does not grow, competition for greater shares becomes more intense. In the 1980's the competition became so intense that at times it was labeled "trade wars." The origin of such competition can be seen in figures such as the following. From 1979 to 1982, employment in major sections of American manufacturing declined: automobiles down 34 per cent; steel down 48 per cent; clothing down 23 per cent; shoes down 24 per cent. For this same period, foreign imports in each of these sections were increasing: automobiles up 43 per cent; steel up 46 per cent; clothing up 45 per cent; shoes up 29 per cent.[7] Valid or not, it was all too easy to draw the conclusion that the increase in imports caused the decline in employment.

Economists for over 200 years have argued that, over the long run, free trade is the best guarantor of economic growth. Free trade encourages each country to make what it can make most efficiently. For the same amount of resources and effort, more goods are produced. If a country tries to keep out "cheap foreign imports" (and it is only the cheap ones we worry about) by adding a tax called a "tariff," then it only raises the prices of those goods to its own citizens. Its own workers may manufacture these goods instead, but because they cost more, fewer of them will be made and fewer will be bought. The country as a whole will suffer a decline in living standards. Protectionism, as the application of tariffs and other barriers to imports is called, protects only the economic interests of the few in the industries involved while penalizing everybody else in the country.

The way in which protectionist measures benefit a small minority is illustrated by the case of automobiles. In the face of rising imports from

Japan, the United States pressured the Japanese to agree to a "voluntary export restraint," holding the number of cars exported from Japan to 1.68 million from 1981 through 1983 (down 7 per cent from the level of 1980) and then to 1.85 million in 1984. One economist estimated that this protectionist measure represented a subsidy by the American consumer of $13 billion. Cars in the United States were more expensive (by $1,500 on the average) because consumers could buy fewer less-expensive imports. The Japanese, limited to a fixed number, exported only their more expensive models. The $13 billion subsidy, as calculated by this economist, broke down as follows: $4 billion to the Japanese automobile manufacturers (and American dealers of Japanese cars); $3 billion to autoworkers, mostly in the form of overtime benefits to those still working (as opposed to the creation of new jobs); and $6 billion to American automobile manufacturers.[8] In 1983, Ford paid 6,035 of its managers an average bonus of $13,000 on top of their regular salaries; General Motors paid 5,807 of its managers an average bonus of $31,000. And autoworkers earned an average of $23 an hour (or $48,000 a year).[9]

Because a country with a protective wall of tariffs will spend more of its resources on its own products, it will have less to spend on imports. But this means that other countries will earn less and so have less money to buy exports. If Americans buy fewer Japanese cars, the Japanese will have less income to spend on American airliners.

If other countries respond to protective tariffs by raising tariffs of their own, world trade quickly declines and everyone's income falls. Such a downward spiral is what followed when in the 1930's the United States introduced the Smoot–Hawley tariffs. Within a few months other countries introduced similar tariffs. Within a year and a half, twenty-six countries had quantitative restrictions. Monthly imports, worldwide, dropped from almost $3 billion (gold) in January 1929 to less than $1 billion in January 1933. Protective tariffs helped turn the recession of 1929 into the Great Depression of 1931–1934.[10]

GATT AND FREE TRADE

To avoid a repetition of such a destructive downward spiral, the leading industrial states of the world in 1948 signed the General Agreement on Trade and Tariffs (GATT). Members of GATT pledged themselves to work for the progressive dismantling of barriers to trade. Foremost among their targets were tariffs. In a series of negotiations between 1947 and 1967, members of GATT reduced tariffs to such an extent that today they constitute only a small part of barriers to trade. Japan, the frequent target of critics, has average tariffs of under 5 per cent.

But GATT has not produced free trade. One reason is that states invariably exempt agriculture from their commitment to free trade. States see agriculture as related to national security; they believe they must keep some farmers in business, no matter how inefficient those farmers are, to prevent complete dependence on foreign supply. Farm groups often have disproportionate influence in the political system and make powerful lobbies.

Thus the United States will not allow food stamps to be used for Polish hams. The Japanese restrict the importation of American oranges and beef. The Europeans subsidize the export of their high-priced grain so it can undersell American grain on the world market.

The issue is an important one for the United States because a high proportion of United States trade is in agriculture products. We often think of ourselves as an advanced industrial country but farm products make up 16 per cent of our exports; their value just about equals the cost of imported manufactured goods.[11]

Another area to which GATT has not been extended is trade in services, such as insurance and banking. Income from such services, called "invisible exports," is important to the United States, yet usually is restricted. For example, the advent of communication satellites and information-processing systems makes it technically possible for United States banks with branches in Brazil to keep all their records in the United States. But Brazilian law severely restricts the ability of these banks to transmit the necessary data out of the country by satellite.[12] Thus an opportunity for United States banks to increase their earnings is lost.

NONTARIFF BARRIERS TO TRADE

The use of nontariff barriers to trade seems to be growing, despite states' declared commitment to GATT. Japan is often accused of pioneering new techniques of protection. An American firm developed a new product in the 1970's, the all-aluminum baseball bat. The bat was well suited for a variety of baseball that used a rubber ball and was played extensively in Japan. Not only was the product innovative; it was one Americans could always produce less expensively than Japanese because the cost of producing aluminum in the United States is so much lower. (Aluminum reduction uses vast amounts of electricity, which costs six times as much in Japan as in the United States.) Yet the Japanese managed to exclude American bats, in favor of their much more expensive aluminum bats, by the device of requiring the approval of the Japan Rubberized Baseball League for any bat used in a league game (which were about 85 per cent of all games played). The league refused to endorse any foreign bat.[13]

Techniques to protect home industry sometimes bordered on the ludicrous. The Japanese at one time required that — for health reasons — Perrier water coming from France be boiled before being shipped to Japan.[14] Then in 1982 the French required that all Japanese videotape recorders enter France through the customs house at Poitiers, where each machine would be inspected individually. The tiny customs station, located in the middle of the country hundreds of miles from the nearest port, was deliberately understaffed, and the number of machines clearing French customs dropped from 64,000 to 10,000 a month.[15]

However much one chuckled at French cleverness, such competition in chicanery did nothing to move either state toward the ideal of free trade both had professed when they signed GATT. The French move outraged other Europeans who believed in the benefits of free trade. Restrictions on imports, wrote the London *Economist*, "underwrite inflation by preserving the costly and the inefficient."[16] The *Economist*, which entitled its editorial "Import or Die," pointed out that Europe depended much more on its exports than did Japan and so stood to lose more in a trade war. Unfortunately there are powerful reasons why more states will follow the practices of the French than will accept the reasoning of the editors of the *Economist*.

DOMESTIC PRESSURES

People today expect their governments to provide prosperity. Economic welfare is believed to be within the power of governments to produce. If they don't produce, they are punished, as recent election results demonstrate. It was not always so. People once thought that economic fluctuations such as "the business cycle" had lives of their own, and governments were no more to blame for recessions than for the eruption of Mount St. Helens. No more. By the Full Employment Act of 1946 the United States Congress declared itself responsible for maintaining full employment.

In general, states today are more democratic, in the sense that governments must take into account what people want. Elections are obviously more important today in Western Europe than they were in the nineteenth century and even (for some countries) in the 1930's and 1940's. But even countries such as Poland cannot ignore the standard of living of the population without disastrous consequences. The lot of the Polish peasant in the nineteenth century was not crucial to the survival of the Polish government; the lot of the Polish farmer and worker became the dominant issue in Poland in 1980.

People demand prosperity of their governments because they have come to expect it. Before World War II, economic performance went up and down;

sometimes economies declined by as much as 7 per cent a year. But once states recovered from World War II, they entered a "golden age" of sustained economic growth. From 1951 to 1973, the advanced economies of the world grew by an average of 5 per cent a year, in real terms.[17] People came to expect continued economic growth. The United Nations went so far as to declare it a human right. The International Covenant on Economic, Social, and Cultural Rights, approved by the General Assembly in 1966, declared that everyone had the right to "the continuous improvement of living conditions."[18]

The golden age came to an end in 1973 with the increase in the price of oil. From 1950 to 1970 the cost of oil, in real terms, fell by 50 per cent. Then, in 1973–1974, the price tripled. From 1974, economic growth in the advanced countries dropped from 5 per cent to 3.5 per cent a year. From 1979 to 1980, the price of oil jumped again, this time by 400 per cent. Economic growth for the 1980's was predicted at around 2 per cent — yet states had discovered that a growth rate of 4 per cent was needed to stop unemployment from rising. After the 1979–1980 oil price hikes, unemployment was rising in the advanced countries at an average of 0.5 per cent a year; by the end of 1982, 30 million people were unemployed.[19]

A SPECIFIC CASE: UNITED STATES VERSUS JAPAN

Many Americans believe the source of their private economic plight is cheap imported goods. It is easy to connect low-priced Japanese color television sets and the closing of television production lines in the United States. A United States Department of Labor study found that the trade imbalance between Japan and the United States in 1980 affected over 500,000 American jobs.[20]

To many people, the cause of the trade deficit seems simple enough: The Japanese are being unfair. Such a conclusion inspires calls for retaliation. We should, said a presidential candidate in 1980, act to strand the Japanese on the docks of Yokohama, sitting in their Toyotas watching their Sonys.[21] On the one hand, these people charge, the Japanese don't pay their workers enough. On the other hand, they use trickery to exclude our products.

The argument about low wages does not hold up under examination. In 1978, when the value of the yen was high on world money markets, total labor costs at Toyota and Nissan were second highest in the world (after the manufacturer of Mercedes).[22] Even after the dramatic decline of the yen (an excessive decline in many people's judgment), it was not the relatively low Japanese wage of $12.50 an hour (versus about $20 an hour in the United States) that made Japanese cars so cheap. According to one study, lower wages and fringe benefits saved the Japanese $550 per car; better management systems saved them $1,398 per car.[23] (For example, it took the average Japanese factory 30.8 hours to build a small car, whereas a United States factory required almost 60 hours.)[24]

The argument about Japanese nontariff barriers is valid but the practice is not limited to Japan. The United States has its own barriers. Chemicals have a moderate tariff but the tariff is calculated according to the "American selling price." Thus a foreign shipment might be sold to a United States buyer for $100 and be liable to a duty of 10 per cent, but because a similar commodity would sell for $300 in America, the duty would be calculated at 10 per cent of $300, and thus the duty would be $30 (or a real tariff of 30 per cent).

The Japanese also point to restrictions such as United States laws that, in the name of national security, make it illegal for them (or any other country) to buy Alaskan oil. But most important among the American barriers to free trade is the "orderly marketing agreement" or "voluntary export restraint." When the United States asked the Japanese to limit export of their cars to 1.68 million vehicles a year, the Japanese agreement to do so was ostensibly voluntary and thus did not violate GATT. But the Japanese had no illusions about the directly protectionist measures the United States would have taken had they not agreed.

Despite the political attention focused on the problem, the United States merchandise trade deficit with Japan continued to grow, from an average of $8 billion a year in the mid-1970's to $15.8 billion in 1981, $34 billion in 1984, and $46 billion in 1985.[25] A major cause of this deficit was to be found not in the area of trade but in the separate although related area of the international monetary system.

THE INTERNATIONAL MONETARY SYSTEM

The major economic questions troubling relations among the advanced industrial states are those concerning the international monetary system and world trade. To some degree all states are interested in those questions, but the less developed countries are more concerned about other issues.

Although it is not a common topic of conversation, the international monetary system has a big influence on our lives. It helps determine whether we have jobs, how much we get paid for those jobs, how much our pensions and other savings will be worth years from now, and how much it costs us to travel in foreign countries when we use those savings for vacations. One important function of the international monetary system is to determine how goods traded between states get paid for.

The.main problem is deciding the worth of one state's currency when it is about to be exchanged for another's. If I am an American car dealer with a $100,000 loan from the bank in dollars, and I want to buy Toyotas, which the Japanese manufacturer has priced in yen, then how many Toyotas will I be able to buy? One of two fundamental methods can be used: *fixed* or *floating* exchange rates. If rates are fixed, then a United States dollar is always worth 300 Japanese yen; if rates float, then a dollar might be worth 300 yen one day, 295 a few weeks later, 290 a month later, 295 a month after that, and so on. Governments among themselves can determine how exchange rates will be set. Each method has advantages and disadvantages.

Fixed exchange rates are thought to benefit efficient manufacturers. They allow reasonable predictions of profits from foreign trade and encourage competition on the basis of price. Japan, for example, under a system of fixed exchange rates could keep on exporting small, fuel-efficient cars at prices United States consumers could afford. This system would work to the disadvantage of the United States, which would risk seeing its automobile manufacturers go bankrupt as Japanese cars took a larger and larger share of the American market. On the other hand, according to the same reasoning, if the dollar floated freely against the yen, then as the American economy became weaker in part due to falling car sales, the yen would be worth more and the dollar less. Instead of 300 yen to the dollar (to continue our hypothetical example), the yen might rise to a rate of 150 to the dollar. Then a Japanese automobile that was priced in Japan at ¥1,500,000 would no longer cost $5,000 (as it would under the old exchange rate of ¥300 = $1); it would now cost $10,000. Fewer people in the United States could afford Japanese cars and many would return to buying American models, thereby restoring the American automobile industry.

Floating exchange rates in theory should help to keep national economies in balance. One disadvantage is that there is a time lag before such balancing occurs, often estimated to be about three years. Another is that if governments themselves have any influence in the setting of exchange rates (as they usually do), they might deliberately try to keep the value of their own currency low compared to other currencies, in order to give their industries the advantage of low prices in world trade. Under such a system, for example, the United States might try to keep the value of the dollar down to a maximum value of ¥150; as a result, the Japanese could never sell any of their products in the United States at prices even close to those of American manufacturers. The Japanese would then try to keep devaluing the yen to make it more competitive with the dollar. Such competitive devaluation would severely hamper world trade.

Another disadvantage of floating exchange rates is that they respond not only to government policies and market forces such as consumer demand but also to manipulations by speculators, who may control billions of dollars in various currencies and can make large profits by creating artificial runs on one currency or another. The growth of international banks, multinational corporations, and rapid means of communication has greatly increased the possibility of manipulating a floating exchange rate. In 1984 world trade was valued at about $2 trillion; international capital flow was valued at $20 trillion to $30 trillion.[26] We are finding that, instead of currency values changing at a measured pace, in response to such long-term economic factors as trade imbalances and different inflation rates, rates between major currencies shift by as much as 1 to 2 per cent a day as currency traders, by pushing buttons on their computers, in milliseconds shift huge amounts of money from one currency to another.[27]

Another element of the international monetary system is reserve assets, which are used to create trust in money. People want to know that their money will be worth as much tomorrow as it is today. If money is only paper printed by the government, the government can overnight print as much money as is already in circulation, thereby making each unit of money worth only half of its original value. The same amount of goods and services would be available, but there would be twice as much money to bid for them, so prices would double; all debts, however, still would be denominated in their original amounts and so suddenly would be worth only half as much — a gain to the debtors but a loss to the lenders. This is *inflation*.

The traditional solution to the problem of trust in money was to find a substance, such as gold, that could not be doubled overnight. But the feature of gold that makes it so attractive — that it can't be rapidly multiplied — can also be a disadvantage, because sometimes a government wants to increase the money supply. If the amount of goods and services available does in fact double (as it will over 20 years even at a modest 5 per cent growth rate), twice as much money is needed to keep the economy going. Otherwise the economy undergoes *deflation*: an increase in the value of existing currency brought on by a decrease in the amount of money in circulation. Although deflation is the opposite of inflation, it has similarly unequal affects on society — some people benefit, some suffer, without much relation to either their own individual productivity or the general good of society. Deflation slows economic activity and impairs everyone's standard of living.

The problem of a reserve asset applies to international economics just as it does to a domestic economy. It is necessary to have a standard that people can trust (like gold), yet that can expand (unlike gold) as world trade expands.

THE BRETTON WOODS SYSTEM

In 1944 these questions about the form of an international monetary system were addressed at a conference held in New Hampshire at an estate called Bretton Woods. At this conference the forty-four major trading states of the Western world devised a system to facilitate their international economic dealings. At the time of the Bretton Woods Conference, neither the Communist countries nor the Third World states were major participants in world trade. Thus the issues considered there and the subsequent conflicts over them have been mainly the concern of the major industrialized states of North America, Europe, and the Pacific.

On the question of an international monetary system the participants at Bretton Woods called for fixed exchange rates among major currencies and the use of gold as a reserve asset, which the economically strongest country (the United States) promised to sell at a fixed price of thirty-five dollars an ounce. Thus, if one of America's trading partners feared that inflation was making United States dollars worth less, it could always ask for gold instead.

Currency rates were firm but not inalterable. During the period of the Bretton Woods systems some countries with weak economies did devalue their currencies — notably Britain, France, and Italy. But such devaluations were permitted only as exceptions; once devalued the currency remained fixed at its new exchange rate. These devaluations were taken with the approval of other participants in the system, after the country that was evaluating its currency had first tried internal measures to increase its productivity and control inflation. The intended effect was to strengthen the particular economy involved and thus the entire system.

Gold did not prove adequate as a reserve asset. Miners in such places as South Africa and the Soviet Union were not able to add enough gold to the world supply to accommodate the surge in world trade, which grew by 270 per cent from 1955 to 1973. But fortunately the United States economy was so strong that it was generating a surplus of dollars. Some of these dollars were sent abroad as foreign aid and as military expenditures. These dollars allowed the Europeans and Japanese to buy what they needed, increase trade, and restore their economies. Other states also could retain dollars as an asset to back their currencies. Although the dollar was theoretically backed by gold, it was in practice backed by the strong United States economy as well. A holder of dollars could reasonably expect always to find something to buy with them, especially as inflation rates were low and dollars retained their purchasing power over time. As a result, two reserve assets came into use: gold and the United States dollar.

The system worked well from 1947 to 1960; then problems began to appear. By 1960 the European and Japanese economies were recovering and offering the United States economic competition. The United States was still the strongest economy in the world, but it could no longer be completely indifferent to measures, such as the devaluation of other currencies, affecting its competitive position. The economic position of the United States continued to weaken until in 1971 it ran its first trade deficit since before World War I.

The wisdom of using gold as a reserve asset also came into question. In 1960, for the first time, there were more dollars in circulation overseas than the United States had gold to redeem. If every foreign country had come to the United States on the same day and asked for one ounce of gold for each thirty-five dollars it had in its possession, the United States could not have paid. Such a state of affairs is not catastrophic; banks regularly keep less money on hand than they would need if all depositors showed up on the same day to make withdrawals. Still, by 1971 United States gold holdings were only $10 billion, and foreign dollar claims on gold amounted to $80 billion.

On August 15, 1971, President Nixon announced that the dollar would no longer be freely converted to gold. The price of a dollar was thus no longer tied to an absolute standard but would rise and fall according to how much financial traders were willing to pay. By the end of the year, the dollar had been devalued through free market trading by about 10 per cent. Thus 1971 marked the end of the Bretton Woods system. By 1973 all major currencies were floating freely against each other.

But it was not only United States weakness that led to the end of the Bretton Woods system. By the 1970's the inflation rate was high everywhere, not responding to the policy discipline that Bretton Woods was supposed to impose. Inflation in the United States had climbed from 1.6 per cent in 1965 to 5.4 per cent in 1969 and then to 6.2 per cent in 1973. With the increase in the price of oil, inflation became widespread, from 7 per cent in West Germany to, at one point, as high as 24.5 per cent in Japan. The sudden increase in the price of oil shifted the economies of the richest countries from a surplus averaging $12.5 billion in the five years before 1973 to a deficit of $11.5 billion in 1974.[28] Such jolts were beyond the ability of a fixed exchange rate system to deal with.

The end of the Bretton Woods system of fixed exchange rates based on gold was not accompanied by the institution of a new system to take its place. After a decade of free-floating exchange rates, it was clear that the international economy was not working well. Currencies fluctuated with no relationship to real sources of value, such as inflation rates, productivity, costs, or prices.[29] In 1971, the last year of fixed exchange rates, the dollar was considered to be overvalued by about 15 per cent. By 1985, after twelve years of floating exchange rates, the dollar was considered to be overvalued by about 30 per cent.[30] Clearly setting currencies free to float was not by itself a solution. It appeared that floating exchange rates made things worse, not better.

The overvalued dollar meant that American goods, which had to be purchased in dollars, were more expensive for the Japanese, whereas Japanese goods were less expensive for Americans. Likewise, a Caterpillar tractor made in the United States was more expensive to a buyer in Brazil or Mexico than was a Komatsu tractor made in Japan. One financial analyst believed that in 1985 the strong dollar gave Komatsu a 20 per cent cost advantage over equipment produced in the United States.[31] In the first half of the 1980's, when the dollar was strong, exports of heavy equipment dropped by 50 per cent; employment in that industry dropped from 188,000 to 80,000.[32] The trade deficit was hurting the American economy, and many people believed that the exchange rate alone accounted for far more of the United States's trade deficit than such factors as lower Japanese wages or higher Japanese efficiency.[33]

The growth of the overall United States trade deficit made the question of exchange rates an important one. In 1971, the year President Nixon abandoned fixed exchange rates, the United States ran its first merchandise trade deficit since the nineteenth century, a deficit of $2.3 billion. In 1983 the deficit was $41.6 billion; in 1984 it was $123.3 billion; in 1985 it was $148.5 billion. And there was some evidence that the United States was not alone in suffering under floating exchange rates. From 1955 to 1971 (under fixed exchange rates), the world economy grew by an average of 4.5 per cent a year and world trade grew by an average of 7.5 per cent a year. From 1973 to 1985 (under floating exchange rates), the world economy grew by an average of 2.8 per cent a year and world trade grew by an average of 3.3 per cent a year.[34] Obviously many factors were involved — the rapid rise in the price of oil, inflation, Third World debt — but economists increasingly saw the international monetary system as an important factor.

Fundamentally, the world faced an international problem but tried to solve it by national means. Without some international mechanism to guide them, states pursued their own interests. The United States dollar was strong in large part because the Reagan Administration was determined to reduce inflation (by setting high interest rates) while reducing taxes and increasing military spending, thereby producing a debt that could be met only by borrowing. The need to induce people to lend money to the United States was another reason to keep interest rates high, but the strategy had the effect of making the dollar more desirable than other currencies such as marks or yen. The stronger dollar had international consequences. It made American products such as Caterpillar tractors less competitive on world markets. It forced other countries to raise their interest rates, in order to attract lenders, but by doing so it made it difficult for borrowers to obtain money to expand businesses and thus it depressed economies. The United States policy, however, was determined largely by domestic considerations, not international ones.

By the time of the annual "summit meeting" of the leaders of the world's seven biggest "free market" economies, calls for a new world monetary system were heard more frequently. The former chancellor of West Germany, Helmut Schmidt, wrote that "the present 'world monetary' system does not deserve the name. At best, it is an unstable constellation."[35] Representative Jack Kemp sponsored several conferences on a return to fixed exchange rates. But despite the talk, nothing was done. Even the most modest proposal — that the central banks of the three largest economies (the United States Federal Reserve System, the Bank of Japan, and the West German Bundesbank) adjust their domestic monetary policies to keep their currencies within a certain range of possible rates of exchange — was not adopted. The potential sacrifice that any individual state might have to make at any one time was too great an obstacle.

In 1984, the United States economy grew at a rate of 6.8 per cent, while European economies averaged only around 2.5 per cent annual growth. The strong dollar attracted Europeans to send their capital to the United States, rather than investing it in their own countries. The strong dollar was generally attributed to the United States budget deficit, an issue that Congress found impossible to come to terms with in 1984 or even through most of 1985. The elected representatives of the American people wanted increased spending on defense, no cutback in social programs, and no taxes. As long as Europeans could be lured by the strong dollar to make up the difference, the Americans could get away with it. But European governments were aware of what was happening and were unhappy about it. In the words of French President François Mitterrand, "Monetary disorders fuel economic wars between friends."[36]

THE NEW INTERNATIONAL ECONOMIC ORDER

Because of the connections between trade and the monetary system, only a comprehensive international effort can produce a lasting solution to the problem of "trade wars." But even a new version of the Bretton Woods system will not be enough. When that system was set up in 1944, world trade was dominated by relatively few countries. Today, many new states are important participants in the international economic system and have priorities quite different from those of the older members.

In 1974 the United Nations General Assembly passed a declaration calling for a New International Economic Order. This declaration clearly defined the most wide-ranging conflict in international economics today, that between the rich states (sometimes called the North, because many are located in the northern hemisphere) and the poor states (the South). The members of each group are fairly easy to identify. The richer states are members of the Organization for Economic Cooperation and Development (OECD), which is made up of the developed market economies of North America, Western Europe, and the Pacific — twenty-four countries in all. The poor states, often called "less developed countries" (LDC's), are members of the Group of 77, an interest group set up at the first UN conference on trade and development held in 1964. The membership of this group has grown to over 120 but it retains the title it adopted when it had only seventy-seven members. Excluded from both groups are the states in Central Europe and Asia with centrally directed economies — the Soviet Union and its allies.

The New International Economic Order (NIEO) foresaw three major changes:

1. Transfer of Wealth from Rich States to Poor Ones. The primary demand was for an increase in official developmental assistance from each of the rich countries to a level equal to 0.7 per cent of their gross national products. (In the 1970's, U.S. foreign aid was about 0.25 per cent of its GNP.) This aid would not be granted directly but would be channeled through the United Nations.

2. Preferential Treatment in Trade. Among several proposals under this heading were demands for controlling the price of commodities — such as copper and cocoa — on which the economies of LDC's often heavily depend. Wild fluctuations in prices can cause the economies of these states to veer from boom to bust. One way of avoiding such fluctuations would be to create international buffer stocks. When demand was low, commodities would still be purchased but would be put into such stocks, to keep prices high. When demand was high, such stocks could then be drawn down.

Another form of preferential treatment would be favorable access for manufactured goods from LDC's. Under such treatment, for example, shoes manufactured in Mexico would not be subject to the same tariffs as those applied to shoes from wealthier countries, even though Mexico itself applied tariffs to keep foreign goods out. LDC's sought such access as a way of expanding their industrial sector and reducing their dependence on the export of primary products.

3. Changes in International Decision-Making Machinery. At present many important decisions in the international economy are made by organizations such as the World Bank and the International Monetary Fund, which

are governed not by the principle of one state, one vote (as is the UN General Assembly) but rather by the technique of weighting each member's vote in proportion to its financial contribution (which means according to the wealth of states). Under the NIEO, LDC's would have a greater if not equal voice in such bodies.

An increased awareness of the extremes of wealth and poverty in the world had by the 1970's created a climate receptive to such demands. When the prime minister of India declared, "The world's resources must be developed to make equitable distribution possible,"[37] her words were heeded because she was leading a country where 30 per cent of the population (175 million people) were living below the official poverty line; when she spoke those words the poverty line in India was set at thirty dollars a year (compared to $3000 a year in the United States).[38] It is easy to see why the leaders of most states found the NIEO more urgent than international monetary issues or free trade.

WEAKNESSES OF THE NIEO

Despite enthusiastic acclaim in the Third World, the NIEO was met with skepticism by many economists and political scientists in OECD countries. After all, for the preceding decades the richer countries had been meeting the first demand: transferring wealth in the form of foreign aid. But foreign aid did not always lead to growth. Some countries (South Korea and Taiwan) received aid and prospered. Others (Mexico, Thailand) prospered without much foreign aid. Still others (India and Egypt) received aid but did not prosper. This mixed record made it hard to argue that more foreign aid would lead to growth.

Advocates of the NIEO could argue on pragmatic grounds that past aid was insufficient or poorly used. Or they could argue on moral grounds that rich countries owed the poor countries aid as reparation for past exploitation. Indeed, some argued that the rich were rich because they had exploited the poor.

The factual basis of such claims is not self-evident. Some European states that had colonial empires (Portugal) are not notably rich. Other European states that are notably rich (Sweden and Switzerland) never had colonial empires. And the attempt to draw up a balance sheet showing the effect of empires on the less developed world leads into thorny problems. A serious problem in many LDC's is that population growth is greater than economic growth, so the wealth per person is declining. But in some measure, population growth is the result of health measures introduced by Western countries when they controlled these regions. The population of the island of

Java, to take an extreme case, went from 4.5 million in 1815 to 63 million in 1960, largely as the result of public health measures introduced when the Dutch controlled the island. Do the Dutch now owe reparations because life is so hard for all these people? Would they owe less if they had not introduced public health measures and had let people die?

The appeal on moral grounds focuses on the suffering of individuals in the LDC's; it seeks to close the "protein gap." But the NIEO is designed to benefit governments; it is intended to close the "development gap."[39] The jealous defense of sovereignty by the LDC's means that the rich countries have no legitimate say as to what happens to aid once it is delivered into the hands of the ruling elite of a poor country. That such aid often does not leave the hands of the elite gave rise to Jimmy Carter's comment during the 1976 presidential campaign that he did not believe in taxing the poor in rich countries to help the rich in poor countries.[40]

Even if the pragmatic argument is rejected because foreign aid hasn't worked in the past, and the moral argument is rejected because right and wrong are not so clear, we must still consider the appeal to self-interest. According to this argument, unless resources are transferred from the rich to the poor, "it is inevitable that we are moving rapidly towards an inter-national catastrophic holocaust in which civilisation as we know it may well be destroyed."[41] The implication is that poor states have it in their power to destroy the present system if they do not get their way.

Such an implied threat, whatever its rhetorical value, would probably not convince a rich state that was realistically calculating its self-interest. It is precisely because the LDC's are weak that they launched the NIEO. In any holocaust it would seem probable that the weak would suffer more. Some-times the LDC's suggest that because they already are poor they could survive better in an impoverished world. One could just as well argue that because they are closest to the brink of starvation, they would be the first to go over.

In fact, the launching of the NIEO coincided with the discovery of a new source of power on the part of the LDC's. The spectacular increase in the price of oil engineered by OPEC in 1973 convinced many LDC's that commodities, often thought of as a source of their weakness, were in fact a source of strength. If producers' cartels spread to other commodities, the LDC's could wield significant power and bargain as equals with the rich states. Such a belief was enhanced by the sort of argument being advanced at the time by the Club of Rome (see Chapter 26, Nonrenewable Resources discussion), which said that commodities were about to become scarce and Western economies to collapse unless major changes were made.[42]

The attempt to come to grips with the commodity issue was the second major feature of the NIEO. Even before the fundamental flaws in the notion of "commodity power" were made clear by the collapse of oil prices, the effort of rich and poor nations to deal with commodity prices ran into difficulties. Contrary to the image of the LDC's as exporters of raw materials and the OECD states as exporters of manufactured goods, world trade is not so neatly divided. Many commodities are abundantly available in rich countries — indeed, agricultural products are among the most important American exports. Higher oil prices might help not only Mexico and Nigeria but also Norway, Britain, and the United States, while harming Brazil. It was also clear that a buffer stock, to level out prices, was not what commodity producers wanted. What they wanted was higher prices. If purchases into a buffer stock helped keep prices up when demand was low, well and good. But if demand rose, the selling off of buffer stocks to keep the price low was not appealing.

Before looking at the fate of "commodity power," let us consider the third demand of the NIEO, the proposal to change the rules of international organizations. Organizations with narrowly defined tasks and highly trained professional staffs, such as the World Health Organization or the World Bank, are among the more successful international organizations. Even representatives of the LDC's acknowledge such organizations' excellence. In the words of a Pakistani advocate of radical change, "Over the last three decades, it [the World Bank] has shown considerable dynamism and brilliant improvisation in the light of changing situations."[43] By contrast, the international organizations following the one state, one vote principle (above all the UN General Assembly) have proved ineffective. How can making effective organizations follow the rules of ineffective organizations improve performance?

THE FATE OF THE NIEO

Rational argument against the NIEO on purely economic grounds addresses only part of the concern of the poor states of the world. Their demands are as much political as economic. But the political realities of the 1980's have made the possibility of a new order recede far into the future. The international recession that followed the oil price hikes of 1979–1980 killed off any hope of transfer of wealth from the rich countries to the poor. As one Third World leader remarked, "We know now that we cannot squeeze blood from stone — we are not going to have one bit of concession from them."[44]

Yet in another way, the world economic upheaval set off by the oil price hikes drew the Third World more closely to the economic system of the OECD countries. While direct transfer payments in the form of official development aid declined, a massive transfer of resources was taking place in the form of loans to the Third World.

THIRD WORLD DEBT

The great oil price increase of 1973–1974 produced a net flow of money to the oil producing states of OPEC. The payments they were receiving were more than their economies could absorb and many of them invested their surplus in banks. The banks, with a sudden increase in money to lend, looked around for new borrowers and found them in the Third World. In the decade after 1973, banks loaned about $500 billion, concentrating on states where the prospects for growth were the greatest.[45] Fifty per cent of all loans went to the "newly industrializing countries" of Mexico, Brazil, Argentina, and South Korea.

But despite the impressive growth rates achieved by these countries, loans were being made at a rate faster than the countries were growing or could reasonably hope to grow. In 1982 the degree to which the banks had overextended themselves became clear when Mexico announced that it would not be able to make payments on its debt of $80 billion. Much of the money was owed to American banks; if Mexico had defaulted, the two largest American banks would have lost 70 per cent of their common equity.[46] The crisis in Mexico was followed by one in Brazil, where one of the largest United States banks had more than its entire net worth in loans and investments. Third World debt was a serious issue for the developed world.

The economic slowdown of the early 1980's caused by the inflationary oil hikes of 1979 – 1980 precipitated the problem. With more unemployment and less buying and selling, the economies of the advanced countries suffered and these states had less money to spend on imports. In a recession, commodity prices (coffee, for example, or copper) are always the first to decline, and many Third World countries depend heavily on one or two commodities for most of their trade earnings.

The economic recession (combined with other factors such as conservation) led to an increase in the supply of oil and consequently pressure to reduce its price. But price reduction of oil brought with it two more problems. Some of the OPEC producers might then want to recall some of their loans, which had made the banks' lending possible in the first place. And some of the major borrowers (Mexico, Venezuela, Nigeria) depended on the sales of oil to repay their loans.

The world economy faced a serious problem. Debtor countries could default on their loans, or come close to it, perhaps in a way suggested by President Alan García Pérez of Peru at his inauguration in 1985: by refusing to use more than 10 per cent of export earnings for debt repayment. At that time, Peru owed a total of $14 billion, with a yearly payment due of $3.7 billion. Peru's total exports earnings for 1985 were estimated at $3.1 billion.

(Notice that even if Peru had not imported a single ton of rice or television set or road grader but had spent every cent to repay its debt, it still would have fallen $600 million short.) Under García Pérez's proposal Peru would have paid only one-tenth of what it owed, although even that $310 million would have been twice what it was paying before García Pérez took office.[47]

Or the debtor countries could have followed Fidel Castro's suggestion that all Latin Americana debtors band together in a "debtor's cartel" and refuse as a group to pay the $380 billion that they owed. Whether undertaken individually or as a group, however, default would harm everybody. Banks and their shareholders would lose directly. The economies of the countries in which the banks were located would suffer disruption — the result of a sudden loss of hundreds of billions of dollars. The countries defaulting would seriously impair their ability to borrow in the future. Their inability to gain credit would cause world trade to drop, further depressing all economies.

Even without default, world trade will suffer. Banks will be cautious about additional lending. A large percentage of export earnings of the debtor countries (estimated at 40 per cent of the total in Latin America) will have to be spent on interest payments. Thus less money will be available in these countries for investment in their own development, reducing unemployment, and improving living standards. The debtor states will cut back on their own imports, hurting exporting countries such as the United States. In fact, when countries such as Mexico and Bolivia cut back orders on heavy equipment, Caterpillar Tractor laid off workers. One writer estimated that 1 million jobs were lost in the United States because of the debt crisis.[48]

States initially responded to the debt crisis with temporary measures. To head off immediate default, wealthy states made extra donations to the International Monetary Fund, which then arranged temporary loans to the countries owing the most. Private banks were pressured by governments into extending new credits. But such measures were capable of preventing eventual collapse only if the economies of the debtor countries grew at an annual rate of at least 3 per cent and only if the debtor countries increased their exports and thereby earned the foreign exchange needed to pay off their creditors. Even if these optimistic conditions were met, banks would still have to keep expanding their lending to the debtor countries year after year at an annual rate of 5 to 7 per cent until 1990.[49]

The debt crisis of the 1980's illustrated the truly international nature of contemporary economic problems. Let us look at just one facet of the problem, the situation faced by Brazil in 1982. Brazil was a major debtor, owing much of its debt to American banks. In this situation, default would have hurt the American economy by causing one or more major American banks to fail, and, in the long run, it would have hurt Brazil as well by impairing its ability to borrow money in the future. So Brazil chose to avoid default in the only way it could, by increasing exports while decreasing imports. This led to a decline in Brazilian standards of living and a jump in Brazilian imports into the United States. Such a jump meant a loss of jobs among American workers both in industries such as shoes that compete with Brazilian imports and in industries such as heavy machinery that export to Brazil, thereby stimulating protectionist measures in the United States to exclude Brazilian imports. Such measures make it more difficult for the Brazilians ever to pay off their debt.

The economies of these countries had become interdependent, yet the mechanism for making economic decisions was still controlled by national governments expected to serve national interests. In such a situation there was a chance of significant movement toward greater international cooperation. But there was also the chance that in the absence of such movement states would become more selfish, take increasingly hostile steps, and end up in a world full of both conflict and misery.

NOTES

1. C. Fred Bergsten, "The Costs of Reaganomics," *Foreign Policy*, No. 44 (Fall 1981), p. 36.

2. *The Economist*, February 19, 1983, p. 11.

3. Lester Thurow, "Other Countries Are As Smart As We Are," *The New York Times*, April 5, 1981, p. F2.

4. Ibid.

5. *The Economist*, July 31, 1982, p. 18.

6. Rupert Pennant-Rea, "International Monetary Reform," *The Economist*, October 5, 1985, p. 31.

7. Clyde H. Farnsworth, "The Democrats Try Protectionism," *The New York Times*, November 7, 1982, p. F25.

8. Yoshi Tsurumi, "They're Merely a Subsidy for Detroit," *The New York Times*, December 16, 1984, p. F3.

9. John Holusha, "Detroit Brings Back the Bonus," *The New York Times*, April 14, 1984, p. 31.

10. Samuel Brittan, "A Very Painful World Adjustment," *Foreign Affairs*, Vol. 61, No. 3 (America and the World 1982), p. 545; *The Economist*, February 26, 1983, p. 28.

11. U.S. Bureau for Economic Analysis, *Survey of Current Business*, June 1981; August 1981.

12. Joan Edelman Spero, "Information: The Policy Void," *Foreign Policy*, No. 48 (Fall 1982), pp. 143–144.

13. Steve Lohr, "How the U.S. Struck Out in Japan," *The New York Times*, October 25, 1981, pp. F1, F17.

14. *The New York Times*, April 14, 1982, p. A16.

15. Paul Lewis, "The Latest Battle of Poitiers," *The New York Times*, January 14, 1983, pp. D1, D3.

16. *The Economist*, February 19, 1983, p. 11.

17. Brittan, p. 563.

18. Article 11, published in *The International Bill of Human Rights* (Glen Ellen, CA: Entwhistle Books, 1981).

19. Denis Healey, "Oil, Money and Recession," *Foreign Affairs*, Vol. 58, No. 2 (Winter 1979–1980), p. 217; *The New York Times*, December 16, 1981, pp. D1, D4; Henry A. Kissinger, "Saving the World Economy," *Newsweek*, January 24, 1983, p. 46.

20. C. Fred Bergsten, "What to Do About the U.S.–Japan Economic Conflict," *Foreign Affairs*, Vol. 60, No. 5 (Summer 1982), p. 1061.

21. John Connally, quoted by Thomas R. Graham, "Revolution in Trade Politics," *Foreign Policy*, No. 36 (Fall 1979), p. 49.

22. *The Economist*, September 23, 1978, p. 88.

23. Thomas L. Friedman, "Autos: Studying the Japanese," *The New York Times*, February 27, 1982, p. Y23; John Holusha, "Why G.M. Needs Toyota," *The New York Times*, February 16, 1983, p. Y29.

24. Steve Lohr, "The Company That Stopped Detroit," *The New York Times*, March 21, 1982, p. F1.

25. US Bureau of Economic Analysis, *Survey of Current Business*, June 1985, p. 48; *The Economist*, June 8, 1985.

26. Jeffrey E. Garten, "Gunboat Economics," *Foreign Affairs*, Vol. 63, No. 3 (1985), p. 543.

27. Leonard M. Glynn, "Have Currencies Floated Too Long?" *The New York Times*, May 8, 1983, p. F12.

28. Rupert Pennant-Rea, "International Monetary Reform: A Survey," *The Economist*, October 5, 1985, p. 17.

29. Brittan, p. 543.

30. Pennant-Rea, "International Monetary Reform," p. 68.

31. Alexander M. Blanton, with Merrill Lynch, quoted in *The New York Times*, September 22, 1985, p. F4.

32. Ibid.

33. Bergsten, "What to Do," p. 1065.

34. Pennant-Rea, "International Monetary Reform," p. 31.

35. Cited in *The New York Times*, May 8, 1983, p. F12.

36. Ibid.

37. Bernard Weinraub, "Mrs. Gandhi Says Rich Lands Owe Debt," *The New York Times*, December 31, 1974, p. 3.

38. A. M. Rosenthal, "A Great Adventure Revisited," *The New York Times Magazine*, May 5, 1974, p. 67.

39. Robert W. Tucker, *The Equality of Nations* (New York: Basic Books, 1977).

40. Richard N. Cooper, "A New International Economic Order for Mutual Gain," *Foreign Policy*, No. 26 (Spring 1977), p. 79 n.

41. Hans Singer and Javen Ansari, *Rich and Poor Countries* (London: George Allen & Unwin, 1977), quoted by Robert W. Cox in "Ideologies and the New International Economic Order," *International Organization*, Vol. 33, No. 2 (Spring 1979), p. 279.

42. Jagdish N. Bhagwati and John Gerard Ruggie, *Power, Passion, and Purpose* (Cambridge: MIT Press, 1984), pp. 23, 50–51.

43. Mahbub ul Haq, *The Poverty Curtain* (New York: NYU Press, 1976), quoted by Cox, p. 282.

44. *The Economist*, March 12, 1983, p. 48.

45. Christine A. Bogdanowicz-Bindert, "World Debt: The United States Reconsiders," *Foreign Affairs*, Vol. 64, No. 2 (Winter 1985/86), p. 261.

46. Brittan, p. 548.

47. *The Economist*, August 3, 1985, p. 32.

48. Bogdanowicz-Bindert, "World Debt," p. 259.

49. Ibid., p. 263.

Chapter 26

Global Issues

Threats to peace can come from the grievances of a specific country. In 1974 Turkey felt its compatriots on Cyprus were being mistreated and so it went to war. In 1971 India wished to relieve itself of the economic burden of refugees by setting up an independent state for them and so it went to war. Even economic competition among states for larger shares of world trade produces countries with specific grievances about other countries. But other problems are not limited to specific countries. We often refer to these problems as *global issues* and in this chapter we will look at a few of them and see how likely they are to cause war.

POPULATION

The number of people in the world is large and growing rapidly. There are more human beings than any other type of vertebrate in the world (human beings having recently pulled ahead of rats for this distinction). What alarms observers is that the number of people is increasing at an accelerating rate. One way to express this rate is to calculate the number of years it takes to add 1 billion people to the earth's population. We estimate that it took until about the year 1750 before total population reached 1 billion; that is, thousands and thousands of years. Another billion people were added between 1750 and 1900, a period of 150 years. A third billion were added between

1900 and 1950, a period of 50 years. The 4-billion mark was passed about 1975, so that the time required to add a billion has been cut to twenty-five years. If the population of the earth continues to increase at this accelerating rate, we will indeed soon have a planet on which there is "standing room only."[1]

But will population continue to increase at an increasing rate? Some people dismiss these predictions as just more in a series of warnings and alarms. They frequently refer to the gloomy predictions of the Reverend Thomas Robert Malthus, an English clergyman who published similar predictions as far back as 1798.[2] In a pamphlet entitled "An Essay on the Principle of Population," Malthus correctly identified the basic principle that causes population growth to accelerate. This is simply that a couple can give birth to many more children than the two needed to replace them when they die. Even if a couple gives birth to only four children (and in the days of Malthus the average number of children was greater than that), and those children reach adulthood, it is reproducing at a rate that will double the population. If each couple in the second generation (usually reckoned as coming thirty years later) gives birth to four children, the population doubles again, making a fourfold increase over sixty years. In another generation at the same rate, population is eight times what it was. Today we call this type of growth "exponential."

At the same time, Malthus wrote, the sources of food for these people (such as arable land) are fixed. As a consequence of his analysis, Malthus predicted great human misery for his country as starvation, disease, and war cut down excessive population.

Today we know that Malthus' prediction was wrong. For one thing, the size of families in England began to drop until it was closer to what population experts call a "replacement rate." For another, providing food and other resources for a much larger population was not as difficult as Malthus had thought. It was not necessary to bring large amounts of new land into cultivation because the amount of food produced on existing farms was increased through machinery, fertilizer, and improved breeds of plants and animals.

But perhaps Malthus was not wrong, only premature. Even with spectacular advances in food yields per acre, sooner or later a population increasing at an exponential rate will outstrip the food supply, simply because land cannot reproduce itself. And though the birthrate has declined in some parts of the world, overall it is still large enough to cause alarm.

When in the 1960's some writers tried to resurrect Malthus' views, others refused to join in the alarm. In nature, these skeptics pointed out, exponential rates of growth never last long. Thus, they predicted, within a decade or so the world would enter "a new phase of history, one with declining rates of growth."[3] And indeed in 1982 the United Nations Fund for Population reported a drop in the rate at which world population was growing, from 1.99 per cent between 1960 and 1965 down to 1.72 per cent between 1975 and 1980.[4]

Yet these world figures are only an average; they mask still very high growth rates in some regions. Furthermore, they indicate only that the *rate* of growth is slowing down; the total population continues to grow. Expanding population will create problems that states must address.

CONSEQUENCES OF POPULATION GROWTH

Uncontrolled population growth is a source of human misery, as the often-cited case of Bangladesh illustrates. Bangladesh is a country the size of Iowa, but whereas Iowa has a population of 3 million, Bangladesh has a population of 94 million. Each year the population of Bangladesh increases by almost the equivalent of Iowa's total population. At the present rates of growth, Bangladesh's population will eventually stabilize at 245 million, or 4,358 people per square mile.

Population growth dilutes the per capita wealth of a society. A 1983 study indicated that in Bangladesh people were consuming less rice than they did twenty years ago, despite large amounts of foreign aid. Eighty per cent of the children under age five were malnourished. In 1983 an Indian nutritionist told a meeting of a World Bank committee that in that year 23 million babies would be born in India. Of that number, 4 million would die in childhood, and 9 million would suffer serious physical and mental disabilities as a result of severe malnutrition. A further 7 million would suffer lesser disabilities from less severe malnutrition. Only 3 million, or 15 per cent, would grow up to be healthy adults.[5]

At the same time, population growth reduces a society's ability to cope with its problems. People have to live somewhere, and so land goes out of cultivation to provide housing. An Egyptian agronomist estimated that Egypt loses 60,000 acres of soil a year just to provide the mud for bricks for buildings. People use fuel for cooking, and in most countries the fuel is wood. People in Kenya burn 27 million tons of wood a year. The population of Kenya is expected to double by the end of the century. At the present rate of consumption there will be no wood left by then and dependence on expensive imported petroleum will be a major drain on Kenya's resources.

In their early years, children are consumers. Money spent to feed and clothe them is money that is not invested in permanent improvements. When the children reach adulthood, they find there are no jobs because there was no investment to provide jobs. In Mexico in 1978 (before the surge in oil prices), it was estimated that 800,000 young people entered the job market each year, but the Mexican economy created only 400,000 new jobs each year.[6]

An obvious consequence for domestic politics in the United States is massive immigration of unemployed Mexicans. But the possibility of war between Mexico and the United States seems remote. This absence of international tension between the two countries seems to contradict the position of some writers, who suggest that crowding by itself is a source of tension. For example, one student of human aggression writes that "to reduce world population, or at least to stem the flood of its increase, is the most important single step which can be taken by mankind to reduce hostile tension."[7] The German expression *Lebensraum* ("living space") is often used in English with sinister implications, in part because it was used by Hitler as a justification for wars of expansion. As the earth becomes more crowded, it is said, there will be wars for Lebensraum.

Perhaps people who use this argument prefer using a term from a foreign language because it gives the appearance of substance to an otherwise very thin argument. There isn't much evidence to back it up. Careful studies of the relationship between population density and interstate aggressiveness have found no significant correlation between the two. For example, a study that was part of the Correlates of War Project, covering the period from 1815 to 1965, found no significant relationship between population density and external wars. Studies of other periods have confirmed this finding.[8]

But it would be premature to dismiss population as having no effect at all on international politics. Population growth or population density might cause conflict in association with other factors. A more technical way of saying it is that there might be an intervening variable between population and war. Consider Japan. In the 1930's the foreign policy of Japan could fairly be described as expansionist, imperialistic, and militaristic. The population density was often given as the explanation for this policy. In the 1950's and 1960's the population of Japan was even denser than it was in the 1930's, yet the Japanese were strongly antimilitaristic. There is a major difference between the two periods: In the 1930's Japanese access to resources was hindered by the United States and other countries. In the 1960's, the Japanese were able to invest, buy, and sell around the world. Although the Japanese case shows that population density alone does not lead to aggression, it suggests that population density will lead to violence if access to resources is hindered. Some confirmation of this hypothesis is found in an analysis of several European states during the forty-five years before World War I. Though the correlation between density and interstate violence was low, the correlation between density and colonial expansion was extremely high.[9] This shifts our attention from the issue of population to that of resources.

FOOD

The first resource that comes to mind when discussing the effects of a rapidly growing population is food. War among the starving over shrinking food supplies is one of the grim visions of the future often held up to us. Many of these predictions (like those of Malthus almost two centuries ago) assert that disaster will occur within a very short time. In 1967 a book appeared with the title *Famine — 1975!*[10] In 1974 the United Nations sponsored a World Food Conference, a forum at which speaker after speaker warned of impending world disaster.

The year 1975 came and went without world famine. In fact, ten years later the most serious problem facing world agriculture was a surplus of grain. Farmers in the United States were being driven into bankruptcy. Fully one-third of the United States wheat harvest each year was going into storage. The attention given to starvation in African countries such as Ethiopia distracted from the fundamental reality that the world had in storage 190 million tons of grain. The famine in Africa was caused by a shortfall of 3 or 4 million tons. Making up the shortfall made no noticeable dent in that enormous reserve.[11]

Countries traditionally thought of as starving showed great gains in food production. From 1982 to 1985 China showed a 15 per cent increase in corn production, 20 per cent in rice, and 40 per cent in wheat; by 1984 China had become the largest producer of wheat in the world, with higher yields per acre than those in the United States. India began harvesting record crops in 1976, the last year it had to import grain. By the 1980's it was looking for export markets, one of the factors driving down the price of grain and devastating the American farmer.[12]

A pessimist might still argue that such surpluses were temporary, as they were dependent on favorable weather. Long-term climate shifts might make some regions of the earth too dry or too hot to continue to produce such large yields. An optimist would probably not be impressed, replying that only one-tenth of the earth's land surface is cultivated, and even this fraction is already producing two and one-half times the amount of food grain needed for direct human consumption. If land were cultivated more intensively, the earth could support a population fifteen times greater than the one it does today; that is, about 60 billion people.[13]

This is not to say there is no food supply problem. It is estimated that out of a total world population of 5 billion, 1 billion people suffer from malnutrition. A person living in southern Asia is likely to consume on the average 1,900 calories a day; an American is likely to consume on the average 3,300 calories a day.[14] The problem is not one of absolute scarcity; it is one of distribution.

The figures show that the world produces two and one-half times as much grain as would be necessary if grain were consumed directly, as cereal, bread, and so on. One problem is that in more affluent societies grain is usually not consumed directly; instead it goes to feed animals and the animals are then slaughtered for meat. But this is a relatively inefficient way to use grain. It takes five times as much in the way of agricultural resources to feed an American on a typical diet of animal protein as it does to feed an Asian subsisting mostly on rice or wheat. In 1974 an average Asian consumed about 400 pounds of grain a year, almost all of it directly. An American by contrast consumed almost 2,000 pounds of grain a year, but only 150 pounds directly; the rest was converted to other forms first (including 100 pounds in the form of alcohol).[15]

An obvious solution would be for Americans to eat less meat and more cereal or, in other words, for American eating habits to become more like those of Asians. But the opposite is happening. The trend in world food consumption has been toward the American pattern. In America itself the consumption of meat has increased greatly over the past thirty years as per capita income has risen. It is considered part of the good life to have steak on the table. Today as income rises in the countries of Europe, in the Soviet Union, and in Japan, consumption of meat is rising with it, repeating the American pattern.

Thus there are two sources of pressure on food resources, rising population and rising affluence. At the same time, land is being lost to agricultural use. Prime agricultural land that lies close to cities is being used instead to house expanding populations. Overgrazing of livestock and other poor land management practices have led to the loss of large amounts of land to desert. Shifting rainfall patterns have led to the gradual movement southward of the Sahara Desert by a number of miles each year. Significant additions to agricultural land through irrigation seem unlikely because most sources of irrigation water have already been tapped. Finally, most of the oceans are being fished at what experts consider the maximum level of a continuously sustained yield.[16]

These trends suggest that even if the earth now produces two and one-half times as much grain as needed, the outlook for the future is grim. But many agricultural experts would not agree that it is. They point out that food yields can be increased by more efficient use of the land now under cultivation; rice yields in India and Nigeria are only one-third of those in Japan, and corn yields in Brazil are only one-third of those in the United States. And these yields are the ones possible under existing technology, not taking into account new developments (such as new varieties of plants) that will undoubtedly come along before present supplies are exhausted.[17]

It might appear that the debate on resources has not changed much since the days of Thomas Malthus. Someone makes a prediction of impending disaster based on a logical projection of a present trend. The prediction turns out to be wrong because of human ability to come up with a technical solution. A France that would have been considered overpopulated with only 40 million people in the 1700's was considered underpopulated with only 40 million people in the 1900's.

But the current debate is different because it emphasizes the connections between factors that in the past were thought of separately: The food supply may be increased by technical improvements but these improvements in turn have direct consequences in such areas as energy supplies, mineral resources, and pollution. The solution of one problem may only make other problems more severe.

Here is a dramatic illustration of this point. Scientists point out that primitive agricultural methods rely mostly on human labor. The yields of primitive farmers may not be very high but these techniques supply from five to fifty calories of food energy for every calorie of energy expended in producing the food. In other words, primitive agriculture produces a *net gain* of calories. The highly industrialized agriculture practiced in countries such as the United States requires five to ten calories of energy just to produce one calorie of food energy. In other words, industrialized agriculture results in a *net loss* of calories. If energy supplies were unlimited, this would not be of great concern. But awareness is increasing that the fossil fuels used to run tractors or even to convert into fertilizer are a nonrenewable resource and supplies will not last indefinitely.[18]

Nor is strain on resources the only harmful consequence of increasing yields per acre. Nitrogen fertilizer is one of the keys to increased yields; the "miracle" strains of grain that have produced the "green revolution" are entirely dependent on high doses of nitrogen. But not all the nitrogen applied to a field can be absorbed by the plants. Some is carried off by rainfall or irrigation water and finds its way into streams or lakes where it becomes food for microorganisms. The resulting growth of these microorganisms rapidly deprives the water of oxygen, making it uninhabitable for other forms of life such as fish. The dead and dying fish in turn make the water unfit for human consumption. Even when this sequence of events does not occur, large amounts of nitrogen in drinking water can be a health hazard to human beings.[19]

NONRENEWABLE RESOURCES

The argument, then, is not simply that we are running out of food but that we are simultaneously approaching limits in many areas — arable land, fresh water, ocean fisheries, fossil fuels, and strategic minerals.[20] Shortages in only one of these areas would have serious consequences in each of the others. This style of analysis first became popular as the result of efforts of an international group of thirty scholars who met in Rome in 1968. The Club of Rome, as they came to call themselves, sponsored a project on "the predicament of mankind." The first report for the Club of Rome's project, published in 1972, was called *The Limits to Growth*.[21]

The Limits to Growth focused attention on a number of issues, especially *nonrenewable resources*. These are substances, unlike food, that cannot be replenished by human effort. The report estimated that if the present trend of steadily increasing rates of use continued, reserves of such basic industrial minerals as copper, lead, mercury, petroleum, silver, tin, and zinc would be exhausted in as little as twenty years.[22] It further calculated that to attain an equilibrium that could be sustained for many years into the future, consumption of these resources would have to be reduced to one-fourth of the 1970 level by the year 1975.[23]

The report of the Club of Rome was successful in stimulating debate on the issue, although less successful in winning unanimous support for the group's position among politicians or academics. Politicians did not inaugurate measures to cut consumption of resources to one-fourth of the 1970 level. Although some academics accepted the conclusions of the report and added studies of their own, others published counterarguments. These critics pointed out that the projections in *The Limits to Growth* are so pessimistic because they depend on *known reserves*, yet known reserves are always relatively low because no rationally run business corporation has any incentive to locate more than a ten- or twenty-year supply. Anaconda Copper will not spend money in the 1980's to locate all the copper ore it will need from 1995 to 2095.[24] Even assuming that reserves are exhausted, these critics argue, prices will rise and this will have three effects. First, companies will then have an incentive to hunt for more reserves (or to use lower-grade ore than was economical before, or to use recycled material). Second, demand will decrease and so the rate of consumption will decrease. Third, people will start hunting for less expensive substitutes. For example, the telephone industry can use glass fibers instead of copper wires to transmit messages.[25] These effects were demonstrated when oil prices rose dramatically in 1973 — exploration increased and new sources were found, prices went up and people used less, and because prices were high manufacturers built more fuel-efficient cars and better-insulated houses. By the mid-1980's oil prices were dropping.[26]

This failure to take into account the possibility of substituting one product for another, the critics say, results from a static definition of what a "resource" is. *The Limits to Growth* assumes that the resources needed in 1972 will be the ones needed in the future. If people had made projections on this basis in 1772, they would have predicted a shortage of wood as a fuel and of iron ore as a manufacturing material, and would have ignored petroleum and aluminum.[27] The neo-Malthusians make projections about the rate of consumption but do not make a similar projection about the rate of technological innovation. One 700-page report devoted 220 pages to the environment but only fifteen pages to technology.[28]

Events since the publication of the first Club of Rome report have not borne out the group's predictions, yet criticisms of the report have not been validated either; the debate between the neo-Malthusian pessimists and the optimists continues. In 1980 a special commission organized by the United States Department of State and the Council on Environmental Quality submitted a report to President Carter entitled "Entering the Twenty-First Century." Known as the *Global 2000 Report*, it claimed that in some areas of the world the population was already exceeding the "carrying capacity" of the earth; it was eroding the land's ability to support life.[29] At present and projected growth rates, the report predicted that the carrying capacity of the entire earth would be reached during the twenty-first century. The writers emphasized the depletion of some resources for which no easy substitute can be found: arable land, water, and petroleum. They predicted that arable land per person would decline to 0.6 acre by 2000, that growing population would cause a 35 per cent decline in water supply, and that nearly 1,000 billion barrels of the world's original petroleum endowment of 2,000 billion barrels would have been consumed by 2000.[30]

ENVIRONMENTAL POLLUTION

The *Global 2000 Report* gave even more of its attention to renewable resources, such as wood and food crops, and the irreversible changes caused by growing numbers of people trying to meet their basic needs from finite cropland, pasture, forests, and water supplies. One kind of change is environmental pollution. Loss of cropland to desert in South Asia and sub-Saharan Africa will lead to increased misery for people living in those areas, but some forms of pollution could have swift, catastrophic consequences for all people, rich and poor alike.

Once again we encounter predictions of impending doom that are difficult to prove. For example, we have heard much about the ozone layer, which is believed to protect the earth's surface from harmful ultraviolet rays of the sun. At times people have come forward with predictions that this layer will be dangerously depleted by such diverse phenomena as supersonic jetliners and the propellant in spray cans, and that loss of the protection that ozone provides against ultraviolet rays of the sun would cause a great increase in skin cancer. Such predictions are usually followed by other discussions meant to show that these fears are greatly exaggerated. In both cases the more serious analysts admit that we know very little about the ozone layer. In fact, we didn't even know it existed until relatively recently.[31] The more aggressive critics of such predictions attack the very methods used in making such prophecies, particularly the projection of present trends into the future. One of the key arguments about the ozone layer depends on a continual rise in the rate at which jet exhausts and aerosols are used. Critics argue that if such methods had been used in England in the 1850's, people studying the increase in population and travel would have concluded that by the end of the century London would be buried under several hundred feet of horse manure.[32]

People who are alarmed about environmental pollution claim that their concern is better founded. They point out that we are confronted today by entirely new circumstances. Many of the products that cause us concern are entirely of human manufacture and, never having existed in the past, have no natural enemies to make them disintegrate and decay once they are discarded. Once nylon or styrene is created, it remains with us virtually forever.[33] Furthermore, many of the effects of these products are not felt until years later. The pesticide DDT was introduced about the time of World War II, yet only twenty-five years later did it begin to kill off brown pelicans in the Gulf of Mexico. Asbestos fibers are now known to cause a painful and invariably fatal cancer of the chest lining, yet death occurs only twenty-five or thirty years after exposure. People who worked with asbestos years ago, even for periods as short as six months, are now finding they were subjecting themselves to a grave risk that was totally unknown.[34] Finally, the rate at which these new products are being introduced has greatly accelerated and even if all of them are first carefully tested, there is no way of testing how they will react with the thousands of other artificial substances already in circulation. For example, adding chlorine gas to water has long been accepted as a safe way of purifying it. Here is a chemical product that saves life without harmful side effects. Yet when traces of acetone get into the water by industrial discharge, the chlorine reacts with it to produce toxic or cancer-causing agents such as chloroform.[35] Thus with each new product the risk of some unforeseen and catastrophic combination increases.

The basic point of the environmentalist is the interrelatedness of many aspects of life. It was one of the contributions of the study for the Club of

Rome to include calculations of the environmental cost of overcoming scarcity. But estimating the cost in money is only part of the problem. If fossil fuels are exhausted, energy may come from nuclear reactors. But nuclear reactors produce highly poisonous waste that may persist for 22,000 years or more. Nuclear reactors may cause an excessive rise in temperature in bodies of water or air used for cooling, changing local weather in radical ways. The waste products of nuclear reactors can be diverted for bombs. These are all undesirable effects but their exact cost is hard to quantify.

We may be able to overcome shortages in food, energy, and resources, but only at considerable cost because of the interrelatedness of all these components of the environment. Yet it is this very interrelatedness that makes the environmental crisis as much a cause for hope as for despair. Because most of the problems of pollution are global, the solution must be global. The acid rain that poisons lakes in Canada appears to come from coal-burning plants in the United States — Canada alone cannot solve the problem. The burning of fossil fuels in all countries appears to be putting large quantities of carbon dioxide into the upper levels of the atmosphere, where it allows rays of the sun to pass through on their way to earth but keeps them from being reflected back into space. The carbon dioxide thus acts like the glass in a greenhouse, with the same potential effect of raising the earth's temperature enough to alter rainfall patterns, make some areas too warm for raising crops, and perhaps even melt the polar icecap. Because this "greenhouse effect" seems to be the result of human activity, it could conceivably be controlled by human activity, but only on a global scale.[36]

It has sometimes been said, half-jokingly, that the only thing that would get the states of the earth to cooperate would be an invasion from Mars. Might environmental pollution become a functional equivalent of invaders from Mars? There are reasons to doubt it. Although it is true that sometimes societies suffering from internal dissension put aside their conflicts in the face of a common enemy, this is not universally so. The German threat to France in 1940, for example, was not enough to bring about unity among the French. But even granting that groups will unite in the face of an outside invader, we cannot be sure that environmental pollution will appear as such a threat. An obvious difference is that pollution presents no readily identifiable person or group of persons on whom we can focus our hatred. As the content of wartime propaganda makes clear, it is the emotion of hatred that pulls groups together in times of conflict. But pollution is not a person or even a force that can be personified into a focus for hatred. The enemy, as Walt Kelly had Pogo declare, is us. Furthermore, the threat to our existence would not come suddenly, as the appearance of Martians would. The threat to life from pollution would be incremental, with only marginal changes from day to day. There is abundant evidence to show that human beings adjust readily to incremental changes. It takes abrupt changes to make people change in a radical way.[37]

It is not even clear that all people in the world would agree that environmental pollution is a real threat to human existence. Our perceptions of the world are shaped by the situations in which we find ourselves and the situation in one country can be very different from that in another. For example, many people in the United States view DDT as a harmful agent. The Audubon Society campaigned to have it banned because of its harmful effects on wildlife. Because such agents disperse themselves widely, such a ban would have to be worldwide to be effective. Yet a country threatened by malaria may view DDT as essential to its national health. In its judgment, the brown pelicans saved by banning DDT would not be worth the human lives lost to malaria.

Cooperation among the states of the world to save the world environment from pollution is certainly one possibility but it is not the only one. It is also possible that people who are rich enough will use their wealth to escape from the worst effects of pollution. They can afford to live in air-conditioned environments, spend their vacations in isolated resorts, even eat "organic" food (which always seems to be higher in price than food grown with pesticides). The result would be a world society more sharply divided between rich and poor. The coming of the industrial age to England brought with it pollution and the result for English society was exactly such sharp division. The wealthy Victorians had country mansions and took trips abroad. The poor worked in hazardous conditions, ate poor-quality food, and breathed polluted air. The coming of environmental pollution on a national scale did not lead to national cooperation in Victorian England. Desirable as it may be, there is no certainty that international cooperation will result from environmental pollution on a global scale.

PREDICTED CONSEQUENCES FOR INTERNATIONAL POLITICS

With the potential scarcity of resources making the question of the distribution of resources more acute, the possibility of war over resources has crossed many people's minds. One observer has written that "'wars of redistribution' may be the only way by which the poor nations can hope to remedy their condition."[38] This prediction, made explicit here, is implied by many of the writers on questions of resources. Although such wars are possible, there are good reasons for thinking that they are not likely.

Even a brief look at past cases shows that states are less likely to go to war when their populations are most miserable. An obvious case is Germany, which was not belligerent during the great inflation of 1923 but rather back in 1914, a period of unparalleled prosperity. The depression of the early

1930's may have helped Hitler come to power but it was not until the late 1930's, with prosperity returning, that Germany went to war again. More recently, Guatemala was threatening its neighbor Belize in the fall of 1975. The threats were forgotten following a devastating earthquake in Guatemala City in early 1976, even though the Guatemalans were clearly more miserable after the earthquake than before.

There are logical reasons for this behavior. During famine and other periods of hardship, people are too weak and too preoccupied with immediate survival to undertake military expeditions. A war between states is not the equivalent of a ghetto riot that ends with the looting of a supermarket. A war requires planning, preparation, training, and resources. Despite the recent emphasis on transnational ties, there are still borders between states and borders (at least those of advanced states) are still effective barriers, particularly against destitute and starving people. Furthermore, famine or other disaster does not come overnight and presumably a government capable of going to war (not all are) would have diverted as many resources as possible to coping with the emergency — factories would build tractors instead of tanks, fuel would go to irrigation pumps instead of jet aircraft, foreign exchange would buy grain instead of missiles. By the time these measures proved inadequate, the ability of the government to solve its problems by military means would be greatly reduced.

The emphasis on the large number of people living in the poor countries of the world creates a misleading impression of the military options available to them. A war of "redistribution" is unlikely and it is even more unlikely that such a war would involve a united front of all the poor countries in the world. Despite the convenience of labels such as "North" and "South," there are great differences among the Group of 77. Some members, such as Brazil, are approaching the industrialized states of the North in per capita income. (Brazil's most severe shortage is oil.) Other countries, such as Iran, are rich in oil, yet short in arable land, water, and minerals. Finally, some countries, such as Bangladesh, are deficient in all respects. It is difficult to imagine a single issue that could lead Brazil, Iran, and Bangladesh to cooperate in a military venture.

This does not exclude the possibility of political instability in a poor country or war between one poor state and another. Large-scale migration by starving people is possible over borders that are today poorly protected or not even well defined, as in much of central Africa. But such migration, which has already occurred along the southern edge of the Sahara Desert, has not been accompanied by violence. Even if it should be, it would be far from the war of South against North that predictions allude to.

A more likely possibility is that some poor states, perhaps only one, will resort not to war but to extortion to solve the problem of scarce resources.

India has already exploded a nuclear device and a number of other states have the potential to do so. Once in the hands of the poor states, nuclear weapons may, as one writer suggests, "be used as an instrument to force the developed world to undertake a massive transfer of wealth to the poverty-stricken world."[39]

This is a possibility that must be taken more seriously than that of a head-on collision in war between rich and poor states. There have been cases in which such tactics have been employed within states. Radical groups in Argentina have forced business corporations to make large donations to hospitals in return for the release of kidnapped executives. In the United States the Symbionese Liberation Army succeeded in extorting a large donation of food from the Hearst family.

Nevertheless, there are reasons for thinking that this course of events is unlikely. Practically, though it may be possible for a poor state to fabricate a weapon, it would be difficult for it to come up with an accurate and reliable delivery system. To achieve its goal of forcing a redistribution of wealth, such a state would have to make an overt threat to use the weapon. But the threat would be a warning and with such a warning, a wealthy state could prepare to defend itself against whatever crude delivery systems (such as converted airliners) might be available. Of course there is a chance that such defensive preparations would fail but the chance of failure might be small enough so that a wealthy state would be willing to take it. Once such a device was used (or even only threatened), the likelihood that the threatened state would then agree to a transfer of wealth would virtually disappear. The citizens of such a state, obviously opposed already to such a transfer (otherwise the threat would not have been made) would self-righteously argue that the "barbarous" conduct of the poor state making the threat was reason enough for refusing to comply. Instead of sending food or other resources, they would be more likely to send bombs.

In the world today a state confronted with massive poverty and starvation would appear to have a better chance of improving the life of its citizens by appealing to the moral responsibility of the rich states rather than trying to stir up their fears. The religious and political values widely shared in the rich countries recognize an obligation to relieve human suffering. Often in the past these countries have been able to avoid acting in accordance with their values because they were able to ignore the problems facing the rest of the world, but such developments as demands for the New International Economic Order have made that less and less probable.

However, although it might be prudent for the leader of a poor state to rely on moral appeals rather than nuclear threats, there is no guarantee that such appeals would meet with success. Indeed, some people have suggested that it will be the rich states that will resort to military force to maintain "the present stratified international system."[40] In this view, the threat to world peace occasioned by diminishing resources will come not from the poor states but the rich.

Asking people to give up what they already have is more difficult than denying them something they never had. A person can think of all kinds of justifications for maintaining an accustomed standard of living. Consider the remarks of President Johnson to American soldiers in Korea, made in 1966: "We don't ask for much, but what we ask for we are going to get, we are going to keep, we are going to hold."[41] Not all Americans agreed with President Johnson's assessment that "we don't ask for much" at a time when the "we" represented only 6 per cent of the world's population but consumed 30 per cent of the world's energy and 50 per cent of the world's manufactured goods; but we cannot dismiss his remarks as coming from an unrepresentative minority. Indeed, President Johnson considered himself, and was considered by others, to be a humane man, genuinely interested in improving the condition of life of poor people. But clearly for him the poor people of his own country had a prior claim on wealth and resources. As the United States' share of world consumption has contracted in the 1980's from 50 per cent to under 25 per cent, Americans are even less willing to put global issues ahead of domestic ones.

AN EVALUATION

Whatever the final judgment of the experts, the belief is widespread that resources are going to be a major source of problems in coming years. There is a fear that resources will become more scarce and an expectation that demands for a fairer distribution of what resources there are will increase. Whatever else, these beliefs about resources will create some new conflicts in international politics. Unresolved but unnoticed questions of boundaries will become sources of conflict if territory is suddenly suspected of containing oil or other minerals. For example, the group of Spratly Islands in the South China Sea became a potential source of conflict among the Philippines, Vietnam, and China because of the possibility of oil fields nearby.[42] The harmonious sharing of resources, possible in the past because there was plenty for all, may become less common as each state tries to guarantee its share of a diminishing resource. For example, the reduction of fish catches led Iceland to lay exclusive claim to the fishing grounds within 50 miles of Iceland, bringing Iceland's coast guard into conflict with British fishing boats and the British naval vessels sent to protect them.[43]

So far the attempts to solve problems of resources cooperatively have had little success. After years of effort the states of the world still have not agreed on laws to govern the use of the sea. In the past the waters called "the high seas" were open to all, because their resources were not considered especially valuable and the means to exploit them were limited. Now that both of these factors have changed, interest in the outcome of international attempts to regulate the high seas is intense. Successful cooperation in this area could lead the way to global cooperation on the other issues of concern — population, food, resources, and pollution.[44]

It is difficult for a writer to avoid being caught up in the temper of the time. But it does appear that the issues discussed in this chapter are new and unprecedented. It does appear that they offer unprecedented opportunities and incentives for a kind of global cooperation never seen in the past. The record of human behavior does not support optimism; it is just as possible that the dire predictions of war or environmental catastrophe will be correct. But perhaps the belief that both the dangers and the opportunities are unprecedented will spur us to unprecedented efforts and we will achieve unprecedented results.

NOTES

1. Carl T. Rowan and David M. Mazie, "Is Population Control Impossible?" in *Politics and Environment*, 2nd ed. (Pacific Palisades, CA: Goodyear, 1975), p. 26. Another set of predictions using "doubling time" is found in Paul R. Ehrlich, *The Population Bomb* (New York: Balantine Books, 1968).

2. For a discussion of Malthus's ideas, see Robert L. Heilbroner, *The Worldly Philosophers* (New York: Simon & Schuster, 1953), Chapter 4.

3. Herman Kahn and William Brown, "A World Turning Point," in *The Next 25 Years*, ed. Andrew A. Sprekke (Washington, D.C.: The World Future Society, 1975), p. 25.

4. *The New York Times*, June 13, 1982, p. Y4.

5. *The Economist*, March 19, 1983, p. 64.

6. *Business Week*, July 3, 1978, p. 44.

7. Anthony Storr, *Human Aggression* (New York: Bantam, 1970), p. 135.

8. Stuart Bremer, et al., "The Population Density and War Proneness of European Nations, 1816–1965," *Comparative Political Studies*, Vol. 6, No. 3 (October 1973), pp. 329–348; John A. Vasquez, "Statistical Findings in International Politics: A Data-Based Assessment," *International Studies Quarterly*, Vol. 20, No. 2 (June 1976), p. 200.

9. Nazli Choucri, *Population Dynamics and International Violence* (Lexington, MA: Lexington Books, 1974), p. 60.

10. William Paddock and Paul Paddock, *Famine — 1975!* (Boston: Little, Brown, 1967).

11. Barbara Insel, "A World Awash in Grain," *Foreign Affairs*, Vol. 63, No. 4 (Spring 1985), p. 904.

12. Ibid., pp. 893, 904.

13. "How to Feed the Third World," *The Economist*, March 22, 1975, p. 72.

14. Ibid.

15. Ibid.; Lester R. Brown, "The Next Crisis? Food," *Foreign Policy*, No. 13 (Winter 1973–1974), pp. 3–33; James Reston, "How to MIRV a Cow," *The New York Times*, July 7, 1974.

16. Brown, p. 9.

17. Ibid., p. 31.

18. John S. Steinhart and Carol E. Steinhart, "Energy Use in the U.S. Food System," *Science*, Vol. 184 (April 10, 1974), pp. 307–316.

19. Barry Commoner, *The Closing Circle* (New York: Bantam Books, 1971), Chapter 5.

20. Willis W. Harman, "Notes on the Coming Transformation," in *The Next 25 Years*, p. 14.

21. Donella H. Meadows, et al., *The Limits to Growth* (New York: Universe Books, 1972).

22. Ibid., pp. 56–59.

23. Ibid., p. 163.

24. Wilfred Beckerman, *In Defence of Economic Growth* (London: Jonathan Cape, 1974), pp. 218–224.

25. Ibid., p. 224.

26. Barry Hughes, *World Futures* (Baltimore: Johns Hopkins University Press, 1985), pp. 105–106.

27. Beckerman, p. 229.

28. Hughes, p. 166, referring to the *Global 2000 Report*.

29. *The Global 2000 Report to the President: Entering the Twenty-First Century*, Gerald O. Barney, study director, Vol. 1 (Washington, D.C.: US Government Printing Office, 1980), p. 3.

30. Ibid., p. 39.

31. "Ozone Damage Overestimated?" *Chemistry*, Vol. 49, No. 4 (May 1976), p. 24.

32. "A Little More Time," *The Economist*, June 29, 1974, p. 16.

33. Commoner, pp. 156–163.

34. Robert Sherrill, "Asbestos, the Saver of Lives, Has a Deadly Side," *The New York Times Magazine*, January 21, 1973, pp. 12ff.

35. "Drinking Water: Another Source of Carcinogens?" *Science*, Vol. 186, No. 4166 (November 29, 1974), pp. 809–811.

36. See the report by 150 scientists from eleven countries, coordinated by NASA, described by Philip Shabecoff, "Altered Atmosphere a Threat to Earth, New Study Warns," *The New York Times*, January 13, 1986, pp. Y1, Y6.

37. For specific application of this observation to international politics, see Robert Jervis, "Hypotheses on Misperception," *World Politics*, Vol. 20, No. 3 (April 1968), pp. 465–466.

38. Robert L. Heilbroner, *An Inquiry into the Human Prospect* (New York: W. W. Norton, 1974), p. 43.

39. Ibid.

40. Dennis C. Pirages and Paul R. Ehrlich, *Ark II: Social Responses to Environmental Imperatives* (San Francisco: W. H. Freeman, 1974).

41. *The New York Times*, November 2, 1966.

42. Fox Butterfield, "Spratly Islands Causing Concern," *The New York Times*, January 25, 1976.

43. Robert Alden, "High Seas Fishing Is No Sport," *The New York Times*, June 3, 1973, Section IV.

44. John Temple Swing, "Who Will Own the Oceans?" *Foreign Affairs*, Vol. 54, No. 3 (April 1976), pp. 527–546.

Conclusion

In the first part of this book we looked at a number of wars that have taken place in the last hundred years or so. Not only have these wars caused great death and destruction and disruption of lives, they have also encouraged development of a military technology that now threatens all human life. Yet for all the importance of war in human life, we have seen that academic scholars can as yet tell us little about its causes. Most of us would readily agree that war is not a very efficient way to resolve disputes. It frequently costs all sides more than any benefit they derive from it. Yet not all war has been futile for all participants. For example, both the Bengalis and the Indians seem to believe that they gained more than they lost from the war with Pakistan in 1971. This occasional usefulness of war in achieving a political goal reinforces the belief among many leaders of states that war is a useful instrument of policy, at least if one has a reasonable chance of winning.

A number of solutions to the problem of war have been proposed. Some remain academic proposals, others have been at least partially attempted. Some of these concentrate on the role of force; others focus on the settlement of grievances. But each proposed approach to peace appears to have one or more flaws that keep us from embracing it with the confidence that here we have at last found the cure to war.

After examining the world as it is today we discover that we cannot simply wait for the problem of war to go away. Tensions between states remain. In some areas they seem to be decreasing (in Western Europe, for example), but in other areas, they appear to be on the increase. The persistence of serious disputes among organized groups of people makes the problem of war as serious today as it was in 1914 or 1939.

But what, you might ask, am I to do now? If the problem is indeed one without a solution, wouldn't it be smarter to abandon the whole subject, take up music or ceramics, and at least have a good time while waiting for the inevitable doom?

The theme of this book has been that there is no simple answer to the question of war and peace and, assuming you have been convinced, how you react to that theme is your responsibility. More than one student has gone from an introductory course in international relations to a major in music or studio art and the world is a better place for the esthetic delight and creative insight that these artists provide. But others are challenged by the intractability of so persistent a problem and seek further study. To say there is no easy answer is not to say there is no answer at all. Libraries offer a variety of books and most schools offer a variety of courses on particular problems of international relations. Such topics as research on the causes of war, the performance of international organizations, and the growth of transnational forces are typical subjects of books being published and courses being offered today. Sometimes these books and courses provide answers, sometimes they suggest further avenues of research. Universities, the United States government, and private organizations (such as the Carnegie Endowment for International Peace) provide career opportunities for people interested in making the study of international relations a life's work.

Or perhaps you disagree with the basic proposition of this book. Perhaps the solution to the problem of war is at hand and all that is needed is more effort at implementation. If you find yourself in strong disagreement with some of the arguments advanced here, an appropriate response would be to work more diligently to further implementation of the proposal that you believe will work to prevent war. Perhaps you believe the answer is international education: The American Friends Service Committee or the Experiment in International Living would be happy to have your help. Perhaps the answer is arms control and disarmament: The Arms Control Association or the Committee for a Sane Nuclear Policy would welcome more adherents. Perhaps your political or religious convictions provide you with an answer to the problem of war: These convictions will be effective in changing the world only if you are willing to act on them.

Even if you do not pursue a career in international relations you can contribute to the furtherance of peace as an informed citizen by giving support to those policies that, if not perfect solutions themselves, are more likely to lead to peace than others. In fact, by looking for a single solution to the problem of war, we may have come to a more pessimistic conclusion than is warranted. If we think not of a single solution but of multiple solutions, the problem may not be nearly so hopeless.

We might for a minute draw an analogy between war and crime. A discussion of the prevention of something called "crime" would not be very helpful. Crime includes a very wide range of behavior: school vandalism, bank robbery, rape, embezzlement, killing game out of season. A remedy for one kind of crime might be no remedy at all for other kinds. Ending compulsory attendance in school might cut down on school vandalism; it would hardly affect the rate of embezzlement. Brighter street lights might discourage rape; it would not stop game poaching.

Lumping very different kinds of behavior under the common label "crime" obscures rather than facilitates the search for solutions. Likewise, putting all kinds of war in one category and then searching for one solution to all of them is almost certain to fail. If we are less ambitious, if we ask only that a given approach to peace prevent some kinds of wars, we have more reason to be optimistic.

But can we break down the general category of war, as we do crime? The most common way in which this is done is to classify wars according to magnitude — total war, limited war, guerrilla war, and others. But this is no more helpful than classifying crime according to the amount of property lost — grand larceny, petty larceny, and others. A more useful way might be to classify wars according to how they start. One could say, for example, that wars start four ways: accident, misunderstanding, miscalculation, and lack of alternatives acceptable to states' leaders. Let us look at each of these and see how well some of the approaches to peace we have discussed might apply.

1. War by Accident. It is easy to imagine such a war, yet hard to find a historical example. Herman Kahn, looking for an example, had to go back to the battle of Camlan in the days of King Arthur, when a knight drew his sword to kill a snake, precipitating a tremendous slaughter between two tense armies that had gathered to negotiate.[1]

The fact that we have had no accidental wars in recent years suggests that in this area at least proposals for peace are working. A number of arms control measures have been implemented over the last twenty-five years and we might credit some of the success in avoiding war to them. Certainly, accidents have happened. The Russians did accidentally launch a missile on a course toward the United States; the American radar did mistakenly interpret a flock of geese as approaching Soviet bombers. Yet in neither case did war result. We probably cannot imagine all possible accidents that can occur, and we probably cannot expect all our arms control measures to function as they are supposed to all the time, but even allowing for such imperfection there is reason to be optimistic that war by accident can be prevented.

2. War through Misunderstanding. Sometimes a war begins when one side misperceives what the other side is doing or misunderstands what the other side is saying. In 1950 the American secretary of state seemed to be saying that the United States would not come to the aid of South Korea, whatever happened. This may have tempted the North Koreans to undertake an attempt to reunify the country by force. There seem to have been a great many elements of misunderstanding in this episode. The North Koreans seem to have misunderstood that much of Secretary Acheson's speech was intended for the American public, not as a signal to them. The Americans seem to have ignored the effect the speech would have on the Koreans.

One useful remedy in such a situation would be diplomacy. At the time the Korean War broke out the United States and North Korea did not have diplomatic relations with each other. It was not possible for the North Koreans to request a "clarification" of Acheson's remarks, nor could the United States explain privately to the North Koreans that Acheson's remarks were directed mainly to domestic concern with China and Taiwan.

One could argue that the beginning of World War II in Europe — the German invasion of Poland in 1939 — was the result of a misunderstanding. Hitler, one could argue, did not believe that France and Britain would go to war on behalf of Poland after refusing only six months earlier to go to war on behalf of Czechoslovakia.[2] French and British diplomats were active but unable to be convincing in the absence of credible armed forces that Britain and France could deploy if diplomacy failed. With the benefit of hindsight it appears that war would have been less likely in 1939 if France and Britain had armed to a level at which they could feel comfortable in confronting Germany. In the absence of disarmament, equal levels of armaments might prevent war.

3. War by Miscalculation. Sometimes the goals and intentions of the other side are well understood by each party to a dispute. Diplomacy can go no further in clarifying the position of each party. Yet war breaks out nevertheless because each party is convinced that it will win. A situation like this seems to have existed in 1971 in relations between India and Pakistan. Even without benefit of hindsight we can see that the Indians had clear superiority. Yet the Pakistanis seem to have cherished the illusion that if it came to full-scale war they could defeat the Indians. The actual combat began with a Pakistani attempt to destroy the Indian air force on the ground, in imitation of what the Israelis had done to the Egyptians at the beginning of the 1967 war in the Middle East. But the Indian planes were dispersed and protected and the Pakistani strike was a ludicrous failure.[3]

Preventing this kind of war is more difficult. Disarmament, even of the most limited kind, could help if it reduced the margin of superiority one side could attain over the other and thus reduced the temptation to think about winning. Both diplomacy and arms control measures could help provide more accurate assessments of capabilities. But none of these are foolproof guarantees against errors in judgment (particularly in times of crisis) by those in positions of responsibility.

4. War Resulting from a Lack of Acceptable Alternatives. The Turkish invasion of Cyprus in 1974 was not the result of accident, misunderstanding, or even miscalculation. The Turkish government, largely for domestic reasons, found the position of the Turkish minority on Cyprus intolerable and the Greek government, also largely for domestic reasons, was unable to compromise and change it. The way to prevent war in such a situation is to provide a mechanism for peaceful change. One can propose such mechanisms in theory: a regional or global organization of states with the power to decide such questions and enforce its decisions; a court of arbitration or adjudication, whose decision would be enforced by other countries; mediation by the representative of an international organization or a major power. Although such mechanisms might increase the danger of war if forced on major powers, they could work quite well if applied to smaller ones. In fact, such solutions have worked on occasion in the past. In 1925 the League of Nations settled a border dispute between the small states of Greece and Bulgaria. Greek troops had actually invaded Bulgaria and were shelling a Bulgarian city when the League of Nations (which was clearly speaking for the major powers in the League) made it clear to the Greeks that if they did not withdraw they would face a naval blockade. The Greeks did withdraw and even paid an indemnity to the Bulgarians. The League was ineffective against major states such as Japan and Italy, but it was able to avert war between minor states.[4]

Such enforcement actions directed only against small powers would be decried as unjust, and so they would be. Yet they would be an alternative to war and in many circumstances some injustice might be preferable to war. Applying such solutions to major powers, however much it might be demanded by small states in the name of fairness, does not seem within the realm of possibility. Yet here we come to one of the paradoxes of the nuclear age. It is for such major powers that war has become an increasingly unacceptable alternative. Turkey and Greece can still consider the option to go to war as a rational alternative. Even if such war becomes an all-out war, using the most destructive weapons either Greece or Turkey possesses, it may still be a useful instrument of policy for them. But all-out war for the United States and the Soviet Union, using the most destructive weapons each of them possesses, is no longer a useful instrument of policy.

There still remains the problem of disputes between major powers and small ones. Drawing in another major power on the side of the smaller power may make the conflict more dangerous but may also help control it. Certainly the support of the Soviet Union for Vietnam was a major factor in the United States decision to withdraw from Vietnam rather than "bomb them back to the Stone Age."

My argument in this book has been that there is no simple approach to peace that will end all wars. But there are many proposals that, if intelligently and diligently applied, could reduce the number of wars and shorten those that do occur. Such proposals are worth applying if for no other reason than to give us time to find more satisfactory solutions. These partial and limited solutions may not prevent all violence among states, but every life they save is a gain for human happiness.

NOTES

1. Herman Kahn, *On Thermonuclear War*, 2nd ed. (New York: Free Press, 1969), p. 525.
2. This is one of the more convincing arguments in A. J. P. Taylor, *The Origins of the Second World War* (London: Hamilton, 1961).
3. International Institute of Strategic Studies, *Strategic Survey 1971*, p. 53.
4. James Barros, *The League of Nations and the Great Powers: The Greek–Bulgarian Incident, 1925* (New York: Oxford University Press, 1970).

Index

Abel, Theodore, 116
ABM (Anti-Ballistic Missile)
  Treaty, 243, 248
  weapons, 212, 214, 215, 232,
    235–236, 260
Accidental war, 233, 241–244,
    328–329, 460–461
Acheson, Dean G., 52–53, 157,
    267, 461
Achille Lauro hijacking, 416–417
Action-reaction, 211–213
Adjudication, 304–308
Afghanistan, 293, 350, 351, 352,
    356, 361
Aggression, definition of, 107, 183,
    192–194, 197, 315–316
Alabama case, 303–304
Albania, 305–306, 309
Allende, Salvador, 351, 368, 370,
    371, 405
Alsace and Lorraine, 17, 28, 31, 120
Ambassador, 147–148, 278–280,
    283
Amin, Idi, 90, 102, 120, 320
Anarchy, 105–109

Angell, Norman, 21
Angola, 200, 351, 361, 376
Antarctica Treaty, 150, 260
Anti-colonialism, 159–161
Appeasement, 34–35, 190–191
Arab League, 199–200, 202
Arbenz, Jacobo, 366–367
Arbitration, 303–304, 305, 309
Argentina, 216, 261, 337, 360, 399,
    407, 413
Aristotle, 112
Arms control, 240–253
Arms races
  and war, 34, 204–207, 215–216
  causes of, 211–215
  definition of, 206–207
  quantitative, 207–208
  technological, 208–211, 217
  US-USSR, 206, 209–213,
    217–218, 352–356
Assured destruction, 227–233
Atomic bomb. See also Nuclear
    weapons, 37–38, 57–58,
    205, 221–222, 365
Attaché, 278–279, 283–284

Austria
 Habsburg Empire, 9–10, 11–17,
  23, 29, 168–172
 modern, 33–34, 288–291, 293
Axelrod, Robert, 274
Ayacucho Pact, 261
Azerbaijan, 42–44

Balance of power, 165–180, 383
Balance of terror, 221–237
Bangladesh, 81–84, 101, 335, 398,
  443
Baruch plan, 267
Beck, James, 26–27
Belize, 453
Berlin, 49, 51, 52
Bernadotte, Count Folke, 301, 324
Biafra, 120, 197, 320, 396–397
Biological weapons, 150, 246, 258
Bi-polarity, 49–50, 173
Bismarck, Otto von, 7, 10–19, 173
Bodin, Jean, 98–99
Bombing, strategic, 37–38, 162, 183
Border disputes, 298, 307–308
Bradley, Omar, 52
Brazil, 107, 304–305, 393, 406,
  407, 436, 437, 438–439
Bretton Woods, 429–430
Brezhnev, Leonid, 349, 350, 352,
  354
Britain. See also England, 27–28,
  34–35, 36–37, 38–39, 43,
  46, 49, 63–65, 67–69, 102,
  168, 206–207, 209, 214,
  215, 303–304, 305–306,
  369, 386, 387, 388
Brodie, Bernard, 365
Brown, Lester, 337
Brzezinski, Zbigniew, 174, 176
Bullock, Alan, 116
Bunche, Ralph, 301, 324
Bundy, McGeorge, 229

Cambodia, 91–92, 136, 149
Cannon shot rule, 161
Cartel. See Producers' cartel
Carter, Jimmy, 279, 281, 359–361,
  364, 368, 370
Catalytic war, 241–242

Central Intelligence Agency,
  366–368, 369, 405
Ceylon (Sri Lanka), 167
Chaco War, 187–188
Chad, 201–202
Chamberlain, Neville, 35, 106,
  194–195
Chamizal tract, 309
Chile, 337, 351, 367–368, 370, 399,
  405
China, 55–58, 102–103, 105,
  176–179, 297, 335, 364,
  373–377
Cholera, 340, 395
Christian Democrats, 384–385
Christian view of war, 110, 112–113
Churchill, Winston S., 36, 42, 44, 48,
  157, 167, 168
Clark, Grenville, 137–138
Clausewitz, Carl von, 7, 17, 39, 90,
  92
Club of Rome, 435, 448–449,
  450–451
Cold War, 41–49, 287–288
Collective security, 181–203
Common Market. See Europe, EEC
Communication, 277–278,
  285–288, 295, 297–298,
  337, 342–343
Conciliation, 300
Congo. See also Zaire, 172–173,
  328–329, 395
Connally Reservation, 309–310
Constantine Plan, 339
"contras," 361–362, 416
Corfu Channel, 305–306
Council for Mutual Economic
  Assistance (CMEA), 50, 393
Cousins, Norman, 133–134, 227
Cruise missiles, 252–253
Cuba, 155, 156, 243, 293, 322, 325,
  351, 360, 392–393
Cutch, Rann of, 303
Cyprus, 84–92, 282, 301–302, 328,
  398
Czechoslovakia, 29, 34–35, 39, 49,
  101, 265, 375

Damage limitation strategy, 231–234
Dante, 127–128

Debt, 437–439
Defense
   concept of, 226–227
   weapons, 258
Defense budget, 1, 212, 213, 217,
      250, 259–260, 364, 365
de Gaulle, Charles, 339, 379, 387
Denmark, 11–13, 122, 141, 288
Deng Xiaoping, 374, 375
Deterrence, 166, 226–233,
      354–355
Diplomacy, 147–149, 277–295,
      305
Disarmament, 29–30, 256–275
Dominica, 100
Domino theory, 195–196
Dreadnought, 209, 266–267
Dulles, John Foster, 50, 52, 68

Eisenhower, Dwight D., 265, 267,
      297, 325, 338, 339, 341
El Salvador, 202, 399
England. See also Britain, 13–14,
      168–171
Enhanced radiation warhead, 247
Espionage, 244–246, 283–284
Ethiopia, 188–190, 192, 200,
      264–265, 395, 398
Europe
   as actor in world politics,
      176–179
   ECSC (European Coal and Steel
      Community), 385–387
   EEC (European Economic
      Community), 386–388
   integration of, 383–388

Fait accompli, 59, 177, 196
Falkland Islands, 399
Fallows, James, 364
Fay, Sidney B., 25, 32
Finite deterrence, 227–237
Fisher, Sir John, 205, 209
Food, 445–447
Ford, Gerald, 281, 368
Fourth World, 393
France, 15–17, 18, 24, 26, 29, 31,
      34–35, 38–39, 131–132,
      168–173, 294, 304–305
Franz Ferdinand, Archduke, 23, 360

Frederick II (the Great) of Prussia,
      168–172, 173, 178, 179
Functionalism, 334–343

Gandhi, Indira, 82, 130, 434
García Pérez, Alan, 437–438
Gas, see Poison gas
GATT (General Agreement on Trade
      and Tariffs), 422–424, 426
Geneva
   Conference on Disarmament
      (1922), 258, 260, 262
   Conference on Indochina (1954),
      302
   Conference on Continental Shelf
      (1958), 304
   Conference on High Seas (1958),
      149, 161
   Convention on Prisoners of War
      (1925), 150, 162
   Gas Protocol (1925), 152, 153, 155
Germany, 7–19, 20–39, 155, 159,
      168–173, 178–179,
      190–191, 207–208, 243,
      258, 282
Gibraltar, 321
Global 2000 Report, 449
Goa, 160, 193, 195
Gold. See Reserve assets
Good offices, 298–299, 323, 324
Greece, 46–47, 48, 84–89
Grew, Joseph, 117, 292, 377
GRIT (Graduated Reciprocation in
      Tension Reduction), 268–270
Gromyko, Andrei, 260, 288
Grotius, Hugo, 99, 161
Group of 77, 393–394, 433
Guatemala, 360, 366–367, 453
Guevara, Che, 266
Guinea, 340

Haas, Michael, 173
Hague Conferences, 27, 149–151,
      184, 261, 304
Haig, Alexander, 347
Hammarskjöld, Dag, 323, 324, 325,
      326, 327, 330
Hassan II of Morocco, 310–311
Hart, Gary, 404, 406
Herter, Christian, 162

Herzl, Theodore, 62
Hijacking, 99, 298–299, 324
Hitler, Adolf, 31–35, 116, 117, 325, 366
Hobbes, Thomas, 96–97
Holsti, K. J., 308
Hot Line, 241–244
Human nature, 112–115
Human rights, 358–361
Hungary, 193, 325
Huntington, Samuel, 216, 217
Hyderabad, 194

Iceland, 204, 455
IGO (Inter-Governmental Organization), 103–104
IMF (International Monetary Fund), 395, 433, 438
India, 81–84, 167, 194, 195, 249, 303, 319, 407, 434, 443, 445
Inquiry, 299
International Court of Justice, 304–308, 309–311
International monetary system, 426–432
Iran. See also Azerbaijan, 279, 283, 361, 363, 369
Iraq, 199–200, 299
Israel, 66–78, 97, 193, 279, 281–282, 303, 319, 327, 331, 341, 342, 400
Italy, 188–199, 288–291, 299–300
ITU (International Telecommunications Union), 342–343

Jackson, Henry, 209–210
Japan, 35, 37–38, 52, 117, 176–179, 185–187, 263, 285–286, 292, 377–383, 423–424, 425–426, 427, 444
Jenkins, Brian, 412
Johnson, Lyndon B., 455

Kahn, Herman, 133–134, 249, 460
Kashmir, 79
Kennan, George, 366
Khrushchev, Nikita S., 241, 291, 349
Kissinger, Henry, 74–75, 250, 251,

282, 286, 291, 292–293, 301
Korea, 50–59, 194, 226, 248, 258, 287
Kurile Islands, 288, 380, 382
Kurth, James, 214–215
Kuwait, 199–200

Law, international, 146–163, 394
League of Nations, 32–33, 46, 184–192, 391, 462
Lebanon, 75–77, 323–324, 328–329, 352
Leibnitz, Gottfried Wilhelm, 100
Lenin, V. I., 25, 118–119
Liberty, 244, 279
Libya, 201–202, 395, 400–401, 415–416
Lin Biao, 374
Lobster War, 304–305
Locust control, 340
Lorenz, Konrad, 112–115
Lorraine. See Alsace and Lorraine

MacArthur, Douglas, 52, 54, 56, 143, 263, 380
McGovern, George, 326, 329
McNamara, Robert, 212, 227–229, 270
MAD. See Assured destruction
Malthus, Thomas Robert, 442, 447
Manchuria (incident of 1931), 185–187
Mao Zedung, 177, 375
Marcos, Ferdinand, 280
Maria Theresa, 168–169
Marshall, George C., 47, 385
Marx, Karl, 21, 25, 118, 348
Marxism-Leninism, 197, 272, 347–349
Mazzini, Guiseppi, 120
Mediation, 300–303, 324, 325
Mediterranean, pollution in, 341
Melman, Seymour, 259
Merchants of death, 116–117
Mexico, 363, 393, 407, 437, 438
Middle East, 61–78
Midgetman, 248
Military planning, 23–24

MIRV (Multiple Independently-targetable Re-entry Vehicle), 211, 250–251, 354
MNE (multinational enterprise). See Multinational corporation
Mobilization, 16, 24
Mobuto Sesu Seko, 200, 395
Monroe Doctrine, 48, 196, 293
Montreux Convention, 286–287
Morgenthau, Hans J., 113
Morocco, 200–201, 284, 310–311
Multinational corporation, 404–408
Multipolar. See Balance of power
Munich (conference), 34–35

Nasser, Abdul Gamel, 67–73, 193, 294, 323
Nation, 97–98, 396, 397–398
National Command Authority, 248
Nationalism, 9, 10, 63, 120–122, 178–179, 398–399
NATO (North Atlantic Treaty Organization), 50, 182
Nauru, 100
Newly industrialized countries (NIC's), 393–394, 406
NGO (non-governmental organization), 403–417
Nicaragua, 202, 307, 310, 361–362, 414, 416
Nicolson, Harold, 287
NIEO (New International Economic Order), 432–437, 459
Nigeria, 120, 197, 320, 363, 395, 396–397
Nixon, Richard M., 49, 117, 130, 174, 176, 200, 202, 218, 226, 230, 280, 297, 349, 377, 430
Nobel, Alfred, 221
Nonaligned nations, 318, 392–393, 400
Non-Proliferation Treaty, 150, 152–153, 185, 250, 266, 288, 399–401
North-South conflict. See NIEO
Norway, 139, 157, 280, 387
Nuclear weapons
   characteristics of, 222–226
   disarmament of, 259, 268–269
   effect on peace, 176, 196, 264
   proliferation of, 214, 399–401
Nuclear winter, 233–234
Nutting, Anthony, 323–324
Nye, Gerald, 116–117

OAS (Organization of American States), 199, 202
OAU (Organization of African Unity), 198–199, 200–202
OECD (Organization for Economic Cooperation and Development), 393
OEEC (Organization for European Economic Cooperation), 385
Ogaden, 200, 351
Oil, 69, 370, 379, 382, 408–411
ONUC (Operation des Nations Unies—Congo), 328–330
OPEC (Organization of Petroleum Exporting Countries), 408–411
Open skies, 265, 267
Osgood, Charles, 268–272
Outer Space Treaty, 150, 260
Overkill, 223–224

Pacifism, 32, 270–272, 350
Pacta sunt servanda, 157
Pakistan, 79–84, 129–130, 249, 303, 395, 398, 399, 400
Palestinians, 75–78, 103, 281, 298–299, 342, 411–412, 414, 416–417
Paquette Habana, 151–152
Partial Test Ban Treaty (1963), 150, 152, 266
Pax Romana, 141
Pearson, Lester, 327
Pérez de Cuéllar, Javier, 332
Permissive Action Link (PAL), 242, 250
Peru, 156, 437, 438
PLO. See Palestinians
Point Roberts, 140
Poison gas, 26–27, 36–37, 150, 155, 162, 190, 243, 246–247, 249, 258–259, 264–265
Poland, 29, 33, 35–36, 39, 42, 47–49, 172, 356, 401

Pollution, 341, 449–452
Population, 441–445
Portugal, 173, 351, 386
Pot, Pol, 91–92, 320
Primordial ties, 397–399
Principles of international politics,
    94–109
Prisoner's Dilemma, 273–275
Producers' cartels, 409–411
Protocol, diplomatic, 286–287
Prussia. See Germany
Psychological distance, 225
Pueblo, 103

Rann of Cutch. See Cutch, Rann of
Reagan, Ronald W., 235, 237, 280,
    350, 361–362, 364–365,
    368, 417
Realism, 17–18, 361
Rearmament, German, 31, 33, 34, 36
Rebus sic stantibus, 158
Recognition, 100–103
Red Cross, International Committee
    of, 325
Regimes, 149
Regionalism, 198–202, 260–261
Reparations, 17, 30–31
Reserve assets, 428
Resources, 448–449
Revisionists, 25–26, 32
Rhineland (demilitarized zone),
    29–30, 33
Rhodes formula, 324
Rhodesia, 321
Richardson, Lewis F., 206
Robbers' Cave, 337–338
Rousseau, Jean Jacques, 105
Ruhr, 31
Rush-Bagot Agreement, 261–262
Rusk, Dean, 117, 288, 373
Russell, Richard, 292
Russia. See also Union of Soviet
    Socialist Republics, 13,
    23–26, 168–171, 172, 175,
    208, 259–260

Saar, 29, 33
Sadat, Anwar, 73, 77, 291, 350, 375
Sagan, Carl, 234
Sahara, 200–201, 310–311, 352

SALT (Strategic Arms Limitations
    Talks), 209–211, 241, 243,
    246, 250–252
Satellite, artificial earth, 245–246,
    249–250, 251–252
Schlesinger, James, 230–234
Schleswig-Holstein, 12–13
Schlieffen Plan, 23–24
Schuman, Robert, 385
SDI (Strategic Defensive Initiative),
    235–237, 365
Sea, law of, 149, 161
Seabed, 150, 260
Security dilemma, 108
Serbia 23, 26, 29
Shaba, 200
Silesia, 168–171, 183
Sinai, 71–72, 75, 328, 331
Si vis pacem para bellum, 204–207
Smallpox, 324–336, 343
Social contract, 336
Sohn, Louis, 137–138
Somalia, 200, 351, 398
Sources of law, 151–152
South Tyrol. See Tyrol
Sovereignty, 98–100, 149, 309–310,
    335, 340, 395
Soviet Union. See Union of Soviet
    Socialist Republics
Spanish Sahara. See Sahara
Spending, defense. See Defense
    budget
Spies. See Espionage
Spratly Islands, 455
Star Wars. See SDI
State, definition of, 95–97
Submarines, 27–28, 151, 157, 162
Sudetenland, 29, 31, 34–35
Suez, 67–68, 72, 73–75, 77–78

Taft, William Howard, 304, 310
Tallinn Line, 211–212
Tanzania, 90–91, 200
Technology, 14–15, 19, 23–24,
    26–28, 36–38, 161, 197,
    211, 256–257, 279–281
Terrorism, 411–417
Test Ban. See Partial Test Ban Treaty
Third parties, 297–311
Third World, 50, 391–401

Threshold, 246–247
Tiran, Strait of, 67, 71, 193
Tocqueville, Alexis de, 338–339, 369
Trade. See World Trade
Treaties, 158–159
Trieste, 299–300
Truman Doctrine, 46–47, 366
Turkey, 45–47, 84–90
Tyrol, 29, 31, 35, 190, 288–291

U-2 aircraft, 244–245
Uganda, 90–91, 102, 200, 412
UNEF (United Nations Emergency
        Force), 69, 319, 327, 330
UNFICYP (United Nations Force in
        Cyprus), 328, 330
UNIFIL (United Nations Interim Force
        in Lebanon), 331
Union of Soviet Socialist Republics,
        35, 38–39, 65, 68, 74, 82,
        347–357, 369
United Nations
    and collective security, 315–316
    and international politics, 53–54,
        65, 318–326, 332
    Charter, 108, 314–315
    in Korea, 316–318
    peacekeeping, 326–332
    Security Council, 54, 314–316,
        374
United States, 303–304, 309–310,
        358–371 and passim
United States Information Agency,
        283
Uniting for Peace Resolution, 317
Universal Postal Union, 184, 340
UNTSO (United Nations Truce
        Supervisory Organization),
        327, 331

Vattel, Emerich de, 99
Vance, Cyrus, 301–302, 325
Venezuela, 159
Versailles, Treaty of, 28–31, 33, 158,
        159, 257
Vienna Congress (1815), 147–148
Vienna Convention (1961), 148–149,
        282–285
Vietnam, 91–92, 302, 373, 407

War. See also name of participant
    causes of, 110–122
    definition of, 2, 7, 17
    laws governing, 108, 149–151
    limited, 57–59
    role in international politics,
        107–108
    termination of, 89, 248
Wars for German Unification
    causes of, 8–13
    destructiveness of, 18–19
    lessons of, 20, 248
Washington Naval Conference (1922),
        259, 262, 265
Westphalia, Peace of, 95, 98
WHO (World Health Organization),
        334–336, 340, 341, 343
Wilson, Woodrow, 46, 119, 257,
        291–292, 362
Wittfogel, Karl, 337
Wohlstetter, Albert, 212–213, 234
World Administrative Radio
        Conference, 342–343
World Bank, 433, 436
World Court. See International Court
        of Justice
World government, 127–144
World Peace Through World Law,
        137–138
World police force, 142–143
World Order Models Project, 160,
        337
World trade, 420–426
World War I
    causes of, 23–26, 297–298
    destructiveness of, 20, 27, 28
    lessons of, 36–37, 184
World War II
    causes of, 31–36
    destructiveness of, 1, 38–39
    lessons of, 38–39, 248
Worst-case estimation, 207–208,
        211–212
Wright, Quincy, 131

Yemen, 202
Yugoslavia, 299–300, 319

Zaïre, 200, 395
Zionism, 61–63